JEFFERSON DAVIS

CONSTITUTIONALIST

HIS LETTERS, PAPERS AND SPEECHES

VOLUME I

AMS PRESS
NEW YORK

JEFFERSON DAVIS

CONSTITUTIONALIST

HIS LETTERS, PAPERS AND SPEECHES

COLLECTED AND EDITED BY

DUNBAR ROWLAND, LL.D.

DIRECTOR OF THE DEPARTMENT OF ARCHIVES AND HISTORY
OF THE STATE OF MISSISSIPPI, SECRETARY
MISSISSIPPI HISTORICAL SOCIETY

VOLUME I

JACKSON, MISSISSIPPI

1923

PRINTED FOR THE

MISSISSIPPI DEPARTMENT OF ARCHIVES AND HISTORY

Library of Congress Cataloging in Publication Data

Davis, Jefferson, 1808–1889.
Jefferson Davis, constitutionalist.

Bibliography: p.
1. Davis, Jefferson, 1808–1889. 2. Confederate
States of America—History—Sources. I. Rowland,
Dunbar, 1864–1937, ed.
E467.1.D2594 1973 973.7'13'0924 [B] 71-163682
ISBN 0-404-02000-3

Reprinted from the edition of 1923, Jackson, Miss.
First AMS edition published in 1973
Manufactured in the United States of America

International Standard Book Number:
Complete Set: 0-404-02000-3
Volume 1: 0-404-02001-1

AMS PRESS INC.
NEW YORK, N. Y. 10003

INTRODUCTION

The belief that no great revolution which occurs in human affairs can be interpreted until the aims and purposes of its leaders are fully understood by those who write history has led to this undertaking, which presents the sources of information concerning a stupendous crisis in the history of the American people.

Up to the present time, with but few exceptions the histories of the War for Southern Independence consist of bitter attack and heated defense, with but little reference in many instances to the great and fundamental principles involved and the motives which actuated its participants. Such unscientific methods, which have been regrettably followed by too many historians, have produced a vast amount of historical literature which cannot survive and must be rewritten. This is the inevitable fate sooner or later of error when in conflict with truth.

Henry Ford was not all wrong when he said that history is "bunk"; much of it is, and particularly that which has been employed by a certain school of historians when writing of Jefferson Davis, the central figure of the revolution for independence by the people of the Southern States of the American Union.

It is unfortunate that the publication of historical source material concerning the government of the Confederate States has n the past been largely of a military nature. Such material should be widely published, but not to the neglect of equally if not more important sources dealing with causes and motives.

The definitive history of the formation of the Confederate States of America and of their struggle for independence as a separate nationality is yet to be written. This is to a large extent due to the lack of published sources of information. The publication of the letters, papers and speeches of Jefferson Davis supplies an extensive and comprehensive collection of historical material which throws new light on that titanic struggle over fundamental principles of government.

Believing that the service to American history would prove valuable and acceptable, the collection of the letters, papers and speeches of the President of the Southern Confederacy for publication was begun May 26, 1908, a century after his birth, a belated task which has been performed none too soon. The first move in the undertaking was the issuance of the following announcements to the press and to the public:

Announcement to the Press.

Department of Archives and History.

Jackson, Miss., May 29, 1908.

"I beg leave to call to your attention the enclosed circular letter which explains an historical undertaking being inaugurated by the Mississippi Department of Archives and History which I trust will call forth your active interest and approval. May I ask you to give it publicity in your publication on June 10, 1908.

"The demand for the collection and publication of the writings and speeches of Mr. Davis has become so insistent among historians that the Mississippi Department of Archives and History has been prompted to collect and publish them as a service to American history.

"The Department will be very grateful for the publication of its appeal, for any editorial comments which you may make, and for copies of the issue containing them," etc.

Announcement to the Public.

"The Mississippi Department of Archives and History has formulated a plan for the collection and publication of the writings and speeches of Jefferson Davis. In order that the undertaking may be successful, it will be necessary to secure the cooperation, not only of the historical societies and patriotic organizations which have original Davis letters, but also of individuals who have preserved them. Up to this time there has been no systematic effort made for the collection in one repository of the letters and speeches of Mr. Davis. These valuable historical materials that are still in private hands, will, in course of time, disappear or be destroyed if they are not collected and preserved in some central repository.

"That the duty of preserving and publishing these records rests upon the Mississippi Department of Archives and History is very evident; and in response to the obligation, the Department issues this appeal for co-operation on the part of those who are interested in the preservation of historical materials, not only in the South, but in every part of the United States.

"The papers of Mr. Davis are not preserved alone in the Southern States; while it is doubtless true that the greater part of them are in the South, it is well known that there are valuable collections in other parts of the country.

"The true story of the Southern Confederacy, lies in the letters, speeches, and State papers of its leaders; and its best justification will come after such historical materials have been made accessible to the truth-loving historian of the future.

"The private and public papers of such Southern leaders as Calhoun, Davis, and Lee will reveal, as nothing else can, the principles for which they contended, and give to posterity the true estimate of their lives and deeds.

"In order that those who are interested may know the kind of papers wanted, it may be well to state that all writings of Mr. Davis, public or private, official or unofficial, in manuscript or printed form, are worthy of preservation and are desired. In other words, any paper in his hand-writing or signed by him, is of value. The papers which are apparently of the least value may give impressions which are of the greatest historical importance. It has been truly said that the account books kept by Washington and Jefferson have afforded to historians an insight into their habits and characteristics which could not have been obtained from the Declaration of Independence or the Farewell Address. It may be gathered from this illustration that the private papers of great men are by no means unimportant to the historian.

"The most valuable historical materials in the United States, relating to the American Revolution, are the original papers of such leaders as Washington, Franklin, Jefferson, and Madison, which are preserved in the Manuscripts Division of the Library of Congress.

"The most desirable form of historical material is the original document. It is often the case, however, that the owner of the original is unwilling to part with it, and an accurate copy is all that can be had. In gathering up the Davis writings and speeches it is the intention of the Mississippi Department of Archives and History to make the largest possible collection of originals that can be obtained. In the event that the original documents cannot be secured, copies, accurately made and certified, can be used to good advantage, and will be gladly accepted; and when any expense is incurred, the amount expended will be returned. Where Davis collections are in the custody of historical societies or other patriotic organizations, or where they are part of the National or State archives, permission to have copies made by persons designated by the officials in charge is requested. In the case of private collections, where the owners are unwilling to give up the original documents, but are willing to furnish, or allow copies to be made, it will be best to allow the original to accompany the copies for the purpose of verification.

"The collection and publication of the writings and speeches of Mr. Davis should strongly appeal to the people of Mississippi among whom his life was spent; this should also have the active co-operation of every patriotic organization in the South, and it is confidently believed that such an undertaking will command the sympathy of searchers for the truth everywhere. The Mississippi Department of Archives and History invites the co-operation of every historical agency in the United States which has Davis writings or speeches in its collections, and it solicits the active aid of those who have in their keeping the archives of the various Southern States in making a worthy undertaking a success. The Department appeals to Confederate Veterans, Sons of the Confederacy, Daughters of the Confederacy, Daughters of Confederate Veterans, and Memorial and Monumental Associations throughout the country to give active aid and support to a movement which has for its motive the preservation of truth.

"Correspondence should be directed to Dunbar Rowland, Director of the Department of Archives and History, Jackson, Miss.

"With the belief that the collection and publication of such historical materials will redound to the honor of the Southern people, and add something of permanent value to the history of the whole country, I am," etc.

The story of the vicissitudes and spoliations through which the papers of Jefferson Davis have passed is told in letters printed in these volumes, which makes it unnecessary to repeat it here. Perhaps no papers of a great man who held high official position have been subjected to such mutations nor to such novel and unusual methods of preservation. Some of the papers ran the gauntlet from Richmond to Florida, where they were buried in a stable, others were carried to New York City by Burton N. Harrison, some found a place of safety in New Orleans, and some were captured by Union soldiers and lost to view. That they were preserved at all during and after the War for Southern Independence is indeed remarkable.

The papers of Jefferson Davis are widely diffused over the United States and are in the keeping of historical societies and departments, libraries, museums, Confederate memorials, private collections and in the files of dealers in autographs and historical manuscripts.

The largest, most valuable and interesting collection of Jefferson Davis papers is preserved in the Confederate Memorial Hall in New Orleans, Louisiana. The collection was placed there by Mrs. Davis when she moved from Beauvoir after the death of her husband. The trustees of the memorial were enjoined not to allow the papers to be examined and used for historical or other purposes until five years after the death of Mrs. Davis. She died in 1906, and in 1911 the papers were for the first time after having been placed in the Hall made accessible to the editor of these volumes.

The Confederate Memorial Hall collection consists of the official letter books and message books of the President of the Confederate States and of official letters to the president. The letters on military subjects in the letter books have been published through the courtesy of Mr. Davis in the "Official Records of the Union and Confederate Armies," the letters published being selected by the representatives of the War Department detailed for that purpose. The rules of exclusion and inclusion by which the copyists were guided are not entirely clear. Much vital material was excluded. A calendar of the letters published in that series will be found elsewhere in these volumes. All letters contained in the letter books of the President of the Confederate States of America are embraced in this publication. Those dealing with subjects other than those of a military character are published for the first time.

The collection of Jefferson Davis papers next in value and interest to the Confederate Memorial Hall collection is in the keeping of the Confederate Museum at Richmond. These papers were preserved by the late Mrs. Margaret Davis Hayes of Colorado Springs, the eldest daughter of Jefferson Davis, and were placed in the Confederate Museum by Jefferson Hayes Davis of Colorado Springs, a grandson of Jefferson Davis. This collection was carefully studied and many of the most interesting letters appearing herein are from that inspiring repository of Confederate history.

The Manuscripts Division of the Library of Congress and

the Old Records Division of the War Department are repositories of Jefferson Davis material of great value and interest; both collections have been extensively drawn on, and some of the most illuminating letters here printed are from these collections.

The collections of the Mississippi Department of Archives and History, both official and unofficial, are rich in Jefferson Davis materials, and from that source comes much that is of special interest. The location of all letters, messages, reports and speeches is given at the beginning of each. This method seems to have the approval of a majority of students of historical sources.

Material of great historical interest relative to Jefferson Davis has been collected by the following historical agencies, and all are represented by letters in these volumes: Virginia State Library, New York Historical Society, Pennsylvania Historical Society, Missouri Historical Society, Wisconsin Historical Society, American Antiquarian Society, New York Public Library, Texas State Library, Iowa State Library, Rhode Island Historical Society, New Hampshire Historical Society, Maine Historical Society, Buffalo Historical Society.

I wish I could adequately express my sense of obligation to the faithful and efficient officials who direct the activities of these cultural agencies. Special thanks for the use of valuable letters are extended to Alexander J. Wall, Librarian of the New York Historical Society, Miss Margaret Wylie of the Pennsylvania Historical Society, Victor Hugo Paltsetts, Chief of the Manuscripts Division of the New York Public Library, Miss Elizabeth H. West, State Librarian of Texas, Edgar R. Harlan, Director of the Manuscripts Division of the Iowa State Library, H. M. Chapin, Librarian of the Rhode Island Historical Society, Miss Annie A. Nunns, Assistant Superintendent of the Wisconsin Historical Society, Mrs. Nettie H. Beauregard, Archivist of the Missouri Historical Society, Miss Edith S. Freeman, Librarian of the New Hampshire Historical Society, Miss Evelyn Langdon Gilmore, Librarian of the Maine Historical Society, Clarence S. Brigham, Librarian of the American Antiquarian Society, and Frank H. Severance, Secretary of the Buffalo Historical Society.

In addition to the use of official collections of Jefferson Davis papers I have been allowed through the gracious and generous courtesy of Jefferson Hayes Davis, of Colorado Springs, Gen. Marcus J. Wright and his son Lt. Col. John V. Wright, U. S. A., of Washington, D. C., Mrs. Floyd Northrop Morenus of Marathon, New York, C. L. Dufour, Esq. of New Orleans, Mrs. Susan Thornton Price of Waco, Texas, Mrs. L. McFarland Blackmore of Hopkinsville, Ky., Hill Ferguson of Birmingham and Robert Fridenburg of New York City to make accurate transcripts of Davis letters in their possession. I thank them heartily for their helpful co-operation.

In the collection of transcripts letters were written to every historical agency in the United States, to scores of dealers in manuscripts and to hundreds of individuals. When it was possible photostat copies of the original letters were taken. In other cases the utmost care was taken in copying, comparing and correcting. The most courteous consideration was extended from every quarter, and generous co-operation followed all requests for the use of important letters. The true spirit of service pervades every historical agency in the United States. It gives me genuine pleasure to express the very warm appreciation I feel for the assistance given me by the following ladies and gentlemen, many of whom are my close personal friends:

To the late Capt. Louis Guion of the Board of Trustees of the Confederate Memorial Hall, and to the late Col. J. A. Chalaron, its custodian, both of whom were gallant Confederate soldiers, I am very grateful for the heartiest co-operation, and to Mrs. H. B. McCants am I indebted for accurate transcription of papers from the Memorial Hall collection.

To Hon. Henry Lewis Stimson, the learned and scholarly Secretary of War, 1911-1913, and Gen. Henry Pinckney McCain, a native of my own State, the gallant and capable Adjutant-General of the United States Army, are the historians of the country indebted for making accessible the historical materials in the Old Records Division of the Adjutant-General's office of the War Department. I am grateful to them for innumerable courtesies. To Dr. Gaillard Hunt, the scholarly Chief of the Manuscripts Division of the Library of Congress, 1909-17, I extend warmest thanks for help and hospitality of the most generous and helpful nature. I am also most appreciative of the consideration given to me in my work in the Library of Congress by Dr. Herbert Putnam, to whom every student and scholar in the United States is indebted. It gives me pleasure to express my obligation to Allan Richards Boyd, John C. Fitzpatrick, and Miss Florence Spofford of the staff of the Library for valued assistance.

I cannot say too much in the expression of my thanks to Miss Susan B. Harrison, House Regent of the Confederate Mu-

seum, and to Miss Ellen M. Ellyson for the careful copying
and collation of the letters from the Davis papers in the Museum. In the beginning of my undertaking in locating letters I
was fortunate in having the cordial help of the late Miss Kate
Mason Rowland who cherished the ideals and traditions of Virginia with a womanly devotion beautiful to see. She died full
of years and honors. It affords me genuine pleasure to record
here my obligations to her.

During the progress of my laborious task I have had the sustaining interest and encouragement of some of the country's
most scholarly and distinguished historians, publicists, jurists
and churchmen to whom I had the honor of submitting my
plans for the publication of ''Jefferson Davis, Constitutionalist, His Letters, Papers and Speeches.'' It affords me
unusual pleasure to add this public acknowledgment of my
gratitude to my appreciation heretofore privately expressed.
I am greatly obliged to the following named eminent ladies and
gentlemen for their generous courtesy: Charles M. Andrews,
James Lane Allen, Edwin A. Alderman, Frederic Bancroft,
Gamaliel Bradford, John S. Bassett, Virginia Frazer Boyle,
Edward Channing, James Alston Cabell, Collins Denny, William
E. Dodd, Worthington C. Ford, Thomas F. Gailor, Clark Howell,
Gaillard Hunt, John S. Kendall, Frances Rawle, James Ford
Rhodes, Mildred Rutherford, Booth Tarkington, Lyon G. Tyler,
Henry Van Dyke, John Sharp Williams and Edward D. White.

Above all am I indebted to my dear wife Eron Opha Rowland,
who for twenty years has been my co-worker in all my historical
undertakings, and who has sustained and inspired me as none
other could have done in times of doubt and discouragement.

The policy pursued in editing is a mean between overloading
the page with notations which may seem pedantic on the one
hand and failing to provide sufficient helps to the investigator
or reader on the other. The needs of the student have been
constantly held in view. The well-known rules for editorial
work which prevail generally with editors of historical sources
have been followed.

On account of the correspondents of Mr. Davis being residents of so many States and some of them being unknown to
fame, it was necessary to secure the help of historians who are
experts in their own State field. I cannot be too profuse in
my expressions of appreciation of the help given by Benjamin
F. Shambaugh, Superintendent State Historical Society of Iowa,
Julius H. Tuttle, Librarian Massachusetts Historical Society,

Lucian Lamar Knight, State Historian of Georgia, Thomas L. Montgomery, Librarian of the Historical Society of Pennsylvania, Solon J. Buck, Superintendent of the Minnesota Historical Society, Mrs. Marie B. Owen, Director Alabama Department of Archives and History, Miss Elizabeth H. West, State Librarian of Texas, R. B. House, Archivist North Carolina Historical Commission, Joseph J. Hill, Assistant Librarian University of California, A. J. Wall, Librarian New York Historical Society, William E. Connelley, Secretary Kansas Historical Society, Miss Stella M. Drumm, Librarian Missouri Historical Society, Mrs. Mary Crittenden Haycraft, Librarian of the Kentucky State Historical Society, L. H. Dielman, Chairman Library Committee, Maryland Historical Society, Clifford R. Myers, State Historian of West Virginia, and William Beer, Librarian, Howard Library of New Orleans. I cannot be unmindful of my obligation to Miss Katharine R. Sanderson and Hermes H. Knoblock, my faithful and accurate copyists. It is a pleasure to thank them for much efficient service.

To Newton D. Mereness, Archivist of the Conference of Historical Agencies of the Upper Mississippi with headquarters at Washington am I greatly indebted for research work in the Library of Congress.

The editor submits ''Jefferson Davis, Constitutionalist, His Letters, Papers and Speeches'' to a generous public with the confident belief that the historical and biographical material contained in these volumes will place the President of the Southern Confederacy in an altogether different light from that in which many have hitherto presented him.

I hope in the due course of time to follow up this publication with a ''Life of Jefferson Davis.'' May I not express the hope that in the meantime other historians on both sides of ''Mason and Dixon's Line'' will devote their talents to the same subject.

DUNBAR ROWLAND.

Department of Archives and History
State of Mississippi
The Capitol, Jackson, Mississippi
May 1, 1922

JEFFERSON DAVIS
1808–1889

Soldier, Scholar, Statesman, Executive, Orator, Author, and Expounder of the Constitution of the United States.

George Washington, Thomas Jefferson, John Adams, James Otis and James Madison were the defenders of the inalienable, constitutional rights of Englishmen of the American Colonies.

Jefferson Davis, Robert E. Lee, "Stonewall" Jackson, Albert Sidney Johnston and John B. Gordon were the defenders of the inalienable, constitutional rights of Americans of all the States of the Union.

These superior and unusual spirits embodied in their ideals of government the deathless principles of democracy which made John Hampden, John Milton, William Pitt, Edmund Burke and Oliver Cromwell immortal.

CHRONOLOGY OF JEFFERSON DAVIS

1808—June 3. Born on his father's farm at the site since marked by the Baptist Church of Fairview, Todd (formerly Christian) County, Kentucky, the tenth and youngest child of Samuel and Jane Davis.

1811—Removes with the family to Saint Mary's Parish, Louisiana.

1812—Removes with the family to a farm near Woodville, Wilkinson County, Mississippi Territory.

1813—Commences attending school, with his sister Mary, in a log-cabin school house, one mile from home.

1815—Enters the Catholic school of Saint Thomas Aquinas in Washington County, Kentucky.

1818—Enters Jefferson College at Washington, Adams County, Mississippi.

1821—October 1. Enters Transylvania University at Lexington, Kentucky.

1824—March 11. Appointed a cadet at West Point.
June 18. Delivers an address on "Friendship" at the junior exhibition, Transylvania University.
September 24. Enters West Point.

1828—July 1. Graduated from West Point and commissioned 2nd Lieutenant of the 1st Infantry.—Stationed at Fort Crawford.

1829—Detailed to superintend the cutting of timber on the banks of the Red River for the repair and enlargement of Fort Crawford.—Stationed at Fort Winnebago.

1831—Superintends the building and management of a saw mill on the Yellow River, contracts pneumonia and returns to Fort Crawford.

1832—In command of a detachment at Galena, Illinois, to remove miners from lands the occupation of which was protested by the Indians; serves in the Black Hawk War and escorts Black Hawk to prison in Jefferson Barracks.

1833—March 4. Promoted to the rank of 1st Lieutenant of the 1st Dragoons.
August 30. Is made a regimental adjutant.

1834—Stationed at Fort Gibson.

1835—June 17. Marries Miss Knox Taylor, daughter of Colonel Zachary Taylor.

June 30. Resignation of commission in the Army goes into effect.

September 15. His wife dies of malarial fever at the home of his sister, Mrs. Luther Smith, Bayou Sara, La. —Recovering from malarial fever, sails for Havana; sails from Havana to New York.

1836—Becomes a cotton planter and a student of political science on Briarfield plantation, Warren County, Miss.

1843—Enters political life as a Democratic candidate for a seat in the Mississippi House of Representatives and engages, on election day, with Seargent S. Prentiss in a notable public debate on the issues of the day.

1844—Makes an effective canvass of his State for the Polk and Dallas ticket.

1845—February 26. Marries Miss Varina Howell.—Elected a member of the national House of Representatives.

December 8. Takes his seat in the House.

December 19. Speaks in the House—his first speech in that body—on native Americanism and the naturalization laws. Offers resolutions with regard to military schools and a mail route from Mobile, Alabama, to Jackson, Mississippi.

1846—January 13. Offers a resolution in the House requesting information from the Secretary of the Navy with regard to the Ship Island channel.

February 6. Speaks in the House on the Oregon question.

March 16. Delivers a strict-constructionist speech on the river and harbor bill.

March 27. Speaks on the bill to raise two regiments of riflemen.

April 8. Speaks on the bill to raise a regiment of mounted riflemen.

May 28. Speaks on the House resolution of thanks to General Taylor.

May 30. Speaks on the bill to alter the pay department of the Army.

June 12. Offers resolutions that medals be awarded in recognition of services rendered by General Taylor and his army at Palo Alto and Resaca de la Palma.

June—Resigns his seat in the House.

July 18. Elected colonel of the first regiment of Mississippi riflemen in the war with Mexico.

July 21. Sails with the regiment from New Orleans for southeastern Texas.

September 21-23. Distinguishes himself for gallantry in the siege of Monterey.

1847—February 22. Wounded while gallantly fighting at Buena Vista.

June 20. Declines an appointment as brigadier general of volunteers on the ground that volunteers are militia, and that the Constitution reserves to the State the appointment of all militia officers.

July 12. Mustered out.

August 10. Appointed to fill a vacancy in the U. S. Senate.

December 6. Takes his seat in the Senate.

December 30. Appointed a regent of the Smithsonian Institution.

1848—January 3. Speaks on a bill to increase the Army.

February 17. Speaks on the resolution of thanks to General Taylor.

May 5. Speaks on the bill providing for a temporary occupation of Yucatan by the United States.

July 1. Speaks in defense of the reputation of General John A. Quitman.

July 12. Speaks on the bill to establish a Territorial government for Oregon.

1849—January 12. Speaks on a petition for the colonization of free persons of color.

January 22. Speaks on resolution by the Legislature of New York with regard to the slavery question.

January 31. Speaks on the bill to aid the construction of a railroad across the Isthmus of Panama.

March 3. Speaks on the bill for the establishment of the Department of the Interior.

December 18. Made chairman of the Senate Committee on Military Affairs.

December 20. Opposes a resolution inviting Father Mathew to a seat in the Senate on the ground of his being an abolitionist agitator.

1850—January 10. Speaks on the resolutions of the General Assembly of the State of Vermont with regard to slavery.

February. Elected to the Senate for a term of six years.

February 8. Speaks on the question of receiving a petition for the dissolution of the Union.

JEFFERSON DAVIS, CONSTITUTIONALIST

February 12. Speaks on the subject of the extension of slavery to the Territories.

March 18. Speaks in defense of Buchanan's position on the slavery question.

May 1. Delivers a strict construction speech on the joint resolution providing aid to search for Sir John Franklin.

May 2. Objects, in a speech, to the granting of public lands to corporations.

May 8. Presents "the report and resolutions of the Legislature of Mississippi, on the subject which distracts and divides the people of the Union, and which threatens, unless checked in its onward course, to produce consequences fatal to the cause of human liberty, as secured and advanced by the Constitution of the United States."

June 13. Speaks on the bill to grant to Arkansas the swamp lands in that State.

September 28. Speaks on a proposition to abolish flogging in the Navy.

January-September. Speaks many times on Clay's compromise measures with regard to slavery.

1851—January 22. Speaks on Clay's resolution of inquiry into the expediency of making more effectual provision for the suppression of the African slave trade.

February 18. Speaks on Clay's resolution with regard to resistance, in Boston, to the execution of the fugitive slave law.

September. Resigns seat in the Senate to succeed Quitman as Democratic candidate for governor of Mississippi.

November. Defeated by Henry S. Foote in the Mississippi gubernatorial election.

1852—January. Takes part in the States rights convention at Jackson.

September-October. Speaks in Mississippi and neighboring States for the Pierce ticket.

1853—March 7. Becomes Secretary of War.

July. Speaks in Philadelphia on the Administration's policy with regard to internal improvements, and visits New England.

December 1. Transmits to Congress his first report as Secretary of War.

1854—January 22. Conducts Stephen A. Douglas and some
Southern gentlemen to the White House for an interview with the President on the Kansas-Nebraska Bill.

December 4. Transmits to Congress his second annual
report as Secretary of War.

1855—February 27. Transmits to Congress his elaborate report
on the several possible routes for a railroad from the
Mississippi River to the Pacific Ocean.

December 3. Transmits to Congress his third annual
report as Secretary of War.

1856—December 1. Transmits to Congress his fourth annual report of Secretary of War.

1857—March 4. Re-enters the Senate.

1857-1858—Disabled from service in the Senate and threatened
with the loss of his left eye.

1858—Summers in Portland, Maine, on account of ill health.

July 4. Delivers a speech on board a ship off Boston in
which he pleads for the preservation of the Union.

October 19. Delivers a speech in Faneuil Hall in which
he urges devotion to the Union and obedience to the
Constitution.

December. Speaks in the Senate on his proposed substitute for the Pacific Railroad Bill.

1859—January. Speaks several times on the French Spoliation
Bill.

February 1. Speaks on the agricultural colleges bill.

February 23. Speaks on questions connected with slavery
in the Territories.

December 5. Speaks on a resolution of inquiry into the
John Brown Raid.

1860—February 2. Submits six resolutions defining his position
with regard to the relations of States.

February 29. Speaks on the bill for the admission of
Kansas into the Union.

May 8. Speaks on his resolutions with regard to the
relations of the States.

1861—January 10. Upholds the right of secession.

January 21. Announces that his State has declared her
separation from the United States, delivers a farewell
address, and withdraws from the Senate.

January 25. Commisioned major general of Mississippi
troops.

February 9. Elected Provisional President of the Confederate States of America by the Confederate convention at Montgomery.

February 18. Inaugurated Provisional President of the Confederate States of America.

Appoints Peace Commission to settle differences with the Washington Government without war.

March 3. Appoints General Beauregard to the command of the Confederate forces in and around Charleston.

April 21. Expresses a desire for peace.

May 29. Takes up his residence at Richmond.

October 16. Elected President of the Confederate States of America.

1862—February 22. Inaugurated President of the Confederate States of America.

May 31. Assigns General Robert E. Lee to the command of the immortal Army of Northern Virginia.

December. Makes a tour of the West, reviewing the Confederate Armies.

1863—August 8. After Gettysburg General Lee, on account of adverse criticism, offers to resign his command in a letter which attains to the supremest height of unselfish devotion to country and duty. Mr. Davis in declining to accept the resignation of General Lee pays him a tribute which is a classic of appreciation of the Great Commander.

1864—October-November. Visits Georgia to rally the people to the support of the Confederacy.

1865—Jan. 12. Appoints commissioners to the conference at Hampton Roads.

April 3. Leaves Richmond, Va., in company with the Confederate Cabinet, for Danville.

April 9. Proceeds to Greensboro, N. C.

April 16. Proceeds from Greensboro toward Meridian, Miss.

May 10. Taken prisoner at Irwinville, Ga.

May 19. Confined in the gunroom of a casemate at Fortress Monroe.

May 23. Manacled.

May 26. His irons are removed at the suggestion of his physician.

1866—May. Indicted for treason.

1867—Admitted to bail, visits Canada and sails for New Orleans, via Havana.

1868—Visits Europe.

December. Court divides on a motion to quash his indictment for treason.

1869—February. An order of *nolle prosequi* is entered in his case.—Becomes president of the Carolina Life Insurance Company at Memphis, Tenn.

1870—Presides over the Lee memorial meeting at Richmond.

1875—Urged to accept election to the United States Senate by the State of Mississippi. From 1875 until his death he could have been returned to the Senate on an expression of willingness to accept.

1876—Promotes the Mississippi Society for the purpose of stimulating trade between the United States and South America.

1877—Visits England.

1878—Returns to Beauvoir, Miss., to write his *Rise and Fall of the Confederate Government.*

1881—Completes the *Rise and Fall of the Confederate Government* and visits Europe.

1882—Visits Alabama and Georgia and is received everywhere on his route with unusual manifestations of love and affection.

1884—March 10. Delivers his last address to the Mississippi Legislature. His reception by his own people was remarkable for devotion, loyalty and trust.

1889—October. Completes the manuscript of *A short History of the Confederate States of America.*

December 6. Dies at New Orleans.

AUTOBIOGRAPHY OF JEFFERSON DAVIS.[1]

I was born, June 3, 1808, in Christian County, Ky., in that part of it which, by a subsequent division, is now in Todd County. At this place has since arisen the village of Fairview, and on the exact spot where I was born has been constructed the Baptist Church, of the place. My father, Samuel Davis, was a native of Georgia, and served in the War of the Revolution, first in the "mounted gun-men," and afterward as captain of infantry at the siege of Savannah. During my infancy my father removed to Wilkinson County, Miss. After passing through the County Academy, I entered Transylvania College, Kentucky, at the age of sixteen, and was advanced as far as the senior class when I was appointed to the United States Military Academy at West Point; which I entered in September, 1824. I graduated in 1828, and then, in accordance with the custom of cadets, entered active service with the rank of lieutenant, serving as an officer of infantry on the Northwest frontier until 1833, when, a regiment of dragoons having been created, I was transferred to it. After a successful campaign against the Indians I resigned from the army, in 1835, being anxious to fulfil a long-existing engagement with a daughter of Colonel Zachary Taylor, whom I married, not "after a romantic elopement," as has so often been stated, but at the house of her aunt and in the presence of many of her relatives, at a place near Louisville, Ky. Then I became a cotton planter in Warren County, Miss. It was my misfortune, early in my married life, to lose my wife; and for many years thereafter I lived in great seclusion on the plantation in the swamps of the Mississippi. In 1843 I for the first time took part in the political life of the country. Next year I was chosen one of the Presidential electors at large of the State; and in the succeeding year was elected to Congress, taking my seat in the House of Representatives in December, 1845. The proposition to terminate the joint occupancy of Oregon, and the reformation of the tariff, were the two questions arousing most public attention at that time, and I took an active part in their discussion, especially in that of the first.

During this period hostilities with Mexico commenced, and in

[1] From *Belford's Magazine*, January, 1890.

the legislation which the contest rendered necessary my military education enabled me to take a somewhat prominent part.

In June, 1846, a regiment of Mississippi volunteers was organized at Vicksburg, of which I was elected colonel. On receiving notice of the election, I proceeded to overtake the regiment, which was already on its way to Mexico, and joined it at New Orleans. Reporting to General Taylor, then commanding at Camargo, my regiment, although the last to arrive—having been detained for some time on duty at the mouth of the Rio Grande—was selected to move with the advance upon the city of Monterey. The want of transportation prevented General Taylor from taking the whole body of volunteers who had reported there for duty. The Mississippi regiment was armed entirely with percussion rifles. And here it may be interesting to state that General Scott, in Washington, endeavored to persuade me not to take more rifles than enough for four companies, and objected particularly to percussion arms, as not having been sufficiently tested for the use of troops in the field. Knowing that the Mississippians would have no confidence in the old flint-lock muskets, I insisted on their being armed with the kind of rifle then recently made at New Haven, Conn.—the Whitney rifle. From having been first used by the Mississippians, these rifles have always been known as the Mississippi rifles.

In the attack on Monterey General Taylor divided his force, sending one part of it by a circuitous road to attack the city from the west; while he decided to lead in person the attack on the east. The Mississippi regiment advanced to the relief of a force which had attacked Fort Lenaria, but had been repulsed before the Mississippians arrived. They carried the redoubt, and the fort which was in the rear of it surrendered. The next day our force on the west side carried successfully the height on which stood the bishop's palace, which commanded the city.

On the third day the Mississippians advanced from the fort which they held, through lanes and gardens, skirmishing and driving the enemy before them until they reached a two-story house at the corner of the Grand Plaza. Here they were joined by a regiment of Texans, and from the windows of this house they opened fire on the artillery and such other troops as were in view. But, to get a better position for firing on the principal building of the Grand Plaza, it was necessary to cross the street, which was swept by canister and grape, rattling on the pavement like hail; and as the street was very narrow it was determined to construct a flying barricade. Some long timbers were found, and, with pack-saddles and boxes, which served the purpose, a barricade was constructed.

Here occurred an incident to which I have since frequently referred with pride. In breaking open a quartermaster's storehouse to get supplies for this barricade, the men found bundles of the much-prized Mexican blankets, and also of very serviceable shoes and pack-saddles. The pack-saddles were freely taken as good material for the proposed barricade; and one of my men, as his shoes were broken and stones had hurt his feet, asked my permission to take a pair from one of the boxes. This, of course, was freely accorded; but not one of the very valuable and much-prized Mexican blankets was taken.

About the time that the flying barricade was completed arrangements were made by the Texans and Mississippians to occupy houses on both sides of the street for the purpose of more effective fire into the Grand Plaza. It having been deemed necessary to increase our force, the Mississippi sergeant-major was sent back for some companies of the First Mississippi which had remained behind. He returned with the statement that the enemy was behind us, that all our troops had been withdrawn, and that orders had been three times sent to me to return. Governor Henderson, of Texas, had accompanied the Texan troops, and on submitting to him the question what we should do under the message, he realized—as was very plain—that it was safer to remain where we were than—our supports having been withdrawn—to return across streets where we were liable to be fired on by artillery, and across open grounds where cavalry might be expected to attack us. But, he added, he supposed the orders came from the general-in-chief, and we were bound to obey them. So we made dispositions to retire quietly; but, in passing the first square, we found that our movement had been anticipated, and that a battery of artillery was posted to command the street. The arrangement made by me for crossing it was that I should go first; if only one gun was fired at me, then another man should follow; and so on, another and another, until a volley should be fired, and then all of them should rush rapidly across before the guns could be reloaded. In this manner the men got across with little loss. We then made our way to the suburb, where we found that an officer of infantry, with two companies and a section of artillery, had been posted to wait for us, and, in case of emergency, to aid our retreat.

Early next morning General Ampudia, commanding the Mexican force, sent in a flag and asked for a conference with a view to capitulation. General Taylor acceded to the proposition, and appointed General Worth, Governor Henderson, and myself commissioners to arrange the terms of capitulation. General Taylor received the city of Monterey, with supplies, much needed by his army, and shelter for the wounded. The enemy gained only the privilege of retiring peacefully, a privilege which, if it had not been accorded, they had the power to take by any one of the three roads open to them. The point beyond which they should withdraw was fixed by the terms of capitulation, and the time during which hostilities were to be suspended was determined on by the length of time necessary to refer to and receive answers from the two governments. A few days before the expiration of the time so fixed, the Government of the United States disapproved of the capitulation, and ordered the truce to be immediately terminated. By this decision we lost whatever credit had been given to us for generous terms in the capitulation, and hostilities were to be resumed without any preparations having been made to enable General Taylor, even with the small force he had, to advance farther into the enemy's country. General Taylor's letter to Mr. Marcy, Secretary of War, was a very good response to an unjust criticism; and in the *Washington Union* of that time I also published a very full explanation of the acts of the commissioners, and of the military questions involved in the matter of capitulation in preference to continuing the siege and attack.

General Taylor, assuming that it was intended for him to advance into the interior of Mexico, then commenced to prepare himself for such a campaign. To this end he made requisitions for the needful transportation, as well as munitions, including, among other supplies, large india-rubber bags in which to carry provisions for days, and which, being emptied before we reached the desert of sixty miles, would, by being filled with water, enable his troops and horses to cross those desert plains. These and other details had been entered into under the expectation that the censure of the treaty of Monterey meant a march into the interior of Mexico. Another thing required was a new battery of field-pieces to take the place of the old Ringgold battery, which, by long service, had become honeycombed. When all these arrangements were nearly completed it was decided to send General Scott, with discretionary powers, which enabled him to take nearly all the tried troops General Taylor had, including even the engineer then employed in the construction of a fort, and the battery of new guns to replace the old ones, which were deemed no longer safe, but which, under the intrepid Captain Bragg, afterward did good service in the battle of Buena Vista.

General Taylor, with the main body of his army, went to Victoria, and there made arrangements to send them all to report to General Scott, at Vera Cruz, except the small force he considered himself entitled to as an escort on his route back to Monterey through an unfriendly people. That escort consisted of a battery of light artillery, a squadron of dragoons, and the regiment of Mississippi riflemen. With these he proceeded through Monterey and Saltillo to Agua Nueva, where he was joined by the division of General Wool, who had made the campaign of Chihuahua.

General Santa Anna, commanding the army of Mexico, was informed of the action which had been taken in stripping General Taylor of his forces, and was also informed that he had at Saltillo only a handful of volunteers, which could be easily dispersed on the approach of an army. Thus assured, and with the prospect of recovering all the country down to the Rio Grande, Santa Anna advanced upon Agua Nueva.

General Taylor retired to the Angostura Pass, in front of the Hacienda of Buena Vista, and there made his dispositions to receive the anticipated attack. As sage as he was brave, his dispositions were made as well as the small force at his command made it possible. After two days of bloody fighting General Santa Anna retired before this little force, the greater part of which had never before been under fire.

The encounter with the enemy was very bloody. The Mississippians lost many of their best men, for each of whom, however, they slew several of the enemy. For, trained marksmen, they never touched the trigger without having an object through both sights; and they seldom fired without drawing blood. The infantry against whom the advance was made was driven back, but the cavalry then moved to get in the rear of the Mississippians, and this involved the necessity of falling back to where the plain was narrow, so as to have a ravine on each flank.

In this position the second demonstration of the enemy's cavalry was received. They were repulsed, and it was quiet in front of the Mississippians until an aide came and called from the other side of the ravine, which he could not pass, that General Taylor wanted support to come as soon as possible for the protection of the artillery on the right flank. The order was promptly obeyed at double quick, although the distance must have been nearly a mile. They found the enemy moving in three lines upon the batteries of Captain Braxton Bragg and the section of artillery commanded by George H. Thomas. The Mississippians came up in line, their right flank opposite the first line of the advancing enemy, and at a very short range opened fire. All being sharpshooters, those toward the left of the line obliqued to the right, and at close quarters and against three long lines very few shots could have missed. At the same time the guns of Bragg and Thomas were firing grape. The effect was decisive; the infantry and artillery of the enemy immediately retired.

At the close of the day Santa Anna bugled the retreat, as was supposed, to go into quarters; but when the next sun rose there was no enemy in our front.

The news of this victory was received in the United States with a degree of enthusiasm proportionate to the small means with which it was achieved; and generosity was excited by the feeling that General Taylor had been treated with injustice. Thenceforward the march of "Old Rough and Ready" to the White House was a foregone conclusion.

In this battle, while advancing to meet the enemy, then pressing some of our discomfited volunteers on the left of the field of battle, I received a painful wound, which was rendered more severe in consequence of remaining in the saddle all day, although wounded early in the morning. A ball had passed through the foot, leaving in the wound broken bones and foreign matter, which the delay had made it impossible then to extract. In consequence I had to return home on crutches.

In the meantime a Senator of Mississippi had died, and the Governor had appointed me his successor. Before my return home President Polk had also appointed me Brigadier-General of Volunteers; an appointment which I declined on the ground that volunteers are militia, and that the Constitution reserved to the State the appointment of all militia officers. This was in 1847. In January, 1848, the Mississippi Legislature unanimously elected me United States Senator for the rest of the unexpired term; and in 1850 I was re-elected for the full term as my own successor. In the United States Senate I was Chairman of the Military Committee; and I also took an active part in the debates on the Compromise measures of 1850, frequently opposing Senator Douglas, of Illinois, in his theory of squatter sovereignty, and advocating, as a means of pacification, the extension of the Missouri Compromise line to the Pacific. When the question was presented to Mississippi as to whether the State should acquiesce in the Compromise legislation of 1850, or whether it should join the other Southern States in a Convention to decide as to the best course to pursue in view of the threatened usurpations of the Federal Government, I advocated a Convention of the Southern States, with a view to such co-operation as might effectually check the exercise of constructive powers, the parent of despotism, by the Federal Government.

The canvass for Governor commenced that year. The candidate of the Democratic party was by his opponents represented to hold extreme opinions—in other words, to be a disunionist. For, although he was a man of high character and had served the country well in peace and war, this supposition was so artfully cultivated that, though the Democratic party was estimated to be about eight thousand in majority, when the election occurred in September the Democratic candidates for a Convention were defeated by a majority of over seven thousand, and the Democratic candidate for Governor withdrew.

The election for Governor was to occur in November, and I was called on to take the place vacated by the candidate who had withdrawn from the canvass. It was a forlorn hope, especially as my health had been impaired by labors in the summer canvass, and there was not time before the approaching election to make such a canvass as would be needed to reform the ranks of the Democracy. However, as a duty to the party I accepted the position, and made as active a campaign as time permitted, with the result that the majority against the party was reduced to less than one thousand. From this time I remained engaged in quiet farm-labors until the nomination of Franklin Pierce, when I went out to advocate his election, having formed a very high opinion of him as a statesman and a patriot, from observations of him in 1837 and 1838, when he was in the United States Senate.

On his election as President, I became a member of his cabinet, filling the office of Secretary of War during his entire term.

During these four years I proposed the introduction of camels for service on the Western plains, a suggestion which was adopted. I also introduced an improved system of infantry tactics; effected the substitution of iron for wood in gun-carriages; secured rifled muskets and rifles and the use of Minié balls; and advocated the increase of the defences of the sea-coast, by heavy guns and the use of large-grain powder.

While in the Senate I had advocated, as a military necessity and as a means of preserving the Pacific Territory to the Union, the construction of a military railway across the continent; and, as Secretary of War, I was put in charge of the surveys of the various routes proposed. Perhaps for a similar reason—my previous action in the Senate—I was also put in charge of the extension of the United States Capitol.

The administration of Mr. Pierce presents the single instance of an executive whose cabinet witnessed no change of persons during the whole term. At its close, having been re-elected to the United States Senate, I re-entered that body.

During the discussion of the Compromise measures of 1850 the refusal to extend the Missouri Compromise line to the Pacific was early put on the ground that there was no constitutional authority to legislate slavery into or out of any territory, which was in fact and seeming intent a repudiation of the Missouri Compromise; and it was so treated in the Kansas-Nebraska bill.

Subsequently, Mr. Douglas, the advocate of what was called squatter-sovereignty, insisted upon the rights of the first immigrants into the territory to decide upon the question whether migrating citizens might take their slaves with them; which meant, if it meant anything, that Congress could authorize a few settlers to do what it was admitted Congress itself could not do. But out of this bill arose a dissension which finally divided the Democratic party, and caused its defeat in the Presidential election of 1860.

And from this empty, baseless theory grew the Iliad of our direst woes.

When Congress met, in the fall of 1860, I was appointed one of a Senate Committee of Thirteen to examine and report on some practicable adjustment of the controversies which then threatened the dissolution of the Union. I at first asked to be excused from the Committee, but at the solicitation of friends agreed to serve, avowing my willingness to make any sacrifice to avert the impending struggle. The Committee consisted of men belonging to the three political divisions of the Senate; the State-rights men of the South; the Radicals of the North; and the Northern Democrats; with one member who did not acknowledge himself as belonging to any one of the three divisions—Mr. Crittenden, an old-time Whig, and the original mover of the Compromise Resolutions. When the Committee met it was agreed that, unless some measure which would receive the support of the majority of each of the three divisions could be devised, it was useless to make any report; and, after many days of anxious discussion and a multiplicity of propositions, though the Southern State-rights men and the Northern Democrats and the Whig, Mr. Crittenden, could frequently agree, they could never get a majority of the Northern Radicals to unite with them in any substantive proposition. Finally, the Committee reported their failure to find anything on which the three divisions could unite. Mr. Douglas, who was a member of the Committee, defiantly challenged the Northern Radicals to tell what they wanted. As they had refused everything, he claimed that they ought to be willing to tell what they proposed to do.

When officially informed that Mississippi had passed the ordinance of secession, I took formal leave of the Senate, announcing for the last time the opinions I had so often expressed as to State sovereignty, and, as a consequence of it, the right of a State to withdraw its delegated powers. Before I reached home I had been appointed by the Convention of Mississippi commander-in-chief of its army, with the rank of Major-General, and I at once proceeded with the task of organization. I went to my home in Warren County in order to prepare for what I believed was to be a long and severe struggle. Soon a messenger came from the Provisional Confederate Congress at Montgomery, bringing the unwelcome notice that I had been elected Provisional President of the Confederate States. But, reluctant as I was to accept the honor, and carefully as I had tried to prevent the possibility of it, in the circumstances of the country I could not refuse it; and I was inaugurated at Montgomery, February 18, 1861, with Alexander H. Stephens, of Georgia, as Vice-President.

From this time to the fall of the Confederate Government my life was part of the history of the Confederacy and of the war between the States. It is impossible, therefore, to follow it in detail.

In the selection of a cabinet I was relieved from a difficulty which surrounds that duty by the President of the United States; for there were no "sections" and no "party" distinctions. All aspirations, ambitions, and interests had been merged in a great desire for Confederate independence.

In my inaugural address I asserted that necessity, not choice, had led to the secession of the Southern States; that, as an agricultural people, their policy was peace and free commerce with all the world; that the constituent parts, not the system of government, had been changed.

The removal of the troops from Fortress Moultrie to Fort Sumter, the guns of which threatened the harbor of Charleston, and the attempt to throw reinforcements into that fort—thus doubly breaking a pledge that matters should be kept *in statu quo* —constituted the occasion as well as the justification of the opening of fire upon Fort Sumter. Speedily following this event came the call for a large army by Mr. Lincoln, and the secession of other Southern States as the consequence of this unmistakable purpose of coercion.

Virginia, which had led in the effort, by a Peace Conference, to avert national ruin, when she saw the Constitution disregarded and the purpose to compel free States by military force to submit to arbitrary power, passed an Ordinance of Secession, and joined the Confederate States.

Shortly after this, as authorized by the Provisional Congress, I removed the Confederate capital from Montgomery to Richmond.

Among the many indications of good-will shown when on my way to and after my arrival at Richmond was the purchase of a very fine residence in Richmond, by leading citizens. It was offered as a present; but, following a rule that had governed my action in all such cases, I declined to accept it. I continued to live in Richmond until the Confederate forces were compelled to withdraw from the defences of the capital.

That event was not quite unexpected, but it occurred before the conditions were fulfilled under which General Lee contemplated retreat. After General Lee was forced to surrender, and General Johnston consented to do so, I started, with a very few of the men who volunteered to accompany me, for the trans-Mississippi; but, hearing on the road that marauders were pursuing my family, whom I had not seen since they left Richmond, but knew to be *en route* to the Florida coast, I changed my direction, and, after a long and hard ride, found them encamped and threatened by a robbing party. To give them the needed protection I travelled with them for several days, until in the neighborhood of Irwinville, Ga., when I supposed I could safely leave them. But, hearing, about nightfall, that a party of marauders were to attack the camp that night, and supposing them to be pillaging deserters from both armies, and that the Confederates would listen to me, I awaited their coming, lay down in my travelling clothes, and fell asleep. Late in the night my colored coachman aroused me with the intelligence that the camp was attacked; and I stepped out of the tent where my wife and children were sleeping, and saw at once that the assailants were troops deploying around the encampment. I so informed my wife, who urged me to escape. After some hesitation, I consented, and a servant-woman started with me carrying a bucket as if going to the spring for water. One of the surrounding troops ordered me to halt, and demanded my surrender. I advanced toward the trooper, throwing off a shawl which my wife had put over my shoulders. The trooper aimed his carbine, when my wife, who witnessed the act, rushed forward and threw her arms around me, thus defeating my intention, which was, if the trooper missed his aim, to try to unhorse him and escape with his horse. Then, with every species of petty pillage and offensive exhibition, I was taken from point to point until incarcerated in Fortress Monroe. There I was imprisoned for two years before being allowed the privilege of the writ of habeas corpus.[1]

At length, when the writ was to be issued, the condition was imposed by the Federal Executive that there should be bondsmen influential in the "Republican" party of the North, Mr. Greeley being specially named. Entirely as a matter of justice and legal right, not from motives of personal regard, Mr. Greeley, Mr. Gerrit Smith, and other eminent Northern citizens went on my bond.

In May, 1867, after being released from Fortress Monroe, I went to Canada, where my older children were, with their grandmother; my wife, as soon as permitted, having shared my imprisonment, and brought our infant daughter with her. From time to time I obeyed summonses to go before the Federal Court at Richmond, until, finally, the case was heard by Chief Justice Chase and District Judge Underwood, who were divided in opinion, which sent the case to the Supreme Court of the United States, and the proceedings were quashed, leaving me without the opportunity to vindicate myself before the highest Federal Court.

After about a year's residence in Canada I went to England with my family under an arrangement that I was to have sixty days' notice whenever the United States Court required my presence. After being abroad in England and on the Continent about a year, I received an offer of an appointment as President of a Life Insurance Company. Thereupon I returned to this country, and went to Memphis and took charge of the company. Subsequently I came to the Gulf Coast of Mississippi, as a quiet place where I could prepare my work on "The Rise and Fall of the Confederate Government." A friend from her infancy, Mrs. Dorsey shared her home with me, and subsequently sold to me her property of Beauvoir, an estate of five or six hundred acres, about midway between Mobile and New Orleans. Before I had fully paid for this estate Mrs. Dorsey died, leaving me her sole legatee. From the spring of 1876 to the autumn of 1879 I devoted myself to the production of the historical work just

[1] For a fuller account of my arrest see statements of United States Senator Reagan; W. R. Johnston, President Tulane University; F. R. Lubbock, Treasurer of Texas; B. N. Harrison, Esq., of New York City, all eyewitnesses. Also "The Rise and Fall of the Confederate Government," page 700, vol. II; and for my life at Fortress Monroe, "The Prison Life of Jefferson Davis," by Dr. L. J. J. Craven; New York: Carleton, 1866.

mentioned. It is an octavo book, in two volumes of about seven hundred pages each. I have also from time to time contributed essays to the *North American Review* and *Belford's Magazine,* and have just completed the manuscript of ''A Short History of the Confederate States of America,'' which is expected to appear early in 1890.

Since settling at Beauvoir, I have persistently refused to take any active part in politics, not merely because of my disfranchisement, but from a belief that such labors could not be made to conduce to the public good, owing to the sectional hostilities manifested against me since the war. For the same reason I have also refused to be a candidate for public office, although it is well known that I could at any time have been re-elected a Senator of the United States.

I have been twice married, the second time being in 1845, to a daughter of William B. Howell, of Natchez, a son of Governor Howell, of New Jersey. She has borne me six children—four sons and two daughters. My sons are all dead; my daughters survive. The elder is Mrs. Hayes, of Colorado Springs, Col., and the mother of four children. My youngest daughter lives with us at Beauvoir, Miss. Born in the last year of the war, she became familiarly known as ''the daughter of the Confederacy.''

JEFFERSON DAVIS.

Beauvoir, Miss., November, 1889.

VOL. I

CONTENTS

CONTENTS

CONTENTS

CONTENTS

CONTENTS xxxvii

JEFFERSON DAVIS, CONSTITUTIONALIST
HIS LETTERS, PAPERS AND SPEECHES

Jefferson Davis to John C. Calhoun.[1]

(From New York Public Library Collections.)

Lexington, July 7th 1824.

Transylvania Univer

Sir,

The commission of Cadet granted the undersigned March 11th, and remitted to Natchez, on account of my absence was forwarded here. I accept it.

Am not able to go on before Sept. for reasons I will explain to the superintendent on my arrival.

Yours &c

Jefferson Davis.

J. C. Calhoun.

---

[1] Calhoun, John Caldwell (1782-1850), an American statesman of the States-rights school, was born of Scotch descent, in Abbeville district, S. C., March 18, 1872; was graduated from Yale College in 1804; studied law in Litchfield, Conn., and in an office in Charleston, S. C., and was admitted to the bar in 1807. He was a member of the South Carolina general assembly 1808-1809 and of the national House of Representatives from March 4, 1811, to March 3, 1817; was Secretary of War from December 10, 1817, to March 3, 1825; was Vice President of the United States from March 4, 1825, to December 28, 1832; U. S. Senator from December 12, 1832, to March 3, 1843, and from November 26, 1845, to March 31, 1850; Secretary of State from April 1, 1844, to March 6, 1845. He died in Washington, D. C., March 31, 1850. Calhoun was the author of the South Carolina doctrine of nullification, which conceded to each State the right to nullify any United States law which the State regarded as unconstitutional. He proposed to check the anti-slavery movement by preventing Northern commerce from entering Southern ports and preferred a dissolution of the Union to a submission to the will of the North with regard to slavery. Consult John C. Calhoun, by Gaillard Hunt, 1 Vol., 335 pp., Philadelphia, 1908, and W. M. Meigs, Life of John C. Calhoun, 2 vols., 934 pp., New York, 1917.

Jefferson Davis to Mrs. Susannah Davis

(From the Memoir of Jefferson Davis, by his wife, vol. 1, pp. 33-4.)

Lexington, August 2, 1824.

Dear Sister: It is gratifying to hear from a friend, especially one from whom I had not heard so long as yourself, but the intelligence contained in yours was more than sufficient to mar the satisfaction of hearing from any one. You must imagine I cannot describe the shock my feelings sustained at the sad intelligence. In my father I lost a parent ever dear to me, but rendered more so (if possible) by the disasters that attended his declining years.[1]

When I saw him last he told me we would probably never see each other again. Yet I still hoped to meet him once more, but heaven has refused my wish. This is the second time I have been doomed to receive the heart-rending intelligence of the *Death of a Friend*. God only knows whether or not it will be the last. If all the dear friends of my childhood are to be torn from me, I care not how soon I may follow.

I leave in a short time for West Point, State of New York, where it will always give me pleasure to hear from you.

Kiss the children for Uncle Jeff. Present me affectionately to Brother Isaac; tell him I would be happy to hear from him; and to yourself the sincere regard of

Your Brother,
Jefferson.

Mrs. Susannah Davis,
Warrenton, Warren County, Miss.

Jefferson Davis to George W. Jones [2]

(From the State Historical Department of Iowa.)

West Warrenton Mi
9th Feby 1839

My dear Jones,

If I were a "whig" I should begin this letter by a Phillipic against Amos Kendall, in this, that your much valued favor

---

[1] Samuel Davis, father of Jefferson Davis, died July 4, 1824, and is buried at the Davis farm in Wilkinson county, Mississippi, near Woodville.

[2] Jones, George Wallace (1804-1896), an American political leader, was born in Vincennes, Ind., April 12, 1804; was graduated from the Transylvania University in 1824, studied law and served as clerk of the U. S.

of 16th Dec. '38 did not reach me until the news-papers had brought such intelligence as rendered it probable that my answer would not find you in Washington D. C. the further information received by me induced me to send this to your home, a place hallowed in my memory by associations of friendship and kindly feeling.

I will not pretend that I do not regret the decision of the House of Reps. in the Wisconsin Ty. case, yet my regrets are mitigated by the assurance that your inter-ests will be advanced by your presence at home and that the happiness you will find in the midst of your amiable family will greatly exceed all you could have hoped for at Washington that hot bed of heartlessness and home of the world's worldly.

Although I have seen on former occasions a man's best feelings used as weapons of assault against him, I had not conceived that the disinterested sacrifice you made to support Mr. Cilley and the pain and difficulty you encountered because of your connection with that affair, could be arrayed against you, and I am glad to perceive that you have not recoiled with disgust from a constituency so little able to appreciate your motives.

Doty is too cunning to last long, and the "little man that writes for the news-papers" will probably find himself too poorly paid to play into his hand again—

The President in refusing your appointment as Govr. of Iowa pursued the same shackled electioneering policy that caused him to call an Extra session of Congress and covered the financial part of his last message with the spirit of Banking, a policy which may divide the Democrats take from the banner under which the State right's men would have rallied to their aid, but can never propitiate Bank whigs or Federalists; as the head of the democratic party I wish him success, but he had sowed indecision, a plant not suited to the deep furrows ploughed by his predecessors. You perceive that when I write of politics I am out of my element and naturally slip back to seeding

District Court for Missouri in 1826-1827. He removed to Sinsinawa Mound, Michigan Territory (now Wisconsin), in 1827; served in the Black Hawk war on the staff of General Henry Dodge; was a Michigan delegate in Congress, 1835-1836, and a Wisconsin delegate, 1837-1839; Surveyor General of public lands for Wisconsin and Iowa from January 29, 1840, to July 4, 1841, and from January 3, 1846, to December, 1848; U. S. Senator from Iowa from December 7, 1848, to March 3, 1859; U. S. Minister to Bogota from March, 1859, to July, 1861. Shortly after his return from Bogota Jones was arrested in New York on a charge of disloyalty based on a friendly letter to Jefferson Davis and was imprisoned for sixty-four days in Fort Lafayette, when he was released by order of President Lincoln. He died in Dubuque, Iowa, July 22, 1896.

and ploughing about which I hope to talk with you all next summer.

It gave me much pleasure to hear that I was not forgotten by Dr. Linn [1] and Mr. Allen [2] I esteem them both, and I *love* the Doctor.—I have written to you I scarcely know about what but it all means I am interested in whatever concerns you and wish to hear from you often. My health is better than when we parted, and I hope to visit Sinsinawa next summer looking something less pale and yellow than when we met last winter—

Present my remembrances and kindest regards to your Lady and believe me to be

most sincerely yr. friend
Jeff'n. Davis

Geo. W. Jones
Sinsinawa

Jefferson Davis to William Allen.[3]

(From Manuscripts Division, Library of Congress.)

Warren County Mi., 24th July 1840.

"I long hae thought my honored friend
A something to ha'e sent ye," and though I have nothing now more than my thanks for your kind recollection of me and these in my heart I have often returned to you. I take the occasion of your return from the sphere of your public duties to break perhaps you will say the only repose which those duties leave you to enjoy—well, I bring my offering of thanks, the sacrifice of a pure spirit would always burn. I am willing that mine should be adjudged by that test. I received your speech of Feby. eleventh on the assumption of State debts and could but illy express to you the gratification it gave me as your friend and as such I candidly tell you, I consider it the best

---

[1] Lewis Fields Linn, United States Senator from Missouri, 1833-1843.
[2] William Allen, United States Senator from Ohio, 1837-1849.
[3] Allen, William (1806-1879), statesman, born in Edinton, N. C., in 1806; when sixteen years of age he walked from Lynchburg, Va., to Chillicothe, Ohio, to join his half sister, the mother of Allen G. Thurman; admitted to the bar in 1827; elected to the national House of Representatives in 1832 as a Democrat, was the youngest member of the 23rd Congress; was elected U. S. Senator from Ohio in 1837 at the very early age of thirty-one years, was re-elected in 1843; in 1848 Senator Allen declined a joint offer of the Cass and Van Buren men to make him the Democratic nominee for president, but he refused on the ground that he was the friend and adviser of Cass; elected governor of Ohio in 1873; he died July 11, 1879.

English sample of the Demosthenean style. I recollect you saw
in Mr. Calhoun's speech on the independent Treasy. an especial
likeness to the Grecian orator. I thought he was too senten-
tious, nor indeed could any one opening a question of expediency or dwelling on details of finances speak as Demosthenes
did when he addressed men nearly as well informed as himself
on the subject of which he spoke and addressed them not to
argue but to lay bare before them the true issue and excite them
to action—but perhaps, like the Vicar of Wakefield said to the
lecturer on Cosmogony you may say to me—however with this
difference that instead of once you may have heard all this a
dozen times before and that instead of the second it is the first
time you have heard it from me. Before I quit the subject of
speeches I must tell you of an old democratic friend of mine
who lives some distance back in the hills and who notwithstanding the great increase of post offices is quite out of striking
distance of a mail line. He came to see me in the spring of '38.
I handed him your speech on the independent Treasy. Bill after
reading it. He asked me to let him take it home and show it to
some of his neighbors. I have seen him frequently since but his
"neighbors" have not yet gotten through with it. When Lord
Byron saw an American edition of his works he said it seemed
like to posthumous fame. Recurring to my old friend of the
hills, he states it as a political maxim that "no honest sensible
whig can read Allen's and Benton's speeches without turning
their politics."

I am living as retired as a man on the great thoroughfare
of the Mississippi can be, and just now the little society which
exists hereabout has been driven away by the presence of the
summer's heat and the fear of the summer's disease.

Our staple, cotton, is distressingly low and I fear likely to
remain so until there is a diminished production of it, an event
which the embarassed condition of cotton planters in this section will not allow them to consider. If our Yankee friends
and their coadjutors should get up a scheme for bounties to
particular branches of industry I think the cotton growers may
come in with the old plea of the manufacturers "not able at
present to progress without it."

With assurances of sincere regard and of the pleasure it will
always give me to hear from you and to mark your success
I am yr. friend
JEFFN. DAVIS

To W. Allen
At home

Speech of Jefferson Davis before the State Democratic Convention held in Jackson Mississippi January 3, 1844, for the purpose of sending delegates to the National Convention of the party and for the selection of presidential electors.[1]

(From The Mississippian, January 12, 1844.)

Mr. Davis remarked in substance—Though instructed by the delegation from Warren to cast the vote of our county, in this convention, for Mr. Van Buren, as the presidential candidate, I hope I will be excused for availing myself of the nomination of Mr. Calhoun, to express some of my opinions, as an individual, in relation to the comparative claims these gentlemen have upon us. I would here premise, that I wish nothing which I may say to be referred to a willingness to depreciate the high, just, and often-acknowledged claims of Mr. Van Buren; a democrat who long and severely tried, has never been found wanting— a democrat, than whom there is none I have more implicit confidence—none to whom I would more freely confide in times of difficulty, of danger, and of personal temptation, the safe keeping of the constitution; and in proof of the correctness of this opinion, I will refer to but a single instance: When the "independent treasury" was opposed by a prejudice so fixed and wide-spread among our people, that it was apparent if one had risen from the dead to bear testimony to its merits, he would not have been believed, still did Mr. Van Buren give it his open, decided and unwavering support. Surely it will not now be contended by those who attribute to him so much political shrewdness as to attach to him the name of magician, that he was ignorant of the danger to which an adherence to this measure exposed his political fortune. Upon us, however, it forces itself as conclusive evidence, that he valued truth and the good of his country above power and place, and the conscientious discharge of his duty above personal advancement.

Mr. President, it is not my purpose to attempt an eulogy of Mr. Calhoun. I should be inadequate to the task, and should deem the labor superfluous in the hand of the most able —a long public life of virtue and intelligence, of active and patriotic devotion to the best interest of his country, having shed around his name a halo which it is not in the power of language to brighten. Neither, sir, is it my intention to review

[1] This speech brought Mr. Davis into statewide notice and marked the beginning of his political career. As a delegate from Warren county he favored John C. Calhoun for the presidency.

the political principles of that great statesman; for in comparing him with Mr. Van Buren, I find no exception to that proud and generally just boast of the democracy, that the principles of our party are the same throughout the Union. The points of my preference for Mr. Calhoun will be merely indicated to you; because, resting as they do upon basis so well understood by you, any elucidation of them is uncalled for. First, I will mention "free trade," by which is meant, as I understand it, the most liberal principles of commerce, and from which we may anticipate as a consequence, the freest exchange of the products of different soils and climates, the largest amount of comforts for a given amount of labor. Again, as incident to the freest national intercourse, we may expect the extension of amicable relations, until our canvas-winged doves shall bear us across every sea, olive branches from every land. In addressing Mississippians, who rely upon a foreign market for the disposal of their products, an argument in support of unrestricted commerce is surely unnecessary, and I will close the consideration of this point by saying I consider Mr. Calhoun its exponent.

The annexation of the republic of Texas to our Union, is another point of vital importance to the south, and demanding, by every consideration, prompt action. Daily are we becoming relatively weaker, and with equal step is the advance of that fanatical spirit which has for years been battering in breach the defences with which the federal constitution surrounds our institutions.

Would Mr. Calhoun have less zeal than one less intimately connected with the south, or would he support this measure with less ability? I would answer not less but more. The ardent, able and honest support which he gives to all measures having his entire approbation, enables him more successfully than any one I have ever known, to combat prejudice and error; and I would add that among the many I have known who had enjoyed his intercourse, I recollect not one who had not imbibed some of his opinions.

Again, I believe that Mr. Calhoun could reduce the various divisions of the executive department at Washington to such order, and introduce a system of such prompt accountability, by the various agents, that defalcation could seldom reach that point which would result in loss to the government. That he possesses this ability, I conceive to be demonstrated by his administration of the war department; considered, I believe, of the various departments, that which is most difficult and com-

plex in its disbursements. He found it in great confusion—
he reduced it to an organization so perfect, that it has received
but slight modifications down to the present time, and has been
that department which has afforded but few examples of un-
faithful depositories of the public money.

With the experience he acquired then, and the knowledge
he has acquired since, may we not expect all that I claim for
him on this point?

I will, Mr. President, tax the patience of the convention with
but one point more, and that is one nearly affecting us: it is the
defence of the southern Atlantic and gulf coasts. We have been
treated ungenerously and unjustly, in that the majority has,
through a long course of years, refused to us, the minority,
that protection which it was the duty of the federal government to give us. Having made such appropriations for the
benefit of other portions of the Union, inability has not been
the cause of this failure in duty towards us—a failure which is
aggravated by the recollection that throughout the whole period
of our federal existence, we have contributed, as consumers,
to the revenue, in a higher ratio than that of our representation in the halls of legislation, (by the number of our unrepre-
sented slave population,) and therefore our claim to a share of
those appropriations to which we are all entitled, is something
stronger than our representative rate. Sir, if we institute a
comparison as to the importance, in a national point of view,
between the objects for which we require appropriations and
those for which we have been neglected, still do we find nothing to justify the treatment we have received. Whilst the
northern harbors and cities have been surveyed, and as far as
the ability of the treasury would allow, fortified—whilst navy
yards have been erected along the northern coast—whilst surveys have been made of the sinuosities of our northern lakes,
sometimes where it required the perspective eye of the engineer
to see a harbor, and millions expended year after year, for
these joint purposes, there stand the cape and keys of Florida
unprotected, though by them flows the whole commerce of
the south and west, and though they overlook the straits through
which, in peace or war, is the only maritime communication
between the different portions of our Union, and around which
sweeps a wide curve of circumvallation, extending from the
Oronoko to the banks of the Bahama, from various points of
which, within signal distance, from the batteries of Great
Britain.

Looking further westward, which brings us nearer home—

here upon our own coast lie, wholly unprotected, the islands upon which the British fleet found a safe anchorage and harbor; where British troops debarked for the attack on New Orleans, an event which, though it brought glory to the American arms, and made this day an American festival, does not the less enforce itself as a warning on our government, and should have proved sufficient reason to all who loved their country more than sectional interest, to have guarded against the recurrence of such contingency.

Mr. President, the South has a delicate and daily increasing interest in the navy. She needs her own sons in the navy to represent that interest; she therefore needs in her own waters navy yards, and squadrons at home, on her own waters, to develope the nautical feeling of our youth. A survey made of the Tortugas, by the recommendation of that great man who directed the glorious event to which I but just now alluded as connected with the day on which we are assembled, exhibits a harbor admirably adapted to the purposes of a navy yard. At Pensacola, we have another favorable point, so recognized by our government in building a dock and giving it the name of "navy yard;" and they both have this great advantage over any northern harbor, they are convenient to "live oak," our most important ship timber.

Sir, I will not detain the Convention farther than to urge upon their consideration the necessity we have for a Southern President to advance these measures. The South has borne long; let her be true to herself, that justice may be done.

Jefferson Davis, of Warren, offered the following resolution, which was unanimously adopted.

Resolved, That our delegates to the national convention, in the event of any contingency which shall defeat the purpose for which they are appointed, viz., the nominations of Martin Van Buren for president, and James K. Polk for vice president, that they shall consider as our second choice, John C. Calhoun for president, and Levi Woodbury for vice-president.

Jefferson Davis to William Allen.

(From Manuscripts Division, Library of Congress.)

Hurricane Mi., 25th March 1844.

Hon. Sen. Allen of Ohio,

Dr. Sir,

"The sick man knows the Physician's step," but I assure you that if breaking a long silence to ask a favor of you should expose me to the suspicion of remembering you only because of my trouble, the fact is nevertheless quite otherwise. I am one of the Presidential "electors" for the State of Mississippi and though I do not doubt the democratic character of our people I fear false statements and false issues in the approaching canvass and expect the Whigs to make great exertions.

I wish you to aid me with any statements which can be made available against the charge of *defalcation* and extravagance under Mr. Van Buren's administration, against the present Tariff as productive of revenue, against the U. S. Bank, against the charge of improper removals of officers and if there be such statement the removals in the first year of Harrison & Tyler's administration. Further I should be glad to have the evidence of Mr. Clay's refusal to divide the resolution of censure upon President Jackson for the removal of the deposits and the rule of the senate in relation to the division of questions, Secretary Taney's report on the removal of the deposits from the U. S. Bank, Secretary Poinset's annual report recommending reorganization of the militia and answer to call of the house on the same subject. Was not President V. Buren one of the first to point out the unconstitutionality of the military districts as projected in that answer? I had but cannot now find a speech of yours showing that the U. S. Bank loaned at a time which indicated the purpose, more money to members of Congress than the amount of their pay. Can you send me a copy of that speech?

I have mingled but little in politics and as you perceive by this letter have an arsenal poorly supplied for a campaign. Labor is expected of me and I am willing to render it. I believe much depends on this presidential election, and that every man who loves the union and the constitution as it is should be active.

You will understand what I want or should want better than myself, so far as you can conveniently send such you will greatly oblige me, and any suggestions you may find leisure to make to me will be highly appreciated.

Vy. Respectfully and truly yours

JEFFN. DAVIS

Wm. Allen
Washington
D. C.
P. S.
Address to Warrenton,
Warren County,
Missi.

Jefferson Davis [1] *to Martin Van Buren.* [2]

(From the Library of Congress Manuscripts Division.)

(near) Warrenton Missi.

25th March 1844

M. Van Buren

Ex President of the U. S.

Sir,

Though I have often recurred to the period when I had the honor to enjoy your personal acquaintance and have always remembered it with pleasure, the probability of your having forgotten me is not the less understood—To excuse myself for the liberty I take in thus addressing you, I will state that the democratic convention of this state which decided in your favor as the candidate of the Democracy for the next presidency, placed me on the electoral ticket for the state—and in view of the approaching presidential canvass, and with no doubt of the ratification by the National Convention of so much of our action as refers to yourself, I have determined to call upon you for answers to three points which I expect to be opened and think could not be otherwise as well closed

With great respect I am

etc., etc., yrs.

Jeffn. Davis

(endorsed on Sheet No. 15)

His Excellency M. Van Buren   Jeffn Davis

Ex President of the U. S.   Mississippi

Kinderhook   25th March 1844

New York

---

[1] During a visit to Washington in 1838 Mr. Davis had been a guest of President Van Buren.

[2] Van Buren, Martin (1782-1862), eighth President of the United States, was born, of Dutch descent, in Kinderhook, N. Y., December 5, 1782; was educated in the common schools and Kinderhook academy, studied law in New York City, and was admitted to the bar in 1803. He was a member of the New York Senate, 1813-1820; Attorney General of New York from January 1 to March 12, 1829; Secretary of State from March 12, 1829, to August 1, 1831; Vice President of the United States from March 4, 1833, to March 4, 1837; and President from March 4, 1837, to March 4, 1841. Van Buren was appointed Minister to Great Britain in 1831 but the Senate refused to confirm the appointment. He was defeated in the presidential campaign of 1840 for re-election and was the unsuccessful anti-slavery candidate in 1848. He died in Kinderhook, N. Y., July 24, 1862. Consult Edward M. Shepard, Martin Van Buren, 499 pp., Boston, 1900.

Jefferson Davis to Martin Van Buren.[1]

(From The South in the Building in the Nation, Vol. XI, p. 262.)

Warren County Mi.

M. Van Buren   25th March 1844
Ex President of the U. S.

Sir,

You will oblige me and many other democrats of this section of the country by giving your opinion on the following questions—

First, The annexation of "Texas" to the Territory of the United States

Second, The constitutional power of Congress over slavery in the District of Columbia

Third, The Tariff of 1828 and whether your vote on that bill was entirely the result of the instructions you received—

With great consideration

I am very truly yrs.

Jeffn. Davis

Jefferson Davis to J. A. Quitman.[2]

(From Mississippi Department of Archives and History.)

S. B. Ambassador
11th Dec. 1844

Dear Sir,

Herewith I send you the paper on currency of which I spoke to you when I last had the pleasure to see you—valuable only

---

[1] Mr. Van Buren was a candidate for the presidential nomination at this time, and the Mississippi delegation to the Democratic Convention at Baltimore had been instructed for him.

[2] Quitman, John Anthony (1799-1858), an American soldier and political leader, was born in Rhinebeck, N. Y., September 1, 1799; graduated from Hartwick seminary in 1816; was instructor in Mount Airy college, Penn., 1818-1819; studied law in Chillicothe, Ohio, and in 1821 was practicing law at Natches, Miss. He was a member of the Mississippi House of Representatives 1826-1827; Chancellor of the State 1828-1834; State Senator 1834-1836, serving as president of the Senate and acting governor 1835-1836; served with distinction as brigadier general and as major general in the Mexican war; was Governor of Mississippi 1850-1851; and a member of the national House of Representatives from March 4, 1855, until his death in Natchez, Miss., July 17, 1858. While governor he engaged in negotiations with General Lopez relative to a filibustering expedition to capture Cuba. He was indicted, resigned office, and was tried. The jury disagreed. He was arrested on a similar charge in 1854 but was not tried. Consult J. F. H. Claiborne, Life and Correspondence of John A. Quitman, 2 vols., 792 pp., New York, 1860.

as one of the branches of the besiegers against which we should be prepared to countermine.[1]—

Please offer my respectful regards to your family and believe me very sincerely yrs. &c

Jeffn. Davis

Genl. J. A. Quitman⎱
    Natches   ⎰
Endorsed: Jef Davis Decr. 1845

Jefferson Davis to Editor of the Sentinel.

(From Mississippi Department of Archives and History.)

Brierfield July 5th 1845.

To the Editor of the Sentinel,
Sir,

In your Paper of the 30th ulto. I find a communication calling on me for my views in relation to the Bank act:—commonly known as the "Briscoe Bill."[2] Your correspondent attaches

[1] During the presidential campaign of 1844 Jefferson Davis was one of the candidates for elector on the Democratic ticket.

[2] Says S. H. Fulkerson in his "Random Recollections," describing the times following the speculative collapse of 1837, "Litigated cases were very numerous owing to the financial troubles of the day, and though circuit court would hold for four weeks, the docket was never cleared." After judgment was rendered the attorneys would resort to writs of supersedeas and certiorari, and after the passage by the legislature of the State, in 1843, of what was known as the Briscoe bill, the writ of quo warranto would be invoked in the bank cases, of which there were many.

The farmers who visited Fulkerson as deputy clerk called the latter "the curanter." The writ of quo warranto was of course nothing new, but the Briscoe bill gave it special sanction against the banks, which were not able to redeem their bills. Under the Briscoe bill "proceedings by quo warranto were instituted against nearly every bank in the State to have them dissolved and thus to get rid of the debts due to them." (Mayes.) The bill was introduced by Briscoe, of Claiborne, and amended by Judge Guion to protect creditors. The bill passed July, 1843, over great opposition. Fulkerson points out the curious coincidence that there was a Briscoe proposition before the house of commons in 1693 for supplying the king with easy money and exempting the nobility from taxation by a national land bank. But it was the collapse of a scheme of this kind that the Briscoe bill applied to.

At the January term, 1846, of the High Court of Errors and Appeals, Justice Clayton delivered an opinion sustaining the Guion amendment to the Briscoe bill; Chief Justice Sharkey concurred, and Justice Thatcher dissented. The sections of the law against which the contest was made required "that when a judgment of forfeitures is entered against a bank, its debtors shall not be thereby released from their debts and liabilities, but that the court rendering such judgment shall appoint one or more trustees to take charge of the banks and assets of the same—to sue for and collect all debts due it—to sell all its property and apply the same as

to my opinions a value to which they are not entitled and attributes to me an influence I certainly do not possess. Others as I have been informed also desire from me such a statement and as I have no opinions which I wish to conceal they are herein submitted, with no other hesitation than that which arises from an unwillingness to appear before the public, and with no other request than that this answer shall not be construed into an admission of my being a candidate for any office. Of the question, in its strictly legal character I am not able to judge, and will not offer an opinion. As a measure of policy and justice, every man's political right constitutes him an umpire and every man's conscience must dictate his decision. It seems to me that the question has been changed from its true nature, the rights of Creditors against the obligations of Debtors, into an issue of the Banks against the Country, and its Laws. Were the latter the true question, I certainly have no favor for the Banks which could draw me from my duty to the country. From my earliest inquiries into the policy of a paper currency, I have believed it to be an unqualified evil to an agricultural people, especially one like ourselves engaged in the product of a staple of export. As we sell for the currency of the world, if we have a local currency which is cheaper, we must pay the enhanced price for all that we buy, and thus lose the difference. Its action may be likened to selling by a large measure and buying by a small one. To show that my opinion on the subject of Bank forfeitures is free from the bias of any personal interest, I will state that I have never owned a share of Bank stock nor borrowed a dollar from a Bank. The various opinions in relation to this question may be arranged in three classes. 1st,—those who hold that when forfeiture is adjudged against a Bank all debts to and from it shall be expunged, the personal effects ("escheat to") become the property of the state and the real estate revert to the original grantor. 2nd,—that after forfeiture the state shall appoint a receiver to collect the assets of the Bank for the benefit of the state. 3rd,—that after forfeiture of franchise, trustees shall be appointed under penal restraints, and with sufficient security, to collect the assets and dispose of the property of the corporation for the benefit of the creditors and stockholders. Among

might be thereafter directed by law, to the payment of its debts.'' The opinion of the court sustained this law.

About the same time the legislature voted against the proposed repeal of the quo warranto law, but the bank-indebted interest obtained the passage of a new law which was regarded by many as much worse than the original Briscoe bill.

the third class, Sir, I arrange myself. No one has openly contended for special legislation to relieve Bank debtors; but it is argued that statutory provision is necessary to give effect to the common law, the operation of which a forfeiture being declared, is asserted to be to wipe out all debts to and from a corporation. The common law is the ancient customs or memorial usages of England and there could have been no such usages in relation to banking corporations for the simple reason that the thing did not exist among them. At the present day, the trade of banking is conducted in that country by private bankers and joint stock companies, deriving their powers and suffering their restraints and penalties, under general acts of Parliament. They do not exist by special grants or charters, and so far as I have learned are proceeded against in the same manner as a mercantile firm which has committed an act of bankruptcy. The bank of England is an exception to this remark, but there the charter provides a mode for terminating its existence, and so far from allowing the government of England to pay its immense debt to that bank by a judgement of forfeiture, expressly provides that the debt shall be paid before the privilege granted be taken away.

Lawyers say that the common law is nothing more than the rules of reason and justice, the definition must be wrong, if the common law will permit an agent to lend out the money of his employers to personal or business friends, and then by an act contravening his duties as an agent, debar the employer from pursuing his money in the hands of the borrower, or if it will permit a banking corporation to throw its notes into circulation and then by refusing to redeem them, deprive the note holders of his remedy against the effects of the bank, or if it will release the debtor from the obligation of his bill given for the notes of the bank and throw the loss upon the note holder who gave the debtor, labor, or property in exchange for the notes, he had borrowed. If this be common law, it is high time it were substituted by statutes accordant with the mandates of reason and of right. Forfeiture, as I have seen it treated in the argument for the first and second class of opinion, constantly carries the mind back to the feudal system, with its Lord paramount.

We have no original grantor of lands retaining reversionary rights, and nothing could be more preposterous than that a man who had sold a house and lot to a banking corporation should claim that the property for which he had been paid, reverted to him as the original grantor, whenever the bank should have forfeited its charter. Equally unjust would I hold an escheat to the state; the grant of the state was a corporate franchise, that, in accordance with the terms of the grant she may reclaim; but it is Anti-American to seize the property of individuals. It is the plundering practice of British confiscation. Our laws provided for the execution of a criminal, but it is contrary to the genius of our government to interfere with the rights of his creditors or heirs. One of the earliest reforms was the expulsion from among us of the English practice of confiscation and attainder. I should be very sorry to see in the minds of any a wish to adopt a measure so germain to the expelled practice, even against the now odious banks. The law as it stands on the statute books is expeditious and seems adequate to protect the rights of all parties, from the time the information is filed; after the bank has been condemned, there is no reprieve, after it has been executed, it cannot be revived.

If the Bill had stopped at the death of the corporation, it is by no means probable that the creditors and stockholders would have abandoned their rights, without a resort to the courts, and long and cumbrous litigation must have been the result. The provision for the appointment of trustees, with the guards and checks it contains, has made the law so far as I can see, all that we want. Already it has received a judicial decision in its favor, the statute stands the adjudicated law of the land and I for one prefer to leave it undisturbed until experience points out its defects. Of the two classes, Creditors and Debtors, the former certainly have the higher claim to kind consideration. Legislation has interfered with the collection of their debts,—thus they were prevented by special law from collecting off the debtors of the insolvent banks, any thing better than the paper of those banks; and at a subsequent period another law was passed prohibiting the banks from transferring its Bills receivable to satisfy the demands of a noteholder. If we should now declare that the forfeiture of a bank charter expunges its debts, well may the creditor complain of our government as having locked up the assets of the banks until it was ready to apply the sponge to all from which he could hope indemnity. Though our present condition forms an exception it is nevertheless a general rule that the few borrow, the many hold the notes of the Banks; it surely must be elsewhere than in the ranks of the Democracy that advocates are to be found contending for the exemption of the few, by sacrificing the rights of the many. Though I have (to answer a position sometimes taken) treated the subject as though a Bank under judgment of forfeiture was a convicted criminal, the reverse is generally known to be the fact. The Quo Warranto is a civil proceeding and a corporation after forfeiture of its franchise is analogous to a deceased person. After the natural death of a person, suits could neither be brought or defended in his name, without a legal provision to that effect, and to my mind the Trustees of a deceased (artificial person) corporation are no more than the administrators or executors of a deceased natural person. This answer, I hope, sir, will suffice for all who thought they were entitled to my opinions, and desired their publication, as well as those who may have wished to submit me to this new political test; and I will now leave the subject where the discussion may be more profitably conducted, in the hands of those learned in the law. If however, it shall be shown that the common law is such as has been represented; I can not yield the opinions herein expressed. My thoughts, my feelings are American,—to England, the robber nation of the earth, whose history is a succession of wrongs and oppressions, whose tracks are marked by the crushed rights of individuals,—to England I cannot go for lessons of morality and justice.

Very respectfully your friend &c.

Jefferson Davis.

Jno. Jenkins Esq.

Sentinel Office, Vicksburg.

(The following communication signed "Cato" is the letter referred to in the foregoing.)

(From Vicksburg Sentinel, June 30, 1845.)

Mr. Editor:—It is with much satisfaction that I learn that the convention on Monday last have determined to present the name of our fellow-citizen Jefferson Davis, Esq., as a proper person to represent our State in the councils of the nation. Those only who know Mr. Davis can properly appreciate him —his urbanity of manners, his gentlemanly deportment, and his kind feelings have justly endeared him to his friends. To know him, is to esteem him highly. His talents which heretofore have been comparatively unknown, owing to the restraints which modesty too frequently imposes, were made manifest in our last Presidential canvass; when some of his speeches for brilliancy, for beauty and force, may be said to have equalled some of the first specimens of modern eloquence. Previously obscure and but little known, at the call of the people, he stepped forth like the fabled goddess, fully armed to do battle for his country; and we all know the result. But Mr. Davis's chief virtue, his pearl of great price, his largest, his brightest jewel, is his spotless integrity; his reputation as an honest man is not only unimpeachable, but above suspicion. And in times like the present when virtue's wand is broken such men are needed. The opinions of Mr. Davis will be listened to with respect, and must have their influence. This is the case in this county; this will be the case wherever he is known.

In view of the influence which his opinions at present exert and are destined to exert to a still greater extent, should he receive the nomination of the coming convention, he will no doubt permit an humble individual who wishes him well through you, Mr. Editor, to request his views on a subject about to be agitated in our next legislative councils and at present dear to the democracy of the Union. I mean what is commonly known as the 'Briscoe bill' in its original form as introduced by the senator from Claiborne.[1] This inquiry will not be con-

THE BRISCOE BILL

[1] *An act to prescribe the mode of proceeding against incorporated banks, for a violation of their corporate franchises, and against persons pretending to exercise corporate privileges, under acts of incorporation, and for other purposes.*

Section 1. *Be it enacted by the Legislature of the State of Mississippi,* That it shall be the duty of each and every district attorney in this State, whenever he shall have reason to believe, or whenever the affidavit of one or more creditable person or persons shall be presented to him, stating that he or they have good reason to believe, and do verily believe that any incorporated bank, located within his district, has been guilty of a violation of any of the provisions of its charter, or has done or omitted to do any act or acts, the doing or omission of which would in law work a forfeiture of its charter, or is commanded or prohibited by its charter, or any statute of the state in relation to banks, forthwith to file a bill in the clerk's office of the circuit court of the county in which such bank shall be located, an information in the nature of a *quo warranto* against such bank, upon the filing of which information, it shall be, and is hereby made the duty of the clerk of such court to issue the proper process against such bank, returnable to the term of the circuit court aforesaid, next succeeding the day on which such information shall be filed.

Sec. 2. That it shall be the duty of each and every district attorney in this state, whenever he shall have reason to believe, or whenever the affidavit of one or more creditable person or persons, shall be presented to him, stating that he or they have good reason to believe, and do verily believe, that any corporation, person or persons are exercising, using and enjoying within the district of such district attorney, without legal warrant and authority, the franchise of being a banking corporation, forthwith to file in the clerk's office of the circuit court of the county in which such franchise shall be so exercised, used and enjoyed, an information in the nature of a *quo warranto*, against the corporation, person or persons aforesaid, upon the filing of which information it shall be, and is hereby made

sidered impertinent when I explain myself. In the first place, although Mr. Davis in the situation which we destine him to occupy, will not be called upon to act in the matter, yet the opinions and views of our public men, on subjects of great political importance, are considered public property, and as

the duty of the clerk of said court, to issue the proper process against such corporation, person or persons, returnable to the term of the circuit court aforesaid next succeeding the day on which such information shall be filed.

Sec. 3. That when process shall be issued against any bank upon information filed under the provisions of this act, the same shall be served by the sheriff or other proper officer, who shall execute the same by delivering a copy thereof to the president, cashier, or secretary of such bank, or if there be no such president, cashier, or secretary, or if the sheriff or other officer is unable to find them, then by leaving a copy of such process at the banking house, or other place of business of said bank; and when process shall be issued against any person or persons, upon information filed in pursuance of the provisions of the second section of this act, such process shall likewise be served by the sheriff or other proper officer, who shall execute the same by delivering a copy to every such person or persons whom he can find in his county, and by leaving a copy for those whom he is unable to find at the banking house or other place occupied for the purpose of exercising the franchises aforesaid.

Sec. 4. That all informations in pursuance of this act, shall be docketed upon the common law issue docket, and shall be tried at the first term of the court after they shall be filed: provided, the process issued against them shall have been served twenty days before the commencement of the court: and provided, that each party shall be entitled to continuance upon the proper showing; said causes shall have priority over all other civil causes upon the docket, and when an issue of fact shall be made up it shall be tried by the ordinary jury in attendance upon the court in the same manner and under the same rules and regulations that govern upon the trial of civil cases.

Sec. 5. That the provisions of this act shall not extend to the funds which legitimately belong to the State of Mississippi, or to the Commercial and rail road bank of Vicksburg, or to the West Feliciana rail road and banking company, so as to affect the rail roads and their operations.

Sec. 6. That upon information being filed in pursuance of the provisions of this act, it shall be the duty of the clerk, as a matter of right, on the part of this state, to issue an injunction or injunctions to restrain all persons from the collection of any demands claimed by said bank or banks, person or persons, or assignees or corporations, and all their officers and agents, or other person or persons, until the said information be finally tried and determined, and said injunction shall have the office and effect of an injunction in chancery; which injunction shall be served by the sheriff or other proper officer of the county in which said information may be filed upon such corporation, bank, assignee or assignees, if any there be, person or persons, or their officers or agents, in like manner as injunctions in chancery are served.

Sec. 7. That none of the provisions of this act shall be so construed as to prevent any bank or corporation, assignee, or assignees, or any of their officers or agents from suing out attachments in the same manner and for the same cause that other creditors are allowed lawfully to do.

[The four following sections constitute the amendments to the original bill.]

Sec. 8. That upon judgment of forfeiture against any bank or banks, corporation or corporations, person or persons, pretending to exercise corporate powers in this state, as contemplated by this act, the debtors of

20   JEFFERSON DAVIS, CONSTITUTIONALIST

such, the people have a right to inquire and expect their inquiries to be answered. Again, when any gentleman of high moral character, having the mind to perceive, and the industry to investigate, who is favorably known and a party leader, favors an important political project and his views become fully known, it thereby acquires a *momentum,* which enables it to overcome all obstacles. Such in a degree may be the effect of the present inquiry.

There is another reason why Mr. Davis should declare his sentiments and make them clearly and unequivocally known: At the convention of Monday last, a resolution was introduced, supposed at the time, and still thought to be adverse to the *bill.* This resolution, if I am not mistaken was advocated by Mr. Davis or claimed to have been so by the enemies of the

such bank or banks, corporation or corporations, person or persons, pretending to exercise corporate privileges, shall not be released by such judgment from their debts and liabilities to the same; but it shall be the duty of the court rendering such judgment to appoint one or more trustees to take charge of the books and assets of the same; to sue for and collect all debts due such bank or banks, corporation or corporations, person or persons pretending to exercise corporate powers, and to sell and dispose of all property owned by such bank or banks, corporation or corporations, person or persons pretending to exercise corporate powers, or held by others for its or their use, and the proceeds of the debts when collected, and of the property when sold, to apply as may hereafter be directed by law to the payment of the debts of such bank or banks, corporation or corporations, or person or persons pretending to exercise corporate powers: provided further, that the notes of any such bank or banks, corporation or corporations, or others pretending to exercise corporate powers, shall at all times be received in payment of any debts due the same.

Sec. 9. That such trustees shall give bond with good and sufficient security, in a penalty to be prescribed by the court or determined by law, conditioned to diligently and faithfully collect the debts due such bank or banks, corporation or corporations, or person or persons pretending to exercise corporate powers, and to sell and dispose of the property belonging to the same, and the proceeds when collected, to pay over as may hereafter be directed by law: provided, however, that the compensation allowed to such trustees shall be paid in preference to all others, but shall in no case be chargeable upon the public treasury.

Sec. 10. That if any trustee shall embezzle or convert to his own use, or fail to pay over to his successor in office, or to others, as may be directed by law, any of the proceeds or assets of any such bank or banks, or other corporations, or person or persons pretending to exercise corporate powers shall, upon indictment and conviction thereof, in addition to the payment of his bond, be imprisoned in the penitentiary not less than two years, nor more than ten, for each and every offence.

Sec. 11. That the foregoing section of this act shall not, nor any part thereof, be so construed as to release any person or persons interested in, or in any way connected with any such bank or banks, corporation or corporations, or person or persons pretending to exercise corporate powers from his individual liabilities, for any fraud or mismanagement of the same.

Sec. 12. That this act shall take effect and be in force from and after its passage.

(From Vicksburg Sentinel, July 11, 1845.)

bill. Some of his friends however, insist that from the confusion that prevailed at the time and the ambiguity of some of the proceedings, his views and feelings have been misinterpreted. Be this as it may, it is right and proper that he should be fully and fairly located, that the people who now see him, *as through a glass, darkly,* may have a clear and distinct view of all his political features. The friends of the measure desire this exposition; its enemies cannot object to it. The fate of Rome and perhaps of Caesar may depend upon it.

Cato.

Jefferson Davis.—Six months ago we expressed the wish of this section of the state to have Jefferson Davis on our next Congressional Ticket. Our wish has been gratified; and triumph and satisfaction rest on the countenance of every democrat among us.

A native of our soil, a free-hearted, open, manly, bold *Mississippian,* and a Democrat to the core, he is destined to be the pride and ornament of our state.

The circumstances under which he has been nominated render his nomination a double triumph, and exhibit a characteristic trait of the man. Upon a minor question of state policy (the Briscoe Bill) he differs from a large portion of the citizens of this part of the state; and that difference he had casually expressed. He was called upon anonymously to express himself publicly on the point. It not being a question in any way touching his acceptability as a member of Congress, (the station to which his friends were anxious to advance him) and the call being anonymous, he might with plausibility have entirely excused himself from replying; and most politicians perhaps, under the circumstances, believing as he did that his reply would inevitably destroy his prospects, would have remained silent. Not so with him. He was determined that no charge should every apply to him that he had kept back his opinions through policy; and under his instructions we, at this office, hastened our press in order that he should lay before the Convention his views upon this question which he thought would cause his defeat. But toleration and harmony—the spirit of casting aside minor and local considerations for the sake of securing soundness and honesty upon great national questions—ruled the hour, he was nominated—and that by the votes of those differing with him upon this.

Doubly triumphant is the securing of such a man in public

life. It is a triumph of straight forward frankness and honesty over the intriguing, non-commitalism, and duplicity which we grieve to say has too much heretofore characterised our public men.

We only bespeak for Mr. Davis the acquaintance of his fellow citizens. We only wish him to be known in other parts of the state as he is at home; and we know that he will become everywhere else as much beloved and esteemed as he is here.

Jefferson Davis to George Bancroft.[1]

(From Confederate Museum.)

House of Reps.
12th. Dec. 1845

To the honble Secy of the Navy,
Sir,

Herewith I have the honor to transmit to you a recommendatory letter which with this I wish you to consider as an application in favor of John Royall Eggleston for a Midshipman's warrant in the U. S. Navy—Descended from a family of some distinction of spotless character the hope may be reasonably indulged that the present promise of the boy will be fulfilled in the man, and the service of the Country be more benefitted than the individual who is hereby offered to it— In addition allow me to add that (if) I am not misinformed) we of Mississippi have had less than our proportionate share of Navy appointments and respectfully asking your attention to the case of Mr. Eggleston, to subscribe myself

yr. mo. obt. sevt.
Jeffer. Davis
M. C. from Mi.

[1] Bancroft, George (1800-1891), an American historian, was born in Worcester, Mass., October 3, 1800; was graduated from Harvard college in 1817, received the degree of Ph. D. from Göttingen in 1820, and studied also at Heidelberg. He was tutor in Greek at Harvard college in 1822-1823; subsequently devoted his attention chiefly to history and political science; and advocated universal suffrage, 1826, as the true foundation of democracy. He was Collector of the Port of Boston from January, 1838, to November, 1841; Secretary of the Navy, 1845-1846; U. S. Minister to Great Britain, 1846-1849; U. S. Minister at Berlin 1867-1874. He died in Washington, D. C. January 17, 1891. As Secretary of the Navy, Bancroft was the founder of the Naval Academy at Annapolis, and gave the orders to the American Pacific Squadron to seize California in the event of hostilities with Mexico. He wrote the History of the United States from the discovery of the American continent (1834-1875). Consult M. A. DeWolf Howe, The Life and Letters of George Bancroft, 2 vols., 658 pp., New York, 1908.

Speech of Jefferson Davis in the House of Representatives, December 19, 1845, on the Subject of Native Americanism and the Naturalization Laws.

MR. DAVIS, of Missouri (?) [1] was opposed to the reference of these resolutions to a select committee on two grounds: and the first was, that, in his opinion, they deserved at the hands of this House no reference anywhere. They called upon Congress to purify the ballot-box. If the ballot-box was impure in Massachusetts, let her legislature look at home. Massachusetts had no right to inquire into its condition in other States. So far as the modification of laws for regulating elections went, it was no concern of Congress.

And why did Massachusetts ask for an alteration in our naturalization laws—laws which had existed since the formation of the Constitution? When this country had declared that a man was not the natural and perpetual subject of the Government under which he was born, and had maintained and established the right of foreigners to expatriate themselves, it contended, of course, in that very act, for their right of admission here. And, if so, why did the gentlemen from Pennsylvania demand a select committee? Such a request proceeded on the presumption that the Judiciary Committee was wanting either in patriotism, fidelity, or legal learning; neither of which allegations Mr. D. had ever heard advanced in any quarter. And, if that committee was possessed of these qualifications, to that, as the law committee of this House, let the resolutions go. This was a question which deeply interested the people of his district. They, too, wanted a modification of our naturalization laws; but it was that they might be simplified, and that the process of naturalization might be more easily accomplished. So far as his own wishes, therefore, were concerned, he should rather be inclined to ask a select committee on the other side of the question.

Much had been introduced in this discussion which was not referred to in these resolutions. A broad field had been thrown open, but here the ancient maxim, *"Medio tutissimus ibis,"* would not hold. We must either make naturalization easy, or we must withhold it entirely; for if we admitted foreigners, and yet denied them the enjoyment of all political rights among us, we did but create enemies to our Government,

---

[1] This appears as "Missouri" in the record, but it is undoubtedly an error and should be Mississippi.

and fill our country with discontented men. Let the principles of Native Americanism prevail, and the foreigner would look in vain for happiness and liberty on the American shore. He detested that party, above all others, for its sordid character and its arrogant assumption.

Mr. D. here referred to a speech which had been made by a gentleman from Massachusetts (Mr. Rockwell) some days since, in which he had maintained that wherever slavery existed there the high moral character and perfectability of man was not to be found. Had the gentleman forgotten that both the Adamses, and Otis, and Gerry, and Hancock, had all sprung from a State which tolerated slavery? Would he deny to these men a high moral character? He had heard it maintained that the way to elevate the character and increase the prosperity of these States was to adopt the policy of excluding foreigners. As a commentary on that doctrine he would refer its advocates to the ancient empire of China, which had for centuries shut out all the world by her great wall and her exclusive laws. And what had been the result? She had been falling back behind all the other nations of the world in commerce and in power, until at last a little British squadron had been able to dictate terms to the most ancient and populous nation on the earth. He stigmatized this doctrine of exclusion as the doctrine of barbarism. Among savage nations a stranger was counted an enemy, and the same word designated both; but as civilization and every humanizing influence advanced and prevailed, the gates of admission were gradually thrown open. Like another celebrated system which had prevailed in this country, this barbarian doctrine of exclusion had been called "the American system." It was no such thing; it was the European system; but even there it was melting away before the dictates of common sense and a more enlightened policy. Even in France, that stronghold of the feudal system, foreigners were now permitted to hold real estate—England alone retained this blot on her national escutcheon. And should we imitate her in that which was her disgrace? Mr. D. here referred to the services of foreigners in our modern revolution; but though he would not affirm that without it we could not have achieved our freedom, still it furnished a strong reason why we should not shut our gates against those who came to us from abroad. Such a doctrine was never heard among the patriots of the Revolution, and never had he been more surprised than when he heard the name of Washington quoted in their support. Washington was born for no age and for no land;

he stood out alone in his native grandeur, and was the boast and the property of the world. His correspondence was still extant in which he referred to his native land as an asylum for the oppressed; and in a letter to Mr. Jefferson had expressed his wonder that those who were oppressed in the Old World did not more frequently take refuge in the New. Was this the man whom Native Americans claimed as the bulwark of their exclusive policy? Much had been said about the Declaration of Independence. Did gentlemen forget that among its signers were to be found eight actual foreigners, and nine who were the immediate descendants of foreign parents? Mr. D. here made a reference, not distinctly heard by the reporter, to the adoption of Washington by the Irish as a son of St. Patrick, although he had no Irish blood in his veins. He concluded by expressing his hopes that the resolutions would not be referred to a committee who were professedly inimical to our foreign population.

Albert G. Brown[1] *to Jefferson Davis.*

(From the Mississippi Department of Archives and History, Letter Book of Gov. A. G. Brown.)

Executive Chamber
Jackson Mi 11 Jany 1846

Col Jeff[son] Davis
  Com Miss[l] Reg[t].
    Mexico
Sir

I send you under advice from the Secretary of War a lot of blank commissions to be used in supplying such vacancies as may be created among the officers under your command by death, resignation or otherwise, You will please advise me when you have occasion to use any of the blanks so that the Register here may be correctly kept—

I sent you some months since a similar package to this by

---

[1] Brown, Albert Gallatin (1813-1880), a political leader, was born in Chester district, S. C., May 31, 1813, removed to Mississippi, studied law and was admitted to the bar in 1834. He was a member of the Mississippi House of Representatives from March 14, 1839, to March 3, 1841, and from March 4, 1847, to March 3, 1853; Governor of Mississippi 1844-1848; U. S. Senator from Mississippi from March 4, 1853 to January 12, 1861; a captain in the 17th Mississippi Volunteers; a senator in the first and second Confederate Congresses. He died at his home near Terry, Miss., June 12, 1880.

mail & as I have not since heard from it fear it has been lost Lieu^t Bradford of the State Fencibles is charged with the delivery of this package.

> Very Respfl
> Your Obt sevt
> A. G. Brown

Jefferson Davis to John Jenkins

(From Vicksburg Sentinel, February 17, 1846.)

Washington, 30th January, 1846.

Jno. Jenkins, Esq:

Dear Sir—I have recently been informed by a letter from Jackson, that a rumor prevails to the effect that I have endorsed the statements made by your correspondent "Veritas," in letters written from this place in December last.

To those who know me, I hope it is unnecessary to say, that I would not adopt such a mode to attack any man, or thus circuitously proceed to guard our State against "intrigue" and "insult." Had there been no other consideration than my own position, it would have been left to time to correct any false impressions which this unfounded rumor may have created; but the so-called "facts" contained in these letters are of a character to excite prejudices in Mississippi which may prove injurious to our common interests; and therefore, without taking upon myself the part of advocate or apologist of any one, I wish to disabuse the public mind by a simple correction of the most prominent mis-statements in the letters referred to.

In the letter of the Dec. 20th, 1845, it is stated that Wm. M. Gwin received a draft for $7,972.24, drawn against an amount of interest decided to be due to the Chickasaw Indians on monies deposited in the Agricultural Bank of Mississippi.

The writer says: "This amount Gwin received while here a few weeks ago. He got the Secretary of the Treasury to allow the claim—had it passed through the several accounting departments; and the Doctor pocketed the snug sum, and hastened forthwith to Mississippi, to attend to Mr. Walker's orders in the Senatorial campaign."

Here is an act asserted to have been performed by the Secretary of the Treasury, and a corrupt motive insinuated for the performance of that act; constituting a charge which might well arouse suspicions, and create fears for the safety of the public funds under the present administration. What are the facts in this case? By the books of the 1st Comptroller, it appears that on the 21st January, 1845, the claim of Wm. M. Gwin, agent for the Chickasaws, was allowed for the sum of $7,992.24, and that sum paid on the same day, by draft on the Bank of Louisiana; the transaction being closed a month and a half before the present administration came into power.

I have learned from the Treasury Department, that shortly after Mr. Walker became Secretary, large claims were presented by Dr. Gwin, agent of the Chickasaws, for allowance and payments; and that under the provisions of the Act of 3d March 1845, they were all rejected, and that no money has been so allowed or paid to Dr. Gwin by the present Secretary of the Treasury.

With regard to the charge of interference in our Senatorial election, made elsewhere more distinctly, and with violent appeal to resent the insult, and resist the attempt at official dictation; I have made inquiries, and been distinctly answered, that Mr. Walker did not write a single letter, or otherwise interfere in the late canvass for a Mississippi Senator.

In the letter dated Dec. 19th, 1845, it is asked, where does the Secretary of the Treasury deposit the public funds in this District? and the writer answers: "Why, he selects the firm of Corcoran & Riggs (brokers and money dealers in this city) as the depositories of the public moneys." The writer does not stop to inform you whether a better selection could have been made, but goes on to tell how "the story runs" that these Bankers "give fine dinners; they dine and wine the Secretary of the Treasury," and that "they also build a fine house for Mr. Walker to dwell in."

Now, sir, this second "fact," this second insinuation of a corrupt motive, is of the same baseless character as the first.

The Bankers were not selected as depositories by the present Secretary of the Treasury, (Mr. Walker.) The security they deposited has been found ample, and they have been continued. If an "Independent Treasury" law should be re-enacted, for which no one has shown greater solicitation than the present Secretary of the Treasury, all future connexion with these Bankers would be precluded. As to the house suffice it to say, Mr. Walker resides in the house he has occupied for years past, and I have been informed that Corcoran & Riggs are not building, nor ever have built a dwelling house in this city.

From these samples you will be able to put a proper estimate upon the many other points which are contained in those letters, and to see the propriety of this move to arrest at once the impression that I was connected with, or responsible for, the veracity of "Veritas."

I will, before closing, notice one other point in the correspondence treated of. In the letter of December 23rd, 1845, your correspondent, ('Veritas,') referring to the circumstances connected with the "Lost Commission," says of the Secretary of the Treasury, "if it does not cost him his seat in Mr. Polk's cabinet, it will at least paralyze his efforts, his aims and desireś for all practical and useful purposes."

Like yourself, I have from the beginning contended that the public had a right to know all that their agents had done in relation to a transaction so important as the appointment of an U. S. Senator. Before this reaches you I hope the correspondence thereon will have been published, and that like many other secrets, its importance will have been lost in the act of disclosure.

In the mean time, sir, I would say that it would be with the greatest reluctance, and the deepest regret, that I would entertain the idea that the efforts of the Secretary of the Treasury are to be paralyzed at the moment when all his energies are directed to the accomplishment of those great objects, "the divorce of Bank and State," and "the repeal of the protective Tariff of 1842."

Am I deceived when I expect Mississippi to nerve the arm engaged in such a contest, rather than to strip it of its power? It is her cause, and her prayers belong to him who enters the lists to sustain it.

The political aspirations of individuals are only important as they are connected with the public good. This is, I think, the case in the present instance. Mississippi has now for the first time in her history, a representative in the Executive Cabinet. We have believed that our interests were unjustly neglected by the Federal Government; we find the Secretary of the Treasury, with his acknowledged ability, laboring for us. Shall he not receive the cheer necessary to sustain the laborer? Shall vague rumors shaped by private spleen—shall dark suspicions anonymously thrown into circulation, be permitted to rob your public servants of the only reward the honest politician seeks, the approbation of those to whom his time and toil have been given?

Please publish this, that it may follow the misrepresentations it is designed to correct.

Very truly yours,

JEFF. DAVIS.

Speech of Jefferson Davis delivered in the House Feb. 6,
1846, on the Oregon question.

Mr. JEFFERSON DAVIS addressed the committee during
the hour. He knew not (he said) whether he more regretted
the time at which this discussion has been introduced, or the
manner in which it has been conducted. We were engaged
in delicate and highly important negotiations with Mexico,
the end of which we had hoped would be an adjustment of our
boundary on terms the vast advantage of which it would be
difficult to estimate. If, sir, (said Mr. D.,) by this exciting discussion we shall hereafter find that we have lost the key to
the commerce of the Pacific, none who hears me will live long
enough to cease from his regrets for the injury our country has
sustained. Again, sir; a long peace has served to extend the
bonds of commerce throughout the civilized world, drawing
nations from remote quarters of the globe into friendly alliance
and that mutual dependence which promised a lasting peace and
unshackled commerce. In the East, there appeared a rainbow which promised that the waters of national jealousy and
proscription were about to recede from the face of the earth,
and the spirit of free trade to move over the face thereof.
But this, sir, is a hope not so universally cherished in this
House as I could desire. We have even been told that one
of the advantages to result from war will be emancipation from
the manufacturers of Manchester and Birmingham.

I hope, sir, the day is far distant when measures of peace
or war will be prompted by sectional or class interests. War,
sir, is a dread alternative, and should be the last resort; but
when demanded for the maintenance of the honor of the country,
or for the security and protection of our citizens against outrage by other Governments, I trust we shall not sit here for
weeks to discuss the propriety, to dwell upon the losses, or
paint the horrors of war.

Mr. Chairman, it has been asserted that the people demand
action, and we must advance. Whilst, sir, I admit the propriety of looking to and reflecting public opinion, especially upon
a question which is viewed as deciding between peace or war, I
cannot respond to the opinion, nor consent to govern my conduct
by the idea, that the public man who attempts to stem the current of a war excitement must be borne down, sacrificed on the
altar of public indignation. Sir, may the day never come when

there will be so little of public virtue and patriotic devotion among the representatives of the people, that any demagogue who chooses to make violent and unfounded appeals to raise a war clamor in the country will be allowed, unopposed, to mislead the people as to the true questions at issue, and to rule their representatives through their love of place and political timidity.

Mr. Chairman, I have been struck with surprise, only exceeded by mortification, at the freedom with which disgrace and dishonor have been mingled with the name of our country. Upon one side, to give notice, and involve the country in a war, is disgrace; upon the other side, not to give notice, to rest in our present position, is dishonor. And my colleague [MR. THOMP-SON] says "notice" is the only way to avoid war; that to extend our laws over our people in Oregon is war—a war of disgrace. Sir, whence comes this decision, this new light upon the Oregon question? The leaders in the Oregon movement, in other times, held different views. And, sir, the discussions upon Oregon, at former periods, would certainly not suffer by a comparison with ours; nor, sir, did the commissioners who negotiated the convention of joint occupancy, either English or American, so understand it.

Mr. Gallatin has recently called public attention to the fact, that in 1827, our plenipotentiary refused to agree to any express provision that, in extending the convention of 1818, neither party should exercise any exclusive sovereignty over the territory. The probability that it might become necessary for the United States to establish a territorial or some sort of government over their own citizens was explicitly avowed. Sir, by discovery, exploration, and possession, we claimed exclusive sovereignty over the valley of the Columbia, and our exclusive possession as against England was admitted by the restoration of our posts in Oregon—the formal, actual surrender of Astoria. The convention for joint right to trade in Oregon did not destroy our exclusive possession of a part, nor limit the rights or powers we might exercise within their former bounds; and that this is the British construction, is sufficiently apparent by the assertion of rights as derived from the Nootka convention over the same territory.

Nothing can be more demonstrable than the unfitness of joint-occupation rights to an agricultural people. It was not designed so to operate, but was designed for a country in the hands of hunters, trappers, and Indian traders.

The Hudson Bay Company, so often represented as colonizing Oregon, has interests directly opposed to agricultural settlements. The fur-trappers have been (if my information is correct) aided in establishing themselves on the south side of Oregon. Fur-trading companies usually require their discharged hands to leave the country, and resist, instead of promoting, colonization—of necessity destructive to their trade. The Puget Sound Company is agricultural, and its settlements are in violation of our convention with England; and the notice required is to forbid such infraction of the treaty. That no right to plant colonies can be deduced from the conventions of 1818 and 1827 is too plain to admit of argument. The claim, if any, must be drawn from the convention between England and Spain, called the Nootka convention. If that convention be still in force, it must be because it was the declaration of rights, not the grant of advantages; and thus, for the sake of argument, I will consider it.

That Spain had the exclusive right of occupation on the northwest coast of America, as far as her discoveries extended, was not denied; but the question was, Had she, without having occupied the country, an exclusive sovereignty over it? Denying this pretension of Spain, Great Britain demanded indemnification for the seizure of British vessels at Nootka sound by the Spanish authorities. This led to the agreement upon which Great Britain has built her claim to territory in the Oregon country. Before entering upon the consideration of the terms of the convention itself, I will refer to the events that led to it.

Long before the voyage of Meares, the port of Nootka sound was known to the Spanish navigators. It was the usual resort of the trading vessels in the north Pacific. Meares, in 1788, visited it, and built a vessel there. For the use of his men, he erected a hut on the shore, by permission of the Indian king, and threw some defences around it, enclosing (according to Vancouver) about an acre of land. Meares, in return for the kindness of the Indian, (Maquinna,) gave him a pair of pistols. In his narrative, he gives a detailed account of the transaction, but does not call it a purchase; that was an after-thought, and first figured in his memorial. Sir, if there had been nothing beyond the narrative of Meares, the temporary character of his location would be fully established. There it appears that when about to sail, leaving a part of his men behind him, he bribed the Indian king, by offering him the reversion of the hut and chattels on shore, to permit his men to remain in peace, and complete the building of the vessel they had commenced.

To show the character of Meares, the purpose of his voyages in the north Pacific, and the country along which Great Britain claimed the right to trade, I will refer to the work of an Englishman, contemporary with Meares, and one of the most enterprising of the navigators of the north Pacific. It is "Dixon's Voyage around the World." Thus it appears that Meares was a fur-trader, and of poor character for his calling; and more important still, it appears that the coast, from Cook's river to King George's sound, was the extent of the region in which British cruisers traded. This, taken in connexion with the 5th article of the Nootka convention, serves to fix the latitude in which joint settlement would be permitted.

The message of the King of Great Britain, communicating the transaction at Nootka, refers only to the seizure of vessels; not a word about lands of which British subjects had been dispossessed.

And when the proposition to vote an address of thanks to his Majesty for the conduct and successful termination of the negotiation, neither in the House of Lords or Commons did any one claim an acquisition of territory; and to the bitter irony and severe assaults of Mr. Fox upon the position in which the territorial pretensions of England had been left, his great rival, Mr. Pitt, then minister, made no reply, but pressed the commercial advantages gained by England.

The only link remaining to be supplied, and which completes the claim of construction, is the examination and final action of Quadra and Vancouver, when sent as commissioners to carry out the first article of the convention.

If, then, no tracts of land could be found which had been purchased by Meares; if no buildings of which he had been dispossessed, and the Spanish flag was never struck to that of Great Britain, Spain still maintaining her settlement at Nootka; the parallel north of which the joint right of settlement exists must be drawn through the northern extremity of Quadra and Vancouver's island; the established rule of nations being, that settlement on an island is held to extend to the whole of the island.

Oregon territory, then, is divided into a portion where we have possession above the treaty, and over which we can exercise all the rights not inconsistent with the trade permitted to England; another portion, in which, admitting the Nootka convention to be still in force, we have, with England, a joint right of trade and settlement; this being limited to the south by a line down through the head of the Quadra and Vancouver island. Between these portions, if there be any territory, it is in the condition of a joint right in England and the United States to occupy for fur trade, and the agricultural settlements are in violation of the spirit of the treaty.

Whenever the joint right by convention ceases, we must at once assert our exclusive right, or thenceforward possession matures into right on the part of Great Britain. During the continuance of the convention the title remains unimpaired; we are in possession; can establish over the undisputed part of the territory whatever regulations may be necessary to promote good order, and encourage emigration of agriculturists. Between England and the United States, the party having bread in Oregon must triumph.

No army can be sustained there for any considerable time by either country if the food must be transported from abroad to support it.

Never had man better right to cry "save me from my friends" than the President of the United States on this occasion. His positive recommendation has been made subordinate to his suggestion. He has urged to extend protection to our citizens in Oregon, but advised that notice be given to terminate the treaty of joint occupancy for reasons given. All this has been reversed, and the positive, unqualified declaration of a perfect title to the whole of Oregon up to 54° 40′ comes strangely from those who claim to support an Administration that has offered nearly the same compromise line which had been time and again proposed by his predecessors. Sir, for the honor of my country, I hope that we have not been for thirty years negotiating when there was no conflicting claim; and for past as for the present Executive, I utterly deny that they have ever proposed to cede away a part of the territory, when our title was complete, to appease the voracious demands of England. It was a difficult and doubtful question; it was the adjustment of an undefined boundary. If the President should find himself compelled to close this question in twelve months, without any appropriation, without any preparation, he will be constrained to choose between compromise or war measures with the country unprepared. This will be the result of our action; and if he should effect a treaty by such a boundary as will not compromise the honor of the country, I for one—much, sir, as I wish to retain the whole territory— will give my full support as heretofore, and prepare for my share of whatever responsibility attaches. Sir, why has the

South been assailed in this discussion? Has it been with the hope of sowing dissension between us and our western friends? Thus far, I think it has failed. Why the frequent reference to the conduct of the South on the Texas question? Sir, those who have made reflections on the South, as having sustained Texas annexation from sectional views, have been of those who opposed that great measure, and are most eager for this. The suspicion is but natural in them. But, sir, let me tell them that this doctrine of the political balance between different portions of the Union is no southern doctrine. We, sir, advocated the annexation of Texas from high national considerations; it was not a mere southern question; it lay coterminous to the Western States, and extended as far north as 42d degree of latitude; nor, sir, do we wish to divide the territory of Oregon; we would preserve it all for the extension of our Union. We would not arrest the onward progress of our pioneers. We would not, as has been done in this debate, ask why our citizens have left the repose of civil government and gone to Oregon? We find in it but that energy which has heretofore been characteristic of our people, and which has developed much that has illustrated our history. It is the onward progress of our people towards the Pacific, which alone can arrest their westward march; and on the banks of which, to use the idea of our lamented Linn, the pioneer will sit down to weep that there are no more forests to subdue. Sir, the gentleman from Missouri has, in claiming credit to different States for services in time past, wandered round Mississippi, and passed over it unnoticed. I wish not to eulogize my State, but, thus drawn to my notice, let me tell him that at Pensacola, at Bowyer, in the Creek campaigns, and on the field to which he specially alluded, (New Orleans,) the people of Mississippi have performed services that give earnest for the future, and relieve her sons of the necessity of offering pledges for her. It was Mississippi dragoons, led by her gallant Hinds, that received from the commanding general the high commendation of having been the admiration of one army and the wonder of the other.

It is as the representative of a high-spirited and patriotic people that I am called on to resist this war clamor. My constituents need no such excitements to prepare their hearts for all that patriotism demands. Whenever the honor of the country demands redress, whenever its territory is invaded, if then it shall be sought to intimidate by the fiery cross of St. George—if then we are threatened with the unfolding of English banners, if we resent or resist—from the gulf shore to the banks of that great river—throughout the length and breadth, Mississippi will come. And whether the question be one of northern or southern, of eastern or western aggression, we will not stop to count the cost, but act as becomes the descendants of those who, in the war of the Revolution, engaged in unequal strife to aid our brethren of the North in redressing their injuries.

Sir, we are the exposed portion of the Union, and nothing has been done by this Government adequate to our protection. Yet, sir, in the language of our patriotic Governor on a recent occasion, if "war comes, though it bring blight and desolation, yet we are ready for the crisis." We despise malign predictions, such as the member from Ohio who spoke early in these debates, made, and turn to such sentiments as those of another member from that State, the gentleman near me. In these was recognised the feelings of our western brethren, who, we doubt not, whenever the demand shall exist, will give proof of such valor as on former occasions they have shown; and if our plains should be invaded, they will come down to the foe like a stream from the rock.

Sir, when ignorance and fanatic hatred assail our domestic institutions, we try to forgive them for the sake of the righteous among the wicked—our natural allies, the Democracy of the North. We turn from present hostility to former friendship— from recent defection, to the time when Massachusetts and Virginia, the stronger brothers of our family, stood foremost and united to defend our common rights. From sire to son has descended the love of our Union in our hearts, as in our history are mingled the names of Concord and Camden, of Yorktown and Saratoga, of Moultrie and Plattsburg, of Chippewa and Erie, of Bowyer and Guilford, and New Orleans and Bunker Hill. Grouped together, they form a monument to the common glory of our common country. And where is the southern man who would wish that monument were less by one of the northern names that constitute the mass? Who, standing on the ground made sacred by the blood of Warren, could allow sectional feeling to curb his enthusiasm as he looked upon that obelisk which rises a monument to freedom's and his country's triumph, and stands a type of the time, the men, and the event that it commemorates, built of material that mocks the waves of time, without niche or moulding for parasite or creeping thing to rest on, and pointing like a finger to the sky to raise man's thought to philanthropic and noble deeds.

Albert G. Brown to Jefferson Davis.

(From the Mississippi Department of Archives and History, Letter Book of Gov. A. G. Brown.)

Executive Chamber
City of Jackson Mi
3rd March 1846

Sir

Please find enclosed a memorial of the Legislature of this State, which I have the honor to transmit, relative to the improvement of the navigation of certain Rivers therein named. You have a Legislative request that it shall receive your influence.

Very Respfl
Your obt. Servt
A. G. Brown

Hon. J. Davis
M. C.

A copy sent to each of our Senators & Representatives in Congress.

Remarks of Jefferson Davis on the bill to raise a regiment of mounted riflemen, March 8, 1846.

Mr. J. DAVIS said, with no unfriendliness to the object of the gentleman from Virginia; (for he thought it was one of the great objects to be accomplished in connexion with Oregon —the establishment of a regular mail to that territory,) he must object to the gentleman's amendment, and he hoped no amendment would be incorporated into the bill. Immediate action was essentially necessary; any amendment which sent this bill back to the Senate, would produce such delay as would almost defeat the object of the bill.

Mr. HOPKINS (Mr. D. yielding for explanation) said, the amendment which he had sent to the Chair was not likely to delay the final action of Congress upon this subject. It was an amendment in direct conformity with the bill already reported to the Senate by the Committee on the Post Office and Post Roads of that body, which was likely to meet with favorable consideration there. The bill of the Senate differed from this amendment only in this, that it proposed to give to the President of the United States the power to have this mail transported to Oregon by detachments from the army of the United States, while his amendment was specific in its provisions, and referred directly to the regiment they were about to raise by this bill—a regiment assigned to this particular line. His amendment, therefore, had that peculiar merit over the bill of the Senate, and would doubtless be concurred in in that body without delay.

Mr. DAVIS resumed. The bill, as it was now before them, (he said,) had passed the Senate. To attach any amendment certainly would beget the delay of sending it back; if the Senate would act immediately upon it, it might not be so objectionable; but they were now so involved in the discussion which was now occupying their attention, and over-riding everything else, that there was no certainty when it would be reached, if sent back there again.

Again, he held that there could be no necessity of giving in the law authority to the President of the United States to direct that these troops shall escort the mail, since he had that authority now over every existing regiment in the army.

Mr. HOPKINS (Mr. D. again yielding for explanation) stated that, without this amendment, there was no law authorizing the establishment of a post office in Oregon; there was no law authorizing the President of the United States to send the mail of the United States to Oregon; and any mail sent there would have to be entrusted to somebody or other whose duty it was not made by law to distribute it, and it would be equal or worse than no mail at all. It would be better to put the whole line under the direction of the general post office law and the Postmaster General. And he understood that the President, though he had not conversed with him on the subject, was exceedingly anxious to have this provision incorporated in the bill, that he might send the mail to Oregon.

After some further conversation on this point between these two gentlemen,

Mr. DAVIS resumed. He attached much weight, (he said,) as a friend of the Administration, to its recommendations, when they came before Congress in a proper form; and he considered the providing facilities for the transportation of this mail highly important, but he considered this regiment still more important. By the 20th of next month, the emigration would commence. Then it was necessary that this regiment should be organized and ready for action, which could be accomplished alone by passing this bill into a law without delay. This was the only way of raising a proper military force for this service: let the officers of this regiment—the company officers—go into the western country to enlist the men to serve under them, where there are men competent to ride, hunt, and acquainted with the dangers and hardships of the service to be found; and with the state of feeling that now exists, let it be known that the regiment was intended expressly for this Oregon route, and there would be no difficulty whatever in finding sufficient recruits, which difficulty would exist, to some extent, in recruiting for the army generally.

As to taking for this service a portion of each company as it now exists, all must be aware that it could not be accomplished. A man would object to being transferred, if he was eminent in his regiment; and such men only would answer for this service.

Again: it would be extracting from every company the picked men of the company, and leaving the rest scarcely fit for the service in which they were now employed.

They had constantly heard about the ability of the President to mount a regiment for this particular service. The President had no such power, unless they gave it to him by law. There was no regiment of infantry not now employed; and we knew not how soon we might be called to increase our army now in Texas.

As to expense, he considered that it was usually much over estimated. While in service on this route, the men would nearly support themselves upon game, and their horses would subsist on the grass at their feet. It was only when they returned to garrison to be recruited, that the expenses for forage, &c., were incurred to any great extent.

He touched upon the question of nativeism, opposing the amendment of Mr. LEVIN, and arguing while the West was principally to be relied on to furnish the men and officers, fitted by education and experience for this peculiar service, that the discretion should be left to select from among foreigners, as well as elsewhere, those who were best qualified. He spoke in high terms of the value and efficiency of service of many foreigners, and instanced the case of an Englishman, (of whom he gave some anecdote,) who was the best dragoon he had ever seen.

He concluded by appealing to his western friends, especially, who knew the necessity of this bill, and that the force proposed under it should be raised and ready for service by the 20th May, to reject amendments, which would embarrass the bill, and pass it without delay.

Remarks of Jefferson Davis on the bill to raise two regiments of riflemen delivered in the House March 27, 1846.

Mr. JEFFERSON DAVIS said he did not intend to enter into a wide discussion with reference to the tariff, to Oregon, to Texas, or to the improvement of the rivers and harbors of the country. The House had under consideration a proposition to raise two regiments of riflemen. The only questions to be determined were: first, the necessity of the increase; and, second, the mode in which it should be made. There were two great propositions imbodying different modes: one to increase the army by increasing the number of regiments; the other, to add to the rank and file of the existing regiments. Our organization under a peace establishment is designed only to be the skeleton of an army; we organize our regiments not so much with a view to their present efficiency as on the arising of an emergency which shall require them to enable us to fill them up and render us the greatest service. We who were literally the rifle people of the world, who were emphatically skilled in the use of the rifle, were now falling behind France, England, and other nations, who were paying attention to it, and now actually had no rifle regiment. For this reason, if there were no other, he would vote to raise a rifle regiment to perfect our organization, and add the wanting bone to the skeleton of our army.

Another reason in behalf of this bill was, that it was recommended by the President of the United States. [Mr. D. read that part of the Message recommending the establishment of stockade forts on the route to Oregon, &c.] It did not depend upon the notice, upon future emigration, but was necessary to protect the emigration now passing to Oregon. He pointed out the dangers from the attacks of nomadic hostile Indians, to which the traveller across the prairies is exposed, the necessity of mounted riflemen for their protection, and the superiority in very many respects of mounted to unmounted riflemen for this service. He agreed with the gentleman from Kentucky, [Mr. Boyd,] who, in his amendment, proposed to make it discretionary with the President whenever, in his opinion, the public interests shall require, to mount such portions of these regiments as he may deem necessary. He (Mr. D.) hoped that at least half of them would be mounted; for it was perfectly idle to send infantry to guard emigrants against Indians who live on horseback, who rob all companies not sufficiently strong to resist them, and fly with their booty as on the wings of the wind.

He denied the correctness of the position of Mr. RATHBUN, that this bill was intended for raising troops to transport our men, women, and children to a territory over which we dared not assert our rights; and said that the President had recommended mounted riflemen to protect the emigration which is now going on; we needed it before emigration commenced, and emigration has only increased its necessity. He urged the importance of this measure, and the advantages and facilities which would be extended to emigrants to Oregon, by the erection of a line of stockade forts on their route. In further reply to Mr. R., he vindicated the qualifications of western men for this particular kind of service, acknowledging that they would be loth to submit to military punishment, but assigning their habitual subordination to the laws of the country, and their patriotic and gallant devotion to its interests, as the means by which they would avoid subjecting themselves to it. In the course of his remarks, he adverted to the necessity of the Military Academy in reference to the attacks from time to time made upon it, maintaining the unquestionable necessity of a military education to prepare a man for command in the army; which education, he said, was only to be obtained at a military academy, or piece by piece to be picked up, at the hazard of loss of property and life, by the officer, after he was commissioned and under heavy pay. Mr. D. also touched briefly upon one or two other points.

Speech of Jefferson Davis in House on April 17, 1846 on the Oregon question.

Mr. JEFFERSON DAVIS said, the closing remarks of the gentleman who had preceded him certainly invited a reply; but in consideration of the little time which remained of that allowed for this discussion and the number of gentlemen anxious to address the committee, he would only say, in answer to these remarks, that he repelled the assumption, that all who differed from the gentleman in his opinions upon Oregon, were so wanting in wisdom or patriotism as ignorantly or timidly to sacrifice American rights. Not always was it found that those who most readily entered into quarrel, bore themselves best after they were in. Sometimes the first to get into a row are the first who wish themselves out.

He declined to enter into the question of title. The ancient voyages of Spain—the ancient conventions in relation to the

Northwest coast of America—seemed to him so little connected with the subject before the committee, that he had listened to such speeches with the feelings of the Vicar of Wakefield, when he met the sharper of the fair in prison, and he commenced his recital on cosmogony. Stop! said the Vicar, sorry to interrupt so much learning, but I think I have heard all that before.

He would point out his most prominent objections to the bill, and before closing, would offer a substitute for its provisions. He said, the title of the bill met his entire approval. Our citizens in Oregon had a right to expect our protection. It was gratifying to him to witness the fact, that though they had gone beyond the exercise of our jurisdiction, they looked back and asked that the laws of their father-land might follow them; they invited the restraints of our legislation; thus giving the highest proof of their attachment, and paying the richest tribute to our institutions.

There is sufficient unanimity as to the propriety of extending our laws over American citizens in Oregon, to justify me in omitting that branch of the subject, and proceeding at once to inquire by what mode this may be effected. By the bill under discussion, it is proposed to extend the jurisdiction of the supreme court of Iowa, and the laws of said Territory, as far as applicable to that portion of the territory of the United States which lies west of the Rocky Mountains, and also over a belt of country east of those mountains and west of the Missouri river, and lying between the fortieth and forty-third parallel of north latitude.

Who here knows what the laws of Iowa are, still less what they may be; but this much we all may know, that from the difference in the condition and wants of the two countries, the one must be very poorly calculated to legislate for the other, and great confusion must ensue in the attempt to apply the wants of one to the other. He referred to the mining character of Iowa, which gave to her people and local legislation a character peculiar and inapplicable to Oregon. He denied the propriety of extending the laws of Iowa over the Indian country, considered such extension a violation of the principles which had heretofore controlled our intercourse with the Indian tribes, the principle which had been characteristic of our Government, contradistinguishing it from those of Europe, who had had intercourse with the aborigines of America. Our Government had always recognised the usufruct of the Indians of the territory possessed by them. Our jurisdiction over Indian country has heretofore been confined to regulating trade and intercourse with the Indian tribes, and serving process upon our own citizens within the Indian territory. This is to give force to the laws of Iowa over all the Indian country therein described; to wrest, without the just and liberal compensation we have heretofore paid for the extinguishment of Indian title, a belt of country on this side of the mountains, from the tribes who possess it, and, by the strong hand, to seize all which lies beyond.

He said, gentleman had frequently addressed us upon the rights of Great Britain and the conflicting claims of that Government and ours in the Oregon territory. By the conventions of 1818 and 1827, the title as between these two Governments was in abeyance. Let us strictly regard all our treaty stipulations with that rival claimant; but most especially let us respect the rights of the more helpless occupant, and more rightful possessor—the savage who originally held the country.

To this end, he said, he had drawn up, and would submit a substitute for the bill, violative of the rights of no one, in strict accordance with the usage of this Government, and, as he believed, most effective to preserve peace and order, and extend to our citizens in Oregon the benefits of our republican laws and institutions. It was the application, so far as suited to the circumstances, of the ordinance of 1787, for the government of the territory of the United States northwest of the Ohio river, and of the law of 1789, to render it more effectual. Under these, our citizens in the various territories of the northwest had passed from the condition of Indian country to the second grade of government. No question could arise in their application which had not been already adjudicated; and, therefore, in adopting this plan, we could distinctly see, and accurately judge, of the results it would produce. In view of the peculiar condition of the Oregon territory, he expected, by a proviso, that portion of the ordinance which refers to a general assembly; also substituted for the freehold qualification of officers required by that instrument the qualifications prescribed in the territory of Iowa, where no freehold is necessary, and had added a section securing to the British subjects in Oregon all the rights and privileges they derive from existing treaties, so long as those treaties shall continue. By this substitute it is proposed to provide for the appointment of a Governor, who should be *ex officio* superintendent of Indian affairs, and three judges. These officers appointed by the President, by and with the consent of the Senate, are to receive the same compensation as officers of a like grade in the Territory of Iowa. They are to be authorized to adopt such laws from the statutes of the different States of our Union as may be applicable to the condition of that country, the whole to be subject to the revision and approval of Congress.

Thus, sir, we shall be guarded against the dangers of extending the laws of a territory existing, and hereafter to be enacted without our knowledge, and above our control, likewise from any improper legislation which might result from a representative assembly in a mixed and unsettled colony. The officers of the Government thus constituted are authorized by proclamation to define the limits of the settlements of our citizens in Oregon, to which the Indian title has been, or may be extinguished, and within such settlement to locate the seat of government for the territory. Until the Indian title has been legally extinguished in some portion of the territory, it is a violation of the policy we have heretofore observed, and which stands upon our history a proud monument of humanity and justice, to locate our courts, and assume territorial jurisdiction in that country.

Having a point upon which to rest our territorial government, its process can thence extend into the Indian country around it to persons found therein, and subject to our jurisdiction. Now, by the act of 1834, a criminal might be arrested in the territory of Oregon, brought over to our courts in Missouri or Iowa for trial, as they are frequently arrested, and brought to trial from the Indian country east of the mountains.

From the various instances of erecting a territorial government in the manner proposed, he would detain the committee by a reference to but one—that of Wisconsin.

The United States held free from Indian title the small tract of land at Green Bay. Upon this they located their territorial officers; here the laws were administered: and hence a process issued into the remainder of the territory occupied by Indians.

The only difference between Wisconsin and Oregon, if any difference exists to vary our practice on this point, must arise from the joint-occupancy convention between England and the United States. To my mind this offers no obstacle.

Our settlements in Oregon are entirely within the limits within which we have actual, legal possession—our possession recognised by the Government of Great Britain before the joint convention was formed which is now said to impose upon us limitations.

Pending the negotiation of 1827, Mr. Gallatin informs us the American Plenipotentiary declined to agree to any convention containing an express provision against the exercise of any exclusive sovereignty over the territory. He says, in his letter dated January 22, 1846, referring to the negotiations of 1827, in relation to the territory west of the Stony Mountains, "The probability that it might become necessary for the United States to establish a territorial, or some sort of a government, over their own citizens, was explicitly avowed." Great Britain, through her mercantile corporation, the Hudson Bay Company, extends her laws over Oregon. We have none other than political corporations, through which to effect the same object on the part of the United States. The proposition he submitted was through a governor and judges, as the head of a territorial incorporation, to transmit the laws of the United States to her citizens residing beyond the practical extension of her organized jurisdiction.

This, he contended, we had a right to do under the existing convention with Great Britain; this was our duty to our own citizens, to the Indian inhabitants of that territory, and, as he believed, essential to the preservation of order, and the maintenance of our treaty obligations. This policy was unconnected with the termination of the convention of the joint occupancy with Great Britain, and should have been adopted long ago. It was necessary to limit the British act of 1821, which has found an excuse, in the absence of all other law, or "civil government," for an extension invasive of our rights, and injurious to our people.

With this brief explanation, and relying on the familiarity of the committee with the subject-matter it contained, he submitted his substitute to their consideration.

Substitute bill on the Oregon question offered by Jefferson Davis in the House of Representatives on April 22, 1846.

The bill having now been gone through with,

Mr. JEFFERSON DAVIS proposed the following as a substitute therefor:

"That from and after the fourth day of July next, the territory of the United States, lying west of the Stony Mountains, 'shall, for the purposes of temporary government, constitute a 'separate territory, by the name of Oregon.

"SEC. 2. *And be it further enacted,* That there shall be 'established, within the said territory, a government in all respects similar to that provided by the ordinance of Congress, 'passed on the thirteenth day of July, one thousand seven hun-

'dred and eighty-seven, for the government of the territory of
'the United States northwest of the river Ohio, and by an act
'passed on the seventh day of August, one thousand seven hun-
'dred and eighty-nine, entitled 'An act to provide for the
'government of the territory northwest of the river Ohio;' and
'the inhabitants thereof shall be entitled to, and enjoy all and
'singular the rights, privileges, and advantages granted and
'secured to the people of the territory of the United States
'northwest of the river Ohio by the said ordinance: *Provided,*
'That a legislative assembly shall not be organized in said terri-
'tory of Oregon, until the same shall be authorized by an act
'of Congress.

"SEC. 3.   *And be it further enacted,* That the officers for
'said territory, who, by virtue of this act, shall be appointed
'by the President of the United States, by and with the advice
'and consent of the Senate, shall respectively exercise the same
'powers, perform the same duties, and receive for their services
'the same compensation, as by the laws of the United States have
'been provided and established for similar officers in Iowa
'Territory; and the duties and emoluments of Superintendent of
'Indian Affairs shall be united with those of Governor: *Pro-
'vided,* That the qualifications for office shall be the same as in
'Iowa Territory.

"SEC. 4.   *And be it further enacted,* That the Governor and
'judges of said territory shall, by proclamation, define the limits
'of the settlements of American citizens in said territory to
'which the Indian title has been or may be extinguished; and
'the seat of government of said territory shall be located at
'such point within the limits of said settlements as the Gov-
'ernor and judges, or a majority of them, shall select.

"SEC. 5.   *And be it further enacted,* That provision shall
'hereafter be made by law to secure and grant to every white
'person, male or female, over the age of eighteen years, three
'hundred and twenty acres of land; and to every white person,
'male or female, under the age of eighteen years, one hundred
'and sixty acres of land, who shall have resided in the said
'territory described in the first section of this act for five
'consecutive years, to commence within three years from the
'passage of this act.

"SEC. 6.   And be it further enacted, That nothing contained
'in this act shall be construed to deprive the subjects of Great
'Britain of any of the rights and privileges secured to them by
'existing treaty stipulations during the continuance thereof.''

Which substitute amendment was *rejected.*

Jefferson Davis on The War with Mexico.

(From Port-Gibson Correspondent, June 3, 1846.)

Washington, May 12, 1846.

The Oregon controversy will scarcely be settled, by negotiation, and when the joint convention shall be abrogated conflicts with England will probably ensue. Before that time we ought to close all questions with Mexico, and have the ship overhauled for action on a larger scale. Let the treaty of peace be made at the city of Mexico, and by an Ambassador who cannot be refused a hearing—but who will speak with that which levels walls and opens gates—American cannon.

I signified to our friend John Willis that in the event of war I should like to command a Warren Regiment. My position here forces upon me the recollection of all which is due to those who sent me here. Yet I look to the movements of our forces on our Mexican border with a strong desire to be a part of them. My education and former practice would, I think, enable me to be of service to Mississippians who take the field. If they wish it, I will join them as soon as possible, wherever they may be.

JEFFERSON DAVIS.

Remarks of Jefferson Davis on the resolution of thanks to Gen. Taylor, May 28, 1846.

Mr. JEFFERSON DAVIS said, as a friend to the army, he rejoiced at the evidence now afforded of a disposition in this House to deal justly, to feel generously towards those to whom the honor of our flag has been intrusted. Too often and too long had we listened to harsh and invidious reflections upon our gallant little army, and the accomplished officers who command it. A partial opportunity had been offered to exhibit their soldierly qualities in their true light, and he trusted these aspersions were hushed—hushed now forever. As an American, whose heart promptly responds to all which illustrates our national character, and adds new glory to our national name, he rejoiced with exceeding joy at the recent triumph of our arms. Yet it is no more than he expected from the gallant soldiers who hold our post upon the Rio Grande—no more than, when occasion offers, they will achieve again. It was the triumph of

American courage, professional skill, and that patriotic pride which blooms in the breast of our educated soldier, and which droops not under the withering scoff of political revilers.

These men will feel, deeply feel, the expression of your gratitude. It will nerve their hearts in the hour of future conflict, to know that their country acknowledges and honors their devotion. It will shed a solace on the dying moment of those who fall, to be assured their country mourns the loss. This is the meed for which the soldier bleeds and dies. This he will remember long after the paltry pittance of one month's extra pay has been forgotten.

Beyond this expression of the nation's thanks, he liked the principle of the proposition offered by the gentleman from South Carolina. We have a pension system providing for the disabled soldier, but he seeks well and wisely to extend it to all who may be wounded, however slightly. It is a reward offered to those who seek for danger, who first and foremost plunge into the fight. It has been this incentive, extended so as to cover all feats of gallantry, that has so often crowned the British arms with victory, and caused their prowess to be recognised in every quarter of the globe. It was the sure and high reward of gallantry, the confident reliance upon their nation's gratitude, which led Napoleon's armies over Europe, conquering and to conquer; and it was these influences which, in an earlier time, rendered the Roman arms invincible, and brought their eagle back victorious from every land on which it gazed. Sir, let not that parsimony, (for he did not deem it economy,) prevent us from adopting a system which in war will add so much to the efficiency of troops. Instead of seeking to fill the ranks of your army by increased pay, let the soldier feel that a liberal pension will relieve him from the fear of want in the event of disability, provide for his family in the event of death, and that he wins his way to gratitude and the reward of his countrymen by perilling all for honor in the field.

The achievement which we now propose to honor is one which richly deserves it. Seldom, sir, in the annals of military history has there been one in which desperate daring and military skill were more happily combined. The enemy selected his own ground, and united to the advantage of a strong position a numerical majority of three to one. Driven from his first position by an attack in which it is hard to say whether professional skill or manly courage is to be more admired, he retired and posted his artillery on a narrow defile, to sweep the ground over which our troops were compelled to pass. There, posted in strength three times greater than our own, they waited the approach of our gallant little army.

General Taylor knew the danger and destitution of the band he left to hold his camp opposite Matamoras, and he paused for no regular approaches, but opened his field artillery, and dashed with sword and bayonet on the foe. A single charge left him master of their battery, and the number of slain attests the skill and discipline of his army. Mr. D. referred to a gentleman who, a short time since, upon this floor, expressed extreme distrust in our army, and poured out the vials of his denunciation upon the graduates of the Military Academy. He hoped now the gentleman will withdraw those denunciations; that now he will learn the value of military science; that he will see in the location, the construction, the defence of the bastioned field-work opposite Matamoras the utility, the necessity of a military education. Let him compare the few men who held that with the army that assailed it; let him mark the comparative safety with which they stood within that temporary work; let him consider why the guns along its ramparts were preserved, whilst they silenced the batteries of the enemy; why that intrenchment stands unharmed by Mexican shot, whilst its guns have crumbled the stone walls in Matamoras to the ground, and then say whether he believes a blacksmith or a tailor could have secured the same results. He trusted the gentleman would be convinced that arms, like every occupation, requires to be studied before it can be understood; and from these things, to which he had called his attention, he will learn the power and advantage of military science. He would make but one other allusion to the remarks of the gentleman he had noticed, who said nine-tenths of the graduates of the Military Academy abandoned the service of the United States. If he would take the trouble to examine the records upon this point, he doubted not he would be surprised at the extent of his mistake. There he would learn that a majority of all the graduates are still in service; and if he would push his inquiry a little further, he would find that a large majority of the commissioned officers who bled in the actions of the 8th and 9th were graduates of that academy.

He would not enter into a discussion on the military at this time. His pride, his gratification arose from the success of our arms. Much was due to the courage which Americans have displayed on many battle-fields in former times; but this courage, characteristic of our people, and pervading all sections and all classes, could never have availed so much had it not been combined with military science. And the occasion seemed suited to enforce this lesson on the minds of those who have been accustomed, in season and out of season, to rail at the scientific attainments of our officers.

The influence of military skill—the advantage of discipline in the troops—the power derived from the science of war, increases with the increased size of the contending armies. With two thousand we had beaten six thousand; with twenty thousand we would far more easily beat sixty thousand, because the General must be an educated soldier who wields large bodies of men, and the troops, to act efficiently, must be disciplined and commanded by able officers. He but said what he had long thought and often said, when he expressed his confidence in the ability of our officers to meet those of any service—favorably to compare, in all that constitutes the soldier, with any army in the world; and as the field widened for the exhibition, so would their merits shine more brightly still.

With many of the officers now serving on the Rio Grande he had enjoyed a personal acquaintance, and hesitated not to say that all which skill and courage and patriotism could perform, might be expected from them. He had forborne to speak of the General commanding on the Rio Grande on any former occasion; but he would now say to those who had expressed distrust, that the world held not a soldier better qualified for the service he was engaged in than General Taylor. Trained from his youth to arms, having spent the greater portion of his life on our frontier, his experience peculiarly fits him for the command he holds. Such as his conduct was in Fort Harrison, on the Upper Mississippi, in Florida, and on the Rio Grande, will it be wherever he meets the enemy of his country.

Those soldiers to whom so many have applied deprecatory epithets, upon whom it has been so often said no reliance could be placed, they, too, will be found in every emergency renewing such feats as have recently graced our arms, bearing the American flag to honorable triumphs, or falling beneath its folds as devotees to our common cause to die a soldier's death.

He rejoiced that the gentleman from South Carolina [Mr. BLACK] had shown himself so ready to pay this tribute to our army. He hoped not a voice would be raised in opposition to it; that nothing but the stern regret which is prompted by remembrance of those who bravely fought and nobly died will break the joy, the pride, the patriotic gratulation with which we hail this triumph of our brethren on the Rio Grande.

Remarks of Jefferson Davis on the bill making alterations in the pay department of the army, May 30, 1846.

Mr. JEFFERSON DAVIS said there were two positions taken in relation to the bill which he thought incorrect: first, that it became necessary from the war existing with Mexico; second, that it was designed to relieve the paymasters from oppressive duty. By referring to the report of the Paymaster General, which accompanied the President's Message at the commencement of this session of Congress, it will be found, that before this war commenced, and in reference to the then condition of the army, an increase of the paymasters was desired; and in the close of his report a convincing statement was made for the necessity of an Assistant Paymaster General—not, as has been assumed, to reside here, but to superintend payments in the military district of the Southwest; and this was enforced by the fact that he was then compelled to station a senior paymaster at headquarters of the army in Texas to discharge the duties of assistant to the Paymaster General. Sir, it is not to relieve the paymasters from fatigue, but to insure prompt and regular payments to the troops, that this increase was asked. If the number of paymasters be half of those required to make payments to the army at the regular periods, which is every two months, it follows that the payments will be delayed, and occur every four or every six months. The hardship would fall entirely on the troops to be paid, not on the disbursing officers who pay them. And as to the amount of service which the paymasters can be required to perform without destroying the efficiency of the department, I think gentlemen should allow the Paymaster General to be a better judge than ourselves. But to aid us in a conclusion, he has given the fact, that to pay at all the posts and arsenals as often as the law requires, would require travelling to exceed 100,000 miles per annum. This referred entirely to the state of things as they existed prior to a war with Mexico.

The second section of the bill changes the tenure, which is now an anomaly in the service, either land or naval. Quartermasters, commissaries, officers of the engineer department engaged in the construction of works, are charged with disbursements which cannot be so closely supervised as those of the pay department. It is the same case with pursers in the navy, yet all these hold their offices during the pleasure of the President; which, by practice, is considered equal to during good behavior.

This bill seeks to place paymasters on the same footing with other disbursing officers of the army; and I see no reason why they should be made an exception to the rule. Their attendance upon a marching army requires that their commissions should not expire during a campaign, as much as that a purser's commission should not expire on a voyage; and the tenure of their office should be fixed in reference to this, perhaps the most important, portion of their duties. The proposed change of tenure could not impair their efficiency or weaken their responsibility under ordinary circumstances, whilst it would adapt them to the extraordinary condition of war. The liability of all disbursing officers of the army to be removed by the President is constant; it is expected to follow immediately on a failure quarterly to account for funds placed in their hands, and with the amendments to require new bonds every four years, the present bill seems very free from well-founded objections.

The gentleman from South Carolina has so ably covered the whole ground that it is unnecessary to go further into it.

Mr. D. referred to remarks made yesterday by Mr. JOHNSON, of Tennessee, which were particularly directed against himself. He said, among those to whom he had been long known no explanation could be necessary; but here, having been misunderstood, it seemed to be called for.

Once for all, then, he would say, that if he knew himself, he was incapable of wantonly wounding the feelings, or of making invidious reflections upon the origin or occupation of any man.

He had, two days since, in a reply to the gentleman from Ohio, endeavored to correct this misunderstanding; it seemed, however, he had not succeeded. That gentleman [Mr. SAWYER] had, on a previous occasion, expressed his want of confidence in those officers of our army who had been cadets, and said, for the defence of the country we must look to the farmers and mechanics.

Mr. D. said, in answering that position he had referred to the service lately rendered by our army on the Rio Grande—had pointed out the results of skill and military science, and asked if such achievements could have been expected from men who had not the advantage of a military education.

He named two of the trades of civil life, not because they were less useful or honorable than others, not that either one or the other could disqualify a man from acquiring the other. On a former occasion, and for a similar purpose, he had made an extended allusion to many trades and professions, to all he had not thought it necessary again to refer. His opinion, in all its bearings, was no more than this, that war, like other knowledge, must be acquired. A military education did not qualify for the civil pursuits of life, nor did preparation for any of the civil pursuits, in itself, qualify for the duties of a soldier.

Was it necessary for him to say that a citizen might acquire the knowledge of arms, might become a distinguished soldier? Surely no one can deny it. He referred to the commander-in-chief of our army in terms of high commendation as a scientific soldier; said he had once been a lawyer, but had ceased to be so, and his military fame since he had become a soldier had almost swallowed up the remembrance of his earlier profession.

Jefferson Davis to the People of Mississippi.

(From Vicksburg Sentinel, July 21, 1846.)

Fellow Citizens: I address you to explain the cause of my present absence from the seat of the federal government.

Those of our fellow-citizens who, in answer to a call of the President, had volunteered to serve the U. S. in the existing war with Mexico, have elected me for their Colonel, and the Governor has furnished to me a commission, in accordance with that election. Having received a military education and served a number of years in the line of the army, I felt that my services were due to the country, and believed my experience might be available in promoting the comfort, the safety and efficiency of the Mississippi Regiment in the campaign on which they were about to enter. Such considerations, united to the desire common to our people to engage in the military service of the country, decided me unhesitatingly to accept the command which was offered. The regiment was organized and waiting to be mustered into service preparatory to a departure for the army of operation. Under such circumstances, I could not delay until the close of the Congressional session, though then so proximate that it must occur before a successor could be chosen and reach the city of Washington.

It was my good fortune to see in none of the measures likely to be acted on at this session such hazard as would render a single vote important, except the bill to regulate anew the duties upon imports. The vote on this was to occur very soon (in two days) after the receipt of my commission as Colonel, and I have the satisfaction to announce to you that it passed the House the evening before I left Washington; and I entertain no doubt of its passing through the Senate and becoming the law of the land. An analysis of the votes upon this bill will show that its main support was derived from the agricultural and exporting States. To these in a pecuniary view it was the measure of highest importance. But whilst I rejoice in it for such considerations, because tending to advance the great staple interest of our State, and thus to promote the prosperity of all industry among us, I am not less gratified at it as a measure of political reform. In adopting the ad valorem rule and restricting its operation to the revenue limit, the great principle of taxing in proportion to the benefits conferred is more nearly approximated, and the power to lay duties is directed to the purpose of raising money, for which alone it was conferred in the constitution of our confederacy. Thus it was exercised by the fathers of our Republic in the first tariff enacted under the federal constitution; when for the benefit it would confer upon American producers and manufacturers they chose to raise revenue by imposts rather than direct taxation. Since then, as in the bill of 1842, (to be substituted by that lately passed through the House of Representatives,) the collection of revenue has been the subordinate; the benefit to particular classes, the main object of duties. And the extent to which this was pursued was concealed by specific duties and minima valuations—rendering the law unintelligible on its face, and in many cases wholly prohibitory in its operation—destroying revenue but leaving taxation. A tariff ''for protection'' must discriminate against the necessaries of life to favor manufactures in a rude or ''infant'' state; a tariff for revenue may, and generally would, impose its highest duties upon luxuries, for reasons so just and equalizing in their practical effects, that one could have no inducement to conceal the policy or shrink from its avowal.

Commercial changes and the wants or superfluities of the treasury must require occasional modifications in the rates of duties upon imports; but a salutary check is held by the people so long as all modifications are made by changing the rate per cent. on enumerated articles, by which it is seen at once what tax is imposed upon consumption, and whether or not the limit of revenue is passed.

I trust we shall never again witness the spectacle, so revolting to every idea of self government, of a law in which, by specific duties and minima valuations, the purpose and effect is as absolutely concealed as in the edicts of the ancient tyrant, which were written in a hand so small and hung so high as to be illegible to those upon whom they were to operate.

During this session, as your Representative, I have acted upon all measures as seemed to me best to accord with the principles upon which I was elected, and most likely to correspond with the wishes and interests of the people of Mississippi. Thus my support was given to the law for the separation of the fiscal affairs of the general government from all connection with banks. The bill passed by the House of Representatives will, it is confidently expected, pass the Senate of the United States probably with an amendment extending the time at which it is to go into full effect. This is supposed to be necessary to prevent an injurious revulsion in the trade of the country, consequent upon the sudden contraction of the discounts of those banks, which have extended their accomodations upon the government deposits. Evils however positive, cannot always be immediately abated; and in this extension of the time it is only designed to make a temporary concession of policy, that by an easy, gradual change the prosperity of trade may be secured and monetary derangement be avoided. These two, the "tariff" and "Independent Treasury," are the measures which seem to me most deeply to involve the interests of Mississippi. Without mountain slopes, and mountain streams to furnish water power; without coal mines permanently to supply large amounts of cheap fuel at any locality, we cannot expect, in competition with those who enjoy either or both of these advantages, ever to become a manufacturing people. We must continue to rely, as at present, almost entirely upon our exports; and it requires no argument, under such circumstances, to maintain the position that the interest of our State will be most advanced by freeing commerce from all unnecessary burthens, and by measuring the value of our purchases by the standard used in our sales—the currency of the world.

By the active exertion of our Senator Speight, a bill was passed through the Senate, granting to the State of Mississippi alternate sections of land to aid in the construction of the proposed Mississippi and Alabama rail road. It is scarcely to be hoped that the House will act upon this measure at the present session, but placed upon the calendar of unfinished business, I think it will become a law at the next session of this Congress. I have also hoped that at the same session, a law would be passed to enable the Postmaster General to make contracts for a long term of years with rail roads under construction, by which the government would be secured from the exorbitant charges monopolies have it in their power to impose, and such certainty conferred upon the value of rail road stock as would greatly aid in the completion of an entire chain of railways from the Mississippi at Vicksburg to the Atlantic, and to the metropolis of our Union—a chain like a system of nerves to couple our remote members of the body politic to the centre of the Union, and rapidly to transmit sensation from one to the other; or like great sinews, uniting into concentrated action the power of the right hand and the left—the valley of the Mississippi and the coast of the Atlantic—when ever the necessities of one or the other shall require the action of both.

Much has been done during the past winter to adjust suspended and conflicting claims to land purchased from the U. S., and it is to be hoped that the action of this Congress will relieve our people from the uncertainty and harassing delays under which so many of them have labored for years past.

The bill to graduate and reduce the price of the public lands, will no doubt become a law; and we may expect from it an important increase to our population and State wealth; such as has been the result in the northern portion of our State, where under the Chickasaw treaty, a graduation system has been in operation, it is to be supposed, will be the result of a similar graduation in those districts where the public land has remained long unsold. The coast survey, now in progress along the Gulf of Mexico, cannot fail to have an important influence upon that portion of our State which borders on the Gulf, by giving correct charts of the channels and points of entrance safe for coasting vessels. Beyond this, I anticipate that the survey will establish as a fact that the best point west of Cape Florida for a navy yard to repair or construct vessels of the largest class, is the Harbor of Ship Island; and further, that it will lead to the speedy establishment of the necessary lights along the Coast and upon its adjacent Islands. The difficulty of obtaining appropriations for these has heretofore been greatly increased by the want of official information. The Legislature of our State memorialized Congress upon the propriety of re-opening the Pass Manchac. I was fully impressed with the propriety of the claim. Under more favorable circumstances, an appropriation for the purpose might have been obtained; and I yet hope that we shall get a survey and report for the contemplated work, in time for action at the next session of this Congress.

Since I took a seat as your Representative in Congress, the country has been disturbed; its political elements agitated and thrown into confusion; its peace with England seriously endangered by a question of boundary in what is known as the Oregon Territory. We have now satisfactory reason to believe that this question is amicably adjusted. The exact terms of the agreement have not transpired; but in general language it may be stated as settled on the basis of the 49th parallel of north latitude, with a temporary permission to the Hudson's Bay Company to navigate the Columbia River. That there should have been a desire among our people generally to hold the whole Territory was but natural, and this not merely from a wish to extend our territory, but also from a more creditable desire to reserve as far as we might, the North American Continent for republican institutions. As few will contend that this desire would have justified our Government in waging a war for territorial acquisition, the question was narrowed down to this: how far our rights clearly defined, and how shall we best secure what is clearly our own, and upon what terms shall we compromise for what is disputable? There were some who claimed for the parallel of 54° 40′ N. L. a talismanic merit—that it was the line to which patriotism required us to go, and short of which it was treasonable to stop. This opinion could only rest on the supposition that by purchase from Spain we acquired a perfect title. But this was to assume too much. The assumption carried with it the element of its own destruction. The Spanish claim extended as far as the 61st degree. If the boundary had been well defined, and the title perfect, then there was no power in our Government to surrender any part of it, and the Convention with Russia is void. But if, as must be generally admitted, the line of 54° 40′ was a compromise with Russia growing out of the fact that our title was imperfect and the boundary unsettled, then was 54° 40′ merely a line of expediency, as any other parallel would have been—good only as against Russia, and subject on the same principle to further adjustment with the other claimant in that territory.

The history of our past negotiations with Great Britain in relation to that territory gave little foundation for the expectation that we could get amicably, the whole country we have now secured south of the 49th parallel of latitude; and if the information I have derived from the officers who have explored different portions of that country be correct, a few years will satisfy our people that we have obtained nearly all which would have been valuable to us—a territory extending further north than the most northern point ever occupied by any portion of our people, and if the term "Oregon Territory" was properly applicable to the valley of the Columbia, or

Oregon River, a territory far more valuable than could be claimed in the valley drained by that stream and all its tributaries.

In the south we had another question of boundary unsettled; and though all proper efforts were made to adjust it amicably, they proved abortive. The minister sent to Mexico under a previous understanding that diplomatic relations should be renewed, and invested with full powers to treat of all questions in dispute, was rejected, without even being allowed to present his credentials. It could not be permitted to our rival claimant thus to decide the question, and though the insult would have justified an immediate declaration of war, in spirit of forbearance, the administration refrained from recommending this measure, and merely moved forward our troops to take possession of the entire territory claimed as our own, when there was no longer a prospect of adjustment by negotiation. This led to such hostilities as rendered it necessary to recognize the existence of war. Our government made the declaration in the mode provided by the constitution; and proceeded steadily to supply the means for a vigorous prosecution of the war into which we have been so unexpectedly drawn. In this connection it is worthy of remark that before a declaration was made on our part, the President of Mexico had made a similar declaration, and the appointments of the Mexican army which crossed the Rio Grande to attack the forces of General Taylor clearly show that it had advanced on that frontier for the purpose of invading the State of Texas.

The zeal shown in every quarter of the Union to engage in the service of our common country—the masses who have voluntarily come forward in numbers far exceeding the necessities of the occasion—attest the military strength of our Republic, and furnish just cause for patriotic pride and gratulation. I regret the disappointment felt by so many of my fellow-citizens of Mississippi at not being called into service; and I have not failed to present the case fully to the Executive of the U. S. Your patriotic anxiety is well appreciated; nor is the propriety of your conduct in waiting until regularly called for, forgotten; and if the war should continue, as further supplies of troops be required, there is no doubt but that our State will be among the first looked to for new levies.

There are several subjects connected with the local interests of Mississippi upon which it would have been agreeable to me to have said something, but the great length to which this letter is already extended, induces me with a few remarks bearing more particularly upon myself, to terminate it.

Unless the government of Mexico shall very soon take such steps as to give full assurance of a speedy peace, so that I may resume my duties as your Representative at the beginning of the next session of Congress, my resignation will be offered at an early day, that full time may be allowed to select a successor.

Grateful to the people for their confidence and honor bestowed upon me, I have labored as their representative industriously. Elected on avowed and established principles, the cardinal points to guide my course were always before me. How well that course has accorded with your wishes; how far it is improved by your judgment, it is not for me to anticipate; but I confidently rely on your generous allowance to give credit to my motives, and for the rest, as becomes a representative, I will cheerfully submit to your decision.

JEFF'N DAVIS.

Steamer Star Spangled Banner,
Mississippi River, July 13, 1846.

Jefferson Davis to Robert J. Walker.[1]

(From New York Historical Society Collections.)

Mouth of Rio Grande
24th Aug. 1846

Honble R. J. Walker
        Dear Sir,
    A part of our Regt. has started to Camargo, I embark in a few hours with another detachment making a total of five Companies— We have met delay and detention at every turn, the quartermasters at New Orleans have behaved either most incompetently or maliciously, and I am now but two days

---

[1] Walker, Robert James (1801-1869), an American political leader and financier, was born in Northumberland, Penn., July 23, 1801; was graduated from the University of Pennsylvania in 1819 and began the practice of law in Pittsburg in 1822. He removed to Mississippi in 1826; became prominent as a lawyer and land speculator; was a member of the U. S. Senate from March 4, 1835 to March 5, 1845; Secretary of the Treasury 1845-1849; Governor of Kansas from April to December 1857. He died in Washington, D. C., November 11, 1869. Walker was firm against the nullification doctrine of 1832-1833; was the author of the tariff bill of 1846, a revenue and not a protectionist measure; negotiated a loan in Europe for the United States 1863-1864; impaired the European financial credit of the Confederacy, and came to the rescue of the Alaska purchase treaty. Consult W. E. Dodd, Robert J. Walker, Imperialist, 40 pp., Chicago, 1914.

in possession of the Rifles ordered forward before I left Washington. But don't give the quartermaster's Dept. credit for that, my acknowledgements for having them *now* are due to your naval Militia—Maj. Roach despairing of the q.M. Dept. applied to Capt. Webster of the revenue service who placed the arms on the cutters "Ewing" and "Legare" and brought them to the Brazos Santiago. The ammunition and accoutrements sent from Baton Rouge to be forwarded by the quarter Master have not arrived and the ordnance stores on the frontier above have a very insufficient supply of Rifle ammunition. All this arises from having a bundle of papers and prejudices against Volunteers charged with the duties of quarter Master at New Orleans—viz. Lt. Col. & Asst. Qr. Master Hunt of the U. S. Army.

I must acknowledge the debt due from the Missi. Volunteers for service timely and courteously rendered by Capts. Webster and Moore Comdg. the Cutter "Ewing" and the Captain Comdg. the "Legare." If you can notice their conduct, I hope we may so use the rifles as to show the service was not to us alone.

Maj. Roach informs me that the surveyor of the port of New Orleans Mr. Hayden gave him kind assistance and feeling that it was done as a favor to your friends causes me to regret that I heard the statements in New Orleans which were communicated to you.

The mouth of this River has but little to invite one seeking the Land of promise to enter it the banks are low and without trees, but the current meets the sea with such force as to keep the entrance generally smooth, and it has been to me a matter of surprise that goods bound up the river were not brought ashore here, instead of being carried over the breakers at the Brazos in lighters & then brought in other lighters here. The anchorage is said to be equally good and the entrance habitually more quiet, though somewhat more shallow. I have not received the letter you intended to send me but hope always a brave and cheering us onward leads to the expect a letter from at Army Head Qrs. (Letter torn in this sentence).

"Claiborne" went off on the Louisiana Volunteers, (as I understand it a mere pretext) for the fact is they were sick of the job, and but very (few) of all I have seen wished to remain longer in this country. Our Regt. have suffered much from disease, had transportation been furnished promptly we would (have) gone with a full Regt. and what is more important with men full of zeal, and vigor, into the Campaign—

Though we pick the mill stone we can't see through it, if ever I find a hole it will give me pleasure to communicate to you the wonders found within.

Present me to Mrs. Walker in the kindest terms and give my remembrances to my young friends your Children—

With great regard I am

Yrs &c ——

Jeffn. Davis

Albert G. Brown to Jefferson Davis.

(From the Mississippi Department of Archives and History. Letter Book of Governor Brown.)

Executive Chamber
Jackson Miss. 29th Aug. 1846

Col Jeffr Davis
Com 1 Regt. Miss Volunteers
Army of Invasion

Sir

The Secr of War has forwarded to me the letter of resignation of Lt Burrus of the Yazoo Volunteers under your command, with an intimation from the Adgt Genl U. S. Army endorsed thereon that the resignation should have been tendered to the Governor of Missi. The Secr forbears to decide as to the correctness of the Adgt Genl intimation but says the consent of the Prest & the Dept is given to the withdrawal of Lt Burrus from the service.

I enclose several blank commissions to be used by you as occasion may require not doubting that they will be safe in your hands— This is done to facilitate the operations of your command to relieve you from any embarrassment growing out of deaths and resignations among your officers — In every case when a resignation is tendered and accepted by you, my approval is hereby given, and you have my consent to issue a commission to a successor from the inclosed blanks— I shall expect you of course to make a return to the adjt Genl of this State or to myself and also the Dept at Washington of the name of the officer succeeding together with the date of his commission. I have communicated the contents of this letter to the Secr of War

Very respfl
Your obt servt
A G Brown

HONOR TO OUR VOLUNTEERS.

(From Vicksburg Sentinel, November 10, 1846.)

The *Vicksburg Volunteers,* and *Southrons,* and the *Warren Cavalry,* have tendered a COLLATION to be given at the Southron's hall in Vicksburg, on Tuesday evening next, at 7 o'clock, to those who have returned from Mexico, on Furlough, and on account of ill health.

It is intended as a Compliment to Col. Jefferson Davis, Capt. George P. Crump, of the Volunteers—Capt. John Willis, of the Southrons, and *all* the returned Volunteers of said Companies. As the members returned are dispersed through the County, it is impossible for the Committee to reach them by private communication, and they are hereby specially invited to be present on the occasion.

The Committee also take great pleasure in tendering invitations, without distinction, to all those gallant Volunteers belonging to other Companies of the Mississippi Regiment who have returned, and who can make it convenient to honor the Collation by their presence, to partake with their comrades in arms.

MILES C. FOLKES,
ALEX. H. ARTHUR,
ALEX. M. PAXTON,
DANIEL S. MERCEIN,
ISAAC G. BIBBY,
JAS. H. McRAVEN,
C. A. MANLOVE,
E. G. WALKER,

Vicksburg, Nov. 6, 1846.   Committee.

Jefferson Davis to John Jenkins.

(From Vicksburg Sentinel, November 24, 1846.)

Brierfield, Nov. 16, 1846.

Jno. Jenkins, Esq.—Sir—My ideas of military propriety prevented me from publishing any statement of the conduct of the Mississippi Regiment in the siege at Monterey.

Secure in the consciousness of its gallant and valuable services, even without such restraint, I should probably have remained silent and allowed the official reports of commanders to reach an unbiassed public.

But by the publications of others a question has been prematurely raised as to the capture of the first Fort at the east end of the city of the 21st Sept. Deferring to some subsequent period a full account, I will now only present some of the main facts bearing upon this event.

In the forenoon of the 21st Sept., a part of Gen. Twigg's division made a demonstration upon the advanced work at the east end of Monterey—Gen. Butler's division from the position occupied heard the firing of small arms, but were not in sight of the combatants, when three Regiments, to-wit, the Tennessee, the Mississippi and the Ohio, were put en route in the direction of the firing, which was obliquely to our left and front.

After we had proceeded a short distance, the Ohio Regiment was diverged to the front, and the Tennessee and Mississippi Regiments continued their line of march in the order named, and moving by a flank.

During the whole march we were exposed to a cross fire of artillery. A round shot raking the Tennessee Regiment made great havoc, but did not check the advance.

The firing of small arms which had attracted us, ceased, and when we halted before the Fort and fronted to it, a small body of troops in the undress of our "regulars" was standing in such a position as to mask the right companies of the Mississippi Regiment. I pointed out the fact to Brig. Gen. Quitman commanding in person, and the closing or other movement of the Tennessee Regiment having created an interval on our left, it was agreed that I should occupy it. We were within the effective range of the enemy's fire but beyond that of our Rifles. I therefore executed a movement which gained ground to the front and left and when the Regiment was again formed into line, the troops who had stood upon my right were gone.

The attacking force now consisted of the Tennessee and Mississippi Regiments. The latter on the right, was directly in front of the Fort.

A deep, wide embrasure (which seems to have been used as a sally port, was immediately before our fifth company, numbering from the right; the piece of artillery which belonged to this embrasure was run behind the parapet. We commenced firing, advancing; the men were directed to select their objects and aim as sharp shooters. Their fine rifles told upon the enemy so that in a short time, say ten minutes, his fire was so reduced as to indicate the propriety of a charge. I had no instructions, no information as to the plan, no knowledge of any sustaining troops except the Tennesseeans on our left, and seeing nothing to justify delay, gave the order to charge.

Lieutenant Col. McClung led the company before the embrasure at full speed upon it, the flanks ran, converging to this line of approach, which was over a smooth piece of ground from which the corn had been lately cut. When the movement commenced, I saw Col. Campbell directing his Regiment in some flank manoeuvre; thereafter I do not recollect to have looked back, and did not see him; but I have been informed that he led his Regiment by a flank.

When I crossed the ditch our Lieutenant Col. was the only man upon the parapet. I sprang into the embrasure beside Lieutenant Patterson of our Regiment. The defence of the place was abandoned; the last of its garrison were crowding out of the sally port at the other extremity; we pursued them, firing upon them as they fled to a fortified stone building in rear of the Fort and across a stream to a fort still further to the rear.

When I saw Col. Campbell's letter (recently published) claiming for his Regiment the credit of storming this fort, carrying it at the point of the bayonet, and giving to the Mississippi Regiment the merit of only having sustained him, my surprise at such an arrangement of the Regiments, was only equalled by that which I felt at learning that the bayonet had been put in requisition. No one could go upon the ground, examine the position of the Regiments and the condition of the parapet and ditch of the fort, and the surface over which it was necessary to approach, without coming at once to the conclusion, that our Regiment must have entered the fort first, or faltered in the charge. Why this claim has been put forth it is not for me to determine. It is improbable, unjust, injurious to us, and unnecessary to our comrades in that attack, when the conduct of the whole was the property of each. As a duty to my Regiment, I will follow this question, raised by others, until a mass of concurrent testimony from a variety of witnesses shall incontestably establish our claim to whatever credit attaches to the storming party on that occasion.

Your friend, &c.,
JEFFERSON DAVIS,

Jefferson Davis to the Editor of the Washington Union
(From Washington Union, Feb. 11, 1847.)

Victoria, Tamaulipas, Mexico.
January 6, 1847.

Dear Sir: After much speculation and no little misrepresentation about the capitulation of Monterey, I perceive by our recent newspapers, that a discussion has arisen as to who is responsible for that transaction. As one of the commissioners who were entrusted by General Taylor with the arrangements of the terms upon which the city of Monterey and its fortifications should be delivered to our forces, I have had frequent occasion to recur to the course then adopted, and the considerations which led to it. My judgment after the fact has fully sustained my decisions at the date of the occurrence; and feeling myself responsible for the instrument as we prepared and presented it to our commanding general, I have the satisfaction, after all subsequent events, to believe that the terms we offered were expedient, and honorable, and wise. A distinguished gentleman with whom I acted on that commission, Governor Henderson, says, in a recently published letter, "I did not at the time, nor do I still like the terms, but acted as one of the commissioners, together with Geenral Worth and Colonel Davis, to carry out General Taylor's instructions. We ought and could have made them surrender at discretion," &c., &c.

From each position taken in the above paragraph I dissent. The instructions given by General Taylor only presented his object, and fixed a limit to the powers of his commissioners; hence, when points were raised which exceeded our discretion, they were referred to the commander; but minor points were acted on, and finally submitted as a part of our negotiation. We fixed the time within which the Mexican forces should retire from Monterey. We agreed upon the time we would wait for the decision of the respective governments, which I recollect was less by thirty-four days than the Mexican commissioners asked—the period adopted being that which, according to our estimate, was required to bring up the rear of our army with the ordnance and supplies necessary for further operations.

I did not then, nor do I now, believe we could have made the enemy surrender at discretion. Had I entertained the opinion it would have been given to the commission, and to the commanding general, and would have precluded me from signing an agreement which permitted the garrison to retire with the honors of war. It is demonstrable, from the position and known prowess of the two armies, that we could drive the enemy from the town; but the town was untenable whilst the main fort (called the new citadel) remained in the hands of the enemy. Being without siege artillery or entrenching tools, we could only hope to carry this fort by storm, after a heavy loss from our army; which, isolated in a hostile country, now numbered less than half the forces of the enemy. When all this had been achieved, what more would we have gained than by the capitulation?

General Taylor's force was too small to invest the town. It was, therefore, always in the power of the enemy to retreat, bearing his light arms. Our army—poorly provided, and with very insufficient transportation—could not have overtaken, if they had pursued the flying enemy. Hence the conclusion that, as it was not in our power to capture the main body of the Mexican Army, it is unreasonable to suppose their general would have surrendered at discretion. The moral effect of retiring under the capitulation was certainly greater than if the enemy had retreated without our consent. By this course we secured the large supply of ammunition he had collected in Monterey—which, had the assault been continued, must have been exploded by our shells, as it was principally stored in "the Cathedral," which, being supposed to be filled with troops, was the especial aim of our pieces The destruction which this explosion would have produced must have involved the advance of both divisions of our troops; and I commend this to the contemplation of those whose arguments have been drawn from facts learned since the commissioners closed their negotiations. With these introductory remarks, I send a copy of a manuscript in my possession, which was prepared to meet such necessity as now exists for an explanation of the views which governed the commissioners in arranging the terms of capitulation, to justify the commanding general, should misrepresentation and calumny attempt to tarnish his well-earned reputation, and, for all time to come, to fix the truth of the transaction. Please publish this in your paper, and believe me your friend, etc.,

JEFFERSON DAVIS.

Memoranda of the transactions in connexion with the capitulation of Monterey, capital of Nueva Leon, Mexico.

By invitation of General Ampudia, commanding the Mexican army, General Taylor accompanied by a number of his officers, proceeded on the 24th September, 1846, to a house designated as the place at which General Ampudia requested an interview. The parties being convened, General Ampudia announced, as official information, that commissioners from the United States had been received by the government of Mexico; and that the orders under which he had prepared to defend the city of Monterey, had lost their force by the subsequent change of his own government, therefore he asked the conference. A brief conversation between the commanding generals, showed their views to be so opposite, as to leave little reason to expect an amicable arrangement between them.

General Taylor said he would not delay to receive such propositions as General Ampudia indicated. One of General Ampudia's party, I think, the governor of the city, suggested the appointment of a mixed commission; this was acceded to, and General W. G. Worth of the United States army, General J. Pinckney Henderson, of the Texan volunteers, and Colonel Jefferson Davis, of the Mississippi riflemen on the part of General Taylor; and General J. Ma. Ortega, General P. Requena, and Señor the Governor M. Ma. Llano on the part of Gen. Ampudia, were appointed.

General Taylor gave instructions to his commissioners which, as understood, for they were brief and verbal, will be best shown by the copy of the demand which the United States commissioners prepared in the conference room here incorporated:

Copy of demand by United States Commissioners.

"I. As the legitimate result of the operations before this place, and the present position of the contending armies, we demand the surrender of the town, the arms and munitions of war, and all other public property within the place.

"II. That the Mexican armed force retire beyond the Rinconada, Linares, and San Fernando, on the coast.

"III. The commanding general of the army of the United States agrees that the Mexican officers reserve their side arms and private baggage; and the troops be allowed to retire under their officers without parole, a reasonable time being allowed to withdraw the forces.

"IV. The immediate delivery of the main work, now occupied, to the army of the United States.

"V. To avoid collisions, and for mutual convenience, that the troops of the United States shall not occupy the town until the Mexican forces have been withdrawn, except for hospital purposes, storehouses, &c.

"VI. The commanding general of the United States agrees not to advance beyond the line specified in the second section before the expiration of eight weeks, or until the respective governments can be heard from."

The terms of the demand were refused by the Mexican commissioners, who drew up a counter proposition, of which I only recollect that it contained a permission to the Mexican forces to retire with their arms. This was urged as a matter of soldierly pride, and as an ordinary courtesy. We had reached the limit of our instructions, and the commission rose to report the disagreement.

Upon returning to the reception room, after the fact had been announced that the commissioners could not agree upon terms, General Ampudia entered at length upon the question, treating the point of disagreement as one which involved the honor of his country, spoke of his desire for a settlement without further bloodshed, and said he did not care about the pieces of artillery which he had at the place. General Taylor responded to the wish to avoid unnecessary bloodshed. It was agreed the commission should reassemble, and we were instructed to concede the small arms; and I supposed there would be no question about the artillery. The Mexican commissioners now urged that, as all other arms had been recognised, it would be discreditable to the artillery if required to march out without anything to represent their arm, and stated, in answer to an inquiry, that they had a battery of light artillery, manoeuvred and equipped as such. The commission again rose, and reported the disagreement on the point of artillery.

General Taylor hearing that more was demanded than the middle ground, upon which, in a spirit of generosity, he had agreed to place the capitulation, announced the conference at an end; and rose in a manner which showed his determination to talk no more. As he crossed the room to leave it, one of the Mexican commissioners addressed him, and some conversation, which I did not hear, ensued. Gen. Worth asked permission of Gen. Taylor, and addressed some remarks to Gen. Ampudia, the spirit of which was that which he manifested throughout the negotiation, viz: generosity and leniency, and a desire to spare the further effusion of blood. The commission reassembled, and the points of capitulation were agreed upon. After a short recess we again repaired to the room in which we had parted from the Mexican commissioners; they were tardy in joining us, and slow in executing the instrument of capitulation. The 7th, 8th, and 9th articles were added during this session. At a late hour the English original was handed to Gen. Taylor for his examination; the Spanish original having been sent to General Ampudia. Gen. Taylor signed and delivered to me the instrument as it was submitted to him, and I returned to receive the Spanish copy with the signature of General Ampudia, and send that having Gen. Taylor's signature, that each general might countersign the original to be retained by the other. Gen. Ampudia did not sign the instrument as was expected, but came himself to meet the commissioners. He raised many points which had been settled, and evinced a disposition to make the Spanish differ in essential points from the English instrument. Gen. Worth was absent. Finally he was required to sign the instrument prepared for his own commissioners, and the English original was left with him that he might have it translated, (which he promised to do that night,) and be ready the next morning with a Spanish duplicate of the English instrument left with him. By this means the two instruments would be made to correspond, and he be compelled to admit his knowledge of the contents of the English original before he signed it.

The next morning the commission again met; again the attempt was made, as had been often done before by solicitation, to gain some grant in addition to the compact. Thus we had, at their request, adopted the word *capitulation* in lieu of *surrender;* they now wished to substitute *stipulation* for *capitulation*. It finally became necessary to make a peremptory demand for the immediate signing of the English instrument by General Ampudia, and the literal translation (now perfected) by the commissioners and their general. The Spanish instrument first signed by Gen. Ampudia was destroyed in the presence of his commissioners; the translation of our own instrument was countersigned by Gen. Taylor, and delivered. The agreement was complete, and it only remained to execute the terms.

Much has been said about the construction of article 2 of the capitulation, a copy of which is hereto appended. Whatever ambiguity there may be in the language used, there was a perfect understanding by the commissioners upon both sides, as to the intent of the parties. The distinction we made between light artillery equipped and manoeuvred as such, designed for and used in the field, and pieces being the armament of a fort, was clearly stated on our side; and that it was comprehended on their's, appeared in the fact, that repeatedly they asserted their possession of light artillery, and said they had one battery of light pieces. Such conformity of opinion existed among our commissioners upon every measure which was finally adopted, that I consider them, in their sphere, jointly and severally responsible for each and every article of the capitulation. If, as originally viewed by Gen. Worth, our conduct has been in accordance with the peaceful policy of our government, and shall in any degree tend to consummate that policy, we may congratulate ourselves upon the part we have taken. If otherwise, it will remain to me as a deliberate opinion, that the terms of the capitulation gave all which could have followed, of desirable result, from a further assault. It was in the power of the enemy to retreat, and to bear with him his small arms, and such a battery as was contemplated in the capitulation. The other grants were such as it was honorable in a conquering army to bestow, and which it cost magnanimity nothing to give.

The above recollections are submitted to Generals Henderson and Worth for correction and addition that the misrepresentation of this transaction may be presented by a statement made whilst the events are recent and the memory fresh.

JEFFERSON DAVIS,
Colonel Mississippi Riflemen.

Camp near Monterey, October 7th, 1846.

The above is a correct statement of the leading facts connected with the transactions referred to, according to my recollection. It is, however, proper, that I should further state, that my first impression was, that no better terms than those first proposed, on the part of Gen. Taylor, ought to have been given, and I so said to General Taylor when I found him disposed to yield to the request of General Ampudia; and, at the same time, gave it as my opinion that they would be accepted by him before we left the town. General Taylor replied, that he would run no risk where it could be avoided—that he wished to avoid the further shedding of blood, and that he was satisfied that our government would be pleased with the terms given by the capitulation; and being myself persuaded of that fact, I yielded my individual views and wishes; and, under that conviction, I shall ever be ready to defend the terms of the capitulation.

J. PINCKNEY HENDERSON,
Major General Commanding the Texan Volunteers.

I not only counselled and advised, the opportunity being offered the general-in-chief, the first proposition; but cordially assented and approved the decision taken by General Taylor in respect to the latter, as did every member of the commission, and for good and sufficient military and national reasons—and stand ready, at all times and proper places, to defend and sustain the action of the commanding general, and participation of the commissioners. Knowing that malignants, the *tremor* being off, are at work to discredit and misrepresent the case, (as I had anticipated,) I feel obliged to Col. Davis for having thrown together the material and facts.

W. J. WORTH,
Brig. Gen. commanding 2d division.
Monterey, Oct. 12th, 1846.

Terms of the capitulation of the city of Monterey, the capital of Nueva Leon, agreed upon by the undersigned commissioners—to wit: General Worth, of the United States army; General Henderson, of the Texan volunteers; and Col. Davis, of the Mississippi riflemen, on the part of Major General Taylor, commanding-in-chief of the United States forces; and General Requena and General Ortego, of the army of Mexico, and Señor Manuel M. Llano, Governor of Nueva Leon, on the part of Señor General Don Pedro Ampudia, commanding-in-chief the army of the north of Mexico.

Article 1.   As the legitimate result of the operations before this place, and the present position of the contending armies, it is agreed that the city, the fortifications, cannon, the munitions of war, and all other public property, with the undermentioned exceptions, be surrendered to the commanding general of the United States forces now at Monterey.

Article 2.   That the Mexican forces be allowed to retain the following arms—to wit: The commissioned officers, their side-arms; the infantry, their arms and accoutrements; the cavalry, their arms and accoutrements; the artillery, one field battery, not to exceed six pieces, with twenty-one rounds of ammunition.

Article 3.   That the Mexican armed forces retire within seven days from this date beyond the line formed by the pass of the Rinconada, the city of Linares, and San Fernando de Pusos.

Article 4.   That the citadel of Monterey be evacuated by the Mexican, and occupied by the American forces to-morrow morning, at 10 o'clock.

Article 5.   To avoid collisions, and for mutual convenience, that the troops of the United States will not occupy the city until the Mexican forces have withdrawn, except for hospital and storage purposes.

Article 6.   That the forces of the United States will not advance beyond the line specified in the 3d article, before the expiration of eight weeks, or until the orders of the respective governments can be received.

Article 7. That the public property to be delivered, shall be turned over and received by officers appointed by the commanding general of the two armies.

Article 8. That all doubts, as to the meaning of any of the preceding articles, shall be solved by an equitable construction, and on principles of liberality to the retiring army.

Article 9. That the Mexican flag, when struck at the citadel, may be saluted by its own battery.

W. J. WORTH,

Brig. Gen. U. S. A.

J. PINCKNEY HENDERSON,

Maj. Gen. commanding the Texan volunteers.

JEFFERSON DAVIS,

Colonel Mississippi riflemen.

J. M. ORTEGA,
T. REQUENA,
MANUEL M. LLANO,

Approved: PEDRO AMPUDIA,
Z. TAYLOR,

Maj. Gen. U. S. A. commanding.

Done at Monterey, Sept. 24, 1846.

Jefferson Davis to C. S. Tarpley and others.

(From Vicksburg Weekly Whig, June 9, 1847.)

Monterey, May 7, 1847.

Gentlemen—Your letter of the 5th ult., conveying the resolutions of a public meeting held in the capital of our State, on the 3d of April, 1847, has just been received.

For the approbation thus conferred on the officers and men of the 1st Mississippi Rifles, I feel most sincerely thankful. For myself, and for those whom it has been my honor and good fortune to command, I will say, that in such manifestations of regard and esteem of our brethren at home, is contained the reward for whatever we have borne of toil, privation or loss; for whatever we may have achieved of honorable service in the cause of our country.

The necessary directions will be given, to place your letter on the records, and ensure its reading at the head of each company of our Regiment.

For the very kind and highly complimentary terms in which you, as the organ of the meeting have presented its resolutions, I am truly sensible, and offer my grateful acknowledgements.

Cordially, I am your friend and fellow citizen,

JEFF'N DAVIS.
Colonel 1st Mississippi Rifles.

Messrs. C. S. Tarpley, Jno. D. Freeman, Jas. J. Deavenport, H. Stuart Foote, C. R. Clifton, Charles Scott, Daniel Mayes, Jno. I. Guion, A. Hutchinson, Jno. Mayrant,—Committee.

Albert G. Brown to Jefferson Davis.

(From the Mississippi Department of Archives and History. Letter Book of Governor Brown.)

Executive Chamber
Jackson Mi 17 May 1847

Col Jeff^n Davis
Com 1st" Miss Rifles,
Sir

I have the honor to enclose a copy of a letter written by me to the Secretary of War requesting that officers & men in your Regiment be allowed to retain their arms on retiring from the service or that said arms be issued to Mississippi as a part of her *quota* from the Genl Government. The Secr. has not yet replied to the letter, but it is not doubted by me that he will at least yield to the last request. Expecting to be absent from home for some weeks I have instructed the Sec of State to forward Gov Marcy's answer to you when it is received. Should either of my requests be complied with, you will allow the men under your command to retain their arms when you disband them. If they are issued to the State, I cannot render a more acceptable service to the people for whom your ever glorious Reg't has won such imperishable honor than to say in their name "there shall be no divorce between the gallant soldier & his Gun."

Very Respy
Your obt. serv't
A. G. Brown

James K. Polk [1] *to Jefferson Davis.*

(From Vicksburg Weekly Whig, October 20, 1847.)

Washington City, May 19, 1847.

My Dear Sir:—The Secretary of War will transmit to you, a commission as Brigadier General of the United States Army. The Brigade which you will command, will consist of volunteers called out to serve during the war with Mexico. It gives me sincere pleasure to confer this important command upon you. Your distinguished gallantry and military skill while leading the noble regiment under your command, and especially in the battles of *Monterey* and *Buena Vista,* eminently entitle you to it. I hope that the severe wound which you received at the latter place, may soon be healed, and that your country may have the benefit of your valuable services, at the head of your new command.

I am very faithfully, your friend,

JAMES K. POLK.

To Brigadier-General Jefferson Davis, U. S. Army, in Mexico.

Jefferson Davis to John M. Chilton and others.

(From Vicksburg Weekly Whig, June 16, 1847.)

New Orleans, 11th June, 1847.

Gentlemen—Your letter of the 31st of May, conveying in the most kind and complimentary terms the wish of the citizens of Vicksburg and Warren county to receive the 1st Mississippi Rifles at a Barbecue, was received at this place.

We most sensibly feel your flattering attention to our ap-

[1] Polk, James Knox (1795-1849), eleventh President of the United States, was born in Mecklenburg county, North Carolina, November 2, 1795, graduated from the University of North Carolina in 1818, removed to Tennessee, studied law, was admitted to the bar in 1820, and began practice in Columbia, Tenn. He served in the Tennessee House of Representatives 1823-1825; was a member of the national House of Representatives, 1825-1839; Speaker, 1835-1839; and Governor of Tennessee 1839-1841. He was President of the United States, 1845-1849. During his administration the annexation of Texas (1845) involved the country in aggressive war against Mexico (May, 1846-September, 1847) which resulted in the acquisition of California and other cessions from Mexico. A dispute with the British government about the boundary of Oregon was settled by the Treaty with Great Britain signed June 15, 1846. President Polk retired from office in March, and died at Nashville, Tenn., June 15, 1849.

proach, and hope to have the pleasure of meeting you at Vicksburg on Tuesday morning, the 15th inst.

To you, gentlemen of the committee, for the pleasing manner in which you welcome our coming, I return, on the part of the Regiment, the sincerest thanks. Very truly, yours,

JEFF'N DAVIS.
Colonel Mississippi Rifles.

John M. Chilton, Ch'n., A. H. Arthur, T. E. Robins, W. H. Johnson, N. D. Coleman, E. J. Sessions, W. C. Smedes, J. Jenkins, M. C. Folkes, N. B. Batchelor, C. J. Searles.

Reception in honor of the First Regiment Mississippi Volunteers, War with Mexico at Natchez, Mississippi, June 15, 1847.

(From Natchez Weekly Courier, June 16, 1847.)

Yesterday was a day which will long be remembered in our annals—a glorious day, alternately illuminated by sunshine or darkened by clouds, and one of the hours of which will be deeply traced with every sentiment which could do honor to an admiring people, or to our glorious returned volunteers, "the bravest of the brave"—who have so gallantly won and so nobly worn the brilliant chaplets of fame which adorn their brows. It is to be regretted that our city of the bluffs was not honored by all the companies of the regiment, although those who were present had performed deeds, worthy, if possible, (which could not be) a reception more enthusiastic. But, it is useless to talk about *that*. No reception could have been warmer, more whole-souled, or more heart-inspiring. It was a sight to make the pulse throb, and the heart beat with accelerated motion to see those gallant soldiers—those glorious boys of our own State—the "Star Regiment" of Gen. Taylor's army—THE MEN who had stormed the rocky steeps of Monterey, and met with unquailing hearts the iron storm that raged in that doomed city—now a glorious monument of their valor. There were the men who had breasted unflinchingly the crimson tide of battle at Buena Vista. There were the men who had never faltered in the fiercest of the death struggle and when frightened fugitives were frantically flying from the sanguinary conflict, *they* remained as firm and unmoved as the rock which for ages has breasted the surges of the billows of ocean. There were their ever-glorious commanders,—the noble Davis, the fearless McClung—scarred with honorable wounds—yet suffering from the injuries they had received in their country's service—but full of patriotic devotion and with spirits unsubdued, and with hearts as free and souls as high as when they first responded to the call of their government and flew to the field of conflict. They were, officers and men, a spectacle which reminded us of the times of our revolutionary ancestors—of the "times that tried" the "souls" of the men who were led to battle by Washington, Montgomery, Greene, and many others, whose names illumine as with a glorious stream of sunlight, the history of that eventful epoch,—and they were evidently from the same stock, for *such men* could not have sprung from any other stock.

But, to the arrival of our laurelled volunteers. The shades of night had scarcely yielded to the bright beams of morn, ere the loud-toned cannon thundered forth the signal, announcing to the citizens of our city and the country round about, the apporach of the pride and glory of our chivalrous State. The whole city was moved as if with one mighty inpulse,—citizens from the country flocked in in thousands—stores and other places of business remained unopened, and one general thrill of joyous enthusiasm appeared to animate the vast mass of moving and excited humanity which crowded our streets and thronged the bluffs of the mighty river which flows past our city, to render "honor to the brave."

At about 9 o'clock, the companies of our First Regiment of Rifles were formed at the landing, and at about the same time the fine military companies of our city—the Fencibles, the Light Guard, the Natchez Guards, the Jefferson College Cadets and the Natchez Cadets,—marched under the hill to escort them to our city. The military was formed in the following order: the Fencibles and Light Guard on the right, the Rifles in the centre, and the College Cadets and Natchez Cadets and Natchez Guards in the rear, and thus the long line moved up upon the bluff.

The procession then moved up Main street to Pine street, and down Franklin street to the bluff, where preparations on a scale commensurate with the importance of the occasion, had been made to receive our honored guests.

When we arrived upon the Bluff, a scene of rare and surpassing beauty, never excelled and rarely equalled, burst upon our sight. The Promenade ground was thronged with the bright and beautiful, and wherever he turned a blaze of loveliness was sure to dawn upon the vision of the beholder. But of all the scenes that pleased us in the highest degree was that presented by the pupils of the Natchez Institute—*six hundred in number* —who, under the admirable supervision of the Principal of the Institute, Mr. Pearl, were formed in two lines on each side of the central promenade—the young ladies immediately in front and the boys in the rear. Each young lady held in her hand a boquet of beautiful flowers, and, as the war worn veterans, with their bronzed visages and toil-hardened frames filed slowly past them, presented each with a boquet. It was a touching as well as a soul inspiring spectacle and deeply did this manifestation of respect strike into the hearts of the toil-tried sons of gallant State. We heard dozens give expression to sentiments of high gratification. It was an offering from the young, the lovely and the guileless, that came from bosoms untainted with the vices and strifes of the world, and went directly home to the inmost cores of the hearts of these well-tried veterans. It was a beautiful sight, and which would inspire any man with feelings of the liveliest satisfaction that he lived in a State that possessed such men to send forth to the field of glory and victory, and such hands to strew with flowers the pathway of their return to the State that sent them forth to perform their daring and brilliant deeds.

After performing various military evolutions, the Rifles and our volunteer companies were formed in mass around the rostrum prepared for the reception of the officers, committees, orator of the day, and other distinguished citizens. At this point the presence of the crowd was intense. No consideration of personal convenience appeared to operate upon the nerves of any, either ladies or gentlemen, in endeavoring to get within hearing distance. When all the arrangements were completed, the orator of the Day, Col. Adam L. Bingaman, arose and delivered the following address—an address sparkling with the highest coruscations of genius, and abounding with the brightest attributes of intellect—an address to the purpose, eloquently delivered, and which went home to the hearts of the brave men whose gallant deeds and glorious achievements he was recounting.

We will not attempt to give a description of the address—for that would be a work of entire supererogation. The speech will be found below and will rivet the attention of every reader.

Col. Bingaman's Address.

Col. Davis, Lieut. Col. McClung—Officers and Soldiers of the First Mississippi Rifles:

Veteran Volunteers—the Star Regiment—men of Monterey— men of Buena Vista! Never was there assigned to any one, a more grateful duty, than that which has been conferred, by the partial favor of the citizens of this city and county upon the individual who now addresses you: the office of expressing to you, feebly though it be, the warm and gushing sentiments of heartfelt pride, gratitude and congratulation, with which they throng to hail and welcome you, on your safe return from the fields of your, and their country's glory. All that surround you—the hale and the infirm—the aged and the young—the Fair—those discriminating and devout admirers of the brave, who constitute, at once, the resistless incentive to gallant deeds, and the priceless reward of those who have passed through the purifying baptism of fire,—all, all, with one sympathetic and enthusiastic accord, press forward to join in the general jubilee of triumph and exultation:

> "While from the scaffolds, windows, tops of houses
> Are cast such gaudy show'rs of garlands down,
> That e'en the crowd appear like conquerors,
> And the whole city seems, like a vast meadow,
> Set all with flowers, as clear Heaven with stars."

High, as had previously been, the character of Mississippi for deeds of noble daring, when, under the chivalrous Hinds, on the plains of Chalmette, her cavalry excited the "astonishment of one army and the admiration of the other," *you* have exalted that character to a still higher pitch of glorious elevation. The first to carry a fortress in Monterey,—at Buena Vista, a small but determined band of less than 300, you held in check an assaulting column of 6000 men. Calm, steadfast and immovable, as a rock firm-seated against the innumerable and impetuous billows of the ocean, you held the enemy, as with the iron grasp of Destiny, steadily to his place; until, upon the coöperation of the gallant Bragg and the death-storm of his artillery, by your joint efforts, you drove him headlong and howling from the field. Upon our corps of artillery, too much praise cannot be bestowed. Always, in the language of your Commander-in-chief, in the right place at the right time—they mainly contributed to the achievement of the most glorious victory, which emblazons the annals of our country. Like the Legio fulminatrix, the fulminating legion of Aurelius, their *appropriate device* should be, a winged thunderbolt; denoting, at once, celerity of motion, unerring certainty of aim, and irresistible and all-overwhelming power. Nor will our feelings of *national pride* permit us to pass by in silence, the gallant bearing of the soldiers of our sister States. Louisiana, nobly prodigal of her men and her treasure,—Kentucky, the State of the bloody ground—Tennessee, Illinois, Texas—Americans all—all generous competitors for the prize of honor—all resolute, as Spartans, to return crowned with laurels or borne on their shields. Never, even in the palmiest days of chivalry, did more stalwart and devoted knights enter the lists of the proudest tournament;—never were the interests and honor of a country entrusted to more valiant and determined hands. Why, it was like the fire races of the ancients. From officer to officer—from man to man—from county to county—from State to State—from regulars to volunteers—the torch of glory was passed in such bright and rapid succession, that the horizon of the whole Union has become radiant and burning with the blaze.

But while we exult with the living, let us pay the merited tribute of our tears—of proud, though bitter tears—to the memories of the glorious dead. Tearing themselves from the enjoyment of ease, comfort and competence,—from the blessings of family and friends,—from all that man holds dear, save *Honor,*—they rushed, with you, to the rescue of their fellow citizens, in a distant and hostile land. To the citizen soldier the voice of his country is always imperative.

> Say that it is his country's will
> And there's the foe,
>
> He has nae thought but how to kill,
> Twa at a blow.
>
> Nae cauld faint-hearted doubtings tease him;
> Death comes, wi' fearless eye he sees him;
> Wi' bluidy hand, a welcome gies him:
> And when he fa's
> His latest draught o' breathin' lea'es him,
> In faint huzzas.

Such were McKee, and Hardin, and Yell, and Clay, and Watson, and Lincoln, and all, *all* who bravely and nobly fell, striving in the front ranks, to uphold the honor of our flag; and to wrest from the hands of chance, the evergreen chaplet of victory. Pained, heart-stricken, as we are, at the loss of such men, there are yet mingled with our regrets, consoling sentiments of proud and patriotic exultation. Great, invincible, deep seated in the affections of its citizens must that country be, upon whose altars are laid such priceless victims, as free offerings.

To live with fame,
The Gods allow to many! but to die
With equal lustre, is a blessing, Heaven
Selects from all the choicest boons of fate,
And with a sparing hand on few bestows.

Honored and cherished were they in their lives. Embalmed in our memories, they ever shall be. Death has made them immortal. Hallowed, to all future time, be the earth in which repose their honored bones; and woe to the head that would counsel, or the hand that would sign a surrender of one inch of soil, which has been appropriated by the precious blood, and made sacred by the sepulture of an American soldier.

To your Commander, fellow citizens of the Star Regiment, highly as we appreciate his merits as a soldier, and grateful, as we are, for the honor he has conferred on our State,—we must beg leave, on this occasion, to express our additional thanks, for an act of disinterested and noble generosity. When the terms of the capitulation of Monterey were assailed—when reproach was attempted to be cast upon him, who is first in honor as the first in place—when a stigma was sought to be fixed upon the Hero of the age—on that man of iron will, upon whose sword sits Victory laurel-crowned—whose praise, Time with his own eternal voice shall sing—when "the Eagle of his tribe" was hawked at by mousing owls—and when it was attempted to drug with poison the chalice of congratulation—when the serpent of defamation was cunningly concealed in the chaplet of applause;—who? disinterestedly, nobly, in the frank and fearless spirit of a true soldier; who, generously, manfully and effectively stood forward in defence of a brother soldier? Who was it, that did not only scotch, but killed; aye, and seared the reeking fragments of the lurking reptile? Col. Jefferson Davis, of the Mississippi Rifles. Thanks, honor, to you sir! for such noble conduct. Your own conscience approves the act; and the voice of a grateful country sanctions and sustains the approval.

When I look upon that country, supported and sustained by the heroes of Palo Alto, Resaca de la Palma, Monterey, Cerro Gordo, Sacramento, and the American Marathon, Buena Vista! —when I see hosts, armed and accoutred, spontaneously springing from her soil, as if sown with dragon's teeth;—when I see heroes, bursting forth in full and glittering panoply, as sprang Minerva from the front of Jove—she seems to me like the revered Cybele, the Mother of Gods,

"Omnes Caolicolae! omnes supera alta tenentes."
I see her seated upon her triumphal car, drawn by trained lions, patient alone of the curb of discipline, and on her head a turret-like attire, the emblem, at once, of independent strength, of deep-seated security and of offensive, defensive and self-avenging power. Honor then to the banner of the Union! Honor to the men who have upheld its honor! Welcome! thrice welcome the victors returned from the fields of their fame! Glory to the heroes of Monterey! Glory to the heroes of Buena Vista! And in the language of your own McClung, "Three cheers for General Taylor—the stout-hearted old soldier—the Blucher of America—who *gave* the battle—and three cheers for the gallant hearts that *won* it."

Col. Jefferson Davis, on behalf of his regiment and himself, delivered a most beautiful and heart-thrilling response to the complimentary allusions to the heroic deeds and gallant conduct of himself and his command. We much regret that it has been out of our power to obtain even a sketch of his eloquent and appropriate remarks. Being indisposed nearly the whole of yesterday, we have labored under great disadvantage in giving a description of yesterday's proceeding. Col. Davis' remarks were eloquent and apt, in the highest degree. After paying a deserved tribute to the unflinching bravery of his men,—to their discipline,—to the unquailing courage with which they manfully stood up and fought when the odds against them so fearfully preponderated that defeat seemed certain and ruin inevitable,—he gave a most glowing description and paid the merited meed of praise to the second in command—the undaunted Alexander K. McClung—who first charged home upon the first taken Mexican fort in Monterey. These remarks were received with unbounded applause by the vast concourse within the hearing of his voice. He then rapidly passed over a retrospective view of the situation and condition of the army under Gen. Taylor at the capitulation of Monterey—described the destitution of means of transportation and provision under which the commanding general labored—defended the capitulation and impressed upon his hearers convincingly, its necessity, its policy, and the general benefit which the American arms and government had derived from it—spoke of old *Rough and Ready* as the great captain of the age, and one whose deeds of generalship and noble devotion to country entitled him to the gratitude of the people of the United States in as great a degree as he had excited the admiration of the world At every mention of the name of Gen. Taylor, the applause of the assemblage made the welkin ring. Col. D., in his address, displayed not only the frankness and honesty of the veteran soldier, but the fearlessness and zeal characteristic of true heroism, in standing up and vindicating his glorious old commander from foul aspersion and base insinuation. Would that Jacob Thompson had heard *that* speech. We again reiterate our regret at not being able to furnish a full synopsis of this most eloquent address. Indisposition and other causes, have, however, placed it out of our power, but if we can obtain a copy of it we shall enjoy both pride and gratification in laying it before our readers.

After the applause occasioned by the speech of the gallant Davis had subsided, the name of McClung was shouted forth, as if the lungs of the whole vast assemblage were put in requisition to echo that glorious name. Lieut. Col. McClung responded to the call in a strain characteristic of true heroism and of the well-tried gallantry of the veteran soldier. He was most happy and appropriate in his remarks, and his tones reminded us of an occasion, perhaps not as interesting, but fully as important, when his clarion voice rang like a trumpet through the land calling upon the people to vindicate their just rights and to rebuke all aggressions that were attempted to be practiced upon them. He disclaimed, as far as he was concerned, any laurels that might be attempted to be entwined around his brow for the successful storming of Monterey. He claimed no more credit for that glorious achievement than that which was due to every officer and private in the whole regiment. Here the gallant and war-scarred soldier was most eloquent and happy in his remarks. He declared that every man fought as though the laurel crown of immortal glory was within his own grasp—as though the brightest wreath of fame and the everlasting glory of the victor was extended only for him to reach and clasp it. He rendered to all—subordinate officers and privates, that meed of praise to which the universal acclaim of the nation was allowed them. He spoke feelingly of the trials and of the services of our gallant Riflemen, and while he claimed for himself no more than he yielded to the humblest private in the ranks, he was grateful for the indications of respect and esteem which his fellow citizens had profusely lavished upon him. At the conclusion of his remarks the gallant Colonel was greeted with loud and prolonged applause.

At the conclusion of Col. McClung's address the crowd generally dispersed to different parts of the promenade ground and to the city. After a short interval the Rifles and the escort volunteer companies were mustered and marched to the tables for the purpose of taking needful refreshment, after the fatigues of the day. And here it is proper to say that the sumptuously loaded board, and tastefully arranged arbors reflected the greatest degree of credit upon the Committee of Arrangements. When we take into consideration the shortness of the time they were allowed to perfect the organization necessary to ensure success, it is really wonderful that they accomplished so much.

When the eatables were removed and the cloth cleared, toast and sentiment sped merrily around the board. Doctor L. P. Blackburn, acted as President, assisted by Josephus Hewett, Esq., as Vice President. We give below the regular toasts and as many of the volunteer ones as we could procure. The lateness of the hour and want of room prevent us from giving details. It is enough to say, however, that the mere mention of the name of old Zack Taylor was the signal for thundering applause and a sure index to the strong hold he has upon the affections of the people. The sentiments to Davis, McClung and Bradford were greeted with that approbation which a grateful people always bestow upon true merit.

The regular and volunteer toasts (as far as we have been enabled to obtain them) will be found below:

REGULAR TOASTS

1st. *Our Country.*

2nd. *The President of the United States.*

3rd. *The Army and Navy of the United States.*

4th. *Major General Zachary Taylor.*—His Country relies on him. *"He never surrenders."*

5th. *Major General Winfield Scott.*—The Hero of Lundy's Lane and Cerro Gordo. Skilful in plan, terrible in execution.

6th. *Col. Jefferson Davis.*—In counsel, the ready defender of the noble and meritorious against the foul vituperations of myrmidons; in battle, the unyielding bulwark of his country's glory.

7th. *Col. Alex. K. McClung.*—Mexican ramparts proved no obstacle to his onward march to fame and renown; Mexican balls could never crush his bold and daring spirit.

8th. *Major Alex. B. Bradford.*—His undaunted bravery, and unflinching patriotism has placed him high in the estimation of his countrymen. With propriety we may style him the modern Putnam.

9th. *The Officers, Non-Commissioned Officers and Privates of the First Mississippi Regiment.*—True to the lead of their gallant Officers, as their unerring rifles to the mark;—unswerving in battle, as the shore to the sea, they proved at Monterey that ramparts may be stormed without regulars. At Buena Vista. that Cavalry may be repulsed without the bayonet.

10th. *The First Mississippi Regiment.*—In making and receiving a charge, unsurpassed and unsurpassable. Overwhelming as the Ocean's wave—immovable as the Mountain rock.

11th. *Old Kentucky.*—Her fallen brave proves too melancholy that she too was in the field.

12th. *The brave Officers and Men who fell at Monterey and Buena Vista.*—Though their bodies be in the soil of their enemy, their deeds shall live in the recollection of their countrymen.

13th. *The Ladies.*—First to cheer the soldier on—first to welcome him back. Cherished be the dear ones who strew the soldier's path with roses.

VOLUNTEER TOASTS

By R. M. Gaines—The First Mississippi Rifles. They have acted out the spirit of that mother who told her son to bring back his shield or be brought back upon it. Their fame is the property of their country, but especially of the state which sent them forth to battle. They are as "a city set upon a hill which cannot be hid."

By Dr. L. P. Blackburn—Cols. McKee and Clay. Twin brothers in honor and chivalry, they sleep together the sleep of the brave, the mention of one awakens melancholy recollections of the other.

By J. Hewett, Esq.—The Birth-day of Washington and the Victory of Buena Vista—Glorious deeds on a glorious day.

Col. Doniphan.—His unprecedented marches and brilliant achievements have stamped his name with the seal of immortality.

By J. L. Mathewson, formerly of this city, now of New Orleans, an invited guest, after some remarks relative to the kind reception given him, gave the following toast:

Major General Jno. A. Quitman—Mississippi has honored him—he has in return honored Mississippi.

By Dr. Bowie—Lieut. Col. Alex. K. McClung.—The Hero of Monterey.

By Lieut. Col. McClung—The Ladies of Natchez. Although the chivalry of this beautiful place were in spite of their exertions prevented from going with us to battle, yet our reception by its beauty has repaid us for their absence.

About five o'clock in the afternoon the volunteers returned on board the steamers which were to convey them to Vicksburg, their point of debarkation, escorted by our volunteer companies and by a large concourse of citizens, the bands playing their merriest tunes,—and amid the thundering of cannon and the shouts of the spectators, these brave men departed from among us bearing with them the warmest wishes and most ardent desires for their future welfare and happiness of our whole community of the city and county.

Yesterday was a day the memory of which will long be cherished by our citizens. It was a proud day for Old Adams, and well did her sons maintain the reputation of their ancient hospitality. The sun set in glory in our western horizon, but his beams shed less splendor upon the state from which he was withdrawing his light than had the glorious deeds of the gallant volunteers who were leaving us.

Below will be found the letter of the "Committee of Invitation," and the letter of acceptance from Col. Jefferson Davis.

(Letter of Invitation.)

To the First Mississippi Regiment:

The undersigned, a committee, appointed at a meeting of the citizens of the city of Natchez and county of Adams, to tender to the *First Mississippi Regiment* an invitation to partake of the hospitalities of their city and county, have the honor to discharge that pleasing and grateful office.

In the name of the city and county, the committee present their most respectful and pressing invitation to their gallant fellow-citizens of the First Mississippi Regiment to visit them upon their return to their homes, and to allow them an opportunity to express in some degree the warm gratitude, admiration of pride, which fills all hearts for those brave men who have so nobly sustained and increased the glory of our beloved State by courage, constancy and gallantry, unsurpassed in the history of any country.

> A. L. Bingaman,
> J. S. B. Thacher,
> J. T. McMurran,
> C. L. Dubuisson,
> Wm. P. Mellen.

Natchez, May 31st, 1847.

(Letter of Acceptance.)

New Orleans, June 11th, 1847.

Gentlemen,—From the hands of R. M. Gaines, Esq., I had the honor to receive your invitation to the 1st Mississippi Rifles, to partake of the hospitalities of the City of Natchez and County of Adams.

On the part of the Regiment, allow me through you, gentlemen, to offer the sincerest thanks to our fellow citizens, whom you represent, for this manifestation of their regard and kind appreciation. In the resolutions passed at your public meeting, we found, not the measure of our merit, but the extent of Mississippians' fraternal affection and received most gratefully this over-approbation of those whose censure we could not have borne.

On Monday, the 14th inst., we hope to have the pleasure of meeting you at Natchez.

To you, gentlemen of the committee, for the very pleasing manner in which you have conveyed to us the flattering intentions of our fellow citizens, I offer our most thankful acknowledgments.

With the highest personal regard, please accept the best wishes of your friend and fellow citizen.

Jeff'n Davis,
Colonel Miss. Rifles.

To Messrs. A. L. Bingaman, J. S. B. Thacher, J. T. McMurran, C. L. Dubuisson, Wm. P. Mellen, R. M. Gaines, and Wm. Stanton

Jefferson Davis to Jos. B. Cobb and others.

(From The Southron, July 16, 1847.)

Brierfield, Miss., 29th June, 1847.

Gentlemen:—I have the honor to acknowledge the receipt of your very kind and complimentary letter of the 21st inst. inviting me to a public dinner to be given to the "Tombigby Volunteers," who have recently returned from Mexico. The prospect of meeting my many kindly remembered friends of your vicinity, would at any time create in me the most pleasing anticipations, but on the present occasion such anticipations are more than ordinarily excited by the very gratifying terms of your invitation, and the opportunity you offer of meeting embodied, perhaps, for the last time, those of my brethren in arms appropriately termed by you, "the remnant of that gallant corps the Tombigby Volunteers." Circumstances deprive me of the pleasure of being with you in person on this occasion, and of enjoying the proud satisfaction of seeing you bestow upon my late comrades the only reward which they ever could have expected, the only incentive worthy of their conduct: the gratitude of their fellow citizens, the approval of those whom they especially represented in their country's service, the "well done" of those whose good name was entrusted to their keeping.

Through you gentlemen of the committee, permit me to return my thanks to your fellow citizens of Lowndes County, for their flattering attention, and to express the sincere regret I feel at not having been able to accept their invitation. To you for the kind and most pleasing terms in which you have addressed me, I am deeply obliged.

With sincerest regard I remain
Your friend,
JEFFERSON DAVIS.

To Jos. B. Cobb, and others.

Jefferson Davis to James K. Polk.

(From Vicksburg Weekly Whig, October 20, 1847.)

Warren County, Miss., June 20, 1847.

To the President:

My Dear Sir:—Your very kind and complimentary letter of the 19th May last, was received in New Orleans, together with the commission to which you therein referred.

To be esteemed by you as one whose services entitled him to promotion, is to me a source of the highest gratification; which will remain to me undiminished, though my opinions compel me to decline the proffered honor.

I will this day address to the Adjutant-General of the U. S. Army, an official note informing him, that the commission has been received, and is declined. To you I wish to give an explanation, being too sensibly affected by your expression of honorable estimation and friendly regard, willingly to run any hazard of a misapprehension of the motives which have decided my course. You inform me that my command will consist of volunteers. I still entertain the opinion expressed by me, as a member of Congress, in May and June, 1846, that the "volunteers" are militia. As such they have a constitutional right to be under the immediate command of officers appointed by State authority; and this I think is violated by any permanent organization made after they have passed into the service of the United States; by which they lose their distinctive character of State troops, become part of a new formation, disciplined by, corresponding and only recognised through the head, which the federal government has set over them.

Such I consider the organization of Volunteer regiments into Brigades, under Brigadiers appointed by the President, as provided for in the law of June, 1846; and entertaining this opinion, my decision, as stated to you was the necessary result.

For the gratifying notice you have taken of myself and the regiment I had the honor to command; for the distinction you have been pleased to confer upon me by this unsolicited appointment; and for the kind solicitude you express for my welfare, receive, Sir, my sincerest thanks.

Very truly, your friend,
JEFFERSON DAVIS.

Jefferson Davis to W. L. Marcy.

(From Mississippi Free Trader, Aug. 4, 1847.)

Warrenton, Mississippi, June 29, 1847.
Hon. W. L. Marcy, Secretary of War:

Sir—Several companies have been raised in this State, composed partly of the men of the Regiment I commanded in Mexico. Applications have been made to me for information as to the mode by which they can be received into General Taylor's army, and obtain transportation thither. The greater part of them prefer to serve as mounted men; they are willing to engage for the war, and if authority were given, I have no doubt would soon fill up the incomplete Regiment called from Texas. I believe it would require but a short time to raise another Rifle Regiment to take the place of that lately disbanded, if this be desirable. Those who have spoken to me attach great importance to the difference between volunteers as originally called out, and the organization provided for those, who after the expiration of their twelve months term should re-engage, because the first class have the right of electing their own officers whenever vacancies occur.

Please inform me whether companies or a battalion or a regiment of Riflemen will be received; if so, will they be allowed to go out as mounted men, or will they be received as foot under the act of May 13, 1846.

Very respectfully,

Your most Obed't serv't,

(Signed)   JEFFERSON DAVIS.

Jefferson Davis to Stephen Cocke.[1]

(From Mississippi Department of Archives and History.)

Brierfield, Mi.
15th July 1847.

Chancellor Cocke,

Dear Sir, When we parted I hoped by this date to have been able to leave home free from the inconvenience and disagreeable exposure of hopping on crutches.[2] My foot has not improved much and though just now its appearance is flattering I have been so often disappointed that I await further evidence.

I thank you for the interest you take in the appointment of U. S. Senator and am really obliged to Gov. Brown for feelings which by others I had been led to believe he did not entertain towards me.

With the hope that I will soon have the pleasure of seeing you I am as ever very sincerely your friend

Jeffrn. Davis.

W. L. Marcy to Jefferson Davis.

(From Mississippi Free Trader, Aug. 4, 1847.)

War Department, July 16, 1847.

Sir: I am directed by the President to inform you, in reply to your letter of the 26th ultimo, that he will accept of such a Battalion of Riflemen as you suggest, to serve during the war, to be raised in the State of Mississippi. You indicate the employment of them under Major General Taylor, but it is probable that the more active operations will be with the column under the command of Maj. Gen. Scott, and their services may

---

[1] Chancellor Mississippi Superior Court of Chancery from 1846 to 1853.
[2] Col. Jefferson Davis and his regiment of Mississippi Riflemen saved the army of General Taylor from defeat at the battle of Buena Vista. He was painfully wounded in the foot during the engagement; and after returning to his plantation at "Brierfield" in June 1847 he was disabled for some time. It was during this period that he was appointed United States Senator from Mississippi by Governor Brown.

be required in connection with that column. Presuming that they will prefer the most active service, and that a different destination from that mentioned by you will not impede the raising of it, I shall send forthwith a request to the Governor to aid in the organization thereof.

In regard to your suggestion that the Battalion should be mounted, I would remark that the mounted force already called out is deemed to be sufficient for the service which may be required of that description of force, and it is not now proposed to add to their number.

Very respectfully, your obd't serv't,
W. L. Marcy, Sec'y of War.

Col. Jefferson Davis,
  Warrenton, Mississippi.

Jefferson Davis to John Jenkins.
(From Vicksburg Sentinel, August 18, 1847.)

Brierfield, Mississippi.
4th August, 1847.

John Jenkins, Esq.—

Dear Sir: I send you herewith the correspondence between the Secretary of War and our Governor, in relation to the arms of the first Mississippi Rifles.

One of the letters passed out of my possession at New Orleans, to satisfy the United States Mustering officer of our right to retain the Rifles, and has been recently recovered, or I should have presented this correspondence to you earlier, and asked its insertion in your paper. The prompt and early attention of Gov. Brown to a feeling so deep in our Regiment, has received as it deserved, our especial thanks; and it has seemed to me worthy of being made public.

Very respectfully,
Your friend, &c.,
JEFFERSON DAVIS.

A. G. Brown to W. L. Marcy.
(From Vicksburg Sentinel, August 18, 1847.)

Executive Chamber,
Jackson, Mi., 20th April, 1847.

Hon. Wm. L. Marcy, Secretary of War.

Sir: A number of the volunteers in the first Regiment from this State have expressed a very natural anxiety to be allowed to retain the Arms they have borne in Mexico. The attachment which a soldier feels for his gun may easily be imagined. The Mississippians of the first regiment will return home in the course of a few weeks. The reluctance which many of them have expressed, and all of them feel to *giving up their guns,* induces me to request an order that they be allowed to retain them. If this request cannot be granted, I then request that the arms in the hands of the volunteers belonging to the first Mississippi Regiment may be issued to this State as a part of the quota due her, in which event the State will present them to the volunteers. The Regiment will feel gratified, as well as the citizens of Mississippi generally, if a piece of ordnance taken at Monterey, were presented to the volunteers on their return home as a trophy of that victory, which the Regiment from our State assisted in achieving.

Very Respectfully,
Your obedient servant,
A. G. BROWN.

W. L. Marcy to A. G. Brown.

(From Vicksburg Sentinel, August 18, 1847.)

War Department,
May 11th, 1847.

Sir: I have the honor to acknowledge the receipt of your letter of the 20th ultimo, representing the anxiety felt by a number of the volunteers in the first Regiment from your State to retain the arms they have borne in Mexico, and requesting that an order might be issued to that effect. In answer, I regret to say that the Department has no power to dispose of the public property confided to its charge, in the way here proposed. But with a view to gratify the natural desire of the volunteers as far as may be consistently done, the Department takes pleasure in adopting the suggestion of your Excellency, and has accordingly directed that the arms in the hands of the volunteers belonging to the first Mississippi Regiment be issued to the State as a part of her quota under the act of 1808, agreeably to the report of the Ordnance Department herewith enclosed.

It would give me sincere pleasure to comply with your request in relation to presenting to the gallant Mississippi Volunteers a portion of the trophies won at Monterey, but I regret that I have not the right to dispose of them, even to those by whose valor they were acquired. The right to dispose of them is in Congress, and I cannot doubt they will readily and cheerfully gratify the wishes of your brave fellow citizens as soon as it shall be made known to them.

I have the honor to be, very respectfully,
Your obedient servant,
W. L. MARCY,
Secretary of War.

His Excellency,
A. G. BROWN,
Governor of Mississippi,
Jackson, Mississippi.

G. Talcott to W. L. Marcy.

(From Vicksburg Sentinel, August 18, 1847.)

Ordnance Office,
Washington, 5th May, 1847.

Hon. W. L. Marcy,
Secretary of War:

Sir: In relation to the letter of the Governor of Mississippi, referred to this office, asking that certain Volunteers from that State be allowed to retain the arms which they have used so efficiently in Mexico, I have the honor to report as follows: With every disposition to gratify the rational desire of the soldier to retain in his possession the weapon, with which he has so successfully fought and gained imperishable renown, there is no power in this Department to thus dispose of public property. One thousand Percussion Rifles were issued to the Regiment commanded by Col. Jefferson Davis. How many have been lost or destroyed in service, is not known. The alternative proposed by Governor Brown, that these arms be issued to the State of Mississippi under the law of 1808, as a part of her quota, may be adopted provisionally, and the whole number stand charged to that State until the losses are ascertained, or until legislation shall be had in the case.

The number of muskets usually apportioned to the State is about three hundred and fifty, so that it would absorb the allotment for three years, were the whole number issued to remain charged to the State.

The letter of Governor Brown is returned herewith.
I am, sir, respectfully,
Your obedient servant,
G. TALCOTT,
Lt. Col. Ordnance.

W. Hemingway to Jefferson Davis.

(From Vicksburg Sentinel, August 18, 1847.)

Jackson, Miss., 21st May, 1847.
Office of Secretary of State.

Sir: Enclosed you will receive copies of letter received at the Executive Department, and which, it is, doubtless, the desire of the Governor you should have as soon as possible.

With the highest respect,
And most sincere consideration,
I am you obedient servant,
W. HEMINGWAY.

Col. Jefferson Davis,
Comd'g 1st Mississippi Regiment.

Albert G. Brown to Jefferson Davis.

(From the Mississippi Department of Archives and History. Letter Book of Governor Brown.)

Executive Chamber
Jackson Mi. 10th August 1847

Col Jeff^n Davis
Warrenton Mi.
Sir

I have the honor to enclose you a commission as U. States Senator to fill a vacancy occasioned by the death of the late General Speight.[1] The people have experienced deep and sincere regret in the mournful event, which deprived them of a faithful friend and long tried public servant. In this feeling I have participated to the fullest extent. The event has given us all an opportunity which we embrace with melancholy pleasure of testifying our high appreciation of your valuable services as a member of the twenty-ninth Congress, and your more valuable and distinguished services at the head of the 1st Miss. Reg^t in Mexico. The people will never cease to remember with pride and gratitude that to you, Sir, and the brave Mississippians under your command, is our State indebted for honors as imperishable as the soil on which you won them; honors, which shall last as long as chivalry is respected or valor has a

[1] Jesse Speight, 1795-1847. Born in Greene County, N. C. Congressman from that State. U. S. Senator from Mississippi Dec. 1, 1845 to May 1, 1847, the date of his death.

place in the hearts of men. They expect me to offer you this commission, and it gives me sincere personal pleasure to gratify that expectation. It is the tribute which a grateful people speaking through their representative pays to heroic deeds of disinterested patriotism. In returning to the arena of politics you may have it in your power to counsel your Government in regard to a people whom you have aided in conquering whose weaknesses & follies you have learned to appreciate from personal observation, and to whom I am sure you are willing to give an honorable peace whenever they and their rulers shall have the good sense to accept it.

Very Respectfully
Your ob't serv't
A. G. Brown

Jefferson Davis to A. G. Brown.

(From Mississippi Free Trader, Sept. 8, 1847.)

Warren County, Miss.,
15th August, 1847.

Gov. A. G. Brown, of Mississippi:

Sir—I have the honor to acknowledge the receipt of your very kind letter of the 10th inst., accompanying the commission (which you have conferred upon me) of U. States Senator to fill the vacancy occasioned by the death of the late Senator Speight.

In the deep and sincere regret experienced at the loss of our tried and faithful representative, none can sympathize more truly than myself; none more fully realize the calamity we have sustained, in the death of this pure politician, this fearless exponent and vigilant guardian of the interests of our State.

It is with a grateful sense of the distinction bestowed, and a high estimate of the responsibilities which I am about to assume, that I accept the commission you have tendered, with so much of delicate and gratifying encouragement.

The approbation which you convey of my services in the twenty-ninth Congress is especially pleasing, because therein was manifested my fixed opinion on the taxing and expending powers of the federal government, my uniformly entertained and often avowed creed of strict construction for the constitution of our Union.

I cannot express adequately my thanks for the high commendation you bestow on the services rendered in Mexico by the first Mississippi Riflemen. As the representative of the people give us that meed of praise, which is the great incentive, the only reward of the citizen soldier for all which he may suffer or do in the cause of his country. As State troops, under your organization we entered the service of the United States. Proud of the name of Mississippi; proud of her former achievements in war; anxious to burnish on the battle field her shield, rusted in the repose of peace; it was my wish, it was my effort to preserve my distinct organization, our State individuality; that thus we might bring back whatever of honorable distinction we should have the good fortune to acquire, and lay it at the feet of Mississippi, as our contribution to the joint property of her citizens, the reputation of the State.

You have justly anticipated my views in relation to a peace with Mexico; an event to be desired not merely from its influence on our domestic policy, but also to save from monarchial alliance, or entire prostration, a republican confederacy, which, despite our caution and magnanimous forbearance has forced us into war. The common desire of our countrymen to see the principle of self-government extended over this continent and recognized as the policy of America, has justified past administrations in tolerating past offences by Mexico, and still seeking to cultivate friendly relations. This desire has, I doubt not, led to a general approval of the course pursued by the present administration, in its steady efforts to open negotiations for a treaty of peace.

Should these efforts continue to be unsuccessful, we will have the satisfaction to know that our government has acted as became the United States, in avoiding unnecessary injury to a weak, though perverse and offending neighbor. Sincerely thanking you for your kind expressions and generous confidence, I promise all which zeal and industry can effect in the duties of the high station to which I am assigned.

Very respectfully, Your obedient servant,
Jeff. Davis.

Jefferson Davis to C. J. Searles.

(From Washington Union, October 12, 1847.)

Brierfield, Sep. 19, 1847.

C. J. Searles, Esq.—*My dear sir:* Your highly valued letter of the 3d inst. came duly to hand, but found me quite sick, and I have not been able at an earlier date to reply to it. Accept my thanks for your kind solicitude for my welfare.

Your past conduct enabled me to anticipate this from you, and I am therefore doubly grateful.

The political information you communicate was entirely new to me, and it is only under the belief that the crisis renders important the views of every southern man, that I can account for any speculations having arisen about my opinions as to the next presidency. I have never anticipated a separation upon this question from the democracy of Mississippi; and if such intention or expectation has been attributed to me, it is not only unauthorized but erroneous.

It might become necessary to unite us southern men, and to dissolve the ties which have connected us to the northern democracy, the position recently assumed in a majority of the non-slaveholding States has led me to fear. Yet, I am not of those who decry a national convention, but believe that present circumstances with more than usual force indicate the propriety of such meeting. On the question of southern institutions and southern rights, it is true that extensive defections have occurred among northern democrats; but enough of good feeling is still exhibited to sustain the hope that as a party they will show themselves worthy of their ancient appellation, the natural allies of the south, and will meet us upon just constitutional ground. At least I consider it due to former associations that we should give them the fairest opportunity to do so, and furnish no cause for failure by seeming distrust or aversion.

I would say, then, let our delegates meet those from the north, not as a paramount object to nominate candidates for the presidency and vice presidency, but, before entering upon such selection, to demand of their political brethren of the north a disavowal of the principles of the Wilmot Proviso, an admission of the equal right of the south with the north to the territory held as the common property of the United States, and a declaration in favor of extending the Missouri compromise to all States to be hereafter admitted into our confederacy.

If these principles are recognised, we will happily avoid the worst of all political divisions—one made by geographical lines merely. The convention, representing every section of the Union, and elevated above local jealousy and factious strife, may proceed to select candidates, whose principles, patriotism, judgment, and decision indicate men fit for the time and the occasion.

If, on the other hand, that spirit of hostility to the south, that thirst for political dominion over us, which, within two years past, has displayed such increased power and systematic purpose, should prevail, it will only remain for our delegates to withdraw from the convention, and inform their fellow-citizens of the failure of their mission. We shall then have reached a point at which all party measures sink into insignificance under the necessity for self-preservation; and party divisions should be buried in union for defence.

But, until then, let us do all which becomes us to avoid sectional division, that united we may go on to the perfection of democratic measures, the practical exemplification of those great principles for which we have struggled, as promotive of the peace, the prosperity, and the perpetuity of our confederation.

Though the signs of the times are portentous of evil, and the cloud which now hangs on our northern horizon threatens a storm, it may yet blow over with only the tear-drops of contrition and regret. In this connexion it is consolatory to remember, that whenever the tempest has convulsively tossed our republic and threatened it with wreck, brotherly love has always poured oil on the waters, and the waves have subsided to rest. Thus may it be now and forever. If we should be disappointed in such hopes, I forbear from any remark upon the contingency which will be presented. Enough for the day will be the evil thereof, and enough for the evil will be the union and energy and power of the south.

I hope it will soon be in my power to visit you and other friends at Vicksburg, from whom I have been so long separated.

I am, as ever, truly your friend,
JEFFERSON DAVIS.

Jefferson Davis to John Jenkins.

(From Vicksburg Sentinel, September 29, 1847.)

Brierfield, Sept. 21st, 1847.

John Jenkins Esq:

Dear Sir:—In your paper of the 1st inst., I observed a notice of a long article in the "Mississippi Advertiser," being an attack upon my "friends" in general, and myself in connection with the fact, that the 2d Mississippi Regiment, had offered to elect me their Colonel, and that I declined to accept. Much stress is laid upon a paragraph in a number of your paper issued whilst I was in Mexico, referring to a rumor that I would probably become the commander of the 2d Mississippi Regiment.

I saw the paragraph, and at the same time a notice of it in a New Orleans paper, which treated the rumor as ridiculous. Either or both views seemed to me very unimportant, as no vacancy existed, and there was no prospect that one would happen. Col. R. Davis left his Regiment on leave of absence, not to resign, but to make such arrangements as would enable him to return to his command, and remain during the war. This information communicated to me, by himself, I frequently gave to others, to correct an impression that he would not return.

He rejoined his Regiment very soon after I left Monterey. Ill health has subsequently compelled him to resign, and a vacancy thus unexpectedly occurred. In the mean time your paragraph, which the Advertiser considers as so effective, had become old,—if you can bear the supposition, perhaps Sir, it was forgotten in the 2d Regiment; the more supposible, as the report you noticed came from them, and could acquire no additional importance by travelling back. The "Advertiser" says: "The announcement of the rumor of some circumstances, had time to reach the camp of the 2d Regiment in Mexico, and also the refusal of the tender of the Brigadier Generalship." Now, Sir, I have just said I thought the announcement had too much time, and I have some reason to believe the refusal had not enough. A Physician formerly a member of the 1st Mississippi Regiment, now on duty in the medical staff of the division which includes the 2d Mississippi Regiment, wrote to me from camp Buena Vista, on the 10th July; five days before the letter of the committee, from whose letter I make the following extract: "The 2d Mississippi, leave for Augua Nueva, in a few days, and more troops are expected up. We were all delighted to hear that you have been promoted to Brigadier, and would take command of this Division."

The idea of electing me Colonel of the 2d Mississippi Regiment, I have been informed by some of the officers, was as old as its organization; and repeatedly when we were at Monterey, members of the 2d Mississippi Regiment, expressed a wish, in the event of their Colonelcy becoming vacant to have my services in that capacity. These will remember, whilst I acknowledged the compliment, the extent to which I always discouraged the proposition, and will recognize in the third reason of my letter to their committee a principle they have heard me more fully present. By them my reply might have been anticipated, yet if they supposed I could not resist an invitation so generously and unexpectedly given, they were not far wrong. Had

I been physically able, and free to accept, they would probably have been right.

Now, Sir, to return to the article of the "Advertiser," having gratuitously made the supposition, that the invitation of the 2d Regiment, was procured to subserve some purpose, and be refused, the editor with all the solemnity of an indictment proceeds: "If Col. Jefferson Davis has, at any time, or in any form," &c &c, to instruct me what it is requisite for me to do in the case. To the low suspicion, I have nothing to reply. It must find its rebuke in every ingenuous mind, and its refutation must come from my friends of the 2d Mississippi Regiment, who best know the degree of its falsehood. How an unprejudicated mind could originate such things, it is difficult to conceive. Nor is it more easy for me to imagine whose vanity has been wounded, whose envy excited, whose jealousy has prompted him to this misrepresentation of a free offering, an honorable distinction, which my fellow citizens of the 2d Regiment, have been pleased to confer upon me.

At the close of the Advertiser's article, is a call for information as to the ground on which I declined the proffered command. Those who volunteer advice, ought to have a great deal of information, and I am happy to have it in my power to contribute any. I therefore send you for publication the correspondence in relation to this transaction. It is comprised entire, in two letters herewith enclosed. No. 1 the letter of the committee, No. 2, a copy of my reply.

Very truly your friend,
JEFFERSON DAVIS.

A. McWillie and others to Jefferson Davis.

(From Vicksburg Sentinel, September 29, 1847.)

Buena Vista, Mexico,
July 16th, 1847.

Genl. Jefferson Davis—Sir:—As you will doubtless have learned before this reaches you, the office of Colonel of the 2nd Mississippi Rifles will be vacated on the 1st of September next, by the resignation of Col. Reuben Davis.

Feeling a deep interest in the selection of his successor, the officers held a meeting on last evening to ascertain, if possible, who was the choice of the regiment.

Knowing and appreciating the high reputation you have acquired as commander of the 1st Mississippi Regiment, there was on the part of the meeting a unanimous expression of opinion in your favor, and the undersigned were appointed a committee to ascertain the preference of the whole regiment, to communicate with you upon the subject, and to know if you would accept the command if tendered to you. We have made such enquiry among the men, and we are happy to be able to state, that you are the *unanimous* choice of the whole regiment. We therefore request that you will communicate to us at the earliest practicable period, what your views are upon the subject, so that we may communicate the same to the regiment.

Permit us to indulge the hope personally that it may not be incompatible with your wishes and interests to assume the command, and that we may soon have the pleasure of greeting you as our leader.

We have the honor to be,
Very respectfully,
Your ob't serv'ts,
A. McWILLIE,
Capt. 2nd Miss. Rifles,
E. DOWSING,
1st Lieut. 2nd Miss. Rifles,
F. AMYX,
1st Lieut. 2nd Miss. Rifles,
A. J. TRUSSEL,
2nd Lieut. 2nd Miss. Rifles.

Jefferson Davis to A. McWillie and others.

(From Vicksburg Sentinel, September 29, 1847.)

Brierfield, Warren co., Miss.,
August 19th, 1847.

Gentlemen:—I have the honor to acknowledge the receipt of your most gratifying letter of the 16th ult., conveying to me the information that my esteemed friends of the 2nd Mississippi Riflemen unanimously offer to elect me their regimental leader.

The honorable post you offer has every thing to commend it to me; it is the free gift of Mississippians; it invites me to field service in a region where the energy and health of the troops will not be impaired by the climate, and it assures me of being in the column of the general in whom I have unmeasured confidence.

Your proposition under all the circumstances which attend it, is an honor of which the highest reputation might well be proud, and for which I feel more grateful than I have power to express. In declining a station so honorable, so acceptable to my tastes, feelings and associations, and offered in a manner so highly complimentarily, I have three reasons to submit to you in justification of my decision:

1st. I have not so far recovered from my wound as to be able to travel immediately; the probable date of your advance admits of no delay in one who would join you in your present position, and the anticipated character of your movement, in the event of an advance, renders it doubtful whether an individual could join you on the march.

II. Before the receipt of your letter I had accepted a commission to fill a vacancy in our Representation in the U. S. Senate.

III. I have held that vacancies occurring in the field afford opportunities to reward merit among yourselves, and that policy dictates, and esprit du corps demands, that promotions should thus be made. I feel that your kindness has made me an exception to a rule, and that I best show myself worthy of your generosity by declining to take advantage of it.

Though I shall not be with you to share the glory, it is permitted me to hope that at no distant day the fortune of war will give you an opportunity to fulfill the expectations of you, so early and confidently announced by myself, in common with your many friends and admirers.

To you alone now is Mississippi's standard confided. Rent and blood-stained it may be; but in your hands, can never be dishonored. It may droop with the cypress, but will be crowned with the laurel.

For yourselves, gentlemen, please receive my sincere thanks, for the grateful terms in which you have conveyed the flattering wishes of my friends and fellow citizens of the 2nd Mississippi Rifles, to whom I pray you make my acknowledgements acceptable.

With assurances of the deep interest I will always feel in your prosperity and fame, and with the hope that under the blessing of peace we may be early reunited at home. I am very cordially,

Your friend and ob't serv't.

JEFFERSON DAVIS.

Messrs. Capt. A. McWillie, Lieut. E. Dowsing, Lieut. F. Amyx, Lieut. A. J. Trussell, committee 2nd Mississippi Rifles.

Jefferson Davis to C. G. Forshey.

(From Natchez Courier, October 6, 1847.)

Brierfield, Miss., Sept. 24, 1847.

C. G. Forshey, Esq., of Com. of Invitation:

Dear Sir—When I received the letter of your committee, inviting me on behalf of the citizens of Concordia, to a Barbecue to be given on the 30th inst., as a compliment to the character and gallant services of Gen. Z. Taylor, I hoped it would have been in my power to meet you on an occasion to me so interesting, and grateful to the warm personal attachment I feel for the patriot hero whom you propose to honor. Valuable and brilliant as have been the public services of Gen. Taylor, attracting the admiration and gratitude of his countrymen throughout our broad Union, those who have known him best will equally remember and honor him for the purity, the generosity, and unostentatious magnanimity of his private character. His colossal greatness is presented in the garb of the strictest republican simplicity; and to this no doubt in a great degree may be referred the feeling you describe when you say, "we are learning to regard him with a filial affection."

To speak of Gen. Taylor as one who has known him long and well, I will say, that his life has been devoted to the service of his country for no other reward than the consciousness of serving it well—and that for many years past, the goal of his desires has been a private station, as soon as his official obligations would permit, to retire to the enjoyment of a sovereign citizen of the United States.

Before closing I will refer to a recent and characteristic exhibition of his disinterested patriotism, which has not received all the attention, I think it deserves. He was called on by the administration for his opinion as to the best mode of prosecuting the war with Mexico. In view of the embarrassments which surrounded Gen. Scott, and the importance of the operations in which he was engaged, Gen. Taylor recommended that a portion of his own command be sent to reinforce the Southern column. For the good of his country, he sacrificed his long deferred hope of an advance at the moment of its fulfillment, and doomed himself to the worst punishment of a soldier—inactivity on a line of defence. For the good of his country all personal ambition, all rivalry were forgotten—he gave his vest also to the man who had taken his coat, and left him exposed to the storm of "Buena Vista."

Permit me to offer you for the occasion:

General Taylor—The soldier who "never surrenders;" the citizen whose love is "for the country, and whole country;" the man whose sacrifices are all of himself.

Accept for yourselves, gentlemen of the committee, and please tender to those whom you represent, assurances of my high esteem and the regret which I feel at not being able to meet you as invited.

Very respectfully, yours,
Jefferson Davis.

Jefferson Davis to Albert G. Brown.[1]

Reports of the Battles of Monterey and Buena Vista.

(From the Mississippi Department of Archives and History.)

Brierfield
3^d Oct. 1847

Govr. A. G. Brown

Sir,

Herewith I have the honor to transmit to you the reports of the Regimental officers of the Battles of Monterey and Buena Vista, as far as the same were in my possession. I had hoped

---

[1] At the election of officers of the First Mississippi Regiment of Volunteers War with Mexico July 18, 1846, Capt. A. B. Bradford, who had been a soldier under Jackson in 1812--15 and Colonel of a regiment of Tennessee volunteers of Armstrong's mounted brigade under General Call in Florida, 1836, and was known as "the hero of Withlacoochee," was supported by the northern counties for Colonel and received 350 votes to 300 for Jefferson Davis, who was a graduate of West Point, had been a Lieutenant in the regular army in the Black Hawk war, and Adjutant of the Dragoons in a Comanchee war, and was at the time a Representative of Mississippi in Congress. R. N. Downing also received 135 votes, W. L. Brandon 91, and A. G. Bennett 37. Bradford declined to consider the election his, although it was sufficient in militia elections, unless he had a majority of the regiment. On the second ballot Davis received a majority of 147. A. K. McClung, R. E. Downing and Major-General Duffield were candidates for Lieutenant-Colonel and McClung was elected on the second ballot. On a subsequent day Bradford was elected Major. McClung commanded the regiment until after it reached New Orleans,

The staff officers were: Richard Griffith, Adjutant; Seymour Halsey, Surgeon; John Thompson, Assistant Surgeon; Charles T. Harlan, Sergeant-Major; S. Warren White, Quartermaster-Sergeant; Kemp S. Holland, Commissary; Stephen Dodds, Principal Musician.

Colonel Davis, then at Washington, D. C., arranged that the regiment should be armed with rifles instead of the ordinary infantry musket. On this subject he said later in life: "General Scott endeavored to persuade me not to take more rifles than enough for four companies, and objected particularly to percussion arms as not having been sufficiently tested for the use of troops in the field. Knowing that the Mississippians would have no confidence in the old flint lock muskets, I insisted on

before this to have received full information in relation to the number of Rifles for which our state will be justly responsible and to have sent you a consolidated return; but regret to say that no company return has been made to me, since that of which I advised you.

It was my purpose to have made a report to you, which should have been a history of our Campaign in Mexico, but ill health at last compels me to abandon the design. A wish on the part of the Company officers to have their reports published, has been communicated to me by one of their number, and I have replied that they would be furnished to the Executive.

Very Respectfully
yr. mo. obt. svt.
Jeffn. Davis.

Jefferson Davis to John A. Quitman.[1]

(From the Mississippi Department of Archives and History.)

Monterey. 26th Sept. 1846.

Gen Quitman,

Comdg 2d Brig. 1st Div. Vols,

Sir, In conformity with your instructions I have the honor to report such facts in relation to the conduct of the Regiment of Missi. Riflemen on the 21st and 23d Insts. as came under my immediate observation, and will add such explanations as may seem necessary. When on the morning of the 21st the 1st Division was drawn up in order of battle before the city of Monterey, you will remember that the position of the Regt. under my command was thought to be too much exposed, and that it was detached to the left. Separated from the division, I did not hear the orders by which it was put in motion, but seeing the other Regt. of your Brigade, (Col Campbell's) moving towards the enemy, I ordered the Missi. Riflemen to advance by the left of the Battalion and follow it.

Thus when the Regts. of your Brigade were united their natural order was inverted. In this order under a cross fire of artillery, we advanced in front of the fort upon our left,

their being armed with the kind of rifle then recently made at New Haven, Conn., the Whitney rifle. From having been first used by the Mississippians, those rifles have always been known as the Mississippi rifles.'' The arms were sent to the regiment by ship, to New Orleans. They were without bayonets, there having been no time to make them. Colonel Davis, traveling by way of Wheeling, joined his command at the camp near New Orleans July 21, 1846.

[1] In command of brigade of which Col. Davis' regiment was a part.

to a point within the range of the enemys musketry but beyond the effective fire of our rifles. Under your orders to fill an interval which had been created upon my left, I ordered the Mississippi Riflemen to advance obliquely, by the left of companies to a line which I estimated as effectively near to the enemy, and then ordered the Battalion into line. The companies being directed when formed, to commence firing as in open order. In a few minutes the fire of the enemy had so far diminished as to indicate the propriety of a charge, and being without instructions, it was accordingly ordered. Lieut. Col. McClung sprung before his old company, and called on them to follow him. The call was promptly answered. In an instant the whole regiment rushed forward, the flanks converging to an open embrasure which lay nearly before our centre, and it became a contest of speed who first should reach the fort. The enemy fled from the rear sally porte as we entered the front, leaving behind him his artillery, a considerable number of muskets, his dead, and wounded. Passing immediately through the fort we found the enemy flying in disorder, some to a fortified stone building immediately in rear, others across the stream to the fort which stands beyond it. Our pursuit was so close that we reached the gate of the stone building before it was secured, and upon forcing it open the men inside fled behind the pilasters of the portico, and held up their hands in token of submission. An officer offered me his sword, and announced the surrender. I received it, and retired to select an officer to take charge of the prisoners, and receive their arms. Lieut Townsend of company "K" was directed to discharge this duty, and the pursuit of the enemy was immediately resumed. Leading those who had come up across the ford, we advanced within rifle range of the fort beyond the stream, and opened a fire upon such of the enemy as showed themselves above the wall, the intention being to storm the fort as soon as a sufficient number of our regiment came up. In this position we received no fire from the enemy's artillery, and his musketry had not proved destructive up to the time when I was ordered to retire.

Until after we withdrew I knew nothing of the position, or cooperation of the forces on our right. In accordance with my instructions, and expecting to find the main body of my Regt. I passed up the street to our right, with the force just withdrawn across the stream. We soon became mingled with other troops which we found along the wall, and after rallying my command for a forward movement, I found it much reduced. Capt. Cooper had kept, say twenty of his company together;

with these, and about ten others of our Regt. I advanced until we met with Capt. Field of the U. S. Army, who led me to a point where he had discovered a considerable body, probably one hundred of the enemy; on our approach they fled beyond a street which was enfiladed by the fire of a strong party sheltered behind the Tête du Pont of the principal bridge.

Capt. Cooper with the party accompanying us was posted in an interior building to act as sharp shooters against the men of the Tête du Pont, until we should be sufficiently reinforced for more offensive operations. After a brief period we were joined by Major Mansfield, of the U. S. Engineers, with a small party of the 1st infantry under his command. Whilst the men were resting we reconnoitred the position and decided on a plan of attack. At this instant we were joined by Gen. Hamer with a portion of his brigade; and from him we received orders to retire, as I was afterwards informed to give protection to a battery of artillery, threatened by Lancers, in the rear.

In the meantime a few individuals, but no organised portion of my regiment had joined me, and we followed in rear of Gen. Hamer's column. After having proceeded the half of a mile or more, the enemy's cavalry appeared on our left and the troops in front began to close and form on a chaparral fence in advance of us. The men under my command had undergone such severe fatigue that their movements were necessarily slow, and some of them fell behind. A party of Lancers dashed forward to attack the rear. I ordered the Riflemen to face about, and returned to the relief of our comrades. The movement was readily executed, and though the files were in loose order their effective fire soon drove the enemy back leaving several dead behind him.

Soon after this, I was joined by Maj. Bradford with the portion of our Regt. which had served under his orders a great part of the day, and for whose conduct during that period, I refer to Maj. Bradford's report accompanying this statement.

We were now on the ground where for the third time during the day we had been under the cross fire of the enemy's batteries; when I learned from you the position of another portion of my Regt. and received your orders to join, and consolidate it. Were I to mention all the instances of gallantry, and soldierly firmness which came under my observation, this statement would extend beyond a convenient limit.

I saw no exhibition of fear, no want of confidence, but on every side the men who stood around me were prompt, and willing to execute my orders. I cannot omit to mention the gallant bearing of Lieut. Col. McClung.[1] At the storming of the fort, he first mounted the parapet, and turning to the Regt. waved his sword over his head in token of the triumph of our arms; leaving him in that position to cheer the men on to further danger, it was my misfortune soon after to lose his services. At the fortified stone building he was dangerously wounded.

I must also mention Lieut. Patterson who sprung into the open embrasure as Col. McClung mounted parapet, and fired the first American piece within the work of the enemy. Capt. Downing in whom is happily combined the qualities of a leader, and commander, was severely wounded whilst (among the foremost) cheering his company to the charge, and I felt severely the loss of his services. Corpl. Grisham of Capt. Taylor's company "I" fell near me, after we had crossed the stream and were advancing upon the fort beyond it. He had fired his rifle several times, and was advancing—firing with exemplary intrepidity, when he fell pierced by two wounds, and died as he had fought, calmly, silently, and with his eye upon the foe. Lieut. Calhoun attracted my attention by the gallantry with which he exposed himself, and the efforts he made to shelter others.

Pleased with the enthusiasm and dashing spirit of all, I was yet more struck with instances of coolness, which verged upon indifference to danger, but which the limits of this communication will not allow me specially to notice.

Subjoined is a list of the killed, and wounded in the action of the 21st Sept. 1846

Very Respectfully

Jeffn. Davis

Col. Missi. Riflns.

note

A condensed statement of the casualties of the 21st 22d & 23d will be appended, instead of the separate lists.

J. D.

Endorsed:

No. 1

Col. Davis' report of the transactions of the 21st Sept. 1846

---

[1] McClung, Alexander Keith, a soldier and lawyer, and a nephew of Chief Justice Marshall, was born in Fauquier County, Va. He was educated in Kentucky, entered the navy and settled in Mississippi in 1832 where he opened a law office. He was a Whig in politics, but was never in an important office. About 1844 he established a Whig newspaper, the True Issue, at Jackson. During the Mexican War he served as Lieutenant Colonel of Jefferson Davis's regiment. He died by his own hand about 1857.

Jefferson Davis to John A. Quitman.

(From the Mississippi Department of Archives and History.)

Additional Report.

Gen Quitman,
    Comdg. 2 Brig. 1st Div. Vols.

Sir, omitting to notice those occurrences which transpired whilst with you holding the fort on the 22nd I resume my statements at the point when ordered out to reconnoitre the movements, and position of the enemy on the morning of the 23d. My command consisted of Co "H" commanded by 1st Lieut Moore, Co. G, commanded by 1st Lieut. Greaves, and two Companies of Col. Campbell's Regt. under the command of Lieut. Col. Anderson. Having been deprived of the very valuable services of Adjt. Griffith of the Riflemen by an injury received in his shoulder which compelled him to remain in camp, Lieut. Cook, at a time when the duty we had to perform was considered both difficult, and perilous offered me his services, and rendered great assistance. As we advanced into the town armed bodies of men fled through the streets at our approach. Having turned the flank of the Fort we found it evacuated & the artillery removed, as I suppose under cover of the night. We took possession of it, but as it was commanded by the forts in the rear of it, and the têrre pleine exposed to their fire it was necessary to take shelter upon the outer side. At this time I was accompanied by and received valuable assistance, and advice from Lieut. Scarrett of the Engineers. After a reconnoissance still further to the left, I received your orders to advance to what my examination induced me to believe a better position, and my command was changed in relieving Co "G" by Capt. Cooper's Co "B" of our Regt. and substituting one of the companies of Col. Campbells Regt. by Co "D" of the Missi Riflemen commanded by 1st Lieut. Russel. Finding no enemy within our range at the next position we advanced to a breastwork thrown across the termination of a street to our left. Whilst examining it I was twice fired at by sharp shooters; the files of my command nearest to me stepped forward to punish the assailants, and in a few moments we were in action. Our fire was effective upon the right, but the enemy posted upon the top of a large building on our left, continued to fire from his place of security and killed one of our men whose gallant conduct had I remembered attracted your attention. Private Tyree of Co

"K", whose company being in rear, had voluntarily come up, and joined us. We had (I think) done all which we could effect from that position when you directed us to a place of greater safety to which you had ordered the remaining companies of my Regt. to advance. Capt Taylor, and his company were not relieved from the duty with which I had charged him, that of holding a post in the rear which was very important in the event of our being compelled to retire. I had found him so efficient on the previous occasion, and his company so prompt and gallant that I regretted his absence. After we were joined by the Texas Volunteers under Gen Henderson I derived great support from them; as well from their gallantry, as their better knowledge of the construction of Mexican houses.

We continued to advance, and drive the enemy by passing through courts, gardens, and houses, taking every favorable position to fire from the house tops, which from their style of architecture furnishes a good defence against musketry. Until near "the Plaza" where we found all the streets barricaded, and swept by so severe a fire that to advance from our last position it became necessary to construct a defence across the street, for this purpose we used the baggage, and pack saddles found in the houses, and though under a fire of artillery, as well as musketry had more than half finished the work when we received orders to retire. This was done in good order though I regret to say that the enemy, emboldened by the first retrograde movement followed our retreat by a cross street, and wounded several of our party among others Lieut. Howard of the Missi Riflemen who was bringing up the rear. As on the former occasion to name those whose conduct equalled my highest expectations, and hopes would be to furnish a list of the officers, and men engaged in the action.

I wish to mention for your notice two gentlemen who joined my Regt. and served in the ranks as volunteers on the 23ᵈ viz. Maj. E. R. Price of Natches, and Capt. I. R. Smith late of the Louisiana volunteers, they were both conspicuous for their good conduct on every trying occasion, always with the advanced detachment, and as prompt in the observance of orders as in the encounter of danger.

Whilst I cannot mention all who deserve commendation, and feel that you will bear me out in claiming the highest credit for each, I cannot forbear from naming Capt. Cooper, Lieuts. Moore, Russell,* and Cook, and Sergeant Major Harlan, who

* The names of *Posey, Greaves, & Hampton* should have been here inserted,

being especially under my observation, and generally out of your view, might otherwise pass without that notice, which their soldierly conduct so well merits. The conduct of Regimental Surgeon Seymour Halsey is worthy of the highest credit, and claims especial notice. On the 21st he was on the field of battle, and exposed several times to much personal danger, whilst giving early relief to the wounded, and has effected much by his attention since. To his vigilance and skill it is fair to assign the fact, that not a case of amputation has yet occurred in our Regiment. Herewith is a List of the killed and wounded on the 22^{d} and in the action of the 23^{d} Instant.

Very Respectfully
Jeffn. Davis
Col. Missi. Rifln.

note,

The Casualties will be found in the condensed statement annexed—

J. D.

Endorsed:

No. 2.

Col. Davis'

Report of transactions of the 23^{d} Sept. 1846

Jefferson Davis to A. G. Brown.

(From the Mississippi Department of Archives and History.)

Govr. A. G. Brown,

Sir,

From the preceding report much was omitted which would have been supplied had it been originally written for one who was not himself an actor in the events described. Some portion of the facts thus omitted I deem it proper here to append.

Having as stated in my report of the transactions of the 21st been marched at the close of that day to our encampment at the Walnut Springs, the regiment was dismissed to its quarters for the night. In the morning of the 22^{d} I was warned that our regiment was required for field service. The Companies were formed and marched to the regimental parade. The severe service of the previous day had reduced the number, but had in no degree impaired the ardor or energy of our men. I announced the duty for which the regiment was drawn out and marched it from the encampment. The report that we were off for another fight brought out all who were able to march, and I have often recurred with pride to the recollection, that when I subsequently counted the files for the issue of ammunition, we had forty seven men more, than when we formed on our Regimental parade.

By directing our march through some fields which concealed us from the view of "the Citadel," we reached the plain above "fort Teneria", the work which we had taken on the previous day, before we came under the enemy's fire. Here his artillery in the fort "el Diablo" opened upon us, and before we reached fort "Teneria," one shot took effect, killing Private Dubois and wounding Private Gregg of Company "H."

In conjunction with the Tennessee Regiment, under the command of Lt. Col. Anderson, we relieved the guard found in "Fort Teneria," and under the assignment of Brigadier Genl. Quitman took post for further orders. This work, "La Teneria", was composed of two field entrenchments and a stone house; the salient, was a circular redoubt, mounting four guns, one at an open embrasure, and three in barbet; the next, was an irregular redan resting on the stone building; on the top of the stone building was a breast work of sand bags, from behind which the defenders had an upper tier of fire against their assailants, and at the last moment a plunging fire into the interior of the works below.

The Tennessee Regt. was placed in the round work, the Mississippi Riflemen with Major Ridgely's battery in the redan and stone building. From the top of this house I made frequent observations during the day upon the positions and movements of the enemy at the east end of the town, without acquiring any other valuable information, than that he had a large force at the north east angle of his defences.

Working parties were detailed throughout the day, and under the direction of Maj. Mansfield and Lieut. Scarrett of the Engineers, threw up a traverse to connect the round work with the redan, and made some additions to the more defective part of the breast work. From the fort "el Diablo" and "the Citadel", the enemy continued throughout the day to throw shot and shells at us; by constant vigilance we avoided injury from them, though the walls of the intrenchment were much too low to defile the interior of the work. At the approach of night Capt. Taylor's company was posted in the north-west part of the stone building, the same in which we had taken the prisoners on the preceding day, with instructions to defend the gates in the event of a night attack, and by sentinels on the roof and at other suitable places to keep vigilant watch upon the enemy. The other companies were distributed along the breast work of the redan.

We had left camp without preparation, were in light clothing and entirely without food. Our Quarter Master had been directed to bring out the blankets and the day's rations for the companies, he informed me subsequently that he made several ineffectual attempts to do so, and failed from being unable to get an escort for his wagon, across the plain, where it would have been exposed to attack. Thus unprovided, rain and a norther came together upon us. The work which we occupied was rudely constructed and unfinished, earth had been taken from the inside of the parapet, the rain collected in holes and men already shivering with cold had to stand in the water when called to the breast work. We were so near the enemy as to hear his guard calls, and the turning out of his cavalry patrols. His signals indicated that some concerted movement was to be made during the night; as he ought to have attacked us it was therefore to be expected, and we remained at the breast work, though the exposure was extremely severe.

Thus passed the night of the 22^d. At dawn of the 23^d our sentinels on the house top reported that very few persons were visible in the fort "el Diablo," my own observations connected with the events of the night induced me to believe that the greater part of the garrison had been withdrawn. I communicated these things to Genl. Quitman, Commanding the post, who authorized me to make a sortie with four companies, two of Missi. riflemen and two of Tenn: Infantry. We entered the suburbs of the city, and saw the enemy retreating rapidly before us. Having passed on sufficiently far to secure an approach on the gorge of the fort, and thus to avoid the fire of artillery if that arm had not been removed, the column was headed to the left and marched rapidly upon the fort. We found it's garrison and armament had been withdrawn, the traverse at its gorge had been dug down so as to render it more untenable by us, and the men who had been seen in it claimed to be noncombatants. With a small party of Riflemen commanded by Lieut. Hampton, I then proceeded with the assistance of Lieut. Scarrett of the Engineers to examine the ground and a redoubt upon our right. It had been also evacuated, and the houses in it's vicinity, which had been pierced with loop holes, were generally abandoned. In this reconnoissance we took some fifteen prisoners who informed us that the enemy had retired to the main Plaza. Lieut: Scarret proposed to report these events to Genl. Taylor and to apply for sapping tools to advance into the city. For this purpose he soon after left us, and circumstances prevented his returning, as was desired. With the prisoners taken we returned to the fort "el Diablo."

I next proceeded with a few riflemen commanded by Lieut. Moore to reconnoitre the positions to our left. The first was a tenail connected by a line of abattis with a stone wall, in it's rear, thence the defences were continued along the bluff of the city, by houses, the stone walls of yards, and the barricades constructed at the ends of the streets, to the South-eastern angle of the Town, where an old Hospital, standing out in a salient position to the rest of the line, had been fortified and garnished with guns, to command one of the principal entrances to the Town, that by the Cadareita road. All the works along this line had been abandoned except the last mentioned, and from the obstinacy with which it was maintained, it is probable that the enemy then had in contemplation a retreat by that route, the only one then open to him on which he could have carried *artillery*.

When returning from this reconnoissance to the fort "el Diablo" I saw Lieut: Greaves with his Company, on the plain below the City, the facts connected with the duty he was performing will be found stated in Lieut. Greaves' report.

After our return to the fort "el Diablo" one of the Missi. Companies "G." was relieved by Company "B." and returned to the "Teneria." Company "D." was then ordered up, and my original command was changed, as noticed in my report to Genl. Quitman of the operations of the 23ᵈ. With Companies "B." Capt. Cooper & "D." Lieut. Russell & "H." Lieut. Moore, and one company of the 1ˢᵗ Tenn. Volunteers, I advanced under Genl. Quitman's orders. As the line, upon this side of the enemys defences, was a system of detached field works they were each of course untenable by us as long as the enemy could hold those in their rear, we therefore proceeded, over the ground I had reconnoitred, to the block of the city, where the enemy first contested our progress, and the action commenced, as described in my report of the 23ᵈ.

The chief preparations of the enemy had been made against an attack upon the northern and eastern side of the Town. We were expected to approach by the Marin or Cadareita road, and from the enceinte of outworks to the main plaza, nothing had been omitted to increase the resistance upon these approaches. Barricade, succeeded barricade, along the streets; the dwellings were supplied with ammunition, and prepared for its use. Infantry posted on the tops of the houses were securely sheltered by the stone parapet which surrounds their flat roofs, and though forced from these positions it must be conceded that they firmly resisted. The Mississippi and Texas Riflemen were vastly their superiors at sharp shooting and drove them back but they slowly retired from house to house and from square to square, obstinately defending the crossing of every street. We continued to advance until abreast of the Cathedral of the main plaza, here we seized a two story house, and maintained a contest, under the converging fire of the enemy, which lasted several hours, he was finally driven from every exposed position within the range of our rifles. The command at this position consisted of the advance of Col. Woods Texan Rangers, under Genl. Henderson; and the advance of the Missi. Riflemen.

The prisoners taken in our reconnoissance of the morning, and a Mexican found in our second reconnoissance, to the left, concurred in stating that the Main plaza was a square to the right of the Cathedral, but we now found that the Cathedral was upon one side of the plaza, and that our direction had been too far to the right. On the next square, immediately before us, was an unusually high house, from which it seemed a plunging fire could be thrown into the Plaza.

To this house, after consultation with Genl. Henderson, it was decided to advance, and secure it as a position to be held through the night. The task was more difficult than any we yet had performed. Throughout the day we had been under the fire of the enemy's artillery, generally throwing shells, but now we were close upon his field guns, which covered by a permanently constructed barricade swept the narrow pebble paved street over which we had to pass. The deadly efficiency of artillery in such a situation rendered it necessary to construct a shelter for our men whilst crossing the street. For this purpose we had to rely on such material as the neighboring yards and houses contained, of which we were fortunate in getting enough and in form as convenient as would probably be found among articles not designed for such use.

Whilst engaged in this construction, I dispatched Sergeant Major Harlan to the rear, to inquire of Genl. Quitman what had become of the field piece which he had said would cooperate with us; and to direct Major Bradford, with the portion of the Regiment under him, to join me. Sergt. Maj. Harlan returned and informed me that all the troops in our rear had retired, and that he was told the order to withdraw had been three times sent to me. He also informed Genl. Henderson that a like order had been sent by the commanding Genl. to him.

This intelligence was received with regret by all. As the resistance of the enemy became more obstinate, as the danger and difficulty of advancing increased, the energy and resources of our men rose with the demand, and all their views were onward. To none is this remark more applicable than to those who had encountered the greatest hardship, the men of Company "H." This company after the exposure and fasting of the previous day and night had marched out with me early in the morning, before the supplies had been received from our encampment, and had been actively engaged ever since. I regret that, their gallant leader, Lieut. Moore had not made a report of this day (23^d Sept. 1846) when he fell in the Battle of Buena Vista.

As we retired the enemy who had passed to our rear, kept up a constant fire upon us, especially at the crossings of the streets. We found no support in our rear until we reached the suburbs of the city, the first was Capt. Bainbridge with a company of the 3d U. S. Infantry and a piece of light artillery.

About five o.Clock having been actively engaged the whole day, we rejoined the other part of our Regiment, at the Fort we had left in the morning, and the whole were soon afterwards ordered to the encampment at the "Walnut Springs."

Early in the morning of the next day, a flag was sent out by the enemy, asking for a truce, and a conference, from which followed without further hostile operations the "Capitulation of Monterey."

Very Respectfully,
yr. obt. svt.
Jeffn. Davis.

Brierfield
20th Sept. 1847.

A. B. Bradford [1] to Jefferson Davis.

(From the Mississippi Department of Archives and History.)

Camp near Monterey, Mexico
Col. Jefferson Davis,   September 26, 1846
        Sir,

I was called upon by you last evening to make such report of the conduct of the Mississippi Riflemen as came within my

---

[1] Bradford, Alexander, a lawyer, made his home at Holly Springs, Mississippi, and was well known as a successful lawyer. During the Seminole War, in 1836, he seems to have rendered important service as a soldier. In the Mexican War he was major in Jefferson Davis's regiment. He was a candidate for Governor of Mississippi in 1847 against Joseph W. Matthews.

immediate observation during the battle of Monterey, and in conformity thereto I herein send you a statement which I vouch to be correct as far as it proposes to detail. On the morning of the 21st Inst. our Brigade under the command of Genl. Quitman moved out in the direction of Monterey; the Tennessee Regiment on the right. When we arrived opposite the city, we halted a short time, and then were ordered to move south by the left flank, the Tennesseeans still being in front. A brisk cannonade was kept up upon us until we had moved our Regiment with its whole front nearly opposite the Lower Fort or Redoubt of the Town, the Tennesseeans still being on the left. At this moment a most destructive fire opened from the Fort of Grape, Canister and musketry—raking our whole line from right to left. We instantly received orders to charge and they were as promptly executed, and the Fort carried by storm. As far as my attention was directed to the first occupation of the Fort by our troops, I can say that Lieut. Col. McClung of our Regiment was the first on the wall, followed immediately afterward by others of the Regiment. At this moment I heard Adjutant Griffith proclaim we had taken the Fort. As to the conduct of the officers and soldiers of the Regiment on this day, I say with pleasure they did their duty nobly. On the 22d Genl. Worth on the part of the American Army had the field, and we had but little to do except to receive such shots at the lower Fort, which was in our possession, as the enemy thought proper to send at us.

On the morning of the 23d you were ordered out by Genl. Quitman with two companies of our Regiment, and two companies of the Tennesseans to take the Fort No. 3 opposite to our then position, which you promptly did. In about an hour thereafter I was ordered by Genl. Quitman to move out quickly with the balance of the Regiment, except Capt. Taylor's company, which was ordered by you to remain and guard the Fort, to sustain him in an attack made with the detachment under your command on the lower part of the Town. We instantly moved out, and immediately after passing the creek, a heavy fire of grape and musketry opened, by which we were annoyed and exposed to for several hundred yards; yet it was met with admirable firmness by the Riflemen until their arrival in Town, where a warmer salute awaited them, which was received with equal spirit by the whole Regiment. We remained some time under cover of the houses, during which time a portion of the Regiment joined your command, and a portion remained with me. We were afterwards ordered by Genl. Quitman to charge on the Town, and the command was executed with almost unparalleled firmness. We carried the Street here for several hundred yards under a continued shower of grape and canister shot, accompanied with musketry, and took a position in the heart of the Town and maintained it firmly for several hours under a most galling fire the whole time, and until we were ordered by the commanding General to draw off, and then retired in good order.

The officers with me of the Mississippi Riflemen, as far as now recollected, were Capts. Willis & McManus; Lieuts, Patterson, Townsend, Wade, Arthur, Bradford and Markham, who all behaved with great presence of mind and courage, as did every soldier who accompanied us. Indeed their gallantry was conspicuous throughout, and met my entire approbation. I cannot close without making mention of Capt. Bennett of the 1st Tennessee Regiment under Col Campbell, and Capt. Hewitt, of the 2d Regiment of Texas mounted men under Col. Woods, who voluntarily served with my command and under my orders. They both together with their companies behaved with great gallantry, and from them I received most efficient aid. Dr. Veech, Quarter Master of Col. Woods' Regiment was also with me the whole time, and with his great coolness and courage rendered me essential service. All reflected on themselves the highest honor.

> I have the honor to be
> Your most obdt. svt.
> A. B. Bradford Major
> Miss. Riflemen.

(Copy)

> R. Griffith, Adj't
> Regt. Miss. Riflemen }

Endorsed:
> No. 4
> Major A. B. Bradford's
> Statement

D. H. Cooper to Jefferson Davis.

(From the Mississippi Department of Archives and History.)

Statement of Capt. D. H. Cooper of Co.[1] "B" Missi Vols. in regard to the battle of the 21st Sept. 1846.

The Brigade under Gen Quitman approached the round fort, near the distillery at the South Eastern corner of Monterey, by

[1] Company B, Wilkinson Volunteers—Capt. D. H. Cooper, Lieutenants Carnot Posey, James Calhoun, Sam R. Harrison.

LETTERS, PAPERS AND SPEECHES   117

a file movement by the left flank. The column formed by the Missi. Regt. filed to the right, and then formed by company into line, the left file of each arriving first upon the line. The fire upon the fort commenced upon the left of the Regt. and was taken up successively by each company as it arrived on the line. Being in command of the extreme right of the Regt. I arrived on the line after the firing had commenced.

My company formed, fired, and by some mistake of the men fell back perhaps ten paces, loaded, and were again brought up to the former position & fired obliquely to the left at the fort. The noise, and confusion at this time was great, and I could not hear any command from the field officers, but observing a forward movement, I gave the command to advance, which was executed rapidly. When I arrived close enough to the breastwork to see anything distinctly the first thing I observed was Col. McClung waving his sword upon the fort. I called out to my men to hurry in, pointing to Col. McClung. When I reached the ditch, the Missi Riflemen were running into the fort, many of my men were in the fort before I could get over the ditch, and up the embankment. When I jumped into the fort men from different companies of our Regt. were pouring in from all sides, and around on the embankment. I passed on immediately out at the rear of the round fort, and on to the right across the branch which runs between the distillery and the 3ᵈ fort, with some of my own company, & some of other companies of the Regt. inclining to the right, up the creek or ditch under the hill upon which the 3ᵈ fort stands.

I have no recollection of seeing any soldiers but the riflemen in the fort when I passed through it, and do not believe any others got in before the enemy were driven out by the Missi. Riflemen. Those immediately with me were close upon the heels of the Mexicans firing upon them as they ran over to the 3ᵈ fort & into the bushes along the creek. After recrossing the creek, about where I previously crossed it, some few, perhaps 20 riflemen were conducted by Col. Davis to the right still further, until we reached the corner, where the first street to the right of the fort, intersects the road leading from the distillery to the right. I posted the Riflemen behind a house, and wall within a garden on the corner. A considerable number of regular troops, and a portion of Gen. Hamer's command had by this time collected in the lane near the corner. The Mexican guns raked the street on our right. Col. Davis endeavored to prevail upon the officers in command of the troops with which we were thrown to charge the battery on our right, under cover of the fire of our rifles.

But we were ordered out, and retired across the street, and into the fields without again returning to the fort. We were exposed to the fire of the cannon in crossing the fields, and were threatened with a charge from the Mexican cavalry. After remaining for a considerable time exposed to fire from the forts, towards evening the remainder of the Mississippi Regiment under Maj. Bradford joined Col Davis. We were then ordered to go to the relief of Gen. Taylor at the fort, and distillery. After advancing part of the way under a raking fire from the enemy's Forts, we were ordered to retire to Camp. Having crossed the range of the cannon I think four times, in marching and countermarching across the fields.

(Signed)   D. H. Cooper [1]
                              Comdg. Co. "B" 1st Missi Vols.

Statement of Lieut Carnot Posey (of Company "B") of the charge of the Missi Riflemen on the South Eastern fort of Monterey—21st September, 1846.

On the morning of the 21st Brig. Gen Quitman's Brigade approached the south eastern corner of the town, after two or three volleys were fired, the order was given to the Missi Riflemen to charge the fort, which was forthwith, and unhesitatingly obeyed, when I arrived within twenty or thirty paces of the fort, I observed Lieut. Col. McClung waving his sword on the top of the breast work, and calling on the men to rush on. As I reached the brink of the ditch, I turned and called on Co. "B" to rush on, calling their attention at the same time to their Lieut. Col on the top of the fort. In turning to call on our company I was particular to look round me, and did not see any men near the fort except the Missi. Riflemen, of this I am certain. I threw myself, and crossed the same, passing round the "Round fort" to the second fort, by the distillery. When I approached the second fort, I observed two officers of the

[1] Cooper, Douglas H., a soldier, was a resident of Mississippi at the opening of the civil war, was sent by the Confederate Government to form alliances with the Cherokees, Creeks, Choctaws, and Chickasaws. He was colonel of a Choctaw-Chickasaw regiment under General Albert Pike, at the battle of Pea Ridge, in 1862, and was promoted brigadier general May 2, 1863. At the second invasion of Missouri by Sterling Price, he was entrusted with the operations against Fort Smith and Fort Gibson, in cutting off communications. His command was composed of the 1st Choctaw and Chickasaw, the 2nd Choctaw, the 1st and 2nd Cherokee, 1st and 2nd Creek, and Cherokee, Seminole and Creek battalions, Howell's Texas Battery. He settled in the Indian Territory and died there about 1867.

Mexican army, holding up the hilts of their swords, and surrendering to our men. I immediately turned to our men calling on them not to shoot, as the fort had surrendered, and observed none except the Riflemen near me. Not entering either fort, I passed, and crossed the creek beyond the fort pursuing the flying enemy. Col Davis, and Capt. Cooper being with me, with men from each company. After crossing the creek we turned to the right, being about two hundred yards from the third fort, and approaching the same we crossed a ditch to the right, and then turned to the left up a lane or street, being continually exposed to a shower of bullets, the men returning the fire of the enemy from every hut and wall. When in the act of charging the third fort, we were called on to retire from the town which was done under a continued, and heavy fire from the enemy. After reaching the field, we were charged by the cavalry of the enemy, which were repulsed by a few volleys. Col. Davis was then joined by Maj. Bradford with the rest of the Regt. when the Regt. was ordered to the assistance of Gen. Taylor. Before reaching the town, the Regt. was ordered to return to the camp, which was done, being under the cross fire of the enemy's cannon for some time.

(Signed)   Carnot Posey 1st Lieut. Co. "B."
Endorsed :
        No. 5 Compy "B"
        Statement of
        Capt. Cooper
        and of
        Lieut. Posey.

John Willis [1] to Jefferson Davis.

(From the Mississippi Department of Archives and History.)

                        Steamer Galveston, Novr. 1st 1846.
Dear Sir,
    I herewith hand you a report of such occurrences of the battles of the 21st & 23d of September as I witnessed.
    On the morning of the 21st the Missi. Riflemen under your command and a Regiment of Tenn. Volunteers commanded by Col. Campbell marched out of Camp under Genl. Quitman

---

[1] Of Warren county, Mississippi. In after years lived in Sharkey county, Mississippi, a planter of large holdings.
    Company C, Vicksburg Southrons—Capt. John Willis, Lieutenants Henry F. Cook, Richard Griffith, Rufus K. Arthur.

towards the city of Monterey. When within about a mile of the "Citadel" the Brigade was halted in a hollow, where we found Capt. Ramsey with a heavy mortar firing shells at the City. We remained a short time and took up our line of march in the direction of the eastern part of the City, where we had heard the report of small arms. Our Regt. marching by the left flank and following the Tennesseeans, who marched by the right flank.

We continued to advance in this order under a heavy cannonade, which cut down a number of Tennesseans and a few of our men, until within about three hundred yards of the Mexican Forts, when our Regiment was by your order thrown into column of companies and the whole moved by left of companies for a short time, and then formed in order of battle, bringing the centre of our Regt. directly opposite the fort.

Then it was the action commenced—our men by your orders advancing & firing with great coolness. The Regiment still continued to advance on the Fort, and when within some eighty yards of it, I heard Lieut. Col. McClung who was near to me call to the men to follow him and he moved rapidly towards the embrasure of the Fort, mounted the parapet & waved his sword several times. A number of our Regiment passed into the Fort immediately & followed the enemy who were retreating to their forts beyond the creek. The remainder of the Regt. followed in a run, took possession of the Fort and a large & very strong stone distillery immediately in the rear of it and strongly manned by the enemy.

So far as the capturing of these works are concerned I am satisfied that it was all accomplished by our Regiment without the assistance of the Tennesseeans who were too far removed from them to assist in the assault. On the morning of the 23ᵈ you marched out of the fort with three companies and took possession of a strong fort, evacuated the night previous by the Mexicans. You then advanced into the Town & commenced an attack on the enemy strongly posted on the hospital & other strong buildings. After you commenced the attack Maj. Bradford was ordered to your assistance with four companies, my own among the number. After we had reached the town we were joined by the eastern Regiment of Texan Rangers, and in company with them moved down into the city several squares, exposed to a severe fire from the Barricades thrown across the streets. From our position in town we were ordered to retire, which was done, and we returned to the Fort which you took possession of in the morning—remained there a short time and then retired to the fort & distillery taken by us on the 21st.

I neglected to mention in its proper place that after our attack upon the Fort & distillery on the 21st, many of our Regiment passed down to the creek & several across it in pursuit of the enemy and were ordered to retire, by whom I do not know.

I am very respectfully
your obt. servt.

(signed)   Jno. Willis
Comdg Com. "C"
1st Missi. Riflemen

Col. Jeff: Davis
    Comdg. Regt.
        Missi. Riflemen
Endorsed:
    No. 6   Compy "C"
        Statement of
        Capt. Willis

Daniel R. Russell [1] to Jefferson Davis

(From the Mississippi Department of Archives History.)

Camp near Monterey
26th Sept. 1846.

Col Jefferson Davis,
        Dear Sir

At your request, I send you a hurried account of such occurrences of the battle of the 21st inst as came within my own observation.

About ten o'clock in the morning of the 21st whilst your Regiment was lying down under cover upon the left of the Tennessee Regiment, both Regiments being in front of the town, and nearly a mile to the right of the fort which was first taken that morning, a very sharp firing of small arms was heard proceeding from the direction of the last mentioned Fort. You exclaimed they are getting the start of us, and in a few moments your battalion was ordered up, and marching by the left flank moved towards the Fort. The rear of the column near which was my company, it being the third from the right, marching

---

[1] Of Carroll county, Miss. Auditor of the State, 1851-1855.
    Company D, Carroll County Volunteers—Capt. Bainbridge D. Howard, Lieutenants Daniel R. Russell, Louis T. Howard, E. W. Hollingsworth, Thomas J. Kyle, Leon Trousdale.

in double quick time. The Tennessee Regiment being upon your left was now the head of the column. Meantime the Fort towards which we were moving kept up a heavy fire, while a large Fort upon the right of the town, and in front of which we had just been posted (under cover) threw a number of heavy shot upon the column. The head of the column was moving diagonally upon the Fort, when filing to the left the Brigade was thrown into line right in front upon a line parallel with the front face of the Fort, and about one hundred and forty yards from it. Your Battalion was placed immediately opposite to the Fort, the Tennessee Battalion ''Col Campbell'' being in a straight line further to the left. Col Campbell's Battalion suffered a heavy loss from killed, and wounded while advancing as I judged from the numbers of his command whom I observed lying upon the road side. The first firing from the Brigade upon the Fort which I observed proceeded from your left companies who began to fire as they formed upon the line of battle. By the time my command arrived within 50 or 60 yards of that line order had disappeared, and the movement of the companies in front of me was a rush upon the line. Mr. Griffith, the Adjutant, directed me to my place in the line, my attention was then confined for a time to the movements of my men under the direction partially of the Adjutant and yourself. The attempt was made to make the firing regular but it was futile for every man loaded and fired with the utmost rapidity. I observed and was cheered by the presence, and coolness of Mr. Griffith, and by your usual presence as your duty brought you near my position. You at length, in five minutes from the time we halted (say ten, but it was quick work.) demanded ''why do not the men get nearer the fort'' ''why waste ammunition at such a distance''? I then moved my men some thirty or forty yards nearer, those of my men most advanced being some twenty yards still nearer. It was but a moment before I was aroused from the side of a wounded man over whom I had bent for a moment by your voice above the din of the battle shouting loudly for a charge. I arose and saw you fifty yards before the general line with your sword upraised waving over your head cheering on the Battalion to charge upon the fort, for the men were now in a position which they had never been before brought to occupy in line and the most advanced were some fifty yards ahead of the more laggard. Not wishing to be left I rushed to the head of my company, and found myself in the midst of your command en route (with the fury peculiar to an American charge in battle) for the Mexican Fort. Lieut. Col. McClung of your command was the first man

I saw upon the wall of the Fort, he leaped upon it, and waved his sword in triumph. You were immediately afterwards within the Fort, I think you passed Col McClung before he left the wall. I am sure when I arrived at the Fort that I was in the midst of the men of your Battalion. I am sure with a certainty that cannot err that none but the men of your Battalion preceded me into the Fort, and I am sure that I had spent some moments after getting within the Fort in silencing the guns of our own men by the command of some superior whose name I now forget, and had partially succeeded, almost entirely, when I observed the front wall of the Fort to be covered by Col. Campbell's men who reopened the fire upon such of the enemy as presented themselves to view. I appealed to an officer of that command to silence his men, and left the Fort for the city.

While we were before the Fort, and firing from the line the shot, as I suppose grape, and from small arms fell thick upon us. I forgot to mention that a large house, strongly fortified in rear of the Fort was manned, and fired small arms upon us. Previous to the charge there was firing from the chapparel between the right of your Battalion and the Fort. I was at one time directed by a field officer of your command to fire upon the men thus placed supposing them to be the enemy, but I did not do so, and never knew who they were.

I have thus hurriedly related such facts as I now remember connected with the attack upon the Fort.

Yours respectfully
(signed)   Danl R. Russell
1st Lt. comdg Co "D' 1st Regt
Miss Volunteers.

Supplemental report of Lieut Russell,
    18th Oct. 1846,
        Camp Allen—

Daniel R. Russell to Jefferson Davis.

(From the Mississippi Department of Archives and History.)

Col Davis,
Dear Sir

In my statement made in my communication to you under date 26th ultimo. I say nothing of the occurrences of the 21st after relating the capture of the Fort by your Battalion. Being at leisure I will now further add such facts as I observed afterwards.

124   JEFFERSON DAVIS, CONSTITUTIONALIST

I cannot say how many men remained in the Fort, or the large house (a distillery I believe.) in the rear of the Fort, after the surrender. I saw you pass out from the Fort towards the city a very few moments after I entered the Fort. Men of your command were constantly leaving it in your footsteps. As I left the Fort Gen Twiggs, (as I think it was,) appeared mounted shouting "go on, go on, secure your victory" &c. There were a goodly number of Americans now in the Fort, but the movement was general for the city. While under the walls of the distillery my attention was called by one of my company to two Mexican officers standing upon the roof of the building, behind the parapet holding up their swords, the hilts upward. One of the officers held a small white flag in one hand. I stopped and attracted their attention, and by signs sought to obtain a sword, one of the officers was shot at this moment, and the other darted down from his dangerous position. Passing on a few paces, I discovered Lieut Col Mc-Clung evidently wounded, Lieut Kyle of my company was in the act of raising him from the ground, this was immediately opposite and near to the only entrance upon that side to the distillery. The entrance was a double gate. The route which you had taken led by the above mentioned double gate down a small hill, and crossing a creek which was about knee deep at the ford led on to another Fort. We crossed the creek which I suppose is an hundred and fifty yards from the second Fort, and proceeded some fifty or sixty steps when the men who were with me took cover behind a small hillock immediately upon the road side, and to the left. They were twenty or twenty-five in number, perhaps some company officers were among them but I do not remember, ten or twelve of them were of my company. I now saw you for the first time since I saw you go out of the first fort. At this time to my right, and rear behind a chapparel fence were some twenty more Riflemen, many were scattered over the open plain to the left pursuing the retreating Mexicans, and some were to the right in an old field shooting at the retreating enemy. Some of those who had left the Fort went to the right into a street which is now known as the lane. There were I think, when I first saw you beyond the creek fifty men in view, and about you. You told me on my asking for orders that we could take that Fort, pointing to the second Fort, in five minutes, and ordered me to form my men. I asked you where, you said where we stood. While I was engaged executing your command I again met you (you had disappeared for a few moments) you were cursing bitterly, you ordered me to retire from my position to recross the creek and form in the lane. You said you had been ordered to withdraw your men, and repeated you would have taken the Fort in five minutes if you had been allowed to proceed. The firing upon us while in the position last spoken of, that is between the creek, and the fort was extremely hot but from small arms alone, as the guns from the Fort did not bear on us. I saw several men shot around me. We retreated to the other side of the creek wading it where it was waist deep. I again saw you in the lane, and my men following me went with you to a small house which protected us from the firing. There, being exhausted, we sat down, and rested for the first moment since we arose from our position, and moved upon the first Fort. While sitting down Gen Quitman rode up, and dismounted. I went to him and telling him I had been ordered to withdraw, desired to know what was the order, to what place we were to retire. He told me to stand where I was, and stop every Rifleman, and bring up the rear of the Brigade as it left the town. Capt Cooper with Lieuts Posey, and Calhoun were there, and some twelve or fifteen of their men, a good many regulars, some twelve or fourteen of my company with Lieut Kyle, and stragglers from several other companies of your Regiment. From behind a small house in the lane which we had passed, some fifteen or twenty Riflemen, and a few musketeers were firing upon the Fort. While behind the house where I saw Gen Quitman, my attention was attracted by a sharp fire of musketry in the lane upon my right as I faced the Fort. I saw Gen Hamer's Brigade were in line behind the low stone wall, and firing. They fired several volleys, and in a few moments formed a column, and moved off from the town. Before their rear passed us you rejoined us, and taking command of the Riflemen brought up the rear of the column.

Here I insert an extract from my official record of the occurrencies in my company book noted down a day or two after the battle to wit "at length Gen Hamer's Brigade withdrew from the town, and some fifty Riflemen, a part of Capt. Cooper's company, with Capt Cooper. Lt Posey and Lt Calhoun a part of my own company with Lt Kyle, and myself under Col Davis brought up the rear by order of Gen Quitman. We left the town passing to the westward of the Fort we had taken, and crossing the first battle field directed our march to some fields of corn surrounded by chapparel fences. Our men were tired down, some of them wounded, and unable to keep well up were straggling behind the column, some of them fifty yards from the rear of the close column. Upon our left as we were retiring was a chapparel fence beyond was an open plain extending to the "Black Fort" or "Citadel". It was discovered that a Regiment of the Enemy's Lancers had sallied out from the Citadel and were evidently intending to attack us. As many Rifle men as we had with us were immediately thrown into line, and ordered to reserve their fire. . . . The Ohio Brigade had been faced to the front, and posted behind, and along the fence. . . . The left of their line was fifty yards or more to our right—we abandoned the muskets, and prepared our little band to receive the Lancers. They came up gallantly, their fiery little chargers prancing, and rearing handsomely.

We now saw that about fifty of them had passed around our left flank, and were approaching through the corn upon our rear. A volley from a few of the Rifles upon those in front seemed to check their headway. Our men faced about, and moved down towards those who had passed to our rear. Two of the enemy rode up to within about sixty or seventy yards of us, just to the edge of the corn. They were both brought from their saddles by shots from our rifles. . . . We were then marched for a reason most probably known to Gen Hamer . . . backwards, and forwards within the compass of half a mile in range of a heavy cross fire of cannon from three forts five times. At length most of our Regiment coming up in small detachments, we abandoned Gen Hamer, and under our own Col were withdrawn. It was now within an hour, and a half of night when we were again brought out to be fired at by said cannon by Gen Quitman, and halted. He said Gen Taylor had sent for the Brigade that had done the service during the day, and we must go back to town. We again turned our faces Montereyward, and after marching a few hundred yards, were again halted, and finding our ammunition was exhausted were marched to camp. I have written this very carelessly, and hastily, only seeking to be correct and explicit

Yours &c.
(signed)   Danl. R. Russell

Endorsed:

No. 7

Compy. "D."
Statement of
Lieut. Russell

J. L. McManus [1] *to Jefferson Davis.*

(From the Mississippi Department of Archives and History.)

Camp Allen near Monterey,
18th Oct. 1846

Col J. Davis,
Sir,

Owing to my indisposition ever since the battle I have not been able to comply with your request sooner.

I will endeavor to give you a plain and succinct account of everything that occurred, or came under my immediate attention during the engagements, as nearly as I can now remember.

On the morning of the 21st Sept. we took up the line of march on the road leading into Monterey, when we arrived in about one mile and a half of the city, we were ordered to halt, and remain under cover of a small hillock, to protect us from the batteries, that were occasionally playing upon us, we had not remained in this position long before we heard a quick firing of small arms, about one mile upon our left, very soon thereafter you ordered us down in the direction of the firing. Gen. Quitman's Brig. moved off there. The Tennessee Regt. in front, your Regt. marching by the left flank; whether the Tennesseeans were marching by the left flank, I know not, we proceeded in that direction in double quick time, running over some armed troops, who they were I have never learned, nor have enquired since. We marched on under a heavy fire of artillery all the way when in about two hundred yards of the fort we commenced our fire, we advanced slowly, and fired. About this time I discovered the Tennessee Regt. was in some confusion, which caused us to get the start of them. I turned my attention to my own company, and did not see what became of them afterwards. When we arrived within fifty or sixty yards, I heard you order the charge, and exclaim about the same time "now is the time, Great God, if I had thirty men with knives I could take that fort." This seemed to encourage the men, and they rushed forward immediately upon the fort. Lieut. Col. McClung ran in front of Capt. Rogers' company, and called upon them by name to follow him, there was then a general foot race to the fort. Col. McClung arrived first

[1] Of Hinds County, Mississippi.

upon the fort, soon followed by Lt. Patterson and some others
I do not now recollect. We passed through the Fort where I
discovered you, Lt. Col McClung, and Lt. Patterson some short
distance ahead of me. I lost sight of you as you passed round
the west end of the second fort, when I arrived there I was
met by some five or six men, bearing Col McClung out of the
fort severely wounded. I stopped and pulled off my coat to
bear him away, which threw me some distance in your rear.
When I saw you again you were upon the opposite side of
the stream, that is in about sixty yards of the Fort. I turned
up the stream, and took shelter with several others behind some
Ranches, we remained here some time firing at the Fort, until
we were ordered to retire by Maj. Bradford, during all this
time we were under a continual fire of artillery, and small arms.
We returned to camp that night. On the 22nd, wearied, and
worn down we started to the Fort we had already taken. We
arrived at the fort with but little loss, and remained there all
day, and night.

On the 23d you took a detachment of two companies one commanded by 1st Lt. Greaves, the other 1st Lt. Moore, and took
the third fort, meeting with no resistance. You, proceeded on
towards town where you did meet with resistance, the remaining companies under Maj. Bradford were ordered to your support, we succeeded in getting into town, under a heavy fire
of musketry—we extended our line along the street until we
advanced some two or three hundred yards, where I first met
with you, we were separated again. Major Bradford ordered
me to form my company, and follow him up the street. Lt
Bradford and myself with some fifty, or sixty men, followed him,
nothing of much importance occurred on that day, the fire was
kept up about five hours.

Yours respectfully,
(signed) J. L. McManus.[1]
Capt. Company "E." 1st Regt Missi Riflemen.

Endorsed:
> No. 8
> Co. "E."
> Statement of
> Capt. McManus

---

[1] Company E, State Fencibles, Hinds County—Capt. John L. McManus, Lieutenants Crawford Fletcher, J. H. Hughes, C. M. Bradford.

R. N. Downing [1] to Jefferson Davis.

(From the Mississippi Department of Archives and History.)

Camp near Monterey, Sept. 26th 1846

Col. Jeff: Davis,

Sir: At your request I send you a brief statement of the storming of the Mexican Battery on the morning of the 21st so far as the same came under my observation.

When the attack on the Mexican Battery commenced, the Company under my command was on the extreme left of the Mississippi Regiment, and next to the Tennessee Regiment. It appears that the Tennessee Regiment, under the command of Col. Campbell moved forward to the attack by the right flank, which, when they halted and faced the enemy, owing to the position in which they were placed, threw their (then right) left in front.

The Mississippi Regiment moved by the left flank, and consequently when they halted, and fronted the enemy's battery, the left was in front. The fire of the enemy was tremendous and most destructive; and I suppose continued for thirty minutes before the charge began. When the charge was ordered, I ordered my company to cease firing, load and charge. At this time Col. Campbell rode up to the left of his Regiment, next to me, and ordered them to charge. The company on the extreme left, rose from the Chaparral and grass where they had been firing, and commenced advancing on the Battery at shoulder arms, in a walk. The Mississippi Regiment now commenced the charge in double quick time, and in advance of the Tennessee Regiment who were moving to the charge by a flank; and when the Battery was stormed and the whole force of the enemy driven from it, and the Mississippi Regiment in complete possession of it, the company on the left of the Tennessee Regiment, which was in advance of that Regiment had not yet reached the Battery, and were firing to the left, on the retreating Mexicans as they were attempting to reach the second Battery, beyond the Fort. I, with several other officers of the Mississippi Regiment were calling on the Tennesseeans to cease firing as they would shoot our men, who were then passing the fort in pursuit of the retiring enemy. Col. Campbell was riding by the side of his Regiment, and also called to his Command to cease firing. At this time the Tennessee flag was

[1] Of Hinds County, Mississippi.

unfurled by their standard bearer on the Battery. Before, however, the Tennesseeans got into the Battery, the Mississippians were in possession of the Fort, where Col. McClung was shot.

I am very certain that Col. McClung was the first man on the Breast works, and that the Mississippians had taken the Battery and Fort before the Tennesseeans arrived

Yours respectfully
(signed)   R. N. Downing [1]
Comdg. Compy. "G"
1st R. M. Vols.

In addition to the above facts, when you ordered the charge sounded, which was simultaneous to the order of Genl. Quitman, the whole regiment moved promptly & together to the execution of the order

R. N. Downing

Camp Allen, near Monterey
October 18th 1846

Sir,   At your request, I herewith furnish you, with a short statement of what occurred, under my observation, on Wednesday the 23d of September, in Monterey.

Soon after you had taken possession of the Field-work,—in rear of the old Fort, which commanded the entrance to the City of Monterey, Genl. Quitman ordered me to take the Raymond Fencibles,—Company "G"—and advance upon the city, to see what effect it would have upon the enemy. I did so immediately, and approached within a few paces of the fortifications which had been thrown up by the Mexicans, around that end of the City.

I soon discovered that the enemy had abandoned them, and by approaching the breast-works, and looking along the streets, I could see them moving on towards the Grand Plaza, where, I was informed by some Mexican prisoners taken by Lieut. Hampton—they had assembled to make the last resistance. From this place, I discovered, to my left, some Mexicans standing upon the top of a large stone building watching our movements, through a *spy glass*. I moved up, with the company, within rifle shot of the building, when Genl. Quitman ordered me to halt. I did so, and remained within the range of the

[1] Company G, Raymond Fencibles—Capt. Reuben N. Downing, Lieutenants Stephen A. D. Greaves, W. H. Hampton, F. J. McNulty, Samuel B. Thomas.

fire of that building for fifteen or twenty minutes. A company of Tennesseeans had been ordered up by Genl. Quitman to support me, & had halted some two hundred yards in our rear.

The enemy to my astonishment, did not fire upon us; although, I believe, they could have done so with effect. I was then ordered back to the Field work occupied by our troops; & did so, slowly and in order.

During our halt in front of the enemy, I discovered, a few paces to my right, where they had mounted a cannon, but which had been taken away, as I supposed the night previous, and planted on the Plaza. Very soon after, the attack was made on the city of Monterey; and my command had the honor & gratification of sharing the Danger and glory of that day. As we approached the City, the fire of the enemy was exceedingly warm. I noticed, a well directed fire was kept up from the large stone building, which I had approached so near, an hour before. In advancing upon the city, we were all entirely exposed to the fire of the enemy who were concealed in stone houses, & protected from our fire. As soon, however, as we had passed over their strong fortifications, and entered the City of Monterey, we entered their houses where the doors were open, and broke those down that were closed. We continued to fire upon them, from house to house, & from square to square until ordered to retire from the city by Genl. Taylor, late in the evening. We advanced following *your* lead,—within a square or two of the Grand Plaza, near the Cathedral; where the enemy made a most desperate and obstinate resistance. The men under my immediate command fought gallantly throughout the day, as did others, whom I had an opportunity of seeing.

The scene was exceedingly inspiring, when Lieut. Bragg entered the city, late in the evening, with his train of flying Artillery, & commenced firing along the streets, & driving the enemy back upon the Plaza. That end of the city was then in the possession of the Americans, who were in almost every house firing upon the enemy. As soon as our troops saw him enter the streets of Monterey, galloping fearlessly at the head of his artillery, they commenced cheering & seemed to enter into the fight with more spirit and enthusiasm. Just after him, came Ex President Lamar of Texas, on horse back, at full speed, with his sword drawn, cheering on the men, & urging them to battle nobly for Texas and the United States.

Fortunately, I did not lose a man that day, I did not even have one wounded, I think, we entered the City of Monterey, about 9 O.Clock in the morning, & retired from it, about 5 O.Clock in the evening. The fire, during these eight hours, was uninterrupted

Your's

Respectfully

(Signed)   S. A. D. Greaves 1st Lieut.[1]

Commanding Co. "G."

Endorsed:

No. 9 Compy "G."

Statement of

Capt. Downing

and

Lieut. Greaves

James H. R. Taylor [2] to Jefferson Davis.

(From the Mississippi Department of Archives and History.)

Camp before Monterey.

Sept. 27th 1846

Col Jefferson Davis

Dear Sir.

Allow me to make known to you through this report all things that fell under my immediate observation during the battle of the 21st at Monterey. Early in the morning Genl Butlers division moved from the camp, and were posted behind the mortar planted about a mile and a half from the city. While the division were thus stationed an engagement was brought on to the left of the City by the third, and fourth Infantry, and Baltimore Battalion. Genl. Butler's division was ordered into action to their support. The Tennessee Regiment commanded by Col Campbell filed by us. In consequence of the other Regiments (Genl Hamer's Brigade) not being loaded, the Mississippians closed up upon the Tennesseans. A Brisk cannonading was kept up upon us from the Fort to the right of the City, and also from the Fort attacked by the troops first mentioned. For before we had arrived within musket shot of the Fort the firing had ceased or nearly so. The Tennesseeans passed in column to the left of the Fort while the Mississippians were brought up in line immediately opposite, and in direct line with the main embrasure.

---

[1] Of Hinds County, Mississippi.
[2] Of Marshall County, Mississippi.

The third and fourth Infantry as well as the Baltimore Battalion retiring on the right as far as I could judge. Here the action brought on in earnest, and continued with increasing heat for some time. One or two of the companies were a few paces in advance of the Regiment and Genl. Quitman rode down the line and ordered an advance alignment upon them. About the time the column reached that point, I heard the command to charge. The person who gave the command, must have been very near me, or else amidst the roar of the cannon, and small arms I should not have been able to have heard it. At the time the command was given you yourself was the nighest officer to me being amongst my company encouraging them on. Lieut: Col: McClung was the first person upon the battlement of the Fort followed closely by the main body of the Mississippians. I remained in the fort a few seconds for the purpose of collecting my company, during which time I saw no bayonet within the Fort, and I stand convinced that none passed in before me. From there we were led on past the second Fort which surrendered about the same time of the first. There Lieut: Col: McClung who had acted with so much gallantry was seriously wounded.

Passing the second Fort—we were led on by yourself across the creek to make a charge upon the third Fort. Here a heavy fire was gallantly sustained by those who had crossed the creek. The numbers across the creek were minutely increasing while you were arranging a charge upon the third Fort when you were ordered back by Gen Quitman. After we recrossed the creek I encountered many of the Tennesseeans filing up the lane leading to the right of the Fort. In this lane all the troops acted with great firmness, and courage being exposed to ball, grape, cannister, and musket shot from the Fort, and a heavy fire enfilading the street. I would further state that from an examination of the ground across the creek, had your command advanced forty yards further the Fort would have been at their mercy. For even in the position that we occupied the enemy could not depress their cannon so as to bear upon us, and a few yards further we would have been sheltered by an embankment that led entirely up to the fortification.

The remainder of the Mississippi Riflemen were upon the bank of the Creek and crossing when they were ordered back. Allow me to recommend to your notice the conduct of both the officers and men under my command, who acted with great courage and daring. I cannot conclude this report without mentioning the conduct of Joseph Heatron who fell advancing upon the first fort, and, dying, encouraged his comrades to the charge. I would further bring to your recollection the conduct of Corporal Grisham of my company who fell, under your own eye, across the Creek. He fell in advance of all and every one advancing on the third fort.

Respectfully
(signed)   James H. R. Taylor [1]
Comdg. Com. "I" 1st Regt.
Missi. Volunteers
Marshall Guards

Endorsed:

No. 10 Compy. "I."
Statement of
Capt. Taylor

W. P. Rogers [2] *to Jefferson Davis.*

(From the Mississippi Department of Archives and History.)

Camp near Monterey, Sept. 26, 1846.

Col. Jefferson Davis

Sir: I was in twenty paces of fort on the 21st Sept. when it was mounted by Lieut. Col. McClung the Col. was followed instantly by crowds of the Mississippians.

My means of judging whether the Riflemen were followed by the Tennesseeans or not was limited, for I stopped but a moment in the fort to gather my men and then passed on. I remember however to have seen a few say four or five Tennesseeans in the fort—and I think these men were with the Mississippians during the remainder of the fight. By far the greatest portion of those who crossed the creek in advance upon the second fort were Mississippians—

Respectfully
(signed)   W. P. Rogers

Camp near Monterey
Oct. 12th 1846

Col. Jefferson Davis

Sir: Having prevented by sickness from making a full report of the conduct of the Company (I have the honor to command)

---

[1] Company I, Marshall Guards—Capts. Alexander B. Bradford, succeeded by James H. R. Taylor; Lieutenants Christopher H. Mott, Samuel H. Dill, W. E. Epps.

[2] Lowndes County, Mississippi.

before Monterey on the 21st of Sept. I now ask to report as follows.

I marched from Camp on that morning with thirty eight non commissioned officers and privates. The position of my company when the firing commenced was directly in front of the centre of the fort which we were attacking, which position we maintained, except that we advanced upon the fort, until I heard the order to charge, from Lieut. Col. McClung, (he being the only field officer near me at the time) which order was given, as am credibly informed, by Col. Davis in several different forms on the right, and extended up the line.

The order to charge was promptly obeyed by my company, and I entered the fort followed by a majority of my company fifteen or twenty paces behind Col. McClung. Lieuts. Patterson & Townsend followed by eight or ten others entered the fort, immediately behind Lieut. Col. McClung. Lieutenant Wade during this entire time occupied his proper position with the Company and gallantly urged it to the charge. During the charge and previous thereto four of my company were wounded. Two but slightly and two very badly. We halted but a moment in the fort and passed out in pursuit of the flying enemy. In this chase we passed the sugar House or Distillery, which the enemy had converted into a fortification, in rear of the fort, crossed the creek a short distance beyond it, and reached a position fifty or seventy five yards beyond the Creek. We were, temporarily, halted by your command. You immediately returning to the creek, as I supposed to urge the remainder of the Regiment to follow. We being then in charge upon the second fort into which the enemy had taken shelter, and from which they were now pouring upon us a galling fire. This position we maintained some ten or fifteen minutes when we received the order to fall back to the right and rear and advance up a lane or street. This we did, when I recrossed the Creek and advanced a short distance up the street. I fell under the command of Major Bradford, you having passed on. We advanced slowly up the lane, all the time exposed to a galling fire from the enemy, which was returned with equal warmth. We advanced up this lane one or two hundred yards, occupying it for several hours when we returned to the fort, from which place we were marched out in order across the plain for a mile or possibly further when we rejoined the portion of the Regiment with you. I would be doing injustice were I to individualize, any single one of the officers or men under my command. All acted bravely and all did their duty.

On the morning of the 22ᵈ I marched from camp with twenty eight non commissioned officers and privates. We were marched to the breast works in front of the sugar House, where we remained. At night I returned to Camp by the permission of yourself, and Genl. Quitman. I was not in the engagement of the 23ᵈ—

Respectfully your's &c
(signed) W. P. Rogers
Comdg. Co. "K." 1ˢᵗ Regt. Mi. Vols.

—————— , ——————

Camp Allen, Oct. 18ᵗʰ 1846

Col. Jeff: Davis

Sir, At your request, I proceed to inform you of the action of Compy. "K." of Missi. Riflemen in Battle in the Town of Monterey on the 23ᵈ Sept. 1846.—On Wednesday morning about a half hour after sun rise, you left us in the fort at the Distillery with two companies under your command and took possession of the *small fort* that had been evacuated the night previous. About 10 o.Clock we received orders from Genl. Quitman's aid de Camp to march immediately to your support, you having commenced an attack upon the Town with the small force under your command. ——————— Company "K" being the first formed and ready to move we marched off, Compy. "C." I think followed next to us. We crossed the Creek in this order and entered the Town opposite the small fort under a very heavy fire from the small arms of the Enemy. At this point we got into action in connection with Compy "B."

Shortly afterwards the Texan Rangers joined us, & a very warm fire was kept up on the enemy during the day. We had only their heads to aim at as they would show them over the stone walls to fire at us. I cannot therefore state the amount of damage sustained by the Enemy from our Rifles. We forced them however from one square to another, until we got very near the *Church,* at which time we had orders to retire to the fort, we obeyed this order with much reluctance.

The loss sustained by Comp: "K" on this day was Private Snedicor who was mortally wounded while crossing a street, and Private Tyree who had strayed off from his Company early in the morning, & at the time the action commenced joined the Vicksburg Vols. He was shot dead, I believe in the presence of yourself and Genl. Quitman.

I have the honor to inform you that the Officers, non Com.
officers and Privates all showed great coolness and bravery
on this day.

Very Respectfully your's &c

(signed)   Wm. H. H. Patterson [1]

1st Lieut. Comdg. Co. "K."

Missi. Riflemen.

Endorsed:

> No. 11
> Compy "K."
> statement of
> Capt. Rogers
>   and
> Lieut. Patterson

C. T. Harlan to Jefferson Davis.

(From the Mississippi Department of Archives and History.)

Statement of C. T. Harlan Sergeant Major of the 1st Miss Riflemen in
the battle of Monterey Sept. 23, 1846

Col. Davis

Sir: In reply to Your call for a statement of Occurrences
during the 3rd day of the battle of Monterey, particularly those
connected with the special duty to which I was assigned by
You, I have the honor to state that:—

——The first Miss Regt on the 22nd Sept were in garrison at the
fort attacked by them on the preceding day that at day break
on the morning of the 23rd you discovered that the enemy had
evacuated or partially so the Second of the line of forts which
protected the entrance to the lower part of the City of Monterey
— Selecting two Companies You led them to its occupation—
from there You entered the town. About 8 O clock Major
Bradford with the remaining Companies was ordered to your
support as also Col Wood's Regt. of Texan Rangers. In the
desultory strife through the City I became separated from this
reinforcement and found myself close to a position occupied
by Genl. Quitman and Yourself having with You a few Tennessee troops and Your two Companies of Rifles—with Your

---

[1] Company K, Tombigbee Volunteers—Capt. Alexander K. McClung,
succeeded by William P. Rogers; Lieutenants William H. H. Patterson,
William P. Townsend.

Command alone You struggled through several squares of the City—In a short time you were joined by Genl Henderson with a portion of Col. Woods Regt. and together You forced Your way to within a few squares of the plaza. The Miss Regt remained disunited throughout the day. There were no bayonets with us and two pieces of artillery attempting an advance had fallen back from want of efficient support after firing a few discharges along the streets— The sun was fast declining— Genl Henderson now Consulted You as to the Course to be pursued, a further advance required a increase of the forces under your commands, indeed nothing but the enemies ignorance of your numbers and unsupported position could have prevented your destruction. After the Conference I was.ordered to bear a message from Genl. Henderson to Genl. Taylor, and from Yourself to Genl. Quitman. I could not find those Commanders or the portion of the Miss Regt. under Major Bradford—in the pursuit of this object I arrived at the extreme edge of the town, where I found a detachment from I think Capt. Braggs battery. From its officer I learned that our forces had fallen back—At this moment Mr Ezra Price (serving with but not attached to the Miss Regt.) met me. He came from the Commanders to whom I had been sent, bearing orders for all our troops to retire from the town, and although these Chiefs were not distant more than ½ mile, Yet as the night was fast closing I thought it proper for me to immediately convey to you the commands as delivered by Mr. Price—On returning I found you alone, the ammunition of Your Command had been reduced to a few rounds, the men had not partaken of food for 36 hours had been under arms all night without even the protection of a blanket from a chilling rain which had fallen during the time, and had been subjected to a most arduous day's duty— It was under these Circumstances the order was delivered to you, and gathering Your men together You retired from the town though not without opposition.

The foregoing remembrances are respectfully submitted and I am

Yours Very respectfully
C. T. Harlan

Endorsed:

No.

Statement of Sergeant Major C. T. Harlan
Monterey——

A.D. 1846

Memoranda of events connected with the Mississippi Riflemen during the siege of Monterey, New Leon, New Mexico.

By Jefferson Davis

On the 19th of Sept. we were encamped with Genl. Taylor's main Army in the wood of San Domingo about a league to the north of the City.

On the 20th Genl. Worth was detached with a division to take position on the west end of the city and occupy the main Saltillo road.

On the 21st the remaining force except a camp guard was marched out to make a demonstration upon the East end of the city, which would serve to attract attention from the movements of Genl. Worth and which it was also hoped might lead to more substantial results. This force was composed of two divisions, the 1st commanded by Genl. Twiggs and the 3rd commanded by Maj. Genl. Butler. The Mississippi Regt. formed part of Genl. Butler's Division, and with the Tennessee Regt. under Col. Campbell constituted the left Brigade commanded by Brig. Genl. Quitman.

Genl. Butler halted his division in a ravine about a mile from the City and then occupied by our shell battery. The Kentucky, Ohio, and Tennessee Regts. were formed in line on the right of Cap. Ramsey's Mortas. The Mississippi Regt. was detached to the left—There the whole division lay under cover of a ridge which protected it from the Enemy's shells—In the meantime Genl. Twiggs' division was ordered to the left and in a short time we heard a rapid fire of small arms in the direction of a Fort at the East end of the City and which I had discovered whilst examining the ground to the front and left of the position of the Missi. Regt. Soon after the commencement of this firing, I saw a movement in Genl. Butler's division from which we had been detached so far, that I did not hear the order which produced it. The Tennessee and Ohio Regts. moved by a flank towards the left inclining to the front. The Kentucky Regt. was left in position. Being a portion of the command to which these Regts. belonged and seeing that their march was in the direction of the firing, I moved the Miss. Regt. by advancing from the left and filed in at the head of the Ohio Regt., and in rear of the Tennessee Regt., claiming that position from Col.

Mitchell of the Ohio Regt. because the Mississippians and Tennesseeans were of the same brigade. The Ohio Regt. was subsequently filed off to the front. The firing ceased. Our Brigade continued to march obliquely to the left and front exposed to a cross fire of Artillery until we halted in front of the advanced work of the Enemy on the East end of the City.

When the Mississippi Regt. fronted (about three hundred yards from the Fort) I observed a small body of Troops before the right companies of my Regt. and asked Genl. Quitman if I should not take some space on our left which had become vacant since we halted, and as we were exposed to the enemy's fire, but not yet within the range of our rifles—I determined in taking the ground to the left, also to advance in a mode which would expose the men less than a movement in line. The companies were ordered to advance by left then to incline to the left, and then the Battalion was formed into line when about one hundred and eighty yards from the fort—the companies to commence firing. The movement brought the left company first into line and the firing extended to the right. Two Companies having been left as a garrison at Seralno, we had eight on the field. The fort before us was a round work with a low, wide embrasure which formed the easiest entrance to the fort. This embrasure (which I think was now as a sally porte) was immediately in front of our fifth company numbering from the right. The men were cautioned to fire only when a distinct object was presented and steadily to advance firing. Their accuracy of aim seemed to intimidate the enemy, their artillery was silenced, the fire of their small arms was so diminished as to indicate the propriety of a charge. I had no orders, no information as to what was designed. The troops who had been on my right were gone, and except Tennesseeans on the left, I had no knowledge of any supporting force. A charge could have been made on the right or on the left of the fort whilst the enemy were occupied with our fire, but seeing nothing, hearing nothing, to warrant the expectation of such a movement, and believing the moment was passing which should not be lost, I gave the order to charge.

I expected but little resistance, I announced to the men my conviction of the ease with which we could storm the place, by saying that twenty men with butcher knives could take it.

The Regt. was advancing firing, the formation had thus become loose, I was passing from the centre towards the right directing and bringing forward the men, when Lt. Col. McClung, who had been on the left sprung before the fifth Company, of which he was the former Captain, and I heard him call on the men to follow him, and at their head he dashed rapidly off towards the Fort, so rapidly that who should reach it first was a question to be decided by speed and position at the start. I have said that the fifth, Capt. Rogers Company "K" was in front of the entrance, the left Co. which was next to the Tennessee Regt. though the Capt. R. N. Downing made his utmost efforts, could not be first because they had further to go. As to the position of the men and of the Companies at the Fort, I consider the result of their position in line of battle, and as all equally struggled for the first place full credit is due to all.

I crossed the ditch with the advance of the Mississippi Regt. Lt. Col. McClung first mounted the parapet, Lieut. Patterson sprang into the embrasure and shot down a Mexican in the fort, I stepped by Lieut Patterson's side, the garrison had abandoned the defence of the place, and the last of their men were crowding out of the sally porte in rear of the work, upon the parapet the only person visible was our Lt. Col. who stood looking to the rear and waving his sword in token of the triumph of our arms. Intent on the pursuit, I only paused to glance around the fort and then led through it. When the Missi. Regt. commenced its charge I saw Col. Campbell near the flank of his Regt. directing some movements, the nature of which I have since learned I did not understand, and I did not see his Regiment afterwards.

Having passed through the fort we found the Mexicans flying some to a stone building which was fortified by a breast work of earth in front and one of sand bags upon its top; others fled across a stream in rear of this building to a Fort which stood beyond it.

Between the fort which we had captured and the fortified building in its rear, I saw Genl. Twiggs, he was alone, and after I passed him, heard him call to our men, and in his striking, peculiar manner point out the advantage of a close pursuit. The enemy made no attempt to enter the stone building by its front, but passed on to an entrance on the right side of the building. I was so close behind the last who entered that as they closed the heavy door, I ran with all my force against it, before it could be barred and threw it open. The enemy, some twenty odd in number, ran under a portico on the left side of the inner court and held up their hands in token of submission. An Officer announced their surrender and approached me and delivered his sword. I then passed out closing the door to prevent any one from firing through ignorance of the surrender, and looked among the bystanders for an officer to whom I would entrust the duty of receiving the arms and taking charge of the prisoners. The duty was assigned to Lieut Townsend of Co. "K" and I immediately renewed the pursuit of the enemy. With some twenty or thirty men crossed the stream and from such cover as the ground afforded opened a fire on the fort to which the enemy had fled. Our position was favorable, the enemy having no artillery posted to bear upon it, and our advance upon the fort in the direction of its gorge would have been sheltered for a great part of the way by the natural declivity of the ground, so as to compel the enemy in firing upon us in the then condition of his wall to expose a great part of his person.

I was standing in the road near the ford calling and making signals to the men in rear to follow me, when I received an order from Genl. Quitman through his aid de Camp Lieut. Nichols, directing me to retire, and soon afterward General Quitman came in person and rode into the stream whence he called to me to renew the order.

I believed then, as now, that the enemy were panic stricken, and that the men who were coming to me with those already across the stream would have taken the fort with very little loss. I obeyed the order reluctantly as did the men who were with me; but cannot censure an order which could spring alone from a desire to save our men, and a belief, though never realized, that the same could be more easily attained.

After recrossing the stream, as directed, we moved through a street to the right, when we again joined the Ohio Regt. posted under a deadly fire and so far as I could see without any commensurate advantage in the position. There Col. Mitchell fell severely wounded a moment after having given me his congratulation on my safety, here and very nearly at the same time Genl. Butler was wounded, and here we lost a number of men especially from the Ohio Regt. Though the works of the enemy were detached, their relation to each other gave to this position the disadvantage which would belong to attacking the curtain of a bastion front. After a hasty examination I indicated to Genl. Butler a route by which the salient on our right could be attacked, he seemed preoccupied, and after speaking to the other Genls. on the ground, I called the attention of Inspector Genl. A. I. Johnston to the movement I proposed, he suggested to me to commence it, with as many of my Regt. as I could collect, we proceeded to the right a short distance, when we met Cap. Field (accompanied by but one man) he had discovered a party of the enemy moving on our rear, and led us to their position. Though at least three times our number, we attacked them and drove them back until they crossed a street enfiladed by the Tete du pont which was the salient of the system of works we were attacking. There we were joined by Maj. Mansfield of the Engrs. with a party of the 1st U. S. Infy. Capt. Cooper, the senior officer with me, was placed with the men of our Regt. in a stone house on the left side of the street to pick off the enemy whenever he appeared above his parapet. Maj. Mansfield selected the opposite side of the street and commenced cautiously crossing his men over to advance on the right whilst we advanced on the left side of the street. At this time Gen. Hamer, Division Comndr., Genl Butler having left the field, came up with a large body of volunteers and directed us to retire. Against the advice of Maj. Mansfield and my own opinion distinctly expressed, but as I have understood by the consent of his Comndg Genl. he withdrew the troops from their position. We were now conducted a half a mile or more to the rear. When passing out of a cornfield, the line was threatened by the enemy's Cavalry. The Mississippians were in rear, the exertions of the day had been so severe that when the troops in front of us began to move rapidly to form under cover of a brush fence, our men could not keep up with them. A detachment of the enemy's Cavalry, say fifty men, dashed over the broken fence in our rear and attacked the persons who were in the corn behind us. I called on the men of my Regt. to return and make a counter attack, they did so with their usual spirit and drove the enemy back, killing four of his men. After various counter marches we were joined by Genl. Quitman, the Brigades were reorganized as well as might be and we took a position to which ammunition was directed, but before the arrival of the Rifle cartridges, were marched back to our encampment.

On the 22nd with the Tennessee Regt. commanded by Lt. Col. Anderson took post in the Round Fort. The Mississippi Regt. held the work in rear and the stone building to which it was attached. We had gone out without preparation, and remained without food, or other than the very light clothing we wore, through the night exposed to a severe north wind and penetrating rain. It was too dark to see anything except the signal rockets and fires of the enemy, but we could, from time to time, hear Cavalry moving, and owing to the great superiority in numbers which the enemy possessed over us, and his intimate knowledge of all the approaches, were kept constantly on the alert. At daybreak I saw enough to convince me that the enemy were withdrawing from the works near us, but couldn't perceive that he had removed his Artillery, this was communicated to Brig. Genl. Quitman Comdg. and I was sent out with two Mississippi and two Tennessee Companies to reconnoitre and gain any advantage which should be offered. We passed to the right and crossing a deep irrigating canal, entered the gorge of the fort known as "Del Diablo" and found it evacuated.

With Lieut. Scarrett of the Engineers and a small party of Riflemen, I examined the proximate flanking works and agreed with him that they were untenable in their then condition, but with slight labor and some pieces of artillery could be made very available in future operations. This report I made to Genl. Quitman whom I found, on my return to the "Fuerte Del Diablo" and Lieut. Scarrett went to report to Genl. Taylor. During this reconnoissance we took some thirty prisoners who said they were peasants.

My reconnoissance was extended to the left, the Command was changed to three Mississippi and one Tennessee Companies. Lieut. Col. Anderson remained in charge of the "Fort Del Diablo" and I advanced upon the flanking works to the left until fired on by the enemy who seemed to be advancing to dispute the possession of a barricade on which I was standing. My Command formed on the reverse side of the barricade and drove the contending party back with the reported loss of fourteen. We lost one Mississippian, than whom there was none more gallant. We were still exposed to a fire from a building which was beyond the range of our Rifles, and known to be occupied by a large force. I therefore withdrew the men and placed them under cover and awaited the arrival of reinforcements. The remainder of the Mississippi Regt. (except one company on duty in the rear), came up, a part of Col. Wood's Regt. of Texas Rangers having dismounted joined us as Riflemen. We now advanced into the town from house to house, passing generally through the Court Yards and driving the enemy steadily back from house tops, each of which formed a place for attack and furnished a very secure defence. The advance was composed in about equal numbers of Mississippians and Texans, and we were abreast of the main Plaza on the evening of the 23rd when we received orders to retire. I had sent the Sergt. Maj.

of the Mississippi Regt. back to find Genl. Quitman, and that
portion of the Regt. which I had left with Maj. Bradford, to
inquire also what had become of the piece of Artillery which
had been sent to cooperate with me. He returned and informed
me that orders had been sent sometime before to Genl. Henderson and myself to withdraw and that all the troops in our rear
had retired. About this time we were engaged in forming a
barricade to cross a street which was literally swept by the
fire of both Artillery and small arms, this we had nearly completed using such material as was found in the neighboring
houses, and it had been agreed between Genl. Henderson (Commanding the advance of Col. Wood's Texan Regt.) and myself,
with the advance of the Missi. Riflemen, that we would take possession of a stone house in our front, which from its height
would enable us to fire down into the main Plaza in which the
great body of the enemy's troops had been collected. In that
building we had determined to pass the night. It is to be
attributed to the fact that we were so far in advance that but
little was known of the advantages we had gained that the
order to withdraw was sent to us.

To this may be added the influence which reports of sorties
against us, and false rumors of the loss we were sustaining, must
have produced. The enemy did not again take possession of the
advanced position from which he had been driven, probably because they had withdrawn their Artillery and feared again to
risk it, or to go out without it, therefore our withdrawal had no
evil consequences.

On the morning of the 24th a flag of truce was sent in by
the Mexicans' Commander to ask for terms of capitulation. A
conference was granted and the well known capitulation was
the result.

As to the wisdom of the course adopted in this capitulation,
men did and probably will differ; for myself, I approved it when
it was done, and now reviewing it after the pact, I can see much
to confirm me in the view I originally took. We gained possession of a Fort large and well constructed. We had neither a
battering train nor trenching tools to reduce it, to carry the
work by storm must have cost us many men, when we had
not one to spare. We gained a large amount of powder and
fixed ammunition. Much of this was stored in the main Cathedral and the fire of our mortars directed against that building
must have produced an explosion which would have destroyed
the ammunition, a great number of houses, which have been use-

ful to us, and with the enemy's troops in the plaza, must have destroyed many of the advance of our own forces.

Jefferson Davis

6th April 1885

Copied in part by Varina Anne Davis his Aunt and Godmother, and Varina Davis his Grandmother for Jefferson Addison Hayes when he was six months old.

The forgoing, down to the signature "Jefferson Davis" is a copy of a memorandum, made by me in 1846, of events connected with the 1st Mississippi Regiment which I commanded in .the siege of Monterey. It was, with other papers lost when my library was pillaged from the place where it was deposited in Hinds Co. Missi for safety during the war between the States. Genl. W. T. Sherman was in command of the troops a detachment of whom were the pillagers, and he has recently claimed consideration as having had possession of the stolen papers. In the month of Jan. last, the Revd. F. M. Bristol, of Chicago, Illinois, informed me that he had possession of a paper which he described purporting to have been written by me and which he desired to have verified. Hoping to recover the report which I had made to the Gov. of Mississippi of the operations in which the Missi. Regt. I commanded had been conspicuous, and which report had been abstracted from the State Library at Jackson, Missi., I asked Mr. Bristol to send the paper to me for verification or condemnation, also requesting, if it was a true paper, that I might be permitted to copy it. With his assent, the foregoing copy has been made and the original returned to him as an innocent holder.

Jefferson Davis.

Beauvoir Miss.
6th April 1885

> To write this tale, until its course was run,
> It took three faithful scribes, instead of one.
> The first could tell of battles, lost, and won
> The next whose love through war, and pain could last
> The third who spell-bound hears these stories of the past.

V. A. Davis.

RETURN OF THE KILLED, WOUNDED AND MISSING OF THE 1ST REGIMENT OF MISSISSIPPI RIFLEMEN COMMANDED BY COL. JEFFERSON DAVIS IN THE BATTLES OF THE 21ST, 22D AND 23D SEPTEMBER, 1846, BEFORE THE CITY OF MONTEREY, MXO.

RANK	COMPANY	NAMES	KILLED	WOUNDED					MISSING	REMARKS
				Mortally	Dangerously	Severely	Slightly	Very slightly		
Lt. Col.		A. K. McClung			1					
Private	B	Wm. H. Miller			1					
Private	B	A. Lanehart				1				
Private	B	J. L. Anderson					1			
Private	B	J. H. Jackson			1					
Private	B	G. H. Jones						1		
Private	B	R. W. Chance		1						Died Sept. 25th
1st Lt.	C	H. F. Cook						1		
3d Lt.	C	R. K. Arthur						1		
Corpl.	C	J. B. Markham				1				
Private	C	L. M. Turner	1							
Private	C	H. B. Thompson					1			
Private	C	P. W. Johnson				1				
2d Lt.	D	L. T. Howard				1				
Sergt.	D	E. W. Hollingsworth					1			
Private	D	George Wills				1				
Private	D	W. Hoffman				1				
Private	D	O. W. Jones				1				
Private	D	Alpheus Cobb			1					
Private	D	Wm. Orr					1			
Private	D	D. Love					1			
Sergt.	E	Jo. H. Langford				1				
Private	E	H. W. Pierce			1					
Private	E	W. H. Fleming				1				
Private	E	Wm. Shadt			1					
Private	E	A. P. Burnham		1						Died Sept. 24th
Private	E	Jacob Fredericks					1			
Private	E	John Coleman					1			
Private	E	Wm. P. Spencer						1		
Private	E	M. M. Smith						1		
Private	E	James Kilby						1		
Private	E	Silas Meechem	1							
Private	E	J. N. Williams							1	Since returned unhurt
Captain	G	R. N. Downing			1					
Private	G	J. Williamson			1					
Private	G	Warren White			1					
Private	G	A. W. Teague			1					
Private	G	Robert Bowen			1					
Private	G	Saml. Potts							1	Supposed to be dead
Private	H	Jos. P. Tennille	1							
Private	H	Danl. D. Dubois	1							
Private	H	Fredk. Mathers		1						
Private	H	B. F. Roberts					1			

RETURN OF THE KILLED AND WOUNDED — *Continued*

RANK	COMPANY	NAMES	KILLED	WOUNDED					MISSING	REMARKS
				Mortally	Dangerously	Severely	Slightly	Very slightly		
Private	H	Avery Noland						1		
Private	H	Robt. Grigg						1		
Sergt.	I	Francis A. Wolf			1					
Private	I	Jos. Heatron	1							
Private	I	Jos. Downing	1							
Corpl.	I	Wm. H. Grisham	1							
Private	I	C. F. Cotton				1				
Private	I	G. Williams				1				
Private	I	Nat. Massie						1		
Sergt.	K	Wm. H. Bell			1					
Private	K	E. B. Lewis			1					
Private	K	D. B. Lewis			1					
Private	K	Chas. Martin			1					
Private	K	Jas. L. Thompson					1			
Private	K	John Stewart						1		
Private	K	John McNorris						1		
Private	K	John M. Tyree	1							
Private	K	Platt Snedicor		1						Died Sept. 24th
Private	D	Dr. G. W. Ramsey		1						Died Sept. 23d
		Total	8	5	13	13	10	11	2	Grand total 62

Attest

      R. GRIFFITH, Adj't.
           1st Regt. Miss. Riflemen

                Camp near Monterey, Mexico,
                  Friday, Sept. 25, 1846.

Endorsed

        No. 12

        Report of the Killed, Wounded and
Missing of the 1st Regt. Miss. Riflemen,
Sept. 21st, 22d, and 23d, Monterey, Mxo.

Jefferson Davis to W. W. S. Bliss.[1]

(From the Mississippi Department of Archives and History.)

Saltillo, Mexico
2[d] March 1847

Sir:—

In compliance with your note of yesterday, I have the honor to present the following report of the service of the Mississippi riflemen on the 23[d] ultimo.

Early in the morning of that day the regiment was drawn out from the Head-quarters encampment, which stood in advance of, and overlooked, the town of Saltillo. Conformably to instructions, two companies were detached for the protection of that encampment, and to defend the adjacent entrance to the town. The remaining eight companies were put in march to return to the position of the preceding day, now known as the battle-field of Buena Vista. We had approached to within about two miles of that position, when the report of artillery-firing, which reached us, gave assurance that a battle had commenced. Excited by the sound, the regiment pressed rapidly forward, manifesting upon this, as upon other occasions, their more than willingness to meet the enemy.

At the first convenient place the column was halted for the purpose of filling the canteens with water, and, the march being resumed, was directed towards the position which had been indicated to me, on the previous evening as the post of our regiment. As we approached the scene of action, horsemen recognised to be of our troops, were seen running, dispersed and confusedly, from the field, and our first view of the line of battle, presented the mortifying spectacle of a regiment of infantry flying disorganized from before the enemy. These sights, so well calculated to destroy confidence, and dispirit troops just coming into action, it is my pride and pleasure to believe, only nerved the resolution of the Regiment I have the honor to command.

Our order of march was in column of Companies advancing by their centres. The point which had just been abandoned by the regiment alluded to, was now taken as our direction. I rode forward to examine the ground upon which we were going to operate, and in passing through the fugitives, appealed

[1] Son of Capt. John Bliss, U. S. A. Was graduated from West Point 1833. Presented by the State of New York with a gold medal for gallant services in War with Mexico.

to them to return with us, and renew the fight, pointing to our regiment as a mass of men behind which they might securely form. With a few honorable exceptions, the appeal was as unheeded as were the offers which, I am informed, were made by our men, to give their canteens of water to those who complained of thirst, on condition that they would go back.

General Wool was upon the ground making great efforts to rally the men who had given way. I approached him, and asked if he would send another regiment to sustain me in an attack upon the enemy before us. He was alone, and after promising the support, went in person to send it.

Upon further examination, I found that the slope we were ascending was intersected by a deep ravine, which, uniting obliquely with a still larger one upon our right, formed between them a point of land difficult of access by us; but which, spreading into a plain towards the base of a mountain, had easy communication with the main body of the enemy. This position important from its natural strength, derived a far greater value from the relation it bore to our order of battle, and line of communication with the rear. The enemy in number many times greater than ourselves, supported by strong reserves, flanked by cavalry, and elated by recent success, was advancing upon it. The moment seemed to me critical, and the occasion to require whatever sacrifice it might cost to check the enemy.

My regiment having continued to advance was near at hand. I met and formed it rapidly into order of battle; the line then advanced in double quick time, until within the estimated range of our rifles, when it was halted, and ordered to "fire advancing."

The progress of the enemy was arrested. We crossed the difficult chasm before us under a galling fire, and in good order renewed the attack. The contest was severe,—the destruction great upon both sides. We steadily advanced, and as the distance was diminished, the ratio of loss increased rapidly against the enemy; he yielded, and was driven back on his reserves.

A plain now lay behind us—the enemy's cavalry had passed around our right flank, which rested on the main ravine, and gone to our rear. The support I had expected to join us was nowhere to be seen. I therefore ordered the regiment to retire, and went in person to find the cavalry, which after passing round our right, had been concealed by the inequality of the ground.

I found them at the first point where the bank was practicable for horsemen, in the act of descending into the ravine—no doubt for the purpose of charging upon rear. The nearest of our men ran quickly to my call, attacked this body, and dispersed it with some loss. I think their commander was among the killed.

The regiment was formed again in line of battle behind the first ravine we had crossed; soon after which, we were joined upon our left by Lieut. Kilbourne with a piece of light artillery; and Col. Lane's, the 3ᵈ Regiment of Indiana volunteers.

Lieut. Kilbourne opened a brisk and very effective fire: the enemy immediately receded; we advanced, and he retired to the mountain. No senior officer of Lieut. Kilbourne's corps being present upon this occasion, it gives me pleasure to bear testimony to the valuable services he rendered, and to express my admiration of the professional skill and soldierly qualities he manifested.

We now occupied the ground where the Mississippi Regiment first met the enemy. A heavy fire was opened upon us by a battery, which the enemy had established near the centre of his line. The Indiana regiment was most exposed and passed from the left into the ravine upon our right. The artillery retired to the battery from which it had been drawn. I had sent forward some parties, to examine the ground on which we had fought in the morning, for the purpose of bringing in the wounded: when these parties had returned, our regiment retired by its left flank, and marched along the bank of the ravine, heretofore noticed, as being on our right. The Indiana regiment, moving down the hollow, was concealed from the view of the enemy, who was probably thereby encouraged to make an attack.

We had proceeded but a short distance, when I saw a large body of cavalry debouche from his cover on the left of the position from which we had retired, and advance rapidly upon us. The Mississippi regiment was filed to the right and fronted, in line across the plain; the Indiana regiment was formed on the bank of the ravine, in advance of our right flank, by which a reentering angle was presented to the enemy. Whilst this preparation was being made, Sergeant Major Miller, of our regiment, was sent to Captain Sherman for one or more pieces of artillery from his battery.

The enemy who was now seen to be a body of richly caparisoned lancers, came forward rapidly and in beautiful order— the files and ranks so closed, as to look like a solid mass of men and horses. Perfect silence, and the greatest steadiness prevailed in both lines of our troops, as they stood at shouldered arms waiting an attack. Confident of success, and anxious to obtain the full advantage of a cross fire at short distance, I repeatedly called to the men not to shoot.

As the enemy approached, his speed regularly diminished, until, when within 80 or 100 yards, he had drawn up to a walk, and seemed about to halt. A few files fired without orders, and both lines then instantly poured in a volley so destructive, that the mass yielded to the blow, and the survivors fled. Captain Sherman having come up with a field piece from his battery followed their retreat with a very effective fire, until they had fled beyond the range of his gun.

Soon after this event, a detachment of our artillery and cavalry moved up on our left and I was directed to cooperate with it, in an attack upon the enemy at the base of the mountain.

We advanced parallel to this detachment, until it was halted. I then placed our men under such protection, as the ground afforded, from the constant fire of the enemy's artillery, to which we were exposed; to wait the further movement of the force with which we were to act. At this time, the enemy made his last attack upon the right, and I received the General's order, to march to that portion of the field.

The broken character of the intervening ground concealed the scene of action from our view; but the heavy firing of musketry formed a sufficient guide for our course. After marching two or three hundred yards, we saw the enemy's infantry advancing in three lines upon Capt. Bragg's battery, which, though entirely unsupported, resolutely held its position, and met the attack, with a fire worthy of the former achievements of that battery, and of the reputation of its present meritorious commander. We pressed on, climbed the rocky slope of the plain on which this combat occurred, reached its brow so as to take the enemy in flank and reverse, when he was about one hundred yards from the battery. Our first fire—raking each of his lines, and opened close upon his flank—was eminently destructive. His right gave way, and he fled in confusion.

In this the last conflict of the day, my regiment equalled—it was impossible to exceed—my expectations. Though worn down by many hours of fatigue and thirst, the ranks thinned by our heavy loss in the morning, they yet advanced upon the enemy with the alacrity and eagerness of men fresh to the combat. In every approbatory sense of these remarks, I wish to be included a party of Col. Bowles' Indiana regiment, which served with us during a greater part of the day, under the immediate command of an officer from that regiment, whose gallantry attracted my particular attention, but whose name I regret is unknown to me.

When hostile demonstrations had ceased, I retired to a tent upon the field for surgical aid, having been wounded by a musket ball, when we first went into action. Our regiment remained inactive until evening, and was then ordered to the encampment of the previous night, under the command of Major Bradford.

We had seen the enemy retire; but his numerical superiority over us would scarcely admit the supposition that he had finally retreated. After my arrival at our encampment, which was some time after dark, I directed Capt. Rogers, with his Company "K." and Lieut. Russell, commanding Company "D." to proceed with their commands to the field of battle, and report to the commanding General for orders. These were the two companies which had been left as a guard at Headquarters encampment as stated in the beginning of this report. They had been threatened during the day by a strong detachment of the enemy's cavalry; and had performed all the duties which belonged to their position, as will be seen by the accompanying statement of Capt. Rogers, in a manner creditable to themselves and their regiment; but they were disappointed, because they had not been with us in the battle of the day, and were gratified at the order to march upon night service, and probably to a dangerous post.

Every part of the battle having been fought under the eye of the commanding General, the importance and manner of any service it was our fortune to render, will be best estimated by him; but in view of my own responsibility, it may be permitted me to say in relation to our first attack upon the enemy, that I considered the necessity absolute and immediate. No one could have failed to perceive the hazard. The enemy, in greatly disproportionate numbers, was rapidly advancing. We saw no friendly troops coming to our support, and probably none except myself expected reinforcement. Under such circumstances, the men cheerfully, ardently entered into the conflict; and though we lost in that single engagement, more than thirty killed, and forty wounded, the regiment never faltered, nor moved except as it was ordered. Had the expected reinforcement arrived, we could have prevented the enemy's cavalry from passing to our rear, results more decisive might have been obtained and a part of our loss have been avoided.

To enumerate the instances of gallantry, and good conduct, which I witnessed, would exceed the limits proper to this communication, and yet could not fail to omit very many which occurred. I will therefore attempt no other discrimination than to make an exception of the two privates who were reported as "missing," and who have since been returned by the enemy, taken prisoners without a wound. Upon all others both officers and men, I have the pleasure to confer my unqualified commendation.

To Major Bradford, I offer my thanks for the prompt and creditable manner in which he executed all the orders I gave him, and would especially refer to the delicate duty assigned him, of restoring order among the files of another regiment, when rendered unsteady by the fire of the enemy's artillery.

Adjutant Griffith rendered me important aid, as well in his appropriate duties, as by the intelligence and courage with which he reconnoitred the enemy, and gave valuable information. I must also notice the good conduct of Sergeant Major Miller, and Quarter Master Sergeant White, of the regimental staff.

First Lieut. Mott acting assistant Commissary of subsistence, joined his Company, (Capt. Taylor's) and performed good service throughout the day.

Second Lieut. Slade acting assistant Quarter Master, was left, in charge of his train, at our encampment. It has been reported to me, that when the enemy's cavalry threatened our encampment, he formed his teamsters and others into a party, mounted them on waggon horses, and joined Lieutenant Shrover of the artillery, in his brilliant sortie, by which the enemy was driven from his position on our line of communication.

Captain Sharp's Company "A." and Captn. Delay's Company "F." having been on "detached service" when the battle of Monterey was fought, seemed anxious on this occasion to bring up any arrears in which they might be supposed to stand to the regiment. They formed the first division, and did their duty nobly.

Three of the companies were by unavoidable causes, deprived of the presence of their Captains on this occasion, viz.

Company "C." commanded by Lieut. Cook, whose gallantry at the storming of Monterey received my notice, and whose good conduct on this occasion is worthy of the highest commendation.

Company "E." commanded by Lieut. Fletcher, who showed himself equal to all the emergencies of that eventful day.

Company "H." commanded by Lieut. Moore, who so gallantly led it on the 23^d of September, in the storming of Monterey. Cool, brave, and well informed, he possessed my highest respect and entire confidence. He fell in our first engagement, and on our most advanced position. The command of the company then devolved upon 2^d Lieut. Clendennin (Captain elect) who continued to lead it during the battle.

Captain Taylor of Company "I." was present with his command throughout the day, and, as on former occasions, proved himself worthy to be the leader of that gallant company.

Captain Cooper, with his company "B." upon the left flank of the regiment, seized every opportunity which his position gave him, and rendered distinguished service.

Captain Downing joined his company "G." on the 22^d at Buena Vista. He had heard at the Rinconada that we were about to be attacked, and though the road was beset by "Rancheros," he hastened forward, and took command of his company in the morning. In the first engagement of the 23^d, this company was particularly distinguished, and fulfilled the expectations which its high state of discipline warranted. Second Lieut. McNulty was killed when leading a portion of the company to the charge. First Lieut. Greaves and Second Lieut. Hampton for their gallantry in battle and uniform good conduct, deserve the highest consideration.

There were many instances of both officers and men, who after being wounded remained upon the field, and continued to discharge their duties until active operations had ceased. Such was the case with Captain Sharp; who though shot through both thighs, evinced so great reluctance to leaving the field, that he was permitted to remain and follow his Company on horseback. Lieuts. Posey and Corwine, and Stockard were wounded, but set the valuable example of maintaining their posts.—Such also, was the conduct of Sergeants Scott, of Company "C." and Hollingsworth, of Comp. "A." of Private Malone of Company "F;" and of others whose names have not been reported to me.

In addition to the officers already commended in this report, I would mention as deserving especial consideration for their gallantry and general good conduct, Lieuts. Calhoun, & Dill, and Arthur, and Harrison, and Brown and Hughes.

It may be proper for me to notice the fact, that early in the action Col. Bowles of Indiana, with a small party from his regiment, which he stated was all of his men that he could rally, joined us, and expressed a wish to serve with my command. He remained with us throughout the day, and under all circumstances, displayed much personal gallantry.

Referring for the casualties in my Regiment to the list which has been furnished, I have the honor to be very respectfully,

yr. mo. obt. svt.

Jeffn: Davis

Col. Missi. Rifln.

Major W. W. S. Bliss⎱
  Asst. Adjt. Genl. ⎰
Endorsed:
    No. 1
        Col Davis
        Report

A. B. Bradford to Jefferson Davis.

(From the Mississippi Department of Archives and History.)

Saltillo March 2nd 1847

Col Jefferson Davis
Comdg Miss Riflemen,

Sir: late this evening I was called upon for a report of such transactions as took place at the Battle of Buena Vista on the 23rd Ult. which have immediate connection with our Regiment. If I had been called on sooner it would have given me pleasure to have went into detail, but time will not admit, and I shall therefore confine myself to the more important occurrences of the day. Your Regiment was on the field of Buena Vista on the 22nd, & remained there until near sundown when we was ordered down to this place that night as I understood to guard the city which was threatened, & to return to the field as soon as practicable next morning. Some time before we moved off on the evening of the 22nd there was a brisk fire of small arms on General Taylors left between his troops and the enemy which lasted until some time after Dark & then ceased with but little damage to either side as I am informed. On the night of the 22nd Your Regiment encamped on the right adjacent to this city, & as soon as the troops breakfasted on the morning of the 23rd you took up the line of march for the field of action,—and when in about two miles of it the battle again commenced on General Taylors left, & by the time we arrived on the Ground the action had become General. Immediately before we took our position the Second Regiment of Indiana troops under the command of Col Bowls gave way on the right of our Regt, & many of them was leaving the field in Route, when I succeeded in stoping a portion of one of the companies opposite to our line, who fell in with us, & they together with their brave Col fought with us through the battle. We formed rapidly on the Right flank, and at this moment the fortunes of the day seemed against us. There was a heavy column of Infantry of about 4000 of the enemy that had completely turned General Taylors left & were moving to fall on his rear, & many think if it had not been checked by the Mississippi Riflemen, might have lost our arms the brilliant victory which followed.

You perceived the critical position in which the army at this crisis was placed and determined to move forward upon them rapidly keeping up a fire upon them as we advanced, and arrest their progress if possible. You gave the word and like veterans the Regiment moved off, under one of the heaviest fires I ever saw, which was returned by our Regiment with equal spirit, until we came to a deep ravine which impeded our progress for a short time as its banks were from 10 to 15 (feet) high and very abrupt, yet this did not check the ardour of the men; they very soon crossed it & steadily advanced upon the enemy keeping their fire, until the enemy began to give way; a heavy body of Lancers seeing this, bore down on our left, and we were about being overwhelmed between these two columns, till your timely direction to fall back by the right down a ravine. We retired under the circumstances in good order, & formed on the opposite side of the ravine which we had crossed in our advance movement with the utmost promptness. Never did troop behave with more unflinching courage than did the Riflemen in this dangerous, but necessary movement. I crossed the Ravine with them, and moved in their midst, & altho they were rapidly falling on all sides, each officer & soldier seemed to present a gallant and noble bearing till the moment the order to retire was given. At & beyond the ravine towards the enemy we lost between 80 & 90 officers & men—there the brave Lieuts Moore & McNulty were killed, & Captain Sharp wounded. I can say with pride & pleasure that I have never witnessed any entire body of troops display such unwavering courage as did the Riflemen on this occasion. Shortly after we took position a second time the third Indiana Regiment commanded by Col Lane a portion of the 2nd Indiana & some stragglers from other Regiments took position on our left for mutual protection. The enemies battery opened upon us, & at the same time the Lancers made a demonstration on us from the Left, at which the troops above named seemed to take a panic, and a portion of them were rapidly giving away; seeing the imminent danger we were in if they left their position, I threw aside military etiquet for a moment, & rode around them & exhorted them to rally and return to their ranks & sustain their Eagle; they moved back to the line, & their brave officers with my humble exertions succeeded in again forming them.—The Indianaians changed position very soon from our left to right flank, & we formed at a right angle on the left. In the meantime the ruthless Lancers not satisfied with the slaughter they had made amongst us thought by one desperate effort to exterminate us prepared to charge us & in a few minutes advanced rapidly in column upon us; and when they arrived in proper distance we poured in altogether such a volley upon them as to sweep off all their entire front and they retired in the utmost disorder. Our Regiment flanking Col. Lanes Regiment, some time before the close of the action, made a handsome & very destructive charge upon the enemy who were pressing a portion of our troops on our right & repulsed them with great loss on their part. After this our Regiment was ordered to flank the Artillery & did so until we were ordered to leave the field which was not until the enemy had ceased firing & were with drawing their forces. I cannot distinguish between the gallant officers of our Regiment, as to who are most deserving to be named All are worthy of a place in a report, but I respectfully suggest that as Captain Taylor of the Guards & his Subalterns were not named at the battle of Monterey, & Captain Sharp & Delay and their Subalterns were on detached service and did not participate in the honour of that day, that for their distinguished conduct on the field of Buena Vista, they may be named in your report.

In conclusion I am pleased to say that I observed with pride the devotion you manifested toward your Regiment & your country, by remaining for hours after receiving a severe wound on the field indeed that you did not retire until the close of the battle.

All which is respectfully submitted

I have the honour to be your

Most obt Servant

A. B. Bradford Maj

Miss Riflemen

Endorsed:

No 2

Maj. Bradford.

Amos B. Corwin to Jefferson Davis.
(From the Mississippi Department of Archives and History.)

Camp near Saltillo, Mexico, March 1st /47

In obedience to the request of Col. Jeff. Davis, I submit the following report:

On the morning of the 22ᵈ ultimo, information having been received by the commanding Genl. that the enemy was advancing, the 1st Regt. Miss. Riflemen, together with the other troops attached to Head Quarters, was ordered under arms, and, after the necessary preparation, took up the line of march from its encampment near Saltillo, to *Buena Vista.*

The incidents of that day were trivial and unimportant, & our Regiment not getting into action, it was ordered back to camp late in the evening. The next morning, however, at an early hour, it again repaired to *Buena Vista.*

Arriving upon the field, a scene of the greatest consternation presented itself to our view—Some of the troops belonging to Genl. Wool's division were seen retreating before the enemy in great confusion the enemy having succeeded in making his way around the left wing of our line and secured a position at the base of the mountain which gave him greatly the advantage over us and rendered the fortunes of the day somewhat problematical. At this critical crisis our regiment was ordered up to a point where the enemy in great numbers had drawn up in line ready to give us battle.

We were marched up by the right flank and when within suitable distance of the enemy were halted, brought into line and then advanced in the same position, by the front—Col Davis giving the order to fire advancing. A deadly fire was poured upon the enemy which greatly thined his ranks and caused him to retire in great confusion.

In this charge Capt. Sharp was wounded in both legs, and from the serious nature of his wounds, the command of the company necessarilly devolved upon me, although he remained on the field the greater part of the day encouraging his men by his presence and appeals to "stand to their arms."

After making this successful charge, which I regret to say, was attended with heavy loss on our side—many of our most gallant and skillful officers and bravest men having fell—Col. Davis, perceiving a large body of Cavalry approaching our left, gave the order for us to retire, that we might gain a more advantageous position and receive support.

In a short time the 3d Indiana Regt. commanded by Col. Lane, and our piece of Light Artillery from Capt. Bragg's Battery, commanded by Lieut Kilbourne, came to our assistance. Col. Davis then gave the order to again advance which was promptly obeyed; and at the approach of the Cavalry halted his command and cautioned it to stand fast and reserve its fire until the nearer approach of the enemy. Col. Lane did the same to his command, which was on our right and front—the two regiments forming a half-square. As the Cavalry came near us, a heavy and deadly fire was directed at their ranks which caused them quickly to disperse, with great loss. The brilliant achievements of the day were at length crowned with success by another charge of our regt. supported by the 3d Indiana, upon the heights of the ravine on our right, upon a column of infantry who were completely driven from their position, which they had just before gained.

The conduct of my command generally was so meritorious that I forbear mentioning individual instances of gallantry lest I do injustice to others.

It may not be improper here to mention that a fragment of Col. Bowls' 2d Indiana Regt. who had been rallied by the exertions of Major Bradford and Adjutant Griffith, after the route in the early part of the action, put themselves under my immediate command, and their conduct throughout the day was commendible in the highest degree. There were from 16 to 18 of them. I regret that I cannot procure their names, as such an exhibition of bravery is rarely met with—their comrades having been driven from the field in dismay, whilst they, but a handful, were left to bear the brunt of battle with comparative *Strangers!*

Amos B. Corwin, Lieut.

Com'd'g. company "A." 1st Regt.

Miss. Riflemen

Endorsed:

No. 3 Com. "A."

Lieut. Corwin's

Statement

D. H. Cooper to Jefferson Davis.

(From the Mississippi Department of Archives and History.)

Saltillo March 1st 1847

To Lt. Richard Griffith

Adjt. Miss. Riflemen

Sir: In compliance with your request, I have the honor to report for the information of the Colonel commanding, such facts as came under my own observation during the recent operations against the enemy at this place & Buena Vista & which may not be known to him.   Having been left in command of the Camp guard, consisting of my company, (B) & (E) Company, Lt. Fletcher Commdg on the 22nd Febry. the operations of that day, of course, are not within my personal knowledge. Nothing of any moment occurred at camp, except the appearance of some two thousand of the enemy's cavalry, who came through a mountain pass on the east side of Saltillo, & marched down to the Factory near the Monterey road; where they remained during that day & night.   Apprehending an attack their appearance was at once communicated to Gen Taylor & towards night, dispositions of the wagons & artillery (one piece under Lt. Shover) were made with a view to the defence of the camp & baggage.   The wagons were parked under the direction of Capt Sibley Qt. Master assisted by Lt Slade Regimental Quarter master.   Lt Slade also rendered great assistance in visiting the videttes & communicating with other points near the camp.   Mr. Wetmore Sutler was also very active as a vidette.   Capt McManus 'tho' unable to undergo any fatigue, was constantly present and ready to render whatever aid in his power.   The men remained under arms all day & exhibited great coolness & determination, when momentarily in expectation of an attack.   On the 23rd my company was ordered out to the field; & being directly under the eye of the Col. it is unnecessary for me to say any thing as to our movements on that day.   I cannot refrain however from bearing testimony to the gallantry of Lts. Posey Calhoun & Harrison during that trying time.   My admiration was also excited by the very brave and gallant bearing of Lt. Greaves of Capt. Downing's Company—in the first charge upon the enemy.   Sgt. Maj. Miller's conduct also fell under my observation, which was cool & every way worthy of praise.

I cannot make any distinction among the men of my company, (with one exception Private Schneider who left the ranks & fell in the hands of enemy on the road to town) where all behaved with great coolness & bravery.   Privates Thos. Titley, Lewis Turberville, William Wilkinson, & Seaborne Jones were found dead, having fallen in the front of the fight.   I have reason to believe some of them were only wounded, at first, but were afterwards murdered by the Mexicans.   It is gratifying to notice the difference between our soldiery in the treatment of wounded.   One case as an example happened with Private Gayden of my company.   A Mexican Lancer's horse had been shot & fallen upon the leg or foot of the man. He was observed struggling, but Gayden would not fire upon him for *fear he might be a wounded man.* Soon however he extricated himself & ran. When Gayden & another man fired the Mexican fell. This illustrates the feeling of our men, even when excited almost to madness by a knowledge of the inhuman barbarity of the Mexican soldiery. I should have mentioned in the proper place that I observed & was struck with perfect coolness under fire, which was exhibited by Capt Downing, Capt Delay & Lt Corwin who was in command after Capt Sharp's wounds forced him to retire from the field. I refer to the short time while we occupied our last position on the hill side near Capt Shermans battery & were fired upon from the enemy's battery near the foot of the mountain. The conduct of the artillery officers Capt. Sherman & Lt. Killburn while with us came directly under the eye of Col Davis & no doubt excited his admiration as it did that of every officer & man present.

Respectfully————
D. H. Cooper
Capt. Miss. Riflemen

Endorsed:

No. 4 Com. "B."
Report——
   Capt Cooper
   Col Davis
   Mississippi Riflemen

H. F. Cook to Jefferson Davis.

(From the Mississippi Department of Archives and History.)

Camp at Saltillo
March 3 1847

Col Davis

I beg leave to submit to you the following report of the Battle of Buena Vista on the 22 & 23rd of Feb. last so far as it refers to C Company Miss Riflemen.

On the morning of the 22 of Feb the Regiment left their camp at Saltillo for the pass of "Buena Vista," when it arrived there, a position was assigned to it in rear of the line of Battle then being formed. We remained in this position during the day, in the course of which we were the silent but anxious spectators of a skirmish in the mountains on the left of our line of battle between a large body of Mexicans & two or three companies of the Kentucky Regiment.

We returned to our Camp at night, and on the next morning the 23rd again left for the approaching scene of action. Before we had reached the field however, we saw that the action had already commenced and that the left wing of our army were closely engaged with a largely superior force of the enemies Infantry & Cavalry. In a short time this entire line gave way & fled from the scene of action leaving the enemy in possession of the field.

The Regiment continued to move steadily forward, marching by the center of companies until within a short distance from the enemy. Then formed into line and marched to the front. When within about two hundred yards of a large body of Infantry you gave the command to "Advance firing."

Unsupported by any other force the Regt faultered not, but continued to advance and fire upon the enemy whose numbers were five times greater than our own.

Crossing a deep ravine whose precipitous banks seemed to oppose no obstacle to their way, they continued their charge until they had gained the opposite bank of another ravine still nearer to their now retreating foe; When at this instant you perceived that a large body of Cavalry were approaching the flanks of the line with the evident intention of cutting of their retreat, and gave the order to the Regiment to retire. This well timed retreat was effected in good order, the men rallied and formed in line without confusion after they had passed beyond the reach of the enemies fire.

The Regiment was then reinforced by a piece of Artillery from Commanded by Lt Kilborne—and in a short time afterwards was further reinforced by a Regiment of Indiana Volunteers, who were formed on the right of our line.

With this form we met and dispersed a large body of Cavalry who were formed for the purpose of making a charge upon us.

Still later in day we were reinforced by ten additional pieces of cannon & Col Mays Dragoons.

With that force we continued to move forward driving the enemy before us, until we had regained possession of the field, which appeared to have been so hopelessly lost to us in the morning.

The day being now far spent & the firing having ceased on both sides, the Regiment returned to Camp, rejoicing over the victory which their arms had so essentially contributed to secure.

The casualties of the Company have already been reported to you.

In conclusion I beg leave to say that the company who were in the action during the day under my command behaved with such uniform gallantry that I refrain from calling your attention to particular individuals, lest others might think themselves slighted by my silence.

All of which is Respectfully
submitted by yrs
H. F. Cook
1 Lieut Comdg C Co
Miss Riflemen

Endorsed:
No. 5
Com. "C."
Col Jeff Davis
Comd Miss Riflemen
Saltillo
Mexico

Crawford Fletcher to Jefferson Davis.

(From the Mississippi Department of Archives and History.)

Camp near Saltillo Mexico
Feby 28th 1847

To Col: Jefferson Davis
Mississippi Riflemen
D Sir

In compliance with your request I Report,

That on the 22d Feby my command with that of Capt Cooper were left to Guard Camp, that during the whole day we were under arms, fearful that the enemy a Body of some two or three thousand Lancers, who were in the neighborhood would attack our Camp, And that my men behaved remarkably well obeying all orders with the greatest alacrity being desirous of meeting the enemy.

That on the 23rd Feby 1847 my Company with others of the Mississippi Regt under your immediate Command took up the line of March for Buena Vista, that about nine o clock we arrived on that field, where the day to all appearances was lost, the Enemy having turned our left flank and defeated one of the Indiana Regt driving the greater portion of them off the

Field. The Lancers in hot pursuit of our Cavalry who were retreating before them and coming down upon our Camp supported by their infantry a body of six or seven thousand men, Just at this particular crisis, joined by a few Indianaians under the Command of Col: Bowles who rallied and came to our support we Commenced the attack upon the Enemy and succeeded in Stopping their onward Course for a short time; Being attacked by the Lancers on the right and the Infantry moving down upon us in front supported by a very large body of Lancers, I received your orders to retire and in doing so lost six of the best men in my Company all of them were wounded in the first charge and left on the field and afterwards murdered in cold blood by the Mexicans and six wounded who were carried off the Field.

That after retreating a short distance I rallied my men aided by Lieut J. H. Hughes and lyned the Regt by the side of a deep ravine. One Regt of Indianians under Comd of Col Lane and a piece of artillery under comd of Lieut Kilburn Coming to our support resisted the charge of a very large body of Lancers, who were repulsed with a considerable loss, that my Command in Company with others of the Regiment under your Command made several other attacks upon the enemy at different points and places, and always succeeded in carrying our points, About three o clock we received orders to support the Kentucky Regt under Comd of Col: McGee & Col Hardings Regt of Illinois troops who were retreating before the Enemy, we did so, and repulsed them (with) considerable loss recapturing two pieces of Artillery they had taken, they ended this day work,

That the men of my Company individually and as a body behaved with the greatest coolness and courage I noticed many instances of daring courage & gallant conduct on their part Lieut: Hughes the only commissioned officer of the Company who was in the action besides myself always assisted me in rallying the men and came to my aid on all occasions behaving nobly and Gallantly.

I regret exceedingly that Captain McManus whose long debility & severe illness prevented him from participating in the action of the day as also Lieut Bradford who is absent on Furlough.

Crawford Fletcher 1st Lieut
Comdg Comp "E" Miss Riflemen

Endorsed:

No. 6 Com. "E."

William Delay to Jefferson Davis

(From the Mississippi Department of Archives and History.)

Report

Of the operations of Company F. of the first Regiment of Miss Riflemen on the days of the 22d & 23d of Feb. 1847, in *the* Battle of *Buena Vista*.

On the morning of the 22d Feb. '47, this company encamped with its Regiment at Saltillo, received orders to prepare each member with one days provision and march immediately with the Regiment to the Pass Buena Vista about 6 miles from our then encampment. This order was immediately executed, and at the signal to form the Regiment each member of the company appeared in his place excepting 3 one left sick in hospital at Monterey, one sick in camp & one on extra duty as Wagoner, the two latter both manifested much anxiety to join their company and march The Regiment took up the line of march and after arriving within one mile of the above named Pass no guns had been heard fire as yet but an immense column of the Enemy was seen a few miles beyond the Pass advancing. As the Regiment was advancing near the pass by the right flank, by order of the Col it filed to the left and marched 2 or 3 hundred yards and formed on the left of an Indiana Regiment, which position it held until dark. At 27 minutes past 3 P. M. a cannon was heard to fire from the Mexican Army, and soon after several others in succession but none from our army that I knew of. At about an hour & a half by sun P. M. a large party of Mexicans had ascended a ridge of the mountain on our left flank and opened a brisk fire upon a portion of our troops (I learned was the Kentucky Cavalry who had ascended another Ridge in the Mountain) which fire was briskly returned by them; the firing was kept up by both parties until after dark when our Regiment returned to Camp. Early next morning (23d) we heard a report of a cannon from the Enemy and so soon as it was sufficiently light we could see that the firing was resumed upon the Mountain; the Regiment took up the line of march as the morning previous,—when we arrived in about a mile and a quarter of the scene of action we heard a number of cannons in quick succession with a multitude of small arms, we then marched hurriedly until we arrived at the scene of action,—we filed to the left as the day previous, to take our position on the left flank. As we advanced near, we discovered a considerable portion of the troops on the left flank of our Army retreating and a large column of the enemy of both Cavalry & Infantry passing through A number of the troops retreating passed our Regiment rapidly while we were hurriedly advancing, and I was told they were the 3d Indiana Regiment. I heard many voices in our Regiment soliciting them to return which some of them did, though but few. We had now arrived in plain view of the whole Mexican force which had passed through which looked to be between 6,000 & 8,000 in numbers. I saw no other Regiment or piece of Artillery to support ours in a charge So soon as the Regiment arrived in shooting distance with Rifles of the enemy we opened a fire upon a Column immediately in our front, which column I discovered turn to retreat.—We were then ordered to charge and after crossing a deep Ravine, we continued our fire for a short time, when it was discovered that the enemy were firing upon us from three different directions—on our right in front & on our left flank. We were then ordered to retire a short distance to Rally again; Whilst retiring I learned that Sergeant Hagany, Corporals Blakely & Butler, & privates Donovant, Jones and Garrott of my company were all killed & that Bigbie, Simpson, Morris and Courtney of the same were severely wounded & Malone and Lieut Stockard slightly wounded. 3 members of the company were dispatched to take the wounded to hospital, all the wounded went except Lieut. Stockard & J. T. Malone who kept their places in the company during the whole day— 2 of the three who went back with the wounded returned to their places in time for the next charge, the other one did not return during the day. Each of my Lieutenants had Rifles, and I noticed them firing frequently during the day at the Enemy. Every member of the company then present kept his place until the company with the Regiment returned to camp at night.

The many interesting scenes which transpired during the latter part of the day, I leave for others more competent to depict

Your Obt Servt
Wm. Delay Capt
Comp F 1st Reg Miss Riflemen

Endorsed:

No. 7 Com. "F."
The Adjutant
of the
1st Reg Miss. Riflemen

R. N. Downing to Jefferson Davis.
(From the Mississippi Department of Archives and History.)

Camp 1st Regt Mississippi Riflemen

R. Griffith Adjt   Saltillo 1st March 1847
     1st Regt Missi Riflemen
Sir
     I herewith submit a statement of the operations of the first
Regiment of Mississippi Riflemen commanded by Col Jeff Davis,
and G. company, same regiment, in the battles of Buena Vista
fought near this place on the 22nd & 23rd ultimo. I assumed
the command of G company on the evening of the 22nd when the
troops were being arranged in order of battle near the ranch
of Buena Vista, at the pass of En Cantada, for a conflict with
the enemy who was advancing with a large and superior force.
Whilst engaged in arranging the order of Battle, skirmishers
became engaged with the enemy in the mountains on the left
of the line, and continued a brisk fire until night fall, without
any material result on either side when our regiment which
was in reserve was ordered to return to Camp at this place,
a distance of near eight miles. Early in the morning of the
23rd we returned to the battle field. As we approached the
roar of cannon & the heavy discharges of musketry were distinctly heard, giving assurance that the battle had earnestly
commenced. As we approached nearer rumors of every character reached our ears, the most alarming, that the day was
going against us—that our left wing had been turned & that
the enemy were pouring into the plain to attack us in rear. Our
regiment moved forward & not a man did I hear expressing any
fear or alarm as to the result. When we arrived in sight, we
discovered the left wing had broken & were flying in every
direction, & were being pursued by a large & overwhelming force
of the enemy. We met many of our friends flying in haste
from the field. We endeavoured to rally them but in vain—
but few could be rallied, who joined us & fought gallantly
through the day. The enemy were following the fugitives cutting them down at every step. Our arrival on the field arrested
their attention. I counted six heavy armed regiments of Infantry & four detachments of Cavalry of the enemy, in echelon
at the base of the mountains and on the Plain. Our regiment
in column command moving rapidly in the direction of the
enemy having a ravine on our right, I looked behind to see what
assistance we would receive. I could see none. When we arrived in proper distance we deployed into line, gave three hearty

cheers & rushed impetuously on the enemy's lines. Such was the impetuosity of the onset, one regiment of the enemy retired rapidly to a heavy reserve in their rear. At this time my attention was directed to a large body of Lancers, approaching us on our right, evidently with the intention of attacking us in rear. I called all the riflemen I could around me, crossed the ravine in the direction of the enemy placed them in a safe posi- & commenced a fire on the head of their column, when I received orders to retire, which was done, the enemy firing down the ravine at us, retiring & we returning the fire. Two riflemen were killed near me in retiring. On emerging from the ravine I discovered the Lancers had retired, as also their Infantry & took a position near their reserve During this time we had received no assistance from any arm in the Service. At the moment we commenced the rapid movement on the enemy, he was evidently making his disposition to advance on the open plain, (which was altogether open to him) & attack our army in rear, he was waiting for the arrival of the heavy body of Lancers who made the demonstration on our right to make the movement. The charge on our part checked their movement effectually & compelled them to fall back on their heavy reserve. Our regiment retired about two hundred yards to the rear, & rapidly formed a line, when an Indiana Regiment came to our support, together with Lieut Kilborn with one piece of light artillery. We commenced moving slowly upon the enemy with the artillery in the centre. This piece was admirably served & with such effect, that Col Davis perceived a demonstration on the part of the enemy to charge us. This we prepared for by changing the line, forming in right angle, the Indiana Regiment on our right, their flank protected by a deep ravine & our left by artillery. As we had finished making this disposition the enemy's Lancers came down upon us in gallant style to within sixty or one hundred yards, when they received a fire from the whole line which was so destructive it caused them to wheel & retreat rapidly from us. Being reinforced at this juncture by Capt Sherman & three pieces light artillery & Col May with the dragoons, we continued to advance upon them, with the artillery, Col May with the dragoons moving up on our left, making a demonstration to charge, the Infantry & artillery moving directly upon them, had the effect of dispersing them in the mountains or driving them entirely from the field. After resting from the fatigues of the charge we were ordered to the front near the centre of our line, to assist our friends who were gallantly struggling against terrible odds,

When advancing to their relief we discovered a large body of Mexicans, charging in fine style down the hill on the artillery. We opened a fire upon them at the distance of two hundred yards which arrested their progress. We gave many hearty cheers & charged them—the enemy broke & fled over the point of the hill, we pursuing—we perceived a Mexican Battery to our left next the mountains which commanded this hill. I ordered my company & those of the Riflemen, who followed, to pass with me rapidly over the point of the hill, to the next ravine where I supposed the enemy were—This was performed by a portion of the regiment & the enemy commenced retreating from the ravine, we received a raking fire from their Battery, & were ordered to retire, which was done, not however until we had succeeded in killing and dispersing this force of the enemy. Nothing further occurred worthy of mention during the remainder of the evening. We had been engaged with the enemy near eight hours. The conflict for the day was over, the enemy had been driven from all our line, & we remained victors of the day. Towards night our regiment was ordered to return to camp & after the nights repose, we again prepared ourselves for the field, when we received intelligence that Genl Santa Anna with all his forces had retreated in the direction from which he came, in great haste & apparently in great confusion.

I take pleasure in mentioning the good conduct of Lieuts Greaves & Hampton who were very efficient & rendered good service throughout the day. Also the good conduct of the non commissioned officers of G Company & Sergeant McNair of E company who acted with me a portion of the day, & *all* the men of my company. Of the four corporals one was killed & three were wounded, Corporal Atkinson, Privates Thompson, Neely, Gibbs, Sanders, who were wounded, continued the fight during the day. Lieut. McNulty fell while leading a portion of the company against the enemy in the morning. Private James H. Graves, Bond, Felts, Parr, Seay, L. A. Cooper & Corpl Alexander, also fell in the first conflict with the enemy in the morning   Very Respty
yr obt Svt
R. N. Downing
Capt Comdg 1st Rgt M. R.

Endorsed: No. 8 Com. "G."
R Griffith Adjt [1]
1st Regt Missi. Riflemen

[1] Richard Griffith, Brigadier General, C. S. A. Killed at Savage Station, Va., June 29, 1862.

J. S. Clendenin to Jefferson Davis.

(From the Mississippi Department of Archives and History.)

R. Griffith

Dear Sir

On approaching the field of action, in the morning of the 23rd the left wing of our army which had been engaged by an overwhelming force was giving away and heavy columns of the enemy, both of infantry and cavalry, were turning our flank. The fate of the day seemed already to be irretrievably against us, and our regt, without being halted, was moved with all possible speed against the enemy who, were triumphantly advancing in immense masses from our left flank, in direction of the rear of the main body of our army. After a few minutes rapid advance we engaged the foe in terrible conflict, but our advance and fire upon them were unfortunately for us interrupted by a deep ravine, which we had to cross, and which gave to the enemy in addition to their far superior numbers, an advantage over us, too great to be resisted with immediate success; yet we gained position across the ravine and renewed a fire upon the columns of the enemy which halted and confused them. But being unable to sustain so unequal a combat long, and being entirely without any support whatever we retired from the then contested ground, until we were joined by a few pieces of light artillery which were wisely ordered to our assistance. This junction soon being formed we advanced against a tenfold force of the enemy, and opening a most destructive fire upon them, they soon became the retreating party. After this we were joined by a portion of the Indiana troops who had been rallied and formed at our side. They in connexion with our regiment (the credit of which belongs to the latter) successfully and without loss repulsed a large body of Lancers who during the engagement of the day came down upon us in solid column. Our regiment during the day, frequently engaged large bodies of the enemy and drove them, with great slaughter to themselves but with inconsiderable loss to us. Nearly the entire loss of the regiment in killed and wounded, was in the first conflict. It was then that my own company suffered its entire loss in killed and the number afterwards (wounded) were but two. It was then that 1st Lieut R. L. Moore fell while nobly serving his country. In the death of Lt. Moore our Regiment and the service have lossed a brave and worthy officer. His cool courage and his capacity to command, united to a rigid determination to do that which (was) right rendered his services almost beyond estimate. Near

him fell three privates of the company who, left behind them
no better soldiers than they were themselves. Of my own company who were with me on the field I could not speak of one in
higher terms than another. All did their duty bravely and
well. Whether in resisting a charge of cavalry or in the hot
fire of infantry coolness and courage characterized them. It is
also due to 2nd Lt. J. J. Poindexter to say in this report that
the services rendered me by him in the command of the company
on that trying (occasion) were most eminent and worthy of
notice. The officers of the regiment as far as met my observation
behaved with courage & capacity.

I submit the above with due respect and

am

Yours &c

J. S. Clendenin Capt

Commanding Company

R Griffith

Camp near Saltillo March 2nd 1847

Endorsed:

No 9 Com. "H."

J. H. R. Taylor to Jefferson Davis.

(From the Mississippi Department of Archives and History.)

Col: Davis

In pursuance to your request I will attempt to give a report
of the action of the 23rd at Buena Vista so far (as) the Regiment or rather my company as forming a part of the Mississippi
participated in the engagement of the day. Early in the morning of the 22nd Feb the Regiment was put in motion from Saltillo to Buena Vista in quick time a distance of six miles. On
reaching the heights occupied by our troops we were drawn up
in line of battle during the day. Towards evening a scattering
fire was brought on at the base of the mountain at the extreme
left flank of our army. About five o clock in the evening the
fire became much Greater Clearly showing that the Mexicans
had largely increased were attempting to Gain the heights next
to the Mountain. Some time after sun set our Regiment was
put in motion for our Camp at Saltillo. Early on the following
morning we were en route for scene of action Before reaching
it however a heavy fire commenced on the left flank of the
Army the enemy having succeeded in Gaining the desired
heights. Our Regiment moved directly to the scene of operations in double quick time. On coming near the engaged forces
we discovered the Indianians routed and retreating in great

confusion. It seemed to be the desire both of our officers and men as they passed us to rally them to the fight. Col Bowles joined us without a Command so also Lieut: Lewis with a few men and here let me add that through out the day Lieut Lewis rendered his country efficient service and Col Bowls distinguished himself for his bravery and gallantry. In the face of the Mexican forces were we led single hand without artillery to back or other troops to sustain us. Flushed with their success the Mexicans moved against us at a rapid stride but with dressed ranks onward the Mississippi Regiment moved until within one hundred and fifty yards when we were ordered by you to fire and advance. The Regiment advanced steadily upon the enemy until we came to a deep ravine forty or fifty feet deep and almost perpendicular. Here we were ordered to march on and no sooner ordered than your Regiment had descended and scaled the opposite precipice and were advancing upon the enemy, they giving away. In this charge the most gallant I can say on record the enemy suffered great loss as well as many brave and gallant Mississippians fell. The Regiment was advancing when the order to fall back was given for just then we were almost surrounded by the enemy and a large body of lancers were endeavoring to get possession in our rear. The Regiment with you at its head fell back to the ravine and down the ravine and repulsed a heavy body lancers that had formed above us. In gaining a favorable position the Regiment was halted and formed by Battalion front. We had then been joined by the Indiana Regiment commanded by Col Lane And to Maj Bradford belongs great credit for the rallying that regiment to sustain a charge about to be made upon us by a large body of approaching us on the left. The Lancers charged up within about fifty yards of our line and there every officer did his duty exhorting the men to their duty. The Lancers were repulsed with great loss. From early in the morning until late in the evening even until sun set the Mississippi Regiment were hotly and actively engaged and it were idle for me to undertake to enumerate the many regimental feats of daring and the many undertakings bold and fearless It is useless for me here to state that my company shared its fatigues, dangers and achievements. I can make no distinction—like a band of brothers each did his duty emulating the good example. I would recommend to your notice my brave Lieuts Moll & Dill. The officers all did their duty they in particular were prominent. As for my heroic dead their deeds are their epitaphs. Sergt Anderson, Henry Trotter, A. Collingsworth & John

Branch and J. Peas were distinguished in the fight and fell as far that day as a Mississippian dared go.   To you Col: Davis here permit me in behalf of my Company to express our thanks for your remaining with your regiment though wounded early in the action and our high esteem for coolness and foresight during the day   Obt yours I remain

J. H. R. Taylor
Capt Comdg Com "I" Miss :
Riflemen

Endorsed : No 10 Com. "I."
Col Jefferson Davis
Saltillo Mexico

W. P. Rogers to Jefferson Davis.

(From the Mississippi Department of Archives and History.)

Camp near Saltillo, Mxo
March 6th 1847

Col Jeffn. Davis,
Comdg. Miss: Riflemen
Sir,

It affords me pleasure to call your attention to companies "D" and "K" of the Mississippi Regiment which were left in Camp at Head Quarters on the 23d Ult: for its defence and protection, under my command

Early on the morning of the 23d, a large body of the enemy were seen on the plain two or three miles east of our Camp. They were mounted men, and evidently threatened an attack upon camp, which disposition was apparent at a later hour of the day.   Soon after you had led your regiment to the field of Battle, a large number of American Soldiers were seen flying from the field of battle toward my post in great disorder and confusion.   With the assistance of Lieut: Russell, who was in command of Com. "D", and other officers under my command, I succeeded, after great exertion in rallying about two hundred of them.   Those of them who were on foot I placed under the command of Captain McManus,—to whom I am indebted for assistance on that occasion.   Those on horses I placed under the command of Lieut: Slade.

Soon after these dispositions were made the enemy appeared in large force on the road leading from Saltillo to "Buena Vista" about one mile from camp and between my post and the main Army.   I now deemed an attack certain, and after striking tents, formed my command in rear of the Gun under the command of Lieut. Shover, who instantly opened a heavy fire upon the enemy. Soon after this Lieut. Shover ran his gun out half mile more and continued his fire, which soon drove the enemy from their position. In the mean time however Lieut: Slade gallantly led his mounted men on in support of the Gun, which followed the enemy a mile or more from my post, and drove them from the field.

I cannot fail to mention the cool and intrepid conduct of the officers and men under my command, and the ready willingness evinced by all to meet the enemy as much probably from a desire to divide the dangers of the day and withdraw a portion of the enemy from the main field as from a personal disposition to share in the glories of the battle of ''Buena Vista.''

On the night of the 23d in obedience to your orders I reported the two companies under my command to the Comdg General whom I found at the advanced post of our Army, and by him was ordered to a position in rear of Captain Sherman's field Battery, where I remained until the morning of the 24th when it was found that the enemy were gone. We then gave *three cheers* for the American flag and *Genl: Taylor,* and by orders I rejoined my regiment.

Respectfully yours
Wm: P. Rogers
Captn: Com. ''K''
Miss: Riflemen

Official

    R. Griffith, Adjt.

Endorsed:

    No. 11 Com. ''K.''

RETURN OF THE KILLED AND WOUNDED OF 1ST REGIMENT OF MISSISSIPPI RIFLEMEN COMMANDED BY COL. JEFFERSON DAVIS IN THE BATTLE OF THE 23D OF FEBRUARY, 1847, ON THE PLAIN OF BUENA VISTA, MEXICO

RANK	COMPANY	NAMES	KILLED	Dangerously	Severely	Slightly	
Colonel		Jefferson Davis			1		
Captain	A	J. M. Sharp			1		
Lieutenant	A	A. R. Corwine				1	
Sergeant	A	Theo. Ingram	1				
Sergeant	A	D. M. Hollingsworth				1	
Private	A	Geo. Brook		1			
Private	A	D. H. Clark			1		
Private	A	W. H. Stubblefield			1		
Private	A	S. P. Stubblefield				1	

RETURN OF THE KILLED AND WOUNDED — *Continued*

RANK	COMPANY	NAMES	KILLED	Dangerously	Severely	Slightly	
Private	A	R. L. Shook			1		
Private	A	C. O. Sullivan	1				
Lieutenant	B	Carnot Posey				1	
Private	B	Seab. Jones	1				
Private	B	Thos. H. Titley	1				
Private	B	L. Turberville	1				
Private	B	W. H. Wilkinson	1				
Private	B	J. M. Miller			1		
Private	B	G. H. Jones			1		
Private	B	Solomon Newman			1		
Private	B	J. M. Bonnelly				1	
Private	B	W. A. Lawrence				1	
Sergeant	C	W. H. Scott				1	
Corporal	C	J. A. McLaughlin				1	
Corporal	C	Howard Morris			1		
Corporal	C	Saml. C. Suit				1	
Corporal	C	J. W. Collier				1	
Private	C	D. H. Eggleston	1				
Private	C	Wm. Couch	1				
Private	C	James Johnson	1				
Private	C	Jno. Preston	1				
Private	C	J. M. Barnes				1	
Private	C	J. C. Cown			1		
Private	C	Levi Stevens				1	
Sergeant	E	W. W. Philips	1				
Sergeant	E	J. H. Langford	1				
Corporal	E	F. M. Robinson	1				
Corporal	E	Jas. C. Reville	1				
Private	E	Robt. A. Joyce	1				
Private	E	Wm. Sellers	1				
Private	E	Richard Claridy			1		
Private	E	Jno. Keneday				1	
Private	E	J. C. Laird				1	
Private	E	A. B. Puckett			1		
Private	E	Robt. Fort			1		
Private	E	Jas. Waugh			1		
Captain	F	J. P. Stockard				1	
Sergeant	F	B. Higany	1				
Corporal	F	Jas. W. Blakely	1				
Corporal	F	D. L. Butler	1				
Private	F	P. Dunivant	1				
Private	F	Stephen Jones	1				
Private	F	Enos Garrett	1				
Private	F	J. N. Bigby		1			
Private	F	Thomas Courtney				1	
Private	F	J. W. Morris			1		
Private	F	J. L. Simpson			1		
Private	F	T. J. Malone				1	
Lieutenant	G	Francis McNulty	1				

RETURN OF THE KILLED AND WOUNDED — *Continued*

RANK	COMPANY	NAMES	KILLED	WOUNDED Dangerously	Severely	Slightly	
Corporal	G	J. M. Alexander	1				
Corporal	G	A. B. Atkinson				1	
Corporal	G	P. Sinclair				1	
Corporal	G	G. W. Harrison				1	
Private	G	Jas. H. Graves	1				
Private	G	J. S. Bond	1				
Private	G	L. A. Cooper	1				
Private	G	W. M. Seay	1				
Private	G	Robert Felts	1				
Private	G	Richard E. Parr	1				
Private	G	P. Burnit				1	
Private	G	B. F. Edwards			1		
Private	G	J. Hammond				1	
Private	G	C. W. Gibbs				1	
Private	G	A. J. Neely				1	
Private	G	J. Thompson				1	
Lieutenant	H	R. L. Moore	1				
Sergeant	H	A. M. Newman				1	
Corporal	H	Henry Land			1		
Corporal	H	J. E. Stewart			1		
Private	H	W. D. Hamson	1				
Private	H	Pat. Randen	1				
Private	H	Jacob Locke	1				
Private	H	Thos. White	1				
Private	H	Wm. Winans				1	
Private	H	S. D. Carson				1	
Private	H	S. Edwards			1		
Private	H	Jno. Dart				1	
Private	H	W. H. McKenny				1	
Sergeant	I	P. M. Martin			1		
Sergeant	I	Gan. Anderson	1				
Private	I	H. G. Trotter	1				
Private	I	I. S. Branch	1				
Private	I	Jno. Peas	1				
Private	I	A. Collingsworth	1				
Private	I	T. D. Randolph			1		
Private	I	J. Hudspeth		1			
Private	I	T. O. McClanahan				1	
			39	3	22	31	Total 95

(*Signed*) JEFFERSON DAVIS
Col. Mi. Rifln.

Endorsed

No. 12

Return of Killed and (wounded)
in the battle of Buena Vista

Jefferson Davis to A. G. Brown.

(From the Mississippi Department of Archives and History.)

Brierfield
24th Oct. 1847

Govr. A. G. Brown
    Dr. Sir,
    Some time since I had the honor to send you such reports as were in my possession of events in the Mexican campaign of the 1st Mi. Rifln. Since then I have received a statement of Sergeant Major Harlan referring to a special service with which he was charged on the third day of the attack on Monterey. It contains information possessed by no one other than himself, and I enclose that it may be filed with the Monterey reports heretofore furnished, it will follow the report of Co. "K" and be I believe number 12—
    With congratulations on the hearty reception given to you in the east, and my best wishes and highest regard
                    I am yours
                    Jeffn. Davis

N. D. Coleman and others to Jefferson Davis.

(From Vicksburg Sentinel, November 17, 1847.)

Vicksburg, Nov. 2, 1847.

    Col. Jeff'n Davis—*Dear Sir:* It is the desire of your friends of this city and Warren county, to make some manifestation of their regard for you before your departure to take your seat in the United States Senate. They therefore trust it may suit your convenience to name a day before your departure when you will accept of a public dinner.
    In tendering you this slight testimonial of our esteem we assure you, that it proceeds from an abiding admiration for your character as a man, and gratitude felt towards yourself and the officers and soldiers of the First Mississippi Regiment, in consequence of the distinguished honor which has been shed upon our State by their and your glorious conduct at the Battles of Monterey and Buena Vista.
    With sentiments of the most sincere friendship, we subscribe ourselves,
    N. D. Coleman, Jno. Jenkins, D. S. Mercien, W. Peck, S.

Garison, Cha's E. Smedes, W. V. Davenport, William Porter-
field, R. M. Martin, Joe Sellers, A. L. Yeiser, H. Hendren,
R. R. Randolph, F. Steigelman, V. Dodge, J. H. Dupree, Shep-
herd Brown, E. G. Cook, Cha's J. Searles, P. Fletcher, John
Hebron, Geo. K. Birchett, Jno. Rabb, W. T. Balfour, E. S.
Crawford, E. Hansford, T. A. Marshall, W. A. Lake, Tho's M.
Green, F. Lightcap, Miles C. Folkes, Alex. H. Arthur, A. B.
Reading, Girard Stites, L. R. Coleman, E. D. Downs.

Jefferson Davis to N. D. Coleman and others.

(From Vicksburg Sentinel, November 17, 1847.)

Vicksburg, Nov. 2, 1847.

Gentlemen—I have the pleasure to acknowledge the receipt
of your most gratifying letter inviting me on the part of my
friends of this city and of Warren county to name a day when
I will accept a public dinner. My feeble health and the near
approach of my departure from home, compel me to decline
the proffered honor. In doing so I take the occasion to express
the sensibility with which I receive this new manifestation of the
regard of my neighbors, from whom I have so often experienced
unmerited consideration and kindness; and to say that I enjoy
the proudest satisfaction, the sweetest reward for any efforts
made in the public service in the general approbation of those
among whom I live and who know me best.

No compliment could have been dearer to me than that which
you bestow on my late comrades. For such approval they
toiled, suffered, bled and gave to their country's cause many of
the best and bravest of our number. It were enough to satisfy
the highest ambition, that the people of Mississippi should
accord to us to have sustained her honor and military reputation,
to have proved ourselves worthy to be the successors of the men
who on the ever glorious field of New Orleans, won for the
banner of Mississippi the inscription, "The wonder of one army
and the admiration of the other."

Thanking you gentlemen most sincerely for your kind attention and offering you at our parting my most cordial wishes
for your prosperity and happiness.

I am cordially your friend
And fellow-citizen,

JEFF'N DAVIS.

Messrs. Coleman, Jenkins, Searles, &c., &c.

Jefferson Davis to Stephen Cocke.[1]

(From Department of Archives and History.)

Washington, 30th Nov. 1847

Chancellor Cocke,

My dear friend, your very kind letter of the 7th has just reached me having been forwarded by my Brother. I truly thank you for the interest you manifest in my election, which is of course a subject upon which I now feel greater interest than I should have done had I remained at home, because to be beaten under present circumstances is to be recalled.[2]

Genl. Foote[3] mentioned to me this morning that he had received a letter informing him that Thompson's[4] friends were endeavoring to excite a feeling in the North by stating that I had opposed his election. My opinion of Mr. Thompson is known to you and if I had been in his district I should certainly have opposed his nomination, but my notions of propriety caused me to refuse when requested to write to some of my friends and urge them to put him aside by a renomination at a new convention. Briefly, I never interfered in the contest. The report may be of no importance, if however it should appear to you advisable you can say thus much to any of our friends in the legislature whose opinion may be affected by the underground attack.

The President is in good health & fine spirits, feels confident of being able to discomfort the enemy as signally at home as abroad. The Southern and Western Whigs are understood to be with us on the War question, which will be in the beginning at least the chief ground of contest. I think the Wilmot Proviso will soon be of the things which were. Cass is heartily with us, and says he always was but saw the necessity last

[1] Cocke, Stephen, a lawyer, was born in East Tennessee. In 1818, when his father settled at Columbia, Miss., as Choctaw agent, the boy was very young. He became clerk of the Agency, under his father, and was then elected circuit court clerk. In 1835 he was a member of the Mississippi Senate, and from 1845 to 1857 he was Chancellor of the State.

[2] The appointment of Colonel Davis to the Senate by Governor Brown held only to the following session of the legislature. Jacob Thompson, at that time a congressman from Mississippi, was an aspirant for the position in opposition to Senator Davis.

[3] Henry S. Foote, United States Senator from Mississippi.

[4] Jacob Thompson, representative in Congress from Mississippi.

spring of caution, lest the fire which would go out if let alone should be kindled by attempting to extinguish it too suddenly.

I have not been able to find the books and papers which I left here and have no list of correspondents. I wish at your leisure you would from time to time send me names especially of those we met in our joint canvass.

With great regard I am

Yr. friend

Jeffn. Davis.

Give my respects to Messrs Price and Fall.[1]   I will try to write to them this evening—if not ask them to send me the Mississippian, which request I did not make because I took as granted they would know my wish upon that point.

Jeffn. Davis.

Remarks of Jefferson Davis on bill to increase the army. In the Senate Jan. 3, 1848.[2]

Mr. DAVIS, of Mississippi.   I deem it proper to say, as one of the Military Committee, that this bill was pre-passed by a committee, under the impression that more troops were necessary to be raised immediately. The chairman of the committee, in accordance with the views of a majority of said committee, announced his intention to bring it up at the first possible moment, and press it to its speedy passage. And it is now one week, I believe [Mr. CASS: Two weeks]—one week was enough for the purpose; but it seems two weeks have elapsed since the announcement was made. We had hoped that one week would have been sufficient to have secured its passage; for we believed that a great and pressing emergency existed.

It appeared plainly manifest to us, that if any military movements took place in Mexico—that would naturally excite the military ardor of the people of the United States—it would require all the intervening time between the present period and the time when the yellow fever would set in, to organize and forward the drafts of troops necessary to carry on active opera-

---

[1] Publishers and editors of The Mississippian, one of the leading Democratic newspapers of Mississippi.
[2] Senator Davis took his seat in the Senate December 6, 1847.

tions. The Senator from Florida is not wrong in supposing that there is ground for apprehension in regard to our troops in Mexico, and that further soldiery will be required in the battle-field. For what has been the cause of so much loss of life already? I would ask, if it has not been owing, in a considerable degree, to the tardiness in furnishing the supplies, as well as the deficient quantity? But for the small amount of forces furnished, the battle of Buena Vista would never have been fought; and if General Scott, sir, had had a powerful army, with which to have followed close upon the heels of retreating Santa Anna, no fortifications would have been thrown up, and no fighting would have taken place, or resistance been made, before the walls of Mexico. What induced Santa Anna at Buena Vista to attack General Taylor, but the belief that his troops were numerically exhausted, and were not sufficient in number to repel such an attack. Shall we, by a repetition of these errors, invite similar attacks again?

Sir, all history has taught us, that where civil governments at home assume to direct military operations abroad, ruinous evil has been the result. Shall the Senate delay to decide whether it is necessary to send additional forces to Mexico? The Executive, with the information that he has in his possession, has been induced to call for these additional forces. If it be so—if the same delay is again to take place in the transmission of troops—we must then expect to see, what we have seen, a few of our gallant soldiers outflanked by a superior force, and obliged to fight their way through the serried ranks of the enemy. May it not be so again? Then, why expose the lives of your countrymen, while disputing upon questions that have no practical bearing? We are all anxious to hear the sentiments of the distinguished Senator from South Carolina, not that I am of opinion that the fate of this bill can be affected by any vote upon his resolutions. I can accept his resolutions, and still vote for this bill. If, indeed, we do not wish to annex Mexico—if we wish her to maintain an independent government, and to conclude this war by a honorable peace—I ask, why hesitate to pass this bill, and grant an adequate force and sufficient supplies? But the Senator wishes to be heard upon this question. If other gentlemen wish to answer him, these resolutions can be laid upon the table, the public service attended to, and then a wide discussion can be entered upon—a discussion which I, for one, would be inclined to listen to with much interest.

J. W. Matthews [1] to Jefferson Davis.

(From the Mississippi Department of Archives and History. Letter Book of Governor Matthews.)

Executive Chamber
Jackson Miss. Feby 14th 1848

Honr Jefferson Davis
    Washington City
Dr Sir

I have the honor of transmitting herewith a copy of a joint Resolution of the Legislature of the State of Mississippi to the Congress of the United States relative to the condition of the Second Mississippi Rifles, and the Battalion in New Orleans
    With Sentiments of the highest esteem
        I remain your Obt Servt
            J W Matthews

To the Hon. Jefferson Davis, a Member of the Senate of the United States.

(From the Washington Union, Feb. 17, 1848.)

Sir: I shall make no apology for the use of your name in a letter intended to vindicate the constitution, the government, and the honor of the nation. No more appropriate medium of communication on these subjects could be chosen. I know you well. Gifted with an enlightened mind, devoted to popular liberty, uniting in your character the ardor of the patriot with the disciplined courage of the soldier, the sympathies of your heart cannot fail to be enlisted in whatever concerns the welfare of your country, or the glory of her arms.

I have read, sir, with unfeigned astonishment and sorrow, a letter purporting to have been recently addressed to a gentleman in Ohio by an associate justice of the Supreme Court of the United States. My first impression was, that it was a forgery. I could not believe that any judge of the Supreme Court

[1] Matthews, Joseph W. (1812-1862), a governor of Mississippi, was born near Huntsville, Ala., in 1812, received only a limited education, and settled in Mississippi, as a land surveyor. He became a planter in Marshall County, was active in politics, as a Democrat; was a member of the Mississippi House of Representatives in 1840; a member of the Mississippi Senate, 1844-1848; and governor of the State, 1848-1850, after which he held no public office. He died, on a journey to Richmond, Va., at Palmetto, Ga., August 27, 1862.

of the United States could advance the unconstitutional opinions which that letter contains; much less could I suppose that an eminent magistrate, clothed in the pure ermine of justice and law, would, amidst the conflict of arms between his own country and a foreign power, come down from the bench to take part against his own government, and to pervert the constitution for the purpose of weakening its arm in the prosecution of that conflict.

But, sir, I fear, from some expressions in the letter, that it is the genuine production of that distinguished jurist. I have heretofore heard of his denunciations of "this miserable war" —I have heard of his flaunts at "military glory"—and, coupled with his long-unconcealed ambition to become the President of the United States, my surprise is diminished that he should, at this crisis in the presidential contest, have allowed himself to be betrayed into the position of an echo of the sentiments of the Lexington orator, and of a rival for the favor and suffrage of the whig party. My early and inveterate personal respect for the eminent judge—my still unabated kindness for him—my regard for the republican principles with which he first came into public life—unite in making me deplore the course he has thought fit, on this occasion, to adopt. Nor would I, sir, to subserve any other human purpose than what I devoutly believe to be the present and permanent welfare of my country, consent to indulge in any public animadversion upon the letter which constitutes the subject of this communication. Nothing personal or disrespectful shall tarnish this animadversion.

This war has been glorious in all respects. It has been characterized by skill, judgment, indomitable energy and courage. It has been distinguished by the humanity with which the vanquished enemy has uniformly been treated. It has been unchequered by a defeat, or by an act of cowardice, on the part of any portion of the American army. It has brilliantly developed the military capabilities of the country. It has been illustrated by more than twenty-five American victories. It has elevated the tone of American patriotism and of the national feeling. It has taught Europe to appreciate our strength, and to see our capacity for defence, as well as for aggression. If it has been dashed by the heroic blood shed in its progress, that is the inevitable incident of all wars. And if this be the ground for the judicial denunciation of this as a miserable war, the same denunciations might have been uttered against the war of the revolution.

The commencement of the war was that of invasion, attack,

and bloodshed against us. It was a war waged by a set of military Mexican usurpers, sustained by their rabble army, composed of the mixed and adulterated blood of the negro, the native Mexican, and Spaniard. And the government of the United States would have been recreant to their plighted faith to one of the States of this Union—recreant to the American people—recreant to the national honor, if it had not promptly adopted the means to repel the threatened invasion and hostility of the Mexican enemy.

Before our army took a position in any part of the territory of Texas, as soon as Texas was admitted into the Union, our friendly relations with Mexico were sundered by her own act. Her minister had demanded his passports, and terminated the peace of the two nations. The Mexican government had proclaimed its determination to consider the annexation of Texas as a declaration of war on our part. It had actively commenced its preparations for war. It claimed—not what a faction here has of late denominated the disputed ground, but the whole of Texas, from the Rio del Norte to the Sabine. All these demonstrations occurred before General Taylor marched to Corpus Christi. And, with a knowledge that the Mexican government had marched an army towards Texas, General Taylor was ordered to the Rio Grande. He had no sooner arrived there, than he found a Mexican army on the opposite shore of the river. Before he had fortified his positions at Point Isabel and opposite to Matamoras, the Mexicans had crossed the river. They had murdered Colonel Cross; they had attacked a small detachment of American troops, killing and cutting off the greater number of them. They were rapidly increasing in numbers. Their formidable force menaced the entire destruction of General Taylor and his gallant little army.

Under these circumstances, and with the intelligence of the meditated hostilities of the Mexican enemy, if the executive government had not foreseen, anticipated, and instructed the military officer commanding our troops to proceed as he did, it would have violated its constitutional duty—it would have given to the Mexicans every advantage—it would have exposed the whole of Texas, a member of this confederacy, to invasion and conquest—it would have exposed a small American army to slaughter, capture, and disgrace. And the opposition at home would have been the first and the loudest in their condemnation of the criminal imbecility of the President. The successful defence of Fort Brown, the glorious battles of Palo Alto and Resaca de la Palma, would never have taken place.

The Mexican enemy would have marched to the Sabine, and for a time occupied the whole of the State of Texas, then and now constituting a part of this Union. It is the constitutional duty of the Executive, in all emergencies, to be ever ready to defend the country, and at all times to maintain its honor abroad. It is the duty of the judiciary to administer justice fairly and impartially at home.

I shall now, sir, proceed to show more conclusively that, with the intelligence possessed by the President of the intentions and movements of the Mexican government and army, the constitution and law required him to prepare, as he did, by all the military means at his disposal, for the defence of the nation, and for the repulsion of threatened invasion.

It has never been doubted that for these purposes the President has the power to employ any portion of the army. In pursuance of a provision of the constitution, the law enacts that whenever the United States shall be invaded, or in imminent danger of invasion from any foreign nation, the President shall call forth the militia of the States most convenient to the place of danger, or the scene of action, according to his judgment of the necessities of the emergency, to repel it.

Aware of the preparations of Mexico, her movements, claims, and declarations in regard to the invasion of Texas, and considering that State, a part of the United States, to be in imminent danger of invasion, the President, as by the law under the constitution authorized, ordered General Taylor first to take a position at Corpus Christi; and, the danger becoming more imminent, he then ordered him to advance, and take such a position for defence of the left bank of the Rio Grande as his judgment should consider the best. Orders, as true forecast and foresight dictated, were also given to him, whenever the exigency might happen to require it, to call upon the States nearest to the place of danger, to supply him with such a force of militia as he might need to meet and repel the danger. All this was strictly within the competency of the executive power; and all this alone was done by the President prior to actual hostilities. The President neither desired nor made any declaration of war. The war was commenced—the first blow was struck by the Mexicans, arrayed in large military force on the Texan side of the Rio Grande.

The constitution of Texas comprehended as within her limits all the territory to the Rio Grande. The President had no power to consider that any portion of it down to that line was not a part of Texas. The act of annexation rendered the formation of the State of Texas subject to the adjustment by our government of all questions of boundary that might arise with other governments. No such adjustment had occurred. No disposition had been shown by Mexico to negotiate on that or any other point. And the President was not at liberty to consider any part of Texas embraced within her own constitutional boundaries, as excluding him from the lawful power and duty to repel its invasion by any foreign power. He was bound to recognise the whole of the territory, down to the left bank of the Rio Grande, as a part of the United States, until, by negotiation and adjustment, a different boundary should be established. Until then, he was as solemnly bound to defend the left bank of that river, to repel invasion from it, as he was to defend and repel the invasion of the right bank of the Sabine. The war was not commenced by the President. It was commenced by Mexico.

These are the incontestable facts of the case. What, then, becomes of the judgment of the eminent jurist, that this war was unnecessarily and unconstitutionally commenced? To establish this position, he must search the constitution of Mexico. He must discover in it the unconstitutionality of the power of the military usurper of the executive government of Mexico to commence the war upon us. He must show that on his part there was no necessity for it. He will then demonstrate his proposition, that the war was unnecessarily and unconstitutionally commenced—not by the President, but by the Mexican usurper. But the learned judge intended to advance the charge against his own government; and, in my judgment, I have repelled the charge as triumphantly as Gen. Taylor repelled the invasion of Texas.

Congress, so far as we are concerned, declared the war. Congress declared its existence by the act of Mexico. Congress provided specific means to prosecute the war to a speedy and successful termination. And now, before the war has been terminated, Congress is invoked, by a high judicial functionary, to force the President to bring it to a close by the unconstitutional measure of prescribing to the Executive the terms on which peace shall be made; by the still more unconstitutional proceeding of prescribing these conditions in the appropriation bills; and by the daring advice, that Congress should, in the event of the President exercising his constitutional power to refuse his sanction to an unconstitutional and disgraceful military appropriation bill, require the army to take up such positions as shall carry out its views.

Congress is advised by this high judicial functionary to assume the command of the army of the United States! The constitution vests in Congress no such power. That power is exclusively vested in the President of the United States.

But if these unconstitutional recommendations should fail to effect a fair or disreputable peace, then Congress must, forsooth, refuse to issue any more treasury notes, limit the terms of loans in such a manner as to prevent their accomplishment, and force the administration to resort to a system of direct and internal taxation, to render the war unpopular, and to coerce the Executive into any sort of a peace that Mexico may think proper to grant to us!

If the distinguished judge had simply advanced the proposition, that Congress had the power to devise the mode which it thought best, of raising money for the continued prosecution of the war, subject to the final sanction of the President, his doctrine would have been constitutional. But the coercion of the Executive, by the unconstitutional exertion of congressional power to compel him to make peace on terms to be prescribed by the federal legislature, constitutes the basis, object, and end of his argument. Where is the authority of Congress to make or compel peace to be found in the constitution? It is nowhere to be discovered. It is a power which, in the government from which we derive most of the principles of our institutions, belongs to its executive branch. It is a power which, by our own constitution, is expressly vested in the President, subject to the advice and consent of two-thirds of the Senate in its executive capacity.

It is said that the late war with England was nobly sustained by the people. It was. The present war is as nobly sustained by the people. But the late war, like the present, was factiously resisted in its commencement, and throughout its progress. It was then declared to be the war of the President, unnecessary and unconstitutional in its commencement and in its continuance. More than a year elapsed, after it was declared, before any direct taxes were laid. And it was not until two years and a half after the beginning of the war, that an efficient system of direct and internal taxation, devised for its more vigorous prosecution, was, under the influence of the bold and able financial genius of Alexander James Dallas, passed and put into operation. I speak by the book. I speak of affairs known to me at the time, and a part of which I was.

The adversaries of the war and the government then prophesied the certain unpopularity of taxation. The people, nevertheless, did nobly sustain the system. They were then ready, as they are now, to bear any burdens to support the success of our arms and the honor of their country. It is a libel upon them to say that an attempt to tax them would wind up the war in sixty days. I am astonished that any man would indulge in such a vaticination. I am astonished at the allegation, that a people who have sent their sons in battalions and brigades, in hundreds and thousands, to the battle-fields in Mexico—who have themselves, in hosts, rushed to the standard of their country, to sustain its flag and its fame on foreign ground, for just, American purposes— will not freely pay their money to support the glorious conflict, but will compel the government to wind up the war in sixty days, if it should attempt to raise the means by taxation for its further necessary prosecution.

But what is military glory—what is national honor—when they interpose obstacles to the gratification of aspiring ambition? And war, however necessary—however unavoidable—however conducive to the prosperity and fame of the nation—must be resisted, traduced, brought to a disgraceful close; lest, in its progress, it should confer celebrity and renown upon a patriot hero, the splendor and magnificence of whose achievements might surround his name with a circle of radiant glory, by which the flickering lights of civic life would be extinguished. This possible result of war, this probable contingency in its operations, are to justify an unholy opposition to the manly assertion of our rights and interests by the sword!

BRUTUS.

February 17, 1848.

Remarks of Jefferson Davis on the resolution of thanks to Gen. Taylor. Feb. 17, 1848.

Mr. DAVIS, of Mississippi. The Senate will not expect that I intend to enter into this discussion. Indeed, I regret that the discussion has been thought necessary by any one; and I hope, with the Senator from Kentucky, that we will return immediately to the resolutions from which we never should have wandered. It should be allowed to remain on the ground assumed, a simple vote of thanks, in which the justice of the war, its policy, the wisdom of the legislature on the subject, cannot, with any propriety, be at all involved. Officers have no other right than to refuse to obey an unconstitutional order. The power to declare war was vested by the Constitution in the Congress of the United States, and when they declared the war, it cannot be unconstitutional. The officer obeys the order he receives as an executive officer, and, upon the vote of thanks, involving only the consideration whether he has faithfully discharged his duty, we might expect the union of which the Senator from Kentucky has spoken—the union of the whole country on a question which has but two sides—the side of our country, and the side of the foreigners with whom we are at war. Party lines cannot enter into the consideration of such a question, whilst patriotism exists. There may be a faction—there will be a faction—in all times there has been a faction, that would raise its croaking voice, when the people, with one accord, send up their pæans of thanks or prayers for success Yes, sir, the American people, rejoicing over their independence, just acquired—exulting in the possession of civil liberty, at the close of our Revolution, returned their thanks to Almighty God, who had held them in the hollow of his hand, and yet, in the emphatic and classic language of Patrick Henry, one croaker was found whose discordant voice attempted to disturb the harmony. The good sense of that day turned in loathing and disgust away. Why not do so now? Why shall we pause to enter into this long discussion about foregone conclusions before the question was raised? Must President-making, too, be involved in a resolution of thanks to gallant officers? If so, and if the great result which has been deprecated is to come, and the army is to make your President, I would rather receive him from them than from the hands of fanatics. But there stands a soldier whose life has been wholly devoted to his country—whose services accumulating one by one, have become a pyramid, as beautiful for its simplicity as it is sublime for its grandeur—one which can stand like the commemorative monument of Bunker Hill, a plain and noble obelisk, with its head amid the clouds, and despising the assaults of the creeping things that crawl around its base?

I trust that the feelings of gallant men will not be assailed when the country comes to thank them for services done to the whole country. I trust, sir, that the Senate will no longer engage in a discussion, not one point of which bears upon the question at issue; and that, leaving whatever of croaking there may be to disturb the harmony of the people's thanks, we will test the question by a vote of the Senate, allowing those who refuse to yield their thanks to the gallant soldier to go before the country in the issue.

Jefferson Davis to Robert J. Walker.

(From New York Public Library Collections.)

Private

Washington
18th March 1848

R. J. Walker
        My dear Sir,
    Wm. B. Howell is an applicant for the appointment of Post Master at Natches. He has sent me a recommendation signed by many of the business men of that city which has been submitted with a letter from Govr. Brown and myself.
    If agreeable to you I wish you would address a note to the appointing bureau P. O. Dept. in favor of the appointment of Mr. Howell. You can appreciate the solicitude I feel about this matter and may anticipate my gratitude for any service rendered.

As evr yr. friend
Jeffn : Davis

    The appointment is asked as successor to Wren when his present appointment expires. The Dept. I am informed will not recommend Wren for reappointment.

Remarks of Jefferson Davis on the Mexican War. In Senate March 21, 1848.

    Mr. DAVIS, of Mississippi. The Senator from Louisiana [Mr. JOHNSON] has expressed his conviction of the certainty of an immediate peace, and on that he based his argument in presenting his motion to recommit the bill, with instructions. I have just received a letter from Mexico, which certainly does not encourage me in the prospect of peace. This letter states that the road from Vera Cruz to Mexico is infested by guerilleros, and that a party for Orizaba had been attacked by them, and been compelled to return to Vera Cruz. Though reported that the Mexicans had been dispersed, yet the American party left their dead on the field, and all their property fell into the hands of the guerilleros. Those reports which we have had of Santa Anna asking his passports, and leaving the country, are all pretext. Instead of leaving the country, it is said that he is now recruiting his forces, and looks to future operations.

Perhaps he is raising nothing more than an escort—but peace
is not his object. I beg to say to the honorable Senator from
South Carolina, that that party in Mexico to which he alludes,
as being neither unfriendly nor inimical to us, is the party
on which Santa Anna is falling back for support in his hostile
movements—the party of Puros, which invited him to return
to Mexico, as the enemy of monarchical government, in order
to overthrow Paredes.

I cannot, for myself, approve of any such policy as that
spoken of by the Senator from South Carolina, nor can I at all
conceive why he should regard the raising this additional force
in the light of mere braggadocio. We propose to raise it for
the moral effect which it may produce on Mexico. We may
with great propriety pass this bill in order to give Mexico to
understand that if she do not give us peace willingly, we
will coerce a peace. But that gallant army which has performed so many glorious deeds is rapidly wasting away. The
yellow fever has appeared in Vera Cruz, and our troops are
dying in the interior of other diseases. The volunteers are becoming daily more and more dissatisfied with the service; and,
in my opinion, the spirit of the contract under which they entered the service justifies their discharge as soon as active
hostilities cease. They entered for the war, but they believed
that on the cessation of active hostilities they would be discharged. Already the question is mooted whether, if there
can be war without a declaration of war, there may not be peace
without a treaty.

But the honorable Senator from South Carolina not only
directs his attention to the present measure, which he repro-
bates as mere braggadocio, but this goes back to an old subject—
the removal of the army to the banks of the Rio Grande. He
says:

"The whole affair is in our own hands. Whether the treaty
fails or not, we still have the complete control, if we act with
wisdom and firmness, and avoid, what I detest above all things,
a system of menace or bravado, in the management of our negotiation. I had hoped that that system had been abandoned
forever. It nearly involved us in a war with England about
Oregon. It was only prevented by the wisdom and firmness
of this body. It was resorted to in our negotiations with Mexico,
and the march of the army under General Taylor to the Rio
Grande, was but intended to sustain it. Unfortunately, the
circumstances prevented the Senate from interposing as in
the case of Oregon, and this war was the consequence."

Now the President has clearly the right to move the army of the United States into any portion of its territory.

Mr. CALHOUN (in his seat.) Certainly not into disputed territory.

Mr. DAVIS. The Senator says that the President has not the right to move the army into any disputed territory. When we annexed Texas, we left this boundary question open for negotiation. The Administration sought assiduously to settle the question by negotiation. What, then, is the argument of the Senator? When the opposite party refuse to settle the question by negotiation, are we to be estopped? Are we to allow the enemy to wrest from us the dominion which we claim as ours of right? If so, what is this but a broad invitation to every land to dispute the boundary with us? But I would ask the honorable Senator, how comes it, that even before the annexation of Texas, the navy of the United States was ordered to the Gulf of Mexico for the protection of Texas?

Mr. CALHOUN. The answer is obvious. The Gulf of Mexico is the common property of all nations. It is not disputed. But though we had a right to lay off Vera Cruz, we had not the right to enter the harbor of Vera Cruz.

Mr. DAVIS. Was it not the gentleman's own order to make a naval demonstration against Vera Cruz?

Mr. CALHOUN. I have no knowledge of such an order. Will the Senator permit me to notice another point? He indicated that the President had a right to march the army into any disputed territory. Am I right?

Mr. DAVIS. I do not consider it disputed territory.

Mr. WESTCOTT. I beg to remind the Senator that Mr. Jefferson and Mr. Madison seized upon the country west of the Mississippi.

Mr. CALHOUN. Oh! that was a trifling case. You could cover the whole country with a blanket.

Mr. DAVIS. I repeat, that I cannot perceive on what grounds the Senator will justify the order sending the navy to the Gulf of Mexico, whilst we were negotiating the annexation of Texas, and yet deny that after annexation was completed——

Mr. CALHOUN. They were issued when Congress was in session. If any attack had been necessary, application would have been made to Congress for authority.

Mr. DAVIS. The whole case is matter of record; and we know as well as the actors in it, that our navy did stand off and on the coast, looking into Mexican harbors, to keep our Government advised of any hostile movements, and be pre-

pared to act, if necessary, for the protection of Texas. For the
like purpose, a large portion of our army was concentrated upon
the border, and put in correspondence with the President of
Texas. The Senator from South Carolina, then Secretary of
State, communicated to the Texan Government this disposition
of our land and naval forces, and announced it to be the purpose
of the President, as a duty under the then existing circumstances,
to use all his constitutional power to protect Texas from foreign
invasion. If the whole power to grant the protection thus
offered, consisted in asking for authority by an act of Congress, it was a promise likely to be filled with hope deferred.
In view of the delays which would probably have attended the
passage of such an act, what justification can there be for
so early a movement of the army and navy to the immediate
proximity of anticipated operations. Does the Senator deny
the power of the President to order the army into any part of
the United States?

Mr. CALHOUN. He has no right to order it into disputed
territory.

Mr. DAVIS. What! shall a foreign Power dispute our territorial limits—refuse to settle the boundary by negotiation—
seize, by force, territory rightfully ours, and our Executive
stand powerless by and see the enemy gain the advantage of
occupying all the commanding positions of the country. This
would be an alluring invitation to every coterminous Power
to select their opportunity and dispute our boundary. At another time, during the recess of Congress, according to the
Senator's general position, the territory thus disputed could
be seized with entire safety. Upon the question of the northeastern boundary, to which the Senator alluded, my recollections are different from his. I think by both the Committee
on Military Affairs and by the Committee on Foreign Relations
reports were made at the time, recognizing the power of the
Executive to use the military force of the country—to call out
the militia—to protect the territory claimed by Maine from
hostile invasion, or an attempt by military force to exercise exclusive jurisdiction within the disputed territory. But I was
about to say, when I yielded to the honorable Senator, that
after Texas became a part of the American Union, and we
failed by negotiation to adjust the boundary with Mexico,
the question became closed against us, and the United States
had no other mode by which to determine the territory of Texas,
than by reference to her limits, as defined before annexation
to the United States; all which having been asserted and

maintained, we were bound to insist on and defend from forcible seizure. By annexation, Texas lost the power to negotiate or to carry on the war; and coextensive with this surrender were the obligations imposed upon the United States. The President did what every man of patriotic impulses will say he should have done—afford to Texas that protection which a State had the right to demand; and in ordering the army to the Rio Grande, he did no more than might have been done in the case of the northeastern boundary, when that was an open question. But the Senator has laid down the position that this was done to intimidate Mexico. Not so. Our army was encamped at Corpus Christi, which had been made a port of entry. Was that, then, in the disputed territory? Where was the disputed territory? Mexico claimed up to the Sabine. She has continued to assert that claim; and any intermediate line between the Sabine and the Rio Grande, is of our suggestion, and not of Mexican origin. When, at a recent period, Santa Anna returned to Mexico, he promised to restore the severed territory of Texas, and to gather laurels on the banks of the Sabine, and lay them at the feet of the Supreme Government. A right to the whole of Texas, a determination to restore it to Mexico, has, by her soldiers and her statesmen, been uniformly asserted —adhered to with the pertinacity characteristic of the Spanish race. The whole of Texas, then, was included in this disputed territory, and if the President had no right to march the army to the Rio Grande, he had no right to order it across the Sabine. Mexico claimed the whole of Texas. In the controversy on the part of Mexico the question was not whether the Nueces or the Rio Grande was the boundary, but whether Texas was a part of the United States or not. Upon the part of the United States that question was closed, forever closed. Before her army was ordered into the territory of Texas, nothing was open but the adjustment of boundary. This was sought by negotiation with Mexico, and our advances were insultingly repelled. That the boundary of revolutionary Texas was the Rio Grande—at least the lower part of that river—has been too often and too conclusively demonstrated to require more than a passing notice. Without adverting to the mass of evidence which has been presented here on other occasions, I will refer only to that on which I mainly rely. After the battle of San Jacinto, and when Santa Anna was a prisoner in the hands of the Texans, General Filisola, commanding the Mexican army, wrote to his Government, communicating the fact of President Santa Anna's capture, and giving the saddest account of the condition of the troops under his command. The President *ad interim* replied, and gave the General authority to do whatever should be necessary to procure the release of the captive President, and to save his troops and munitions of war. These results were obtained by treaty. General Filisola was one of the parties to that treaty, and the consideration given to Texas for the vast benefits thus secured was the recognition of the Rio Grande as a boundary, and the immediate withdrawal of all Mexican troops beyond it. It is true this treaty was never formally ratified by Mexico, but having obtained the full benefit of all its stipulations, I submit whether the moral obligation was not complete henceforth and forever to recognize the Rio Grande as the true boundary. That is the only argument on which I have ever found it necessary to rest this point.

Not being a lawyer, I will not attempt to discuss a legal question with the eminent jurist on the other side of the Chamber, [Mr. WEBSTER,] but cannot forbear from expressing my surprise at the view which he, in connection with the distinguished Senator on his side of the Chamber, [Mr. CALHOUN,] takes of the legitimate rights of our army when invading a foreign country. They would restrain our army from the moment it enters a hostile country, so as to prevent it from availing itself of any of the public funds—they would restrict it to such contributions as they might wring from the citizens. Now, one of the evidences of the advancement of civilization in the conduct of war has been seen in that very procedure on the part of an army which these distinguished Senators condemn. Instead of wringing from poverty, from the agricultural citizen, the means of maintenance, our army have seized only upon the public resources of the country, and have thus illustrated the intelligence, the chivalry, and humanity of the American people.

The Senators contend that legislation is necessary to appropriate the public revenues of Mexico to the maintenance of our army, whilst they admit the right to seize private property for its use. Sir, I had thought our war was waged against the general government of Mexico, and that our policy was as far as possible to relieve the peaceful population from the ordinary sufferings of war. Sir, I am at a loss to conceive how we could properly legislate upon a country which had not been conquered—for a people in open war against us—or how the laws, if enacted, could be properly executed under such circumstances. The foreign government must have been displaced by our arms, before there was space for our legislative and judicial departments to flow in; and the roar of those arms must have been hushed, before the voice of the lawgiver could be heard. The Constitution of the United States makes provision for the organization and maintenance of our army and navy, and for calling out the militia by legislative enactments. It makes the President the commander-in-chief of the army and navy, and the militia, when called into service. Congress declared that war existed. It passed laws for raising men and money. The President, as commander-in-chief, assumed the command of the army; and, as has been stated by the Senator from Michigan, from that moment all the rights which appertain to a state of war, attached to the army. The exercise of legislative rights only follows when Congress takes possession of a conquered country. Up to that point nothing but the power of the Executive department flows in. The power belongs not to the President merely, but to the Executive department; and, without orders from the President, every officer in the army could exercise it. The right is conferred by war, and the only difference between the action of our army and that of any other, has consisted in this, that ours has demanded less, and taken nothing by force. It has not committed pillage. The government opposed to us has been deprived of power, and the resources by which it was sustained naturally flowed to the army which took the country and people in charge. In laying duties —in collecting taxes, they have collected but a portion of the revenue which would have flowed to the Mexican Government if it had not been displaced by our arms. Both could not exist together. Such is the plain, common sense view of the matter. The legal view I must leave to others. The honorable Senator from South Carolina fears that if the President exercise this power, immense abuses may follow—that armies may be raised, and treaties may be made with other countries; and that, he says, would be in violation of the Constitution of the United States. The Constitution of the United States is a temple, gradually extending itself, and covering acre after acre, State after State, spanning rivers and mountains, but not yet gone to foreign lands. It is still limited to the United States. It cannot be violated in Mexico. It does not extend to Mexico, and God forbid it ever should It is the Constitution of our own Union and our own people, and none but territory annexed to our Union can claim to be under that Constitution. If the President has violated the Constitution, in the progress of this war, you must prove that he has failed to comply with the law which declared the war and authorized him to prosecute it, giving him men and money for that purpose. Until that be shown, the

President cannot have violated any provision of the Constitution in Mexico.

But the main purpose for which I rose, sir, was to speak of the effect of the passage of this bill in Mexico. We had information from a special agent sent to Mexico in 1844 that he had commenced preliminaries, and had the prospect of a settlement by negotiation, of all the difficulties then pending. On the fourth day after the negotiation had been opened, two celebrated letters published in that year reached Mexico. One dated at Raleigh, and the other at Lindenwold. On the arrival of these letters, forwarded, it is said by the Mexican minister at Washington City, the negotiation was immediately suspended. Again, Mexico probably intended to enter into a negotiation for the settlement of the questions then in dispute, when Mr. Black received intimation, in the terms so often referred to here, of a willingness on the part of Mexico to receive a commissioner; though I think that there has been altogether a misunderstanding of the language in which the note was written. *Commissionado* was the term employed, meaning one commissioned, empowered to settle the question in dispute. Now, they may have meant no other questions than those growing out of the annexation of Texas; but, as the Senator from Michigan remarked, they sought refuge in the subterfuge of the distinction between the terms "minister" and "commissioner," and thus evaded the obligation of the contract into which they had voluntarily entered. And why? Because, at that time a controversy had arisen with regard to the boundary in Oregon. The Mexicans then cherished the hope that there would be war between this country and England, and that, with the latter as an ally, they would be able to regain Texas. The old hope was thus revived. They refused to enter into negotiations. And now, if they have their hopes revived again with the prospect of a refusal here to supply men and money to prosecute the war, they will again reject negotiations in the expectation that a new administration may come into power in the United States more favorable to them. If we change the policy which we have heretofore pursued, there can be no doubt they will refuse to ratify the treaty.

In our intercourse with Mexico, if we have erred, it has been in undue consideration and misplaced leniency. For a long term of years we have borne national insult, and left unredressed the personal outrages and pecuniary injuries done to our citizens by Mexico. We have passed unnoticed the offences repeatedly offered in their official correspondence; it was the strong rendered patient, with the captiousness of the weak, by the consciousness of his ability to punish. This course, so long observed by our Government, has surely not been departed from by the present Administration.

I cannot conceive, sir, how the President could have exhibited greater forbearance towards Mexico. He sent out a minister to treat with her on the first intimation of any desire on her part to enter into a negotiation for the purpose of restoring amicable relations. Acting in the forbearing and friendly spirit of the power, who had taken that infant republic by the hand when it first essayed to walk, we studiously avoided collision. Collision, however, from the causes to which I have alluded, became at last inevitable. Yet it is gravely asserted, that the President had determined to extend the territory of the United States to the Rio Grande, "peaceably if he could, forcibly if he must;" most certainly not to extend the territory of the United States, but to settle the question of boundary; and had we been the aggressive party, as it has been alleged—had we been reckless of the feelings, rights, and interests of Mexico, we certainly never should have incorporated a provision in the terms of annexation, securing to us the right of settling the limits of Texas—that was done to guard against the possibility of a collision with Mexico; we did not adopt the extreme claims of Texas, but reserved to ourselves the right to settle the question of boundary. Nothing could have been done more indicative of the friendly spirit which we entertained towards Mexico.

At this late hour, I certainly shall not attempt to enlarge; but I must take occasion to say, that I do not think that Mexico is about to cede any territory to the United States; I think that we are about to retrocede territory to Mexico. I hold that in a just war we conquered a larger portion of Mexico, and that to it we have a title which has been regarded as valid ever since man existed in a social condition—the title of conquest. It seems to me that the question now is, how much we shall keep, how much we shall give up, and that Mexico cedes nothing.

Mr. WEBSTER was understood to inquire if that view was in accordance with the terms of the paper?

Mr. DAVIS. I have seen papers in English and Spanish, and I think in none was the term cede employed. As a moralist I would not undertake to defend the seizure of country from the inhabitants, but the question was settled long before the oldest member of the Senate entered it. These very Mexican people settled it when they conquered the ancient Aztecs. If they had the right to take the territory from that people, who did not cultivate it, the argument is equally good against them now. They produce little to that which the country is capable of yielding; and year by year the amount is steadily decreasing. The country is going to waste, villages are depopulated, fields once highly productive in all that nature in her bounty yielded to the industry of man, now lie uncultivated, and marked only by the remains of the irrigatory ditches by which they were formerly watered. The exuberant wealth of Mexico once flowed out to sustain the American colonies of Spain—the governments of Louisiana and Florida received contributions from her. Turn, now, and contemplate the change which the difference of government has wrought, and tell me whether all the arguments of utilitarianism and of humanity may not now be more successfully applied to the Mexican than by them against the Aztec population.

The Senator says this war is "odious." Odious! Odious for what? On account of the skill and gallantry with which it has been conducted? Or is it because of the humanity, the morality, the magnanimous clemency which has marked its execution? Odious! Why, in any newspaper which I take up, I find notices of large assemblages of the people gathered together to do honor to the remains of some dead soldier brought back from Mexico; or around the festive board to greet the return of some gallant member of the army. The conductors of the press, without distinction of party, express the highest approbation of the conduct of the army. Where is the odium? What portion of our population is infected with it? From what cause does it arise? It cannot be on account of the origin of the war, the extraordinary unanimity with which it was declared by both Houses of Congress, the eagerness with which our citizens pressed to the service, forbid that conclusion. A long and unbroken succession of victories has satiated the public appetite for military triumph. There may be a surfeit, for more has been offered than needed for a feast. An over anxiety for immediate peace is the natural result; with this I sympathize; beyond this I am not prepared to believe the popular feeling of the country extends.

We have cause to be proud of the record this war will leave behind it—a monument more lasting than brass. We, the actors of to-day, must soon crumble to dust; the institutions we now maintain, and hope will be perpetual, may pass away; the Republic may sink in the ocean of time, and the tide of human events roll unbroken over its grave; but the events of this war will live in the history of our country and our race, affording, in all ages to come, proof of the high state of civilization amongst the people who conducted it—proof of the intelligence which pervaded the rank and file who fought its battles—proof of the resources of such a Government as ours, wholly unembarrassed in the midst of war, conquering one nation and feeding another! Where, sir, are the evidences of evil brought upon us by this "odious" war? Where can you point to any inroad upon our prosperity, public or private, industrial, commercial, or financial, which can be, in any degree, attributed to the prosecution of this war? All that is yet to be shown, and I confidently await the issue.

Remarks of Jefferson Davis on the bill to pay the California Claims. April 28, 1848.

Mr. DAVIS, of Mississippi. In the progress of this discussion allusions, which I consider equally unjust as unkind, have been made in relation to the conduct of the committee —by whom this bill and amendment were reported. It was within the knowledge of the committee that indeterminate claims against our government for supplies furnished to the battalion of Colonel Frémont, existed in California, and that the failure to make payment in these cases had produced a dissatisfaction which could not be otherwise than dangerous to whatever interests we may have in that remote country. To silence complaint, to appease discontent, and to secure our Government against fraud, and the future annoyance of manufactured claims, the plan which the committee have adopted was presented to the Senate. It approximates as nearly as the present state of the case will allow the established usage, and the bill as amended seemed to us beyond the reach of constitutional objection. It has been said that the word "appoint" was carefully avoided. Sir, the purpose of appointing officers was not entertained; and it therefore required little care to avoid the use of any word which would convey such an idea. Claims which could not be settled by the accounting officers of our Government were presented to our consideration. We believed them to constitute a just demand against us, and a bill was introduced to legalize them. The first and controlling question is, will Congress declare them to be valid? If this be decided in the affirmative, payment must be ordered as a consequence; and there remains but the minor consideration, the manner of discharging the admitted obligation. A portion of the debt is established by regular vouchers, which it is ordered shall be paid as ascertained claims. If Congress receive the testimony to these cases as sufficient, and order payment thereon, have we not the same right to specify how the validity shall be determined of those which are denominated unascertained claims? Surely the decision can be made by us as to what testimony shall be deemed sufficient to establish whether a claim be a debt of this Government or not; otherwise it would be idle for us to entertain any proposition to examine a claim presented to our consideration.

The Senator from South Carolina treats this as an ordinary case of army disbursement, and seems to me to confound the rights of those who furnish supplies to our troops with the accounts of the disbursing officers of the army. It is the latter which are adjusted, as he states, in the auditing offices here. The payment for the supplies furnished to our army is ordinarily made in the field by the appropriate officers, and first heard of here through the accounts of those by whom the disbursements were made. If the commissary and quartermaster, and paymaster, to this battalion in California had been supplied with funds, these claims would have been paid as they arose. The whole case was an irregular one, and if deemed worthy, requires an unusual course in relation to it. Hence the proposition for special legislation. The officers named in the bill were those under whose orders, or by whom the debts were contracted; they have ceased to be officers, and it is proposed to revive their functions so far as may be necessary to complete their vouchers, and to determine how far, by their former official acts, they have rendered their Government responsible. It is not only true that they are best qualified to do justice between the parties, but it is further true that they alone can give to these claims the form which will admit of their being finally audited by the United States Treasury.

The commanding and purchasing officers of the California battalion, and they only, can reduce these claims to the established forms, and give to them their appropriate character. But those who held such positions in this case are no longer in the service; to give force to their acts, it is necessary by law to revive the functions of their expired offices. That it is proposed to do to the extent required, for the purpose declared, and no further. Those who deny the justice of these claims— those who refuse to acknowledge the responsibility of our Government for the debts contracted by the persons named in the bill, when they were officers of the California battalion, may properly refuse to extend the functions of these ex-officers to the end that they may perfect their accounts; but such as admit our obligation to pay for the purchases they made for the use of that battalion, are, I think, constrained to grant to them such powers as will enable the Government justly to discharge its obligations to its creditors. The connection of the persons named in the bill with the transactions out of which the claims arose, instead of being an objection, as has been assumed, constitutes the only sufficient reason for having named them. Such is the connection which all commanding and disbursing officers necessarily have to army expenditures and purchases. Had the campaign been regularly ordered and supplied, these persons would, in their official character, have made purchases and payments upon just such accounts as it is now proposed to authorize them to prepare. That payment may be made by an officer of the Government, who is to be provided with funds for that purpose. The supposition that the check imposed by the auditors in other cases is to be here dispensed with, is entirely erroneous. A power is given to the persons named in the bill, which will enable them to perfect their accounts; but as they have ceased to be officers, it is not proposed to intrust them with funds for payment. If the President shall choose to avail himself of the means provided in this bill, he will give his instructions; —and it is fair to suppose that they will require all accounts to be as fully vouched as they would have been had payment been made by these persons when they were officers. The disbursing officer who may be sent out will, of course, only make payment upon fully authenticated vouchers, and his accounts will be subject to the same revision here as would have been made had the claims been paid originally. The amount, though certainly important, is small, compared to the disbursements which have, in the progress of this war, been made by individual quartermasters. The paying officer in this case will give to the Government the same assurance of integrity and accuracy which is possessed in other cases where officers are intrusted with sums vastly disproportionate to their bond. The good faith which has heretofore been kept in our army disbursements does not warrant apprehension upon the present occasion.

To maintain the credit of the Government, so as to exclude distrust from entering into the calculations of those who sell to our officers, is an obligation which it requires no argument to enforce; but more than usual care is demanded when, as in this instance, our dealing has been with those who have the best means to know our intentions, and who may be supposed most ready to suspect our integrity. Nor should time be allowed to accumulate, and the value of the claims to depreciate in the hands of original holders, or be transferred to others who seek to speculate on the fears or necessities of those who have become creditors of the Government. At the present session of Congress the committees of both Houses have reported a case of deferred payment of a claim growing out of supplies furnished to our troops in Florida, that a decision which placed the rights of the claimant under the rules applicable to a disbursing officer was not reputable to our Government. Disreputable and truly unfortunate will it be, sir, when those who supply our army with food, or clothing, or transportation, shall be required to wait until the purchasing officer shall have submitted his accounts to the scrutiny of the auditing officers of his Government, with hopes and fears dependent upon the decision, but with the certainty, if it be adverse, that his property is gone, and that no redress is left to him.

The question which contains all others is, will you legalize the "California claims?" If so, then the direct and just mode is, to send those in whose official action these claims originated to collect the vouchers and perfect their accounts, to the end that prompt payment may be made.

Jefferson Davis to Stephen Cocke

(From the Mississippi Department of Archives and History.)

Washington
18th. June 1848

My Dear Sir,

Mr. Featherston [1] showed me your letter and draft of a bill in the case of Gordon Boyd and others. I read and approved of it and asked Mr. F. what his views were. He said he was in favor of it and would introduce it as it had been sent to him. I of course left it in his hands. Had it been with me I would have presented it in the Senate. Mr. F. told me some time since that he had failed to get it before the House, would continue his efforts to do so, and that he would write to you on the subject.

---

[1] W. S. Featherston, a member of the House of Representatives from Mississippi.

I have to apologize for not having addressed you earlier in answer to yours of the 24th. Ult. The Patent report shall be sent to you as soon as received. The printing is much behind its ordinary state at this period of the session.

Very truly yr's

Jeffn. Davis.

Jefferson Davis to James K. Polk

(From the Mississippi Department of Archives and History.)

Washington, 23 June, 1848.

To the President,
          Sir:

I reluctantly trouble you but a sense of duty, of obligation to an injured friend requires it.

Lieut. L. B. Northrop of the 1st. Dragoons an officer of many years service and of acknowledged merit, when engaged in a difficult and dangerous service was wounded by the accidental discharge of a pistol, the ball could not be extracted and he was disqualified for service. When he became convinced that he was permanently disabled, he wrote to the Adjt. Genl. asking for three years leave of absence stating his intention to study medicine, which would increase his usefulness as an officer if he should recover and join his regiment; also stating that if permanently disabled so that he could never again resume his duties, he intended to seek a support by the practice of medicine, as he was unwilling to remain a charge upon the army list. It will be seen by the correspondence upon the files of the Adjt. Genl's. office that before the expiration of the named period he sought for duty on the staff, for which he believed himself competent though unable to bear constant exercise. After the expiration of the period for which he had asked leave of absence, a construction was placed upon his application by which he was reported for dismissal and he has been accordingly "dropped" from the rolls of the army.

Briefly I will present my view of the case as it now stands. He has been dropped because he had received a long "leave of absence" granted under the understanding that he would resign at the end of that "leave." I deny that Lt. Northrop's application warrants the idea of a contract, or obligation to resign. I deny that an officer's commission can be made the subject of such sale or purchase. I deny that Lt. Northrop received any peculiar indulgence, or advantage over other officers in like situation, he like others had to report himself monthly and show his inability to return to duty. He has been dropped, but others continue to report and are permitted to remain upon "sick leave." A nice sense of propriety a delicacy of honor caused him to feel and to express an unwillingness to remain in commission if unable to do duty; but for this the Adjt. Genl. informs me he could like others have remained upon "sick leave," and unquestioned have continued to draw his pay.

I submitted the case to the Secretary of War who has sent me copies of the Adjt. Genl's. report &c., upon which the decision to drop Lt. Northrop was based.

The case was presented, that the errors of the Adjt. Genl. might be corrected; and the order rescinded by which a gallant and crippled officer had been stricken from the rolls of the army, because he avowed intentions creditable to him as a gentleman and a soldier. He has been disappointed, his wound has not been healed and his general health has become worse, he is therefore unable to support himself as he had hoped, and unless restored to his commission is debarred from any provision which may be made for a retired list of disabled officers. Soliciting your attention to the case of Lt. Northrop, I am very truly, Your friend, Jefferson Davis.

Endorsed: This was rewritten on account of defective arrangement and style, the second sent at date.

Jefferson Davis to William C. H. Waddell

(From Mississippi Free Trader, Aug. 2, 1848.)

Washington, D. C. June 29, 1848.

Wm. C. H. Waddell.

Dear Sir:—I have the pleasure to reply to yours of the 26th inst., enclosing an extract from a letter dated San Angel, Mexico, April 26, 1848.

The censure cast upon Gen. Lewis Cass on account of a bill which was reported from the Military Committee of the Senate, during the present session, "to provide clothing for volunteers in the service of the United States," is in every sense unjust. That bill, now a law, was drawn from a bill to authorize the President to call out twenty thousand volunteers for the further prosecution of the war with Mexico, which last was prepared in the War Department and sent to the Military Committee of the Senate. For the benefit of the volunteers, the committee unanimously decided to report the section providing for the issue of clothing to them, as a separate bill, and thus obtain for that measure more speedy action than was anticipated for the bill, of which it was a section.

On my own motion the committee changed the phraseology so as, in their opinion, to render the position of the volunteers in the matter of clothing less identical with that of the regular army; and the section thus modified was reported by a member of the committee, (not Gen. Cass,) and the Senate concurred without division or amendment. I enclose to you a copy of the act, by the terms of which you will perceive that the purpose was to authorize the volunteers to buy clothing from the army stores up to the amount of money allowed under existing laws. Regulars are allowed $2 50 per month on account of clothing. If the soldier drew less clothing than is equal to that amount, the balance is credited on the muster and pay rolls, to be paid him in money. Volunteers are allowed $3 50 per month on account of clothing. The bill enclosed allows them to purchase army clothing at the same rates as "regulars," but does not require them to purchase more than they require. In the field, troops use fatigue clothing, a full allowance of which does not cost two and a half dollars a month. "Regulars," therefore, under such circumstances, are expected to have a monthly balance in their favor on account of clothing. Any one familiar with these facts, must have anticipated that a part of the allowance to volunteers would be paid in money; and no one, with a proper sense of justice, could have desired or have attempted to reduce the allowance to volunteers for clothing, which formed as much a part of their contract as did their monthly pay.

The law received a construction at the Adjutant General's office which led to an order directing that the future pay of volunteers should be made out on the basis of an allowance of $2 50 per month *on account of clothing.* As soon as informed of this order, I brought the matter before the Military Committee. Gen. Cass and all the members of the committee declared that no such result was intended or believed to be deducible from the terms of the act and resolved that it must be corrected or counteracted.

The order has been countermanded, the original allowance of $3 50 has been continued, and the cause of dissatisfaction has been removed.

With great respect, yours, &c.,
JEFF'N. DAVIS.

Zachary Taylor [1] *to Jefferson Davis.*

(From New York Public Library Collections.)

Baton Rouge Louisiana
July 10th, 1848.

My dear General,

Owing to some cause either by accidents in the mails &c, I have not yet been notified by Govr. Morehead that I had been nominated by the National Whig Convention which recently assembled at Philadelphia as their candidate for the presidency at the coming election, which he was requested to do & no doubt has done; but as I have been absent from here during the last month at my plantation in Mississippi, & during the whole of this in N. Orleans until yesterday, it may have failed to reach me at one or the other place by being forwarded; as my friends express great anxiety in regard to this matter, I have written Governor M—— on the subject requesting him to forward me a duplicate with as little delay as practicable, & as I do not know where to address him, not knowing what portion of the State of North Carolina he resides in, I have taken the liberty of inclosing my letter for him to you, & have to request you to give it the proper address & forward it with as little delay as practicable——

I received the notice of my nomination while on my plantation soon after it was made, it having been brought by Telegraph to Memphis, & from there by the Steam Boat Genl. Taylor, Capt. Morehouse; altho, highly gratified at the honor done me, & no one could be more so, by that enlightened, pure & patriotic body, yet I am free to say I felt neither pride or exultation at the moment the information was communicated to me, nor have I done so up to this time, & if I know myself when the time arrives, my feelings would not be changed in the slightest de-

---

[1] Taylor, Zachary (1784-1850), twelfth President of the United States, was born in Orange County, Va., September 24, 1784; removed with his parents to a farm near Louisville, Ky., in 1785; and there remained until his 24th year acquiring only such an education as was available on a frontier. He was commissioned a first lieutenant in the 7th U. S. Infantry in May, 1808; was made a captain in 1812, a major in 1814, a lieutenant-colonel in 1819, and in 1832 fought in the Black-Hawk War with the rank of colonel. On Christmas day 1837 he inflicted a severe defeat on the Seminole Indians in Florida, and in recognition of this service he was brevetted brigadier general. In the War with Mexico he won the battles of Palo Alto and Resace de la Palma, captured Monterey and was crowned with military glory by his success at Buena Vista. Commonly known as ''Old Rough and Ready'', Taylor became President of the United States March 4, 1849, and served until his death in Washington, D. C., July 9, 1850. Consult O. O. Howard, General Taylor, 386 pp., New York, 1892.

gree was I to receive notice of my election to the office in question neither should I be mortified was I instead of my own, to hear of the success of my adversary; for as the time approaches & the prospects increase for my reaching that high office, I find my disinclination to embark in it, & to undertake the important duties connected with it greatly to increase. The honor done me by that Convention in which there were so many Fathers of the land, have laid me under obligations which I can never repay, & created feelings of gratitude which I have not language to express; that they should during high political party excitements have nominated me an humble individual personally unknown to nearly the whole of them, as a suitable candidate for the first office in the gift of a great & free people, or I may say the first in the word, in fact to rule over them & our country, without requiring pledges or promises of any kind, have manifested a confidence in my honesty, truthfulness & integrity never surpassed & rarely equaled since the days of the Father of his country, which confidence I hope to retain by continuing to merit it at which I know I feel more or as much elated should it be my good or bad fortune to reach the presidential office. I went to N. Orleans the last of the past month to meet the Volunteers on their arrival in the city from Mexico, where I remained ten days. A few of the Regts. had got there previous to my arrival, & nearly the whole if not all who were to come there had done so while I was there, & proceeded to their homes where many ere this have arrived. It was truly gratifying to me to have the opportunity once more of meeting many old friends & comrades & more so, to find those from the lower line had passed through Vera Cruz without suffering seriously from yellow fever, or from any other infectious disease; they for the most part expressed themselves both officers & men delighted to get back to their own Country again. I met among others with Col. Clark & many of the officers & soldiers of the 2d Mississippi Regt. What was left of them generally returned in good health; I met with Col. Crittenden, & many other of your warm friends.

While in the City met your neighbour & friend across the river, Judge Perkins from whom I was truly gratified to hear your excellent brother his & your excellent ladies had all gone North & would take Washington in then write when they would turn over the latter to you, remaining themselves some days with you, which I was more than gratified to learn, as I know it will be gratify(ing) to all, to be together even for a short time, & I believe your brothers required to reestablish his health not only relaxation & rest from his labors but a change to a more northern & less relaxing climate than Mississippi, & if benefitted by visiting the most desirable places in other portions of our Country in regard to their reputation for restoring invalids from the South, & is benefitted by a few months residence there, which I truly & sincerely hope will be the case, he ought to go North every season, as the preservation of his health & life, is of more importance to his family, friends & country than all the wealth he could accumulate for the former; particularly as he has already enough to make them all more than independent.

I feel under my dear Genl. the greatest obligations for the continued interest you feel & have taken in my reaching the first office as the gift of the American people, in which you & other dear friends I am confident take much more concern than I do; the statement you made to the Honl. Senator from N. Jersey, Mr. Dayton, in regard to my course in the event of my election has added an other to the many acts of kindness I am indebted to you; the smallest portion of which I greatly fear I will never have it in my power to repay.

I again repeat I have your own advancement more at heart than my own, You are now entering on the stage of action, while I must soon retire from it; you must therefore pursue that course which your good judgment will point out, as far as your honor & the good of the country is concerned, without regard to advancement; it is sufficient to me to know that I possess your friendship, which is all I ask or wish.

Judge Perkins informed me the corn crops were never better in Louisiana & in Mississippi, & the Cotton promising along the river, but had somewhat been damaged by long and heavy rains, but no doubt there will be more made in the country than can be disposed of; in fact the appearances abroad as regards prices are very gloomy.

Please present my kindest regards to your better half, & to your kind brother & his excellent lady should they be with you, or should you meet them before their return South, & wishing you all continuing health & prosperity

I remain
Truly & sincerely
Your Friend

Genl. J. Davis   Z. Taylor
  U. S. Senate
    Washington City—
      D C

Remarks of Jefferson Davis on the bill to establish a territorial government in Oregon. July 12, 1848.

On motion of Mr. BRIGHT, the Senate proceeded to the consideration of the special order, being the bill to establish a Territorial Government in Oregon; when—

Mr. DAVIS, of Mississippi, addressed the Senate. He commenced with a reference to the importance of the bill, the twelfth section of which discourses abolition. He denied that there was any intention to force slavery on Oregon. The South only desired to show the ground on which she has stood from the commencement of the Confederacy to this moment; and further, that she should be let alone. He stated that the Missouri compromise had obtained its validity from the consent of the States. Congress might enact laws on the subject, or make compromises; but without the consent of the States interested, they would have no validity.

As to the introduction of slavery into Oregon, no southern Senator had ever asked it. The fact that the slave is property, which its owner may carry with him into any part of the Union, was that which they were desirous to see recognized. The clause in the Constitution relative to the regulation of commerce was a constitutional admission that the slave is property. It is because slaves are considered property that the importation of slaves from Africa has been carried on under the sanction of this clause in the Constitution. The words "slave, or any other property," in the Constitution, are conclusive on this point. If the existence of the slave as property be admitted, what power has Congress to interfere with it? He denied that there was any such power in Congress. What powers Congress possesses, he showed by reference to the Constitution itself. Congress had no power to change the condition of slavery, or to strip the master of his right in his property. Entering a Territory with this property, the citizen has a right to its protection.

On the acquisition of territory, the condition of slavery was not changed. The Government acquired no new power over it, but stood merely in the position of an agent for its protection. He spoke depreciatingly of the persons who had assumed in Oregon the right to make laws for the Territory, contending that they were without qualifications for the task. They were far inferior in intelligence, in morals, and in personal wealth, to the population lying south of the Oregon boundary.

As to the inviolability of the law which prevailed in a Territory when acquired, he admitted that until abrogated, the existing law or municipal regulation must remain in force within the territory itself. He denied that there was any power in Congress, or in the people of the Territory, to interrupt the slave system. He gave his views as to the motives which induced Virginia to cede the Northwestern Territory, which originated in a patriotic and generous feeling on the part of the mother State. He regarded the course pursued by the northern States in relation to fugitive slaves as an outrage on justice, and a violation of that principle of the equality of the States which is guarantied by the terms of that instrument. The owner of a slave, when he entered some of these States, if he took his slave with him, was either exposed to the mortification of seeing his slave seduced from his side, or seized and carried away by violence.

He went into many other views, which, from indisposition, the reporter felt himself utterly unable to report.

He stated that if the opponents of slavery wished to emancipate the slaves, they were taking the wrong course. Slavery could not be abolished without a long series of preliminary preparations; and during these preparations, great dangers would menace the peace of the South. The most judicious course was to let the institution alone, and permit it to spread itself through the adjacent States, so that it may assume a new and more liberal character. The practical and useful emancipation of the slave will not be the labor of one generation. The slave must be made fit for his freedom by education and discipline, and thus made unfit for slavery. And as soon as he becomes unfit for slavery, the master will no longer desire to hold him as a slave.

What remedy has been proposed by the opponents of slavery? What good have they done? They have abducted slaves, but emancipated none. Do they expect to persuade the South to give up slavery? It is probably for the political advantage of the section in which the agitation against slavery originates. The spirit of concession exhibited by the South had failed to produce a corresponding spirit in the North. The latter still continued to assail the South as influenced only by a desire to increase the slave power, and obtain still greater political influence in the scale of States.

He insisted that the disorder and agitation which prevailed in the southern States, was not of domestic origin, but came from New England and from Great Britain.

He asserted it to be the duty of the United States to protect the property of a slave-owner during the transit from one State to another. The resolutions of the States who favored abolition were adopted entirely with a view to obtaining additional political power, and imposed on the South the strongest obligation to rise in self-defence. He referred to the fraternal feeling which induced the southern States to make common cause with the North in the war of the Revolution. The South had no especial cause of complaint; it was flourishing by its trade with Great Britain. But it was actuated by fraternal feeling and principle to take up arms; and now, was she to be asked to give up her domestic institutions? The South asked for no new guarantee, no new security; but she desired that the Constitution should be preserved from violation.

If the spirit of the Missouri compromise was to be invoked, as was proposed by his friend from Indiana, [Mr. BRIGHT,] he had a right to ask that the South should be placed on a basis of permanent security, so that there may hereafter be no new agitation on the subject. He was willing to go far, as far as his principles would permit, to meet the North. But if nothing would satisfy the North short of the destruction of this institution, then was the time for dissolution come; but let us separate peacefully, and with good feelings towards each other. Let not the battle-fields of our country be stained with the blood of brother fighting against brother. He trusted the danger would pass away, and that this agitation would turn out to be nothing more than a temporary struggle between politicians.

Jefferson Davis to H. R. Davis and Others

(From Mississippi Free Trader, Oct. 26, 1848.)

Warren County, Mi. Oct. 6, 1848.

Gentlemen: I have the honor to acknowledge your complimentary letter of the 3d, inviting me to a mass meeting on the 14th inst. to be assembled at Cold Springs, and to be composed of both the political parties of your county. Domestic affliction confines me at home, and I decline your invitation with a regret proportionate to the pleasure it would give me to meet my fellow citizens of Wilkinson, the county with which my earliest recollections and dearest associations are connected.

Seldom, if ever, has there been a period in the history of our confederacy, more critical and momentous than the present. Questions of ancient origin and slow growth, have recently hastened to maturity, and present issues which, to be met successfully, must be met promptly. At such a time, it would be especially agreeable to confer with you about the future, and to render to you an account of my past conduct as a representative of Mississippi.

The choice of a president, which from your letter, I infer will be the special subject of consideration at your proposed meeting, must depend upon the policy we adopt and the party with which we decide to affiliate for the future. Who shall be president, is a question of passing and minor importance except as connected with the principles which will govern and the measures which will follow his administration: These, under the political organization of our day, are to be judged by the party which sustains his election and upon which he must rely for support when in power. There has been a change in the dress in which measures are presented, but parties are divided as heretofore on principles; the difference is radical, and is to be decided by the same reasons which have influenced different minds, and in times gone by, drawn them from the same premises, to opposite conclusions; forming among our people two great classes of political opinion. We are called to choose between the whig and democratic parties of the United States, and as there is no well founded personal objection to either of their candidates for the presidency, we are free from this disturbing influence, and left to decide upon the measures and principles they avow.

Separating myself as far as possible from the prejudice I may very naturally feel for the creed of my entire political life, it seems to me evident and demonstrable, that the South should fraternize with the Democracy. This is the party of strict construction, of checks and balances, and constitutional restraints. We of the South are the minority and such we must remain; our property, our security in the Union depends upon the power of the constitutional curb with which we check the otherwise, unbridled will of the majority. So long as the Federal government limits its interference with the currency to the constitutional grant of power to coin money, and regulate the value thereof, the minority have little to fear from its abuse; so long as duties are laid for no other purpose than to provide money as a means to execute the specific grants of the constitution, the weak have little to fear from the class legislation of the strong; or one section nothing to dread from the power of another, by indirect taxation, to drain its substance for the improvement of rivers, the construction of roads, canals, and harbors for that other's benefit. Let me not be understood as claiming unanimity of the Democratic party upon these great principles, but only that they find their support and must rely for their success on the ranks of the democracy. Among the checks provided in our federal compact the executive veto is prominent, as well for its popular nature, as for the beneficial effects which it has produced in past times and for the salutary influence it may be expected to exert hereafter; especially in protecting the constitutional rights of the minority.

For the first consideration, it well becomes the democracy to advocate its preservation and use, for the latter consideration it might have been expected, that all Southern men would insist upon its remaining with all its original scope and power. Though in our form of government, politicians can never become a class, warring against the people, they may nevertheless have private interests controlling their public conduct, and it is a truth established by many examples that representatives do not always reflect the will of their constituents; in some such cases the executive veto has been exhibited in its popular character, but its great object and use is to restrain irresponsible majorities from unconstitutional aggression on minorities, No power could be less liable to abuse because no corrupt or ambitious motive could induce to its exercise; neither one nor the other would bend to the strong, take protection under the legislative expression of popular will, instead of braving a dominant majority to protect the weak or to maintain a principle. The veto of the president gives to a considerable minority a power which may be relied on to shield it from legislative invasion of a vital right. For instance, the wide spread, settled and increasing hostility in the north to our domestic slavery must be expected to manifest itself in every form in which that institution can be assailed. In the present division of parties it is in the power of the South, if united, to dictate terms to one party or the other and to elect, by co-operating with it, a president, pledged, by his constitutional veto, to prevent he passage of a law which would violate a right, paramount with us to all other considerations.

Upon the right of slaveholders to migrate with their property into territory belonging in common to the States of the Union, you have been presented, by the north, with an issue as offensive to your self-respect as unjust to your constitutional rights.

It has been assumed, that domestic slavery is a moral and political evil, and from this hypothesis of those who are practically ignorant of the subject, the conclusion is drawn that its further extension should be prevented. In the face of all historical truth it has been in the same quarter, asserted that slavery is the creation of local law. As property is regulated by law—but where are the statutes creating it? Traced to the time of the law giver Moses, we find it then treated as an established state of society, and regulations made for it as such. So it is viewed in our federal compact. Its condition or existence is to be decided by state sovereignties only, being beyond the range of federal legislation, and above the power of territorial government. This issue, in the form in which it is presented, admits of no compromise; one or the other must yield before there can be any basis for adjustment. The southern states have to some extent shown a willingness to consider the Missouri compromise as a compact, and to extend and continue it; but this cannot be acceded to by those who contend for the total exclusion of slavery from the territories, resting as it must upon our rights as joint proprietors of the public domain. In deciding the question, with which of the two great parties of the Union, should the south affiliate, it is important to inquire how they stand affected towards us upon this grave issue.

So far as shown by their representatives in congress it does not appear that either of the parties in the north are fully with us, but there is this important difference, so far as fraternal feeling was manifested by the non-slave-holding states, it was found in the ranks of the democracy. Denounced and divided at home because of their support of the constitutional rights of the south, shall they be suspected and repulsed by us? Have we reached the point at which no northern man can be trusted to administer the government; if so, we have reached the limit beyond which our union ceases to be a blessing.

For what, under such a state of facts, and with the avowal of such a position can a sectional minority hope.

In viewing the progress of the present canvass at the north, we find the nominee of the Baltimore convention opposed by a portion of the old democratic party, whose watch word, is opposition to the extension of slavery. What higher recommendation could he have to your confidence? It is not necessary, nor would the limits of a letter permit, that I should discuss the characters, qualifications, and services of men so well known as Cass and Butler. As little can it be required that I should testify to you my intention at the approaching presidential election, to vote, as on past occasions the democratic electoral ticket.

Having already extended this letter beyond my original design, I will only further trouble you, gentlemen, with a request that you will make my apology to such of our friends as may have expected my attendance, and with the ardent hope that our canvass will be conducted with the harmony and conciliation becoming men, who have common interests which lie beyond, and are of paramount importance to it. Allow me to offer to you, individually, my thanks for your kindness and best wishes for your prosperity.

Very truly your friend,

JEFFERSON DAVIS.

Messrs. H. R. Davis, B. Killgore, J. H. King, W. J. Hodge, R. Philips, H. Strong—Committee, of Invitation.

Remarks of Jefferson Davis on a petition on the subject of colonizing free negroes. Jan. 12, 1849.

Mr. DAVIS, of Mississippi. It is really to be regretted, Mr. President, that from day to day those who assemble here for the purpose of discharging their constitutional duties in legislation, should find themselves beleaguered by irritating questions forced upon them by individuals whose piety is so great that they must always be appropriating to themselves other men's sins. When did the South ask for this vicarious repentance, and whence do you derive your power to instruct her in her moral duty? Answer me these questions satisfactorily, or cease this perfidious interference with the rights of other men. But, sir, of all the clap-trap that ever issued from the lips of the advocates of such a policy, that which relates to the question of the right of petition is the greatest. What did the Constitution guaranty at the time that right was introduced, and for what purpose was it introduced? When these States were infant colonies, who ever denied the right of the colonists to petition? That was a right granted them. The right to assemble was the only right that was ever interfered with, and the right of petition carried with it the idea of the suppression of a grievance. Those rights are fully maintained in the Constitution. But what grievance is there to any non-slaveholding State if other communities think proper to keep slaves? And does that circumstance interfere with their right peaceably to assemble, guaranteed to them, under the Constitution? Sir, does this poor right to beg, as it has been described, carry with it the obligation to grant? This is the whole question before Congress. Shall we receive, entertain, and discuss petitions upon a subject which every one recognizes we have no right to grant, upon which we have no power to grant anything? It is an idle waste and a base abandonment of the duties of members upon this floor thus to squander the time which should be devoted to some useful purpose. Sir. it has been stated, in the progress of this debate, that the course of southern men, in objecting to these petitions, has created all this excitement. Let those who entertain this opinion refer to the action of the House of Representatives, and they will there find a decision against them. In the House, where this question has been made, where these petitions have been received, referred, and discussed, abolitionism has gone on step by step, steadily progressing; whilst in the Senate, where the wiser and more dignified rule has been adopted to lay the question of reception on the table without discussion, there was scarcely an allusion to the topic, until some over-zealous, over-pious, latterday saints have come into the Senate and forced the subject upon us. We are told by them, sir, that they are for enlarging the circle of human sympathy; and it does appear, with many of these advocates of the enlargement of such circle here, that they cannot rest satisfied in any other circle than that of affection for the negro race. It begins, and ends, and has its middle with the negro race. I can hear of nothing else, sir; I can hear of nothing which is progressive in human reform, nothing which does not concentrate itself in this question concerning the African race. And what is the proposition, sir, now before us? Why, it is to take money from the treasury and bestow it upon a certain class of passengers to another country. What right, I ask, have you thus to distinguish between one class of passengers and another? None, sir. And when the Senator from Kentucky appealed to the North for their support, he should have said, You were the men who imported these negroes into this country; you enjoyed the benefits resulting from their carriage and sale; and you, having reaped the largest profit accruing from the introduction of the slaves, should of course contribute to carry them back whence they came, and not lay a new and oppressive burden upon the already burdened South. As to any influence that may be exerted upon the State of Kentucky, I not only agree with the Senator from Virginia, but go further, and say that I would be unwilling to allow any influence to operate upon the convention of Kentucky, believing that they are able to take care of themselves upon this subject, and it is their right so to do.

If the people of Kentucky wish to emancipate their slaves— though I should regret such a course—I would interpose no obstacle by saying that we would not make appropriations to transport their slaves, any more than I would offer an inducement by assuring them that we would make such appropriations. It would be better, sir, if these pious personages who cry out "Good God" were, instead, to cry out "Good devil," when their whole purpose is to scatter the seeds of dissension and disunion; and it would be much more to their credit if, instead of indulging in lamentations about the evils resulting from slavery, they were to look upon the other side of the picture, and ascertain if it has not prevented evils. Has it made any man a slave any more than he was a slave without this institution, or reduced any man from liberty to slavery? That is the question, sir; and I answer, it has not. Under laws older than the records of history men were taken captives in war, and held as slaves. These slaves were purchased from contending warring bands who held their captives in slavery, and the slaves thus purchased were saved from a more ignominious and degrading slavery than they would be subject to on this side of the Atlantic. It benefits them, in removing them from the bigotry and the heathen darkness which hangs like a cloud over the country in the interior of Africa to the enjoyment of all the blessings of civilization and Christianity. Slavery brought with it commerce, sir; for it occasioned the necessity of enlarging our productions; and what is commerce but the parent of civilization, of international exchanges, and all those mighty blessings that now bind the people of the most remote quarters of the globe together? These are some of the fruits, sir, that are to be considered before you judge the tree. It is our tree, sir; and it is only to answer these libelous imputations cast upon an institution with which I am practically acquainted, and about which the aforesaid libelers speak ignorantly and presumptuously, that I deign to enter upon a discussion of this character.

I thank the Senator from Illinois for the fearless manner in which he met this question; and if all those of equal intelligence, representing like constituencies, would thus speak to the men they represent, I feel there is patriotism and good sense enough in the country to recall us from this wandering career, which will terminate in naught but evil. This, sir, is the question which is to destroy our republican institutions, if indeed they are to fall; and now is the time for those men who love the Union better than they love place—still better than they love the negro race—to speak plainly to those whom they represent, and tell them that when they raised the question of the restriction of slavery, it was an issue of their own—a mistaken one—and that they are bound first to promote the issue of non-interference with the rights of the slave States, or the disunion of this glorious

Confederacy will follow, causing the destruction of all the bright hopes of liberty based upon its continued establishment. With this issue in mind, let our northern friends appeal to their constituents, and, if they are true descendants of such sires as Hancock and Adams, they will refrain from all further interference with southern rights.

Jefferson Davis to John J. Crittenden.[1]

(From the Library of Congress Manuscripts Division.)

Senate Chamber
30 th Jany 1849

My dear Govr.

I have been long intending to avail myself of your kindness by writing to you, but you know the condition of a Senator during the session of Congress and may be able to estimate the condition of a lazy man thus situated. It is I hope unnecessary for me to say that my sympathies have been deeply enlisted in the case of Maj. Crittenden and what is more important my conviction complete that he has been unjustly treated.

You know Mr. Polk and your view of the manner in which he should be dealt with as shown by your letters has very closely agreed with my own. Wearied by this hesitation I have called for the proceedings in the case and if he holds out it is a case in which the weaker goes to the wall. I think I will beat him and so you may say in confidence to your gallant Son.

My boy Tom, in which style I hope you will recognize Col. Crittenden has been discreet and I think efficient in a cause where feeling might have warped the judgement of an older man.

I regret exceedingly to see that Mr. Clay is to return to the Senate, among many reasons is one in which I know you will

[1] Crittenden, John Jordan (1787-1863), a political leader, was born near Versailles, Ky., September 10, 1787, and graduated from William and Mary College in 1806. He was Attorney-General of Illinois Territory in 1810; served in the War of 1812 on the staff of General Isaac Shelby; was a member of the Kentucky House of Representatives 1811-1817; U. S. Senator from March 14, 1817, to March 3, 1819, from March 4, 1835, to March 3, 1841, from March 31, 1842, to June 12, 1848, and from March 4, 1855 to March 3, 1861; U. S. district attorney 1827-1829; Attorney General of the United States from March 5 to September 13, 1841, and from July 2, 1850, to March 3, 1853; Governor of Kentucky 1848-1850; a member of the national House of Representatives 1861-1863. He died in Frankfort, Ky., July 26, 1863. Crittenden was one of the stanchest champions of Union in the Southern States and during the Civil War exerted his influence to keep Kentucky in the Union. Consult Mrs. Chapman Coleman, the Life of John J. Crittenden with selections from his correspondence and speeches. 2 vols., 781 pp., Philadelphia, 1871.

sympathize, the evil influence he will have on the friends of Genl. Taylor in the two houses of Congress. Many who would have done very well in his absence will give way in his presence. This will also introduce a new element in the selection of the Genls. Cabinet. It must be composed of men of nerve and of no Clay affinities. One instance to illustrate my meaning Berrien of Ga. though well enough without Clay's shadow, would not do under it. You see that I disregard Mr. C s- pledge to support the administration, he may wish to do so, but can his nature react so much. The Englishman Baker, who came from the Rio Grande to draw pay, mileage and a year's stationery as a member of Congress is here, with recommendations from legislatures for the post of Secty. of War. What would Genl. Taylor say to such impudent dictation and indelicate solicitation. Butler King wants to be Secty. of Navy you know the little Yankee Andrew Stuart wants to be Secty. of Treasy. the man who proved wool to be a vegetable. I hope you will talk fully with Genl. Taylor he knows very little of our public men personally and will have very little opportunity to observe them after his arrival.

Clayton is true and talks right, has he the necessary nerve,— how would Birney of Philad. do for the Treasy. A. Lawrence is not a Lawyer and is a manufacturer, how would Mr. Lawrence do for Navy, how would Gadsden do for War, how will a Post Master Genl. be selected—

The Genl. will need you and I hope to see you here— Loose and hurried as my remarks are, written in the midst of much "noise and confusion" you may from intimate knowledge of all I have treated of, unravel what would be unintelligible to one less informed—Your friend

Jeffn: Davis

Remarks of Jefferson Davis in the Senate Jan. 31, 1849, on the bill to aid the construction of the proposed railroad across the Isthmus of Panama.

Mr. DAVIS, of Mississippi. I agree with the Senator from Delaware in a part of what he has said, and differ very widely with him in relation to other portions of his remarks. I think, if there is any ground for mortification in regard to this matter, it is that this Republic, the mother of the republics of the American continent, does not contemplate the transportation of the property of the Government and of the citizens of the Republic within her own limits; that she does not construct for herself, if she have the constitutional power to undertake such work at all, a road from the valley of the Mississippi to the western limit of the territorial possessions of the United States. If I were to contemplate the idea of constructing a road, either through the instrumentality of the Government exclusively, or by advances of money made to contractors for that purpose, I should make the line of road pass through the territory of the United States. Such a road I would regard as more advantageous to the interests of this country and its citizens. I would consider it preferable in a commercial point of view, and still more so upon political considerations, that our citizens and their property, instead of being separated from the country in their transit from one portion of the United States to the other, should be kept within our own limits; and that the connection with our remote possessions should be as direct as possible. It is not that I have any want of confidence in the attachment of any American citizen to the Government of the United States; for I have an abiding confidence in that attachment. I believe that it is not to be broken off, however widely they may be separated from the Government. But, if anything is calculated to invite or lead to a forgetfulness of that attachment, it would be for our citizens to find themselves on the shores of the Pacific a powerful people, having an extensive commerce with Asia, without any communication with the United States, and with the legislature sitting here to fix the laws governing their intercourse, both domestic and foreign. If that people are to be bound permanently to this Union, if it is to be made their interest in all time to come to remain a portion of the United States, then I say it is necessary that a ready and accessible means of communication should be afforded them; and the links of communication must be continuous; towns, villages, and hamlets, must extend along the line of communication, from the seat of the General Government until we stand upon the shores of the Pacific. This must be our ulterior object, and all other measures in reference to this subject must be considered as temporary expedients only.

I am not willing to see this Government permanently coupled with any work outside of the United States, and if we are to have any connection whatever with this proposed Panama road, let it be temporary, and let it be in dollars paid for heads and tons conveyed, and let them bear the charge of making the road. I am not willing to pay any stipulated sum to this company in prospect, or when they have perfected the work, other than that which they may receive upon a contract for carrying public stores or for carrying persons, when they are in readiness to perform such work. It is with this view that I have presented the amendment. And, adopting the bill in that form, we shall be equally ready to avail ourselves of the road across Tehuantepec, if one be constructed there. I believe that the route proposed will be subject to interruptions from foreign countries, especially in time of war. I believe with the Senator from Delaware, that the Tehuantepec route would connect itself more intimately with the interests of the United States; but there are other considerations which should not be lost sight of. We have no right of way, and the time must be remote when a road will be constructed there, unless the Government of the United States expend a large sum of money in the construction of a road through the Republic of Mexico. Notwithstanding the amusing definition which the honorable gentleman gave of the name of Tehuantepec—and which, I suppose, was given by him more in jest than seriously—I will tell him that, although there are northwest winds sometimes prevailing along that coast, such as he has described, rendering the approach of vessels extremely hazardous, yet there are deep indentations in the coast where vessels may safely enter, the force of the waves being broken by the jetting head-lands which extend for a considerable distance into the sea. So far, then, as those two routes are concerned, the advantage is decidedly in favor of Tehuantepec. But it is not my purpose to enter into this question at all. We have nothing to do with one or the other of them; they are foreign routes; we neither propose to determine the route nor to build the roads; but if they are built, and their services are afforded to us at reasonable rates, then let us avail ourselves of them, whether the road be through Tehuantepec or Panama. I therefore say again, that I am opposed to any proposition to expend even the hundredth part of the sum stated by the Senator from Delaware in the construction of a road. I wish to confine the expenditure of any money for the establishment of a communication with the Pacific within our own country, taking such a course as will lead in a direct line through the valley of the Mississippi to the Pacific. Wherever the passage of the mountains may be most advantageously made, let the road be there constructed, and let us look finally to the accomplishment of a direct passage across the continent, within the limits of the United States, from one sea to the other. If I succeed in the proposition which I have made to amend the bill, by striking out all that relates to the rates of compensation, in the form of annual payments to be made to the company, and all limitations, it shall then be followed by an amendment which shall stipulate that the Government of the United States shall pay for transportation a rate which shall not exceed that fixed in the second section of the bill upon the persons and property of American citizens. The Government certainly will be able to make contracts with the company for the transportation of persons and goods upon more favorable terms than the tariff we would be authorized to fix. And I have no reason to believe, from any computation that I have been able to make, that the sum thus annually to be paid by the Government would reach the amount which is contemplated by this bill. But, whatever the amount, be it more or less, it should be compensation for services rendered. As the bill stands, if it should come to pass that we should wish to abandon that road, having another communication open to us, we must still continue our payments in the same manner as though we received services. This is a distinction which I would give to no road in our own country, and certainly not to a road without the limits of our own country. Opposed to internal improvements by the Government, I cannot become the advocate of external improvements. They rest upon the same principle, and, so far as that principle is to be extended to give advantage to any one, it should be to those who seek to open internal communication, and to give commercial advantages to the United States. I have never myself, in any examination of the bill as amended, believed that the language bore the construction which has been placed upon it; but, such being the construction, I wish to get rid of the difficulty, and it is for that purpose that I have offered the amendment.

Jefferson Davis' report from the committee to announce to Gen. Taylor his election as President of the United States. Feb. 27, 1849.

Mr. DAVIS, of Mississippi, made the following report:

The committee appointed on the part of the Senate, jointly with the committee on the part of the House of Representatives, to wait on Zachary Taylor and Millard Fillmore, and notify them of their election as President and Vice President of the United States, report:

That they have performed the duty assigned them; and that the President elect, in signifying his acceptance of the office to which he had been chosen by the people, evinced emotions of the profoundest gratitude, and declared his distrust of his ability to fulfill the expectations upon which their confidence was based; but gave assurances of a fixed purpose to administer the Government for the benefit and advantage of the whole country.

In alluding to the fact to which his attention had been drawn —that the chairman of the committee represented a public body a majority of whom were opposed in political opinion to the President elect, and accorded with that majority, he recognized in it the deference to the popular will constitutionally expressed, on which rest the strength and hope of the Republic; and he said that it was to have been expected of the Senate of the United States.

He expressed an ardent wish that he might be able in any degree to assuage the fierceness of party, or temper with moderation the conflicts of those who are only divided as to the means of securing the public welfare.

He said, having been reminded that he was about to occupy the chair once filled by Washington, he could hope to emulate him only in the singleness of the aims which guided the conduct of the man who had no parallel in history, and could have no rival in the hearts of his countrymen.

In conclusion, he announced his readiness to take the oath of office on the 5th March proximo, at such hour and place as might be designated.

And the committee further report, that the Vice President elect, in signifying his acceptance of the office to which he had been chosen by the people, expressed the profound sensibility with which he received the announcement of his election, and said, that deeply impressed with the obligations which it imposed, and the distinguished honor it conferred, he should do injustice to his feelings if he failed to express his grateful thanks for this manifestation of confidence; that he should accept the office conscious of his want of experience, and distrustful of his ability to discharge its duties, but with an anxious desire to meet the expectations of those who had so generously conferred it upon him.

Mr. DAVIS then submitted the following resolution; which was considered and agreed to:

Resolved, That there be appointed a committee of the Senate to make the necessary arrangements for the reception of the President elect on the 5th of March, and to apprise him of the same.

On motion of Mr. DAVIS, of Mississippi,

Ordered, That said committee be filled by the Chair.

The VICE PRESIDENT named Mr. JOHNSON of Maryland, Mr. DAVIS of Mississippi, and Mr. DAVIS of Massachusetts.

Remarks of Jefferson Davis on the bill to establish the Department of the Interior. March 3, 1849.

DEPARTMENT OF THE INTERIOR.

Mr. HUNTER, from the Committee on Finance, to which was referred the bill from the House of Representatives to establish the Home Department and to provide for the Treasury Department an Assistant Secretary of the Treasury, and a Commissioner of the Customs, reported it with amendments.

Mr. UNDERWOOD moved to take up the bill to establish a Home Department.

Mr. KING hoped that the bill would not be taken up. He thought it would lead to a very extended discussion.

Mr. UNDERWOOD said he was perfectly willing to vote and to say nothing about it.

Mr. CAMERON thought, from indications around him, that the bill would be very fully discussed. He knew gentlemen who were resolved upon entering largely into the discussion whenever the bill should come up, and he believed it would consume the whole day.

Mr. DOWNS hoped the bill would be taken up. It was a very important measure, and he thought it would not take long to dispose of it.

Mr. BRIGHT. I hope the motion will not prevail. There is a great deal of very important business that ought to be attended to, and I think, from the disposition that is manifested in various quarters to enter largely into the discussion of this bill, that, if it be taken up, very little, if any, business will be done. All, or at least a large portion, of the important bills now ready for the action of the Senate, will have to be passed over if the motion of the Senator from Kentucky shall prevail.

If Senators think that this bill can be passed without a thorough examination and full discussion of its merits, they are mistaken. I hope, therefore, that, if it is to be taken up this session at all, it will not be taken up until all the more important business shall have been disposed of.

Mr. DAVIS, of Mississippi. I do not suppose that any Senator is going into a long speech upon this bill at a moment like this. We are all equally interested with the Senator from Indiana [Mr. BRIGHT] in the speedy disposition of the important bills which remain yet unacted upon. If Senators wish to express their views in relation to the measure, they can do so without occupying much time, if they choose. If objections to the bill exist, they can be briefly stated. All that I have to say, I can say in a brief space. If we seek only to elicit the truth, to ascertain the facts of the case, to legislate for the good of the country, it will not take long to dispose of this bill.

The establishment of a Home Department has been recommended by one whose name will be honorably remembered as long as our Treasury Department stands. This illustrious man, who is about to close his labors in that department, which he filled with such high honor to himself, and such signal benefit to his country, after mature deliberation, after that investigation which no man not at the head of the department could have made, proposed the bill which is now before the Senate, having passed the House. He is convinced that it was absolutely necessary in his administration of the department to have such a division as is proposed by this bill; and that it will be more so during the next four years, and for every succeeding four years during all coming time. I feel a very peculiar interest in this measure, as every one who comes from a new State must feel. We are peopling the public lands; the inhabitants of the old States are the people of commerce. The treasury belongs to us in common. The Secretaries of the Treasury must be taken from those portions of the country where they have foreign commerce, and therefore they are men who are not so intimately connected and acquainted with the relations and interests of the public lands in the new States as those who control those relations and interests should be, in order to protect and foster the interests of the new States.

Again: no feature is more common in our form of government than its checks and balances—one department checking and guarding the other. Why, then, shall we not carry out that principle to its legitimate extent? Why, then, have we, and why shall we continue an organization which violates that principle? It was a departure from that great principle to put in the same hands in the organization of our Government the collection and the disbursement of the revenue. The one should check the other. The officer who is charged with finding the ways and means to carry on the Government properly, never should have been charged with the disbursement of those ways and means. And this division of the Treasury Department I consider essential to the rigid economy and just accountability which belongs to our Government.

On same subject later on in the debate on the measure.

Mr. DAVIS, of Mississippi. The debate upon the measure

under consideration has assumed a character so different from that which was anticipated when I addressed the Senate in advocacy of the bill, that I am compelled again to ask the attention of the Senate. In doing so, I will express the reluctance I feel to consume any part of the little time which now remains to close the legislation of the session.

Had the measure been opposed directly, and discussed upon its merits, I should not have considered it necessary to reply; but remarks have been made calculated to prejudice the bill, and also those who support it. The Senator from Virginia [Mr. MASON] has presented the question in a form as new as it was unlooked for, and to which it is more disagreeable than difficult to reply. He rests his objection upon party ground, refers to the support given to the bill on the opposite side of the Chamber, seeming thence to draw the conclusion that it deserves opposition from those who, like him and myself, sit upon this. Sir, this argument could only weigh with me in the absence of all reason, when, groping in the dark, without light to direct me, I should find myself reduced to the necessity of following the call of those whose voices assured me of the direction followed by my friends. He says the measure has become popular on the other side, and finds favor with some upon this side of the Chamber. I enter not into the consideration of time when this measure found favor with my political opponents; neither will I scan the motives which may by others be attributed to them as prompting their action. Believing it to be right, I find on the threshold a satisfactory cause for all the support which the measure receives, and am proud to be numbered among the "some upon this side of the Chamber" who support a measure from higher purposes than party advantage or individual benefit; who find in the necessity, the propriety of the act, its justification, and who will not defeat a public measure because the patronage which attaches to it will inure to the benefit of others; still less, far less, because the efficiency it will bring to the executive departments will relieve from embarrassment an administration of the Government by those to whom we are politically opposed.

Sir, I have been surprised to hear it asserted that this is a new proposition, suddenly presented to the Senate. The bill, after debate, passed the House of Representatives, and has been for some time before the Senate. The main proposition is nearly as old as our Government. The first Secretary of the Treasury recommended a division of the Treasury Department, and subsequent experience has brought from time to time additional recommendations for a measure the propriety of which was so soon perceived in the practical working of our Treasury Department, until the bill now before us was prepared by the present Secretary, Mr. Walker, whose fortune it has been to have charge of the department when expanded territory, enlarged commerce, and a war conducted in a foreign country, brought unprecedented burdens and difficulties upon the department, and fully exemplified the necessity for a new organization. To divide, to classify the official functions, so as to give expedition and simplicity, increased checks and accountability, is the purpose and operation of the bill. Yet it is said to be an extension of the Federal power, a measure repugnant to Democracy.

Sir, I have no occasion to climb the house-top and proclaim my own democracy; I have grown with it, and all who know me recognize me best in the only political mantle they have ever known me to wear. Nor, sir, do I believe my democracy so feeble a plant that it requires to be surrounded with props, and is in danger of falling if left alone. But on the present occasion there is no want of supports the highest and most honored. A measure, the principle of which bears the sanction of Washington, Madison, Monroe, and Secretary Walker, could scarcely endanger a democratic reputation which was worth preserving, though these names may render it necessary, if Democracy be the basis of opposition, to trumpet it loudly, lest the fact should not be known. It is a strange confusion of ideas which identifies the creation of a new department, the appointment of new officers, with an extension of Federal power. In the progress of our Government this had been a frequent occurrence; and in its future growth and ramification must continue to occur. One Secretary, at an early period of our national history, had charge of both the Navy and Army Departments. It has been necessary to divide them, and to erect many bureaus in each; the agents have been multiplied, that the powers might be well executed. Extended intercourse with the Indian tribes has required new agencies and superintendents; the expansion of our population has produced, with each village which rose as the forest fell, the necessity of new post routes and offices, new judicial districts, new collection districts—enlarged the patronage, increased the action of the Federal Government; but will it thence be contended that its constitutional power has been magnified, that functions not delegated have been usurped?

Sir, my belief has been, and is, that the Constitution of the United States would suffice for any extent of territory which should be covered by people sufficiently honest and intelligent to administer it; but, with widened surface, and multiplied population, there must be a lengthened list of agents too; nor did it ever occur to me that in this the Constitution would be violated, or Democracy overthrown.

Mr. President, there are two modes in which this bill may be defeated—either by amending it, and causing it, for the want of time, to be lost between the Houses of Congress, or by consuming the time which remains of the session in discussing the merits of a bill upon which the opinion of the Senate has been clearly expressed. To prevent the first, I will vote against all amendments, and to avoid the second will be as brief as circumstances will justify.

I always feel respect for a voice which is raised against the encroachment of the Federal Government, and always feel ready to cooperate with those who declare a purpose to restrain it to its constitutional limits; but, sir, to restrain is not to cripple or to destroy. Within their sphere the powers of the General Government are supreme, entitled to the respect and support of all; to be maintained and defended with the same zeal with which encroachment upon the reserved rights of a State should be resisted. If there be one class which, more than all others, owe this respect and support, it is that which is especially devoted to guarding against encroachment. I was, therefore, surprised to hear the Senator from Virginia, [Mr. MASON,] whilst arguing for restraint upon the Federal Government, assert that it had nothing to do with our domestic relations. Under what other head than domestic relations will he place the district courts, the transmission of the mails, the collection of revenue, the intercourse with Indian tribes, the disposal of the public lands, the protection of frontier inhabitants, and the many other duties of the General Government to the people of the United States?

Mr. MASON. If the honorable Senator will allow me, I will explain. I did not say that the Federal Government had nothing to do with domestic relations. I said the Federal Government was created to provide for foreign relations; but if it was necessary to give it some share of power over our internal relations, over the Patent Office, Indian bureau, the public lands, &c., it should be subordinate. Being formed to take charge of our exterior relations, we should not extend its power to our interior relations any further than was absolutely necessary.

Mr. DAVIS. It was not my memory, but my hearing which was at fault, as appears by reference to the note I made of the

Senator's remarks when delivered. I am very glad to be corrected, and to know his opinion accurately.

Mr. President, this bill has been denounced as a "federal measure." Its origin is democratic, its purposes are democratic, if it passes it will descend as part of the fruit of this Democratic Administration, and I shall claim it as a Democratic measure. The *ad valorem* duties of the tariff of 1846 have created many questions which had to be referred, and which have augmented the labors of the Secretary of the Treasury and increased the necessity for a division of the department as proposed. These questions are incident to that mode of levying duties, and believing it to be the only equitable mode, I am anxious to remove every cause which might serve to impair its usefulness or injure it in public estimation. By the provisions of this bill much of the delay which has occurred from the mass of business thrown upon a single head of department will be avoided, and by prompt decisions great injury to individuals and to the Government will be avoided. Thus will be removed part of the objection to a feature in the present tariff, which I consider particularly democratic, and which I am most anxious to preserve. The argument against transferring the management of the public lands from the Secretary of the Treasury is based upon a supposition that the public domain is to be viewed as property for sale, and disposed of for revenue purposes alone. This may be conclusive to the mind of the Senator from Virginia, but with me one of the strongest inducements to the support of this bill is the provision to separate the disposal of the public lands from the office charged with providing the ways and means to support the Government. It is due to those who tame the wilderness and open new sources of national prosperity and strength, that their interests should be regarded through a purer medium than pecuniary gain. It is due to permanent and general advantage, and to the acquiescence of the new States in the narrow policy which has heretofore obtained in relation to the public domain, that higher and more liberal considerations should govern hereafter. It is not to be expected that the Secretary of the Treasury, intent upon supplying revenue, will consider the public lands otherwise than as a source from which money is to be drawn; he would be more than human if he could divest himself of the influence which his position would exercise in the decision of questions which might seem to militate against his great purpose to supply means to the treasury. In him we would naturally find an opponent to preemption privileges, grants to States, and graduation laws, and such other enactments as justice to frontier settlers would dictate, and a policy broader than annual receipts would recommend. These are considerations which deeply interest those States in which the General Government is a great landed proprietor, and to which we of those States have a right to ask respectful attention.

Mr. HUNTER. And have a second treasury.

Mr. DAVIS. A second treasury, if the Senator chooses so to term a division of the department which will separate the disposal of the public lands, and the conduct of those measures which principally concern those who settle upon them, from the general system of collecting revenue for the Government. If to provide further means to secure a wise administration of this trust—to place relations between the Government and a highly meritorious and useful class of the people in hands more likely to direct them to the ends of justice—be to establish "a second treasury," sir, let it be established.

I stated this morning, in argument for this transfer, that we had seldom seen a Secretary of the Treasury taken from a section of the country where the operations of the land laws could be practically observed and understood. In future, this will probably be still more the case, as settlement advances from the commercial ports and removes the unsold domain yet further from the places of commerce. The Secretary, chosen on account of his capacity for the more important duties of his station, will usually be from the neighborhood of the great depots or thoroughfares of trade, and, in the progress of events, be more removed from an opportunity to learn the true policy to be adopted in relation to the public lands. Such was my argument for transfering their management to one whose whole duties would indicate a selection from the citizens of the interior; the men who, by information and sympathy, would have the ability and the will wisely and justly to discharge the duty. I esteemed it fortunate that the bill had been prepared by the present Secretary, who possesses an an intimate knowledge, practically and theoretically, of the management of the public lands. No man could better estimate existing and probable difficulties, and none could better suggest remedies and preventives. Upon this and other matters of his department, provided for in the bill under consideration, I said the Secretary of the Treasury was so much better informed than myself that I would adopt his details to carry out principles which I approved—would take them on faith. This the Senator has strangely misconstrued into a declaration on my part that he should not express an opinion opposite to that of the Secretary, and that my creed was to adopt anything which a Secretary should recommend. I said nothing to justify his inferences or to warrant his construction. It was not for me to question the right of that or any other Senator to entertain and express an opinion upon the policy of any measure. I paid a just tribute to the information and honest zeal of the Secretary, and stated how far his opinion would influence my own, but did not claim from the Senator the confidence I felt—certainly did not assume to dictate to him. I felt as little inclined to do so as to adopt his assertions in opposition to the opinions of the Secretary. My remarks were confined to this case, applied to this Secretary of the Treasury, and bore upon my own conduct only. I made no general proposition, stated no opinion as to the weight to be given to the recommendations of secretaries, nor will I follow the Senator in remarks which have no bearing on the subject under discussion. How far my own opinion will be governed by department recommendations will be shown when propositions are presented to which I am opposed. The only answer which it is necessary to give to the statement that this measure will give but little relief to the treasury is, that who has administered the department, and whose opinions have the advantage of experience and the credit due to a position which must render him personally disinterested, has most emphatically stated the reverse. The relief to be given is not to be measured by the number of items of business transferred, but by the labor of each. This mode of showing the amount of relief is like that of Governor Von Twiller, who adjusted account books by weighing them against each other.

The Senator from South Carolina, [Mr. CALHOUN,] from whom I always regret to differ, and to whose opinion upon a question of organization I would especially defer, objects to the plan of the new department because of the incongruity he discovers in the subjects referred to it, and especially objects to the transfer of the Indian bureau from the War Department. When our intercourse with the Indian tribes was held under the protection of troops, and wars and rumors of wars came annually with the coming of grass, it was proper to place Indian relations under the War Department. Happily for them, honorably for us, the case has greatly changed, and is, I hope, before a distant day, to assume a character consonant with the relations of guardian and ward, which have been claimed by us as those existing between our Government and the Indian tribes. After having been partially civilized and prepared for agricultural life, tribes have been removed to the western fron-

tier. It is now equally a duty to them and ourselves that we
should, as far as we can, prevent them from lapsing again into
barbarism. By our recent acquisition from Mexico we have a
class of Indians industrious and inclined to depend upon the
white race, rather than, like sons of Esau, to plunge into the
wilderness and live by the chase. These and other changes in
their condition recommend a corresponding change of administrative organization. War being the exception, peace the
ordinary condition, the policy should be for the latter, not
the former condition. To the objection that incongruous things
are to be brought into one department, I reply that there is no
greater incongruity than exists at present, whilst there is the
gain of unity in having all those subjects which are purely
interior separated from those which are exterior. Why, to
take a case which has been selected for objection, should patents
for invention be connected with the State Department? What
congruity is there between patent rights and diplomatic intercourse? None, sir; and so different has been the character and
qualifications of individuals required for the two, that the connection has been nominal, and the bureau of patents has been
steadily growing into an independent department. So far, sir,
from perceiving the danger referred to from the further extension of the Patent Office as an agricultural and statistical bureau, I think the reverse would be the effect of this measure;
because the office would be brought more under the supervision
of the new Secretary than it could be under that of the Secretary of State, and, as it is controlled by one having other objects of interest, other channels through which to reach national reputation, so will the tendency to wander from subjects
legitimately belonging to it be diminished.

As a measure of accountability, it is proper that whenever the
duties of an officer increase beyond his ability, such division
should be made as will afford responsible agents, instead of
having functions delegated to clerks for which an officer is
held responsible without the power to know how the duty is
discharged. A large part of the labor of the Secretary of the
Treasury, as the department is now organized, is purely me-
chanical. This is the necessary result of confiding duties to
those who have not power legally to perfect the papers. Such
is the labor of signing treasury warrants and correspondence
relative to disbursements. This will be remedied by the appointment of an Assistant Secretary, as provided in the bill,
to whose office, as an appropriate duty, I suppose will be trans-

ferred the signing of warrants and other papers of like character.

Cases arising under the revenue laws will have, by the creation of a Commissioner of Customs, a distinct and appropriate place of reference, and the delays which have occurred, it is to be hoped, will be avoided, and the extra labor which has been performed by the officer charged with these cases as a part of his many duties, will be spared to his post in future, from which dispatch of other business must follow as a consequence.

Those who hear me know how heavily the labors of the Treasury Department have borne upon him who is soon to close his official connection with it, and they will remember how near it came to proving fatal to him. From such bitter experience does he speak in recommending this relief for those who are to succeed him. This is done when he sees his mantle about to fall from his shoulders, and knows it must descend to one not merely unconnected with, but opposed to him politically. It is no common merit, under such circumstances, to have sought to perfect the administrative details, so as to relieve his successor from evils with which he had stoutly struggled, over which he had gloriously triumphed. It was the conduct of one who values the prosperity of his country so much above party considerations, that he would lend a laboring hand to smooth obstructions from the road of his opponent, and wish him the success which is identified with the welfare of our common country.

Mr. President, in the formation of our Constitution, the advocates of popular right looked for safety in providing checks and balances which should restrain the usurpation of power; and nothing in the progress of government has more distinctly marked the two great parties of the country than the advocacy or opposition to centralization. By this bill, it is sought to divide the collection and disbursement of revenue, to separate considerations as to the mode of raising money from the manner of paying out—operations which should not be connected, but which, if distinct, form the proper and efficient checks one upon the other. Let those whose democracy leads to centralizing power and shielding public officers from public scrutiny, denounce this as a federal measure; let those who would restrain emigration to the untamed soil of the West, contend for keeping our public lands under policy and rules which have no other object than to extract the greatest amount of money from the hardy pioneers who, as joint owners of the public lands, have settled upon them; let those who would prolong, indefinitely, the landed proprietorship of the General Government in the new States, insist upon keeping the disposal of the public domain in hands the least apt to advocate a policy which would hasten their settlement and cultivation: my purposes are the reverse of these; and, from a desire to promote them has arisen the interest I have taken in this bill. Believing it to be a measure of public utility, and that to amend, at this late period of the session, would be to defeat it, I shall vote for the bill as it passed the House of Representatives, and leave to the future the correction of such imperfections as may, in its operation, be found to exist. Fully assured of the correctness of the main features of the bill, I wish to secure the adoption of the measure by passing it. If, as some suppose, it will not serve the main purpose I have in view, because of defects in detail, when time permits I will unite with them in supplying such deficiencies.

Jefferson Davis to Col. Edwards.

(From New York Public Library Collections.)

Col. Edwards, please inform what if any decision has been made on the application of Geo. D. Williamson, a private of Capt. Willis' Co. "C" 1st Regt. Missi. Vols. and oblige very truly yours,

Jeffn. Davis
U. S. S.

15th March 1849

Speech of Jefferson Davis in the Democratic State Convention.[1]

(From Columbus Democrat, Aug. 1, 1849.)

Fellow-citizens—Brother Democrats!—. It gives me sincere pleasure, after so long an interval, again to meet you assembled in fraternal reunion. It gladdens my heart and gives earnest of the future, to see here so many of those identified with our past trials and triumphs, and among them the fathers of our political church, whose presence and approving co-operation are proof that we have not departed from the way in which we were trained to go.

To have remained fixed in the midst of change, to have stood the test of time and varied circumstances, offers no weak assurance that our creed is founded on the immutable basis of

[1] Held for the purpose of nominating state officials.

truth, and will descend from generation to generation, such as it came to us. Temporary excitement, faction or error, like enveloping mists, may obscure it for a while, yet it will stand, as the house which the wise man built on a rock.

Since our last State convention a presidential election has transferred the executive department of the general government to our political opponents. The federal patronage is therefore an element to be calculated against us. I do not refer to the gain or loss of individuals by appointment and removal, but the more important consideration, the influence which is thus brought to bear upon the politics of the country, the effect which is thus produced upon the measures through which our principles have their practical application. The change which has occurred in the chief magistracy creates additional necessity for strenuous exertion. You can no longer rely upon the executive veto to preserve them. Your safety is to be found in a majority of the representatives. There all the modifications which have been found necessary in the practical working of those measures can be introduced, and the government be left to the quiet and steady exercise of its functions under a system which is daily growing in popular favor. You have already secured the great measures of your creed; it is only required to perfect and preserve them. You have a majority of the Senate, all you need is a gain of five members to give you a majority of the House of Representatives. Cannot Mississippi contribute one? Alabama, Tennessee, Kentucky and Indiana, if they emulate the example of Virginia, will more than complete the number. Then you will merely have lost by the Presidential election the federal patronage, a loss which will soon be forgotten in the joy of seeing our chief measures preserved. The most signal victories of the democracy have usually followed a defeat; they rise like the son of Terra, invigorated by a fall. With the hope that it will now be thus elsewhere, let us make it thus at home. Bring the lost district to the democratic fold—let Mississippi again be heard to speak with one voice in the halls of Congress.

From the foundation of our government the people have been divided into political parties; they represent antagonistic principles; are separated by an essential difference; and however we may regret the bitterness to which the controversy sometimes rises, it is not to be expected that it will permanently cease. It sleeps but does not die, and wakes to renew the contest; it may be with new phrases, new issues, with changed names; but with the same radical difference as before. Then take your old armor, it has been proved; your old banners, they have never been disgraced; and go to the new fields, where your old battles have to be fought over again. As your conviction that our policy is identical with the permanent welfare of the country is thorough, and without such conviction politics sink to a trade and elections become an unworthy struggle for place; as you believe your measures to be valuable; as your principles are dear, so should we be united as one man, in the support of our ticket. Surely we have not assembled merely to determine who should be presented for the honor and emolument of office, but for the more dignified purpose of securing concert of action for the advancement of those principles and measures which we believe promotive of the public good.

If, then, any feeling of friendship has been wounded by the defeat of candidates; if any hope of personal ambition has been disappointed; if individual rivalry, or hostile reminiscences obtrude before any part of the ticket; bring them as a peace-offering, a sacrifice meet for the altar of principle. If any local expectation, founded upon the idea of sectional distribution, has been thwarted, you will know best how to account for this. You can appreciate the circumstances and motives which have influenced the convention: to explain them and remove any dissatisfaction which may be created will be your useful and grateful task. Or if this cannot be done, then, as you can justify the motives, to strip the dissatisfaction of the sense of intentional wrong, and throw over the error the mantle of brotherly love. I will say here what I have often said, that I think it proper and conducive to successful administration to select nominees for the offices from different parts of the State. Yet, if a ticket is framed otherwise, I would not therefore give it a less zealous support. If I know myself, my interest would not be diminished, though every nominee were taken from one county, and that county should be the one most remote from my own residence.

Mississippi has no conflicting interests; are we not one as Democrats? bound through good and evil to maintain a common cause. To a party having well defined principles—one policy and one interest—adhesion like this is but a natural consequence. To him who follows as a guiding star the motto of our creed, "measures not men," the difficulties which obstruct the political path can neither check his progress nor divert him from his course. But among these difficulties there is one which we are sometimes called upon to meet, which is far harder to overcome than any which I have enumerated.

It is when we see in the candidate of our opponents, one who is entitled to our gratitude, commands our respect and possesses our confidence and personal affection. To sink personal hostility in political coincidence is an easy task, compared to its opposite, the sacrifices of personal ties because of political difference. Of this I can speak experimentally, having been submitted to the test in the late presidential canvass; and though in my course on that occasion I find nothing to regret or repent, it was not permitted to pass without misconstruction and misrepresentation; it may therefore be proper for me to refer to it. In the candidate of the opposite party, I recognized a personal friend, to whom gratitude was due for his public services, and who had claims upon myself and others of my fellow-citizens which if they were not of a higher, were of nearer and more binding character than those. Honored as a patriot, admired as a soldier, trusted and loved as a man, yet I opposed him as a political candidate; and as the leader of our adversaries feared his success, in proportion to the influence, which his military services, his elevated qualities, and many virtues would give him, for the advancement of a policy which I believe to be wrong. Therefore, whenever I addressed the people during that canvass, whilst I acknowledged the debt of gratitude which was due to Gen. Taylor for the services which from youth to age he had rendered to the country, a debt which the democracy have not been wont to pay with stinted measure or reluctant will, and admitted all which his political supporters said of his private virtues, I, nevertheless, warned the democracy against trusting political power to their adversaries because of the personal confidence they might feel in him who would thus become the head of the administration. On all such occasions I appealed to them to give a united supported to the democratic ticket, and cautioned them against the danger of transferring the care of their measures not yet perfected, in truth an infant system, to the hands of a nurse who would probably strive to strangle it.

Weary of party strife, trusting to the delusive representatives of partizans that the long contested issues were not to be revived; that it was only sought to administer the government as in the earlier days of the republic; that political tests were no longer to be applied to the officers of government, and attracted by beautiful theories, which have died with the canvass, many democrats were drawn from the support of their own ticket. Captivated by the idea of a political millenium, won by the ad captandum appeals of the "outs," who desired to be "ins," they followed after false prophets, and are now learning in the hard school of experience the impracticability of the promises with which they were flattered. Existing circumstances forbid the idea of any one reaching the Presidency except as the candidate of a party: until this is otherwise, or until we see a successful party disregarding the offices which have been brought within its reach, we must expect with every change of administration to see something like that which we have recently witnessed. The great and unexpected loss which we sustained in the popular vote of this State, was but the forerunner of more decisive losses elsewhere.

The result is history; the consequences are being rapidly developed, and the new policy has almost ceased to be the subject of conjecture. With the unfolding of that policy, the democracy have awakened as from a dream; stimulated by the reality which has succeeded the vision, like one refreshed by slumber they come with increased strength to the present contest. They have reviewed the lesson learned in 1841, and I trust have now learned it so well, that they will never again be drawn into the snare; though one should rise from the dead to testify, that they will not believe. I honor the whig party, openly avowing and supporting their creed, though I believe it to be wrong—I grant all which I claim, sincerity in their opinions, and accord the patriotism which commands respect. But the "no party party" I consider a cunning device to undermine the majority, and always to be regarded with the distrust which attaches to the pursuit of political power without the avowal of the purpose for which it is sought. Does any one now believe that our political opponents will not revive, at least in part, the old issues upon which the country has been so long divided, if they shall have a majority in the next house of Representatives? I hope every democrat will have this in view, at the next Congressional election, and that he will remember the difference between one pledged to a special vote, and another who it is known will cordially, zealously, directly, and indirectly support our great measures. To illustrate my meaning, I will suppose that a candidate pledges himself to vote against a protective tariff, or even to support an ad valorem tariff, yet, if he would vote for a speaker friendly to the policy against which he was pledged, and who would organize committees to promote it, he would thus contribute to establish the very measure against which, as a candidate, he was pledged to vote. There are many other ways which will readily occur to you, through which even an unintentional aid may be given to the party with which even the member has a general coincidence.

They all tend to enforce the idea that to maintain your policy, and measure, you must have agents who fully agree with yourselves. Upon the question of internal improvement by the general government, the fears which I expressed last fall have in no degree abated. I yet believe whatever party may be in power, that this corrupting system will prevail, will run its course through political, sectional, and individual combination, with all its demoralizing consequences to public and private virtue, until it becomes odious by the creation of a great national debt. Then public scrutiny will be directed to the millions which have been squandered, and with the reaction will come the inquiry, what have we received for the money expended? The nature of the answer, it is possible to divine from the history of the twenty-eight millions, which in 1837, the general government transferred to the States, and by reference to the appropriations which have, from time to time, been made for works of internal improvement, the local character of which it has been vainly attempted to disguise, and the sectionality of which is too glaring to be denied.

It is the characteristic of all legislation for specal interests that the benefits inure to the strong; thence it has ensued that appropriations for internal improvements have mainly been made at the North and East. We who have contributed to the national treasury in a much greater ratio than that of our property or representation, have been but in a very minute degree, the beneficiaries of the large sum which the general government has expended on public works.

Henceforward we must become relatively weaker in the national legislature, and therefore rather expect an increase than cessation of the unjust discrimination heretofore made against us.

This question as before said, is one on which I expect the democracy to be divided, but from our friends, it will receive its opposition; if beaten, we will maintain the doctrine, keep the holy fire alive until a happier day shall enable us to place it again on the democratic altar.

In reviewing the events of the last four years, the democracy have cause to be proud of their position, and surely never had higher incentives than now to be firm and united.

After many years of contest; we have established our revenue and treasury policy. At its inception it was exposed to the severest tests to which such measures can be submitted, and has evinced a capability surpassing the expectation of its most sanguine friend. Before time was allowed for the perfect organization of the "Independent Treasury" or for the commercial changes which were relied on as consequences of the more liberal tariff of 1846, the government became involved in a foreign war, requiring disbursements new in their character, and extraordinary in their amount. The ad valorem tariff and independent treasury have sufficed to supply the means, and to make the disbursements required. We have had the two-fold gratification to see the revenue increase whilst the duties, that is the tax on consumers, was decreased, and the fiscal operations of the government conducted like its other functions by responsible agents. These measures having shown themselves equal to the wants of the government even in war, the plea of necessity can no longer be urged for their repeal.

By the constitution and laws of our State, all political power rests with the majority of citizens, who practically possess entire political equality, and the principles of democracy must always prevail wherever the issue is fairly presented. You have met for this purpose. From this, as a centre, let the spirit go forth which will arouse the attention, and secure the union of our party. Then the democrats will come in their strength next November to recover their old domain, and the ramparts which the whigs have erected during their slumber, will be levelled by their tread, as the returning tide of the ocean sweeps the cobwebs from its beach.

Restored to our position of 1845, instead of the meager majority of last fall; to political unity in the different Congressional districts of the State, instead of the divided representation of the last Congress, your representatives, possessed of the moral force which belongs to decided majorities, and united in political creed, will speak in the name of the State with the authority and decision warranted by such unanimity among their constituents.

Fellow-citizens, I have addressed you as a democrat, answering to the invitation of a democratic Convention, and have forborne to allude to a question of vital interest, because it is above party and should be kept separate from it. Need I say my reference is to the spirit of aggression manifested by the Northern towards the Southern States of the Union. As a representative of the State, deeply impressed with the importance and urgency of the sectional issue which is forced upon us, it is my purpose, to such extent as circumstances will permit, to visit my constituents and confer with them, as to the future of this momentous question. On this occasion I have only alluded to it, to express the hope that in political controversies during the approaching canvass, difference in political creed will not be allowed to disturb the fraternity, or impair the unanimity which exists among us, in all which relates to the maintenance of our domestic institutions and rights as a people. To preserve the Union as established under the constitution, and our equal rights and privileges in it, is our highest hope. I believe the united, decided, energetic action of the South will ensure success, whilst divisions among ourselves will entail consequences from the contemplation of which every patriot must recoil. We must be harmonious to be respected, and united to be safe. Then whilst we should relax nothing of proper exertion to secure our political ascendency, we should forget that we strive with our brethren, and however we may differ about measures of policy or principles of administration, should never lose sight of the fact, that we are one people, and in the defence of our domestic rights, recognize no difference of creed.

I thank you for the courtesy and kindness which has permitted me to address you in this family meeting, assembled in accordance to our time honored custom. My anticipations in relation to the next election in our State are little, if at all, short of my hopes. To fulfil both, can only require the concert and action of the democracy. In ploughman's phrase, "God send you speed" and entire success to the cause for which you are laboring. It is the cause of truth, justice, the union & the constitution from which it sprung and which it cannot survive.

Jefferson Davis to Stephen Cocke.

(From the Mississippi Department of Archives and History.)

Brierfield, 2d. Aug. 1849.

Dear General.

I have the pleasure to acknowledge your kind letter of the 30th. ult. by our friend Harris. I do not know how it happened that I did not answer your letter of last spring to which you refer, and can only speak of the feelings which have uniformly been entertained towards you and positively decide as to motives which could not have influenced me. I have felt and feel such high regard and close friendship for you that I would be as incapable of unkindly interpreting advice from you as from my Brother. I never attributed to you any other considera-

tions than that of kindness for me, and thus as I will hereafter be, not only anxious but expectant for such suggestions
as your experience, your better knowledge of the politicians
of the state, and opportunity for immediate observation will
enable you to offer. To those who were entitled to such consideration I generally replied if they advised or expressed a
hope that I should connect myself with the new administration,[1]
because I disliked the speculation of that kind which I sometimes
saw in the papers, for opinions of the opposite kind I always
felt thankful as evincing the appreciation of me which I desired, and as sustaining a determination as old as the first mention of the subject, and older than the public speculation about
it. To these as to friendly letters a press of business correspondence usually deferred sometimes prevented an answer.
I will look over my file of letters and by the indorsement on
yours will be able to determine whether I wrote an answer and
if not, probably, why it was omitted. Of this Uncle Stephen,
let me assure you, I have no friend on whom I more confidently
rely than yourself, or whose regard it would pain me more
to see diminished. I would lose all the offices to which one like
myself could aspire sooner than such a friend should find me
captious or regardless of his feelings.

Barton[2] I expect to be a candidate for the Senate, his coming to the legislature after refusing a nomination for congress,
without a special question to induce it is as Benton would say
"awfully significant." I noticed that Taylor was beaten in the
nomination of candidates for the legislature by a much younger
and less prominent man. Capt. Taylor is a friend of mine,
not much so of Barton, and this fact connected with the other
makes to my mind a case. I have a respect for Barton and a
high opinion of his native intellect, as a successor I would in-
comparably prefer him to Jake.[3] When I become a sovereign
I shall want an honest servant.

There are many screws which will be tightened on me. The
sectional question as before will be raised and will be stronger
because of the local ticket lately nominated. Quitman will

[1] In the Cass-Taylor presidential campaign of 1848 Jefferson Davis was
confronted with a serious question of party regularity and allegiance.
General Taylor was his father-in-law; and since the storming of Monterey
and the victory of Buena Vista the two men had been on close and intimate terms. In addition he was a Southern planter and slave-holder; and
his position on sectional questions was thought to be more helpful to the
South than that of Cass. Davis, however, remained true to his traditions
and supported the candidate of his party.
[2] Roger Barton of Holly Springs, Miss., an able and resourceful lawyer.
[3] Jacob Thompson.

find his game in pushing the senator as far north as possible. Foote [1] the same. Either may form combinations which you will not require me to say, I will never attempt. The most will be made of the commendations I bestowed on Genl. Taylor as a soldier and my efforts against him as a whig candidate will be kept back, out of sight. I wonder how many of my opponents standing in the relation I did to Genl. Taylor would have endeavored to defeat him for democracy's sake & have refused to walk in the broad way and the open gate to self preferment.

A truce to politics the meanest and most demoralizing pursuit which is followed. Your colts look well and the youngest as is usually the case is thought best. The oldest is light, tall and of the go along figure. She must be 14½ or 15 hands high. [2] I wish you would come to see us and if you will you can also see the colts.

If the health of Mrs. Davis will permit I expect to leave for Aberdeen in the course of this month, and will, as you propose make the circuit and when I chance to find an assembly will be pleased to talk to the people on any subject of interest to them. My heart just now is in union and action of the south against Abolitionism, which may as a generic term include all the associations making war on the slave holding states. Please let me hear from you and believe me as ever your friend

Jeffn. Davis.

Jefferson Davis to W. B. Tebo.

(From Mississippi Free Trader, Aug. 29, 1849.)

Brierfield, Aug. 22, 1849.

Dear Sir: In your paper of the 8th inst., I perceive a reference to myself which is founded in an error, which I have less hesitation in correcting because of the complimentary terms and distinguished company with which my name is connected. I allude to this paragraph:

"There was a time, it is true, when Quitman's position was obnoxious to the democratic party of the State. Previous to the extra session of Congress of 1837, he occupied the position of the patriotic Calhoun and his peculiar friends, a position of temporary disagreement or estrangement from the great body of the democratic party. In this he was associated with many

---

[1] Henry S. Foote.
[2] Senator Davis, like all men of the South, was fond of fine horses.

of the greatest men of the South (democrats too,) and with many in Mississippi who are now, and have long been considered among the firmest and soundest democrats in the State—Judge C. P. Smith, Dr. Lipscomb, Jefferson Davis, Dr. Hagan, T. B. Woodward and the Hon. Joseph W. Chalmers, and the lamented Col. Andrew L. Martin, then of Tennessee.''

At the time referred to I had taken no other part in politics than by casting my vote, and neither before nor since have I had any political associations which placed me in the position of estrangement to the great body of the democratic party. My first vote was cast in favor of General Jackson for President. At subsequent periods I have supported for the same office, Van Buren in 1835, Van Buren in 1840—Polk in 1844— and Cass in 1848.

Political inconsistency is a thing of very little importance to any other than the individual concerned, and except where political principle is involved, is so dependent upon circumstance and association as to afford no evidence of merit.

From my childhood I was attached to General Jackson. My confidence and respect for him increased in after years. My affection and admiration followed him to the grave, and cling to his memory. This feeling induces me to trouble you with the above correction.

Very respectfully,
your friend, &c.,
JEF. DAVIS.

W. B. Tebo, esq.,
Editor of the Free Trader.

Jefferson Davis to George M. Dallas.[1]

(From the Mississippi Department of Archives and History.)

Washington, D. C.
16th Dec 1849

My dear Sir,
It gives me great pleasure to acknowledge your kind favor of the 11th Inst. and to return the thanks of Mrs. Davis and my own for the remembrance of yourself and family.

---

[1] Dallas, George Mifflin (1792-1864), an American statesman and diplomat, the son of Alexander James Dallas, was born in Philadelphia, Pa., July 10, 1792; was graduated from Princeton college in 1810, studied law, and was admitted to the bar in 1813. He accompanied Albert Gallatin, as his secretary, to Russia in 1814; was mayor of Philadelphia in 1829;

I consulted Mr. Pearce in relation to the correspondence of Messrs. Humboldt and Arrago, he thought it would be better that Prof. Bache's name should not be involved in the publication and suggested that the correspondence be published as furnished by Prof. Schumaker to a friend. Prof. Bache seemed to consider the publication only desirable in the event of renewed attack. As to the Missouri Bull and his course we can only say "Quien sabe"; but his numerous engagements will I think scarcely leave him time and temper for the task, heretofore so fruitless.

The question is one of strategy, the only known quantity in equation being the virulent and unscrupulous character of the enemy.

I would be pleased to hear your suggestions and to hear from you on other subjects as often as your leisure will permit.

Please present my most friendly remembrances to Mrs. Dallas and the young Ladies, in which Mrs. Davis cordially unites, and we both offer you our highest regard and assurances of the friendship with which I am as ever your's

Jeffn. Davis.

Remarks of Jefferson Davis in Senate concerning the opinions of Father Mathew, on the resolution to admit him to a privileged seat. Senate Dec. 20, 1849.

Mr. DAVIS, of Mississippi. I am glad to hear the Senator from New York, [Mr. SEWARD] place this movement upon a distinct basis—to know that it is advocated because of the opinions in relation to domestic slavery, which are ascribed to the individual named in the resolution. Yes, sir, I am glad to hear that now avowed.

For years past we have seen our fraternity disturbed, our country torn by domestic contention; even now we see our Government seriously embarrassed by a dissension, the seeds of which were sown by the British emissaries, who assumed the false pretext of philanthropy to mask their unholy designs to kindle the fires of civil war among the United States. There

U. S. district attorney for the eastern district of Pennsylvania, 1829-1831; U. S. Senator from December 13, 1831, to March 3, 1833; Attorney General of Pennsylvania 1833-1835; Minister to Russia from March 7, 1837, to July 29, 1839; Vice-President of the United States 1845-1849; Minister to Great Britain from February 4, 1856, to May 16, 1861. He died in Philadelphia December 31, 1864. Consult "Brief Memoir of George Mifflin Dallas". 18 pp, Philadelphia, 1853.

was a time, sir, when an American feeling pervaded and ruled in this country; when every man worthy to be descended from the sires of our Revolution, repulsed with loathing and scorn the foreign emissary who attempted to distract our nationality. Not even on questions of general policy and common interest would they permit the interference of others.

Has this passed away? Now, when it requires all the forbearance of brotherhood to allay excitement, to calm irritation, to prevent pent up feeling from bursting into strife, are we not only to permit, but to welcome, the intrusion of the stranger into the most delicate domestic question which has ever threatened the peace and safety of our Confederacy? Degenerate and unworthy of the sires from whom we derive our institutions and our union must that son be, who can thus court foreign interference, and grasp the hand in fellowship with which he expects to scatter over our land the seeds of a new and most mischievous species of domestic discord.

Sir, I have no wish to depreciate the labors or to contest the merits of him whose name is identified with the beneficent cause of temperance reformation. The good he has done to a portion of our race deserves the thanks of mankind. The heart pays a willing tribute to the benevolence of a labor like his; and who has not rejoiced in the happy influence his mission has exercised over his unfortunate countrymen? Could it devolve upon the Senate to decide either of these points, there would, I suppose, be but little difference of opinion among us. But it would not thence follow, that as a department of this Government we should give testimonial of our approbation and accordance. Still less can this be claimed for the reason urged by the Senator from New York.

Thus presented, the question is, whether the United States Senate, partly composed of those who represent a slaveholding constituency, shall vote an extraordinary compliment to one known as the ally of Daniel O'Connell in his attempt to incite the Irishmen, naturalized citizens of the United States, to unite as a body with the Abolitionists in their nefarious designs against the peace, the property, and the constitutional rights of the southern States. An act of such obtrusive interference in our domestic affairs, a declaration of opinions so offensive, an attempt so mischievous, requires something more than a temporary silence to justify the unprecedented compliment which is claimed at our hands.

If, as the Senator from Kentucky [Mr. CLAY] intimates, those opinions in relation to African slavery as it exists in this country have undergone a change, why was not such change avowed when an opportunity was kindly offered, as has been stated by the Senator from Alabama? A refusal to do so, under the circumstances connected with it, could not fail to have an injurious effect upon what is recognized as the great object of his visit, and is, therefore, conclusive against the supposition of such a change having occurred. When opinions are gratuitously thrown before the world, it is our right to note them, and, if mischievous, our duty to remember them; this is not to probe private sentiments, but is to see that which is laid before us.

In the present case exceptions have been taken not to the opinions of "Father Mathew" on the subject of slavery, but to his conduct in attempting to instigate his countrymen, naturalized among us, to join in a crusade against institutions of their adopted country. Why, if he came purely as a missionary in the cause of temperance, should he have hesitated to disavow any purpose to interfere with the political relations of any portion of our citizens, or to assail any of the domestic institutions of our country? This was necessary, not to assure us against any supposed danger from his influence—our confidence in the allegiance of our citizens gave full security against that —but was necessary to justify the attentions and courtesy which it was desired to offer. In default of such disavowals, under answers which are said to have been evasive, and with such advocacy as we have just heard, his attitude is that of one who comes covertly as a wolf in sheep's clothing; and I hold the Senator from New York to be the very best authority on that subject.

Mr. President, in opposing this resolution I wish it to be distinctly understood, that I yield all which has been claimed for the success of "Father Mathew" to the cause of temperance in Ireland; and certainly abate nothing of respect and sympathy because of his clerical character and the land of his nativity. If either one or the other had led me into error, it would have been that of compliance, not resistance. Irishmen not allied with O'Connell and abolitionism, take in my sympathies the next place to our brethren; but this feeling is not sufficient to give a controlling influence to the mere name of "Irish patriot." My first duty, my nearest ties, are at home; and I will say of the horde of abolitionists, foreign and domestic, that if I had the power to exclude them all from this Chamber, I would not hesitate a moment to do it.

Remarks of Jefferson Davis on the Vermont resolutions on the subject of slavery. Jan. 10, 1850.

Mr. DAVIS, of Mississippi. Mr. President, I do not know that I should have said anything upon this occasion but for the fact that the Senator from New Hampshire [Mr. HALE] has made several points, and announced them in connection with the fact that he is about to be absent from the Senate. His speech was quite in keeping, sir, with many of the acts I have witnessed on the part of that Senator. It was characteristic with him to make a speech upon this subject just before he was to leave the Senate, that he may avail himself of it, as I suppose, in the region he is about to visit, as food for agitation, and as evidence of his prowess upon the floor. On this occasion, he has taken as his theme the defence of the factory laborer— the intellectual cultivation and excellent morality of his constituents; and in order to produce conviction, I thought it exceeding well, quite prudent, I will not say how necessary, that he should announce that it was his colleague, and not himself, who dwelt among and was to be regarded as the representative of so praiseworthy a population, so high in the scale of humanity, so moral, so intelligent and proper in all things. I thought it well, sir, that it was his colleague whom the honorable Senator located in the midst of such superior samples of humanity.

Mr. HALE. Will the honorable Senator permit me to interrupt him? I stated that my colleague resided in one manufacturing village of the kind I have described, and that I reside myself in another of the same kind.

Mr. DAVIS. I thought the Senator said it was his colleague who resided among these remarkable people; but as he has now corrected the statement, I can only wonder the more that, coming himself from the midst of a population so moral, so accomplished, and instructed, therefore to be supposed so regardful of the rights of others, so regardful of the Constitution as those he has the honor to represent, he should make demonstrations such as he is constantly exhibiting upon this floor. I thought it well, as I understood him first, but now it assumes a more dubious form; and without the high eulogy which he delivered upon that population, and which I suppose he is to take home with him, I should have doubted their claims to such and so numerous virtues. I trust he will take home with him also the speech he delivered the other day upon this floor, in which he announced that all those petitions and memorials are a mere trick, intended for electioneering purposes; that this agitation is a mere game, intended to cajole the people; that it is all a very harmless matter; that it means really nothing, except to keep up an excitement, and secure votes to candidates at election time. I hope that the Senator will repeat that speech to these people when he happens to attend meetings whence these and similar resolutions go forth. When the people in any quarter of this Union are about to be lashed into fury against the institutions of the remaining States by the promptings of fanaticism, and urged to assail that of which they know nothing, I hope that he will rise and tell them how mean a spirit, how corrupt a purpose, and how empty are the declarations which have provoked them to this madness. Let him tell them, as he told the Senator from Vermont, when he referred to the introduction of these resolutions, that it is a convenience to get up resolutions of the sort when a Senator is to be elected. I think, sir, this would be far better than any constitutional argument, or, if such things could be supposed there, than any southern address which could be delivered. I think it would recall the patriotism and the justice even of the Senator's own constituency to a sense of their folly and rashness—recall them from their wild war upon the rights of others, and cause them to reflect how far they had been made the unwilling instruments of mere demagogues, seeking to elevate themselves at their expense and the expense of the country, by means of exciting their jealousy and passion.

But the Senator makes another declaration which surprises me—not being very well informed in relation to his private history—that he is not a member of any of those associations which are operating in the North against the institutions of the South, and that he knows nothing of them. I am glad to hear it; and can now understand his declaration, that he knows of no associations for the purpose of printing incendiary publications, to be circulated at the South. We do know it, and it is strange that he does not. Why, sir, the New York Anti-Slavery Society sends out more publications, I believe, than the Senate of the United States. They are sent not only into the southern States, but, sir, that society has printed numerous publications for the express purpose of circulation in California; and the purpose has been avowed, by means of agents and publications gratuitously distributed, to prevent slavery from being admitted into the constitution of California. Not only this, but they are associated in close affiliation with similar societies in Great Britain and Scotland. They acknowledge the contributions of those societies to be applied to these very objects for which they are laboring, according to their own reports. It is very strange that we, who stand so far off, should know so much more in relation to these matters than the Senator from New Hampshire. Yet, sir, I am glad that it is so—that such is the fact—because it exonerates the Senator from New Hampshire from much of that culpability which we had heretofore assigned to him.

Mr. President, I always enter into the discussion of the slavery questions with feelings of reluctance; and only because I am forced into it by those who, having nothing to do with it, nevertheless indecently interfere in our domestic affairs here, I have done so. Sir, it is a melancholy fact, that morning after morning, when we come here to enter into the business of the Senate, our feelings should be harrowed up by the introduction of this exciting and profitless subject, and we be compelled to listen to insults heaped upon our institutions. Sir, there is no man who comes here to represent his constituency for high and useful purposes, and who feels upon himself the obligation of his oath to maintain the Constitution of the United States, who could thus act, from day to day, for the purpose of disturbing the useful legislation of the country—for no other purpose than to insert another brand into the flame which every reflecting, sober man now sees threatens to consume the fabric of our Government. We of the South stand now, as we have always stood, upon the defensive. We raised not this question; but when raised, it is our duty to defend ourselves. For one, sir, my purposes are to keep down this species of excitement, both here and at home. I know the temper of those whom I represent, and they require no promptings to resist aggression or insult. I know their determination. It is well and deeply taken, and will be shown when the crisis comes. They make no threats against any one, and least of all against the Union, for which they have made such heavy and continued sacrifices. They know their rights, while they feel their wrongs; and they will maintain the one, resent the other, if it may be, will preserve our constitutional Union; but the Union without the Constitution they hold to be a curse. With the Constitution, they will never abandon it. We, sir, are parties to this Union only under the Constitution, and there is no power known in the world that could dictate to my little State a Union in which her rights were continually disrespected and trampled upon by an unrestrained majority. The present generation, sir, will maintain the character their fathers won. They well know how to sustain the institutions which they inherited, even by civil war, if that be provoked. They will march up to this issue, and meet it face to face.

This is our position; you have not respected it. I know yours, and cannot respect it; and knowing it, I came to this session of Congress with melancholy forebodings—with apprehension that it might be the last of our Government. I still trusted, however, in the intelligence and patriotism of the masses, for I have long since said that I put no faith in politicians. I feel that they have raised a storm which they cannot control. They have invoked a spirit which they cannot allay, and dare not confront. And yet I believe that the descendants of the Franklins, the Hancocks, and the Adamses, if they saw our institutions about to be destroyed by a mean and captious exercise of the power of demagogues to press to a fatal extremity aggressions upon our rights by the North, would rise up in their strength, and would enforce the justice and obligations of the Constitution. This is no indication of any confidence which I put in their representatives; with them I am ready to meet this issue face to face; and if the representatives of that people think proper to sow the seeds of dissension, and to inflame the passions and prejudices of one section, whilst they drive the other by every possible provocation to the point of civil war, then all I have to say is, that the representatives of the South, true to their constituency, are prepared to meet the issue here and now. If this is to be the hot-bed of civil war, if from this as a center the evil is to radiate throughout our country, here let the first battle be fought! If gentlemen come here constantly to press upon us, strip us of our rights, move the people of one section of the nation to hostility against the other, I hope that those who have brought the country to this crisis will meet the first test.

Mr. President, it is no part of the business of a southern representative here to deliver panegyrics upon the attachment of his constituents to the Union. We have proved our love of the Union and our devotion to it too often and too long to require such declarations. Let those who feel that it may be doubted make their declarations of fidelity to the Union; we have nothing of the kind to do. If the State of Vermont chooses to send to the Senate of the United States insulting resolutions relating to her sister States, let the Senators and Representatives of that State do their duty in relation to them; and as I say nothing against a sovereign State, I will only say to those

Senators that I regret that Vermont has not now such constitutional scruples as actuated her in the war of 1812, and that she does not keep her resolutions within her own limits, in this war of aggression, as she attempted to keep her troops during that war.

I regret that I shall have to part with many friends with whom I have uniformly acted in the Senate, upon the motion, now pending, to print these resolutions. I would agree to print them, however offensive they might be, if the State had sent them to the Senate. The State has a right to speak to the Senate, and be heard. But I accept the argument of the Senator from Georgia, which has improperly, as it seems to me, been called special pleading, that they are the property of the Senators to whom they are directed, and I perceive no obligation requiring them to have been placed before the Senate. They are instructions addressed to them, with reference to their own duties, and might just as well remain in their own pockets as to lie upon the table of the Senate. I hold them to be unjust, to be untrue, offensive, insulting, treasonable to the Constitution; and I will not endorse them by my vote. I have thus briefly stated my reasons.

Remarks of Jefferson Davis on the bill limiting expense collecting revenue from customs. Jan. 14, 1850.

Mr. DAVIS, of Mississippi. The amendment offered by the honorable Senator removes the objection which I felt to the resolution originally introduced, which was to suspend the operation of the policy of limiting and making specific the appropriation for the collection of the revenue. It is an anomaly in our Government, that the collection of the revenue has heretofore been unchecked by any appropriation from Congress, while all other expenditures have been confined within a fixed limit. It is also most true that it has been impossible, from the reports and estimates, and statements of the Treasury Department, to ascertain what amount of money, paid originally by imposts into the custom-houses, has been detained by orders of the Secretary of the Treasury without any appropriation or any law therefor, and thus consumed in the payment of expenses.

It is somewhat strange that this matter has continued so long unrebuked and unchecked by any administration; and it certainly inures greatly to the credit of the last Secretary of the Treasury, that he was the first who ever asked Congress to take from him a portion of his power; for that is, in effect, what is done, when money is withheld from the treasurer. By the Constitution of the United States, no money can be drawn from the treasury of the United States, except by law; and yet from year to year, here was a large amount of money annually drawn by the Secretary of the Treasury from its natural channel, and appropriated by him at his discretion. This was an evil which I considered to be remedied by the act of March last. It was an evil which was not first suggested in March, 1848, which my friend from Maryland [Mr. PEARCE] seemed to suggest was only carried out in March, 1849, to bear upon the incoming Administration. It was suggested by him in his report at the commencement of his service, and was followed up year after year, until that year when his services were about to close. Then, for the first time, in the year 1848, he omitted it; he passed over the year 1848, and transferred to the year 1849 the action upon this matter. This must be apparent to that Senator, if he recollects the political complexion of the last Congress.

I would prefer, Mr. President, instead of suspending the proviso at all, to increase the appropriation—to increase the sum to whatever limits, by our estimate, may be found necessary to support the expense of the revenue. I do not consider that a case has yet been made out to show that any increase is necessary.

Nor was the sum of $1,560,000 adopted vaguely, without a calculation, as is now intimated. In 1846, a statement was called for of the total amount expended in the collection of the revenue. According to the report of the financial year, ending in June, 1846, the sum total was near two millions of dollars. The same year, Mr. Walker, in two letters, to the Committee of Finance in the Senate and to the Committee of Ways and Means in the House of Representatives, recommended the adoption of just such a law as this. In March, 1846, in writing to the committee, he called upon them to make this report. In May, 1846, he renewed the same recommendation, to which he appended a section, that the amount to be disbursed should not exceed, for the fiscal year ending June, 1847, or for any succeeding year, $1,520,000. In his next report—his annual report—he set forth the various reductions at $500,000, and upon that estimate, and his statements of the expenditures of the previous year, this sum was based.

Now, sir, this sum of $1,560,000 is not the whole sum appropriated to the collection of the revenue. There is to be added to it a further sum of $240,000 or $250,000, on account of the drawback from storage, &c., making a total sum of over $1,800,000, which is directly appropriated. This sum is not equal to the two millions reported in this case. It is about the same originally reported as expended in 1846, because then there was no such drawback for storage, drayage, and labor, which now amounts to two hundred and forty or two hundred and fifty thousand dollars, and which is therefore to be deducted from the sum expended that year. This deduction will bring it down to about that sum.

Then, sir, I do not doubt that the retrenchments have been properly made. I do not expect that any officer of the Government should dismiss his own employees, unless he is coerced to it by specific appropriations. I do not expect that where his predecessor had a certain number of clerks, &c., he will carry his retrenchment into effect by dismissing the employees of his own department. It is not to be expected of any man; and I trust it will not be expected of the present Secretary of the Treasury that he should limit the expenses of the collection of the revenue.

The Senator from Maryland seems to suppose, however, that a new charge, heretofore paid by the Secretary of the Treasury, is to be thrown upon the expenses of collecting the revenue, or upon the importers. Now, I think that is not the case. Heretofore, as I understand, the Government has employed draymen, laborers, and clerks. For all the labor, the drayage, and storage, the Government originally pays, and this is refunded when the goods are taken out. Now, by the act of March 3, 1849, Government will still pay out the amount for labor, storage, and drayage, and when the goods are taken from the warehouses, it will be repaid by the importer; but this sum, thus paid, instead of going back to the general fund, goes to the specific fund. This is all the difference. Now it goes to the specific fund; formerly it went to the general fund. This I understand to be the whole difference.

As to the policy of abolishing the warehousing system, I should oppose it rather more than the change in the collection of the revenue. I believe, sir, that it equalizes the revenue of the country, through different years; that it increases the imports by giving additional facilities to importers, and reduces the expenses of imported articles. This, surely must be the reason of the whole opposition which has heretofore come against it; because it comes in aid of the importer, and because it reduces the price of foreign goods. I, sir, am the advocate of free-trade—free-trade, so far as it is consistent with a revenue tariff. Holding that this warehousing system comes into that general policy, I believe it will equalize the amount collected in two different years, and equalize the number of employees necessary to be kept in the service of the Government. There will necessarily be periods when there will be small importations, followed by periods when there will be great imports. Both of these extremes tend against the treasury, because, when the imports are great, additional clerks are required; and when the imports are small, the clerks are in the employ of the Government, and cannot be dismissed.

I find that the Secretary of the Treasury, in his annual report of this year, states the amount of the additional expenditure at $194,634 66 beyond the storage. Now, sir, I think our attention ought to be attracted to that point. If our public warehouses are to cost so much beyond storage, it is time that we should allow private individuals to keep storehouses. It is a striking fact that this sum should be drawn from the treasury of the United States to support these storehouses, when private individuals can afford to keep public storehouses at the same time and can make money out of it.

But, sir, is this sum of $194,000 properly chargeable to the warehouses? I contend that it is not. I contend that a distinction should be made. There has always been a period when service was required of labor, drayage, &c., just as it is now, and the difference only between that formerly required and that now required is all that should have been charged upon the warehouses. Let us see how far the warehouse system has been increased. The total of foreign exports from the 6th of August, 1846, to the 6th of September, 1848, as I learn from executive document No. 57, adding the balance of the year at the same rate, will be about $104,908,288. In nearly the same time, (for the periods do not exactly coincide,) Mr. Meredith reports a total sum of $87,352,000. Now, the probable duties collected upon this—for the lower price goods do not go into the warehouses—will be the sum of $2,600,000, at 10 per cent. I believe it has been estimated at more than 10 per cent., but I take that as a very low rate. These storehouses increase the revenue, and the balance of $194,000 is not properly charged to them, since they, by facilitating the importations, increase the revenue to a much larger amount.

I am willing to concede, Mr. President, that by the creation of new collection districts, and by the extension of our commerce, some additional expenditure must take place in the collection of the revenue. I am willing, therefore, I say, to support the amendment of the Senator from New York, [Mr. DICKINSON], and increase the sum; though I desire it to be distinctly understood that it is not to be added to the $1,560,000, but to the $1,800,000. Unless the whole proviso is repealed, this will be an addition which will make it $2,000,000. If the Committee on Finance believe that sum to be necessary, I shall not object to it, or to any other specific sum, within any moderate limit; but I shall insist upon preserving the principle of making specific appropriation, by which means we shall know what sum is expended, and by which means we may curtail unnecessary expenditures.

I have no fears, Mr. President, that the turning out of a great number of the employees in the custom-houses, the reduction of the revenue cutters, and the abandoning of many custom-houses, kept up merely for preventive purposes, will be likely to work any great evil. This is a people morally opposed to smugglers; and I know of no other country in the world which can make the same boast. I believe our people reprobate a smuggler, and that very little smuggling has occurred, or is likely to occur. So far as the revenue cutters are concerned, as preventives of smuggling, I do not believe it to be necessary or useful to keep them up. All these, I think, are proper economical reductions of the expenses of the collection.

Nor, on the other hand, am I at all concerned that the duties of the employees of the custom-houses are becoming too onerous, or that the reduction of their salaries would render the offices less an object of pursuit. If such was to be the effect, I should hail it most joyously. If it would reduce that thirst for public office, which I consider now as a great and growing evil in the country, I should hail it as a great benefit. I should be happy to see anything in their reduction, accomplished by legislative reform or otherwise, to rebuke the practice of those who abandon their private pursuits to feed upon the Federal Government. I think that this tendency is inevitable to the greatest political corruption which we have to fear.

Nor, sir, do I object at all to these reforms being very extensively made by the Secretary. It is a part of his duty, as the head of the Treasury Department, that he should report all reforms which he deems to be practicable. He is but discharging his duty. We ought to make the specific appropriation which shall drive the Secretary of the Treasury into reforms he would be unwilling to make otherwise. We should do by him as we do by every other officer, and hold him responsible; limiting the expenditures to a certain number of dollars.

On these grounds, and actuated by no particular reference to the individual who may exercise the functions of this or any other office, I shall give my vote. So far as I am politically opposed to any Administration, I shall not upon such narrow measures attempt to thwart its officers. I am willing to do for this Administration as much as though I politically coincided with them. I understand this to be the policy advocated by the last Administration, and introduced by the Secretary of the Treasury of the last Administration, which comes down to us through the last Congress, where our political opponents held the majority in the House of Representatives, and the same policy applied to every other department and every other expenditure.

Remarks of Jefferson Davis on the resolution of inquiry relative to the appointments by the President in California. Jan. 17, 1850.

Mr. CLEMENS. I am glad to hear the honorable Senator's statement. I am glad that this episode is happily ended; and to the honorable Senator from Mississippi I will take occasion to say that there is no man in this body for whom I have a more sincere respect or kinder feelings. He has, as he has a right to do, presumed on an acquaintance of long standing and many acts of kindness extended to me, to set me right, as he says, in this matter. I may not be right in saying that the entire body of the northern Democracy are against us, but I am not wrong in saying that there is not a Legislature, Democratic or Whig, north of Mason and Dixon's line, that has not instructed its Senators to do what the Legislature of my State has declared to be a cause for the dissolution of the Union.

Mr. DODGE, of Iowa. You are wrong. The Legislature of my State has never done it.

Mr. CLEMENS. I am glad that there are some of them who have not done so. But there are representatives here who do not need to be instructed. It is true, however, sir, that——

Mr. DAVIS, of Mississippi. Will my friend allow me to interpose a single remark?

Mr. CLEMENS. Certainly.

Mr. DAVIS. I would say, then, and I say it to him with the more confidence on account of the high regard I have for him, and the sympathy I have in his present position. I am myself subject to the same feelings of excitement, and especially on this subject. It is a subject on which we all feel, and feel deeply, and on which we are apt to speak strongly. But is it well to re-open the wounds which have already been inflicted in this sectional strife on the Union? Is it well to point to the wrong-doings of others, that they may recriminate on us, and widen the breach which already exists, and increase the danger which already threatens us? I ask my friend to calm himself, in order that his remarks may only be applicable to so much of this discussion as has a bearing on his position in connection with this resolution.

Mr. DAVIS, of Mississippi. The Senator is right. I inter-rupted the Senator just at the point when he was going into the proofs to show how far the Democracy of the North is in-fected with the spirit of abolitionism. What his conclusion would have been, therefore, he has a perfect right to say that no one can know. What proofs he intended to submit, it is impossible for any one to say. I trust, therefore, that advantage will not be taken, to comment upon the few remarks that the honorable Senator did submit in part, as he was induced to give way at that point for the very wholesome purpose of stopping an agita-tion which might lead to still more disagreeable consequences.

I am one of those who have seen northern Democrats stand firm under the most trying circumstances; and I admired them the more for the danger which I believe they encountered in their advocacy of our rights. The Senator from New York [Mr. DICKINSON] has come out more boldly to-day in the expres-sion of his opinions than ever before; and I venture to affirm, that never was he so poorly sustained at home as in the present crisis. I admire him the more that his courage rises the higher, the greater the danger which surrounds him. He expresses hopes which I trust will be fulfilled. I trust that the dangers which now threaten will be removed, and that the further discussion of this question will prove that he is not alone upon this floor.

The PRESIDING OFFICER, (interposing.) Does the Sen-ator from Louisiana [Mr. DOWNS] yield the floor?

Mr. DOWNS. For explanation.

Mr. DAVIS resumed. The Senator from New York has not been alone. Other Senators have been ready to sustain the Constitution, though they may have been against the institution in the abstract. They have frequently taken occasion to avow that although, as an abstract opinion, they were opposed to slavery, yet, in their legislative action, they were ready to stand by the Constitution. Nor is this confined entirely to our own party. Who does not remember the response of the Senator from Vermont, upon the discussion of the compromise bill, and how boldly he sustained the Constitution, notwithstanding the differences of his own private opinion? I must repeat, that it is my conviction that any remarks bringing out again the controversy in which the Senator from Alabama [Mr. CLEMENS] was arrested cannot be otherwise than injurious.

Jefferson Davis and Others to John A. Quitman

(From Mississippi Free Trader, Nov. 27, 1850.)

Washington, January 21, 1850.

His Excellency,

Jno. A. Quitman, Governor, &c, &c,:

Sir—We, the Senators and Representatives in Congress from Mississippi, feel it incumbent upon us to advise you and through you, our common constituents, that we have a well defined opinion, that California will be admitted as a State of this Union, during the present session of Congress. The President earnestly recommended it, and we cannot be mistaken, in supposing that a majority of both Houses of Congress will be found to vote for it—our individual positions have undergone no change. We regard the proposition to admit California as a State under all the circumstances of her application, as an attempt to adopt the "Wilmot proviso" in another form. But separated, as we are, from our constituents, and having no convenient means of consulting them as to their views on the new phase of this perplexing question, we desire, through you, to submit the single fact to the people and the legislature, that California will most likely obtain admission into the Union with her constitutional prohibition of slavery—and we beg leave to add, that we shall be greatly pleased to have such expression of opinion by the legislature, the Governor, and if practicable, by the people, as shall clearly indicate the course which Mississippi will deem it her duty to pursue in this emergency.

Very respectfully, your obedient servants,

(Signed)

Jeff. Davis,
H. S. Foote,
J. Thompson,
W. S. Featherston,
Wm. McWillie,
A. G. Brown.

*Remarks of Jefferson Davis on the reception of a petition against
the extention of slavery to the Territories. Feb. 12, 1850.*

Mr. DAVIS, of Mississippi. I will not detain the Senate long.
The Senator from Illinois has announced that he will prove that
there was a law in Mexico which prohibited slavery in Mexico,
and which is now in force, if that position be controverted. I
wish to give him notice that it is controverted; and I tell him
also that I wish to hear him prove it. I tell the Senator further,
that I spoke advisedly when I said that the abolition of slavery,
not its prohibition, rested on the decree of General Guerrero;
and I will also correct him in his date. It was not in the year
1834 or 1835, but in the year 1837, that Congress legislated, and
then they legislated by the first declaration that slavery was,
or literally remained abolished. The legislation was an admission of the force of the decree—not original legislation bearing
upon the subject. Nor was the legislation in this instance a
prohibition; and I give the Senator from Illinois notice of the
point upon which his position will be controverted, and I expect to hear him prove it.

Mr. MANGUM. Will the honorable Senator postpone the remainder of his remarks in order that the Senator from Georgia
may proceed?

Mr. DAVIS. I do not intend to detain the Senate long, and
certainly I will not trespass upon the honorable Senator from
Georgia more than a minute. I was going to say that the Senator
from Illinois declares that the statement which I made the other
day in the Senate, was a proposition to extend slavery by the
action of Congress into the Territories. It was no such thing.
It bears no such construction; and I was surprised that a
Senator on the other side should have endeavored to put that
construction upon it to sustain his argument. Our position
was from the beginning that the South had a right to go into
any Territories belonging to the United States with their slave
property. This is a right dependent on their joint ownership;
and I then stated, in the spirit of compromise, a desire not
to present any extreme claim, that that pretension would be continued, but insisted on beyond the line of 36° 30′, thus narrowing
down the claim which the South had made.

Nor, sir, was my language susceptible of any such misconstruction as an assertion that it was an irreversible perpetuation
of slavery anywhere; for every sane man knows that in whatever longitude or latitude in these United States a State may be

situated, such sovereign State can decide the matter for itself. A community dependent upon the United States—and of these many such have existed in our history—may not have power to legislate for itself. It is a sovereign State to which I concede that power. The very fact of dependence is against the supposition of such power as is claimed by the Senator from Illinois for territorial communities; while no sane man can deny that it exists in Massachusetts, in Maine, and in hyperborean regions if we had States there.

Speech of Jefferson Davis in Senate Feb. 13 and 14, 1850 on Slavery in the Territories.

The Senate having, as in Committee of the Whole, proceeded to the consideration of the resolutions submitted by Mr. CLAY on the subject of Slavery in the Territories—

Mr. DAVIS, of Mississippi, addressed the Senate as follows:
Mr. PRESIDENT: One of the greatest causes of the apprehension which fills my mind under the existing state of things, is the indifference and incredulity of those who represent the majority of the United States. Yet from every quarter of this broad Union come daily evidences of the excitement which is felt, of the gathering storm which threatens to break upon us. That this Senate chamber should be crowded, that the galleries should be filled, and admittance be sought upon the floor, when men of high national reputation address the Senate, should not surprise any one. But when it is repeated on such an occasion like this, when it must be the cause, and not the advocate, that attracts the multitude, it is time that all should feel there is that within the breasts of the people which claims the attention of the Legislature.

When the honorable Senator from Kentucky [Mr. CLAY] introduced the resolutions now under discussion, I thought it my duty to present my views of what I considered injustice to those whom I represent, and to offer some opposition to the dangerous doctrines which I believed he then presented. Whether it was impatience at finding any of his opinions controverted, or whether it was that he sought an adversary so feeble as to secure an easy victory, I know not, and it matters not to me. He challenged me to this discussion whenever I was ready. I was ready then, and meet him now. It has been postponed at his option, and not mine; and that, when he prepared and delivered his speech before the Senate, I did not immediately follow him, was because I could not obtain the floor. I now come to lift the glove he then threw down, and trust in the justice of the cause in which I stand.

The country has been induced to expect—and notwithstanding all previous evidence against it, even I had cherished the hope— that the great power of that Senator, and his known influence in the country, would have been exerted in a crisis so dangerous as this, with the high and holy purpose of preserving the Union. I had hoped from him a compromise that would have contained the spirit of that which, in another dangerous period in the history of this country, brought calm and sunshine, instead of the gloom which then lowered over us. In this hope I have been disappointed—grievously disappointed by the character of the resolutions which he has introduced, and yet more grievously disappointed in the remarks by which they were prefaced. If that great power and influence to which I have alluded, and that eloquence upon which multitudes have hung entranced, and remembered only to admire, had now been exerted in the cause of the weak against the strong, the cause of the Constitution against its aggressors, the evils by which we are surrounded might perhaps have been removed, and the decline of that Senator's sun been even more bright than its meridian glory. But, instead of this, he has chosen to throw his influence into the scale of the preponderating aggressive majority, and in so doing vehemently to assert his undisputed right to express his opinions fearless of all mankind. Why, sir, there was nothing to apprehend, and I presume no one will dispute the right of the Senator to advance his opinions in any decorous language he might choose.

Mr. President, my feelings and my duties run in the same channel. My convictions of what is necessary to preserve the Union correspond with my opinions in relation to the local and peculiar interests which I particularly represent. I have therefore no sacrifices to make, unless it be that personal sacrifice I make in appearing under circumstances like those which now surround me.

The greater part of the Senator's argument has been directed against the right of the southern States to that equality of enjoyment in the Territories to which they assert they are entitled. He has rebuked the spirit of abolitionism as the evil of the country, but, in doing so, instead of describing it as a factious, disorganizing, revolutionary spirit, he has only spoken of it as the offspring of party, the result of passion. Now, Mr.

President, I contend that the reverse is true. I contend that it is the want of party which has built up this faction and rendered it dangerous; that so long as party organization preserved its integrity, there was no place for a third party, and no danger from it. If this were merely the result of passion, I should then have hopes which I cannot now cherish. If it were the mere outbreak of violence, I should see some prospect for its subsidence. But considering it, as I do, the cold, calculating purpose of those who seek for sectional dominion, I see nothing short of conquest on the one side, or submission on the other. This is the great danger which hangs over us—not passion—not party; but the settled, selfish purpose which alone can sustain and probably will not abandon the movement. That upon which it originally rested has long since passed away. It is no longer the clamor of a noisy fanaticism, but the steady advance of a self-sustaining power to the goal of unlimited supremacy. This is the crevasse which the Senator described—a crevasse which he figuratively says is threatening submersion to the whole estate, while the owners are quarreling about the division of the profits. Yes, sir, a moral crevasse has occurred; fanaticism and ignorance—political rivalry—sectional hate—strife for sectional dominion, have accumulated into a mighty flood, and pour their turgid waters through the broken constitution, threatening not total submersion, but only the destruction of a part of the estate—that part in which my constituency, as well as that of the Senator, is found.

What, then, under such circumstances as these, does the Senator propose as a remedy? Does he call all the parties to check the breach which threatens danger to one? Does he lend his own hand to arrest the progress of the flood? No. He comes here, representing those southern interests which are at stake, surrenders the whole claim of the South, and gives a support to abolitionism which no northern man—no, nor every northern man in the Senate—could have afforded. However much we may regret, our surprise must be limited by the recollection that we had some cause to anticipate this. The public press had given us last summer a letter from him, addressed to the Abolitionists of Ohio—a man most notorious among them being upon the committee—in which that very ordinance of 1787 was treated as a great blessing and slavery as a curse. The representatives of the South have never sought to violate that compromise or concession, whatever it may be called, that was made in 1787. The representatives of the South have not entered into arguments upon the blessings and evils of slavery. They have said, from time to time, that it was a domestic institution; that it was under their own control; and that they claimed for it only the protection which the Constitution accords to every other species of property. Less than that they can never take, unless they are willing to become an inferior class, a degraded caste in the Union.

A large part of the non-slaveholding States have declared war against the institution of slavery. They have announced that it shall not be extended, and with that annunciation have coupled the declaration that it is a stain upon the Republic— that it is a moral blot which should be obliterated. Now, sir, can any one believe, does any one hope, that the southern States in this Confederacy will continue, as in times gone by, to support the Union, to bear its burdens, in peace and in war, in a degree disproportioned to their numbers, if that very Government is to be arrayed in hostility against an institution so interwoven with its interests, its domestic peace, and all its social relations, that it cannot be disturbed without causing their overthrow? This Government is the agent of all of the States; can it be expected of any of them that they will consent to be bound by its acts, when that agent announces the settled purpose in the exercise of its power to overthrow that which it was its duty to uphold? That obligation ceases whenever such a construction shall be placed upon its power by the Federal Government. The essential purpose for which the grant was made being disregarded, the means given for defence being perverted to assault, State allegiance thenceforward resumes its right to demand the service, the whole service, of all its citizens.

The claim is set up for the Federal Government not only to restrict slavery from entering the Territories, but to abolish slavery in the District of Columbia, to abolish it in the arsenals and dockyards, to withdraw from it the protection of the American flag wherever it is found upon the high seas; in fact, to strip it of every protection it derives from Government. All this under the pretext that property in slaves is local in its nature, and derives its existence from municipal law. Slavery existed before the formation of this Union. It derived from the Constitution that recognition which it would not have enjoyed without the confederation. If the States had not united together, there would have been no obligation on adjoining States to regard any species of property unknown to themselves. But it was one of the compromises of the Constitution that the slave property in the southern States should be recognized as property throughout the United States. It was so recognized in the obligation to restore fugitives—recognized in the power to tax them as persons—recognized in their representation in the halls of Congress. As a property recognized by the Constitution, and held in a portion of the States, the Federal Government is bound to admit it into all the Territories, and to give it such protection as other private property receives.

I do not propose to follow the argument of the Senator from Georgia, [Mr. BERRIEN.] I will not mar its beauty or weaken its force by anything which I can say. I believe that his argument upon that point was so conclusive, as to require no addition, if I had the power to make it. It becomes us, it becomes you—all who seek to preserve this Union, and to render it perpetual—to ask, why is this power claimed? Why is its exercise sought? Why is this resolution to obstruct the extension of slavery into the Territories introduced? It must be for the purpose of political power; it can have no other rational object. Every one must understand that, whatever be the evil of slavery, it is not increased by its diffusion. Every one familiar with it knows that it is in proportion to its sparseness that it becomes less objectionable. Wherever there is an immediate connection between the master and slave, whatever there is of harshness in the system is diminished. Then it preserves the domestic character, and strictly patriarchal relation. It is only when the slaves are assembled in large numbers, on plantations, and are removed from the interested, the kind, the affectionate care of the master, that it ever can partake of that cruelty which is made the great charge against it by those who know nothing of it, and which, I will passingly say, probably exists to a smaller extent than in any other relation of labor to capital. It is, then, for the purpose of political power; and can those who, in violation of constitutional rights, seek and acquire political power, which, in progress of time, will give them the ability to change the Constitution of the United States, be supposed just then to be seized with a feeling of magnanimity and justice, which will prevent them from using the power which they thus corruptly sought and obtained? Man, Mr. President, may become corrupted by the possession of power; he may seek it for pure motives, and be corrupted by its exercise. The reverse of this all history and all reason deny.

Warned by the delusive compromises of the past, we are stimulated by the dangers which surround us to look forward to the issue that has been suggested as the ultimate end—to the day when the power to remodel the Constitution, being possessed, will be exercised; and, therefore, the men of the present

generation are called upon to meet it; they have no right to postpone to posterity the danger which is laid at their own doors;
ours is the responsibility, and upon us devolves the duty of deciding the issue. If, sir, I represented a northern State, however
much it might be opposed to the institution of slavery, I feel
that I should say to my constituents, without a balance of power
such as will enable every interest to protect itself—without such
checks and such restraints as can never exist where any one section is paramount to all others—that the great purposes of this
Union could never be preserved, the Confederacy must be short-
lived, and PERISH by the destruction of the principles upon
which it was founded. That, for such reasons, under the case-
supposed, I would as now, oppose a policy which, if it confer a
temporary benefit on one, must end in the permanent injury
of all.

I believe, Mr. President, it is essential that neither section
should have such power in Congress as would render them able
to trample upon the rights of the other section of this Union. It
would be a blessing, an essential means to preserve the Confederacy, that in one branch of Congress the North and in the
other the South should have a majority of representation. Ours
is but a limited agency. We have but few powers, and those
are of a general nature; and, if legislation was restricted and
balanced in the mode I have suggested, Congress would never
be able to encroach upon the rights and institutions of any portion of the Union, nor could its acts ever meet with resistance
from any part of it. The reverse being the case, who knows
how soon the time may come when men will rise in arms to oppose the laws of Congress? Whenever you take from the people
of this country the confidence that this is their Government, that
it reflects their will, that it looks to their interests, the foundation upon which it was laid is destroyed, and the fabric falls to
the ground. More emphatically in this than in any other—
though it was said by the great Emperor of Europe to be true of
all—does this Government depend upon the consent of the
people. So emphatically is it true, that the laws of Congress
could not be executed in any one State of this Union if that
State was resolved to resist it. So entirely is this the case,
that, whatever law may be passed at this session—and I perceive
a disposition on all sides to pass one for the recovery of fugitive
slaves—I feel that that law will be a dead letter in any State
where the popular opinion is opposed to such rendition. I would
sooner trust it to-day to the sense of constitutional obligations
of the States than to the enforcement of any law which Con-

gress can enact against the popular opinion of those among whom it is executed. I have never expected any benefit to result to us from this species of legislation. I believe upon this, as upon every other subject, that we must rely more on the patriotism, the good sense, and morality of the people, than upon any tribunal to preserve the rights of the southern States. I have said elsewhere, and where there was none to represent them, that I believed, if the wrongs and injuries heaped upon the South were understood by the great body of the people at the North, the whole conduct of their politicians would be rebuked, and peace and harmony would be restored. But, sir, it is the evil of the time in which we live, that the responsibilities which rest upon us—the responsibilities of our day—are sought to be transferred to another. It is the misfortune of the country that men, instead of meeting issues, shrink from them, and, instead of relying upon the sober second thought of the people, are waving to and fro, like reeds before the wind, to the pressure of every popular impulse. We have high and holy duties to perform—duties of which we are wholly unworthy, unless every man here is ready to hazard his political life for the maintenance of those principles which he has sworn to uphold and to preserve.

But, Mr. President, it is my purpose, and I am sorry, even for one moment, to have diverged from it, calmly and briefly to direct my attention to the main argument of the Senator from Kentucky. I claim, sir, that slavery being property in the United States, and so recognized by the Constitution, a slaveholder has the right to go with that property into any part of the United States where some sovereign power has not forbidden it. I deny sir, that this Government has the sovereign power to prohibit it from the Territories. I deny that any territorial community, being a dependence of the United States, has that power, or can prohibit it, and therefore my claim presented is this, that the slaveholder has a right to go with his slave into any portion of these United States, except in a State where the fundamental law has forbidden it. I know, sir, that the popular doctrine obtains, that every community has that power; and I was sorry to hear the Senator from Kentucky, in some portion of his speech, assent to it, though in others he did oppose it. Who constitute the communities which are to exercise sovereign rights over the Territories? Those who, in the race for newly-acquired regions, may first get there. By what right sir, do they claim to exercise it? The Territories belong to the United States, and by the States only can sovereignty be alienated. If a mass of persons, sufficiently great to seize upon one of the Territories of the United States, should, by a revolution, wrest it from us, then they would have sovereignty, and could establish any fundamental laws they chose; but until that high act of revolution is performed, it will not cease, save by their consent, to be a Territory belonging to the United States. The sovereignty rests in the States, and there is no power, save that of the States, which can exclude any property, or can determine what is property, in the Territories so held by the States in common. That power the States have not delegated; it can be exercised rightfully only by compact or agreement of the States. It is, therefore, that I have held and hold that the Missouri compromise derived its validity from the acquiescence of the States, and not from the act of Congress.

The General Government has, as agent, to dispose of the public lands, the power necessary to execute that trust. How far this extends it may not be very easy by fixed standard to determine, but it is easy to perceive that this cannot give sovereignty, or any other than the subordinate functions of government. The Senator from Kentucky, however, claims this from the clause which gives to Congress the power to dispose of and make "needful rules and regulations" for the territory and other property of the United States. I admired his ingenuity when he said Territories. "Territories" is not the phrase of the Constitution; it is "territory," and that territory was the common domain of the United States. That territory—public land—lies within as well as without the limits of the States of the Union. Every new State has been admitted with territory recognized as the property of the United States.

The territory held by the old States was transferred to the United States as a common property. Out of this territory new States have been formed, and the unsold land in these States is still held as the territory of the United States. Does this power, then, to dispose of that territory within the State of Mississippi, for instance, confer upon Congress the sovereignty enabling it to decide what property shall go upon that land, and what shall be the relation of persons subsisting upon it? And if it be not a good argument for a quarter section, or a half section, or a township, it is not good for the vast extent of border which we have upon the Pacific Ocean. It is a power over property, and over property merely. Fully to exercise this will require, where there is no government, that some organization shall be made. Since that has been argued, and so ably argued, by the Senator from Michigan, [Mr. CASS,] it may not need further remark. I regret, however, that I am not able to agree with the whole of the argument of that distinguished Senator. His position and argument carries me to the point where any number of individuals, however small, however unauthorized, may assert that sovereignty which I hold to reside only in the States of this Union. This vagrant power to govern the Territories, located by some in one place, and by others in another, has never been drawn from a source which could not be controverted, except one. That, sir, is the right which the people inhabiting the Territory have to throw off their dependency upon this Government, and to establish a sovereign State by the right of revolution. My argument goes only to the condition of those Territories and those communities, while they are a part of the United States. If the Senator from Michigan, when he asserts the powers of sovereignty to rest in the people of the Territory, and to be derived from Almighty God, means thus to assert as inalienable the right of revolution, and to draw this power from that source, then I agree with him entirely.

It is also, and by very high authority, attempted to draw the right to govern Territories from the treaty-making power. That power does not rest in Congress. It is not a function of the General Government. The treaty-making power vests in the President and in the Senate—the one to negotiate, the other to ratify and confirm. If it is drawn from the treaty-making power, and belongs to that, or grows out of it, then it belongs to the President and the Senate, and not to Congress. The treaty-making power is the means which has been and may be legitimately used to acquire territory; but when it has been acquired, the transferred property is under all the conditions of the Constitution. It is then to be governed according to its principles. It matters not how it was obtained. The Constitution is supreme over it, and there can be no paramount law. The Constitution is the bond between the States—the agreement by which they act in concert. No power can be exercised by any department of this Government, and least of all by its legislative department, which is not derived from that source.

But the Senator from Kentucky did not stop here. If he had paused at this controverted point—if he had only asserted that the Constitution gave power at one place or another—it would not have presented the dangerous aspect it wears in this discussion. But he goes further. He declares—and his position, his high name, may do us great injury by the declaration—that slavery does not exist, that it is interdicted by the law from the Territories acquired from Mexico; and, moreover, that it is excluded by a decree of nature, and of nature's God, from the land. The Senator quoted no law. He referred to a date when there was no law. Upon the point of prohibition I took issue with him, and upon that point I propose to present the proof. I have here, sir, the act of 1824, the decree of 1829, and the act of 1837, in the original language, which, I believe, are all that can be found of action of the Mexican Government, upon that subject; and, by one competent for the purpose, I have had them translated. The act of 1824, is for the prohibition of the traffic in slaves. It declares:

"DECREE OF THE 13TH JULY, 1824.

"*Prohibition by Congress of the Traffic in Slaves.*

"The Sovereign Constituent Congress of the United States of Mexico has thought it proper to decree as follows:
"1. The commerce or traffic in slaves is forever prohibited in the territory of the United States of Mexico, under whatever flag, and coming from whatever Power, (or country.)
"2. Slaves which shall be introduced against the tenor of the foregoing article are free, from the single fact of treading the *territory* of Mexico.
"3. Any vessel, whether national or foreign, in which slaves shall be introduced, shall be irreversibly forfeited, with all its cargo; and the owner, supercargo, captain, master, and pilots, shall suffer the punishment of ten years' imprisonment.
"4. This decree shall have effect from the very day of its publication. But, as to the penalties prescribed in the foregoing article, it shall not have such effect for six months, with reference to the colonists who, in virtue of the law of the 14th October last, as to the colonization of the isthmus of Gonzacoalcos, disembarked slaves for the purpose of introducing them into Mexican territory."

This was a prohibition against taking slaves into California and New Mexico from the United States, while those Territories belonged to the Mexican Republic. This is the only case in which a permanency is declared for the policy avowed, is the only prohibition, and it is now clearly inoperative. Next is the decree of 1829, the decree of a usurper—passed not by forms of law, but in violation of them. It declares:

"15TH DAY OF APRIL, 1829.

"Decree of the Government, in virtue of Extraordinary Powers. Abolition of Slavery in the Republic.

"1. Slavery is (or literally remains) abolished in the republic.

"2. Those are consequently free who were heretofore considered as slaves.

"3. When the condition of the Treasury admits of it, the proprietors of slaves will be indemnified in a manner to be settled by the laws."

That decree was not executed. That some proprietors lost their slaves is not doubted; but that it was not fully executed is clear; from the fact that, in 1837, legislation occurred to carry out the object of the decree:

"5TH DAY, APRIL 4, 1837.

"Law.

"Slavery is (or literally remains) abolished in the republic, without any exception whatever.

"1. Slavery is (or literally remains) abolished, without any exception, in all the republic.

"2. The owners of slaves manumitted by the present law, or by the decree of the 15th September, 1829, (summary of that month, page 2,137,) will be indemnified for the value of the same; this value to be estimated by the valuation of their personal qualities; for which purpose a judge will be named by commissary general, or his representative, and another by the owner, and in case of disagreement, a third, named by the proper constitutional *alcalde,* without interposition of appeal of any kind from this decision. The indemnification of which this article speaks will not be effective as regards the emigrants of Texas that may have taken a part in the revolution of that department.

"3. The same owners to whom will be given gratis the original documents of the valuation referred to in the anterior article will present them to the Supreme Government, who will ordain that the general treasury issue the corresponding bonds for value of the respective amounts.

"The payment of said bonds will take place in the manner which the Government may judge most equitable, conciliating the rights of individuals with the actual state of the public funds."

Here it will be seen, by comparison, that when perpetuity is
intended, a distinct expression is used, as in the act of 1824—
para siempre, forever; this is not found in the abolition decree or
act of Congress. How, therefore, do gentlemen learn the intent,
and how will they proceed to give the stamp of eternal to the
act of a government which furnishes annual revolutions?

This law was never carried out. So far as I have been able to
learn, the appraisement, which was a part of the law, with which
it was to go into effect, was never made, nor in any manner compensation rendered. More, sir; so far as I have been able to
learn, this decree for the abolition of slavery, and the act of
1837, were both in violation of the wishes of the States and
individuals particularly concerned. It was enacted against
their will, by usurpation of power, first on the part of the
Dictator, and secondly on the part of the Mexican Congress.

We have, in our practice and in our principles of government, nothing which can be considered as a parallel to a dictator,
as known in the history of Mexico. The nearest parallel which
I can imagine is, to suppose that in a period of invasion and
imminently great danger, martial law should be declared over
the whole United States. Suppose, in that case, that the Executive of the United States, vested with extraordinary power,
should decree that slavery was abolished throughout the United
States by virtue of the powers which he held under martial
law, does anybody believe it would be submitted to? Will any
man contend that such a decree would have the validity of law
in this Union? Will any man contend that if a future Congress
should legislate in conformity thereto, and to compensate those
who had lost their slaves under such a decree, the owner would
be thereby compelled to submit to the decree? Or does any man
believe that even if the right were conceded to our Congress
to pass an emancipation act, providing that the slaves should
be liberated by paying for them, the passage of such an act
would be obligatory upon the owners before the compensation
was made? All these points failed in the Mexican case. So far,
then, as I can view this case, with my notions of constitutional
construction, it was void in the beginning, and remained void
to the end.

But suppose it was a law. However informal the enactment,
that supposition may be made from the fact that slavery did
not exist in Mexico at the time we acquired the territory. Suppose it be conceded that by law it was abolished—could that
law be perpetual?—could it extend to the territory after it became the property of the United States? Did we admit terri-

tory from Mexico subject to the constitution and laws of Mexico? Did we pay fifteen millions of dollars for jurisdiction over California and New Mexico, that it might be held subordinate to the law of Mexico? In the discussion upon that treaty by which we acquired the territory; it was a very general opinion that we should get jurisdiction, and jurisdiction alone; that all the land would be found to be covered by grants which had become valid, so that we should not get public domain. Under the present construction, it seems that we did not get jurisdiction either.

The argument made here and elsewhere for the continuance of the laws of Mexico is drawn from the laws of nations in relation to a conquered territory. I do not intend to go into that discussion. It is gratifying to every one, and marks the progress of civilization, to observe step after step taken to soften the rigors of war, and to ameliorate the condition of the subjugated. But, sir, this is not a conquest. This people came not to us as a conquered race. We acquired the territory by purchase and treaty, and we got from Mexico only that which she was willing to sell. The negotiation of the treaty shows that our commissioner endeavored even to get a small strip off from Sonora, and was refused upon the ground that they would not interfere with the limits of a State. They sold us that which they were willing to part from; and whatever it was worth to us, we paid them much more than it was worth to them.

It is not to the law of nations, it is not to the moral feeling of the age, in relation to a conquered people, that we are to look. It is to the treaty, to the terms of the treaty, and to the principles of the Constitution of the United States. Of the two articles—the 8th and 9th—the one secures all the rights of property to the Mexicans in the territory at the time of its acquisition; the other guaranties a further admission to the rights of citizenship:

"ARTICLE VIII.—Mexicans now established in territories previously belonging to Mexico, and which remain for the future within the limits of the United States, as defined by the present treaty, shall be free to continue where they now reside, or to remove at any time to the Mexican republic, retaining the property which they possess in the said territories, or disposing thereof, and removing the proceeds wherever they please, without their being subjected on this account to any contribution, tax, or charge whatever. Those who shall prefer to remain in the said territories, may either retain the title and rights of Mexican citizens, or acquire those of citizens of the United States. But they shall be under the obligation to make their election within one year from the date of exchange of ratification of this treaty; and those who shall remain in the said territories after the expiration of that year, without having declared their intention to retain the character of Mexicans, shall be considered to have elected to become citizens of the United States.

"ARTICLE IX.—The Mexicans who, in the territories aforesaid, shall not preserve the character of citizens of the Mexican republic, conformably with what is stipulated in the preceding article, shall be incorporated into the Union of the United States, and be admitted at the proper time (to be judged of by the Congress of the United States) to the enjoyment of all the rights of citizens of the United States, according to the principles of the Constitution; and in the mean time shall be maintained and protected in the free enjoyment of their liberty and property, and secured in the free exercise of their religion without restriction."

The Commissioners of Mexico had no idea that they were, by treaty, transferring their law abolishing slavery into the United States. They had no conception that we were to be bound by the edicts and statutes of Mexico. And certainly if such an idea had been entertained by the Senate, it could not have been sanctioned by two-thirds of them. But this is not left undecided, or to mere speculation. This question was brought up in the discussion between the Commissioners, and it will be found, by a letter directed to the then Secretary of State (the Hon. Jas. Buchanan) by our agent, Mr. Trist, dated at Tacubaya, February 4, 1847, that the Mexican Commissioners pressed this point, the continuation of their law for the exclusion of slavery, upon Mr. Trist, in the earnest language which was read by the Senator from Kentucky.

But the Senator did not read all that was said in reply to the Mexican Commissioners. I believe it appears in his revised speech. After telling them that such a proposition could not be entertained, Mr. Trist says:

"I concluded by assuring them that the bare *mention* of the subject in any treaty to which the United States were a party was an absolute impossibility; that no President of the United States would dare to present any such treaty to the Senate; and that, if it were in their power to offer me the whole territory described in our project, increased tenfold in value, and, in addition that, covered a foot thick over with pure gold, upon the single condition that slavery should be excluded therefrom,

I could not entertain the offer for a moment, nor think even of communicating it to Washington. The matter ended in their being fully satisfied that this topic was one not to be touched, and it was dropped with good feeling on both sides.''

Then, sir, the people of Mexico cannot expect that their law shall be recognized by our Government. The Commissioner of the United States rejected the proposition as one which could not be entertained.

With this state of facts, the Senate have ratified the treaty. Under the belief that the Constitution of the United States covers all the territory which belongs to the States, under the conviction that the Supreme Court of the United States, sitting in judgment under the Constitution, would sustain us in such rights, we have tried to organize Territorial Governments; we have tried to transfer this question from Congress to the Supreme Court of the United States; we have asked for the establishment of district courts in California, for the simple admission that the Constitution of the United States prevailed over that country, in order to wring from those who opposed our rights under it, some opportunity to test them legally. After all this, and when Congressional agitation has prevailed to prevent the slaveholder from migrating with his property, and sharing in the determination of the fundamental law, we are now told, with patronizing air, that we ought not to object since we have not been prohibited from participation in the Territories by Congress, and that in the case of California we are bound to accept such terms as the inhabitants of the Territory possessing it, under such circumstances, shall think fit to dictate to us. That the will of the conglomerated mass of gold-hunters, foreign and native, is to be taken as the decree of nature, and to be held authoritative for the exclusion of citizens of the United States from equal privileges which the Constitution declares, and was established to secure.

Why, sir, what choice is there between this and the Wilmot proviso? I, for one, would prefer the Wilmot proviso. I demur, sir, after the House had killed the Wilmot proviso, against any claim to a dukedom for him who brings the lifeless corpse into the Senate. I will not agree to grant it, even under the threat of being left to kill all future Percys, without the aid of the knight who found the body by the wayside; least of all, have I any thanks to return to the Senator from Illinois, for the ground which he says he has assumed among his constituents in opposing the Wilmot proviso; that it had no application, because, slavery being already excluded from the Territories, it was wholly unnecessary to prohibit it by new enactment.

Sir, I prefer the Wilmot proviso to that position; I prefer it, because the advocate of the Wilmot proviso attempts to rob me of my rights, whilst acknowledging them, by the admission that it requires legislation to deprive me of them. The other denies their existence.

Mr. DOUGLAS, (interposing.) Mr. President, I do not know what is the intention of the Senator in bringing me into his speech. I am not aware——

Mr. DAVIS. I alluded to the position which you assumed in debate yesterday, for the purpose of answering it.

Mr. DOUGLAS. I stated then, as I have always stated, and as I state now, that I am opposed to the Wilmot proviso, because, in my judgment, it violates a fundamental principle of free government—that all people have the right, derived from God himself, to regulate their own institutions as they see fit.

Mr. DAVIS. If the Senator had been understood by me on that occasion as I understand him now—that he was opposed to the Wilmot proviso because it violated a fundamental principle of our government—I should not have alluded to him.

Mr. DOUGLAS. You will find it so reported in both the journals which report officially for the Senate.

Mr. DAVIS. I did not mean to doubt it, sir. I am always prepared to admit that I am mistaken when a Senator corrects me, in quoting from what he has said. I always permit him or any other gentleman to correct me, when I am stating what his position is, or what I had supposed it to be. I should as soon thing of disputing with him upon the pronunciation of his own name. I presume, of course, that he is right, and I am wrong. And even if he had presented the subject as I thought, and meant to say anything else, his explanation is good with me; the intent, the idea of the speaker, not the language, being that which is valuable. I, perhaps, more readily so understood the Senator from Illinois, because such positions had been taken by the Senator from Kentucky. I think that his earnest, even solemn appeal to the North not to impose the Wilmot proviso, rested solely upon the ground that there was no necessity for it, the exclusion being already complete. If our rights are to be taken away from us, if slavery is excluded from the Territories —and the Wilmot proviso is only intended to exclude slavery— I do think that the honorable Senator from Kentucky presented to the North quite a sufficient argument for not passing that measure. He asks them, for the sake of concord and harmony, for the sake of preserving the Union, to forbear from passing a law for an object and upon a subject which is, according to him, already covered by enactment just as effectual for the purpose intended as that which he asks them to abandon. They must be very unreasonable, if they persist, under such circumstances, in a course of legislation so perilous and so unnecessary; and, I think they might, for a less consideration than the preservation of the Union, consent to a sacrifice which would cost absolutely nothing.

The Senator from Kentucky has not only spoken repeatedly of these resolutions as resolutions of mutual concession, but on one occasion at least he spoke of them as concessions in which the North yields to the South far more than she receives. Where is the concession to the South? Is it in the admission, as a State, of California, from which we have been excluded by Congressional agitation? Is it in the announcement that slavery does not and is not to exist in the remaining Territories of New Mexico and California? Is it in denying the title of Texas to one-half of her territory? Is it in insulting her by speculating upon her supposed necessities, and offering her a sum of money in consideration of a surrender of a portion of her territory? Is it by declaring that it is inexpedient to abolish slavery in the District of Columbia, unless this Federal Government make compensation to the owners of the slaves—a class of property with which this Government has nothing more to do than with any other? Or is it in another condition which places the property of the owner at the mercy of the wayfarer, that is unless consent is obtained from the District, which can doubtless be obtained at some early day, through the great numbers of agents and office-holders the North gives annually to this city as temporary residents? Is this, or either of these propositions, a concession to the South? Are we to fill the Treasury, in order that it may be emptied for the purposes of abolition? Is that one of the purposes for which we submit to taxation, direct or indirect? Can money be appropriated from the Treasury for any other than those purposes indicated in the Constitution? And was this Constitution formed for the purpose of emancipation? Sir, it seems to me that this is a question which gives its own solution—needs no answer.

All property is best managed where Governments least interfere, and the practice of our Government has been generally founded on that principle. What has been the progress of emancipation throughout the whole history of our country? It has been the pressure of free labor upon the less profitable slave labor, until the slaves were transferred to sparser regions, and their number, by such transfer, was reduced to a limit at which, without inconvenience or danger, or serious loss, emancipation of the few who remained might occur. If this Federal Government had been invested with a trusteeship to take charge of the negroes of the United States, and provide for their emancipation, then I would admit that appropriations of money might be made out of the Treasury for purposes of abolition in the District of Columbia, but not otherwise.

But, sir, is it true that the State of Maryland alone has any interest in this question? Is it true that there is no implied faith towards other States than Maryland not to disturb this question? The citizens of other States who helped to build up this capital and these public edifices expected it to be neutral ground, upon which they might all come with their rights equally recognized, each as in the different sections of the Union. Was there no implied faith to them? Should we stand upon an equal footing? in this District, the common property of the several States, if slavery were abolished and the southern man were not permitted to bring with him a species of domestics to which he is accustomed and attached, and which are therefore necessary to him? Would he have the same privileges in this District as those who have domestics of another sort? If not, then I say it ceases to be the common property of the United States, in which the citizens of every State have equal privileges.

I will now, sir, in this connection—because it is so much more pointed than anything which I could offer on the subject—refer to the remarks made by the honorable Senator from Kentucky, when formerly a member of this body, upon this very subject, the abolition of slavery in the District of Columbia. He then said:

"The following is the provision of the Constitution of the United States, in reference to this matter:

" 'To exercise exclusive legislation in all cases whatsoever over such District (not exceeding ten miles square) as may by cession of particular States, and the acceptance of Congress, become the seat of Government of the United States.'

"This provision preceded, in point of time, the actual cessions which were made by the States of Maryland and Virginia. The object of the cession was to establish a seat of Government of the United States, and a grant in the Constitution of exclusive legislation must be understood, and should be always interpreted, as having relation to the object of the cession." *   *   *

"If it were necessary to the efficiency of this place as a seat of the General Government to abolish slavery, which is utterly denied, the abolition should be confined to the necessity which prompts it—that is, to the limits of the city of Washington itself. beyond those limits, persons concerned in the Government of the United States have no more to do with the inhabitants of the District, than they have with the inhabitants of the adjacent counties of Maryland and Virginia which lie beyond the District." * * * * * * * * *

"The grant in the case we are considering, of the territory of Columbia, was for a *seat of government.* Whatever power is necessary to accomplish that object is carried along by the grant. But the abolition of slavery is not necessary to the enjoyment of this site as a seat of the General Government. The grant in the Constitution of exclusive power of legislation over the District was made to ensure the exercise of an exclusive authority of the General Government to render this place a safe and secure seat of government, and to promote the well-being of the inhabitants of the District. The power granted ought to be interpreted and exercised solely to the end for which it was granted."

That I hold to be a more conclusive argument against, than the one which the Senator offered upon this occasion for, the power. We have no right to exercise any authority over the District of Columbia, except for those purposes for which it was ceded to the United States by the States to which it formerly belonged. Until the argument heretofore used is answered more effectively than on this occasion, it is perhaps unnecessary to disturb it. Sir, if the argument of the Senator that slavery was prohibited in Mexico, and that thereby it is prohibited in the Territories acquired from her, were good in relation to slavery, it must equally hold good with reference to some sixty articles of ordinary commerce prohibited by Mexican law. In a letter from the Secretary of the Treasury, March 30th, 1847, he states that about sixty articles of ordinary commerce are embraced in the acts of prohibition in Mexico, including many of the most common articles of trade, such as cotton and cotton fabrics, salt, tobacco, coarse woollen cloths, grain of all kinds, and most kinds of leather, and other manufactured articles. If the right of the slaveholder to migrate into the Territories, and to carry this species of property there, is prohibited by Mexican laws, so is the right of the ordinary trader to enter there with any of those sixty articles of commerce likewise prohibited, and the privilege which every citizen now freely exercises of free trade in the Territories does not exist of right. But the right of free trade throughout the United States is derived from the Constitution, and resulted necessarily and instantly from the transfer of the country to the United States. That right equally applies to the transfer of slave property from the domicil of the owner in any of the States to the same Territories; and the Mexican laws are no more in force on this subject than on the other.

But if I am told, by way of answer, that the revenue laws are extended over the Territories, I reply they are extended only by the authority of the Constitution. The Mexican law which abolished slavery had not the same validity—it had not the same formality—not the same binding force as those which prohibited these sixty enumerated articles of commerce. It was because the constitution overrode these prohibitory laws that free trade now exists. It is because the Constitution recognizes property in slaves, and secures equal privileges and immunities to all citizens of the United States, that we claim the abolition of slavery by Mexico to have died with the transfer of those territories to the United States. By the transfer of the territory, the sovereignty of Mexico was withdrawn; the sovereignty of the United States was immediately extended over the country and filled its place; a sovereignty to be measured by our Constitution, not by the policy of Mexico. But let us suppose that it had been referred to the Mexican people, whether they would more readily tolerate the introduction of free trade and of slavery or Protestantism within their boundaries, does any one doubt that they would say, Carry into California and New Mexico any or all of the sixty prohibited articles, and slavery likewise, but spare us the introduction of Protestantism? Does the established religion of Mexico remain in force, is Protestantism excluded from the Territories, or does the freedom of religious worship secured by our Constitution prevail over the land? I hope it will not be attempted to discriminate between the few and the many in cases of constitutional right; that the principles of our compact, sacred to the defence of the minority, will not be stretched and contracted as prejudice or interest may dictate.

The sovereignty of the United States refers to the Constitution. Upon that I am disposed to rest the rights of the South. But, sir, because, on a former occasion, I stated what I believed to be our constitutional rights, but that as there were two great antagonist principles in this country; the one claiming that slavery shall be excluded from all the Territories, and the other contending that slaveholders have a right to go with their property into all of the Territories, and as these two conflicting principles could not be reconciled, as compromise was only to be found in a division of the property, that I would consent to the establishment of a line, on one side of which one of these principles should prevail, and on the other side the other should be recognized—because I stated this, and because I suggested that this common territory, which it seems cannot be enjoyed in peace together, should be divided, I was charged with the desire to establish slavery where it does not now exist. I claimed as our existing right the privilege to go into all the territory, and said I would not recognize your right to exclude us from any portion of it; for one, I was willing to settle the controversy, and incur the hazard of taking the Missouri compromise line as a division, waiving the question of right. I would agree to any compromise adequate to the present crisis which equality and honor will permit. Now, sir, what was the case in the Missouri compromise? That was all slave territory; and to be divided between the slaveholding and non-slaveholding States, it merely required a line to be drawn, and prohibition to be attached to that part which was assigned to the non-slaveholding interest. So in the case of Texas, with the exception that, as the territory was covered by the jurisdiction of a sovereign State, the prohibition could only take effect after Texas withdrew her sovereignty from the part so provided for.

Mr. President, in all the controversy which has arisen about the validity and extent of the Mexican law, no species of property has ever been denied the right to enter the territory we have acquired, except slaves. Why is this? What is there in the character of that property which excludes it from the general benefit of the principles applied to all other property? It is true that gentlemen have asserted that this is local, and depends upon the laws of the States in which it exists; that is was established by municipal regulations. But gentlemen must understand that this slave property, like all other, is not the creation of statute, it is regulated by law like other tenures and relations of society, but like other property, must have existed before laws were passed concerning it; like other property, resulted from the dominion of mind over matter, and, more distinctly than most other species of property, is traced back to the remotest period of antiquity. Following up the stream of time, as far as history will guide us, we find there, in the earliest stage of society, slavery existing, and legislated upon as an established institution. And wherever the hieroglyphics of Egypt have been deciphered, and have told the history of ages not otherwise recorded, they show that the Ethiopian, so far as he has been traced, has been found in the condition of bondage. This kind of property was not established here by law, nor did it originate here. It came into the colonies as all other property, subject to the common law which then governed them; and from time to time laws have been passed to regulate it, but never to establish it. No law has ever been passed to make a freeman a slave, save that which imposes involuntary servitude as a punishment for crimes. Slaves were purchased upon the coast of Africa, and brought to the colonies of the United States, in their earliest history. Those colonies resisted such importations, yet the mother country continued it because it was profitable to her commerce; and after this Union was formed, those States which now insist upon restricting slavery—now most vociferous for abolition—were the same that extended the period to which slaves were introduced into the United States; the same that postponed the date when the custom-house officers of the United States should be required to execute the laws of Virginia, to prevent the further introduction of negroes and mulattoes from the West Indies. Yes, it was northern men who rebuked Mr. Randolph for speaking of the high powers which Virginia might exercise, if the Federal Government should not require her custom-house officers to aid in the execution of that law. This property, after it had ceased to be connected with the slave trade, and no longer served to employ shipping and gratify the avarice of those who had sustained the policy of that trade, became the subject of popular declamation; and those who grew rich in the traffic have been ever since making public demonstration of their horror of the crime, as they denominate slavery. It was, so far as our interest was involved, a sound, wise policy that abolished that trade, and I presume there is no man in the United States who would be willing to revive it.

The slave trade, however, so far as the African was concerned, was a blessing; it brought him from abject slavery and a barbarian master, and sold him into a Christian land. It brought him from a benighted region, and placed him in one where civilization would elevate and dignify his nature. It is a fact which history fully establishes, that through the portal of slavery alone, has the descendant of the graceless son of Noah ever entered the temple of civilization. Thus has been made manifest the inscrutable wisdom of the decree which made him a servant of servants. The slave trade has been the greatest source of permanent blessing to him. It has sent back a population possessed of an intelligence that would have never been reached in their own country. It has established that colony which, if anything can, may lead to the extinction of the slave trade. I say if anything can; for it is a notorious fact, that the slave trade has increased in proportion to the efforts made to destroy it. And the horrors of the traffic have increased in a still higher ratio; not only by the suffering which results from the necessity of using small vessels to escape the vigilance of the cruisers, but also by famine and disease caused by long delay on the coast, the result of difficulty in embarkation, under the watchful vigilance of the observing squadron. From like cause many of the slaves brought to the coast of Africa have been massacred by their barbarian masters. In 1846 the commander of the British ship Actæon wrote to the Secretary of the Admiralty that the native chief of Lagos caused upwards of two thousand of his slaves to be slaughtered. Let this speak to those who suppose that slavery begins with transportation, and that absolute power over the African is a thing peculiar to our continent. But, whatever be the curse or the blessings of the African slave trade, it is a thing which was never introduced or engaged in by the South, and one for which southern men never were and their descendants are not responsible. It is not our province to reply to any strictures which may be made upon it; it is odious among us now, as it was with our ancestors. We only defend the domestic institution of slavery as it exists in the United States; the extension of which into any new Territory will not increase the number of the slaves by one single person, but which it is very probable may, in many instances, produce emancipation. If, during the early settlement of a country, slaves are permitted to enter, the excess of demand over supply of labor will no doubt cause their introduction; but if it prove to be one in which climate and soil are both opposed to their use, then the population of the States which may be erected there, will as certainly decree emancipation, as the same causes produced the emancipation of slavery in any of the northeastern States. It is not, then, for the purpose of emancipation or for the benefit of the slaves that it is sought to restrict it; no, sir, quite otherwise; for it will be remembered that, on the floor of the Senate, it was once avowed that the policy of the extension of slavery was opposed because it would be the means of multiplying their number by increasing their substantial comforts. Yes, sir, we were pointed to the statistics of the North to show that crime, and degradation, and poverty, drew in their train, as a natural result, a check to the increase, and indicated the final extinction of the free blacks resident in that section; and those who said this are the same who, with pretensions of philanthropy, of special regard for the African, are striving for abolition, and attacking the peace of the people with whom they live, and between whom and them exist relations as kind as those which exist between man and man in the ordinary relation of life.

But, sir, the Senator, after declaring that no earthly power could induce him to vote for the recognition of this right to introduce slaves into the territory of the United States, announced that the effort to claim the recognition of it was an effort to propagate slavery, and then, as though it were a convertible term, said to propagate wrong. I do not propose to discuss the justice or injustice of slavery as an abstract proposition; I occupy this seat for no such purpose. It is enough for me to know that here we are not called upon to legislate, either for its amelioration, or to fix the places in which it shall be held, and certainly have no power to abolish it. It is enough for me elsewhere to know, that it was established by decree of Almighty God, that it is sanctioned in the Bible, in both Testaments, from Genesis to Revelations; that it has existed in all ages; has been found among the people of the highest civilization, and in nations of the highest proficiency in the arts. It is enough, if this were not sufficient, to know that it existed in all the States of this Union at the period of the Confederacy, and in all but one at the adoption of this Constitution, and that in one-half of them it continues to exist at the present day. It does not follow, because he believes it demonstrable, that a southern man should enter into argument to justify the right to hold property of this character. Testimony might be produced to show that many blessings spring from it, in proportion to the evils that are so loudly denounced as an inherent part of it. But I ask of those who entertain opinions opposite to mine, is it well to denounce an evil for which there is no cure? Why not denounce criminal laws, declaim against disease, pain, or poverty, as wrong? There are many evils in the condition of man which we would be glad to remedy; but, not being able, we permit them to exist as less than those which would follow an interference with them.

The abolition of slavery in the District of Columbia, so long agitated in both halls of Congress, and which has formed the themes of so many northern lectures, I had hoped, whilst they had so many more important themes, and especially whilst assuring us that there was no intention to interfere with slavery in the States, but only to prevent its extension, would for a season have been permitted to repose, if it be now impossible to return to the sounder opinions of other times. It was formerly the case—I will not say in the better days of the republic, though any that have gone before may prove to be better than these—that northern men, on account of the implied faith of the cession, and for the peace that should exist in the place held for common purposes by a common Government, resisted every attempt to touch the institution of slavery in the District of Columbia. Such, I recollect, was the course of a distinguished Senator once, from the State of Pennsylvania—distinguished then, and more distinguished since—distinguished by his capacity—distinguished by his high attainment—distinguished for his high eloquence—yet more distinguished still for the pure morality of his life, and the stern patriotism of his character. That Senator (Mr. Buchanan, of Pennsylvania,) presented from the people of his own State a petition for the abolition of slavery in the District of Columbia. After a long and able discussion, the prayer of the petitioners was rejected by a vote of 34 to 6. He presented it as a matter of respect to those who had enclosed it to him; but he moved that it be rejected, and made a speech in favor of its rejection. From that speech I will read some short passages:

"The Constitution has, in the clearest terms, recognized the right of property in slaves. It prohibits any State into which a slave may have fled from passing any law to discharge him from slavery, and declares that he shall be delivered up by the authorities of such State to his master. Nay, more; it makes the existence of slavery the foundation of political powers, by giving to those States within which it exists Representatives in Congress, not only in proportion to the whole number of free persons, but also in proportion to three-fifths of the number of slaves."

"Sir, said Mr. B., this question of domestic slavery is a weak point in our institutions. Tariffs may be raised almost to prohibition, and then they may be reduced so as to yield no adequate protection to the manufacturer; our Union is sufficiently strong to endure the shock. Fierce political storms may arise; the moral elements of the country may be convulsed by the struggles of ambitious men for the highest honors of Government. The sunshine does not more certainly succeed the storm than that all will again be peace. Touch this question of slavery seriously—let it once be made manifest to the people of the South that they cannot live with us, except in a state of continual apprehension and alarm for their wives and their children, for all that is near and dear to them upon the earth, and the Union is from that moment dissolved. It does not then become a question of expediency, but of self preservation. It is a question brought home to the fireside—to the domestic circle—of every white man in the southern States.''

Thus he spoke in 1835; and recently, when no longer in the public councils, he answered an invitation from his old friends in Berks county, Pennsylvania, and then, alluding to this same harassing and distracting question, used the following language:

''After Louisiana was acquired from France by Mr. Jefferson, and when the State of Missouri, which constituted a part of it, was about to be admitted into the Union, the Missouri question arose, and in its progress threatened the dissolution of the Union. This was settled by the men of the last generation, as other important and dangerous questions have been settled, in a spirit of mutual concession. Under the Missouri compromise, slavery was 'forever prohibited' north of the parallel of 36 degrees 30 minutes; and south of this parallel the question was left to be decided by the people. Congress, in the admission of Texas, following in the footsteps of their predecessors, adopted the same rule; and, in my opinion, the harmony of the States, and even the security of the Union itself, require that the line of the Missouri compromise should be extended to any new territory which we may acquire from Mexico.''

Now, I have no doubt that if that honorable gentleman was upon this floor, he would vote for the extension of the compromise line to the Pacific, with the admission of our right below the line as distinctly as the prohibition above it. I do not believe he would practice a delusion, but frankly and honestly would say that the application of the Missouri compromise line to the present case would require new terms. It would not be in keeping with the language I have quoted and the opinion I have expressed of him to act otherwise. Is it honest for those who have enjoyed all the benefits of the Missouri compromise, when it was run through slaveholding States and Territories, now to claim that these benefits are not to be extended to others? Who would expect a southern man to accept the Missouri compromise line with the condition of slavery prohibited above it, and nothing said about it below the line? What would be obtained? Would there be a settlement of the question—any peace secured to the country? I ask, is it not offensive to the understanding of any man to suppose he will surrender substantial, essential rights for empty professions? If I am told that it would be implied, but that the feelings of the North will not allow the expression, then, sir, I am offered new evidence of a hostility which is incompatible with the idea of compromise, or the expectation of its faithful observance.

THURSDAY, *February* 14, 1850.

Mr. DAVIS resumed and concluded his remarks as follows:

One of the positions laid down by the honorable Senator from Kentucky, and which he denominated as one of his two truths, was, that slavery was excluded from the Territories of California and New Mexico by a decree of Nature. From that opinion I dissent. I hold that the pursuit of gold-washing and mining is better adapted to slave labor than to any other species of labor recognized among us, and is likely to be found in that new country for many years to come. I also maintain that it is particularly adapted to an agriculture which depends upon irrigation. Till the canals are cut, ditches and dams made, no person can reclaim the soil from Nature; an individual pioneer cannot settle upon it with his family, and support them by the product of his own exertion, as in the old possessions of the United States, where rain and dew unite with a prolific soil to reward freely and readily the toil of man. It is only by associated labor that such a country can be reduced to cultivation. They have this associated labor in Mexico under a system of *peonage*. That kind of involuntary servitude, for debt I suppose, cannot long continue to exist under American institutions; therefore the only species of labor that can readily supply its place under our Government would, I think, be the domestic servitude of African slavery; and therefore I believe it is essential, on account of the climate, productions, soil, and the peculiar character of cultivation, that we should during its first settlement have that slavery in at least a portion of California and New Mexico. It is also true, that in certain climates only the African race are adapted to work in the sun. It is from this cause perhaps more than all others that the products of Mexico, once so important and extensive, have dwindled into comparative insignificance since the abolition of slavery. And it is also on that account that the prosperity of Central and Southern America generally has declined, and that it has been sustained in Brazil, where slavery has continued; that Jamaica and St. Domingo have now, from being among the most productive and profitable colonies, sunk into decay, and are relapsing to desert and barbarism; and yet Cuba and Porto Rico continue to maintain, I might say to increase, their prosperity. I therefore deny what is affirmed by the Senator from Kentucky to be his second truth, and in support of that denial call attention to the wealth and productiveness of Mexico when slavery existed there, and invite a comparison between that and its condition at present. In the great work of Humboldt we find the following statement:

"Mexico, in 1803, after defraying the annual expenses of her administration, $10,500,000, which included the cost of her army of 10,000 Spanish troops, and after remitting to Spain a surplus of $6,000,000 in specie, exhibits the singular spectacle of a distant colony sustaining the other colonies of Spain by the annual remittance to each of the following sums:

To Louisiana	$557,000
To Florida	151,000
To Cuba	1,826,000
To Porto Rico	377,000
To St. Domingo	274,000
To Trinidad	200,000
To Philippine Isles	250,000
Aggregate	$3,635,000

That she might have been called upon to contribute something to the everglades and sands of Florida is not so unreasonable; but that the rich alluvial of Louisiana, with her population industrial, intelligent, established, and engaged in the same pursuits then as now; that the islands of Cuba and Porto Rico, which now, in addition to their own heavy expenditures, contribute to support the Spanish Crown, should then depend on annual contributions from Mexico; and that Mexico has, since the abolition of slavery, become so impoverished that, to derive money for her support, she sold territory to the United States, is proof that cannot be denied of the value of the institution of slavery in a soil and climate like hers. The proof, if not in the whole is certainly in part of California and New Mexico applicable to the same extent as in the rest of the Republic of Mexico. It certainly justifies a claim to trial before the decree is announced.

We do not ask Congress to express an opinion in relation to the decrees of nature, or say that slavery shall be planted in any of the Territories of the United States. We only claim that we shall be permitted to have the benefit of an experiment, that we may have that equal participation in the enjoyment of the Territories which would secure to us an opportunity to be heard in the determination of their permanent institutions. We have only said that we are entitled to a decision of the Supreme Court of the United States, and that we should be allowed to try the institution of slavery, that thus it might be ascertained what the decree of nature is. Both these have been denied to us. We have been denied by Congress an appeal to the Supreme Court; we have been debarred by Congressional agitation from obtaining the decree of nature. We ask that both shall be permitted to us; granted not as a boon, but secured to us as a right—an equal right of the sovereign States of the South. More than this we have not claimed—more than this we do not desire. Instead of insisting upon the expression of any opinion of Congress in accordance with our own, we ask that the expression called for by the Senator from Kentucky shall be suspended. We ask that the decision of the Supreme Court and the decree of nature may intervene; and that Congress shall oppose no legislative influence to the one, and no obstacles to the fair decision of the other. No, sir, we have not sought to rest our rights upon the expression of Congressional opinion, but upon the principles of the Constitution and the laws of nature; least of all do we desire a compromise like that the Senator from Kentucky informs us he brought forward, and which was passed by Congress in 1821—a compromise as devoid of substance as that made by William Deloraine, who, not having learnt his alphabet, being even unable to spell his neck verse, entered into a contract that he would not write. Like this was the Senator's compromise with the State of Missouri that she would not pass laws in violation of the Constitution of the United States—laws, which, if she had passed them, would therefore have been void from their inception. We want something substantial, something permanent; something that will secure to us the peace of which we are now deprived; and something that will protect us from further interruption in the enjoyment of those rights and privileges to which we are entitled; something which promises reason and good feeling, instead of passion and bitterness in the halls of legislation; not a mere verbal, illusory, temporary, fruitless escape from the issue thrust upon us. With this brief notice of what the Senator calls his second truth, I will now proceed to the consideration of the point that I was about to enter upon yesterday when the Senate adjourned.

It is asserted that the Texas boundary is an open question,

and that the Government of the United States has power to close it, and that they derived this power from the terms of the annexation of Texas. I deny that it is an open question. I deny that the Government of the United States ever had, under the resolution of annexation, power to close it. Texas agreed that her boundary should be settled by the treaty-making power of the United States; not by the Government of the United States—not by the Congress of the United States, but by the treaty-making power of the United States; and there is a great difference, as all will perceive, between referring this question to Congress and to the Senate and the President. In referring it to the Senate, Texas referred it to a body in which, at that time, one half of the members had interests like those which she desired to maintain. In referring it to the President, she referred it to a southern man, whose education and associations warranted a reliance both on his information and sympathies. If it had been referred to Congress, her rights would have been in the House of Representatives fully under the power of the North, and this consideration might have entered very largely into the selection of the Senate and President as her advocate, or umpire. There was this difference, so far as her institutions were concerned, between referring it to the treaty-making power and to the law-making power of this Government. The treaty-making power being unable to adjust it, the President of the United States having failed to settle by negotiation, the boundary dispute with Mexico, he then, in conformity with the obligations to defend the territory of every State in the Union, resisted the aggression committed in the invasion by Mexico on the territory of Texas. The boundary which was defined by the Congress of Texas before the annexation, with which definition the United States accepted her, was the only boundary the President could recognize, until a new boundary should be agreed on by treaty with Mexico.

Whatever the United States might have done by treaty with Mexico, as to the boundary of the Rio Grande, it was plain that, when unable to enter into and settle the question by treaty, the United States was bound by every power the Government possessed, to maintain the jurisdiction of Texas, to the extent it was exercised at the date of annexation. The Senator from Kentucky well said that the President of the United States had no right to assume to settle the boundary of Texas. Nor, sir, did that great and good man ever assume such a power; he but discharged the duties which devolved on him as the Chief Executive, to maintain the boundaries of the State, and to defend the Union against foreign invasion. In the discharge of this duty, and in the execution of this high responsibility resting on him, the Mexican war was undertaken for the defence of Texas against Mexican invasion. Then the question arises, shall the United States, after defending the boundaries of Texas, engaging in war to maintain those boundaries, and closing that war by acquiring all the territory claimed, and more besides, present her own claim as opposed to the claim of Texas, and thus falsify the position she assumed when she went to war with Mexico to maintain the boundary of Texas? We must come to that, or admit the boundaries as laid down by her when an independent State, and which we asserted and maintained against the Government of Mexico.

I wish also to call attention to another distinction. We did not acquire Texas as a Territory, out of which a State might be carved. Congress refused to acquire her as a Territory, and she came in as a State. As a State she had sovereign jurisdiction over all her territory; and, save under the qualified power granted in the resolutions of annexation, which must be strictly construed as a contract between the two sovereignties, the United States had no power to touch an acre or a foot even of her territory. I leave the Senator who sits near me, [Mr. RUSK,] and who so ably represents that State, to maintain the boundary of Texas as asserted by her, to lay down the limits over which she has the right to claim sovereign jurisdiction, and further to maintain her title. I promised to be brief, and I am glad to leave the whole question in such able hands.

But the Senator from Kentucky says we have paid $15,000,000 for the acquisition of this territory, and that, therefore, Texas has no right, without paying part of the purchase money, to expect the benefit of the acquisition to the extent of her claim. Well, I am not able to make any distinction between Texas being called upon to make extraordinary contributions to pay part of the purchase money and of the debt incurred in the prosecution of the war to maintain her boundary As a sovereign State of the Union, she pays, through the revenue imposts, her quota towards the defrayment of all the expenses of the Government, whether for peace or war. This purchase money was to acquire territory from Mexico, and though efficient to settle the question between the Governments, which had been complicated by the events of the war, it was not a payment for any part of Texas, surely was not the purchase of a claim to be set up against our own citizens, nor a State of the Union. The boundary of Texas had been maintained by arms, and I cannot admit that

294   JEFFERSON DAVIS, CONSTITUTIONALIST

it was purchased with money. But, if enumerated among the war debts, the sum agreed to be paid by the treaty goes in with all other expenditures incurred in the prosecution of the war. Texas, with no more right can be called on in an extraordinary manner to furnish funds to reimburse the one than the other.

The Senator refers to the liberality of his proposition to give to Texas the territory between the Nueces and the Rio Grande; and, strangely enough, that little strip of country was assumed by him to be nearly equal to the territory of Texas east of the Nueces, and of New Mexico. I presume he meant of the province of Texas as she existed under the Mexican Government. Well, sir, I have a table showing the extent in square miles of the old Province of Texas.

Texas, within her ancient limits, had an area in square
   miles of 148,569
Between the Nueces and the Rio Grande, has.......... 52,018
North of Ensenado, and east of Rio Grande, being the
   part claimed as being in New Mexico,..............124,933
                                                     _____
         Aggregate 325,520

The country west of the Nueces being less than half—not much more than a third—of the size of the old State of Texas.

Texas, as annexed, was not the ancient Province, but the independent State of Texas, as established by her revolution. Her title is now disputed to all that part of her territory which was once within the limits of Tamaulipas and New Mexico— being 177,051 square miles—which leaves 148,569 square miles for the State of Texas; that is to say, more than one-half of the territory she comprises is to be claimed, less than a sixth to be restored; and this is called a liberal concession. But the territory held out as a great boon granted to Texas—that between the Nueces and the Rio Grande—is the very desert once so eloquently described by the Senator from Missouri, who sits near me, as the country through which the dividing line between the United States and Mexico should be drawn. And I now believe that a line drawn through that country would be a better boundary than the Rio Grande. The boundary I desired was the mountain barrier south of the Rio Grande. I wanted all the country drained by the Rio Grande; and I have regretted, from the time that amendment to the treaty failed, to the present day, that we did not decide to amend the treaty by taking from Mexico that portion of her northern possessions which, inhabited by a restless population, was an object of apprehension, and, infested by roving bands of Indians, was useless to her, and might have been highly beneficial to us.

But, sir, the boundary of ancient Texas the Senator from Kentucky, I think, once admitted to be the Rio Grande. I think he once contended that the title to that boundary was as complete as that to the island of Orleans; but now, when he refers to the acquisitions of territory which the United States have made within the last sixty years, he enumerates Louisiana, and Texas, and Florida, all of which he says inured to the benefit of the southern States, save the amount above the line of 36° 30'. Sir, I think the same Senator, in discussing the question of the acquisition of Florida, opposed it on the ground that we gave away the vast domain of Texas, more extended and valuable than the Territory of Florida. I think also that the acquisition of Florida was not a southern measure, and that Mr. Monroe justified himself before southern men for that treaty by the necessity which sectional rivalry had created. It never was a southern measure; the southern men wanted Florida, and were willing to pay a fair price for it. They had long looked forward to the day when she would fall into our hands, as they believed sooner or later, she must; but they did not wish to acquire it at the expenditure requisite at the time it was obtained. Texas, therefore, should not be enumerated again; for she was included in the old Territory of Louisiana, and from which she was separated by a contract unfavorable to the South. Leaving these things—stories twice told, and which are not necessary to repeat—let us take the question as it stands: let us take the Territories north and south of the line 36° 30', and then see where the balance of acquisition has gone. I shall refer to a pamphlet, very widely circulated over the United States, and which has been severely criticised, but I believe the facts set forth have not yet been denied—the pamphlet of Ellwood Fisher. He says:

"When the North American colonies confederated for resistance to Great Britain, the territorial area of the southern portion of them was 648,202 square miles; that of the northern only 164,081, or about one-fourth as large."

In reference to the cession of the Northwestern Territory by Virginia, he says:

"The object of this cession and the ordinance of 1787 was to equalize the area of the two sections. The acquisition of Louisiana in 1803 added 1,138,103 square miles to our territory, of which, by the Missouri compromise, the South obtained only 226,013 square miles, or about one-fifth; the other four-fifths, notwithstanding they came to us as a slaveholding province, were allotted to the North, which thus had acquired more than 700,000 square miles of territory over the South. Florida and Oregon were acquired by the treaty of 1819, by which the South got 59,268 square miles, and the North 341,463, making the North about 1,000,000 of square miles the most. In 1845 Texas was annexed, which added only 325,520 square miles to the South, even if all Texas were included. In 1848 we obtained 526,078 square miles more in the Territories of New Mexico and California. And now the North claims the whole of this also; and not only this, but half of Texas besides, which would make the share of the North exceed that of the South nearly 1,500,000 square miles—a territory about equal in extent to the whole valley of the Mississippi, and leaving the South only about 810,812 square miles, while the North retains 2,097,124, or nearly three-fourths of the whole.''

Estimating all the territory not within the limits of any of the States, it will be found that the part which will inure to the benefit of the North, as against the South, if we extend the Missouri compromise to the Pacific ocean, will be something more than four to one. So much, sir, for the great advantages, territorially considered, which we of the South have derived from the acquisitions of the United States.

But we at the South are an agricultural people, and we require an extended territory. Slave labor is a wasteful labor, and it therefore requires a still more extended territory than would the same pursuits if they could be prosecuted by the more economical labor of white men. We have a right, in fairness and justice, to expect from our brethren of the North, that they shall not attempt, in consideration of our agricultural interests—if that alone be considered—to restrict the territory of the South. We have a right to claim that our territory shall increase with our population, and the statistics show that the natural increase of our population is as great as that of any part of the United States. Take out the accession from foreign immigration, and compare the increase of population in the northern States and the southern States, and the latter will be found a fraction greater. With this increase of population we must require increased territory; and it is but just, and fair, and honest that it sh. uld be accorded to us without any restriction or reservation. I was surprised, then, to hear the Senator from Kentucky, while he admitted that he believed he had voted for the Missouri compromise, which asserted the power and excluded the South from all the Territories she once owned north of 36 degrees 30 minutes, declare that no earthly power should induce him to recognize the right of slavery to go into territory south of 36 degrees 30 minutes where that institution does not now exist. He then said, in emphatic language, that he would not plant the institution of slavery anywhere. That, sir, is not the proposition. Nobody asks the Federal Government to compel its introduction, or to plant slavery in the Territories, or to engage in the slave trade, in order to furnish material for extending the institution into any new territory. All that we assert is the right of the southern people to go with that species of property into the territory of the United States. That, therefore, is the right denied. And, subsequently, while admitting that it was equally right and just if the majority excluded slavery north of 36 degrees 30 minutes, that it should be permitted south of that line, yet, at the same time, he says he could not vote for a proposition that carried slavery into any Territory where it is not already established, though he would yield to such a decision by the majority. If it is equal and just that both rules or neither should be adopted—if it is in the power of the majority to pass one measure, but not their will to pass the other, it seems to be the duty of any one, in the name of equality and justice, to interpose whatever power he may possess to place those equal and just conditions on the whole proposition. In denying our right, however, under the Constitution, to take slaves into the Territories, he stated it to rest on a position somewhat, I think, like this: that slavery did not exist in all the States of the Union, and that, therefore, it was not a property recognized throughout the United States; and in support of that position he supposed a case, that the Northern States should assert that the Constitution abolished slavery because they had no slavery within their limits. Now, to make this an equal proposition, it is necessary to declare that the power to protect is the same as the power to destroy—that this Government is the creator and not the creature of the States—that it is the master and not the servant of the States, and that it created property in slaves and established the institution of slavery. We claim that it is the duty of the Government to protect every species of property—that the Government has no right to discriminate between one species of property and another. It is equally bound to protect on the high seas the slave in the vessel as the hull of the vessel itself; and it is equally bound to protect slave property, if wrecked on a foreign coast, against a hostile assertion of foreign power, as it would be the wreck of the vessel

itself. And to this error—for so I must consider it—this con-
founding of sovereign and delegated authority, is to be attributed
the claim which is set up, of power to abolish slavery, as derived
from the exclusive legislation granted to the Government in this
District. This construction of the word "exclusive" would
render it synonymous with the word "unlimited." That exclusive legislation was necessary for the protection of the seat
of government will be readily conceded. It was essential to the
Government to have exclusive legislation, so that no other
authority might interfere with its functions. But unlimited
legislation surely is not required, and I say it could not have
been granted by the Constitution; nay, more, I hold that the
grant of exclusive legislation does not necessarily extend to the
full power permissible under the Constitution of the United
States, that there are restrictions, and broad distinctions, growing out of the vested rights and interests of others—in this case
not merely of the ceding States, but of all the States of the
Union. The power of the Federal Government extends only so
far as is necessary to secure the seat of government as such, and
to protect therein the public property of the United States. The
Senator asserts, because of the grant of exclusive legislation,
that the Government has equal power over the District with that
which a sovereign State possesses within its limits, applies this
to the regulation of the slave trade, and goes on to declare that
which I will not deny, that the States have full power over this
subject. Yet I could quote himself against this argument, and
could show that he denied this power to the States, and arraigned those who asserted it as being on the side of the Abolitionists. I refer to the case of Groves vs. Slaughter, where the
Senator appeared as counsel, and where the right of Mississippi,
here referred to, the right of a State to exclude the introduction
of slaves as merchandise, was the very matter in dispute, and
where, having argued that the constitution of Mississippi was
directory, and not enacting—that it directs the Legislature to
prohibit the importation of slaves as merchandise, but does not
itself prohibit—he goes on to say:

"The last question in the case is, whether the provision of the
Constitution of the United States which gives to Congress exclusively the right to regulate commerce between the States,
is opposed by the Constitution of Mississippi. The argument for
the plaintiffs in error is on the abolition side of the question.
The counsel for the defendant sustain the opposite principle.

"The object of prohibition in the Constitution of the United
States is to regulate commerce; to sustain it, not to annihilate

it. It is conservative. Regulation implies continued existence
——life, not death; preservation, not annihilation; the unobstructed flow of the stream, not to check or dry up its waters.

"But the object of the abolitionists is to prevent the exercise
of this commerce. This is a violation of the right of Congress
under the Constitution.

"The right of the States to regulate the condition of slaves
within their borders is not denied. It is fully admitted. Every
State may, by its laws, fix the character and condition of slaves.
The right of Congress to regulate commerce between the different States, which may extend to the regulation of the transportation of Slaves from one State to another, as merchandise,
does not affect these rights of the States. But, to deny the introduction of slaves, as merchandise, into a State from another State, is an interference with the Constitution of the
United States. After their introduction they are under the
laws of the States.

"Nor is the power given by the Constitution of the United
States to regulate commerce one in which the States may participate. It is exclusive. It is essentially so; and its existence
in this form is most important to the slaveholding States."

It is not important, however, for the present investigation,
to examine these general positions taken then or now, and I will
not pursue them further. The opinion is adverse, it will be seen,
to the one the Senator stated on this occasion to the Senate. Both
claim extreme powers for the Federal Government, and both
therein I believe to be wrong.

Sir, it has been asked on several occasions during the present
session, what ground of complaint has the South? Is this agitation in the two halls of Congress, in relation to the domestic
institutions of the South, no subject for complaint? Is the
action of the Legislatures of northern States, defeating provisions of the Constitution which are among its compromises for
our benefit, no subject for complaint? Is the denunciation
heaped upon us by the press of the North, and the attempts to
degrade us in the eyes of Christendom—to arraign the character
of our people and the character of our fathers, from whom our
institutions are derived—no subject for complaint? Is this
sectional organization, for the purpose of hostility to our portion of the Union, no subject for complaint? Would it not,
between foreign nations—nations not bound together and restrained as we are by compact—would it not, I say, be just
cause for war? What difference is there between organizations
for circulating incendiary documents and promoting the escape
of fugitives from a neighboring State, and the organizaion

of an armed force for the purpose of invasion? Sir, a State relying securely on its own strength would rather court the open
invasion than the insidious attack. And for what end, sir, is all
this aggression? They see that the slaves in their present condition in the South are comfortable and happy; they see them advancing in intelligence; they see the kindest relations exist between them and their masters; they see them provided for in
age and sickness, in infancy and disability; they see them in useful employment, restrained from the vicious indulgences to
which their inferior nature inclines them; they see our penitentiaries never filled, and our poor houses usually empty. Let
them turn to the other hand, and they see the same race in a
state of freedom at the North; but instead of the comfort and
kindness they receive at the South, instead of being happy and
useful, they are, with few exceptions, miserable, degraded, filling
the penitentiaries and poor-houses, objects of scorn, excluded,
in some places, from the schools, and deprived of many other
privileges and benefits which attach to the white men among
whom they live. And yet they insist that elsewhere an institution which has proved beneficial to this race shall be abolished,
that it may be substituted by a state of things which is fraught
with so many evils to the race which they claim to be the object
of their solicitude? Do they find in the history of St. Domingo
and in the present condition of Jamaica, under the recent
experiments which have been made upon the institution of slavery in the liberation of the blacks, before God, in his wisdom,
designed it should be done—do they there find anything to
stimulate them to future exertion in the cause of abolition? Or
should they not find there satisfactory evidence that their past
course was founded in error? And is it not the part of integrity
and wisdom, as soon as they can, to retrace their steps? Should
they not immediately cease from a course mischievous in every
stage, and finally tending to the greatest catastrophe? We may
dispute about measures: but as long as parties have nationality
—as long as it is a difference of opinion between individuals
passing into every section of the country—it threatens no danger
to the Union. If the conflicts of party were the only cause of
apprehension, this Government might last forever—the last page
of human history might contain a discussion in the American
Congress upon the meaning of some phrase, the extent of the
power conferred by some grant of the Constitution. It is, sir,
these sectional divisions which weaken the bonds of union and
threaten their final rupture. It is not differences of opinion;

it is geographical lines, rivers, and mountains which divide State from State, and make different nations of mankind.

Are these no subjects of complaint for us? And do they furnish no cause for repentance to you? Have we not a right to appeal to you as brethren of this Union—have we not a right to appeal to you as brethren bound by the compact of our fathers, that you should, with due regard to your own rights, and interests, and constitutional obligations, do all that is necessary to preserve our peace and promote our prosperity?

If, sir, the seeds of disunion have been sown broadcast over this land, I ask by whose arm they have been scattered? If, sir, we are now reduced to a condition when the powers of this Government are held subservient to faction; if we cannot and dare not legislate for the organization of territorial governments—I ask, sir, who is responsible for it? And I can, with proud reliance, say it is not the South! it is not the South! Sir, every charge of disunion which is made on that part of the South which I in part represent, and whose sentiments I well understand, I here pronounce to be grossly calumnious. The conduct of the State of Mississippi in calling a convention has already been introduced before the Senate; and on that occasion I stated, and now repeat, that it was the result of patriotism, and a high resolve to preserve if possible, our constitutional Union; that all its proceedings were conducted with deliberation, and it was composed of the first men of the State.

The Chief Justice—a man well known for his high integrity, for his powerful intellect, for his great legal attainments, and his ability in questions of constitutional law—presided over that Convention. After calm and mature deliberation, resolutions were adopted, not in the spirit of disunion, but announcing, in the first resolution of the series, their attachment to the Union. They call on their brethren of the South to unite with them in their holy purpose of preserving the Constitution, which is its only bond and reliable hope. This was their object; and for this and for no other purpose do they propose to meet in general convention at Nashville. As I stated on a former occasion, this was not a party movement in Mississippi. The presiding officer belongs to the political minority in the State; the two parties in the State were equally represented in the members of the convention, and its deliberations assumed no partisan or political character whatever. It was the result of primary meetings in the counties; an assemblage of men known throughout the State having first met and intimated to those counties a time when the State convention should, if

deemed proper, be held. Every movement was taken with deliberation, and every movement then taken was wholly independent
of the action of anybody else; unless it be intended by the remarks made here, to refer its action to the great principles of
those who have gone before us, and who have left us the rich
legacy of the free institutions under which we live. If it be attempted to assign the movement to the nullification tenets of
South Carolina, as my friend near me seemed to understand,
then I say you must go further back, and impute it to the State
rights and strict construction doctrines of Madison and Jefferson. You must refer these in their turn to the principles in
which originated the revolution and separation of these then
colonies from England. You must not stop there, but go back
still further, to the bold spirit of the ancient barons of England. That spirit has come down to us, and in that spirit has all
the action since been taken. We will not permit aggressions.
We will defend our rights; and if it be necessary, we will claim
from this Government, as the barons of England claimed from
John, the grant of another *magna charta* for our protection.

Sir, I can but consider it as a tribute of respect to the character for candor and sincerity which the South maintains, that
every movement which occurs in the southern States is closely
scrutinized, and the assertion of a determination to maintain
their constitutional rights is denounced as a movement of disunion; whilst violent denunciations against the Union are now
made, and for years have been made, at the North by associations, by presses and conventions, yet are allowed to pass unnoticed as the idle wind—I suppose for the simple reason that
nobody believed there was any danger in them. It is, then, I say,
a tribute paid to the sincerity of the South, that every movement of hers is watched with such jealousy; but what shall we
think of the love for the Union of those in whom this brings
no corresponding change of conduct, who continue the wanton
aggravations which have produced and justify the action they
deprecate? Is it well, is it wise, is it safe, to disregard these
manifestations of public displeasure, though it be the displeasure
of a minority? Is it proper, or prudent, or respectful, when a
representative, in accordance with the known will of his constituents, addresses you the language of solemn warning, in
conformity to his duty to the Constitution, the Union, to his
own conscience, that his course should be arraigned as the
declaration of ultra and dangerous opinions? If these warnings
were received in the spirit they are given, it would augur better
for the country. It would give hopes which are now denied

us, if the press of the country, that great lever of public opinion, would enforce these warnings, and bear them to every cottage, instead of heaping abuse upon those whose case would prompt them to silence—whose speech, therefore, is evidence of sincerity. Lightly and loosely representatives of southern people have been denounced as disunionists by that portion of the northern press which most disturbs the harmony and engenders the perpetuity of the Union. Such, even, has been my own case, though the man does not breathe at whose door the charge of disunion might not as well be laid as at mine. The son of a revolutionary soldier, attachment to this Union was among the first lessons of my childhood; bred to the service of my country from boyhood, to mature age I wore its uniform. Through the brightest portion of my life, I was accustomed to see our flag, historic emblem of the Union, rise with the rising and fall with the setting sun. I look upon it now with the affection of early love, and seek to maintain and preserve it by a strict adherence to the Constitution, from which it had its birth, and by the nurture of which its stars have come so much to outnumber its original stripes. Shall that flag, which has gathered fresh glory in every war, and become more radiant still by the conquest of peace—shall that flag now be torn by domestic faction, and trodden in the dust by petty sectional rivalry? Shall we of the South, who have shared equally with you all your toils, all your dangers, all your adversities, and who equally rejoice in your prosperity, and your fame—shall we be denied those benefits guaranteed by our compact, or gathered as the common fruits of a common country? If so, self-respect requires that we should assert them; and, as best we may, maintain that which we could not surrender without losing your respect as well as our own.

If, sir, this spirit of sectional aggrandizement, or, if gentlemen prefer, this love they bear the African race, shall cause the disunion of these States, the last chapter of our history will be a sad commentary upon the justice and the wisdom of our people. That this Union, replete with blessings to its own citizens, and diffusive of hope to the rest of mankind, should fall a victim to a selfish aggrandizement, and a pseudo philanthropy, prompting one portion of the Union to war upon the domestic rights and peace of another, would be a deep reflection on the good sense and patriotism of our day and generation. But, sir, if this last chapter in our history shall ever be written the reflective reader will ask, whence proceeded this hostility of the North against the South? He will find it there recorded that the South, in opposition to her own immediate interests, engaged with the North in the unequal struggle of the Revolution. He will find again that, when Northern seamen were impressed, their brethren of the South considered it cause for war, and entered warmly into the contest with the haughty Power then claiming to be mistress of the seas. He will find that the South, afar off, unseen and unheard, toiling in the pursuits of agriculture, had filled the shipping, supplied the staple for manufactures, which enriched the North. He will find that she was the great consumer of Northern fabrics—that she not only paid for these their fair value in the markets of the world, but that she also paid their increased value, derived from the imposition of revenue duties. And if, still further, he seeks for the cause of this hostility, it at last is to be found in the fact that the South held the African race in bondage, being the descendants of those who were mainly purchased from the people of the North. And this was the great cause. For this the North claimed that the South should be restricted from future growth —that around her should be drawn, as it were, a sanitary cordon to prevent the extension of a moral leprosy; and if for that it shall be written the South resisted, it would be but in keeping with every page she has added to the history of our country.

It depends on those in the majority to say whether this last chapter in our history shall be written or not. It depends on them now to decide whether the strife between the different sections shall be arrested before it has become impossible, or whether it shall proceed to a final catastrophe. I, sir—and I only speak for myself—am willing to meet any fair proposition—to settle upon anything which promises security for the future; anything which assures me of permanent peace, and I am willing to make whatever sacrifice I may properly be called on to render for that purpose. Nor, sir, is it a light responsibility. If I strictly measured my conduct by the late message of the Governor, and the recent expressions of opinion in my State, I should have no power to accept any terms save the unqualified admission of the equal rights of the citizens of the South to go into any of the Territories of the United States with any and every species of property held among us. I am willing, however, to take my share of the responsibility which the crisis of our country demands. I am willing to rely on the known love of the people I represent for the whole country, and the abiding respect which I know they entertain for the Union of these States. If, sir, I distrusted their attachment to our Government, and if I believed they had that restless spirit of disunion which has been ascribed

to the South, I should know full well that I had no such foundation as this to rely upon—no such great reserve in the heart of
the people to fall back upon in the hour of accountability.

Mr. President, is there such incompatibility of interest between the two sections of this country that they cannot profitably live together? Does the agriculture of the South injure
the manufactures of the North? On the other hand are they
not their life-blood? And think you if one portion of the Union,
however great it might be in commerce and manufactures, was
separated from all the agricultural districts, that it would long
maintain its supremacy? If any one so believes, let him turn
to the written history of commercial States; let him look upon
the mouldering palaces of Venice; let him ask for the faded
purple of Tyre, and visit the ruins of Carthage; there he will
see written, the fate of every country which rests its prosperity
on commerce and manufactures alone. United we have grown
to our present dignity and power—united we may go on to a
destiny which the human mind cannot measure. Separated, I
feel that it requires no prophetic eye to see that the portion of
country which is now scattering the seeds of disunion to which
I have referred, will be that which will suffer most. Grass will
grow on the pavements now worn by the constant tread of the
human throng which waits on commerce, and the shipping will
abandon your ports for those which now furnish the staples of
trade. And we who produce the great staple upon which your
commerce and manufactures rests, we will produce those staples
still; shipping will fill our harbors; and why may we not found
the Tyre of modern commerce within our own limits? Why
may we not bring the manufacturers to the side of agriculture,
and commerce, too, the ready servant of both?

But, sir, I have no disposition to follow this subject. I certainly can derive no pleasure from the contemplation of anything
which can impair the prosperity of any portion of this Union;
and I only refer to it that those who suppose we are tied by
interest or fear, should look the question in the face, and
understand that it is mainly a feeling of attachment to the
Union which has long bound, and now binds the South. But, Mr.
President, I ask Senators to consider how long affection can be
proof against such trial, and injury, and provocation as the
South is continually receiving.

The case in which this discrimination against the South is
attempted, the circumstances under which it was introduced
render it especially offensive. It will not be difficult to imagine
the feeling with which a southern soldier during the Mexican

war received the announcement that the House of Representatives had passed that odious measure, the Wilmot proviso; and that he, although then periling his life, abandoning all the comforts of home, and sacrificing his interests, was, by the Legislature of his country, marked as coming from a portion of the Union which was not entitled to the equal benefits of whatever might result from the service to which he was contributing whatever power he possessed. Nor will it be difficult to conceive of the many sons of the South whose blood has stained those battlefields, whose ashes now mingle with Mexican earth, that some, when they last looked on the flag of their country, may have felt their dying moments embittered by the recollection that that flag cast not an equal shadow of protection over the land of their birth, the graves of their parents, and the homes of their children so soon to be orphans. Sir, I ask northern Senators to make the case their own—to carry to their own fireside the idea of such intrusion and offensive discrimination as is offered to us—realize these irritations, so galling to the humble, so intolerable to the haughty, and wake before it is too late, from the dream that the South will tamely submit. Measure the consequences to us of your assumption, and ask yourselves whether as a free, honorable, and brave people, you would submit to it?

It is essentially the characteristic of the chivalrous that they never speculate upon the fears of any man, and I trust that no such speculations will be made upon the idea that may be entertained in any quarter that the South, from fear of her slaves, is necessarily opposed to a dissolution of this Union. She has no such fear; her slaves would be to her now as they were in the revolution, an element of military strength. I trust that no speculations will be made upon either the condition or the supposed weakness of the South. They will bring sad disappointments to those who indulge them. Rely upon her devotion to the Union, rely upon the feeling of fraternity she inherited and has never failed to manifest; rely upon the nationality and freedom from sedition which has in all ages characterized an agricultural people; give her justice, sheer justice, and the reliance will never fail you.

Then, Mr. President, I ask that some substantial proposition may be made by the majority in regard to this question. It is for those who have the power to pass it to propose one. It is for those who are threatening us with the loss of that which we are entitled to enjoy, to state, if there be any compromise, what that compromise is. We are unable to pass any measure, if we propose it; therefore I have none to suggest. We are unable to bend you to any terms which we may offer; we are under the ban of your purpose; therefore from you, if from anywhere, the proposition must come. I trust that we shall meet it, and bear the responsibility as becomes us; that we shall not seek to escape from it; that we shall not seek to transfer to other places, or other times, or other persons, that responsibility which devolves upon us; and I hope the earnestness which the occasion justifies will not be mistaken for the ebullition of passion, nor the language of warning be construed as a threat. We cannot, without the most humiliating confession of the supremacy of faction, evade our constitutional obligations, and our obligations under the treaty with Mexico, to organize governments in the territories of California and New Mexico. I trust that we will not seek to escape from the responsibility, and leave the country unprovided for, unless by an irregular admission of new States; that we will act upon the good example of Washington in the case of Tennessee, and of Jefferson in the case of Louisiana; that we will not, if we abandon those high standards, do more than come down to modern examples; that we will not go further than to permit those who have the forms of government, under the Constitution, to assume sovereignty over territory of the United States; that we may at least, I say, assert the right to know who they are, how many they are—where they voted, how they voted —and whose certificate is presented to us of the fact, before it is conceded to them to determine the fundamental law of the country, and to prescribe the conditions on which other citizens of the United States may enter it. To reach all this knowledge, we must go through the intermediate stage of territorial government.

How will you determine what is the seal, and who are the officers of a community unknown as an organized body to the Congress of the United States? Can the right be admitted in that community to usurp the sovereignty over territory which belongs to the States of the Union? All these questions must be answered, before I can consent to any such irregular proceeding as that which is now presented in the case of California.

Mr. President, thanking the Senate for the patience they have shown towards me, I again express the hope that those who have the power to settle this distracting question—those who have the ability to restore peace, concord, and lasting harmony to the United States—will give us some substantial proposition, such as magnanimity can offer, and such as we can honorably accept. I, being one of the minority in the Senate and the

Union, have nothing to offer, except an assurance of coöperation in anything which my principles will allow me to adopt, and which promises permanent, substantial security.

Jefferson Davis to W. H. Bissell.[1]

(From Natchez Courier, March 15, 1850.)

Washington, D. C., Feb. 22, 1850.

Sir: I am informed that in yesterday's debate you asserted that at the time it was claimed for the Mississippi regiment, on the field of Buena Vista, to have passed through the scattered files of the 2d Indiana regiment, and to have met the Mexican forces, who had routed and were pursuing that regiment, the Mississippi regiment was not within one mile and a half of that particular spot.

Not having been able to find a "report" of your remarks, and being the proper person to answer any charge which a responsible man may make against the Mississippi regiment referred to, I take this mode of asking whether the information I have received is correct. Yours, respectfully,

Jeff. Davis.

Hon. Mr. Bissell.

W. H. Bissell to Jefferson Davis.

(From Natchez Courier, March 15, 1850.)

Washington, Feb. 22, 1850.

Sir: In your note of this date, you enquire whether I asserted, in yesterday's debate, that "at the time it was claimed for the Mississippi regiment, on the field of Buena Vista, to have passed through the scattered files of the 2d Indiana regiment, and to have met the Mexican forces, who had routed and were pursuing that regiment, the Mississippi regiment was not in one mile and a half of that particular spot?"

The best answer I can give to your inquiry is to state what I did say, which was this: That "at the time the second Indiana regiment gave way, the Mississippi regiment was not within a mile and a half of the scene of action." This, sub-

[1] Soldier in the War with Mexico, Congressman from Illinois in the Thirty-first, Thirty-second and Thirty-third Congresses; governor of Illinois 1856-1860.

stantially, was all I said in reference to the Mississippi regiment. I also said that the 2d Kentucky, the 2d Illinois, and a portion of the 1st Illinois regiments, were the troops that, at that time, met and repulsed the advancing columns of the enemy. In my remarks, I referred to what occurred at "that particular spot" at that point of time.

Having answered your inquiry, I deem it due, in justice alike to myself and the regiment, to say that I make no charge against that regiment, but I am willing to award them the credit due to their gallant and distinguished services in that battle. My only object was to do justice to the character of others, living and dead, whose conduct fell under my own observation on that occasion—a duty imposed upon me by remarks previously made in the course of the same debate.

Very respectfully, yours, &c.,

W. H. BISSELL.

Hon. Jeff. Davis.

Remarks of Jefferson Davis on March 8, 1850, on Compromise resolutions concerning slavery.

Mr. DAVIS. The Senator from Wisconsin has referred so frequently to the Senator from Mississippi, calling my attention to what he was about to say, that I think it necessary, without intending fully to reply to him, to show how unfairly he has treated what I said in the Senate on a former occasion.

Mr. WALKER. I beg to assure the honorable Senator that I did not intend to treat him unfairly.

Mr. DAVIS. I will say to the Senator from Wisconsin, that I am glad to hear his statement, that he did not intend to do it; and yet his presentation of what I said is such as to do me great injustice; but, it being unintentional, without commentary or preliminary remark, I will merely read those passages of the speech upon which his argument was founded, and will leave what I have said heretofore to answer what has been said by him in relation thereto on the present occasion. It will show that he has not quoted what I did say, but something that he has assumed me to have said.

Mr. WALKER. The most material part of what I quoted from him was from a different speech from the one he holds in his hand, published in the *Union* of the 30th.

Mr. DAVIS. The Senator heretofore referred to what I had said in relation to the Missouri compromise. I answered him on that occasion; and on receiving the pamphlet edition of my remarks, to avoid the possibility that he had misunderstood me, I assured myself that he had a copy of my speech, and called his attention to it, as containing a full explanation of my views upon that subject. And if, knowing my opinions, he has represented me otherwise, I leave it to him to explain. In this speech, when treating of what was claimed by the North, as the proper action of the Federal Government, in relation to the exclusion of the slaves of the southern States from the territories, and the grounds upon which it was done, I said:

"All this under the pretext that property in slaves is local in its nature, and derives its existence from municipal law. Slavery existed before the formation of this Union. It derived from the Constitution that recognition which it would not have enjoyed without the confederation. If the States had not united together, there would have been no obligation on adjoining States to regard any species of property unknown to themselves. But it was one of the compromises of the Constitution that the slave property in the southern States should be recognized as property throughout the United States. It was so recognized in the obligation to restore fugitives—recognized in the power to tax them as persons—recognized in their representation in the halls of Congress. As a property, recognized by the Constitution, and held in a portion of the States, the Federal Government is bound to admit it into all the territories, and to give it such protection as other private property receives."

That was my argument. I appeal to the Senator whether his remarks upon that portion of my speech are fairly applied to the text.

Mr. WALKER. If the Senator pleases, I did not quote from that speech.

Mr. DAVIS. Then again, in speaking of the right under the Constitution, after having acquired this territory from Mexico, to carry any species of property into that territory, notwithstanding any law having a prior existence, which prohibited its introduction, I said:

"If the right of the slaveholder to migrate into the territories, and to carry this species of property there, is prohibited by Mexican laws, so is the right of the ordinary trader to enter there with any of those sixty articles of commerce likewise prohibited; and the privilege which every citizen now freely exercises—of free trade in the territories—does not exist of right.

But the right of free trade throughout the United States is derived from the Constitution, and resulted necessarily and instantly from the transfer of the country to the United States. That right equally applies to the transfer of slave property, from the domicil of the owner, in any of the States, to the same territories; and the Mexican laws are no more in force on this subject than on the other.

"It was because the Constitution overruled these prohibitory laws, that free trade now exists. It is because the Constitution recognizes property in slaves, and secures equal privileges and immunities to all citizens of the United States, that we claim the abolition of slavery, by Mexico, to have died with the transfer of those territories to the United States. By the transfer of the territory, the sovereignty of Mexico was withdrawn; the sovereignty of the United States was immediately extended over the country, and filled its place—a sovereignty to be measured by your Constitution, not by the policy of Mexico."

The Senator surely did not answer to that position, but to a position which he seems to have imagined I assumed in relation to the Missouri compromise. The Senator spoke as though I was claiming something extreme, demanding a recognition of a right which we had not heretofore asserted, and taking some ground higher than the South has heretofore maintained. Now, I will make no other argument than to read a part of the speech to which he referred. I had been previously misconceived. It had been asserted, that I had claimed that Congress should establish slavery in some portion of this territory, and that I had previously to explain this point. I said:

"But, sir, because, on a former occasion, I stated what I believed to be our constitutional rights, but that, as there were two great antagonist principles in this country, the one claiming that slavery shall be excluded from all the territories, and the other contending that slaveholders have a right to go with their property into all of the territories, and as these two conflicting principles could not be reconciled, as compromise was only to be found in a division of the property, that I would consent to the establishment of a line, on one side of which one of these principles should prevail, and on the other side the other should be recognized—because I stated this, and because I suggested that this common territory, which it seems cannot be enjoyed in peace together, should be divided, I was charged with the desire to establish slavery where it does not now exist. I claimed, as our existing right, the privilege to go into all the territory, and said I would not recognize your right to exclude us from any portion of it—for one, I was willing to settle the controversy, and incur the hazard of taking the Missouri compromise line as a division, waiving the question of right. I would agree to any compromise, adequate to the present crisis, which equality and honor will permit.''

I then go on to state what was the case when this Missouri compromise line was applied to the Territory of Louisiana, which was slave territory. The line of 36° 30' was drawn through the territory, and when slavery was prohibited north of that line, the division was complete. It was unnecessary to say anything about the country below, because, saying nothing, slavery existed as theretofore. It was decided by making a division of the territory between the slaveholding and the non-slaveholding States. I have said that, in this case, where the whole territory is in dispute, there should be a distinct application to the one side and to the other, in order that we might have the full benefit of the spirit of the Missouri compromise, in a case unlike that for which it was made; that the citizens of the United States were engaged in controversy as to the right to take a particular species of property into the territories; that this controversy—so painful, injurious, and dangerous in its tendency, and seemingly so irreconcilable—might be adjusted, without compromise of principle, by a division of the territory between the two sections of the Union—the one to have sole possession above, and the other to have equal possession below, the line —for, sir, when you admit slavery into the territory, you do not exclude the white laborer. It is a great fallacy, which has been repeatedly here promulgated, to suppose so. No, sir; slave labor forms the substratum on which white labor is elevated, and he who seeks for that portion of our country where, in fact, as in theory, political equality does exist, must be pointed to the slaveholding States. Such, at least, I know to be the case among all the white men where I reside, and such I cannot believe to be the case where, as in the non-slaveholding States, white men are sunk to menial occupations.

But, sir, the Senator has noticed some closing remarks of that speech, which I hoped would have had a tendency rather to quiet than to excite controversy. Expression was given to the feelings which I have always entertained, of an abiding love for all portions of the country; and no petty sectional hostility toward any, has ever found shelter in my breast. Even that portion of my remarks, the Senator has thought proper to comment on, and, as I think, unkindly. I indicated as the cause of sectional strife—it might be, of the destruction of our happy and happiness-conferring Union—the poor, the despicable antipathy to the South, because of her institution of African bondage. To this he replies, that there is no hostility toward us of the South, because we hold the African race in bondage; but that it is only to the extension of the territory in which the African may thus be held. He has no hostility, then, it appears, to the fact of our holding the African race in bondage in one place, but he has insuperable objections to our doing so in another. Why is this? Is it for the benefit of that race itself? Not at all; for every man must understand that diffusion, not concentration, is for the benefit of the slave. Is it for the benefit of the white race? Not at all; every one must understand, that as the white population predominates over the black, the safety and happiness of both are secured; and, further, all must understand, that if final emancipation is ever to ensue, it must come when the slaves are few in proportion to the whites inhabiting the country. The number of slaves is rapidly increasing, in a ratio probably equal to the natural increase of the white population in any part of the United States. There is no policy which would perpetuate and rivet that institution forever on this country, so surely as that which confines the slaves to the present limits in which they are held. There must—to render emancipation practicable —be a door opened, by which they may go out; and that door must be toward the equator. All who understand their habits and constitutional peculiarities, must admit this. And yet, the policy is here advocated, day after day, by those who claim to be the peculiar friends of emancipation, to draw around us a barrier to prevent the exodus of the slaves, and dam them up in the small territory which they occupy, where, increasing in number year by year, the impossibility of emancipation will augment also, until he only can deny that the system must be perpetual, who is prepared to see the slave become the master, to convert a portion of the States of this Union into negro possessions, or, to witness the more probable result, of their extermination by a servile war.

A word or two more as to another remark made by the Senator. He assumes that the Mexican States were the creation of the Federal Government, and not the Federal Government the creation of the States. Now, sir, the Mexican Republic, like our own, passed from the colonial condition into one of national independence; and when they organized a Government, after throwing off the dominion of Spain, they stated—I read from "White's New Recopilacion of the Laws of Spain, and the Indies," &c., &c.:

Title of the Constitutive Acts of the Mexican Federation.

"ART. 1. The Mexican nation is composed of the provinces formerly known as the viceroyalty of New Spain, the captain-generalship of Yucatan, and the internal provinces of the East and West."

"ART. 5. The nation adopts for the form of its Government a popular representative and Federal Republic."

"ART. 6. Its integral ports are free, sovereign, and independent States, in as far as regards exclusively its internal administration, according to the rules laid down in this act, and in the general constitution."

"ART. 9. The supreme power of the Federation is divided into the legislative, executive, and judicial, and two or more of these powers can never be united in one person or corporation, nor can the legislative power be entrusted to a single individual."

"ART. 171 of the federal compact—the written constitution of the United Mexican States—ordains those articles of this constitution and of the constitutive act which establish the liberty and independence of the Mexican nation, its religion, form of government, liberty of the press; and the division of the supreme powers of the Union and of the States can never be changed."

Mr. BALDWIN. I wish to ask the Senator whether, by the constitution of Mexico, California and New Mexico were States or Territories?

Mr. DAVIS. Territories, I think.

Mr. WALKER. That I may give the Senator the advantage of this position, I will ask him a question. Suppose the Government of Mexico had been established on the plan of Iguala, and that afterward the Congress created under that plan had taken our Constitution and adopted it literally, changing things that absolutely required it, as, for instance, the names, would that constitution have had the same effect there as it would here?

Mr. DAVIS. That involves a great many questions.

Mr. WALKER. I wish him to view it merely in this light: taking the consolidated Government, which was in fact the plan of Iguala, and proclaimed to be the constitution of Mexico, I wish to know if the Congress created under that plan had adopted our Constitution, would it have had the same effect there as here?

Mr. DAVIS. Certainly not; but I only speak of the case as presented. Thus, by revolution, the viceroyalty fell, and a confederation of States, free and independent, rose upon the site it had occupied. The Constitution adopted, defined the powers of each department of the Federal Government there, as here, the depository of the general trusts. I can only answer for things as I understand them to exist, not to supposed cases and their effects.

I had occasion to state to the Senator, on a former occasion, the fact, that the slave being a person, and recognised in a twofold aspect as a person and as property, the laws of the State from which he is carried may follow him, and affect his condition in the State to which he may be migrated. The slave may have, by law, a right to his liberty at a certain age; and if he be carried away before he reaches that age, he does not become a slave for life. The decisions of the courts of Mississippi have been most liberal in this respect. Our juries are prone, in cases involving a supposition of fraud upon the personal rights of a negro, to shield him with a generosity proportionate to his weakness. I believe it will always be found, that among us both the juries and the courts have given to the negro the amplest protection of our laws. This is the natural result of that sympathy and generosity which the relation of master and slave is apt to produce. It is the public opinion of the country—somewhat suppressed, it is true, but not destroyed by the offensive and mischievous interference of our northern brethren with a domestic relation which they do not understand and cannot appreciate. I remember a case in point, that of an African who was supposed to have been brought in after the year 1808, having been captured in some of the constant wars of those barbarian tribes. He was purchased by subscription, and, with a sufficient outfit, was sent back to his native country.

It is no uncommon case for questions to arise, growing out of the laws of the State from which a slave may be brought, and I think this has probably led the Senator into an erroneous construction of judicial decisions.

In replying to my remarks, the Senator from Wisconsin treats my position as an assertion, that slavery results from a natural right. I did not say that. This is the passage from my speech:

"I do not propose to discuss the justice or injustice of slavery, as an abstract proposition; I occupy this seat for no such purpose. It is enough for me to know, that here we are not called upon to legislate, either for its amelioration or to fix the places in which it shall be held, and certainly have no power to abolish it. It is enough for me elsewhere to know, that it was established by decree of Almighty God; that it is sanctioned in the Bible, in both Testaments, from Genesis to Revelation; that it has existed in all ages, has been found among the people of the highest civilization, and in nations of the highest proficiency in the arts. It is enough, if this were not sufficient, to know that it existed in all the States of this Union at the period of the Confederacy, and in all but one at the adoption of the Constitution, and that in one half of them it continues to exist at the present day.''

That is the passage, I believe, on which the gentleman relies. Now, sir, I never spoke about a natural right. I am not very sure what a natural right is. The only natural right I comprehend, is that of force—I know of no other natural right. The Senator owns a hat, not by a natural right, but by law. So he owns land, not by a natural right, but by law. I did not use the term natural right, and yet he founded his argument upon that assumption.

Mr. WALKER. I said that the honorable Senator had traced it to the law of God; and I maintained that that certainly was as much as a declaration that slavery was founded on the laws of nature.

Mr. DAVIS. Well, sir, I did assign it to the decree of God, and I was a little surprised to hear the Senator read the *dicta* of judges of human law to show that it is not the decree of God. I do not know why he went to the reports of judicial decisions to determine what is the decree of God. He should go to the inspired writings, and not to the theories of natural right. Let the gentleman go to Revelation to learn the decree of God— let him go to the Bible, and not to the report of the decisions of courts. I said that slavery was sanctioned in the Bible, authorized, regulated, and recognized from Genesis to Revelation.

Genesis, chapter 9, *verses* 25, 26.—''And he said, cursed be Canaan, a servant of servants shall he be unto his brethren. And he said, Blessed be the Lord God of Shem, and Canaan shall be his servant.

''God shall enlarge Japheth, and he shall dwell in the tents of Shem, and Canaan shall be his servant.''
Genesis, chapter 12, *verse* 7.—''And the Lord appeared unto Abraham, and said, Unto thy seed will I give this land.''

This land being the plain of Moreh, then inhabited by the Canaanite.

Verse 18.—''The same day the Lord made a covenant with Abraham, saying, Unto thy seed I have given this, from the river of Egypt unto the great river, the river Euphrates.''

And then various tribes inhabiting the country were enumerated.

And he who is said to be the father of the faithful, of whom it is said the Lord delighted to honor, Abraham, was given the country of Canaan as his possession; and after many years of oppression, the people of Israel returned to the land of the Canaanites—the land of promise. The Mosaic law regulated slavery as an established institution, drawing the broadest distinction between slavery and servitude, or involuntary and voluntary servitude, making a distinction between the bondsmen who should be of the heathen, and the temporary service of the Jews.

Slavery existed then in the earliest ages, and among the chosen people of God; and in Revelation we are told that it shall exist till the end of time shall come. You find it in the Old and in the New Testament—in the prophecies, psalms, and the epistles of Paul; you find it recognized—sanctioned everywhere. It is the Bible and the Constitution on which we rely, and we are not to be answered by the *dicta* of earthly wisdom, or more earthly arrogance, when we have these high authorities to teach and to construe the decrees of God.

I was sorry that the Senator alluded to the colloquy between myself and the Senator from Illinois, not now in his seat, and upon whose supposed position I made some strictures, in which I was corrected at the time. I admitted the correction, as I always do that of any gentleman who informs me as to his intent or meaning. I was sorry when the Senator thought proper to quote a portion of that colloquy. If he introduced any of it, he should have given the whole.

Mr. WALKER. I will say to the Senator from Mississippi, that I quoted it for a very different object. I quoted him to show that the admission in regard to my own position, of the non-intervention laws of Mexico being in force, was better for the very claim of the South.

Mr. DAVIS. This is a sad sort of non-intervention, which restricts emigration, and regulates the property of American citizens by the intervention of the laws of Mexico. I say to the Senator that I consider his position worse than the Wilmot proviso. I much prefer the position of him who comes openly with an inhibition of slavery, to that of him who finds an escape from the responsibility and takes shelter under the plea of existing laws of Mexico. I much prefer him who takes from us by force that which we believe to be our own, to him who seeks to do it by constructions and disabilities, which he covertly and obliquely imposes.

As my friend from South Carolina is waiting for me, I will give way for him, with the single remark, that when I heard the

Senator from Wisconsin close his speech with such awful curses on agitators, and those who contemplated a dissolution of the Union——

Mr. WALKER. I said one who should intentionally take the first step toward its consummation.

Mr. DAVIS. Then, sir, I trust the Senator has not intentionally taken that one step to its consummation, by agitating it on the floor of Congress, and shocking the feelings of nearly half the States of this Union. I trust it was not intentional, because, if intentional, the heavy curses which he has multiplied here, will descend upon himself; and when I heard him repeat one curse after another, as long as the curse in Sterne, at every pause, unbidden, rose to my lips the conclusion of, Damn him, Obadiah.

Jefferson Davis to James Buchanan.[1]

(From Pennsylvania Historical Society Collections.)

Senate Chamber
15th March 1850

James Buchanan

My dear Sir, I have delayed for some time a purpose not any time abandoned of writing to you on a matter concerning both of us and yourself particularly.

Soon after you left here, Mr. Cameron called on me and questioned the propriety of my remarks in relation to yourself in connection with the Mo. Compromise. He produced an old newspaper in which an account was given of a mutiny in Lancaster say in 1820—among other resolutions my attention was called to one taking decided ground against slavery especially against the admission of any more slave states—I saw the paper but once and do not very clearly remember its contents.

I informed Mr. C. that I would write to you, as a matter of Justice to you and myself.

And now having commenced I will further say that it is

[1] Buchanan, James (1791-1868), fifteenth President of the United States, was born of Scotch Irish descent, near Mercersburg, Pa., April 23, 1791; was graduated from Dickinson college in 1809; studied law in Lancaster, and was admitted to the bar in 1812. He was a member of the Pennsylvania House of Representatives from March 4, 1821, to March 3, 1831; Minister to Russia from June, 1832, to August, 1834; U. S. Senator from December 6, 1834, to March 5, 1845; Secretary of State in President Polk's cabinet from March 6, 1845, to March 7, 1849; Minister to Great Britain 1853-1856; President of the United States from March 4, 1857, to March 3, 1861. He died near Lancaster, Pa., June 1, 1868. Consult G. F. Curtis, Life of James Buchanan, 2 vols; 1332 pp. New York, 1883.

reported here that you recoiled from the proposition to extend
the Mo. Comp. line with the admission of the right to take
slaves into the territory south of that line—Thus you are un-
favorably compared with Mr. Cass who has it is reported said
to friends that he would go thus far—

As ever your friend

JEFFN. DAVIS.

James Buchanan to Jefferson Davis.

(From Pennsylvania Historical Society Collections.)

Private and Confidential

Wheatland 16 March 1850

My dear Sir

I was in Iowa this afternoon & receiving your letter there I
gave it a hasty answer provoked thereto by the conduct of
Cameron.

So far from having in any degree recoiled from the Missouri
Compromise, I have prepared a letter to sustain it, written with
all the little ability of which I am master.

You may ask why has it not been published? The answer is
very easy. From a careful examination of the proceedings in
Congress, it is clear *that non-intervention is all that will be
required by the South.* Webster's speech is to be the basis of the
compromise;—it is lauded to the echo by distinguished Southern
men,—and what is it? Non-intervention, *& non-intervention is
simply because the Wilmot Proviso is not required to prevent the
curse of Slavery from being inflicted on the territories.* Under
the circumstances it would be madness in me to publish my
letter and take higher ground for the South than they have
taken for themselves. This would be to out-Herod Herod &
be more Southern than the South. It could do no good but
might do much mischief.

The truth is the South have got themselves into a condition
on this question from which it appears to me now they cannot
extricate themselves. My proposition of the Missouri Compromise was at once abandoned by them; and the cry was non-intervention. They fought the battle at the last Presidential election with this device upon their banners. The Democracy of
Pennsylvania are now every where rallying to non-intervention.
They suppose in doing this, they are standing by the South in
the manner most acceptable to their Southern brethren. Our

Democratic Journals are praising the speech of Webster because all the appearances are that it is satisfactory to the South. It is now too late to change front with any hope of success. You may retreat with honor upon the principle that you can carry your slaves to California and hold them there under the Constitution & refer this question to the Supreme Court of the United States. I am sorry both for your sakes and my own that such is the condition in which you are placed.

I say for my own sake, because I can never yield the position which I have deliberately taken in favor of the Missouri Compromise; and I shall be assailed by fanatics & free Soilers, as long as I live; for having gone further in support of the rights of the South than Southern Senators & Representatives. I am committed for the Missouri Compromise; & *that committal shall stand.*

Should there be an unexpected change in the aspect of affairs at Washington which would hold out the hope that the publication of my Missouri Compromise letter would do any good, it shall yet be published.

(Written & crossed out by Buchanan)

~~As a constitutional lawyer I wholly dissent from the opinion.~~ I was about to write more; but this letter is long enough.

It may be and doubtless was the fact that in 1819 or 1820 my name was placed on a Committee which reported the resolutions to which that scamp General Cameron refers. I was then a young man—had a great veneration for the chairman of the Committee as my legal preceptor & probably was under the influence of the excitement then universal in Pennsylvania. I first went to Congress in December 1821; & throughout my whole public career have been uniform in maintaining the just constitutional rights of the South. I have made more speeches on this subject both on the floor of the Senate & at home than probably any other man now living. One of them I now enclose to you *marked* which fell into my hands last evening whilst I was looking for other matters.

I wish you would read my speech through on the Veto Power. It is the only one I ever made which fully pleases myself.

from your friend
very respectfully
JAMES BUCHANAN.

Hon. Jefferson Davis.

P. S. Why did not the Southern gentlemen agree upon a common basis of settlement? Please to let me hear from you soon. I am invited *very specially* to a wedding in Washington & probably I may be there for one day on the 9th April. Would to Heaven! that General Taylor might come out in favor of the Missouri Compromise! I should glory in sustaining him. Endorsed:

> Superscription—16 March 1850 Copy of a letter to Jefferson Davis.

Remarks of Jefferson Davis in Senate March 18, 1850 in defense of Mr. Buchanan's position on the slavery question.

Mr. DAVIS, of Mississippi. I wish merely to refer to the language of Mr. Buchanan, as reported in the Congressional Debates, and will endeavor to keep myself in order, in the few remarks I may offer upon it.

Mr. President, I did not hear the Senator from New Hampshire make the statement which he is reported in the *National Intelligencer* to have made, in relation to Mr. Buchanan. If I had, I should have raised the question of accuracy with him then. I heard the Senator from New York make the statement in relation to Mr. Jefferson, and heard it promptly answered by my colleague and the Senator from Michigan. Certainly it is not true that Mr. Buchanan or Mr. Jefferson have ever announced, that the Democracy of the North were the allies of slavery in the South. That they have announced that the Democracy of the North were the natural allies *of the South,* is true, and it has been my pride to believe them so. I wish I could feel that it were as true now, as in the days when Mr. Jefferson pronounced it. The Democracy of the North are, or should be, the natural allies of the South in this; that strict construction being the basis of their creed, they therefore should protect them in their constitutional rights—the only guaranty that the minority has ever desired, and one of which it can never be honestly deprived, under a confederation like our own. This sort of alliance Mr. Jefferson referred to, and this sort of alliance Mr. Buchanan claimed for the Democracy of the North. If that be all that the Senator from New York meant, he used bad language to state his meaning. If that be all that the Senator from New Hampshire meant, he can find in the speeches of Mr. Buchanan a full corroboration of that opinion. If more, the Senator from New Hampshire, I think, will fail in his researches.

In February, 1842, Mr. Buchanan stated, what I believe he would still maintain if he were here, and what I understand the Senator from Michigan on my right [Mr. Cass] to have maintained the other day. In an argument on the veto power Mr. Buchanan said, at the time to which I have referred:

"Let me suppose another case of a much more dangerous character. In the southern States, which compose the weaker portion of the Union, a species of property exists which is now attracting the attention of the whole civilized world. These States never would have become parties to the Union, had not the rights in this property been secured by the Federal Constitution. Foreign and domestic fanatics, some from the belief that they are doing God's service, and others from a desire to divide and destroy this glorious Republic, have conspired to emancipate the southern slaves. On this question, the people of the South, beyond the limits of their own States, stand alone and unsupported by any power on earth, except that of the northern Democracy."

That is what Mr. Buchanan stated. Let the Senator from New Hampshire produce anything of his inconsistent with this. It was further amplified and powerfully illustrated in the continuation of this speech. To this speech I refer the Senator·from New Hampshire in any researches he may have to make, to sustain his assertion on this subject. I have read from it, because in it I believe Mr. Buchanan went further than in any other, and because I am proud of the position therein taken by that illustrious member of the northern Democracy.

J. A. Quitman [1] *to Jefferson Davis*

(From the Mississippi Department of Archives and History. Letter Book of Governor Quitman.)

Executive Department
Hon. Jeffr. Davis   Jackson April 11 - 1850 -
    Washington City: Dr. Sir
I was not aware until a few days since that it was customary to transmit the credentials of his election to the Senator elect. This will account to you for not receiving the enclosed immediately after the election.
                I remain very respectfully
                        Your obt. Sevt.
                            J. A. Quitman.

The above credentials spoken of, and accompanying letter were this day forwarded to the Honl. Jefferson Davis

[1] Governor of Mississippi.

Jefferson Davis to F. H. Elmore [1]

F. H. Elmore   Washington, D. C., 13th April, 1850

Dr Sir: Since the receipt of your letter we have had some consultation in relation to the proposition you submitted in relation to the Nashville convention. The prevailing opinion is to leave the matter entirely in the hands of the people. My own view is and has been that the convention should meet for preventive purposes. That it is necessary to begin an organization of the South the want of which has left us a divided people, when union and cointelligence was necessary for our safety. The charge which has been made of a design to sever the Southern states from the confederacy but increased the propriety of meeting. If we had no other purpose than to redress past wrongs it would be proper to wait until the measure of our grievances was full; but to check aggression, to preserve the union, peaceably to secure our rights requires prompt action. We should no doubt have greater una[ni]mity, higher resolve if called upon to avenge the blow, than if only required to paralyze the arm upraised to strike. Then it would be the energy of revolution, now it is the preservation of the Constitution.

A postponement is in my opinion, equivalent to abandonment of the Southern convention, and to being hereafter branded as disunionists who were arrested in their purpose. It is needless to add that I cannot aid in the object of postponement. Long since I resolved that if the measure was abandoned it should be by no agency of mine, and have believed that the toryism we now see was only to be put down by the action of the faithful. If a few meet, many will rue the day when they oppose us, and our strength will increase thenceforward—I write freely to you whose aim and feelings I know to be such as I cherish—If a different course be adopted from that which I approve, my cordial wish is that my opinions may prove to have been those of an over excited mind—as ever yr. friend

JEFFN. DAVIS.

Remarks of Jefferson Davis April 16, 1850 on appropriation for the Mexican boundary commission.

Mr. DAVIS, of Mississippi. Mr. President, I wish to move an amendment to the amendment of the Senator from Connecti-

[1] The original of this letter was given to Miss Laura A. White by Miss Ellen Elmore and Mrs. Thomas Taylor, daughter of F. H. Elmore, and is now in Miss White's possession.

cut, [Mr. SMITH.] I will say nothing about the amount of the salary fixed by the Senator. I think it small for the station; but I wish to make a remark about the position assumed by the honorable Senator as to the amount of work which has been executed; I hold that a great deal has been done; I hold that the grand problem has been solved, which was, to determine the initial point and direction of the line which connects the boundary on the Pacific with the junction of the Gila and Colorado. Both extremities have been settled, and it is now a simple operation, which any common surveyor can perform, to connect the two ends of that line. It is the simplest part of the labor which remains to be done. It is a great error to estimate the amount of the labor by the length of the line which has to be run. The Senator is mistaken when he supposes that very little has been accomplished. The difficulty was to establish the initial point and the direction in which the line should run; for this, science and judgment were required. That has been performed upon both ends of the line. Now, it is the simple operation of surveying to complete the line, and then to follow up the river Gila to the point where another constructive line is to be established, to connect the branch of the Gila with the intersection of the boundary line and the Rio Grande. There will occur another high astronomical problem, to be solved as that to which I have referred has been done; the rest is all simple surveying, and this operation may be rapidly performed. I think no more time will be necessary than has been allowed by the Senator's first proposition.

The line that has been determined from San Diego to the junction of the Gila and the Colorado, can be completed as soon as funds have been furnished. The officer in command, who has acted as the astronomer, has directed this to be done by his lieutenant. It is to trace the line, and set up the monuments along it.

The amendment which I propose to offer is to add, after the word "surveyor," in the amendment of the Senator from Connecticut, "and the astronomer," and after the words "dollars per annum," the words "and either of these duties being, or having been, performed by an officer of the army, that his pay during the time of the employment shall be increased to that sum."

I offer this amendment for the following reasons: The duty of an astronomer is quite as dignified, and requires a higher grade of acquirement than that of commissioner or surveyor. The surveyor is in fact a subordinate officer to the astronomer.

The Mexican commissioner and surveyor are officers of high rank and of a high grade of compensation. An officer of our army has heretofore been engaged in performing the duties of astronomer; and, indeed, I do not know where else we should go to get the astronomer; one who combines astronomical with topographical attainments is perhaps nowhere else to be found— certainly not in such position that he would accept this appointment. It may be assumed, then, that we are compelled to select an officer of the army; and when this is done, it is neither just nor politic that he should be expected to support himself on the pay of a captain. Unless the provision herein proposed be made, this will be the case. I have referred to the circumstances by which he will be surrounded. You know the condition of the country. The result is, that the compensation in the case supposed, and which, if this amendment fail, will be the existing case, will be hardly sufficient to have a servant and buy his supplies of absolute necessity. When, therefore, you select an officer competent for this duty, and require him to sacrifice all other considerations to his official obligations, you should give him adequate compensation, and shield his professional and his national pride. You should take into account the station and the associations in contact with which you place him by this extraordinary service. I hope, I feel, that this does not require further argument.

Mr. SMITH. I cordially approve of the amendment suggested by my honorable friend from Mississippi, [Mr. DAVIS.] I wish to call his attention, however, to a provision contained in the House bill, having in view, in part, the very object the honorable Senator has adverted to. The object of that amendment is to vest in the President power to make an extra allowance to officers of the army, when stationed on the Pacific coast, and especially in California, where we all know that their regular pay is not sufficient to cover their expenses; and it may be in consequence of that fact that this provision has been inserted in the House bill, in order that the President may be clothed with discretion in the matter to make such extra allowances as may be just and reasonable to cover the extra expenses of the officers of the regular army that may be engaged in the service. The amendment of my honorable friend applies only to one officer—the astronomer—attached to the commission for running the boundary I suppose he will be from the corps of topographical engineers. There will be other officers of that corps associated with him in that duty. Colonel Emory and some other officers were originally detailed for assistance in the discharge of those duties. I suggest, therefore, that there ought to be a provision, as there is in the House bill, to clothe the President with the power of making such extra allowances to all those officers detailed to the performance of those duties as may seem to be reasonable, in consequence of the extraordinary expense which they must necessarily incur.

Mr. DAVIS, of Mississippi. I have no doubt that there should be such a general provision as has been described by the honorable Senator from Connecticut [Mr. SMITH] for an extra allowance to officers who are stationed on the Pacific coast, in Oregon and in California, as well as on the boundary survey; and I hope that some such provision may be adopted. Yet I do not feel that the amendment which I have offered would be rendered unnecessary even by such a general provision.

The fact, Mr. President, is simply this: An officer is selected for duty on the boundary survey; if he be assigned to his brevet rank, and have a command equal to that rank, he is allowed brevet pay. But when, as at this time, the command is reduced below that due to the brevet rank, I understand the decision to be that he is then reduced to his original pay. The proposition to which the Senator refers is highly proper. Officers serving upon that service, or any other in Oregon and California, should be provided for by some such arrangement; but the case of the astronomer is one of a peculiar kind. The duties are of a high dignity and great importance. He is associated with officers of the Mexican service of high rank and emolument. If he should be a lieutenant, his brevet pay, even if allowed for the highest brevet he would hold, would not be sufficient to place him on an equality with those with whom he would be associated. His pride and ours should not permit him to hold less than an equal position, and equally to sustain it.

Remarks of Jefferson Davis in Senate April 30, 1850, on the bill granting land to Illinois to construct the Central Railroad.

Mr. DAVIS, of Mississippi. I do not agree at all with the Senator from New Jersey in his opinion as to the utility of this road. It has all the characteristics of a useful public highway, because it is constantly changing the latitude and therefore the products through which it passes. Running from Lake Michigan, it crosses the Ohio at its junction with the Mississippi, and then diverges from the Mississippi, passing to the valley of Tombigbee and Alabama rivers. I would say to the

Senator from New Jersey, that, whilst I agree with him that it is impossible to build a road on the banks of the Mississippi which could successfully compete with that river, still a very slight deviation from it will perhaps render this road profitable. I do not pretend to say how profitable. That, however, is a question which those who invest their money in such improvements generally examine more closely and decide more accurately than we can.

I think the proposition of the Senator from Tennessee legitimately flows from one feature in this bill, that which grants land remote from the road, where there is none adjacent. It is a new feature—one never before incorporated in any bill of the kind which I have voted for, and for which I will not consent to vote. If we grant land other than that through which the road is constructed, for the purposes of the road, I see no reason why we should not grant it to aid internal improvements in other States. Nor do I see, in either aspect, any difference between thus granting land or taking money from the treasury to build these works. There is a great distinction between this proposition and one which confines the grant to the land through which the road passes. It is, first, a distinction of principle; for, whilst I deny the power of the Government to appropriate public money for these improvements, it must be conceded the power to dispose of the public lands with certain conditions growing out of the nature of the trust, is fully conferred. For instance, if these lands are unsold or not taken up, we can, by granting a portion of them, construct a road which will bring the adjoining lands into market, as a means proper to execute the trust, to dispose of the public domain for the common benefit of the States. We gain, first, something to the treasury by the sale of lands, which would otherwise be unsaleable, and we gain far more than what is received for the lands, in the revenue which will constantly flow into the treasury, when the lands are occupied and cultivated, by the increased demand for the imports upon which the revenue is raised. This is a reason for granting land which I recognize as within our power and duty as trustee for its disposal. This is the great difference in principle, between a grant of land connected with and remote from the road to be constructed. It carries also two limitations with it. First, it is limited to such grants as are made at the time the lands are unsettled, and in the forest state. It carries a limitation with it then as to time; and by restricting the grant to the land through which the road passes, it carries a limitation as to space. These two restrictions remove from such grants a great many objections which apply to a general appropriation of land or of money from the treasury; the two last being, to my mind, equivalent, so far as the question of power is involved. I therefore consider that the Senator from Tennessee draws his proposition legitimately from the provision in the bill to which I have referred. Both go beyond what I consider expedient or constitutional, and against both, therefore, I shall vote, whatever else may depend upon it. So much of this amended bill as is found from line sixteen, after the word "practicable," down to the word "provided" in the twenty-sixth line, includes the feature of a floating grant, giving the right to go elsewhere than along the road to find the land to build the road, and therefore presents at once the idea that a thickly-settled country may call for grants of land, for the purpose of building roads, where the capital of the people is sufficient to build them, where the grant has no proper connection with the disposal of the public domain, and cannot be expected to bring to the common fund a remunerating result. Such a grant would be equivalent to an appropriation from the treasury. So far as I have supported any of these grants, it has been by placing the Federal Government in the condition of a proprietor of forest lands. An individual so circumstanced would, at least could very well grant a small portion of them to some one who would cut a road, so as to facilitate examination, invite emigration to them, and bring them into market. From a parity of reasoning, the Federal Government may grant land to build a road through its unsettled domain, with a view of bringing it into the market, or rendering it saleable. This is the principle by which I have been governed, and which will guide me in my vote upon this bill. If in order, I move to amend this bill by striking out the clause to which I have referred, so as to leave the bill a simple grant of alternate sections of land along the line of road.

Remarks in Senate on May 2, 1850, on bill granting land to Illinois to construct the Central Railroad.

Mr. DAVIS, of Mississippi, moved to amend section 2, line 26. After "said" insert "provided that the lands to be so located shall in no case be further than fifteen miles from the line of the road, and further."

Mr. KING. This amendment will obviate the objection which has been made to the bill by some gentlemen as to the possibility of these lands being selected all over the State.

Mr. DAVIS, of Mississippi. It is intended by this amendment to bring the provisions of the bill within the principle of making the grant to promote the public interests in the land immediately connected with the road to be benefited by it; for passing through the prairie country of Illinois, there is no doubt that all the land for a greater distance than that will be benefited, and to that extent will be connected with the road. Whilst settlers on these lands have all the elements of production in the soil and climate, these lands must remain valueless so long as the cost of transportation to market is so great as to render the products unprofitable when transported to the place where they are to be sold. In the case where land is really valuable, but is unsaleable in consequence of its remoteness from a suitable market for its products, it will be made valuable by being brought within practicable means of getting to market. My object in offering this amendment is to bring the provisions of the bill within a fair operation of the principle and policy avowed, so as to enable me to vote for it.

Mr. DAVIS, of Mississippi. Mr. President, the Senator from Georgia has assumed his facts and ascribed motives at his own pleasure, and therefore it was very easy for him to reach any conclusion that he proposed, and as easy to apply any censure that he thought proper. The Senator says that there is a purpose of deception. I say, that within my knowledge there is none. I am glad that he uses the pronoun "we," instead of "you." If deceptive purpose exist anywhere, it is not within my breast. Those who feel it, need no accuser. I deny every position which the Senator has taken and assumed to be a fact. I deny emphatically that there is any purpose of deception, to be inferred or by possibility extracted from the motion I have made. So far as I am concerned, this amendment was framed and offered in a spirit any other than that of deception.

Mr. DAWSON. If the Senator will allow me the floor for a moment, I will put him right. It was not the conduct of Senators which I termed deceptive, but the principle that the value of the remainder of the public lands would be increased by giving away a part of them.

Mr. DAVIS, of Mississippi. The manner of the Senator was perhaps more excited than he supposed, at the time he made the charge. But to the question of fact. It is assumed, then, by the Senator, that the land could not be increased in value by having a railroad run within fifteen miles of it. You may have land one hundred or two hundred miles from market,

and some of its products, for the want of transportation, have
no value beyond the demand for domestic consumption; but if
you bring a railroad within fifteen miles of it, instead of having
to go one hundred or two hundred miles to market, you have
now only to go fifteen miles to find means of transportation.
That certainly makes the market more available for the purpose of selling the produce which you may raise upon your
land, than if you had no railroad, and of course makes the
land more valuable. Does not the Senator know, that lands
within fifteen miles of his own navigable streams, which lead
to the sea-ports of the States, or within fifteen miles of his
railroads, are more valuable than they were before the railroads
were built, or would be if that navigable stream did not exist?

Sir, I have not proposed to extend but to restrict the grants
of land to be given for this purpose. Without the amendment
which I have proposed, I would be compelled to vote against
the bill. My proposition was not to extend this grant, but in its
floating character to strip it of the right which it would otherwise have to run all over the State and select lands. I have
proposed not to increase the width of the slip within which
alternate sections are to be given; but to confine its floating
character to within fifteen miles of the road. I think the value
of the lands, within that distance, will be increased by the construction of a means of transporting bulky and cheap com-
modities. The honorable Senator assumes that this is the
same thing as a grant of land for general purposes of internal
improvement. Every feature of the bill denies it. It is denied
by the specific application which is to be made of this grant of
land. It is also denied by the fact that this grant will revert
to the Government, if this railroad is not constructed within
a specific time. All this makes a very different thing from
a general grant of land for general purposes of internal improvement. This road is chartered by the States through
which it is to pass, and is it likely that they would do anything
which they did not think was for the interests of the citizens
of those States?

As I have said before, I have no objection to the freest principle of granting land to actual settlers, but have objections
to granting lands to corporations. Sir, we know that some
years ago a general distribution of the proceeds of the public
lands among the States took place. From all the returns which
have been published, it appears that not one-fifth of the sums
thus distributed ever inured to the benefit of the people, and
so far only because that in some of the States it relieved the

people from taxation for the support of the current expenses of their Government. Why has not Congress since entered upon that scheme? Because it has been condemned by the experience which the country has had of it.

But, sir, a claim is put up for Georgia. I put up none for Mississippi. I supposed it was some great indignation which prompted the Senator from Georgia when he commenced in such a vehement manner—such indignation as one might feel when he found that the Treasury was about to be robbed, fraud to be perpetrated, deception practiced on the public, and that the general interests of the country were about to suffer. But no such thing. He merely attacks the principle we advance lest it be an obstruction to the application for his own State. I make none for Mississippi: I ask no grant of land in this bill; it has been proposed by others, and is connected with the interests of other States as well as those of Mississippi. Sir, Mississippi has never yet asked a favor from this Government for her own exclusive benefit.

The road that is to pass through Mississippi was located by other interests than her own. It was projected at the North and the South, and it passes through Mississippi only because that is the best route. This road is to pass through a region of country in our State, a portion of which is unsaleable, and a great deal of which will remain so; it also passes through a portion of country which is so fertile that not an acre of it belongs to the Government. Our interest in this project is quite small. This road received its direction from Illinois on one side and from Alabama on the other. It comes through Mississippi only as it comes through Tennessee and Kentucky. It bends into our State for some distance, but it does not reach into a portion of it where the land is now vacant and is soon likely to be peopled. When it reaches that fertile country to which I have referred, in the whole of which there is not an acre of land that belongs to the Government, it goes first to the navigable waters of the Tombigbee, and then approaches the navigable waters of the Mississippi. It will, no doubt, be of some advantage to the country through which it passes, but I do not think it will be of any great vital importance to the State of Mississippi. As I have said before, there are some parts of the route so desirable that not an acre belongs to the Government, while, on the other hand, there are other places that for thirty miles on either side are so poor and unapproachable that nobody would buy it, and, consequently, it has to remain on the hands of the Government until greater facilities of transportation, or a lower price, or both, may induce purchasers to take it.

I am sorry, sir, that, notwithstanding the explanation which I made to the honorable Senator from Georgia, he persisted in saying that my proposition was to extend and not to restrict the amount of land to be given for this purpose. I wish the Senator had done me the justice of giving my views as I had stated them, and not according to the interpretation which he chose to put upon them.

Mr. DAWSON. I did not charge the honorable Senator with injustice. I know that his object was to restrict this road. But the ground which I assumed was this: that if you would extend this to fifteen miles, on the same principle you could extend it to fifty miles.

Mr. DAVIS, of Mississippi. Yes, and by a parity of reasoning the Senator might go on to say that you might extend it to five hundred miles on the same principle. I think fifteen miles about the extreme distance, as it is the distance which a loaded team can habitually travel in a day. Some Senators wish to extend the limit further, and some will be in favor of reducing the distance. But I believe I have reduced it as low as a majority of this body will consent to; I believe I have reduced it within the rule originally prescribed to myself. And if this amendment is not adopted I shall vote against the bill, and if it prove that, as I believe a majority of the Senate will be found in favor of the bill without this amendment, I leave to others the responsibility of defeating the restriction, of violating the principle which has been heretofore observed, and of leaving us without guard or check in future grants of this character.

Remarks of Jefferson Davis in the Senate May 1, 1850, on the joint resolution providing aid to search for Sir John Franklin.

Mr. DAVIS, of Mississippi. Mr. President, before the vote is taken, I wish briefly to state the views which decide my course. While I agree with all that has been said in admiration of the enterprise and genius of the lost captain of the British navy, and sympathize with all the feeling which has found expression as connected with this matter, there is a consideration with me that is beyond all this. So far as merchant vessels may enter into this search, they have already sufficient inducement, not merely in the trade which they may prosecute, but in the prospect of the reward which is offered. I have more hope from the enterprise of Yankee whalers than from a national expedition. But it is not of the probability of success that I would speak. This is a proposition that the Government of the United States shall enter into a search for the lost seamen of Great Britain. Now, while we have explorers upon land and sea of our own, whose fate is involved in uncertainty, and who, though not so well known to the world at large, have in their own circle eyes that watch and weep for them as sincerely and anxiously as do others for the more distinguished, and who, having the highest claims upon our Government, are lost—perhaps captives among the savage, and yet remain unsought for —I hope that the efforts of the Government, the means of the treasury, will first be expended for them. The sun of our Government should shine equally upon all its citizens, but constitutionally it shines only upon them—it has no rays to lend to those who owe no allegiance to our flag; surely none until it has lighted all within the proper sphere of its illumination. The British Government has done much—much has been done and is doing by private enterprise—to discover, if possible, the lost navigator. If, happily, he could be discovered by an American merchant vessel within the limit of the recommendation of the Executive, or if he could be discovered by our navy in the proper discharge of their duties, it would be gratifying to our national pride, deeply gratifying to our humane feeling. But an expedition fitted out for this purpose alone appears to me to be beyond the duties of the Government—not the proper service of our navy, and not a constitutional object for the appropriation of money. Having all sympathy of feeling with the widow, and admiration for the noble seaman, I must, nevertheless, consider such a course a very improper exercise of the functions of this Government. I think it is improper to appropriate money for such a purpose; and I can only be convinced of an error in this opinion by being shown that this Government is not a corporation formed by the State for specific objects and with limited powers, but is a great eleemosynary institution with a range as wide as the claims of humanity, unbounded by either sea or land. Until this great change in my creed occurs, I expect to hold that there is no power of this Government, no duty of this Government, that can be brought to bear upon the subject now before us, and therefore to withhold my support from all such propositions. I object not to the fact that these ships are owned by private individuals; though, if this expedition is considered a proper duty of the navy, (and the remarks made by the chairman of the Committee on Naval Affairs seem so to indicate,) then we should build vessels suited for this purpose. If it differs from the general objects of the country, the known national objects—if it is an extraordinary exercise of power, not drawn from the Constitution—then we should have nothing to do with it, in one case or the other.

These are my opinions, Mr. President; and these will control my vote. I will not enter into an extended view of the subject, or attempt to show the remote consequences of this wide departure from strict construction: the anxiety known to be felt to terminate the debate forbids it.

Remarks of Jefferson Davis in Senate May 8, 1850, on presenting the report of the Legislature of Mississippi on the slavery question, and the Nashville Convention.

Mr. DAVIS, of Mississippi, presented a report of a Committee on Federal State relations, accompanied by resolutions adopted by the Legislature of the State of Mississippi, on the subject of slavery, and the question in controversy between the northern and southern portions of the Confederacy growing out of that institution; which were read and ordered to lie on the table.

Mr. D. said: As instructed, I present the report and resolutions of the Legislature of Mississippi, on the subject which distracts and divides the people of the Union, and which threatens, unless checked in its onward course, to produce consequences fatal to the cause of human liberty, as secured and advanced by the Constitution of the United States—consequences destructive to fraternal feeling between the different sections of the Confederacy—and finally to terminate in the wreck of this Republic, the last best hope of free government, of human and social progress and happiness.

In presenting these resolutions to the Senate, I wish briefly to read from the proceedings of the popular meetings which preceded, and probably originated this legislation, both because they illustrate the meaning and intent of these resolutions, and because they have been either greatly misunderstood or grossly misrepresented. The people of Mississippi having seen, in public meetings, in conventions, and in legislative resolutions of northern States, what they deemed to be an assault upon their constitutional rights, looked for protection against these hostile proceedings to the Congress of the United States. When a crisis approached, if it had not arrived, and they saw Congress adjourn, after full discussion of a question dangerous to their peace, their prosperity, and perhaps to their existence, without any action upon the subject, they, as became freemen and the sons of freemen, took the case into their own hands. A primary meeting, after full notice given through the press, assembled at the seat of government in Mississippi on the 7th of May. That meeting called upon the different counties to hold assemblages within their limits, and to elect delegates to a State convention, which should be authorized to take into consideration the means which should be adopted to avert the hazard which seemed to be impending over them. This primary meeting and that State convention have been assailed, either ignorantly or maliciously, and accused of having desired to disturb the fraternity of the nation, if not to dissolve the bonds which hold it together. A complete answer to all such charges is to be found in the proceedings themselves; and I propose now to read to the Senate brief extracts from the journal of the primary meeting, and from the report and address of the convention which assembled in obedience to its call. These extracts, and the remarks with which I propose to accompany them, shall be as limited as the case will allow.

When the meeting assembled, it was organized with all the due forms of a deliberative body, and a committee was appointed to prepare an address and to report it to the meeting. The address thus reported by them reads:

"The committee to whom was referred the subject of controversy between the northern and southern States of the Union have had the same under consideration, and beg leave to report the following as an address to the citizens of Mississippi, together with the accompanying resolutions.

"The subject was approached by them, as it should be by this meeting, in full view of its solemnity and importance; not as a common-place topic—not as a mere question of expediency on a matter of secondary consideration, but as one in which our dearest rights are involved—rights which we possessed as citizens of independent States, and which are reserved to us by the Constitution of the United States.

*   *   *   *   *   *   *   *   *

"We approached the subject, not in anger, but in sorrow. We venerate the Union—we venerate the memory of the illustrious men who cemented us as a family of nations—as one people; and we would hold out as an example to their sons the recollection of the spirit of forbearance—of moderation—of compromise—of equal justice and true patriotism, which governed them in their great work.

*   *   *   *   *   *   *   *   *

"We have met, not only in defence of our individual rights, but in defence of our common country; and we would fondly hope that our timely warning may save our Union unimpaired. We meet not to agitate—not to act but to prepare for action when the occasion may be forced upon us."

Such was the language of those who assembled in this primary meeting. In such terms they called upon the counties to deliberate on the state of the country, and, if found advisable by them, to appoint delegates to meet in State convention, to confer together on the dangers by which they were threatened. A State convention, formed of delegates appointed from the different counties, after full time, and notice, and discussion in primary assemblies, met. The committee of that State convention, appointed to report upon the subjects for the consideration of which they assembled, made the report from which I read:

"We, the delegates to a convention, called by the people of the State of Mississippi, to deliberate on the means to prevent the unfounded pretension that Congress has power to legislate on the subject of domestic slavery, and to prohibit its introduction and existence in the territories of the United States, have duly considered the important subject committed to our charge, and make the following report as expressive of the voice of Mississippi.

*   *   *   *   *   *   *   *   *

"In this unfortunate controversy there are but two alternatives—the one is submission, the other resistance. To the one we cannot, we will not consent; the other, we are reluctant to adopt.

*   *   *   *   *   *   *   *   *

"We have not met to discuss the question of power or expediency; they have been argued and reargued, in and out of Congress, by our statesmen and by our people. We have reasoned and remonstrated in terms of conciliation with our northern brethren, until forbearance has ceased to be a virtue. We have warned them of the consequences of perseverance. They have disregarded our remonstrances and our warnings; they have disregarded the most solemn compromises, in which we yielded too much. They have refused to submit to judicial determination, preferring to decide by the force of numbers. There is no common arbiter; and we, too, must decide for ourselves. That decision is made. We take our stand on the plain principles of the Constitution, and intend to maintain it, or sink in the effort.

"We assert that Congress has no power over the subject of slavery, within the States, or in the Territories; that these States, by the Revolution, by the Declaration of Independence, and by the treaty of peace, became separate and independent sovereignties, with all the political power of separate and distinct nations; that they are still so, except so far as they may have expressly delegated part of their power to the General Government.

*   *   *   *   *   *   *   *   *

"We maintain that the system of slavery was recognized by the Constitution—slaves were recognized as property, the full enjoyment of which was guarded and protected—guarantied by that compact; that Congress has no power over such property.

*   *   *   *   *   *   *   *   *

"The power of Congress to legislate for the Territories is a power to protect the citizen and his property, not to declare what is property."

But, sir, a full answer to those who have charged this convention with any purpose of disunion, is contained in the first resolution passed by that convention, as follows:

"1st. *Resolved,* That we continue to entertain a devoted and cherished attachment to the Union, but we desire to have it as it was formed, and not as an engine of oppression."

This convention appointed a committee to prepare an address to the people of Mississippi; and from that address I will read as briefly as I have from the report:

"The Union must and will be preserved. The slave States, in resisting such dangerous and destructive usurpations of the Federal Government, are defending the Constitution and Union. Their position is wholly defensive—defensive of their domestic relations and their private rights of property; defensive of their laws, upon which these domestic relations and rights of property are founded; defensive of their social and political existence as States; defensive of the Constitution and Union; defensive of law, order, and good government, of the right of the people to govern themselves by governments and laws of their own making throughout the world. It is a cause which cannot fail before the social philosophy.

*   *   *   *   *   *   *   *   *

"Beside and beyond a popular convention of the southern States, with the view and the hope of arresting the course of

aggression, and, if not practicable, then to concentrate the
South in will, understanding, and action, the convention of
Mississippi suggested, as the possible ultimate resort, the call,
by the Legislatures of the assailed States, of still more solemn
conventions—such as should be regularly elected by the people
of those States—to deliberate, speak, and act, with all the
sovereign power of the people. Should, in the result, such conventions be called and meet, they may lead to a like regularly
constituted convention of all the assailed States, to provide, in
the last resort, for their separate welfare by the formation of
a compact and a union that will afford protection to their liberties and rights. In such a crisis, in the language of Mr.
Madison, 'one spirit will animate and conduct the whole.' ''

The last, sir, were not the means chosen, but the alternative
resorted to when all constitutional and legal modes had failed
—to be adopted only when they could not possibly otherwise
secure their rights. After noticing how much depended upon
the Union, how deeply the interests of all sections were connected with it, with what jealousy it was watched, with what
design and purpose at least one foreign power had sought to
sow the seeds of disunion in the United States, the address goes
on to say:

"Our strength as a nation—our success in gaining the commerce of the world—our future growth in wealth and population—the cause of human liberty and the people's rights throughout the world depend upon *our Union as it is*. Let us be true
to our trust. Let us preserve *the Union* and leave slavery to
the natural course of events.''

They have not nor have their representatives ever sought any
other rights than the Constitution gives, or any higher privileges
than our fathers left us as an inheritance. They have never
violated the rights of others, and thus endangered the Union.
They have never disturbed the peace, security, or growing
prosperity of other States, and thus given cause to dissolve
the compact because of its insufficiency or its violation, and still
less have they sought its dissolution themselves.

After these popular proceedings, the Legislature of the State
met. That Legislature, in the resolutions which I proposed
this morning to present, have but responded to the known feelings of the people whom they represent. They have in nowise
departed from the characteristic features of the primary meetings and the popular convention of the State. They have reaffirmed that attachment to the Union which characterizes our

people, and they have reasserted those rights which they value above all earthly considerations, as the birthright of freemen and peers in the Union. Such, sir, has been the action of the State—such has been the action of its Legislature.

I read an extract from a report of the select committee on Federal and State relations, adopted by the Legislature:

"We have arrived at a period in the political existence of our country when the fears of the patriot and philanthropist may well be excited, lest the noblest fabric of constitutional government on earth may, ere long, be laid in ruins by the elements of discord, engendered by an unholy lust for power, and the fell spirit of fanaticism, acting upon the minds of our brethren of the non-slaveholding States; and that beneath its ruins will be forever buried the hopes of an admiring world for the political regeneration of enslaved millions.

*   *   *   *   *   *   *   *   *

"The spirit of forbearance and concession, which has been for more than thirty years manifested and acted on by the slaveholding States has but strengthened the determination of their northern brethren to fasten upon them a system of legislation, in regard to their peculiar domestic relations, as fatal in its effects to their prosperity and happiness as members of the Confederacy, as it is unjust, and contrary to the principles and provisions of the Constitution.

*   *   *   *   *   *   *   *   *

"1. *Resolved*, That we continue to entertain a devoted and cherished attachment to the Union, but we desire to have it as it was formed, and not as an engine of oppression.

*   *   *   *   *   *   *   *   *

"7. That, in view of the frequent and increasing evidence of the determination of the people of the non-slaveholding States to disregard the guarantees of the Constitution, and to agitate the subject of slavery, both in and out of Congress, avowedly for the purpose of effecting its abolition in the States; and, also, in view of the facts set forth in the late "Address of the Southern Members of Congress," this Convention proclaims the deliberate conviction that the time has arrived when the southern States should take counsel together for their common safety; and that a Convention of the slaveholding States should be held at Nashville, Tennessee, on the FIRST MONDAY IN JUNE next, to devise and adopt some mode of resistance to these aggressions.

*   *   *   *   *   *   *   *   *

"*Be it further resolved*, That it is the duty of the Congress of the United States to provide territorial organization and governments for all the territories acquired by the common blood and treasure of the citizens of the several States, and to provide the means of enforcing in said territories the guarantees of the Constitution of the United States in reference to the property of citizens of any of the States removing to any of said territories with the same, without distinction of limitation.''

Now, sir, compare this with the action of those who, striving against the Constitution, and constantly seeking to scatter broadcast the seeds of dissension throughout the Union, yet arraign our defensive measures, which grow legitimately and necessarily out of their own action. Compare the proceedings from which I have read, and the spirit of the extracts from the Mississippi address and resolutions which I have brought to the notice of the Senate, with such tirades as are to be found in the proceedings of Free-Soil conventions. Measure them with the proposition of the so-called Christians for a convention of all the religious denominations of the North and of the West for a crusade against slavery, and to debar slaveholders from communion with the churches.

For the South to have remained passive under all the provocations they have received, non-resistant under all the injuries perpetrated and contemplated, would have exhibited more patience than is consonant with political wisdom, or less spirit than becomes a free and independent people, or less vigilance than is necessary for the preservation of liberty.

We have had cause enough, both in and out of Congress, for all, and more than all, the measures we have ever proposed— warnings, abundant warnings, to have justified more formidable and efficient preparation. Whilst Congress has failed to promote peace and security, by discouraging and refusing in any degree to be connected with fanatical agitation, blank petitions have been sent all over the country to procure signatures asking for such hostile legislation by the Federal Congress as its conduct has permitted evil men to hope for. Instead of giving the repose and the assurance of safety which is a duty of Government, the course pursued here has increased the agitation which a hesitating policy might have been expected to engender when opposed to fanaticism. The senseless cry of the sacred right of petition—surely senseless when there is no grievance complained of, or when no redress is possible—has supported, if it has not created, a morbid desire to exercise the privilege of encumbering the tables of Congress with petitions, which it were uncharitable to suppose had been always examined by the signers. It has become a business of some to multiply the cases of offence to the southern people, to pile higher the mountain of memorials and petitions, abusive of southern institutions, under which the congressional shelves are now groaning.

I read from a document consisting of a number of captions for various petitions, to be distributed for signers in various parts of the country. They are as follows:

"Petition to secure to alleged fugitives the right of trial by jury—to the Congress of the United States."

"Petition for the repeal of all laws, enacted or adopted by Congress, for the support of slavery in the District of Columbia—to the Congress of the United States."

"Petition against the admission of more slave States into the Union—to the Congress of the United States."

"Petition for the establishment and protection of freedom in the territories of the United States—to the Congress of the United States."

On the opposite sheet to that containing these petitions, is the following circular:

"To each friend of liberty in the United States:

"Your prompt attention is earnestly requested to this communication. Please read it with the annexed forms of petitions, and then act efficiently in the premises."

These are sent through the mail, and in due time bear their fruit of public excitement; and when they reach their final destination, the halls of Congress produce that interference with the discharge of our duties which has been recently so often witnessed in the Senate.

Sir, in every form, individually and collectively, through the press and from the pulpit, by associations, by conventions of world-wide delegates, by evangelical alliances—by every known mode, have we been assailed; yes, by State conventions, too. I have before me the proceedings of one, the object of which is to get up a sectional convention. It was held in the State of Rhode Island. The proceedings which have been sent to me bear date of March 16, 1850. With the usual amount of scurrilous abuse of the South, is mingled an attack on a measure now pending in this body—the bill to enforce the constitutional requirement for the rendition of fugitive salves. I will read the introduction, and two of the resolutions:

"FREE SOIL STATE CONVENTION.—The convention was held yesterday in this city at the State House, and was called to order by Joseph Venazie, esq., and was temporarily organized by the election of Walter R. Danforth, president, and John H. Willard and Elisha N. Aldrich, secretaries. A call was made from the chair for certificates of the election of delegates from the several towns, which, being produced, were thus enrolled by the secretaries, as follows:

"Gloucester, Warwick, Exeter, East Greenwich, Providence, Westerly, Hopkinton, Coventry, Cumberland, South Kingstown, North Providence, Burrillville, Newport, and Smithfield.

"*Resolved,* That, if the bill now pending before the United States Senate, "to reclaim fugitives from slavery," becomes a law, we cannot and will not so far degrade our common humanity, mock our professions as lovers of liberty, stultify our convictions of justice, scoff at the plainest teachings of the Christian religion, and deride the instructions of the world's Redeemer, as to refuse to clothe the naked and feed the hungry, panting fugitive, pleading for freedom; or as to become jackals and blood-hounds for man-stealers in pursuit of their innocent victim!

"*Resolved,* That, in our opinion, agitation is essentially necessary to arouse the public mind from its present state of lethargy on the subject of human slavery: therefore we would recommend the call of a New England convention of Free-Soilers, at such time and place as the various State central committees may hereafter determine; and we would earnestly solicit their early attention to the importance of this matter."

Here, sir, is the proposition to assemble a sectional convention for the purpose of violating the constitutional rights of another portion of the Union; yet this passes unnoticed, at least unrebuked, by such as have villified those who have peaceably assembled, not to assail or endanger their neighbors, but to secure their own constitutional rights. They, however, being of the South, therefore are charged with purposes of disunion.

It is not enough that our rights are disputed, our growth and prosperity and equality in the Union attacked as the cause of an enemy, that the burdens and benefits of the Government are distributed with a partial and unjust discrimination against us, but to this, to these, shall the arraignment of our motives be added.

Mr. President, these injuries, positive and negative—these offences against their pride and sensibility—these intrusions upon their domestic relations—these infringements upon their State rights, increasing from year to year in offensiveness, and the strength by which they are sustained—have excited the feeling manifested in the State of Mississippi. But, sir, we have been asked, and asked, too, in the Senate, if this Nashville Convention does not meet for purposes of disunion, why does it meet at all? Mr. President, have we reached that point in the history of our Government when aggression is sanctioned by numbers, and redress can only be obtained by force?—when citizens can not peaceably assemble in convention with other hopes and other prospects than disunion? Sir, this Nashville Convention was founded in the confidence which the people of Mississippi, so far as they recommended it, had in the patriotism, the good morals, and good sense of the North. It was founded in the expectation that the masses of the South could speak to the masses of the North, and gain their attention for useful purposes. It was founded in the hope that fraternity was not yet dead, and regard for the Constitution not yet wholly obliterated among the people, however far politicians may have gone astray. Those who believe that this faith was unjust and this hope was vain, may well ask us, if not assembled there for purposes of disunion, why do we assemble? When those who believe this confidence in the patriotism and fraternity of our co-States of the Union to be unfounded, ask such a question, no answer can be given which to them could be satisfactory.

One of the resolutions which I propose this morning to present, avers it as one of the grievances of which we complain, that Congress has failed to exercise what is an official, a moral, a constitutional obligation, that is, to give government to the Territories, and protection to property going into those Territories. We, the Congress, are the trustees of the public domain. We have failed to exercise the duties of that trust; and why, sir, have we failed? It has been because the power of fanaticism has interfered with our legislation; its influence has been sufficient to control the action of Congress. We have been unable to legislate, unless in accordance with the demands of the anti-slavery party. In this case it is not only a constitutional obligation of the high character which I have stated, but an obligation imposed upon us by treaty, an obligation which we took upon ourselves in the solemn international compact of Guadalupe Hidalgo, by which we received a territory and population of Mexico, and pledged ourselves to give to that population the protection of our laws and our government. We have failed in that treaty obligation, and to the other derelictions have added a breach of national faith by failing to give to the Mexican population accepting the terms of the treaty, that protection which had been guarantied in the contract by which we acquired the territory, to those who chose to remain on the soil and become citizens of the United States.

It is true, sir, that some have proposed to escape from this responsibility by allowing emigrants, drawn from all countries by the attractive force of gold, in conjunction with the resident Mexicans and those who have gone from the United States into California, to execute those powers which it was the duty of this Federal Government in part to have exercised, and in whole to have preserved as the property of the States, until surrendered on their part by competent authority. When we received the territory into the United States, it was the acquisition of the States, and ours the obligation to secure it for the common benefit and to the common use: that we have failed to perform. There was a right in every citizen of the United States to go into that territory, and to find for his property the protection of the law and the Constitution of the United States; that has been denied:—denied for the express purpose of stripping the people of the South of the advantage which even the declaration that the Constitution extended to the territory would have given to the slaveholders who might wish to carry that species of property into the territories. Congress has thus indirectly done that which it has not dared directly to do: it has, by refusing the protection of laws conforming to the United States Constitution, excluded slaveholders from going with their property into the territories as effectually as it could have been done by the odious, abandoned Wilmot proviso. Need we, sir, graver or other causes of complaint to justify a Southern Convention?

If, sir, the people of that territory, coerced by the failure of Congress to give them a government, have assembled and adopted for themselves such governments as they could provide under the circumstances, it was by the action of Congress that they were driven to that necessity. Nay, more, sir: with the knowledge before their eyes, that it was opposition to slavery which prevented the formation of territorial governments, they must have seen, without recurring to the Missouri controversy, that unless they excluded slavery by their fundamental law, their government would be rejected; and thus they were in effect commanded to form a constitution which should exclude slavery from the territory over which they proposed to erect their government. What is this, sir, but two-fold interference with the property rights of one and the political liberty of another portion of the people? What, sir, but dictation to the population of California with regard to the kind of government which they should be permitted to form? If they had a right to form a government at all, they certainly had a right to form it unshackled by extraneous opinions or other limitation than that which the Constitution of the United States imposes. I do not propose now to discuss this question. It is but incidentally involved in the resolutions I present, and belongs properly to a bill which I presume will be soon under consideration of the Senate. I merely wish to suggest to Senators, to ask themselves whether they have given to the people, whom they propose to admit as a State, the free and untrammeled privilege of forming their institutions according to their own will?—whether they have not indicated to them, by their action, that they need not hope to enter this Union save with a prohibition of slavery incorporated into their constitution?

Thus it seems to be sought by the hands of others to do that which the anti-slavery men of Congress have not been able to effect, and thus indirectly, but effectually, to deprive the South of all share in this territory.

The people of Mississippi exercised their right peaceably to assemble—a right which Great Britain denied to our forefathers, and which denial, more than any other one cause, led to the war of the Revolution, which gave independence to these United States. They peaceably assembled. They considered their grievances. They have invited others, like circumstanced, to meet them in consultation upon the subject of providing appropriate remedies. They have not sought by force of arms, nor by force of numbers, to violate the Constitution, or infringe the rights of others. Far from it. They have sought by public opinion, and by a frank expression of their convictions and determinations, to operate upon what they still hope exists— the spirit of patriotism and fraternity—which, in times gone by, animated and governed their fathers, when, united by one Constitution, and marching to a glorious destiny under one banner, they founded the Republic. This is the length and breadth and depth of all the proceedings of the people of Mississippi. Under such circumstances, therefore, they may well scorn the denunciations of those who impugn their motives. They may well rely for their justification against charges of disloyalty to the Union, on the proofs they have heretofore given, and those they are ready hereafter to give, whenever their country may need them, of their devoted attachment to the glory and interests, and their faithful adherence to the Constitution, of the United States. Well may they rely securely upon the purity of their motives, the justice of their demands, and the final judgment of mankind, for a refutation of the charges of those who have attempted to defame them. It is true that the hope and confidence in the justice, the feeling of fraternity, and the sense of constitutional obligation, to which I have referred, have rendered some prone, upon slight evidence, to believe that all danger was past; and if recent events have created thus some division of opinion as to the necessity of the Nashville Convention, let no one presume from that manifestation that there is any purpose of submission, or of abandonment of their friends and neighbors, in case that hope and confidence are disappointed and deceived. The difference, Mr. President, is mainly this: some rely upon the patriotism and good feeling of their fellow-citizens of the North for a full and fair settlement of all matters in dispute; others distrust it. Those who distrust it are in favor of immediate action. Those who feel the reliance to which I have referred are disposed to postpone action, with the hope that it will be rendered unnecessary. I am not one of those who believe the hope to be well founded. It is my opinion that justice will not be done to the South, unless from other promptings than are about us here—that we shall have no substantial consideration offered to us for the surrender of an equal claim to California. No security against future harassment by Congress will probably be given. The rainbow which some have seen, I fear was set before the termination of the storm. If this be so, those who have been first to hope, to relax their energies, to trust in compromise promises, will often be the first to sound the alarm when danger again approaches. Therefore, I say, if a reckless and self-sustaining majority shall trample upon her rights, if the constitutional equality of the States is to be overthrown by force, private and political rights to be borne down by force of numbers, then, sir when that victory over constitutional rights is achieved, the shout of triumph which announces it, before it is half uttered, will be checked by the united, the determined action of the South, and every breeze will bring to the marauding destroyers of those rights the warning, Woe, woe to the riders who trample them down! I submit the report and resolutions, and ask that they may be read and printed for the use of the Senate.

Jefferson Davis to the Washington Union.

(From Mississippi *Free Trader*, June 12, 1850.)

Washington, (D. C.,) May 18, 1850.

Gentlemen: In your paper of this morning I find a letter which, because of its special reference to myself, and still more because of the source from which it emanates, claims from me a notice. For this purpose, I ask the use of your columns, so that the reply and the correspondence to which it relates, may go to the public through the same channel. I refer to the letter of the Hon. Robt. J. Walker, whose name and fame are closely and honorably associated with the constituency I represent, and whose opinions are of high authority throughout our whole country.

To all that is said—beautifully and forcibly said—in favor of our constitutional Union—to every appeal to fraternal feeling, to mutual forbearance and concession—no heart responds more promptly and fully than my own. But my judgment halts at the point where he commences the application of these patriotic sentiments to the so called "compromise bill" now under discussion in the United States Senate. The constitution of the United States, and the will of my constituents, are lights by which I endeavor soberly and conscientiously to examine every political subject upon which it becomes my duty to act. These are concentrated to burning brilliancy upon the question of the equal right of the South as of the North to possess and enjoy the territory belonging to the State of the Union, and with every species of property to migrate to it, without any discrimination injurious to the one or favorable to the other. Has this been enjoyed in California? is it now secured? If not, in what consists the compromise, which, it is said, characterizes our Union, and is marked on our constitution, from the appeal of Franklin in favor of conference and concession, to the close of Madison's record of the debates of the convention which formed the constitution of our Union?

I am told that the Union is in danger, and I am called to the rescue. That summons has been long since received from other quarters, and answered in the spirit of self-sacrifice, of fraternal forbearance, and mutual concession. Time and again have I announced, that to close this conflict of irreconcilable opinion, I was willing to adhere to the compromise line which, by the acquiescence of the States, had acquired a validity Congress could not give, and leaving to each all which pride of opinion could not yield—to divide the territory between the rival claimants, by extending the old line of the Missouri and Texas compromise to the Pacific ocean. Heretofore this compromise had unequivocally operated against the South; now, for the first time, it is a two sided question, and lo! the North rejects it. Who, then, displays uncompromising, ultra, or selfish temper in this controversy? Who, if this Union rests upon the

constitution with all its compromises, limitations, and guaranties, best conduces to its perpetuity—he who resolutely maintains the equality of the State, and of the rights, and privileges,
and immunities of all the citizens thereof, or he who surrenders
to the aggressive spirit of a section.

Together with other southern senators, I have sought to amend
the bill, and strip it of those features which are violative of that
constitutional equality. I have not found any evidence of that
much-lauded spirit of compromise in the provisions of the bill,
and, if it pass without material amendments, can anticipate
only evil as its ultimate result. Under such convictions, and
when, as one of a minority, I was struggling for what I believe to be essential to the Union, and necessary to those whom
I immediately represent, it was with no common regret that
I saw one, so long respected and so much admired, throw his
name into the scale against us, coming forward as a volunteer
to support, by his potential influence, the bill as it is. Nay more:
he invokes to this aid the name of our lamented friend, the late
President of the United States. In answer to the supposition
that Mr. Polk would have given this ''compromise'' his cordial
support, I will quote from the special message of that statesman in relation to the Oregon territorial bill.

After referring to the Missouri compromise and the happy
consequences which resulted from it, and the renewal of the
compromise as applied to Texas, he says:

''The Territory of Oregon lies far north of thirty-six degrees
thirty minutes—the Missouri and Texas compromise line. Its
southern boundary is the parallel of 42 degrees, leaving the
intermediate distance to be three hundred and thirty geographical miles. And it is because the provisions of this bill
are not inconsistent with the laws of the Missouri compromise,
if extended from the Rio Grande to the Pacific Ocean, that I
have not felt at liberty to withhold my sanction. Had it embraced Territories south of that compromise, the question presented for my consideration would have been of a far different
character, and my action upon it must have corresponded with
my convictions.''

The people of Oregon, without authority from Congress, organized a provisional government, and in their fundamental law
excluded slavery. Congress organized a territorial government
out of this provisional government, and gave validity to their
laws, thus, indirectly, through the agency of the provisional
government of Oregon, prohibiting slavery in that territory.
This received the executive sanction, as will be seen by the

extract above, and from other parts of the same message, because it did not violate the Missouri and Texas compromise.

The people of California have, without authority from Congress, organized a government, formed a constitution, and enacted laws; they have prohibited slavery, and the prohibition applies to the country south of 36 degrees 30 minutes; and the question now presented is of that different character which we were told by the late President would have required from him a different action from that of the Oregon bill.

I have elsewhere explained, when it was questioned, the understanding I had of the President's motive for signing that Oregon bill, though I never approved the decision. I honored the motive, as it was stated to me, by which he was prompted, and have endeavored to "save his administration from the obloquy" which its enemies have sought to attach to the act.

Readily admitting the more thorough acquaintance with the views and opinions of the late President which Mr. Walker possesses, it only remains to me to hope that upon reconsideration, he will abandon the supposition that Mr. Polk would have signed such a bill as this we now have under consideration. If I am wrong in the belief that he would have maintained against any and all influences the spirit of the Missouri compromise, then I have been wrong in the only defence I have ever found in any degree acceptable to the democracy of Mississippi, when I have opposed the censure which many bestowed upon his sanction of the Oregon territorial bill. It was not my intention to discuss the merits of Mr. Clay's bill: *that* I may have to do in my place as a senator. Here I wish only to reply to an appeal so made as to put me in a false position, and made by one against whose authority it is to me disagreeable to be opposed.

Very truly, your friend,
Jeff. Davis.

Remarks of Jefferson Davis on bill to establish a branch mint at New York. May 27, 1850.

Mr. DAVIS, of Mississippi. Mr. President, I have been, from the time we acquired this territory, at least from the time that we commenced working these mines, anxious for the establishment of a mint and such assaying offices as may be necessary to secure the interest of the miners, and to secure the benefit of the mining operations of California so far as might be to the commerce of the United States. I am in favor now of the establishment of a mint, and if that may not be, at least of the establishment of two offices for assaying the gold found there. But if a mint is established there—and I am not sure at what point it should be—if it should be established it cannot be at any point which is within striking distance of both the important mines of California. These mines exist in the courses of two rivers, running the one from the north and the other from the south. These rivers meet together at the great port of San Francisco, where this mint is proposed to be established. This is not, however, carrying the mint to the mines, but the gold to the mint, and carrying it a good way in both cases. So far as I have been able to learn, the gold lies in a valley which never approaches that coast, and is from ten to twenty miles wide.

I propose to amend the amendment offered by the Senator from Missouri in the following manner: after the word "silver," in the third line of the first section, insert the words "and two assaying offices, one at Stockton, on the San Joaquin, and the other at Sacramento, on the river of that name;" the object being to bring the assaying offices to the neighborhood of the mines, to the vicinity of the miners, where the dust may be submitted to the assayer and cast into bars prior to the gold being sent to the mint, wherever that may be. The first amendment which I propose will be to strike out the word "one," in the eighth section, and to substitute the word "two," so as to make it "two assayers."

The question was taken on the amendment, and it was agreed to.

Mr. DAVIS. I further move to amend the amendment by changing the word "assayer," in the 13th line of the same section, to "assayers."

The amendment was agreed to.

Mr. DAWSON. I will inquire of the Senator from Mississippi, if two separate buildings will be required for the assayers?

Mr. DAVIS. Of course, buildings and machinery will be required at each place, and I suppose it will cost at least ten thousand dollars at each place.

Mr. BENTON. It is not necessary to alter the amount. Fifty thousand dollars was the amount estimated for one assay office at San Francisco; but as it is proposed to establish two offices in the interior, the same amount may be sufficient for both.

Mr. DAVIS. It may be necessary, to prevent further questions, to amend the amendment in the first section by inserting after the word "branch," in the sixth line, the words "and assaying office." I move so to amend it.

The question was then taken on this amendment, and it was adopted.

The question then recurred on the adoption of the amendment of Mr. BENTON as amended. The yeas and nays having been ordered, they were as follows:

YEAS—Messrs. Bell, Benton, Bradbury, Bright, Clarke, Clay, Cooper, Corwin, Davis of Mississippi, Dayton, Dodge of Wisconsin, Dodge of Iowa, Downs, Felch, Foote, Green, Hale, Hamlin, Houston, Hunter, Morton, Spruance, Underwood and Whitcomb—24.

NAYS—Messrs. Atchison, Badger, Baldwin, Berrien, Borland, Butler, Cass, Chase, Davis of Massachusetts, Dawson, Dickinson, Jones, King, Mangum, Norris, Pearce, Sebastian, Seward, Smith, Sturgeon, Turney, Upham, Walker, Webster, and Yulee —25.

So the amendment was not agreed to.

Mr. WEBSTER. I wish to say to the honorable members from Missouri and Mississippi that I voted against the amendment proposing the establishment of a mint in California because I thought it would embarrass the whole question and cause a great deal of dispute. I am in favor, however, of establishing assay offices, as many as may be necessary, and I think a proposition of that kind would meet with general concurrence.

Mr. MANGUM. I entirely concur with the view just expressed by the Senator from Massachusetts. I voted against this amendment with great reluctance, because I feel the great necessity which exists for the establishment of assaying offices in California, but I do not see the necessity of establishing a mint there.

Mr. DAVIS, of Mississippi. I am sorry to differ with the distinguished gentlemen on the other side of the Chamber on this point. I think now is the time to establish a mint. We have delayed too long to perform those functions which devolved upon us after the accession of the territory, and it is because we have not performed those functions, because we have left them without those provisions to which they were entitled at our hands, that they have taken upon themselves the power of forming a government, and one of the very things which they wished tò attain was a mint, so as to be relieved from those evils which every miner in California now feels. We have been derelict in our duty to the people of California. We have not met the obligations which were imposed upon us by the treaty with Mexico, to provide government for the people of these territories, and with that government also to establish custom-houses and light-houses, and other conveniences and requirements which the people had a right to expect from a Government holding a guardian care over them.

On motion by Mr. DICKINSON, the Senate proceeded, as in Committee of the Whole, to the consideration of the bill to establish a branch of the mint of the United States in the city of New York.

Mr. DAVIS, of Mississippi, offered the following amendment:

SEC. 7. *Be it further enacted,* That there shall be established two assaying offices, one at Stockton, on the San Joaquin river, and the other at Sacramento, on the Sacramento river, in California; for each of which said offices there shall be appointed, on the nomination of the President, and with the advice and consent of the Senate, one treasurer and one assayer, and one melter and refiner, and each of said treasurers shall be authorized to employ and engage one clerk, and as many subordinate workmen and servants for the service of his office as may be provided by law.

SEC. 8. *And be it further enacted,* That each of said assaying offices shall be a place of deposit for such public money as the Secretary of the Treasury may direct, and the treasurer thereof shall have the custody of the same, and shall perform the duties of an assistant treasurer of the United States, and shall be subject to all the provisions of the act approved 6th of August, 1846, entitled "An act to provide for the better organization of the Treasury, and for the collection, safe-keeping, transfer, and disbursement of the public revenue," which are applicable to the treasurer of the branch mint at New Orleans, and shall receive for his services an annual compensation of $5,000.

SEC. 9. *And be it further enacted,* That the assayers and melters, and refiners authorized by this act shall perform such duties, in assaying and fixing the value of gold or bullion in grains or in lumps, and in forming the same into bars, either for individuals, companies, or the Government, as shall be prescribed by the Secretary of the Treasury, and shall each receive for his services an annual compensation of $4,000.

SEC. 10 *And be it further enacted,* That all deposits of gold or bullion in either of said offices for assay shall be with the treasurer thereof, who shall estimate the whole value of each deposit, and deliver to the depositor, under his hand, a certificate of such value, which certificate shall entitle the holder to the gold or bullion so deposited for assay, subject to such charges and deductions, if any, as may be prescribed by the Secretary of the Treasury.

SEC. 11. *And be it further enacted,* That there shall be allowed to each of the clerks authorized by this act an annual compensation of $3,000, and to each of the subordinate workmen and servants, not exceeding twenty, such wages and allowances as are customary and reasonable, according to their respective stations and duties, and as shall be authorized by the Secretary of the United States Treasury.

SEC. 12. *And be it further enacted,* That the officers and clerks herein provided for shall, previously to entering on the discharge of their duties, each of them take an oath, or make affirmation, before some justice of the peace, to support the Constitution of the United States, which oath or affirmation shall be deposited in the Treasury Department.

SEC. 13. *And be it further enacted,* That the sum of $50,000 be, and the same is hereby appropriated out of any money in the Treasury not otherwise appropriated, for the purpose of establishing the assaying offices aforesaid.

Mr. DAVIS, of Mississippi. I do not think the establishment of an assay office in California is incompatible with the establishment of a mint at San Francisco. Indeed, so far otherwise is the effect, that the very amendment, with conditions, was offered as an amendment to the proposition of the Senator from Missouri to establish a mint at San Francisco. It but comes in aid of a mint at San Francisco. It is the establishment of an assay office at the mines, where the miner will have a chance to obtain the true value of his gold dust from an office in the vicinity, instead of being compelled to go himself, or employ an agent to go to San Francisco. It is for the benefit of the laborer in the mines that the office should be established near the mines, and would be a saving to him of not less than two dollars on every ounce of gold dust. It is to relieve the laborer of this great loss that I propose these assay offices. I think the assay offices more necessary than the mint, and that for the interest of the miner the assay offices are indispensable, while for the interest of the Government the mint would also be advantageous. I think there is no greater mistake than to suppose that the gold will come in bars to the United States, and that the coin will flow in the channels of commerce. The reverse is certainly true. If we coin the gold in California, it will have a tendency to come to the United States, and it will only go into foreign countries when it exists in such excess as to cause it to be recoined abroad. The gold bar goes equally into all the world, and the gold bar, much more than the gold coin, will be sent to foreign countries through all the channels of commerce. But this is not a matter of very great importance. I never have desired to see gold accumulated in the United States more than in other countries. I believe that was the cause of the downfall of Spain in the time of Ferdinand and Isabella. I would prefer that the precious metals should not exist in excess here.

In reply to the remark of the Senator from Kentucky, I would say we shall need an assay office if a mint is established at San Francisco, and the gold bars will come to the United States as much as our commerce demands, and beyond that we have no right to it. I would say I think we require three mints only in the United States: one in New York, one in New Orleans, and the other in California, wherever the point may be.

Mr. UNDERWOOD. I did not intend to make at this time any remarks on the merits of this proposition; but after the suggestions of the Senator from Mississipi, I will make one or two. This gold dust, furnished from California, must be carried somewhere, either in the United States or out of the United States. I prefer the coining of it in the United States, giving the American stamp to all the currency which may grow out of the discoveries of gold in California. If it be coined in the United States, the next question which presents itself is, where it is to be coined? I presume most of the Senators will agree with me as to the propriety of having it coined at home. The question will then be, where shall it be coined? It must either be done in California, or it must be brought to the Atlantic shores, to some of our cities here to be coined. Now, it seems to me that it is for the interest of those who dig the gold at the mines to have convenient places where it can be converted into coin. But there must be some limit to these places where it shall be coined. You cannot have a mint in all the various diggings in California. The Government can scarcely be called upon to erect a mint for the accommodation of these people every hundred miles, or every two hundred miles, when we are informed the gold region extends over five hundred miles. What limit shall we prescribe to the erection of mints? Will you have more than one?

Mr. DAVIS, of Mississippi. I do not propose any in this amendment. There is no proposition to establish a mint in California by this amendment; it is to establish assaying offices; and if the Senator will indulge me, I will tell him where the points are which are proposed. The gold region lies in a valley between primitive ridges of mountains, and is from ten to twenty miles in width. The valley in which the gold dust is found is drained by two rivers, one running from the north and the other from the south. Upon each of these rivers it is proposed to erect assaying offices, to which the miners may have access. But between the mines upon these rivers, so draining this whole extent of valley, there is no intercourse, no trade. Each has a trade with San Francisco, but no trade with each other. It is for this reason that the points have been selected which are indicated in the amendment.

Eulogy of Jefferson Davis on the life and character of Senator F. H. Elmore. May 31, 1850.

Mr. DAVIS, of Mississippi. Mr. President, the close personal friendship subsisting between myself and the deceased constitutes at once a disqualification on my part for speaking of him, and an impelling power which will not permit me to remain in silence. My acquaintance with him commenced some twelve years ago; during a part of that time I have been on intimate terms with him, and may be permitted to express my concurrence in what has been said of him on this occasion. He has been truly portrayed as one in whose character was blended firmness and gentleness, wisdom and modesty. These were his characteristics; and above all, directing and controlling all, there was that stern devotion to duty, that single appliance to whatever was the task before him, which constitutes one of the great elements of every public character, distinguished for virtue and public usefulness. It was this devotion to duty in the sphere alluded to by his colleague which no doubt shattered his constitution, and thus terminated his life. On the bed from which he never rose, when wasted by disease and racked by pain, that principle which caused him to devote head and heart to his duty still ruled supreme over physical suffering and exhaustion. I saw him but a short time before his death. His first words to me then were those which pointed to the current business of the Senate, and to those interests of which he felt himself to be more immediately the representative, and of which we know he was so true, so able, and so faithful an advocate. The country loses much in losing such a citizen; the Senate loses much in losing such a member; his State loses much in losing such a representative. But there is a deeper grief, a greater loss, a darker pall spread over his bereaved family. The veil which excludes that sacred grief from public contemplation, yet permits us to offer our hearts' best sympathy with the mourners' affliction.

I feel, Mr. President, that I am utterly disqualified for the purpose of justly describing his many endearing and radical virtues; still more for the set phrase of formal eulogy. I shall not attempt either one or the other. I will leave to other tongues and to other times whatever it may be becoming and proper to say. I cordially second the resolutions presented by the colleague of the deceased.

After a pause—

Mr. DAVIS, of Mississippi, moved that when the Senate adjourns, it adjourn to meet to-morrow at 11 o'clock.

The motion was unanimously agreed to.

The resolutions offered by Mr. BUTLER were agreed to.

Committee Report by Jefferson Davis, June 4, 1850.

REPORTS FROM COMMITTEES.

Mr. DAVIS, of Mississippi, from the Committee on Military Affairs, to which was referred the memorial of Captain F. Britton, asking compensation for extra services in the Commissary's and Quartermaster's Departments, asked to be discharged from the further consideration of the same; which was agreed to.

Also, from the same committee, to which was referred the bill to authorize the Secretary of War to settle the claims of the State of Georgia, for horses and equipments lost by the volunteers and militia engaged in the suppression of hostilities of the Creek, Seminole, and Cherokee Indians, in the years 1836 and 1837, reported back the same without amendment.

Also, from the same committee, to which were referred several memorials in relation to paying moneys advanced by States, reported a joint resolution supplementary to the resolution to refund money to the States which have supplied volunteers and furnished them transportation during the present war, before being mustered and received into the service of the United States; which was read and passed to a second reading.

Also, from the same committee, to which were referred the several memorials of paymasters' clerks, asking an increase of compensation, reported a bill for the relief of paymasters' clerks; which was read and passed to a second reading.

Remarks of Jefferson Davis, June 6, 1850.

INCREASE OF THE ARMY.

Mr. DAVIS, of Mississippi. The Committee on Military Affairs, to which was referred Senate bill to increase the rank and file of the army, which has passed the House of Representatives with an amendment, have had the amendment under consideration, and have directed me to report it back to the Senate without any recommendation. I will state to the Senate that the members of the committee that were present were equally divided as to whether the amendment should be adopted or not, and they, therefore, report it back to the Senate without any recommendation. I would also say to the Senate that this bill provides for the increase of companies serving on our frontier, giving a force which is very necessary at the present time to defend the frontier settlements. I ask for its consideration now.

Mr. CLAY. I object.

So the report was laid over under the rules.

Jefferson Davis to Stephen Cocke.

(From the Mississippi Department of Archives and History.)

Senate Chamber
7th. June 1850

My dear friend

I received your kind and very gratifying letter, have caused your name to be placed on the list of correspondents of the Patent office.

Yesterday I sent you some seeds but could not get any of Chilian Clover. The Commissioner says he has taken measures to get some.

Receive my thanks and my heartfelt regards for you.

In haste and confusion I close this note.

As ever yr friend
Jeffn. Davis.

Remarks of Jefferson Davis on the bill to increase the rank and file of the army. June 11, 1850.

Mr. DAVIS, of Mississippi. I do not entirely approve of the amendment of the House. Indeed, I had expected to oppose it. It is not, however, quite so bad as the Senator from Texas represents. It is a discretionary power conferred on the President to mount such portions of infantry serving on the frontier as he may think proper. In the bill which passed the Senate, and which comes back from the House with this amendment, provision is made to secure the enlistment of western men; and

I may be permitted to say to the Senate that the Secretary of War connected that provision with this amendment, expecting that men would be enlisted in the West who would be suitable for mounted service; and I do not doubt such enlistments may be made, if they have a guarantee that they are to serve on horseback. The Senator from Texas will probably admit that this is an expectation which is well founded. The Secretary of War proposes, then, to select such men from the different companies at various stations on the frontiers, and convert them into mounted men. The companies of infantry will thus have on their muster-rolls men serving on horseback. They are to be equipped and used as mounted men, to act as escorts and to pursue the predatory bands of Indians. Such, I think it due to the Secretary of War to state, was the plan he proposed; and it is, in my opinion, capable of execution, if we may consent thus to disturb the organization of the army. It would require additional remuneration to the men thus to serve on horseback. They would require the pay of cavalry, because their expenses would be increased by such service; and unless they serve permanently, I agree with the Senator from Texas that they would be utterly useless. You could not detail a man unacquainted with his horse, and untrained to riding, and expect him to perform the duty of a soldier of cavalry. He could only use the horse for transportation, to carry him where he had to act, and the chances would be that the man and horse would part company before they got to the place of destination. But if, indeed, the man and horse should together get there and back again—he having no cavalry instruction—no permanent interest or attachment to the horse—would, by his ignorance and carelessness, neglect and abuse the animal. I think, therefore, on the whole, that the provision is not entirely an economical one. I would myself prefer, both for efficiency and economy, to see such mounted force as is required regularly organized. Yet, though the expense would be greater, man for man, as long as it is kept up, according to the proposed plan, it is much easier to get rid of it when no longer required as a mounted force. The infantry could be ordered again on foot, without a law for disbandment, and the horses could be sold. I think with the increase of the army proposed, by increasing the rank and file of the frontier companies, and with the enlistments which can be effected with the guarantee that they are to serve on horseback, that the amendment could be made quite useful, though not so good as a regularly organized force of cavalry. I have always been in favor of having in our army, upon the peace establishment, a nucleus for every branch of the service. We have in recent years added light artillery and dragoons. We have, however, no light cavalry and no lancers. I think a regiment of light cavalry, and one or two squadrons of that regiment armed as lancers, would be a proper addition to the permanent organization of the army, on the peace establishment, and would be the most effective force that we could have for the protection of the frontier.

Mr. DAVIS, of Mississippi. Mr. President, I wish to make a few additional remarks before the question is put to vote. The Senator from Virginia has properly said that this is not a question whether or not we shall perform our duty of protecting the frontier. That has been done by all the means at the command of the Secretary of War, and the employment of rangers in addition to the troops he had at his command. In his report for this year, the Secretary asks for the addition granted to him in this bill, and throws out a suggestion, which is carried out by the amendment of the House, that authority should be given to mount a certain portion of the infantry. That is done to a certain extent usually on the frontier stations. It is done either by hiring or by keeping horses to furnish escorts, and for other detached service. The question to be decided in the amendment is, not whether the infantry ride, if temporarily mounted, as well as the Indians, but whether a force organized as recommended by the Secretary of War can act efficiently against the Indians. I believe they can. I believe that white men, mounted upon our horses, can catch and control these much-vaunted horsemen, the wild riders of the prairie. And this is not a vague opinion. I recollect when my venerable friend behind me [Mr. DODGE, of Wisconsin,] commanded a regiment in which I held an humble post, he pursued the Comanches, followed them, from day to day till he overtook them with a force much smaller than their own; and when by treachery they escaped and fled, he pursued and caught them again, and compelled them to come to terms of peace. Colonel DODGE's men had been but recently enlisted; they had undergone little cavalry instruction; they were just such men as would be enlisted in this instance. There were many of those men brought from the East, from New York, and Pennsylvania, wholly unaccustomed to the frontier; they had not been accustomed to ride from their youth. They were not selected from western recruits, which is the proposition of the Secretary of War. But the Senator from Texas mistakes my purpose. It is not a measure of economy with me. I repeat that I objected to it; and, among other reasons, because I believe it will be more expensive than regularly-mounted men. I believe it will cost far more money than a regularly-organized corps, on account of the great waste of horses and equipments which will result from their irregular employment by this infantry acting as mounted men. I am in favor of the creation of a mounted regiment. I prefer that now to the mounting of infantry; but I do not think this plan so utterly obnoxious as stated by the Senator from Texas. These men, thus enlisted, and thus equipped and mounted, can, I believe, tame the terror of those predatory Indians which infest the borders of Texas. Our race is superior to theirs; our horses are superior to theirs; we are their superiors in every way. As to the skill and horsemanship of the wild men on their little grass-bred horses, it is nothing when brought face to face with our own race, riding our own horses and bearing the weapons which a skilful ordnance corps furnish to our troops.

I will say to the Senator from Texas that there is no one who sympathizes with him more, and few, if any, more willing to remove the difficulties encountered on his frontier. I am ready, and have been anxious to organize a mounted corps of light cavalry and lancers—the organization which I believe peculiarly adapted to that service. This is not my plan. I do not favor it, or advocate it as a measure of economy. It has some advantage, and I thought it due to the Secretary of War, when such strong grounds were taken against his recommendation, that I should state what there is in favor of it. It was an act of candor and of justice due from me as chairman of the Committee on Military Affairs to the Secretary's plan, although I never approved it. But, sir, we are reduced to this point: shall we reject the amendment, and between the two houses lose the whole bill? Shall we deprive the frontier of the advantage which this bill gives it, and stake all on the hazard of raising a cavalry corps? I consider it a very imminent hazard. I agree with the Senator from Texas as to its necessity, and will unite with him in any efforts he may make to accomplish it. But, I tell him now, I believe he will fail. I do not expect the two Houses of Congress to incur expense for a greater increase of the army, or for its increase on a plan other than that recommended by the President and the Secretary of War. I must say that I think something is due to those functionaries I think that the individual placed at the head of a department to execute particular duties, should be allowed to a great extent to select the means for the execution of those duties. For this reason I have felt disposed from the beginning to concede a great deal to the recommendation of the Secretary of War, and to adopt his plan as far as my judgment would allow. I objected to this, however, not merely for the reasons stated by the Senator from Texas, but because I think it destroys the unity and perfection of the organization of the army. I object to it, not for the reason stated by the Senator from Virginia, but because it gives too much discretion. I think we should pass laws which declare what we mean, and not turn over the law, half made, to be finished at the discretion of the Executive. We should, if we want cavalry, say so, and how many. I object to this partition of the legislative power; and it is merely on the score of necessity, urgent necessity for the protection of this frontier, which the Senator from Texas describes as now bleeding from the assaults of predatory bands of Indians, that I agree to the bill. I believe the necessity to be great and immediate, and that this is the only plan by which we can provide for it at this session.

Remarks of Jefferson Davis on bill granting to Arkansas the swamp lands of said state June 13, 1850

Mr. DAVIS, of Mississippi. I have long been an advocate of the graduation of the price of the public lands. I have been an advocate of the surrender to the State of those lands that could not be sold by the General Government within a certain term of years; and in proof of the wisdom of such a policy, I would cite a case that occurred in my own State. The Chickasaws in that State were entitled to receive, instead of an annuity, the net proceeds of the lands from which they removed. The graduating principle was applied to those lands, so as to reduce some of them down to 12½ cents an acre. The lands were sold rapidly, and were got rid of in a short period. These lands netted more than any lands which have been sold by the Government at $1.25 per acre, by being kept in the market a long term of years. The case included in this bill is of swamp lands, which cannot be sold if they have been surveyed, and much of which cannot be surveyed at all, as in Louisiana. Some portions of the lands of Mississippi are in the like difficulty. These lands cannot be sold by the Federal Government. Again, sir, the lands lying contiguous to them—I speak particularly of a portion of the lands of Mississippi—cannot be occupied, and consequently are unsaleable, because they are separated entirely from communication either with the river or the high land, wherever the country is overflowed; and besides, the adjacent country is rendered so unhealthy that lands susceptible of cultivation cannot be occupied. To grant the inundated and unsaleable lands to the State, for the purpose of draining them, is to render the contiguous lands saleable, and of double value. It will secure a rapid settlement, and not merely bring into the treasury the moneys received for the lands, but the customs-revenue from the settlers upon them, which is always far the greater item of profit to the United States Government.

To exclude the fourth section, then, as proposed by the Senator from New Hampshire, would be to restrict the provisions of this bill to limits like those adopted in the bill for Louisiana. The bill for Louisiana was restricted to one State; and upon consideration the bill was passed, and the principle was accepted. It was left alone, that there might be no combination and no confusion about it. Now that the principle is settled, why need you go on and pass a bill for one State after another, enumerating each State containing lands like situated? I think myself that the most appropriate bill would be the fourth section of this bill without the others—to be modified by a clause extending the provisions of the law passed in the case of Louisiana to the other States, embracing all the lands similarly situated. With this modification, the fourth section would contain the whole merit of the bill. The principle would be as correct in one section as in four, if it is sound at all. The bill would require merely that the act of Louisiana should be extended to the other States.

Now, sir, if the fourth section should be separated from the other three, and the fourth section should be lost, I should feel it my duty to bring in a bill allowing Mississippi the same rights that we here grant to Arkansas, the argument for which would equally apply to the lands extending from just below Memphis to the mouth of the Yazoo river. It would be a mere waste of time, and multiply bills, to pass the first three sections and not the fourth, which is the mere application of the same principle to all cases of like import. Surely we would not grant to one and refuse to another.

On the same question September 17, 1850.

Mr. DAVIS, of Mississippi. This is a bill which has been passed through the Senate. If Senators do not understand it now, they should have understood it before the bill passed. The amendments which have been made by the House restrict rather than enlarge the provisions of the bill as it was passed by the Senate. This term, "overflowed land," is a technical expression in the Land Office. It means those lands which the surveyor cannot survey on account of its being low and marshy, and it is therefore returned by the surveyors as "overflowed." That is the character of the land which has heretofore been granted to the State of Louisiana. In regard to that part of Mississippi to which the Senator from North Carolina refers, his argument utterly fails to apply; because there is no vacant land there. We have land there which overflows in time of extreme freshets; but, if the Senator should go there, and undertake to buy it, he would find that he would have to pay fifty or a hundred dollars per acre for it. It is all occupied as private property, and I think he must pass the mouth of the Arkansas river before he will find one acre of the public lands. That is not the character of the land to be affected by this bill. It is the low swamp land, remote from the river; that which is not sold and probably will not be sold. It is upon the smaller streams in the interior. I think it may be that a better class of lands would be included by the phrase "swamp lands," which was adopted by the Senate; as it is a phrase of much larger construction than the phrase "overflowed lands." These are lands which have never been surveyed, and which the Government never attempts to survey. I see no good reason why, if the Senate were well advised when the bill was passed before, we should hesitate about concurring in the amendments which have been made by the House, as they rather restrict the bill which we passed.

Mr. MAGNUM. It is precisely for the reason intimated by the Senator from Mississippi that I desire further consideration of this matter; because I do not understand these technicalities, and the localities, quite so well as those who live on the banks of the Mississippi. I will, therefore, if the motion be in order, move that the bill be referred to the Committee on Public Lands, inasmuch as there is a difference of opinion among gentlemen with regard to the effect of the amendments.

Mr. HALE. When this bill was before the Senate I made some opposition to it; and the Senator from Arkansas, not now present, referred to the very words which the House of Representatives have stricken out as the thing which made the bill definite, and enabled the Senate to see what they were voting away. The objection which I made was, that the provision of the bill was so indefinite that we did not know what we were giving away—whether one, two, or ten millions of acres.

Mr. DAVIS, of Mississippi. Will the Senator from New Hampshire read the words which the House of Representatives have stricken out?

Mr. HALE. They propose to strike out of the first section the words "known and designated in the plats of the General Land Office as swamp lands"; and the Senator from Arkansas said that these lands were designated on the plats in the Land Office. We know now that the House of Representatives have stricken out every clue which we had, whereby we might know what we were voting away. There is nothing to ascertain what these lands are. There is no criterion given; the whole is loose and indefinite, and uncertain; and

Mr. DAVIS, of Mississippi. I agree entirely with the Senator from Tennessee that it is unwise to press this system of leveeing beyond what we have already reached. I have this year endeavored to obtain an appropriation for a minute survey of the delta of the Mississippi. When I say we seek for this, it is not that we may increase the levee system, but that we may provide the means by which the waters of the river may be drawn off to the Gulf, so as to reduce the level of the river, and not to increase it. The extension of the levees everywhere, confining all the waters of the stream, would, I have no doubt, raise the level of the river. But it does not follow that land granted, as is proposed in this bill, will be applied for any such purpose. By no means. I believe that now the people of Louisiana are pretty generally convinced that they require some mode of letting the water out of the channel of the river. The State engineer has so reported. The resolutions of the last Legislature, that have been referred to, address themselves to that end, which they expected would accomplish the result.

It does not follow, then, at all, as the Senator from Tennessee seems to argue, that this land is to be applied to leveeing the Mississippi. It may be applied to cutting out new channels on the right and on the left, to carry water out of the main channel of the river, to act as waste-weirs whenever the river reaches a height above the level of the land. In Arkansas, I take it for granted, they will levee the water out to the whole extent of the river. The honorable Senator from Tennessee knows that is not very great. They will have no opportunity to levee much. It would be only that which passes across the Arkansas river which would pass down the bayous into the Gulf without returning. I do not think, therefore, that the leveeing which might be done in Arkansas would be very material, unless it should be extended to the Missouri.

Mr. BELL. That is what I was afraid of.

Mr. DAVIS, of Mississippi. But that would be more than counteracted if a general system were adopted by which water was to be taken off the river whenever it reached a certain height. That plan might be applied in Mississippi and Upper Louisiana, and particularly in Lower Louisiana. If extensively applied in Lower Louisiana, the danger of an overflow would probably be removed, or at least greatly reduced.

Remarks of Jefferson Davis, June 15, 1850

REPAYMENTS TO STATES.

Mr. DAVIS, of Mississippi, moved that the Senate proceed to the consideration of the joint resolution supplementary to the resolution to refund money to the States which have supplied volunteers and furnished them transportation, during the late war, before being mustered.

The motion was agreed to.

Mr. DAVIS, of Mississippi. I rise for the purpose of making a brief explanation of the resolution. It will be recollected that, by the act referred to in the resolution, provision was made to pay all persons, corporations, or States, any money expended by them in raising or equipping troops for the war with Mexico. It has occurred that some of the States have paid accounts for the raising and equipping of troops without taking their vouchers in a formal manner, and that money has not been refunded to them by the United States. This joint resolution is simply to provide that, whenever an account has been audited by the State authorities, and been paid out of the State treasury before the date fixed in the resolution, the evidence that it has been so audited and paid by the State, for and out of the State treasury, shall be held to be sufficient evidence for refunding the same out of the Treasury of the United States. That is the whole object of the resolution.

On motion of Mr. CLARKE, several verbal amendments were made. The resolution was then reported back to the Senate, the amendments were concurred in, the resolution was ordered to be engrossd for a third reading, and subsequently read a third time and passed.

Remarks of Jefferson Davis on bill granting land to Mississippi to construct the Brandon and Montgomery Railroad.
June 25, 1850.

GRANT OF LAND TO MISSISSIPPI.

Mr. DAVIS, of Mississippi. I ask the Senate to take up Senate bill No. 16, being a bill granting to the State of Mississippi the right of way and a donation of public land for the purpose of locating and constructing a railroad from Brandon to the eastern border of said State, in the direction of Montgomery, Alabama.

The motion was agreed to.

Mr. DAVIS. The committee who reported this bill have reported an amendment, which is to strike out all after the enacting clause, and insert a substitute:

That the right of way through the public lands be and the same is hereby granted to the State of Mississippi for the construction of a railroad from Brandon, in said State, to the eastern border of said State, in the direction of Montgomery, in the State of Alabama, with the right also to take necessary materials of earth, stone and timber, from the public lands of the United States, adjacent to said railroad, for the construction thereof: *Provided,* That the right of way shall not exceed one hundred feet on each side of the length thereof; and a copy of the survey of said road, made under the direction of the Legislature, shall be forwarded to the proper local land offices respectively, and to the General Land Office at Washington city, within ninety days after the completion of the same.

SEC. 2. *And be it further enacted,* That there be and is hereby granted to the State of Mississippi, for the purpose of aiding in making the railroad aforesaid, every alternate section of land designated by even numbers, for six sections in width on each side of said road; but in case it shall appear that the United States have, when the line or route of said road is definitely fixed by the authority aforesaid, sold any part of any section hereby granted, or that the right of preëmption has attached to the same, then it shall be lawful for any agent or agents to be appointed by the Governor of said State to select, subject to the approval of the Secretary of the Interior, from the lands of the United States most contiguous to the tier of sections above specified, so much land in alternate sections or parts of sections as shall be equal to such lands as the United States have sold, or to which the right of preëmption has attached as aforesaid, which lands, being equal in quantity to one half of six sections in width on each side of said road, the State of Mississipi shall have and hold to and for the use and purpose aforesaid: *Provided,* That the lands to be so located shall in no case be further than fifteen miles from the line of the road: *And provided, further,* That the lands hereby granted shall be applied in the construction of said road, and shall be disposed of only as the work progresses, and shall be applied to no other purpose whatsoever: *And provided, further,* That any and all lands reserved to the United States by any act of Congress, for the purpose of aiding in any object of internal improvement, or in any manner for any purpose whatsoever, be and the same are hereby reserved to the United States from the operations of this act, except so far as it may be found necessary to locate the route of the said railroad through such reserved lands.

SEC. 3. *And be it further enacted,* That the sections and parts of sections of land which, by such grant, shall remain to the United States within six miles on each side of said road, shall not be sold for less than double the minimum price of the public lands when sold.

SEC. 4. *And be it further enacted,* That the said land hereby granted to the said State shall be subject to the disposal of the Legislature thereof, for the purposes aforesaid, and no other; and the said railroad shall be and remain a public highway, for the use of the Government of the United States, free from toll or other charge upon the transportation of any property or troops of the United States.

SEC. 5. *And be it further enacted,* That if the said railroad shall not be completed within ten years, the said State of Mississppi shall be bound to pay to the United States the amount which may be received upon the sale of any part of said lands by said State, the title to the purchasers under said State remaining valid; and the title to the residue of said lands shall reinvest in the United States, to have and hold the same in the same manner as if this act had not been passed.

SEC. 6. *And be it further enacted,* That the United States mail shall at all times be transported on said railroad, under the direction of the Post Office Department, at such price as Congress may by law direct.

Mr. DAVIS. The amendment proposed by the committee makes this bill conform entirely with those bills that have already passed the Senate, for purposes similar to that sought to be accomplished by this bill. It is different somewhat from the bill which I introduced into the Senate. The main differences are these: it allows the land to be taken at a greater distance from the road than was originally proposed, and increases the price of the reserved sections to two and a half dollars per acre. I have been opposed to both of these alterations, believing, as I do, that keeping the lands at the minimum price is the most likely way to bring them into market, to cause them to be settled upon and improved, and thus to make them available to the Treasury of the United States. But I shall not, on this occasion, make any objection to the amendment the committee have offered.

The amendment was agreed to. The bill was then reported to the Senate, and the amendment was concurred in.

On the same bill June 27, 1850.

GRANT OF LANDS TO MISSISSIPPI.

Mr. DAVIS, of Mississippi. I now move, Mr. President, that the Senate proceed to the consideration of Senate bill No. 16, being the bill granting to the State of Mississippi the right of way and a donation of public land, for the purpose of locating and constructing a railroad from Brandon to the eastern border of said State, and in the direction of Montgomery, Alabama.

The motion having been agreed to, the Senate, as in Committee of the Whole, proceeded to the consideration of the bill.

Mr. DAVIS. This bill was considered a few days ago, and after I supposed all debate was concluded, the further consideration of it was suspended. I hope it will now be disposed of.

The VICE PRESIDENT. The question is on the motion to strike out the 3d section of the bill.

Mr. CHASE. I moved to strike out that section, believing that the bill would be improved by adopting this amendment. Gentlemen who have charge of this bill seem to think that the rejection of this section would prevent or delay the passage of the bill in the House of Representatives. I am clearly of a different opinion; but I do not wish to embarrass the measure, and I desire simply that the vote may be taken on the amendment.

Mr. DAWSON. If I understand the purport of this amendment, it is to strike out that part of the bill which goes to enhance the price of the sections of land reserved by the Government. Now, sir, the principle on which these appropriations of the public lands have been allowed is, that the Government of the United States loses nothing by it, and that it is not an appropriation for internal improvements directly, nor even a donation. Now, strike that principle from the bill, and what is the principle on which the friends of this bill would ground their request? I appeal now particularly to the Senator from Mississippi, to know if he will consent to the abandonment of the principle on which the majority has acted, in order to secure the passage of these bills?

Mr. DAVIS. I will answer the Senator from Georgia first, and then make a single remark on the amendment itself. I do not believe that it would be an abandonment of the principle which the Senator from Georgia has stated, to strike out this section. I am convinced that it would be a great gain to the Federal

Government either to assign or to sell these lands. They have been from twenty to thirty years in market. They are unsaleable, partly from their poverty and partly in consequence of their remoteness from a market for their produce. Anything that will bring them into market, and facilitate their sale, even if it should not be for more than twelve and a half cents per acre, would be a decided gain to the Government, in enabling us to get rid of the maintenance of various expensive land offices. Nay, I will even go so far as to say that, in my opinion, the Government would be a gainer to give the lands away. However, I will not go into any demonstration of that, because, although I should prefer that this section was not in the bill, it being an amendment of the committee and not in the bill which I presented to the Senate, yet, inasmuch as all other bills for like purposes have contained this provision, and inasmuch as the chairman the other day intimated a general plan for the disposal of these lands when this bill shall pass, and not being disposed to raise the particular question on this bill, I prefer that the section should remain in the bill, although it is against my own convictions of propriety and the interest of the Government itself.

The question was then taken on the motion to strike out the third section, and it was not agreed to.

The VICE PRESIDENT. It is now moved to strike out all after the enacting clause, and insert what has already been read to the Senate.

The motion was agreed to.

Remarks of Jefferson Davis on Compromise Bill of June 27, 1850.

Mr. DAVIS, of Mississippi, said: Mr. President, when I became convinced that this bill could never be so amended by the Senate as to receive my vote, I determined not to trespass further on the patience of Senators with any remarks of mine until the bill should have reached its final stage. I therefore rise now to address the Senate reluctantly, and it shall be done briefly; reluctantly for the reason I have just given, and more reluctantly still because the speech of my colleague requires from me a reply. I would gladly have been spared this task. I have studiously avoided it during the progress of this debate; and had it not been that to-day, with more than ordinary violence, he directed his arraignment against those who entertain an opinion which I had the honor perhaps most prominently to announce, I should have allowed this occasion to pass, like others, without any exhibition on my part of the opposition of opinion between my colleague and myself.

Mr. FOOTE. My colleague must permit me to say, in justice to myself and to the understanding which exists between us, that I did not intend to include him in my remarks.

Mr. DAVIS. I do not intend to charge my colleague with a desire to assail me, but he certainly attacked opinions which I explicitly announced upon this floor, and in language that was offensive. Now he says he is——

Mr. FOOTE. I will state frankly that the opinions which I assailed were first promulgated by the honorable Senator from Florida, [Mr. YULEE,] and my remarks were designed, so far as they were intended to have special application at all, to apply to him.

Mr. DAVIS. I do not claim to have originated the idea; but long before this bill was reported, I announced my *ultimatum* to be the Missouri compromise, with recognition below the line as distinct as the exclusion above it. That I believed to be the *ultimatum* of my constituents, as it is the *ultimatum* which the Nashville Convention, where our State was represented, and which it first suggested, has put forth.

Mr. FOOTE. It is not, as I believe, the *ultimatum* of my constituents.

Mr. DAVIS. The Senator says, "not his constituents." I thought, sir, that he and I represented the same constituency.

Mr. FOOTE made some further remarks.

Mr. DAVIS. I will reach that before I close my remarks, since the Senator makes the issue. But my colleague calls on all those who agreed with Mr. Calhoun when living, and are willing now to adhere to their opinions, to meet the issue, and defies them to answer the argument that he has this day presented. Sir, Mr. Calhoun denied the power of Congress to prohibit or to establish slavery; he asked nothing but the guarantees of the Constitution. That is all I ask now. But the Senator, in his zeal, which surely outruns his discretion, announces that he would scorn to receive protection from Congress for his constitutional rights. What, sir! scorn to receive protection for a constitutional right? For what was this Government founded, then? It is your constitutional right to have trial by jury: would my colleague scorn to receive provisions necessary to secure that? Would he scorn to receive, at the hands of this Government, the execution of the many trusts conferred upon it for the benefit and protection of its citizens at home and abroad? If not, why should he scorn to receive

the protection of Congress for slave property, which will secure to the South the enjoyment in these Territories of those
rights of property, not denied to others, but which now fully
inure to every other portion of the Union? What, sir, is there
humiliating in the attitude of the South, if it claims from Congress legislation to remove the obstruction of Mexican law?
What is there humiliating in the attitude of an American citizen who claims that the Constitution and laws under which he
was born, and which he is bound to support, shall be his shield
upon American soil? Sir, our hardy mariner, who wanders to
the other side of the globe upon which we live, looks back to
the land from which he hails, and claims the shield of its laws
and Constitution still to be over him. It is my pride to claim
and to receive the protection of my constitutional rights at the
hands of the Federal Government. It is my pride to sustain this
Federal Government in the execution of those functions which
make it emphatically the protector of our constitutional rights.

This is my position; and this I consider to be the true position of the South. It is not humbly to beg favors, but to expect
the discharge of duties. ˙My colleague first places the South
in the attitude of opposing the renewal and extension of the
Missouri compromise, and quotes from Mr. Calhoun to establish
that position. He refers then to a conversation between himself
and the Senator from Indiana, [Mr. BRIGHT,] in the presence of
the late President, [Mr. POLK,] to show his own friendship for
that plan of settlement. I recollect well the introduction of that
amendment by a Senator from Indiana; but I do not recollect a
vote which showed the opposition of the South. I was not one
of the southern men with whom my colleague conversed, and
who, he says, were opposed to the Missouri compromise. I
always——

Mr. FOOTE. I did not refer to my colleague.

Mr. DAVIS. I suppose you could not allude to me in that part
of your remarks. But, Mr. President, my colleague must recollect, when he attacks the position upon which I stand before my
constituents, that his remarks are to be, more than those of another, read by those constituents, and that to reply to them becomes, therefore, especially necessary to me. Then, I ask, when
did the South ever show opposition to the Missouri compromise
since it was acquiesced in by the southern States? What vote
establishes that fact? What speeches, made in the Senate or
elsewhere, establish that fact? That proposition was voted
down by northern men in the House of Representatives, when
offered to the Oregon bill by a member from South Carolina; that

proposition has been voted down in the Senate, I believe, every time it has been separately voted on, save once, when the Senator from Illinois [Mr. DOUGLAS] offered it in the terms on which we now advocate it, in the sense and spirit of the original compact. Then it was sustained by the South with unanimity, and then Mr. Calhoun was one of those whose vote is recorded among the ayes.

Mr. FOOTE.   When was that?

Mr. DAVIS.   On the 10th of August, 1848.   He voted then for the amendment of the Senator from Illinois, declaring that the Missouri compromise was to be extended in the sense and spirit of the original compromise.   That is what we want now.   We want the sense and spirit of the original compact honestly carried out.   We do not seek to deceive others.   It is our purpose not to be deceived.   If others are willing honestly to carry out this compromise, and if they will meet the question like men, and say what they mean in unequivocal language, I am willing to meet them on that platform.   But if they seek to delude the country, to conceal their purpose in hollow words, and to bring us into the adoption of a measure that carries nothing conclusively with it, then I have only to say I do not intend to deceive myself, nor to be made the instrument of deceiving or attempting to deceive those whom I represent.

But from this relation of opposition my colleague passes on and puts the South in the position of seeking the Missouri compromise as their choice—their desideratum.   That is not my attitude either.   The amendment now pending before the Senate is an amendment to limit the southern boundary of California by the parallel of the Missouri compromise.   Is that asking the Missouri compromise as our desideratum? or is it not rather claiming that you shall not infringe the Missouri compromise—that you shall not cross it with a State organized because of, and influenced by the anti-slavery feeling of Congress?—driven into their organization and into the prohibition of slavery for the very purpose of gaining admission into the Union?   Surely, Mr. President, that is not sufficient ground for saying that the South now come forward for the Missouri compromise, and that it is their particular choice.   They have taken it as an alternative heretofore, and respected it as a peace-offering on the altar of fraternity.   They now demand that you shall not violate it; but, so far as I know their opinion, and so far as I am any representative of it, they claim now, as they always have claimed, their constitutional rights to be as broad as the Territories of the United States.

But, sir, in a spirit of concession and amity, and for the sake of that Union which is eulogized in such sounding phrases by those who alone disturb its harmony, and who we must therefore suppose do not feel for it with half such intensity as ourselves—in that spirit, and for that purpose, we are willing to restrict our rights—to carry out the compact made by the last generation, at the sacrifice of our rights in a large portion of the Territory. Yes, sir, without asking from our brethren of the North that they should yield one jot or tittle in all the Territory, we are willing to extend the line of 36° 30′ to the Pacific, and give to the North exclusion of slavery in the country above that line, without asking any peculiar privileges in the country below it. All of the territory south of 36° 30′ would remain free from contest or obstruction, open to every man in the United States to go and settle there, with every species of property, in the United States. For this most advantageous arrangement to the North, the Missouri compromise line was drawn in 1820; for this it was extended when Texas was admitted; for this, now, when the admission of California is under discussion, we say we are ready again to extend the line to the Pacific, and close the disturbing question forever.

Mr. President, I could not imagine an association of freebooters so lost to that sense of justice which characterizes mankind, that they would engage in the acquisition of plunder, and then, when those who had stood shoulder to shoulder with them in every struggle, who had furnished a fair share of the means, who had borne a full proportion of the toil and danger and sacrifice of blood, claimed a division, that they should deprive them of all share in the acquired spoils. And can it be, sir, that a band of freebooters have a stronger sense of justice than the Senate of the United States? I will not pursue so offensive a parallel; but I ask every man who hears me, to run the parallel in his own mind, between the case which I have put, and the acquisition which followed the Mexican war, and then ask himself whether, in honor, justice, and good faith, our friends at the North ought to deny to us a fair participation in the acquisitions of that war? I am one of those who claim, that if the territory cannot be enjoyed in common, it should be divided, and that the whole question as to our right to enjoy that portion assigned to us, should be finally determined by the act of division. I want an end of this controversy. I do not wish for an act which will merely change the issue and leave the contest open. I want something which will be final—something which will be truly that which it is constantly assumed this so-called compromise bill is—a settlement of the question.

Let us, when we arrange a settlement, be sure that we reach the point at which controversy cannot again rise. How is that to be reached? Does any man here believe that either section of the Union will surrender its opinion upon the question? Surely not. By what means, then, are you to terminate the controversy so that it shall not be again revived? I say by extending that line, which has now the acquiescence of thirty years in both sections of the Union, a settled construction, and the confidence of the American people, until it reaches the limit of our possessions on the Pacific. By explicitly declaring the rights upon one side and upon the other, you will have terminated the controversy forever. If, according to the opinion of some Senators who have spoken on this subject, no territory shall be found into which any slaveholder would immigrate with his slaves, so be it. We but ask of you a fair opportunity. We ask of you, not all to which we are entitled as your equals, but merely an adherence to the compact which was made with you when the advantage was all on your side. We ask no more, and less than that, I trust, the South will never accept. But, sir, the opinion of Mr. Jefferson, endorsed by Mr. Calhoun, has been referred to in connection with this question. I cordially approve of the position taken by both, in opposition to politico-geographical divisions, and as to the evil of geographical parties. I believe it is a misfortune that the Missouri compromise ever was adopted. Far better if institutions had been left untrammelled to whatever determination the climate, soil, or the character of the people might dictate. Far better that the line had been jagged, and waving, and the localities of different institutions interlocked, so that the people holding, and those not holding slaves, should have been brought in juxtaposition, and have been better enabled to understand each other.

When a parallel of latitude was drawn across our territory, and declared to be the division between the slaveholding and non-slaveholding States, well might Jefferson point to it as an indication of the future disruption of the Union: when the wedge enters, we may anticipate the rending of the oak. But, sir, it has been happily found inadequate to the rending of our Union. Fraternity, patriotism, and good sense triumphed; the compromise has been acquiesced in. The generation has grown up which is now governing the country since that compromise was adopted. We stand now in another and a very different attitude towards the proposition from those by whom it was adopted. Although it was an evil in the beginning, it is now the best resource within our reach, if not the only thing which can produce permanence in the settlement of this vexatious controversy.

It seemed strange to me to hear the supposition that our lamented friend, Mr. Calhoun, would, if living, support the measure before us. That he who has been justly called by my colleague our leader upon this great issue between the North and the South, the champion who was taken away from us like a summer-dried fountain, when our need was the sorest; that he who never shrank from demanding on every occasion the whole rights of the South; that he who opposed the Missouri compromise because it gave to the South less than was her right; that he who was always first of his friends in every contest involving southern interests and southern honor; that he should now be held up as an advocate of that "non-intervention," which leaves in force the Mexican laws prohibiting our entrance into the country, and forbids Congress to remove those impediments which stand in the way of the enjoyment of our constitutional rights, is strange to me, surprising beyond expression. Sir, can any one of those who have served with Mr. Calhoun, or watched his course from however remote a distance, doubt where he would have been found upon this question? Can any one who has read the speech which closed his career in the Senate, doubt as to what were Mr. Calhoun's opinions upon all the points which have been raised in the progress of this debate? Surely none can do it.

But as to the other point, whether or not he would have agreed to the extension of the Missouri compromise with the recognition of slavery below the line, we are not left to mere conjecture. Not only did Mr. Calhoun vote for the Missouri compromise, when offered in the sense and spirit of the original compact, by the Senator from Illinois, and on that occasion indicate his willingness to acquiesce in such a settlement, but he voted for the same proposition, the Missouri compromise line, as contained in what was called the Clayton compromise bill. It is not because one asserts a constitutional right to be higher or broader than the basis of this partition, that it is therefore to be taken for granted he will, in every contingency reject it. Its history gives it a consideration above its merits. It has come down from 1820, renewed in the case of the State of Texas, both times diminishing the territorial strength of the South, and by her has been faithfully observed ever since it became, or was believed to have become, the settled policy in relation to the territories of the United States. But properly enough, the South has stood back to allow those who hold the power to pass or to reject it, to propose the line. It was once proposed by the Senator from Indiana, who now occupies the chair, [Mr. BRIGHT,] and I well recollect the regret I felt on that occasion that it was not made sufficiently explicit and brought to a vote. The same amendment, however, after it was withdrawn by the Senator from Indiana, was renewed by another member of the body, and was further amended by the Senator from Kentucky, [Mr. UNDERWOOD,] who proposed a distinct recognition of the right to carry slaves south of 36° 30′. It is not now, therefore, for the first time that the South has demanded a distinct acknowledgement of her right. At that time I had reason to hope, far, far more than I have now, that the amendment of the Senator from Kentucky would be agreed to, and that the Missouri compromise would be fairly, justly, honorably carried out, in the sense and spirit of the original compact, the line being extended until its trace was lost in the waters of the western ocean.

Mr. UNDERWOOD. I am in favor of the recognition of the right of the southern people to take their slave property south of the line. My amendment was printed also. I am informed by the Senator from Georgia, behind me, [Mr. BERRIEN,] that the Senator from Indiana withdrew his amendment, and that it was renewed by him. But while these amendments were thus pending, the committee of eight was raised, and the bill, with the pending amendments, was referred to the committee of eight. In that committee I introduced my proposition of distinctly recognizing the right of southern individuals to go south of that line 36° 30′ with their slave property, to be protected. Mr. Calhoun made a suggestion to me with regard to the language of the proposition which I submitted, and in the course of our conversation he stated, if it were adopted, he would submit to the line, although it did not meet his views. It was not what he required, but he would acquiesce in it, if adopted. In the committee, he constituted one of the four who voted for the proposition thus offered by myself; but it was rejected by a division of the committee—four to four. These are the facts in reference to the matter.

Mr. DAVIS, of Mississippi. I am glad to have received this minute explanation from the Senator from Kentucky upon a point of history which is valuable. It establishes several main points: First, that this is no new proposition; second, that it received the countenance of half the committee that was engaged on a compromise measure at a former period; and third, that the distinguished southern statesman, long the recognized leader upon all questions peculiarly belonging to the rights and interests of the South, as a member of that committee, acquiesced in the proposition of the Senator from Kentucky, voted for it, and was willing, with that condition, to extend the Missouri compromise line across the continent, and thus close forever the only cause of serious discord between different sections of our Union. It was, therefore, with surprise—these things, at least many of them, being fresh in the memory of all—that I heard my colleague say, that any one had had the infamous falsehood and audacity to assert that southern men had introduced this proposition to embarrass the bill before us, and prevent the adjustment of existing difficulties.

Mr. FOOTE. Will my colleague excuse me? I did not hear the beginning of his remark.

Mr. DAVIS. I will repeat it then. I said that it was with surprise I heard my colleague say, that any one had had the infamous falsehood and audacity to assert that southern men had introduced the Missouri compromise in order to embarrass the bill before us, and to prevent an adjustment.

Mr. FOOTE. I understand my colleague now, and I will simply state that I did not charge any Senator or member of the House with such an intention, but I said that there were individuals elsewhere, who supported the proposition for such a purpose. I cordially acquitted all those with whom I am associated here of any such design; the Senator's words therefore cannot apply to me.

Mr. DAVIS. My colleague might very well have relied on it that they did not. The uniform courtesy with which I have treated him might have assured him that my language was not intended to apply to him.

Mr. FOOTE. I know my colleague did not so intend it, but it might have been so understood by some of those present.

Mr. DAVIS. I do not see how my language could have been so understood. I should be sorry if any one could suppose that I would charge my colleague upon this floor with crimes so degrading as those I was describing. Not at all. He distinctly stated that it was not here but elsewhere that the accusation was made. The accusation is one of those many falsehoods that are now floating through the air. It is a part of the work of that set of scavengers who hang over the Senate, and pounce upon every southern man who advocates the rights and principles of his constituents. It is a part of the work of that class of men among the "letter writers" whose infamous business it is to invent or gather slander, and cater to a vitiated appetite for calumny; one of whom—the vilest Hessian of his class—I am informed is now receiving money to abuse myself and other southern men for the manner in which we have felt it incumbent upon us to represent our constituents here.

Sir, I regret that the introduction of the subject has led me into even a passing notice of such things as these: it is not my habit thus to trespass on the Senate. Proud in the consciousness of my own rectitude, secure in the approval of my own constituents, I allow the presses which here surround us to pour in their artillery without fearing harm from their fire. I have allowed defunct politicians, resurrected for the purpose, to throw in their blows too. I have allowed speeches to go out, one after another, which have placed us in an attitude which does not belong to me, and I have looked upon it with the indifference which belongs to the assurance that I am right, and the security with which the approval of my constituents invests me. I am not prepared to consider the position of a United States Senator so low that he must stand at the mercy of every petty newspaper or degraded letter-writer. I cannot estimate the intelligence of my countrymen so cheaply as to believe I am to be judged by either the praise or condemnation of hired scribblers. I trust my life, which except when in the service of my country, has been spent in the State I partly represent, gives me a character not thus to be destroyed. I have hoped for, not feared the coming of the judgment of my constituents, though, from the very inception of this measure down to the present hour, the country has been flooded with missiles representing all who favor this particular bill as in favor of the Union, and every southerner who opposes it as opposing it for purposes of disunion. Now, sir, when a respectable man shall ever make that charge against me, I will answer him. When any respectable man shall ever accuse me of being a disunionist, I will answer him in monosyllables.

At present I have no wish to enter into an argument to prove that false, which I hope no gentleman will charge, and which my whole life utterly condemns. If I have a superstition, sir, which governs my mind and holds it captive, it is a superstitious reverence for the Union. If one can inherit a sentiment, I may be said to have inherited this from my revolutionary father. And if education can develop a sentiment in the heart and mind of man, surely mine has been such as would most develop feelings of attachment for the Union. But, sir, I have an allegiance to the State which I represent here. I have an allegiance to those who have intrusted their interests to me, which every consideration of faith and of duty, which every feeling of honor tells me is above all other political considerations. I trust I shall never find my allegiance there and here in conflict. God forbid that the day should ever come when to be true to my constituents is to be hostile to the Union. If, sir, we have reached that hour in the progress of our institutions, it is past the age to which the Union should have lived. If we have got to the point where it is treason to the United States to protect the rights and interests of our constituents, I ask why should they longer be represented here? Why longer remain a part of the Union? If there is a dominant party in this Union which can deny to us equality, and the rights we derive through the Constitution; if we are no longer the freemen our fathers left us; if we are to be crushed by the power of an unrestrained majority, this is not the Union for which the blood of the Revolution was shed; this is not the Union I was taught from my cradle to revere; this is not the Union in the service of which a large portion of my life has been passed; this is not the Union for which our fathers pledged their property, their lives, and their sacred honor. No, sir, this would be a central Government, raised on the destruction of all the principles of the Constitution, and the first, the highest obligation of every man who has sworn to support that Constitution would be resistance to such usurpation. This is my position.

My colleague has truly represented the people of Mississippi as ardently attached to the Union. I think he has not gone beyond the truth when he has placed Mississippi one of the first, if not the first of the States of the Confederation in attachment to it. But, sir, even that deep attachment and habitual reverence for the Union, common to us all—even that, it may become necessary to try by the touchstone of reason. It is not impossible that they should unfurl the flag of disunion. It is not impossible that violations of the Constitution and of their rights should drive them to that dread extremity. I feel well assured that they will never reach it until it has been twice and three times justified. If, when thus fully warranted, they want a standard-bearer, in default of a better, I am at their command. This is part of my doctrine of allegiance to the people of Mississippi, and with this feeling my colleague will not be surprised to learn that I regretted to hear him suppose a case, contemplate a contingency, in which he would *scorn* to represent the people of Mississippi.

Mr. FOOTE. My colleague will allow me to say that I am in favor, if possible, of an equitable and honorable adjustment of all these questions; and, under the existing circumstances of the hour, I embrace the opportunity of adjusting them on honorable and fair terms. If a proposal to dissolve the Union should be made, I, for one, could not sanction and sustain it; and if the State of Mississippi should, under present circumstances, assume such a position—which I believe to be impossible—whoever might hold the banner, I would not fight under it. Although I say this, I would not fight against my own State under any circumstances whatever. I have repeatedly said here, and I say again, that in case of any intolerable oppression, placing myself upon the old Jackson ground, I would be as warm and active, and as ardent as my colleague in defence of the rights of my State; but it would be only in a case of *intolerable* oppression that I could think of resorting to a dissolution of the Union, and I do not think that any such case now exists.

Mr. DAVIS, of Mississippi. I will not say what my opinion may be when the bill is brought to its final stage. I have heretofore declined to discuss the merits of the main bill on a mere question of amendment, and I will not do so now. I do not concur in opinion with my colleague. I do not consider it to be an adjustment, or anything approaching it. I consider that nothing is proposed by this bill which can serve to adjust the machine of our Government: it will only be pressed further in the direction to which it was previously leaning. The tendency is all one way; adjustment would require a policy the reverse of this bill, which contributes to the further depression of the weaker side, the South, and to the elevation of that which is already too high, the North. That is my view of it. But, sir, I have no purpose now or at any other time to announce upon what I am ready to go to the ultimate resort of disunion. I have not spoken of disunion to the Senate. No, sir; and whilst I hold a seat here, I shall make no such proposition. I shall never call on Mississippi to secede from the Union, but will remember that I am her representative on the floor of the Senate, and I shall ever leave it to her to judge how long she may require my services here; and when she may need them in a different field——

Mr. FOOTE. Will the Senator permit me for a moment?

Mr. DAVIS. Certainly.

Mr. FOOTE. I have not said that my colleague contemplated disunion at all. The leading Democratic paper in our State, printed in my own county, of the editors of which I will not speak disrespectfully or unkindly, however unkindly I may have been treated by them, has recently published editorial articles, which have been republished in the *Charleston Mercury* and other southern papers of a certain ultra stamp, with glowing commendation—which articles, in my judgment, contain most decided disunion sentiments. I have deeply regretted to see this; and can only attribute such extraordinary indiscretion to a strange and most profound delusion in regard to the true condition of affairs here at the present moment. It is in view of these facts that I deem it my duty to say to-day, and to say distinctly, that I, for one, am opposed to any such project of disunion as seems to have been concerted; and to say further, that the State of Mississippi will never, with my consent, take part in any such dark and dangerous conspiracy against the happiness and repose of this noble Republic. Gentlemen who are induced to figure as disunionists, and who consider the adoption of this bill as justifying a resort to such extreme measures, must act out their own judgments and feelings; but I beg them to allow me, if they please, the humble privilege of observing my official oath and endeavoring to perform my duty as a patriot.

Mr. DAVIS of Mississippi. No doubt there have been articles of this kind in many newspapers and in many places. I have not read the article to which my colleague refers or if I had, I should not think it my duty to defend or reply to it. But it should not excite surprise if, from reading the articles in northern papers, often very offensive to the South, and which are thrown upon them at this time with especial energy, the editor had given violent articles in retaliation. This is but to say that he is human, and influenced by passions liable to be excited. But I say again I am not here to prescribe the terms of secession. I am here to represent the people of Mississippi at the seat of the General Government. My duty is to sustain the Union and the Constitution, and whilst I am here that duty I will endeavor to perform. I have nothing to say about disunion. It is an alternative not to be anticipated—one to which I could only look forward as the last resort; but it is one, let me say, which, under certain contingencies, I am willing to meet; and I will leave my constituents to judge when that contingency shall arrive. I have no suggestion to make to them; for I am not one of those who seek to control the public opinion which they pretend to represent. My purpose is honestly to follow out the wishes of my constituents, as far as they accord with the Constitution I have sworn to support. I have nothing more to say upon that point. What the will of that constituency is, it is well for me to know, but not necessary for me to announce. What the views of our constituents may be relative to the conduct of my colleague and myself on the bill now pending, I preferred to leave without the expression of my opinion. I regret, therefore, that my colleague should have found it necessary, under any circumstances, to allude to the preferences of our constituents; for I certainly should never have alluded to that in relation to him. Notwithstanding the Democratic papers of the State—every one of them that I have seen—come to me with marked expressions of disapprobation of the bill, I chose not to bring the matter before the Senate. Notwithstanding my colleague on a former occasion introduced here resolutions of the Legislature of Mississippi most sternly disapproving the main feature of this bill——

Mr. FOOTE, (in his seat). As a separate measure.

Mr. DAVIS. My colleague says so; then I must read the resolutions:

"Resolutions of the Legislature of Mississippi, approved March 6, 1850.

"Resolved, That the policy heretofore pursued by the Government of the United States, in regard to said territory, [reference was had to the territories acquired from Mexico,] in refusing to provide territorial government therefor, has been and is eminently calculated to promote, and is about to effect indirectly, the cherished object of the Abolitionists, which cannot be accomplished by direct legislation without a plain and palpable violation of the Constitution of the United States.

"Resolved, That the admission of California into the Union as a sovereign State, with its present constitution, the result of the aforesaid false and unjust policy on the part of the Government of the United States, would be an act of fraud and oppression on the rights of the people of the slaveholding States; and it is the sense of this Legislature that our Senators and Representatives should, to the extent of their ability, resist it by all honorable and constitutional means."

So spoke the Legislature who are considered peculiarly the constituency of Senators.

Mr. FOOTE. Will my colleague allow me to explain?

Mr. DAVIS. Oh, certainly.

Mr. FOOTE. I will detain the Senate but a moment. My colleague speaks of his disregard of newspapers. Now, it is well known that I am quite as indifferent to newspaper denunciation as any other man, and that in my public course I have profited more from the revilement of editors than from their commendation. Indeed, I was elected to the Senate with every newspaper in the State against me, or neutral, save one. But if it were a matter of any importance, I could particularize more than two-thirds of the Democratic press of Mississippi who have not taken any hostile stand in relation to me. Most of them are silent, while some are warmly and fully sustaining my course. Almost every Whig paper in the State, it is true, does sustain me upon this question, which I hold to be far above party. More or less warmly, I acknowledge the gratification which I derive from this fact, and I conceive it to be not at all discreditable to me; nor will my colleague, who, at his first election received Whig as well as Democratic votes in our Legislature. Inclined as I am rather to think that the newspapers of the country generally are not very satisfactory representatives of the public sentiment, yet I suppose that, on a question like this, Whig and Democratic papers may be considered as equally good authority, and to be equally relied upon as the exponents of the public opinion of any State. While I am not at war with any of them, and shall seek no controversy with them, still I shall exercise my own judgment freely and independently, holding myself responsible alone to the sovereign people of Mississippi, whose charitable appreciation of my acts I do not at all doubt.

Mr. DAVIS. I have no controversy with newspapers, nor about them.

Mr. FOOTE. A word, if my colleague pleases, in regard to the resolutions.

Mr. DAVIS. Oh certainly.

Mr. FOOTE. These resolutions were adopted by the State of Mississippi while a proposition was pending to admit California as a separate measure, and before even the committee was formed who report this plan of adjustment. And it was in the very spirit of those instructions, and with a view of carrying them out fully and faithfully, that I offered a motion to raise the Committee of Thirteen, with a view, in part, to preventing the separate admission of California, which, but for this same committee, would have been admitted, in my judgment, some time since. I am resolved, when I return to my own home, to explain my own course in connection with these circumstances— to state my motives of action, and to establish by irrefutable proof the fidelity and discretion which have marked my conduct. And I shall be prepared to meet any opposition which may present itself on this question. My colleague, I know, puts a different interpretation on those resolutions of instruction. He conceives that they apply to a state of things not existing at the time of their adoption; that is his opinion. He speaks also of the letters he receives. Well, it is probable those letters are written to him by those who know his feelings on this subject, and his hostility to this plan, and have therefore written to him such letters as they judge will be pleasing to him. Now, I have quite as large a correspondence as any man now in Washington, I believe. I write quite as many letters as it is at all convenient to me to write, and I receive many more letters than I do write. I receive many letters from Mississippi, having correspondents in almost every county; and I have not received more than four or five letters disapproving the plan of adjustment. This state of things only proves that his correspondents think differently from mine, and that the great question between us, in regard to the state of popular sentiment, is only to be decided fairly when we shall both get home. Allow me to say, that among my correspondents in the State of Mississippi is the president of the late Nashville Convention, the president also of the Convention of Mississippi held at Jackson, out of whose proceedings grew the Nashville Convention, and the chief justice of the high court of errors and appeals of the State of Mississippi. That distinguished gentleman has written me a letter, extracts from which I have published, declaring that he approves my whole course in connection with the present measure, and that he does not doubt my being fully sustained in the State. I believe that nine-tenths of our constituents cordially approve this scheme of settlement. My colleague, I know, thinks otherwise, and it is quite a proper subject for an honest difference of opinion. We shall both ascertain the truth upon this head in good season.

Mr. DAVIS. I have no controversy with newspapers or about them. Have no declarations to make about the public opinion to which I am invited, and more than willing to refer our conduct. I should be very sorry to lose my colleague; but am ready to transfer this controversy between us to the arena which he desires, without further remarks on the present occasion than seem to be necessary. I spoke first of Democratic papers, because I was elected with known adherence to the principles of the party called Democratic, and I did not close my remarks upon that point before I was asked to permit an explanation. I had intended to go on and say what I will say now—that the Whig papers and Whig politicians are divided, but that the Democratic papers and politicians are very generally on one side in regard to this subject. As to the matter of correspondence, my colleague is an able and zealous man, bred to the law, speaks freely and fully, and the country knows his opinions. No man could write a letter to him without knowing what would suit him in relation to Mr. CLAY's bill. My own position is entirely the reverse. When the bill was introduced, I chose not to speak upon it at any length, and I indicated, from time to time, that if the bill was amended in certain particulars, it would receive my vote. And, sir, let me say, much as southern men have been denounced for retarding the decision of this measure, that this bill has lived thus long by our courtesy. These southern men thus censured saved this bill from the tomahawk of the northern men when it was first introduced. It has lived thus long at our mercy, and we deserve the thanks instead of the censure of its friends. At any time it was within our power to have consigned it to the tomb of the Senate's table.

And in what spirit has this been met? Amendments have been presented by us, they were declared non-essential, as some said mere surplusage, but we, the particular class of southern men thus arraigned, believed them to be important; and these, sir, have been voted down in face of the fact that your bill lived by our mercy. Now, sir, we have reached a stage in this proceeding when it is time that censure and denunciation here and elsewhere should cease; we have reached a state where further delay and discussion promises nothing desirable, and I am ready to give the vote which shall consign this bill to the table to-day. I have preferred a plan which should involve within its folds the creation of territorial government; for I feared that unless so included, those Territories would remain without governments. And this has been the only reason I have found for seeking to amend this bill, or delaying its final decapitation, if decapitation it is to receive. Is this, sir, the promptings of local prejudice?—is this a sectional consideration? What have we in Mississippi to be advantaged by the creation of territorial governments in Utah and New Mexico—territorial governments which do not recognize our right to migrate with our private property—which do not annul the Mexican laws, but which, as is asserted by the first men of the Senate, leave those local laws in full force over the Territory? I can have no motive save to provide for the people of those remote districts the protection of territorial governments.

But when this measure is coupled with the proposition to sever from Texas a large portion of the territory from which hereafter new slaveholding States are to be created, and to turn it over to the jurisdiction of this Congress, I say, sir, that we deserve especial consideration for the forbearance we have shown; for if this is to be the final form of the bill, far better for me is it, as a southern man, to admit California in a separate bill, and save the whole of Texas for the future increase of southern strength.

As I stated in the opening of my remarks, it was not my intention to have spoken at this time on the bill, and I have already extended my remarks, in consequence, perhaps, of interruptions, longer than I intended. I will not follow further the position of my colleague, because the matter will be transferred to another scene, where he and I can meet in the same kind feeling and good understanding, I trust, which we have here. Far be it from me, here or elsewhere, to seek to make my colleague a victim to what I believe to be his honest error. God knows how much I should have rejoiced to see him retrace his first steps on this question, and stand with me in what I am sure is the advocacy of the interests and will of Mississippi, and in conformity with the policy of the South, as it is now fully established. In relation to the particular amendment under debate, I will make a short statement, for I do not now propose to argue it.

Mr. HALE. It is now late, and I ask the Senator if he will give way to a motion to adjourn?

Mr. DAVIS assenting, the Senate adjourned.

FRIDAY, *June 28, 1850.*

The bill being again taken up,

Mr. DAVIS, of Mississippi, resumed and concluded as follows:

Mr. President: When the Senate adjourned yesterday I was about to offer some statements to Senators in relation to the amendment proposed by the Senator from Louisiana. That amendment is in accordance with a compromise which once gave peace to the country during a period of intense excitement; and resulted from a desire to save the Union from danger, with which it was thought to be seriously threatened. I cannot believe the danger was as imminent then as it is now. Then there were patriotic hearts in Congress from every section of the country that came to the rescue upon this vital question. Does such patriotism exist in the present Congress as was found in that of 1820? Are there not those around me who will meet this question with the devoted patriotism which the crisis demands, and, if need be, sacrifice themselves to the good of their country? If any plan shall be presented which I believe would be final, would terminate this distracting controversy, and restore the fraternity which existed among our fathers, I would make whatever personal sacrifice such a plan would embrace. At an early stage of the present session I indicated my belief that the extension of the Missouri compromise was the best settlement which could be made, and all that has transpired from that day to this has served to confirm me in that opinion. I was among those who supported the raising of this committee—not that the bills then before the Senate should be combined, but with the hope that it would bring in a measure of adjustment, compromise, or settlement which would receive from me an approbation which I could not give to those bills. The hope that something would be presented to us upon which we could all unite has met a grievous disappointment. Though it is not my purpose now to detain the Senate by a general examination of the bill, I may be permitted to say, that I have found in its heterogeneous features nothing to commend it to my support as a southern man, or as one who desires the restoration of fraternity to this Republic. I see in it no termination of those elements of discord which now disturb us. I see beyond it the same questions which now exist. Beyond it I see a higher excitement than that which surrounds us, and the distant vista is enveloped in a gloom from the contemplation of which I turn sorrowfully away. When the Missouri compromise was adopted in 1820, as we were told yesterday, that sage and patriot, Mr. Jefferson, said it was but a reprieve. Such, sir, it has proved. The reprieve has expired, and its extension is denied. Now the measure is considered too extreme a concession from the North which then they enforced on the South. Now we, the minority, are to be brought at once to execution. Shall we submit, or shall we resist? This is a question to which freemen can give but one answer. Whatever may be the result, I, for one, feel myself bound to maintain, by every means at my command, those constitutional rights which I am here to represent. If evil shall result from my course, upon the head of others must rest the responsibility. However sad may be its consequences to myself, if down it is my fate to fall, I shall retain in my misfortune the conscientious conviction of having done my duty as a representative, a patriot, and as an honest man.

In the remarks I propose to offer upon this question, I shall direct myself to other considerations than those broad and general views which have been presented by others, and probably will be presented again. I shall contend for this amendment as a measure of expediency—as a measure which is written by the hand of Nature upon the surface of the country for which we propose to legislate—a measure which is indicated by the character of the people for whom we are about to provide governmental organization, and demanded by soil, climate, and productions, agricultural and mineral. The fathers of this country were neither so unwise nor so profane as to deny the overruling Providence whose interposing hand was often felt in shaping the destiny of the infant Republic. And if there be a special interposition—a guardian care over us still—I think it is manifested in the identity of the geographical and political considerations for the renewal of the compact, the extension of the line of 36° 30′, which is now presented. Never were political considerations more fully maintained by geographical reasons. In looking at the map of California, as it was remarked by the Senator from Louisiana, its unnatural boundaries most forcibly strike the eye. There they are, extending over impassable mountain barriers, including in one government plains which can have no other connection, and embracing the whole sea-coast, as if the frontier were marked out for an empire instead of a State of the Confederacy; as though its purpose was to have a distinct international policy, to assume the command of the whole commerce of the Pacific, and of those vast countries which lie beyond it, and to control those naval stations on the western coast, which greatly tended to create a desire for its acquisition by the United States. There, we see a country, backed by snow-covered mountains, a broad valley, with two rivers to water, and a coast-plain connected with it. This is the natural demarkation of a State. On the one side the Sacramento, and on the other the San Joachin, coming from the north and the south to pour their treasures into the great entrepòt of the country, the harbor of San Francisco, their common and only receptacle. As well might we expect that the country watered by the Sacramento would be united to the valley of the Willamette, and become part of the Territory of Oregon, as that the country south of the waters of San Joachin would be included in the State of California. Other motives no doubt combined wih this reason to induce the Delegates of that part of the Territory to object to the formation of a State constitution—the first operation of which, as I learn from my correspondence in that country, has had such effect that in most of the towns south of San Luis Obispo they have held public meetings for the purpose of petitioning Congress for a territorial organization and government adapted to their condition, such as it now is, and such as from natural causes it must remain.

But to return to the point which I promised to consider—the geographical arguments for this political line of 36° 30′. At the intersection of this parallel with the sea, as I am informed, the coast range of mountains terminates in a bold promontory that overhangs the ocean; thence eastward it passes over desert mountains, crosses the arid plain of the Monterey river, and enters the valley through which the San Joaquin flows south of the permanent tributaries of that river, passing between its southern branches and the Lake Tulares; which, it is represented to me, does not, as is usually shown on the maps, regularly flow into the San Joaquin, but only does so when, in time of freshet, the flats to its north, extending to the San Joaquin, are overflowed. Shut out from the sea breeze, this plain is represented as having almost tropical heat, and as being fully occupied by a quiet, harmless race of fishing Indians, to whom the country is particularly adapted. But if it ever passes into the hands of those who require commercial ports, they must be sought in the south. Distance and facility of route leave no doubt that San Pedro and San Diego, not San Francisco, must be the ports of this section.

Then, am I not sustained when I say that the hand of nature has written this line upon the country in characters which might have been read before it was possessed by man? But, again, the line of 36° 30′ divides the pastoral and agricultural, the semi-tropical country, from the mining and the grain-growing regions of the north. South of this line no mine has proved productive. North of it are the placers, which have, as by magic, drawn together the men who seek to constitute this State. Leaving Monterey, which is about six miles north of this parallel of 36° 30′, and following the valley of the Monterey river, we pass through a country only saved from the name of desert by the dilapidated missions which were established by the kindness of Spain, when the country was under the viceroyalty. For one hundred miles continue high, arid plains, unsuited for cultivation or any other purpose than for wide-ranging flocks and herds. Passing into the basin of Lake Tulares, there is a plain which is watered by small streams from the mountains, and which now supports a considerable population of peaceful Indians, who have a high claim to the protective hand of Congress, which it requires no argument to show may be most effectively extended under a territorial government.

For causes before stated, the climate is such that no white man can work in the sun. This country, now inhabited by an inoffensive, to some extent agricultural people, is unsuited to the white race, unless it possess servile labor. But if we confine our attention to the coast, where the refreshing sea breeze mitigates the climate, then throughout this same extent you find, down to San Luis Obispo, the mountains running close upon the sea; its streams short, and the valleys narrow. Here, then, are scattered, some twenty or thirty miles apart, a few pastoral ranchos, with the agriculture necessary to supply the inhabitants with Indian corn and beans, which seem to be all that the country produces under its present occupation.

To the south, the coast plain widens, the mountains are depressed, gaps are found, connecting the plains above with those which slope down to the sea, until the ridge ceases, and the broad plain of Los Angeles opens to the view. Here, where the keen blasts of the north are checked by sheltering mountains, and the sloping plains face the sun, we pass at once into a tropical climate. This is the land of the grape, of cotton, of maize, of the olive, and sugar cane. Here, so far as cultivation exists, that cultivation depends upon irrigation and upon servile labor. It is a curious fact that we find here a race of Indians who pass at once into servility, and who, from their complexions and characteristics, rather seem of Asiatic origin than to be descended from the same parent stock as the wild and free tribes who were found in the more eastern portion of the United States. The country to the southeast of these mountains has been but little explored; it is in the possession of a more settled and warlike tribe of men; and it is because they have been so warlike and so populous that so little has been heretofore known of the country. Shall we, then, abandon these men, peaceful and prone to servility, or warlike and with fixed habitations, to the laws of California and the aggressions of reckless men? Or shall we extend that protection of the Federal Government over them which a territorial organization will best enable us to give? In times past, the United States have suffered bitter reproaches for their policy towards the natives they found on this continent—reproaches not always just, indeed quite undeserved, as was conclusively demonstrated by the Senator from Michigan, [Mr. CASS,] many years ago, if we compare our conduct with that of other nations, who have exercised control over the aboriginal tribes of this continent.

The strong, far-reaching arm and unbiased policy of the General Government, undisturbed by questions of State sovereignty, may govern to protect these tribes. In the new and even unsettled condition of California, it is to be feared the reverse would be the case, if the country were included in her limits: that aggression would be followed by hostility, to end in their destruction. But, sir there is another race with yet higher claim upon us in the vicinity of the coast. We find that very population, who were by the treaty to have their rights of property when they passed under our protection secured to them; we find the pastoral race of Mexicans who inhabited the country when we acquired it, occupying extensive tracts of lands; and we have reason to believe they are about to be driven from their possessions by the legislation of California. It is not to be neglected or forgotten that the present Governor of California, as we have learned through the press, announced as his policy a taxation of the lands, which would compel these proprietors to sell their possessions. A tax, such as would not be felt in the mining or even a farming district, would be destructive to a pastoral population. This is the natural fruit of legislation by those who have an opposite interest and no sympathy with the others, for whom they make laws. Is this the protection of property which we guarantied in the treaty of Guadalupe Hidalgo? Is this the kindness which those people have a right to claim from the Government of the United States? Or is it not a gross act of injustice to the people, who, ignorant of our institutions, have confided in our guardian care, and whom it is our duty, therefore, specially to protect?

Then Mr. President, whether we consider this question in relation to soil and climate, or in relation to the great characteristics of the physical geography, a division of the country is equally demanded. Whether we consider the question with reference to the present interests or the future interests and well-being of those who now or who are hereafter to inhabit those countries, it is equally clear that South California should be organized into a distinct political community, under laws enacted with reference to their peculiar interests, and the characteristics of the Mexican inhabitants, to whom we owe protection, kind and special, in proportion to their helplessness. For this we ought to retain the powers which a territorial government secures to us over this country, that we may shield it from the inappropriate or hostile legislation of the men of North California.

Mr. President, we are told that it is the will of the people to which we should bow. Do the proceedings of the convention prove that? I know not that any one has full and accurate information in relation to that subject. From such knowledge as I am able to glean, I believe the people of South California were reduced to the alternative of sending delegates to that convention to take part in its proceedings, or seeing it proceed to establish the fundamental law of their country without their coöperation or advice.

And, sir, there is another instructive statement in relation to this matter—that these delegates, when they left their homes to attend this convention, uniformly contended against a State organization, and in favor of a territorial government. We find them, one after another, yielding to different views—under what influences I am unable to say; but it is to be remarked that a large proportion of the members secured advantages, or received offices from the action of the convention to which they were delegates.

But, again, Mr. President, to decide how far this is the will of the people, it is proper to inquire what part of the population took part in those elections. I compare two towns for the purpose of illustrating that fact. Los Angeles, with a population of about five thousand people, gave about seventy-five or eighty votes; while San Diego, a little village composed of about a dozen adobe huts, gave a vote of one hundred and fifty or upwards. Then, sir, the question arises, how did that happen? The answer is two-fold: Los Angeles is one of the districts still inhabited by the population acquired with the country; they did not choose to become parties to this convention; and therefore it was that their vote was so small, although no expedient was left untried, an officer having been sent as a special agent to induce them to take part in the proceeding. All was done that could be done to cause them to vote for delegates, with only such success as is shown by the election return. The explanation in the other case is different. A body of men for the survey of the boundary, and a military escort, had just arrived, and were encamped in the vicinity of the little village, when they heard of an election. True to the instinct of our countrymen, they were ready for a canvass. The boundary commission and the army each put up their candidates; and then the struggle commenced between them to send a delegate to this convention, which was to assume sovereignty over territory of the United States, and to determine the fundamental law of a country they had never seen. The contest was of doubtful issue, when a vessel came to in the offing, and more or less of the crew and passengers were immediately brought in, as I learn, to decide it by their votes in favor of the boundary commission. And then a body of dragoons, stationed some distance in the country, were sent for. They came in; they, too, assisted by their votes to elect a candidate, who was one of the military escort; and thus an officer of the army of the United States became a delegate to the convention which has claimed to measure the rights of American citizens in their own country.

Was this the will of the people? Was this the sovereign will to which it is said that Congress must bow? or was it an unauthorized interference of men who had no legitimate or permanent connection with the matter they presumed to decide?

When, sir, looking into the constituent material of that convention, we meet there, instead of Mexican inhabitants—instead of Americans who had gone there with the intent to remain citizen emigrants, seeking a new home—seven officers of the New York regiment, sent out there by this Government for military purposes, three officers of the United States army, two or three officers of the navy of the United States, a few Mexicans, who could not speak English, and some of our citizens who are said to have gone there to aid in the organization of the government. The residue was composed of persons of whom it may be supposed a part were permanently identified with the country—how great a part I will not pretend to say. But I would ask of Senators how many they suppose of those persons they have known to emigrate to California went there with the intent to remain? It is not enough to say they will probably never carry out their intent to return, because to qualify them to found the institutions of the country, they should have had at the time a fixed purpose in their mind to make that country their home. This could not be the case with those who, a few months before, had gone there merely to collect gold and return to the United States. There is another test: How many had taken their families with them?—that best guarantee of an intent to become permanent residents.

Mr. President, it comes, then, to this: whether sojourners, persons traveling, with no permanent interest or locality in the country—soldiers, sailors, or government employees, who chance to be present—are qualified to lay the foundations of a State, and decide on the institutions which shall prevail among generations yet unborn?

But, sir, there is something further to be offered to those on whom these considerations make no impression. Admitting the population to be as stated in the ordinary estimates, it was only about one-fifth of the population of California which took part in this proceeding, either to elect delegates or to ratify the constitution they formed. What then? Four-fifths of the Americans in the country, and Mexicans, to whom we are bound to extend special protection, had no connection whatever with this convention. Are we still to be told that its proceedings embody the expression of the will of the people of California? These, Mr. President, are the facts which come to light upon an analysis of this remarkable proceeding; and these facts are such as not only amply to sustain, in my opinion, the amendment of the Senator from Louisiana, [Mr. SOULE,] but which would entirely justify us in treating this constitution as a nullity, and proceeding to the formation of a territorial government for the people who inhabit our western territory.

I am not one of those, Mr. President, who can be with any truth described as hostile to these territories. On the contrary, their interest has uniformly received my support. I am one of those who strove most strenuously at the last session of Congress in favor of giving those people a government. I am one of those who was willing then, as I am willing now, to admit them as a State, so soon as they came here regularly with proper qualifications, and asked for admission. But I am one of those who claim a conformity with the precedents which have existed since the foundation of the Government, and which are necessary to secure considerations of far higher importance than any which concern the ascendancy of a particular interest, or political party.

But, Mr. President, I find myself constantly wandering into considerations broader than it was my purpose to enter upon. I have said that this country south of 36° 30′, was separated by nature from the body of what is now called the State of California, and that it claims a political organization separate from the other. The basin of the Lake Tulares, lying immediately south of the parallel of 36° 30′, forms, I think, no exception. A bare inspection of the map, with the slightest knowledge of the mountain ridges and passes, must convince any one that this country belongs to South California. Its ports are San Diego and San Pedro. That all the country back of the Sierra Nevada up to the Salt Lake, must for commercial purposes find its outlet at San Diego and San Pedro, and not at San Francisco, is established now, I believe, beyond controversy. We find the plain extending from the Great Salt Lake, connected by a route over which there is said to be now a good wagon road, with the port of San Diego. Then, sir, nature having determined these connections and divisions, the question arises, what are to be the institutions, if left to natural causes, in the one country and the other? Will they be uniform or diversified? If the latter, why seek to force on them one system of municipal laws?

If, then, as suggested by these considerations, I have been able to show to the Senate, however briefly, that the population, climate, and soil, united with those routes capable of being traveled, all go to sustain this line of 36° 30′ as the natural line of division, I ask whether, in adopting it, we should not be consulting higher considerations than any of mere temporary political expediency? I ask whether reasons of preëminent and general importance do not demand that we should sustain the amendment of the Senator from Louisiana? But, Mr. President, there is still another claim for this amendment. Anterior to the formation of the State constitution by California, Deseret formed a State or territorial constitution, and established her boundary. Deseret, which lies immediately east of California, has no outlet to the sea except through the southern part of California. They find their outlet to the ports of this section which I have mentioned. They have no practical commercial connection whatever with San Francisco. This is most forcibly shown by a fact which has recently come to my knowledge. When Colonel Mason, the military governor of that Territory, wished to obtain troops from the settlement at the Salt Lake, an officer was detached for the purpose; but, instead of being able to go direct, he had to keep down upon the west side of the Sierra Nevada, which stood a snow-covered wall for a distance of more than three hundred miles before he found any opening through which he could pass; after which he had to travel north of the same parallel from which he started. It is best, I think, that this country of South California should stand alone —that it have a distinct organization; but if that is not to be done, then the most proper and desirable thing remaining to be chosen, is to attach it to Deseret, which has claimed a part of it, and to which it belongs by nature more properly than to North California.

But the distinguished Senator from Massachusetts [Mr. WEB-STER] remarked yesterday, that we are reduced to an alternative —that we have to admit California as a State, or that she will be separated from the Union. Mr. President, these words come also from the shores of the Pacific; but what foundation is there, can there be, for them? The people of California knock at your doors for admission into the Union, at the same time we are told that they are suffering for protection and assistance. They have now a State government, and there is no interference to prevent their exercise of all its functions. Indeed, some portions of the army and navy of the United States are kept there for their benefit. They claim, in order to enable them to carry on their State government, the aid of the Federal Government. With what force, then, do they talk, or others for them, of their seceding from the United States and setting up a Government of their own? Why, sir, it is idle. They need the protection of this Government; and I wish them to have it, not the less because they have attempted self-government before they were competent to sustain themselves. With this is connected another inquiry. Why such haste? Were they prompted to form a State government, or was it by their own option? It appears to have been because they were invited to it by one who had no right to the exercise of the civil functions which he assumed, or with which he was improperly invested. They were urged to it by the officers of the army in California. The proclamation under which the convention was convened makes a strange declaration. It asserts that the laws of Mexico made the military commandant *ex officio* civil governor:

"The undersigned, in accordance with instructions from the Secretary of War, has assumed the administration of civil affairs in California, not as *military* governor, but as the executive of the existing civil government. In the absence of a properly-appointed civil governor, the commanding officer of the department is, by the laws of California, *ex officio* civil governor of the country; and the instructions from Washington were based on the provisions of these laws. This subject has been misrepresented, or at least misconceived, and currency given to the impression that the government of the country is still *military*. Such is not the fact. The military government ended with the war; and what remains is the *civil* government recognized in the existing laws of California."

Now, that rests on the doctrine which has been put forward here, that the Mexican laws are in force in the Territories. But, so far as I can learn, there was no such law as that proclamation appeals to. In this same volume is contained a digest of these laws; and I will read one section which belongs to this case, and, I believe, decides it:

"In temporary default of the Governor, another shall be named *ad interim*, in the same manner as the proper one. If the default should be of short duration, the senior (*mas antiguo*) lay member of the departmental legislature shall take charge of the government, as he shall in like manner do during the interval which may take place between the default of the Governor proper, and the appointment of his successor *ad interim*."

Then, sir, it was the oldest member of their legislature who became Governor *ex officio* when the office was vacant. It was the oldest member of the departmental legislature who should have succeeded. If, indeed, the civil government which preexisted the acquisition of that Territory by the United States continued, why should not the Mexican Governor have resumed his duties with the restoration of peace, with their laws in force and their officers restored to their functions? American emigrants would have realized the full force of this doctrine.

But here, sir, is proof of the fallacy of the whole foundation of this argument for the supremacy of Mexican laws. No one relied upon it—no one has yet been willing to follow this argument to the conclusion to which it leads. Else why was not the Legislature of the Department of California called together? The thing has received life from political incubation here.

But the Senator from Massachusetts assumed another position which I wish to notice. He stated, in exact opposition to all those geographical facts which I have presented, that if we had the power to arrange this boundary we could not make a better one than that proposed. Now, sir, it would be very surprising indeed if a convention, without any knowledge of part of the country for which they were to establish a government, should chance to fall upon the best boundary that could be established.

It would be strange if they could do it at the first guess; and it would be stranger still if, after varying with every extraneous pressure they received, they should at last fortuitously settle upon the boundary best suited to the formation of the State. First, in ignorance of the fact that the people of Deseret had formed a government, it was proposed to include that country. Then a boundary was adopted, including a part of the country beyond the mountains, and it appears that the belief existed that the Sierra Nevada run down to the Colorado river. After all this, we are led to the conclusion, by what is found in the debates of the convention, that the boundary finally adopted was selected because it covered the country in which General Riley had ordered delegates to be elected. They considered themselves bound, therefor, to adopt that boundary, and they did not even claim to inquire what limits nature had prescribed. Now, sir, are Senators of the United States to lock up their intellects, to shut out all sources of information, and adopt as the boundaries of the State those which General Riley happened to select as that from which he would call delegates to the convention?

The Senator also says that southern labor could not be profitably used in this country. Why, sir? Do white men work in the burning suns of South Carolina? Are not the products there of that tropical character which, in our more temperate climate, demands slave labor? Or is it because there is too little soil? If the latter be assumed, then I reply: those valleys— now, it is true, to a great extent, desert—were once prolific of products which form the staples of the southern States. Even now, are to be found aqueducts that conveyed the waters from the mountains, and irrigated and fertilized the plains. Wherever water is found in sufficient abundance, our enterprising people will develop the capabilities of the country, and it will again be covered with the profitable productions to which its soil and climate are adapted. It may become the rival for the growth of long staple cotton which is now produced on the sea islands of the United States. So far as we are able to learn, it is, of the whole country of the United States, the best adapted to the growth of the olive and the grape. Why, then, may not this country become great in its agricultural resources, if permitted to introduce that species of labor which can bear the scorching of a tropical sun? Now, they have it in the copper-colored Indians, who readily pass into a servile condition, and serve for the irregular demand which is made upon them for the present limited cultivation. But after those changes, which we must soon anticipate, whence are they to draw the labor required for that climate, save from the slaves of the United States? Without these that country must long remain uncultivated. I will not now repeat what has been heretofore said of our right to transfer this species of labor to that country, and the consequences which would result from it. But, leaving all that where it has been placed, and remains unshaken by argument, I propose to inquire, what is the position in relation to this set of measures which I and those who think with me occupy? We of the South have claimed equality of right in the Territories. Does this bill give it? Does it secure to us anything? Do our opponents, in this sectional issue, concede any point for which they have ever contended? Their assertion is renewed that the local law of Mexico continues in force. With that is coupled the assertion that slavery can only exist by force of local law, and with that is connected, following as effect from cause, the prohibition of the legislature to pass any law for its introduction. Those who hold those opinions, and make that provision, certainly do not intend to concede anything. In what attitude do we then stand in regard to the Territories? We are not prohibited from taking slaves, because the prohibition is believed already to exist. Now, then, if the reverse should prove to be the case, would not the prohibition then be resorted to? But if we are excluded by the Mexican local laws of the land, then the repeal of those laws is refused. This is to organize governments, that we may furnish the officers to execute the laws which would exist without our action. If the laws now there are to remain, the condition after will be very much the same as before our organization. Then where is the merit, the healing power of this great compromise bill? What is there in the whole scheme that a southern man should desire so much as to sacrifice for it all the restrictions of time-honored precedents, should violate all established usages, and his own convictions of propriety? Is it that he may fasten upon his constituents a law which gives them nothing, but takes from them a large portion of Texas, in which they have now an equal right, secured by the jurisdiction of a slaveholding State?

But, sir, on a former occasion I was answered that the laws of Texas would remain in force. Now, let us see in whau position we will stand there. Where is the boundary of Texas? We have called upon Congress again and again to decide that question, and it has again and again shrunk from the duty. When a new line is drawn, who shall say whether the land beyond it was in or out of Texas before that line was drawn? Being now undetermined—the dispute being as to whether that country is New Mexico or Texas—I ask what assurances we have that we shall not be answered finally, that the local laws of New Mexico exist in these Territories, and not the laws of Texas? Then, sir, we are to surrender to the control of an anti-slavery Congress this vast domain, without having obtained a recognition of boundary, or an admission that the Texas laws are over it. Thus we are to turn it over to the tender mercies of the anti-slavery majority of Congress, whose mercy to the South is as the mercy of the winds and waves.

It is not necessary for me to multiply arguments like these to sustain my decision as to my own action, or justify the vote I intend to give to my constituents; nor can I believe it necessary for me to multiply such arguments to justify myself in the mind of every patriot who loves his whole country more than his own section. Sir, I know that the weakness of human nature renders man prone to view his own case through a different medium from that through which he views it when it is another's; but, if I can judge what would be my feelings if the case were reversed, I may say I would stand by the minority, whose rights were about to be stripped from them— would stand by the Constitution and justice, against any popular feeling that might press upon me from any quarter, however respected.

Sir, so far as I am concerned—and, I think, so far as the South generally is concerned—every assertion that we have opposed the admission of California, because of the prohibition of slavery, is unfounded. I am one of those who have uniformly avowed the doctrine that the people, in forming a State constitution, have a right to determine for themselves whether they will have slavery or not. I am willing to follow that doctrine to any conclusion to which it may lead. But, sir, the doctrine does not carry with it the right of every band of wandering men in any section of country, who may choose to assemble together and adopt a so-called constitution, to bind us to recognize its validity and their sovereignty. Such a right is not implied in the doctrine I avow. We object, sir, mainly to this provision, because it does not come from the permanent population of the country, and because it was inserted, as is too plainly apparent, to yield to the anti-slavery dictation of the American Congress. What would it advantage the South, if we could insert in this constitution a provisionary clause to admit slavery, if it be true that the people, the soil, the climate, are all opposed to it? What could it, under such circumstances, advantage us, or what could it injure you? If, under such a condition, any man should undertake to go to such a country with slaves, it would follow, of course, that he would lose his property. And to those who so ardently desire the emancipation of the slave, what better guarantee could they ask than that they should be sent to a country where the population, the soil, the climate, the productions, are all opposed to slavery? Sir, there is a want of sincerity somewhere. Those who assert so unqualifiedly that slavery cannot exist there must, I say, be wanting in sincerity when they so furiously oppose the idea of leaving the decision of the question to time and the future population. Men do not, from week to week and from month to month, battle against a mere abstraction. No doubt some southern men believe that slaves would not be taken to that country, and yet contend for it as a constitutional right. That is a different question. A constitutional right is a substantial thing, because of its sacred character, and the possible consequences of permitting a breach at even the least important point. But the man who opposes, as a matter of policy, the exercise of the right to introduce slave property from States of this union, and at the same time asserts that it could not exist, that no law could introduce it and keep it there, must have a strange mode of reasoning, or a want of that sincerity which we have a right to expect in discussion here. But suppose that the constitution of California had contained a clause permitting slavery: how then would the case stand? Would those who, at the last session of Congress, opposed the organization of a territorial government unless the slavery prohibition were contained in the act, have voted for the admission of a State into the Union with such a constitution? Would those who refused that the Constitution of the United States should be extended over the country, lest it should give some advantage to slaveholders in the Territories—would they, I say, with such a provision in the Constitution as I have supposed, have voted for the admission of California? No, sir; their past conduct too plainly shows the contrary. Yet these are the same who arraign southern men for a position assumed upon different ground, and attribute to them the purpose to exclude it because slavery is prohibited. Now, as heretofore, I claim that our attitude is defensive; I maintain that we are merely contending for our constitutional rights, and contend for even less than our constitutional rights, when we ask that the contract under which we have existed for thirty years shall be renewed. That position, however, is denounced as ultra. Ultra in what? Is it beyond the faith heretofore pledged to us—beyond the compact made for the advantage of your section to our disadvantage? Is it beyond the Constitution which secures equal privileges to every citizen? What is it beyond? Will any man tell me it is ultra to assert our constitution rights?—ultra to ask that a compact heretofore made and renewed shall be again extended?—ultra to claim that we are equals in the Union, and should enjoy equal rights? And, in keeping with this idle and unsubstantial charge, we are told that the extremes here meet.

It is charged here and elsewhere that the ultras of the North and the South have met, and this great and important measure of settlement and compromise is to be destroyed by that conjunction. Well, sir, upon what grounds have the extremes met? They meet upon the ground that it is proper to say what they mean—to tell the country plainly, honestly what their purpose is; and upon that ground men of any opinion may meet me at all times. And in such a conjunction, being an attempt to say what we mean, to say nothing unintelligibly, and to defeat all illusory schemes, I am willing to be found with men of any opinion, however repulsive. Beyond this there is no conjunction. Any insinuation that there is any cointelligence beyond this, that there is any caucusing, to use a phrase well understood here, I pronounce, so far as I am concerned, to be false. I stand upon my own ground—that which I have uniformly announced to the Senate. Let those who choose to vote with me do so for whatever reasons may be satisfactory to them. God forbid that I should ever have such feelings of repugnance to any Senator, that I should change my vote for fear of being found thus connected with him. But, sir, I am not cheered or encouraged by the aid thus given to our opposition to this bill. On the other hand it constitutes, to me, one of the most alarming indications of the times. What more can be wanted by our extreme opponents than this bill gives them? It is not enough for them to seize the whole matter in dispute, but must they insist upon doing it in the most offensive form? Is this the worse alternative we are called on to avoid by adopting this bill? I reject the inducement, and find in the argument an answer to the promises of peace which are offered us by those whose faith embraces things not seen.

We are told that this bill is to bring pacification and settlement; but who can show how this is to be effected? Settled, it is true, by the admission of California into the Union—by the taking from Texas her just domain. But what power has any one to say that agitation will not continue in the country, in relation to the Territories? Unless the South is effectually excluded by this bill, that this discord may not hereafter disturb us; that the same strife may not go beyond this measure? No one can say thus, who does not shut his eyes to passing events around him; for he must see that this very measure is productive of new elements of discord, without healing one of those five wounds that we have had held up before us. I desire pacification; I desire settlement; I wish to see the legislation of the country go on again in its peaceful channel. I wish again to stand with my brother Senators without a conflicting opinion of such a character as to disturb kind relations. I wish again to look upon this broad land without seeing the people of one portion of the Union discussing the affairs of the other in such manner as to destroy the fraternity which is the strongest support, the only reliable bond of our Union. Do not many things which daily pass around us foreshow a growing distrust of one section for the other? Are we not sufficiently warned that we stand upon the verge of civil war? Is not the smallest item in the account of sectional differences which I have stated the growing alienation, not to say sectional hostility, between the citizens of this Union, enough to fill every American's heart with the desire to come to the rescue, in order that he may aid, by head, hand, and heart in the adoption of some plan for the final settlement of this question; so fruitful of evil and so threatening in its present aspect? Could such a plan be brought forward, I would be one of the first to labor for it, and one of the last to grow weary of toil in such a cause.

Resolution offered by Jefferson Davis, July 3, 1850.

Mr. DAVIS, of Mississippi, submitted the following resolution; which was considered and agreed to:

Resolved, That the Secretary of War be directed, if within his possession and not incompatible with the public interest, to furnish the Senate with a copy of the report made to General Riley by Lieutenant E. O. C. Ord, of a reconnoissance between Los Angeles and San Diego, in California.

Remarks of Jefferson Davis on the Compromise Bill, July 18, 1850.

Mr. DAVIS, of Mississippi. Mr. President, I will trouble the Senate with but a very few remarks. Not having heretofore discussed the subject of disunion, I do not propose to do it now. I said on a former occasion that I was not here to dissolve the union and therefore I am not here to decide when or for what the Union is to be dissolved. I have said before, and I repeat it now, that, as the representative of a sovereign State, I am here truly to maintain her interests and honor, as far as I can consistently with my obligation to the Constitution and the dictates of my conscience. When that State shall find disunion necessary, this post will no longer become me, and she can call me hence, to use me wherever my mother State may require my unimportant services. I have nothing, therefore, to say here as to what should or should not determine the State to dissolve her connection with the Union. I repeat, that is a question for her decision, not mine. But my colleague has incorporated me with others, with so many others, and all of them so superior to myself, in arraigning those who entertain a particular opinion, that I hardly know what share of his remarks is due to myself. It may be but an atom, but it must be some portion. He arraigns me with others for having heretofore asserted that the Constitution repealed the Mexican laws, and for having abandoned that position. Now, he was unfortunate in his mode of stating it.

Mr. FOOTE here made an inquiry, which was not distinctly heard by the Reporter.

Mr. DAVIS, of Mississippi. My argument was the reverse in its application to what my colleague supposes. He treated it as an argument against the municipal laws of Mexico. New Mexico and California I suppose he referred to in this case. Not so. The argument was against the general, the political laws of the Republic of Mexico. Whatever it was worth, it was to that my argument must have been directed. I was confident then, and am confident now, that I stood upon true ground. But is it abandoning this ground that I should refer to these opposite opinions of the most eminent jurists of the land as a motive for legislation—as a reason why no man would hazard his property whilst this threatening cloud hung over his rights? Is it an abandonment of this opinion that I should insist that Congress should remove the obstructions which were considered insurmountable obstacles by some of the best lawyers in the Senate, and which, if they exist, interfere with—yes, sir, deny to us the exercise of—our constitutional rights? This was no new opinion with me, nor is it peculiar to this place, or to the persons named.

I was glad to hear my colleague say that he would stand by every position that our State has taken, as this may bring us into the conjunction I desire. Our Legislature have passed two series of resolutions—one presented to the Senate by my colleague, and one by myself. From the first one of them I will read to establish that this ground of opposition to the prominent feature of this bill has an origin more commanding than that which has been assigned. Our Legislature passed a series of resolutions, approved March 6, 1850, from which I will read the following:

"Be it further resolved, That it is the duty of the Congress of the United States to provide territorial organization and governments for all the Territories acquired by the common blood and treasure of the citizens of the several States, and to provide the means of enforcing in said Territories the guarantees of the Constitution of the United States in reference to the property of citizens of any of the States removing to any of said Territories with the same, without distinction or limitation.''

That, sir, is what we claim, here and now. We claim that the Federal Government shall provide the means of enforcing our constitutional rights, of protecting us in our property, as guarantied by the Constitution, within those Territories to which the States have surrendered the control to the central Government. This is not begging the Federal Government to come to the protection of the States. This is not inviting the Federal Government to infringe the limits of sovereign States; but demanding that she should perform those functions which have been confided to her in regions from which the States have withdrawn their right of control. I have heretofore answered the position of my colleague that there is something humiliating in this. I will not repeat what I have said—will not weary the Senate by a thrice-told tale.

The resolutions which my colleague presented equally uphold the same position. They were approved upon the same day, but are a different series, and refer to the question before us. After referring to California and the government for New Mexico, the resolutions go on to say:

"*Resolved,* That the exercise by the Government of the United States of a silent and passive jurisdiction over the Territory of California, in consequence of the failure by Congress to provide laws for the government of said Territory, and for the equal and indiscriminate protection of all the citizens of the United States removing to said Territory with their property, is in the highest degree unjust towards the people of the slaveholding States, by deterring them from going to said Territory with their slaves, and is calculated, and is intended, to deprive them of an equal participation in the common property of the people of all the States.

"*Resolved,* That the policy heretofore pursued by the Government of the United States in regard to said Territory, in refusing to provide territorial governments therefor, has been and is eminently calculated to promote, and is about to effect indirectly, the cherished object of the Abolitionists, which cannot be accomplished by direct legislation, without a plain and palpable violation of the Constitution of the United States."

Here is a complaint of the Federal Government that it does not give the protection due, and that it avoids a plain and palpable violation of the Constitution of the United States, that it may effect the same purpose by indirect means. That has been the burden of the argument of those who have acted with me against this bill, and that has been the main ground against the admission of California. Having been thus deprived of

equality of enjoyment in the Territory, it is now proposed
permanently to exclude us by admitting it as a State with a
constitution that was framed to answer the views of an anti-
slavery Congress, and which was neither formed nor adopted
by the majority of the inhabitants of that Territory. This is
the position of our State, and I think that it has fairly and
fully maintained the position those with whom I am connected
here, have taken upon this subject. I have too humble an opinion of my own judgment to have any great pride of consistency.
If convinced of error, I hope that I would at any moment change.
But I must ask that gentlemen will wait till I do change before
they attach to me the charge of inconsistency. I maintain
now, as I have always maintained, that the Constitution gives
us a right to go there with any kind of property, and I ask
the Federal Government to provide the necessary means to
secure the enjoyment of that right.

The proposition of the Nashville Convention, my colleague
says, was not an ultimatum. I will not argue about the meaning of that word. The proposition of the Nashville Convention
was to divide the Territory by the parallel of 36° 30′, with
a right to carry slaves below that line as the least that they
would take. Yes, sir, as an *extreme concession* by the South,
it was agreed to propose such a division; I thank you for the
expression. I have read the letter of ex-Governor Brown, of
Tennessee. That is his position. He says he does not stand
upon that line alone—and who does? He says that he will
take nothing less than the division by that line, as proposed
by the Convention—and what man, with a due regard to the
interests of the South, would for a moment think of doing
otherwise? To propose to renew the compact based upon a division by that line is not to assert that it has any magic virtue
in it, though it may well be insisted on as preferable to a new
line, because of the acquiescence of the States in it, and because
of the prescriptive claim it has, and the respect it enjoys among
the people as a measure sanctified by time, and still more by
the blessings it brought to our country at a time of serious,
even alarming, agitation. To me it offers the last hope of immediate, radical, permanent, satisfactory adjustment to the
only question which disturbs the peace of our countrymen and
threatens the overthrow of the high hopes from our Union, so
grateful to the pride and so near to the heart of every true
American.

I have stated on other occasions, sir, that as an original question I doubted the right of Congress—indeed I do not believe

that Congress has the constitutional power—to pass such a bill as the Missouri Compromise; but I have said that in consequence of the acquiescence of the States during a succession of years, I do not consider it now an original question, standing upon the same grounds as it did at the date of its adoption, and I have been willing to renew and extend it, not because it gives us all we are entitled to, but because I hoped that it might be a measure of pacification—permanent, substantial pacification of the country.

Mr. FOOTE. I trust the Senate will bear with me while I make a few more remarks in explanation of this matter. I did not expect to call my colleague up.

Mr. DAVIS, (in his seat.) Had you not referred to me by name, I should not have got up.

Mr. FOOTE. My intention certainly was to refer to him in the kindest manner, and to avoid all collision with him, especially after the understanding between us on the subject.

Mr. DAVIS. I will tell my colleague frankly, that though he referred to me sufficiently pointedly, I should not—in consideration of the understanding to which he refers, and of a general desire to avoid controversy with my colleague, in the belief that the interests of our State would be militated against by it —had he not referred to me specially by name, have made the remarks which I did.

Mr. FOOTE. I did not desire to depart from the understanding between myself and colleague; but, after all, I do not see why we may not discuss these topics of general interest together, as well as any other gentlemen, observing, as I know we shall, the rules of courtesy.

Mr. DAVIS, (in his seat.) I have no objection.

Mr. FOOTE. And in accordance with this view of the matter, I shall proceed to make a remark or two in reply to my colleague. I understand him to say, that whenever Mississippi was prepared for disunion, he was prepared to unite with her—

Mr. DAVIS, (in his seat.) My colleague will please use my language.

Mr. FOOTE. I will with great pleasure, if I can recollect it; but what I have recited is according to my memory of what he actually said.

Mr. DAVIS. I said that I was here to represent the State of Mississippi at the Federal Government; that I had therefore no propositions to make in relation to disunion, no opinion to express when disunion should be resorted to; but that when the State of Mississippi should resolve on disunion, and summon me hence, I had no right to remain here longer, and that I was then at her service.

Remarks on Compromise Bill June 18, 1850.

Mr. DAVIS, of Mississippi. Is that the amendment to divide California into several States?

A SENATOR. Yes, sir.

Mr. DAVIS, of Mississippi. It strikes me to be rather premature. There is no State of California yet; still less are limits determined for the territory within which we may constitute her a State. If it is proposed to divide her territory before we know what is its extent, it is taking time rather too far by the forelock. The proposition presupposes everything, and is so much in advance, that I do not think it proper to consider it.

Mr. HALE. Precisely the same objection raised by the Senator from Mississippi will apply to the stipulations in regard to Texas. At that time her boundaries were unsettled, and she was not a State.

Mr. DAVIS, of Mississippi. Yes.

Mr. HALE. She was not a State of this Union, and her boundaries certainly were unsettled; and just the same objections would have applied to her then as are applied to this proposition in regard to California now.

Mr. DAVIS, of Mississippi. No; the cases are very different. Texas was an independent State, with a certain part of her territory undisputed. Some part was in dispute; but the part undisputed, and which must finally remain of the State of Texas, was still large enough to be divided to justify, indeed in accordance with, the original policy of the confederation to require divisions.

Mr. BERRIEN. There certainly is a diversity between the case of Texas and California, as is suggested by the Senator from Mississippi. The boundaries of Texas were unascertained, however, and the United States had the right to ascertain them. Now, the other objection made by the Senator from Mississippi would be operative with me, if the provision now attempted to be inserted in the bill could not be cotemporaneous with one describing and limiting the boundaries of California. But they are to go together, and one does not at all anticipate the other. I hope, therefore, that the Senator from Mississippi will not urge his objection to the amendment, which, it seems to me, having been presented in this form, it is desirable should be adopted.

Mr. DAVIS, of Mississippi. The proposition calls on me to

vote in relation to this matter before the bill is passed; therefore my vote will not be cotemporaneous with the admission of California as a State: it must precede that order of business. Then, again, I hope, when California is admitted, it will be with the exact limits she should have as a State, and no more. I, for one, certainly cannot consent to admit an empire on the Pacific, with a prohibition of slavery in its constitution, so that future States may be carved out of it under the moulding influence of that constitution. It is but another mode, and a more effectual one, to accomplish the same end, sought to be attained by the famous Wilmot proviso.

Mr. DAVIS, of Mississippi. In offering this amendment, I endeavored to present, and thought that I had presented, my proposition in terms so plain that it must be intelligible to every Senator. I was willing, therefore, that a vote should be taken upon it without saying anything to explain or enforce it. But the honorable Senator from Kentucky seems, strangely enough, to misconstrue this amendment, as he did the amendment which I offered in an earlier stage of this discussion. By that amendment I sought to provide police regulations and other remedies for protecting all rights of property in the Territories; and although it was modified several times, from a wish to make it conform to the taste of Senators most friendly to this bill, as far as was consistent with the object of that amendment—to secure to the territorial legislature the right to provide for the protection of slave property by such laws as are indispensable wherever slaves are held—still that simple right, that lowest possible demand which a southern man could have made, was finally rejected Now, sir, I ask that these local laws pre-existing in the territory which we have acquired, and which abridge or obstruct in those Territories the rights of the citizens of the United States as they are derived from the Constitution and laws of the United States, shall be held to be repealed. I agree entirely with the position taken by my colleague, that the Constitution does repeal all such laws. But, sir, is the holder of one species of property to be compelled, when he goes into that Territory, to establish his right to hold that property there by a law-suit? And is the Senate here gravely enacting a law to increase litigation? Will the Senate declare that our Constitution and our laws are supreme wherever our territory extends, or will they leave that to be decided after suit by the courts of the United States? That, sir, is the simple question; and let those who shrink from a declaration in favor of our own constitutional laws now do so. In the spirit of the Senator from Mas-

sachusetts, [Mr. WEBSTER,] so forcibly and beautifully exhibited
to the Senate on Saturday, I say: "I am an American. No
local feeling controls my heart; and my attachment is as broad
as my whole country. My good wishes are coextensive with our
wide domain, reaching from sea to sea. I ask no local advantage; and I hope that no sectional discrimination will be imposed upon me. I do not seek the first, and shall certainly oppose the last." The Mexican law excludes various species of
property; and yet no one proposes to continue it so as to exclude any property under the operation of our laws, except those
who seek to exclude property in slaves. Sir, I was prepared to
see some exhibitions of fanatic opposition to slavery connected
with the amendment; but I was not—am not prepared to see
the American Senate refuse to acknowledge the Constitution of
the United States supreme, and the shield of American citizens
upon American soil. Sir, have we expended so much blood and
treasure to acquire Territory that the fundamental laws of
Mexico may govern it? Have we conquered and paid for a
territory which a part of our citizens cannot enjoy—over which
our jurisdiction cannot extend? Or do you say that a citizen of
the United States must go through the process of a lawsuit before
he shall be fully entitled to the protection of the Constitution?
Sir, I feel that it is our duty to look rather to the limitation than
the extension of lawsuits. I propose not to abrogate the local
laws, as the Senator from Kentucky seems to suppose. Such a
supposition is not to be drawn from the amendment. I propose to repeal them, so far as they interfere with the rights of
American citizens, and leave them to whatever effect they may
have hereafter on the private relations of those whom we found
in the country, and on contracts made before the transfer of
the territory. I ask not to interfere with any contract made
heretofore; and surely no one would claim that any future contract made in these Territories should be under the operation
of Mexican laws. Whatever rights they had under the laws of
Mexico they will still retain, so far as that amendment is concerned. But certainly, sir, we who own the Territory have a
right to go into that Territory under the shield of our own Constitution and laws, unrestricted by the laws of Mexico. If not,
what have we acquired?

Mr. President, I have not at this stage of the bill chosen to
enter into a general debate upon it. The few remarks I have
made since its introduction have been specially directed to
pending amendments. I have waited in order that those who
have the power might perfect the bill, and then I shall most

probably give my opinion upon it. I stated in the beginning that neither myself nor those with whom I am bound to act had made or would make any factious opposition. We merely ask to supply what we consider defects in the bill, and to remove what we consider most objectionable. We told you in the beginning, that when you gave us that which it was our duty to ask as representatives, we had no further objection to interpose; and if you refuse it, the path of duty to those whom I represent lies before me, and is one which I shall, even if alone, follow without hesitation. If the American Senate are prepared to declare that the provisions of the Constitution of the United States only apply to these Territories so far as the Supreme Court shall determine, let it be said. I would be willing to submit that question to any part of the American people I have ever known. If this anti-slavery feeling controls Senators of the United States so far, let them announce that they intend to maintain the *lex loci* of Mexico, and thus to abrogate the rights of American citizens who go into that territory with slave property; and when they have thus plainly spoken, we shall then know what course to take.

Mr. DAVIS. I will tell my colleague why I cannot concur with him. This is an amendment which I had prepared to meet what I considered the impediment or difficulty which we might and should by law remove, if it existed. Whether, under the Constitution, we had a right to take slaves into a territory where slavery had not been established by the local law, was the question on which I was willing at a former time, and now, to rest on the Supreme Court. The amendment is to another consideration entirely. This is the reason why I introduced this amendment, which was shown to my colleague yesterday; and I supposed we then agreed.

I am not now holding my colleague to any test of consistency, or any obligations of an understanding which I believe he and I had yesterday. His proposition now would go to the extent of an amendment which would be declaring what our constitutional rights are. I could not admit that power to be in Congress.

Mr. FOOTE. I conceived there was some ground for supposing that something might be accomplished by this amendment. Such an amendment I have heretofore opposed in this body, because I conceived it opposed to the general principle of the bill.

Mr. DAVIS. Then my colleague suggests to me an amendment, to which he himself is opposed; in that opposition we at least agree. I have not asked that Congress should declare what our rights in the Territories are, and, as I have more than once stated, have no disposition—no, sir, never could consent—to allow the Congress to decide what are the constitutional rights of the South, and how far they extend. I claim those rights, privileges, and immunities to which every American citizen is entitled. I only ask that such laws of Mexico as obstruct these rights shall be removed. That seems to me to be a very different proposition from asking the Senate to declare what our constitutional rights are. Now, sir, when he who I believe is considered the first lawyer in the Senate, the first in the United States —I refer to a Senator not now in his seat—has informed us that it is his opinion that the local law does remain, I, as a modest man, must feel some doubt, however well assured I am in my position. When the Senator from Kentucky, [Mr. CLAY,] whose authority is certainly high in this body, and high all over the country, asserts that the *lex loci* does remain, it belongs to younger and humbler men somewhat to hesitate as to the correctness of their own opinions; and if not as to the correctness of their opinions, they at least should consider what effect such dicta may have upon the property-holder, who would migrate with his slave property into that Territory. This is the most delicate species of property that is held; it is property that is ambulative; property which must be held under special laws and police regulations, to render it useful or profitable to the owner, or that it may not be injurious to the community under which it is held. Then, sir, the local law in these Territories either continues or it does not; and this is a question on which the ablest lawyers disagree. But, if there be any doubt as to whether it continues, I ask what slaveholder will go into that country with his slaves? None, unless it may be for the purpose of testing the question at law, and of obtaining a final decision of the Supreme Court of the United States. I wish to place the holders of this kind of property under the protection of the Constitution and laws of the United States. I wish to remove all obstruction to the constitutional right, to simplify the question before the courts, if it shall be the subject of a suit, so that they may go directly, and without the intervention of collateral considerations, to the great question of constitutional right. I think that all the amendment proposes is to remove foreign obstructions to the enjoyment of constitutional rights by American citizens within the limits of our own country.

Mr. DAVIS. I want to say a word or two to the Senator from Louisiana. I think the whole answer in his case is simply this:

that prohibition of the constitution of California is void until it receives our sanction; to possess it must derive validity from Congress; and therefore it becomes indirect intervention, as stated by the Senator from Georgia.

Mr. DOWNS. It is the act of Congress.

Mr. DAVIS. The Senator says it is an act of Congress. That is his own definition, which would make it direct intervention. But what is non-intervention seems to vary as often as the light and shade of every fleeting cloud. It has different meanings in every State, in every county, in every town. If non-intervention means that we shall not have protection for our property in slaves, then I always was, and always shall be, opposed to it. If it means that we shall not have the protection of the law because it would favor slave-holders, that Congress shall not legislate so as to secure to us the benefits of the Constitution, then I am opposed to non-intervention, and always shall be opposed to it. So far as I have favored non-intervention, it was the doctrine which restrained the Federal Government from interfering with private property, and from determining what our constitutional rights in this respect are. Then, Mr. President, I come down to the case in point. Non-intervention as applied to this amendment, would be to leave the Mexican laws in force, so that the United States may acquire territory, but the Constitution and laws of the United States shall not go there; but that laws repugnant to the rights of American citizens shall remain in force, and that Congress cannot repeal those laws. Every feeling of my heart is opposed to such an idea. Every respect I feel for the Constitution under which I was born, and the laws I have sworn to support—all, all make me discard such a doctrine as that—reject it at once— as a thing which I hope never to hear of again. Sir, I had supposed that non-intervention, when it was contended for as part of the Democratic creed, was to leave to every section of this broad land its rights under the Constitution. But, sir, if, it meant to bring this Government into subserviency to the laws of Mexico, as far as was transferred soil from Mexican to United States dominion, or at former times to those of France, when we acquired Louisiana, or those of Spain, when we acquired Florida, then as an American, proud of my country, and ready to sustain her institutions at any sacrifice, once for all, I eschew, and forever, the odious, horrible doctrine.

Mr. DAVIS, of Mississippi. There are some things which must be done at the time, or they are not worth doing at all. I hardly know, since my colleague has insisted on speaking before me, whether it is worth while for me to notice some errors which the Senator from Louisiana [Mr. Downs] fell into in relation to my position. I rose immediately after he concluded, for the purpose of correcting those errors, and I will do it now. The Senator from Louisiana fell into the error, first, that I had abandoned my position that the Constitution extended over the Territories acquired from Mexico, and was supreme therein over the laws of Mexico. He paid me a very unmerited compliment, when he referred to an argument made by me in support of the opinion that by the Constitution all citizens of the United States have an equal right with any property held by them to occupy the territories of the United States, and which he described in terms I could not realize as due to any effort of mine, which he said convinced him of the truth of that position then maintained by me. Now, I have not changed my opinion. I entertain the same conclusion still; but I referred to authorities so high, and to intellects and acquirements so much superior to my own, that I thought it justified doubts, and certainly would create doubts in the minds of persons who had their property at stake. That was my position, and the Senator surely misunderstood me. Then, again, he misunderstood me about non-intervention. I certainly have not said that my understanding of non-intervention is the establishment of slavery, or peculiar legislation for the protection of slavery. Yet I have said that non-intervention is not a doctrine opposed to the repeal of foreign laws which interfere with the constitutional rights of the slaveholder in this species of property. The non-intervention which I recognize and uphold is non-intervention with constitutional rights. I state again that I was, and I hope I always will be, for intervention which shall repeal any foreign laws within the Territories of the United States, if such laws can there exist, which interfere with the rights of American, citizens on American soil.

Now, sir, a word as to the argument of my colleague, [Mr. Foote.] The Senator from Georgia [Mr. Berrien] has shown so clearly and fully the difference between our position now and when the Clayton compromise was adopted, that I could only add to his argument to weaken it. I will say, however, that the cases are not at all alike. Then it was before emigration, and when the whole territory was open to settlement from every section of the Union. Now, after the better portion of the territory has been turned over, or will by this bill, if it pass, be turned over, to a State government that prohibits slavery, and the balance of the territory has been to a large extent occupied by immigration influenced by anti-slavery agitation, it is another case, and there is no right to expect us to take the same terms. The cases are so wholly dissimilar, that the same proposition cannot possibly apply to them both. Do you expect any man to be fixed in an opinion which only involves expediency, the disposal of matter, even after you have taken that matter away? Shall we now be content with the same terms in relation to the remnant of territory for which we contended when the whole was open? Shall we be satisfied ten years hereafter, when it is peopled, and the whole of it is about to become States, except, perhaps, some sand desert that was voluntarily excluded from the limits of the adjacent State? Shall we be satisfied then, and admit that we had our equal rights in the Territories, when the whole has been swept away, because you do not impose the Wilmot proviso on this sand desert? Sir, such an argument as that is not worth further or graver answering. It can impose upon no one; it certainly cannot govern the opinions of any one to whom I am responsible for my action here.

I am sorry, however, that my friend from Louisiana has so greatly mistaken my argument. I am sorry, indeed, that he should suppose that I was advocating here the doctrine that Congress should establish slavery anywhere, when time after time I have announced before the whole Senate that I should oppose it to the end, on a principle which I never would yield. I did not expect, at this late day, to be so misunderstood. Nor can I feel, because I wish to remove Mexican impediments, or because I bow to the weight of authority—because I admit that authority to be so great as to throw a cloud over the rights of citizens, and to affect them, when they shall contemplate migration with their slave property into these Territories—that I have therefore surrendered my own opinion in favor of our constitutional right. If I have one defect which stands out more prominently than the rest, I fear it is that I adhere to my own opinion when others believe that arguments enough have been offered to warrant a change, rather than that my opinions vary as rapidly as the definitions some of our friends give of ''non-intervention.''

On Compromise Bill July 24, 1850.

Mr. DAVIS, of Mississippi. I think that all the gentlemen who have addressed the Senate on the precedent quoted and drawn from the Territory of Mississippi have left out one, and certainly the most delicate of all the points that entered into negotiation, and that reason which above all others required commissioners. That Natchez district, to which the Senator from Georgia referred, was, as all must be aware, claimed by Great Britain as a part of West Florida; she had her grants of land running along the Mississippi river as high as Yazoo. But when, during the revolutionary war, Spain, as the ally of the United States, conquered Florida from the possession of Great Britain, she then set up her claim as far as the Mississippi river, as a part of West Florida. It was a controversy, therefore, not between the United States and the State of Georgia only, but between the United States and Spain also; and Spain held possession of this country long after the cession by Georgia, and was finally deprived of possession by a revolutionary movement of American citizens, who had settled in the country; and after that revolutionary movement was successful, Mr. Madison recognized it, and took possession of the country as part of the territory of the United States. That was the question involved as to this part of West Florida or part of Georgia, which formed the greatest and most delicate question. I think, therefore, that, for all the purposes for which it was used by my friend from Georgia, [Mr. Dawson,] the precedent is utterly valueless, as much so as was the case between Iowa and Missouri, which was, as it has been described, simply a question of what the act meant. It was, in fact, to decide the question whether the Des Moines rapids were to be found in the Mississippi river or in the Des Moines river. The Territory of Iowa claimed that falls in the Mississippi river were the Des Moines rapids; on the other hand, if I recollect rightly, Missouri set up a claim that falls in the Des Moines river itself were the Des Moines rapids. There was this contest between the two, and it was to establish where the Des Moines rapids were that these commissioners were to be appointed, and that point was to be determined according to the act of Congress. Neither of these precedents bear upon the case which is before us. This is not a proposition to send commissioners to find a line, not to demark a line, but to make a line, to establish a new boundary for the State—a boundary which the State never asserted. It is to send commissioners to mark out a line so as to coerce Texas to a cession—not, as in the case of Georgia, to determine where the cession was which Georgia had made. It is a different proposition altogether; and when the Senator from Georgia [Mr. Dawson] speaks so emphatically of his attachment to that section of the Union which he and I both in part represent, let me ask what is to be our fate? By whom are these commissioners to be appointed? and with what view must they be appointed? To sustain the claim of the United States against Texas. And, sir, on the other hand, how is the claim of Texas to be satisfied? How are the commissioners of Texas to be induced to recede from their extreme demands, and yield to the extreme demands of these commissioners appointed adverse to the claim of Texas? By large offers of money. Then, sir, on the one hand, the section which the Senator and myself represent is to lose land, and, on the other hand, their unequal burden of the taxation is to furnish the money for it. Sir, what controversy is to determine? To turn over territory to the United States, to be subject exactly to the same temptation and controversy as the other territory which was recently acquired from Mexico —is this desirable? Is it likely to stop the controversy between Texas and New Mexico, or is it not at once an intimation to Texas that her boundary is not to be recognized, will not be established by Congress, the only power by which it can be done. And are we, who represent every section of the Union; are we, who stand here, I hope, to some extent at least, above mere sectional prejudices; are we to surrender so great and delicate a question as this into the hands of commissioners to be appointed in the manner proposed in this amendment? Sir, it seems to me a two-edged sword, and both edges are cutting the South. This is a mode by which we are to lose our right to territory in Texas, and the mode by which our taxation is to be increased to furnish the means by which we are to be deprived of the territory. I cannot conceive, therefore, how my friend from Georgia can couple a proposition of this kind with a declaration of his intention to maintain to the last the interests of the section which he and I represent.

On motion of Mr. CHASE, the Senate then adjourned.

On Compromise Bill July 25, 1850.

Mr. DAVIS, of Mississippi. Mr. President, nearly all who have spoken on this subject agree on one thing—they are disposed to protect all the claim of New Mexico—and the argument seems to be, how they can effect that object. For myself I have never been able to perceive of what importance it is now to inquire where the boundary of New Mexico is. We acquired this territory from Mexico, at the end of the war, by treaty and by purchase, and we acquired it as so many acres. It was described, so far as it referred to New Mexico, by its southern and western boundaries. That is the only trace given to the boundary between the United States and Mexico. No other reference was made to provisional boundaries than such as would enter into the question of national boundaries. We acquire this territory as a whole, not as a province.

The question is not the boundary of New Mexico, but the boundary of Texas. That great question seems to me about to be lost sight of. If there be a, rival claim to any territory east of the Rio Grande, it is on the part of the United States, and not on the part of the extinct province of New Mexico. Whatever boundaries she had, were obliterated by the treaty of Guadalupe Hidalgo. It is now a mere unorganized territory of the United States. The only question, to my mind, worthy of inquiry is, where is the line of division between the State of Texas and this unorganized territory? With that purpose, I hold, sir, that the inquiry is closed. We annexed Texas as a sovereign State, with her boundary defined in her statute-book, reserving, as I have said before, merely the right to vary that boundary by negotiations with a foreign country. Failing in these negotiations we went to war, before the civilized world, to maintain the boundary of Texas. And God forbid that I should ever be one of those to falsify the position of my own country, and condemn her in the eyes of all civilized men. We will occupy the unenviable position of having gone to war with a weak power for purposes of spoliation, if we now abandon the position of the deceased President Polk. That seems to be the position in which we now stand; that is, in an attitude of censure towards that deceased statesman. It is a condemnation of our own country which would bring the brand of infamy upon her history forever. I, for one, sir, will never consent to that. I have said time and again that that boundary which was sanctified by the Congress, which declared that a state of war existed by an invasion of our soil on the part of Mexico, that boundary which was consecrated by the blood shed to maintain it, I will never agree to violate for one instant.

Mr. HALE. Mr. President, I have never said anything in all the discussions that have taken place about this boundary of Texas. But a remark of the honorable Senator who has just taken his seat seems to me to require a reply and has induced me to venture a single remark, and it is this: the honorable Senator from Mississippi assumes, and it is not the first time it has been assumed on this floor for I think it has been asserted here a hundred times, that we annexed Texas as a sovereign State, with the boundaries she had assigned to herself.

Mr. DAVIS. I made a reservation. I hope the Senator will state that also.

Mr. HALE. The reservation of the honorable Senator was, the right of this Government to settle any question of boundary which might arise with a Foreign Power. Now, Sir, I undertake to say that if it had been possible for the most astute man in the world, with the greatest degree of philological learning that ever fell to the lot of humanity, to have drafted a resolution that should have excluded that conclusion, it was done by those men who drafted the resolution of annexation. What did we annex to the United States? The resolutions of annexation say "the territory included within, and rightfully belonging to, the Republic of Texas," on the 1st day of March, 1845. That is what was annexed to the United States; nothing more, nothing less. Then it becomes all important to inquire what it was that "rightfully belonged to" and was "properly included within" the Republic of Texas on the 1st day of March, 1845, . . . what was the actual right of Texas, not as it was affected by the treaty of Guadalupe Hidalgo, not as it was affected by her legislative enactment, but by the knowledge of the law of nations in reference to the revolution that was then raging and the war growing out of the revolution then going on between Texas and Mexico. The fact that this seemed to lie at the bottom of this controversy and that it has not been alluded to by several gentlemen who have spoken on it, is my only apology for throwing myself at this late date before the Senate.

Mr. DAVIS, of Mississippi. One word, sir, in reply to the Senator from New Hampshire. According to his argument, Texas is only "rightfully" entitled to that which she possessed on a certain day. I imagine it would take more than twenty years, and require more than three commissioners, to ascertain that fact. Does the Senator know that Texas was a new and frontier State, with its settlements gradually but continually advancing, having controversies pending with the Indians as well as the Mexicans? Does the Senator know that up to one year before the passage of the resolutions of annexation, the Mexicans held possession of the town of San Antonio, now the very centre of Texas? Does he know that the officers of the court were taken captive from the bench, and led from that very town of San Antonio, by the Mexicans, one year before the passage of the resolutions of annexation?

It was not what Texas held in her possession—and it is strange that the Senator should think so after the commendation he has given to the philology of those who drew up the resolutions—but what "rightfully belonged" to her, that was annexed to the United States. Now, the question of right is one which I am willing to try before the proper tribunal—one which I would be willing to hazard before the Supreme Court of the United States. The resolutions of annexation annexed to the United States what "rightfully belonged" to Texas. How is that to be decided? Sir, it is known that the United States endeavored to decide that question by negotiation, and having failed in that, went to war, and, at the close of that war, made a treaty. That treaty closed the war; it closed the question of the Texan boundary, and the right of Texas was complete to the Rio Grande. When the United States went to war and terminated by a treaty the question of boundary, Mexico's rights fell to the ground. And will it be asserted here that the United States, the guardian of that State, its attorney or agent, if you please, having acquired the rights of the client, shall now step in and appropriate those rights to their own use?

Mr. DAVIS, of Mississippi. I supposed that we were engaged in a proposition how to establish the boundary of Texas. So it has been urged from the beginning. This has been one of the great measures of pacification, one of the great features of this compromise bill. We have been warned, time and again, that a feeling of excitement exists in Texas, and that if we delay to settle this question, a collision of arms will take place; and yet we are now offered a proposition to send commissioners, with the understanding that, if their action shall not be satisfactory to the parties standing, it is said, in a belligerent attitude, that nothing is to be concluded by it. Is this worthy of the Senate of the United States? Is it worthy of us on a question of this importance, so immediately pressing, that we should postpone it by a proposition which is absolutely nothing? What though this measure were not passed at all? The rights of the parties would remain as they are. I hold, with the Senator from Texas, [Mr. RUSK,] that Texas has a right—nay, more, I would say it is her duty—to take possession of the territory which is properly within her limits; and I am not one of those who have had apprehension of a collision between the forces of Texas and the troops of the United States. I never have believed, and I do not believe now, that any order or instruction, written or verbal, has ever been sent to the troops of the United States to oppose the legitimate exercise of Texan authority. As I said on a former occasion, I repeat that I believe the Secretary of War has stood strictly upon the ground of neutrality, and the only difference between their present and their former atti-

tude is, that the army was once instructed to aid in the establishment of Texan authority, and that now it is instructed to
be entirely neutral. I do not believe that the officer in command there, or any other officer of the army of rank enough
to command the force now at Santa Fé, would draw out his
troops to oppose a civil officer of Texas, coming with a posse
at his back to exercise a civil function. Such is not the teaching
which officers of the army receive. If there should be a conflict between the people of Santa Fé and the people of Texas, if
anarchy ensues, the destruction of life and property, and the
overthrow of all that is valuable in Government, then it would
be competent, I believe, for the officer in command there to
declare martial law, and to restore and maintain order with
the strong arm; but it is not a contingency which I can
contemplate, in which the troops of the United States can ever be
brought to act on this question. That is my opinion, and it is
my belief that no orders or instructions contrary to this have
been sent to the officer at Santa Fé.

But, sir, we know what the claim of Texas is, and we should
have decided the boundary of Texas; we should have established it, and we should have removed all probability of a collision long since, by declaring the boundary of Texas to be where
it rightfully is. I am prepared now to vote upon the question
of boundary. I am prepared to go further, and to appoint commissioners to find out where the true boundary is. But I am not
prepared to appoint ministers plenipotentiary to go out and
negotiate with Texas as with a foreign nation for territory.
There is a great distinction between the proposition of the
Senator from Virginia and that which is before us. This is a
proposition, not to establish the boundary of Texas, not to establish the boundary of any cession which has been proposed to the
United States by any Power whatever, but it is to agree upon
a line; and it directly charges against the claim of Texas, by
saying that these commissioners shall "begin at the point where
the Red river is intersected by the hundredth degree of west
longitude." Is that the boundary of Texas? Will the Senators from Texas say so? If not, how can they consent to send out
commissioners with instructions to begin at that point within the
limits of Texas, and run the line thence in a straight line to
the Rio Grande? No line can be drawn from that point to the
Rio Grande without cutting off a considerable portion of territory from the State of Texas. Nor, sir, has New Mexico, either
as a Province of the Republic of Mexico, or in any other
form, laid any claim to the portion of country thus cut off.

It is well known that the old Province of New Mexico never extended even to the head-waters of the Rio Grande. New Mexico never had any claim to the territory which it is now proposed by the Senator from Illinois [Mr. DOUGLAS] to take from Texas to give to New Mexico. I liked the candor with which he avowed yesterday that his objection to the proposition was, that it takes too little from Texas; but I was not at all reconciled to his proposition because he said that he was willing to pay for it. I am not willing to transfer territory from the jurisdiction of the State of Texas, and turn it over to the Congress of the United States, because we are to be taxed hereafter to furnish the money to pay for it. My objections are to the amendment, and to the amendment to the amendment. If I understand anything of what is intended by the proposition, it must be that Texas shall stand still instead of exercising her jurisdiction and asserting her authority over the territory which belongs to her. Now, my respect for that sovereign State is too high to believe that she will stand still; my knowledge of the energy, the chivalry, and the decision of her people is too great to believe that she will allow her territory to be wrested from her by mere hollow expressions, that hold her at bay until the United States perfect their title which they now have not, to the territory within the limits of Texas.

Resolution offered by Jefferson Davis, July 24, 1850.

Mr. DAVIS, of Mississippi, submitted the following resolution, and asked its immediate consideration:

Resolved, That the Committee on Commerce be instructed to inquire into the propriety of making the ports of Monterey, San Pedro, and San Diego, California, ports of entry.

The resolution was agreed to.

Resolution offered by Jefferson Davis, July 26, 1850.

Mr. DAVIS, of Mississippi, from the Committee on Military Affairs, reported a bill to provide for the increase of the medical staff of the army of the United States; which was read and passed to a second reading.

Mr. DAVIS, of Mississippi. I beg to offer the following resolution:

Resolved, That the Secretary of the Navy transmit to the Senate copies of the instructions, orders, and correspondence relating to the assemblage of persons on Round Island, and referred to in his letter of the 5th of June last, (Executive document 55,) as having been furnished to the President on the 30th of May last.

This is a resolution calling for papers which, from an error as to the period of the introduction and passage of a resolution of the Senate, have failed to reach the Senate, and the reply refers to papers which, owing to this accident, never arrived. The papers are, consequently, not in the possession of the Senate. It is in order to obtain the first answer that has not reached the Senate that I offer this resolution.

The resolution was adopted.

On Compromise Bill July 31, 1850.

WEDNESDAY, *July* 31, 1850.

The Senate resumed the consideration of the bill for the admission of California as a State into the Union, to establish territorial governments for Utah and New Mexico, and making proposals to Texas for the establishment of her western and northern boundaries.

The President stated the question to be upon the motion of the Senator from New Hampshire [Mr. NORRIS] to strike out from the tenth section the words "nor establishing or prohibiting African slavery." The part of the section proposed to be amended, is as follows:

"That the legislative power of said Territory shall extend to all rightful subjects of legislation, consistent with the Constitution of the United States, and the provisions of this act; but no law shall be passed interfering with the primary disposal of the soil, or establishing or prohibiting African slavery."

Mr. DAVIS, of Mississippi. Before the adjournment of yesterday, I stated that, on account of the character of the debate, I thought it necessary to address some remarks to the Senate. Had I proceeded then, they would have been few; and I trust that they will not be more extended now. It is due to Senators that their kind purpose to relieve me of the necessity of speaking at the close of a protracted session should meet this return. It was not my design then—it is not my intention at this time, or ever again—to enter into any extended consideration of this bill; but being one of those who have advocated the principle of non-intervention, and who adhere to it now, if honestly applied as it was originally understood, I could not allow the remarks which were made yesterday, rendering yet more intangible than before that which had been defined until it became an undefinable, everchanging, shadowy, unsubstantial theory, to pass without some reply, some attempt to set aside a construction so fatal not merely to the principle of non-intervention, but to the great purposes for which all governments are established.

When non-intervention was first promulgated, it was received as a pledge that all citizens of the United States would stand equal and secure upon their constitutional rights. Since then no man could enumerate the number of changes and the varying constructions which it has received, until yesterday it became a doctrine which held the hand of Government powerless for the purpose of giving protection to constitutional rights throughout the United States. To this idea of non-intervention I never subscribed. To this policy no name, however captivating, can allure me. Such non-intervention would be far worse than that which we have been in the habit of considering the last alternative, if not the greatest of evils—disunion itself; for it would leave to the States the burden of a General Government, and strip from them every advantage for which that General Government was created.

The honorable chairman of the committee who reported the bill under consideration—and to whom I never refer except with those feelings of friendship which I have for so many years cherished, and with that respect which he commands from all men—the honorable chairman of the committee, I say, yesterday announced that to deny the power to the Territorial Legislature to establish or prohibit slavery, was to admit full power in Congress over the subject. Shall we, who have from the beginning denied that Congress had this power, when we say that Congress shall not delegate to the Territorial Legislature the power which it has not, be replied to that if we withhold, exclude, or forbid the territorial government we create to exercise this power, we admit that Congress has it? By what species of reasoning such a conclusion is reached I am at loss to imagine. This territorial government is the creation of the Congress of the United States, deriving all its powers and its vitality from the Federal Government; it cannot thence receive—properly it cannot be permitted to exercise—powers which the Federal

Government itself does not possess, though it is the recipient of all the sovereign attributes which the people of the States were willing to surrender. Whence, then, can the Territorial Legislature derive these powers? I may be answered by my friend from Michigan, [Mr. CASS,] as he has answered me once before, that they derive it from God. If so, their power is above ours. They are the sovereigns—theirs the eminent domain. Why speak of the Territories of the United States? They hold the soil and the jurisdiction in their own right, and it is not for us to delegate to them power to use it. Both these distinguished gentlemen yesterday, in arguing this proposition, arrived at the same conclusion, that if we forbade the Territorial Legislature to establish or prohibit slavery, we admitted that the Federal Government had the power to do that which we forbade the Territorial Legislature to perform, and with that came the warning that some day it might be used to ordain and apply the Wilmot proviso. Sir, the conclusion is as obnoxious as the premises are untenable, and the application is a threat to which a reply will be made when its execution is attempted. It now stands a conclusion without an argument to connect it with the main premises, so authoritatively, but by bare assumption, laid down. No Senator, I must believe, would introduce into practical legislation a hypothesis so destructive to the repose of many States of this Union, so offensive to the principles of a Government of delegated powers, or seek to put in execution conclusions and applications which argument cannot justify, and the strength of our Government could not sustain. But the Senator from Michigan especially pointed his argument to a peculiar class of property, and said that to ask protection for slave property was to acknowledge full power in Congress over slavery. We ask only that protection for slave property which is conceded to every other species of property. We have not asked any peculiar legislation at the hands of Congress. We have asked that our constitutional rights to carry every species of property into the Territories should be recognized, and that that right should be protected. For myself, I should much prefer the language of the bill if it prohibited the Territorial Legislature from establishing or prohibiting any species of property held in any of the States of this Union, instead of confining the restriction to African slaves. All that there was offensive to me in it was that species of discrimination between this and other property which is constantly made in argument here. I admit no right thus to discriminate. So far from asking such discrimination, I deny the power to make it. I claim that that species of property stands upon the same general basis with every other. I would not have it otherwise. I would prefer now that the language of the bill should be modified in that respect.

But, sir; when we refer to what has been done in the Senate upon this bill, we are able to understand the meaning of those who oppose the clause it is now proposed to strike out. First, I introduced an amendment to provide that the provisions of the bill should not be so construed as to restrict the Territorial Legislature from passing police laws, and giving other needful protection to the owners of slave property. That was objected to. The Senator from Kentucky, who sits furthest from me, [Mr. CLAY,] found, in his reading of the amendment, a declaration that slaves were there. I never intended to make the declaration. He treated it as a question of fact. I denied it, and I made no reply. Weeks afterwards he denied it again, and still there was no reply. But now I answer that my opinion is, from information I have received partly before that time, but much more since, that slaves have been carried into all those Territories. Though this was my opinion, the amendment intended no such declaration; the fact was not by me deemed of much importance, and the language was purely hypothetical, that if they were there, or should be introduced there, legislation should provide police regulations for them, and remedies as for other property.

That was found objectionable; and though it was, by some who opposed it, declared to be utterly valueless—that neither good nor harm could come from it—yet those who made that declaration most violently resisted it—spoke day after day, and for hours together, against that very amendment which they considered so useless. Finally, in that spirit of compromise for which, on this question, I have received here but little credit, but which I have exercised, as far as my sense of duty would permit, when the Senator from Maryland [Mr. PRATT] proposed to modify my amendment so as to reconcile those friends of the bill who had been most opposed to it, I accepted his modification. What was that modification? It was to prohibit the Territorial Legislature from passing laws to prohibit or establish slavery; and then followed the condition which I had introduced and considered essential, that the Territorial Legislature should have power to pass police regulations and other remedies for slave property.

In the progress of that bill, we have finally reduced that amendment to the small part of it originally proposed by the

Senator from Maryland, by the advice of friends of the bill, as he informed me. That now stands alone—that part of it which was, in the manner I have stated, ingrafted upon my amendment, became separately a part of this bill; and now the proposition is made to strike it out. And this, Mr. President, is a fair example of that spirit of encroachment upon the rights of the South which has marked the history of this country for the last thirty years. It also shows that aggression is moving with an accelerated velocity, and that as it descends along the decline of constitutional right, its flight is increased, and its bounds become longer. Here, in the progress of a single debate, certain gentlemen have changed their position upon this question of vital importance to us, and at the close of the debate appear in opposition to the very thing they ingrafted upon their so-called measure of pacification and satisfactory adjustment. What has produced this revolution in opinion here, or rather this change of position?

Mr. President, we have several times had exhibited to us the policy which seems to control the votes of the peculiar friends of this measure, a policy which I think will not heighten the reputation of the Senate, or exalt the character of its legislation. That policy is, to vote for or against an amendment, as it increases or diminishes the prospects of the final passage of the bill; not whether it is right or wrong, not whether it makes the bill better or worse, but whether it gains or loses votes—a barter with one's own conscience, a barter with the delegated powers of legislation in the Senate of the United States. I use mild language, sir, when I say this will not exalt the character of the Senate or of its legislation. This new policy of controlling the votes of members is introduced upon the bill so emphatically announced as a bill of compromise and adjustment, of fraternization and conciliation, which is to give peace and harmony to this distracted country; is to give satisfaction to those who complain of wrong and aggression, and yet to be shaped not to meet their complaints, but so as to command the largest number of votes in bodies where the interests trodden on are known to be in the minority. What, sir, is government anywhere established for? To protect the rights of the weak against the aggressions of the strong; and that man who fails so to shape his own course as a member of this Government not only violates the purpose of the Government, but strikes a fatal blow at its existence, by destroying that spirit of harmony and fraternal confidence from which this Government sprung, upon which it has been nourished, and by which alone it can exist. What, sir, are the future prospects of the rights of the minority, if, in this early stage of our Republic, legislation is to be wholly controlled by the will of the majority? If that Constitution, which was intended to be a bar to the action of the Legislature—if those checks in the compact between the States, without which they never would have united in common Government—if they are to be swept away at the will of an unbridled majority, I ask you, sir, how long will the minority have their rights respected?—and how long will that minority, descended from sires that under more fearful circumstances severed their connection with the mother country, and announced to the world the determination to maintain their rights, at whatever hazard, and at any cost—how long will that minority remain in this Union? It is not by the denunciation of waiters on popular favor that these sentiments and the declarations of the sons of the sires of '76 are to be arrested or silenced. This Government was formed for high and holy purposes, and those most denounced have contributed most heartily to maintain it in its purity. They have been the balance of this Government and have long held it in its course. But let not gentlemen mistake the signs of the times. Let them not suppose, because men have been true to the principles of the Constitution in peace and in war, true to the Government, and, within its legitimate sphere, are willing still to adhere to it to the last, that they are tame submissionists to surrender the rights they inherited, and to abandon the principles for which their fathers bled.

When we look around us we find, not in the Government alone, but in the ecclesiastical and social condition of the country, much to increase rather than to allay apprehension. Where do we see that spirit of conciliation and fraternity which once governed our deliberations? Who, and with what opinions, have succeeded Franklin and Hancock, and Sherman and Hamilton, and the elder Adams, and many others—the men who heroically rose against the haughty oppressor—men who struggled to maintain the weak against the strong, and staked all upon the issue? The last of these patriots of the Revolution has departed from public employment—their traces have been obliterated, and their places have been more or less filled by representatives of fanaticism and schemers for power, whose policy is at open war with the practice and principles of the Constitution their and our ancestors formed, and of which we now claim the protection.

In keeping with such changes—not to say downward tendency of political principle—we find, day by day, among public men, an increased readiness to disregard, to destroy, to crush the instrument which their fathers created. Now, when we ask that those rights secured by the Constitution shall be protected by legislation, we are told that we abandon a great principle—a principle upon which the whole country stands— meaning thereby, I suppose, the principle that power gives right, that the majority shall construe the Constitution at will, and that the Legislature of the country is to stand powerless before the will of that majority.

When, Mr. President, in the progress of the administration of this Government at a former period, we reached a great sectional controversy, it was not then, as now, a sectional controversy which has for its object to curb and restrain men in the enjoyment of their property; but it was then, as it is partly now, a sectional controversy for political power. When the controversy upon the Missouri question arose, it was not whether a citizen of the United States had a right to introduce his slaves into the territory, but whether new States holding slaves should be admitted into the Union. It was to prevent an accession of political power to the slaveholding States that resistance was made to the admission of Missouri. That one step in itself was insulting enough. And then, if the South had been true to herself—if she had then stood firmly by all her constitutional rights, we should not now require another compromise, to preserve that balance of power which is essential to the preservation of the Confederation itself. The South would have held all the territory acquired by the purchase of Louisiana, stretching to the 49th parallel of latitude, covering by its position all we now possess on the Pacific and thus we should have held now that attitude of commanding strength which belonged to the southern States under the old confederation. Under the influence of coterminous institutions, the policy of the Pacific country would probably have been through all time that of the slaveholding States. But, sir, the South, in her generosity, then, as she had done upon a former occasion, gave away that which was her own. And what has her concession brought? Has it brought peace and harmony? Has it brought a spirit of conciliation? Has it brought a corresponding disposition to yield anything upon the other side? No, sir; but with an increase of power it has brought increased arrogance and aggression. Now we are asked to make a still further surrender—that of equal participation— ay, of any share in the territory acquired from Mexico; and this, too, when that surrender has for its end such disturbance of the political balance between the sections of this Union, that he must shut his eyes who does not see in it, as a consequence, either the degradation of one section or revolution against sectional oppression.

At a still more remote period the southern States yielded that vast territory on the northwest of the Ohio river, to diminish the power of individual States, and to produce that very equilibrium which I contend is as essential now as it was then. The equilibrium then produced is now. about to be utterly destroyed; that Constitution which was framed as a check upon legislation, is now disregarded; and if the South does not take her stand, and if now she is not met in a spirit of fraternity and concession, let gentlemen remember, when the evil day shall come, that it came not from seeds scattered by those who claim the equal rights of southern States, but by those who surrender them, and those who trample upon them.

From that stage of public feeling we have been rapidly progressing, until now, among those very measures which it is claimed are calculated to give satisfaction to the whole country, is included one that is to prohibit the slaveholder from bringing his property into this District, except under certain restrictions, on pain of its being taken from him. The penalty on the owner who brings his slave into this District for sale or future transmission to a slaveholding State, is to be the emancipation of that slave, the seizure and confiscation of property, in violation of that constitutional provision which forbids the Federal Government to take private property except for public use, and then by making due compensation therefor. I but allude to this feature in the grand plan of reconciliation, as connected with that general warning which the political action of the day gives.

Sir, when all these high powers of the Federal Government over property are exercised or proposed to be exercised, when Territories are to be carved out and governments erected; when odious discriminations are made between a slaveholding State whose rights are suspended and a Territory which is to be manufactured into a non-slaveholding State; when it is proposed to emancipate slaves because they are brought into the District of Columbia for sale; when all those high functions of sovereignty are claimed, perhaps to be exercised over private property, if we ask for legislation to protect the slaveholder who goes into the Territory, "Oh, no," is the reply; "that would interfere with the sound, admitted doctrine of non-intervention; that would be an infringement of the principle which the South has maintained." This is the hollow answer of those who assume those high powers over private property. Nay, more: it is the answer of those who are about marching troops into States to compel them to submission—worse still, sir, the answer of one who even yesterday warned us that the power of this Federal Government, through its army, was the means by which Texas was to be prevented from exercising jurisdiction over the territory she claimed when an independent State, and in defence of which the United States waged war with Mexico. That army, supported by the contributions of all the people of the United States—that army in the support of which Texas furnishes her fair quota of money—that army is to be used to prevent a State from exercising the right of jurisdiction within her own territory. And, as if this were not enough, the fame of the commander-in-chief of the army is summoned to show what would be the chance of the youngest sister of the Republic in a struggle against the United States. Yes, sir, the laurels won by Scott at Chippewa and Bridgewater, and on the battle-fields from Vera Cruz to the city of Mexico, which have flourished and grown greater with time, because they have been nourished as they sprung from the blood of his country's enemies—those laurels are laid before the Senate to impress the youngest sister of the Republic with that which every American knows—the prowess of our army's commanding general. Sir, that arm which has been so powerful against the enemies of the United States—that sword which has fallen with such invincible force when it struck in the cause of his country—would lose its edge if uplifted in fraternal strife. That arm would fall powerless by the side of the gallant soldier, who then for the first time would stand unnerved in the presence of danger. Those laurels, which never have faded, would become sere if dipped in a brother's blood. No, sir, no! it could not be. That patriot and soldier who, from his earliest manhood to the present day, has worn the uniform of the United States; whose blood has been a ready offering upon every battle-field where the honor of his country's flag called him—that patriot and soldier would break the sword, dear to him because so long worn in the cause of his country, before he would draw it against his brethren of the Union. Such is the feeling of an American soldier whose love for his country has never been warped by partisan zeal or sectional rancor. It is the feeling which I believe generally pervades the army; and therefore I say, as I said upon a former occasion, I have no fear of conflict between the troops of the United States and the posse of citizens who may be sent to support a civil magistrate of Texas in the discharge of his duties.

I well remember, upon another occasion, when one State stood arrayed against the power of the Federal Government, in the well-known nullification contest, what was the feeling of the army. Though unwilling to refer to myself, yet, as connected with it, I will say that I was then an officer of the United States army, and looked forward to the probability of being ordered to Charleston in the event of actual collision. Then, sir, much as I valued my commission, much as I desired to remain in the army, and disapproving as I did the remedy resorted to, that commission would have been torn to tatters before it would have been used in civil war with the State of South Carolina. Such, sir, I believe to have been and still to be the sentiment of every portion of the United States. Where will you go for volunteers to engage in this fraternal strife? Is it you, or you, who will enlist in such a war?—or who is it? What State, or county, or town, or neighborhood will you go to for recruits? You must raise a foreign army; you must have a Swiss guard when you attempt with sword and bayonet to enforce your laws upon the citizens of the United States. The free-born soldiers of our own country would disdain the task; for they have grown from the cradle with the conviction that this is a confederacy of brethren, which rests for its authority on the consent, and for its support upon the union and harmony and good will of its members. This Union can never be preserved by force.

If I am mistaken in all I have said—if there be those who are so mercenary, so vindictive, or so recreant to the great principles upon which our Federal Government can alone safely repose, that they would march with a cohort to the destruction of a State of this Union for refusing obedience to a law of Congress, let them be warned—to break a link is to destroy the chain; let them be doubly warned—there is a spirit which would not brook the act. An army, such as the imperial Gaul never saw, would be found mustered upon the plains of Texas to drive back any force which corruption or madness should induce the Federal Government to dispatch on a campaign of coercion.

I am not one of those who are likely to be excited by threats of civil war. I believe it to be a phantom of politicians. Some may be startled by the spirits they raise, though called for the alarm of the uninitiated only; but the war is of them and with them—not with the great masses of the people. I believe that if this question to-day, in the form in which it has been fruitlessly argued here, could be referred to the great body of the intelligent people of any section of the country, they would say at once: It is common property, it was acquired at the expense of the blood and treasure of all the people of the United States; and let us divide it fairly as becomes honest men among our partners. Stripped of the little political advantages which it has been sought to derive from this question, I do not believe the difficulties which surround us would ever have existed. We know that in the conflict of parties it has come to pass in many districts of the country that an extreme faction holds the balance of power. The end of this is not to be mistaken. Wherever such is the fact, these extremists will demand full concession from the candidate who gets their support; and the successful candidate must therefore accord in their peculiar tenets with the extreme faction of which he seeks their support. What, then, is the result? That the representatives of a large district, it may be a State, represents neither of the great parties of that State, but the extreme faction which holds the balance of power between the two. Therefore it was that, at a former session of Congress, I said my hope had passed from these halls of legislation to the people of the United States. With them my hope still abides. From them I look for a remedy not elsewhere to be obtained. Now, as on a former occasion, I say I have despaired of ever finding it here.

Mr. President, we had a pecuniary consideration, the subject of free speculation because it was a blank, contained in this bill as reported by the committee. This, it was said, was finally to settle the controversy about the boundary of Texas; that question from which gentlemen choose to anticipate civil war; that question which should have been settled at a previous session of Congress; that question which it was the bounden duty of Congress to settle the moment they had the power—that is to say, the day after the final ratification of the treaty of Guadalupe Hidalgo. Now, sir, in the fluctuation of the opinion of the Senate, and in that "honorable" strife to gain the greatest number of votes for the bill, even this—this one of the great healing measures—is stricken out, and in its place stands something or nothing, as one gentleman or another may construe it. It is no adjustment of boundary. It is not even restricting the commissioners to find the true boundary according to the law and the fact; but it leaves them, in case of their failing to do so, to agree upon a *line of boundary*. They are to be turned entirely loose in the territory of Texas to make a boundary where they please. In case of failing to find the true boundary, these com-

missioners are to do what it seems to have been considered impolitic for the Senate to attempt—to fix the amount of money
to be paid. Thus, at least, I understand the expression, ''And
also to agree upon the terms, conditions, and considerations upon
which such a line shall be established.''

What other considerations than pecuniary considerations,
when a line known not to be the true one is to be run? If any,
I should be glad if any advocate of the amendment would explain. I take it for granted that the pecuniary consideration
contained in the first form of the bill was in the mind of the
Senator who offered this amendment. That pecuniary consideration, which the Senate shrinks from fixing and declaring
openly before the country, these commissioners, in secret conclave, verbally, if they please so to conduct their conferences,
with no supervision and a very imperfect responsibility, are to
agree upon; and then we are to meet the question when it has
been closed, unless we interpose after events which may render
it impossible to restore the question to its present condition.

It is to my mind, Mr. President, not very much short of
turning over the whole power of Congress on this subject to
these commissioners, with a suggestion to negotiate the United
States Treasury against the Texas domain—about equivalent to
that—and therefore contains all that was objectionable originally, when it was to be done by Congress, with the additional
objection that the same thing is to be done by these commissioners as the agents of the Executive.

I promised the Senate, Mr. President, not to detain it long; I
have already spoken longer than I expected, and will only say,
in conclusion, that those gentlemen who are constantly arraying
the dangers of disunion should ask themselves who promotes
that danger, and then remember the threats they have leveled
at the southern States. They should remember the aggressions which those States have suffered, and the denial of justice
with which their complaints have been met. Then they will find
that at their own door rests the responsibility of such danger,
if such danger exists. Give to each section of the Union, justice; give to every citizen of the United States his rights,
as guarantied by the Constitution; leave this Confederacy to
rest upon that basis from which it arose—the fraternal feeling
of the people—and I, for one, have no fear of its perpetuity;
none that it will not survive beyond the limits of human speculation, expanding and hardening with the lapse of time, to
extend its blessings to ages unnumbered, and a people innumerable; to include within its empire all the useful products of the

earth, and exemplify the capacity of a Confederacy, with general, well-defined powers, to extend illimitably, without impairing its harmony or its strength.

Remarks of Jefferson Davis on bill to admit California as a State into the Union. August 3, 1850.

Mr. DAVIS, of Mississippi. Mr. President, as I am one of those who have been considered opposed to this bill, I may say that I have felt the weight of the responsibility very lightly indeed. I did not know before that I had encountered any immense responsibility in opposing the so-called compromise bill. If any portion of the defeat of that bill attaches to me, I feel highly honored. Gentlemen may give me as much of the responsibility as they please, if they only give me an equal share of the honor. I glory in defeating it.

And yet, if a friend of that bill means one who was anxious to modify it so as to vote for it, then I taxed the patience of the Senate so largely with amendments, that I suppose, on that ground, I would be considered a friend of the bill. But, from the beginning, I resolved never to vote for it, unless it was very materially amended. But, when I saw that the bill would not be amended so as to reconcile it to me, from that day forth I was ready to vote to kill the bill at any time, and by any means in my power.

But, sir, in relation to this curtailment of California. Who voted for it? Those southern men who are accused of defeating the "compromise" bill. They voted for it, as a restriction of the extended limits of California. And I think it was straining a point to get them to vote for it; for it was a studied evasion of the line 36° 30', lest that line should carry some "implication" with it. But our friends were generously retiring from that line, on which I think they ought to stand. There was no consideration in relation to the public lands; no consideration of physical geography which justified the southern representatives in receding one degree south. There was nothing, I say, in the line of 35° 30' to commend itself to any except to those who had determined from the beginning to avoid the line of 36° 30', lest it might carry an "implication" with it. We were then conceding a great deal when we took that line. But it was voted down. When it was last offered, I know not under what auspices, an amendment was proposed to recognize the rights of the South in the country below 35° 30'. That was voted down. So we could not get out rights acknowledged in the Territories.

But we are told, time and again, that the line of 35° 30′ would have been agreed to, and the bill passed containing that for the line. This reminds me of a celebrated jumper from Leeds. He was always speaking of how far he had jumped, and how many men he could bring to prove it. Finally, one day some one said to him, "Save yourself the trouble of hunting up witnesses; it would cost ·you much time and expense; just make the jump over again." [Laughter.] Now, sir, if gentlemen have the power to draw that line, let them draw it. The southern men who oppose the bill constitute no obstacle to it. I cannot understand how Senators would to-day vote for a line upon such high principles as should govern any member of this body, and to-morrow, from a little spite, altogether refuse to vote for such a line. I hope no Senator will take that ground. If that line can be drawn, why not draw it now?

Speech of Jefferson Davis, August 5, 1850, in defense of Gen. Taylor, on the resolution of Mr. Cass in relation to the exercise of civil power by the military officers of the United States.

The Senate having under consideration the following resolution, submitted by Mr. Cass on the 27th of June—

"*Resolved,* That the Committee on Military Affairs be instructed to inquire into the expediency of prohibiting by law any officer of the army from assuming or exercising within the limits of the United States any civil power or authority not conferred by an act of Congress, and of providing an adequate punishment for such offence"—

Mr. DAVIS said:

Mr. President: I indicated on a former occasion that I should have something to say on this resolution when it should come up for consideration. This resolution, which was offered by the Senator from Michigan, [Mr. Cass,] proposes to submit to the Committee on Military Affairs the inquiry into the expediency of prohibiting by law any officer of the army from assuming or exercising within the limits of the United States any civil authority not conferred by act of Congress, and providing adequate punishment for such offences. I do not propose to go into the merits of this resolution; yet I would wish to call the attention of the mover of it to the necessity of making it more specific, of directing the inquiry to that which he wishes to reach. As it stands, sir, connected with the history of events which have recently transpired, we should be at a loss to determine whether it was proposed to censure the Congress of the United States, from whose delay the necessity has arisen, or the Executive of the United States—either the last or the present Administration—or the officers of the army. Most probably, sir, the latter; and if the latter, then the censure is imposed on that to which it least justly attaches. It is a fact well known to the whole country that during the war with Mexico we held possession of the district of Santa Fé and the whole Territory of California by the power of the military forces alone. To what, then, were we to refer for the preservation of order? Not to the courts which had just been expelled from the country by military authority; not in the case of California to the legislation of Congress, for they had no power to legislate for it; but necessarily to the military authority, which held it by conquest, and under orders of the Executive of the United States.

The resolution as it stands directs the inquiry to something still more remote—to that great necessity which sometimes occurs and drives an officer to declare martial law—that resort of General Jackson when called to the defence of New Orleans, and without using which the city would have fallen, probably, into the hands of the enemy. The Senator from New Hampshire has proposed an amendment which will render the inquiry more specific, if it be adopted by the Senate, which points the committee to an inquiry into the order given by the last and the present Administration to any officer of the United States conferring authority to be exercised without the limits of the several States of the Union, and to report by whom, and to whom, and by what laws such orders were given. These orders as well as these assumptions of authority depend upon the usages of war—upon the law of nations. They are not derived from the Constitution of the United States, and could not be provided for by the legislation of Congress. If the committee be directed to the inquiry expressed in the original resolution, its terms are either too broad or too narrow. It either restricts the Military Committee from inquiring into those points which may require legislation, and which are connected with the subject under consideration, or else it opens an indeterminate field, without authority to recommend to Congress any provisions for like cases, should like cases occur, which would be to forbid the exercise, as heretofore, of discretionary power, without substantiating any other.

This is one of the contingencies of war. It necessarily results from war that commanders sometimes perform functions not ordinarily intrusted to military officers; it is one of the extreme necessities for which each case has itself provided. As the law now stands each officer assumes it under the high responsibility he feels to prove to his country that a necessity existed which justified the assumption. I do not pretend to say that all which has been done deserves to be approved. Indeed, on other occasions I have said, I believe, that authority had been assumed by officers exercising commands in the territory of the United States, not compatible with the duties of their profession, not required by necessity, and in violation of the rights of citizens of the United States. I hold that it was the duty of the army, when this territory came into our possession, under the orders of the Executive, to hold it for the United States till Congress should provide for it; and such were the declarations and acts both of the administrations of Mr. Polk and General Taylor. Both have absolutely declined to give any decision upon the question of boundary, considering it as a subject over which the legislation of the country could alone exercise control. I will refer to a case before me, which fully maintains my position upon the whole subject. There is a district upon the Rio Grande which lies below the old limits of the province of New Mexico, which was never a part of Texas until it became so by the treaty of San Jacinto, which was, if acquired by the treaty of Guadalupe Hidalgo, in an anomalous condition. It was possessed partly by our own emigrants and partly by Mexicans, and was without law from the date of the treaty of peace and limits with the Republic of Mexico. The commanding officer of the division stationed at Santa Fé directed the officer who held subordinate command over this district, and whose headquarters were opposite to El Paso, to apply what is called the Kearny code, the government provided for New Mexico. These orders were referred to the Executive through the War Department, and I have before me the answer:

"WAR DEPARTMENT,
"ADJUTANT GENERAL'S OFFICE, *March* 8, 1850.

"I am directed by the Secretary of War to state, in reply, that, regarding as he does your orders to Major Van Horne, of December 28, 1849, as manifestly assuming to decide the question of territorial jurisdiction of Texas over the places enumerated therein, and professing to extend a 'code' of laws which had not been accepted by the people even whilst under military authority, it is deemed necessary distinctly to repeat, for your guidance on this occasion, what the department has often stated, that the Executive has no power to adjust and settle the question of territorial limits involved in this case. Other coördinate departments are alone competent to make the decision. The main duties of the army are, to give protection and security on the soil of the United States, and preserve internal peace. Whatever else is done must arise from the urgent pressure of a necessity which cannot be postponed, and to avoid the exercise of any civil authority which is not justified by that necessity. In sending to these people the 'Kearny code,' or other codes, it is proper to remark, that the only regulations which are applicable to their condition are those laws which were in force at the period of the conquest of New Mexico, or Texas may establish. The only exception is, that they be not in opposition to the Constitution and laws of the United States.''

This is in keeping with the messages of the President, three of which now lie before me, and in each one of which he declares it is not for the Executive to determine the boundaries of the Territories, and that the boundary of Texas must be determined by the legislative branch alone. So far as any officer of the army has exercised authority to determine this question, it therefore appears that he is responsible for it.

I will not weary the Senate by reading more that I find quite necessary, and will generally but refer to authorities unless their reading be called for. Either in the case of Santa Fé, California, and the Lower Rio Grande, or in that portion of Mexico which was occupied during the war, there was no civil court. The courts of the enemy could not be permitted to exercise jurisdiction in the country, and Congress had provided by legislation for no courts under the authority of the United States. Offences were constantly committed in and about the army, of which military courts could not take cognizance. This difficulty was early pointed out. The Secretary of War in 1846, in his report accompanying the President's message of that year, called the attention of Congress to it. This necessity increased with the increase of the territory of which we held possession, and finally became the subject of correspondence by General Scott, who prepared a *projet* for the purpose of establishing a commission under military authority to take jurisdiction of those offences of which courts-martial could not take cognizance. General Taylor in his correspondence frequently pointed out this difficulty, and the embarrassment resulting from it, but never assumed to provide a remedy. Thus all of these show the necessity which existed at that time and place for the officers of the army to exercise some authority over the subject which was not strictly professional; and I submit if it should not have been provided for by a law of Congress. If, in the absence of legislation, and under a stern necessity, some civil authority has been assumed, who is to be censured for it? Shall the censure fall upon their Executive, who maintained our authority by the means granted to him, or upon the officers of the army, for the faults which we have committed? The beam is in our eye, and we should not be searching for the mote which is in our brother's. It was not in the power of the Executive, and still less in the power of the officers of the army, to remedy the evil. It was in us; and we have been derelict to our duty. We have created a necessity, and driven these officers of the army to assume an authority which was extra-professional, and from which they would all have gladly been relieved.

With these remarks, which are intended mainly to direct the mover of this resolution to some modification of its terms, or induce him to accompany it with such instructions as will point the committee clearly to what he desires, and which will give it some power to remedy existing difficulties, I will proceed to the consideration of some portion of that argument which has been connected with this resolution. I would be glad if the debate which has arisen upon this resolution would permit me to stop with the expression of those views which belong to the resolution itself. But the remarks of the Senator from Texas involve other considerations, and require a specific answer. At the time when the boundary of his State was the subject of discussion, at the time when Congress threatened to deprive his State of its territory, he wanders from that question which was before us, and which might have called out all his energy and devotion as a Texan, and goes into the remote history of the army upon the Rio Grande, to display his affection for the State he represents. What had the orders and the discipline of the army on the Rio Grande to do with the territorial rights of Texas? And what, I would ask, can the Senator find to justify him upon this occasion, at this remote day, to bring up questions of the discipline of a camp of which he showed himself supremely ignorant, and in the treatment of which he showed himself supremely unjust? When these remarks were submitted to the Senate, I could illy brook the defamation of my old commander, and not very patiently bear the studied detraction from my comrades of that hard-earned reputation which many of them gained at the expense of their lives, and many who live possess with the incumbrance of wounds and disabilities which they will carry to their graves. But happily believing that the fame of one and the other was not to be shaken by such an attack, I was prepared to allow the defence, both of that commander and my comrades, to fall into the hands of those who were not restrained by those political considerations which bore upon me—to those to whom it would be a task equally grateful, and, under the circumstances, perhaps more appropriate. I did not fear to leave their fame without a defence, well assured as I was that their reputation was based upon services of which the country is fully aware, and that their defence might securely be left to history, and to that more imperishable witness, the tradition which springs from the actors in the scenes to which he referred. But that Senator has thought proper, at a more recent period, to reaffirm all he said upon a former occasion—to reaffirm it when the circumstances were changed, when that restraint of political relations to which I have referred as acting upon me had passed away, when political reasons as connected with my old commander had been closed by the grave. Now, sir, if a political opposition ever did disqualify me in the minds of just men from defending the military conduct and character of General Taylor from the assaults of error or prejudice, that disqualification ceases. Now, sir, I am free from these restraints, and come to perform a duty which is equally meet and becoming to my position to execute.

Now, sir, we have reached a point when the material of history is to be collected. Now partisan zeal has reached the limit beyond which honorable men do not extend it, and the scales of justice may be more truly balanced. Under these circumstances, then, I come to save from injury the reputation of a gallant soldier; I come to save from detraction my buried friend; and I expect to prove by the very witnesses which the Senator from Texas himself brought forward the gross injustice of every reflection which he has made, and I expect from his generosity and his manliness, and the benevolence of his character, which I have known so long to distinguish him, that he will retract every aspersion he has thrown upon the fame of that distinguished soldier.

The PRESIDENT. The Senator must not apply a remark of that kind to any Senator. "Aspersion" is a word that should not be so used.

Mr. DAVIS, of Mississippi. I never design to be personal to any member of this body, certainly not to the Senator from Texas. I am but answering his own remark; which remark, under the suggestion of the Chair, I will read, in order that

it may be seen how far my language is applicable. In referring
to the people of the State of Texas, he says:

"The people of that State have been unwarrantably assailed,
traduced, and defamed by the present Executive of the nation,
when a general in the field. If I were not sustained by incontestable authority, I would scorn to impute to any high
functionary of this Government aught that was unworthy of
his station, or of the high position which he occupies; but in this
case I am fully sustained in every word I say, as I will show by
recourse to testimony stronger than the mere assertion of a
political opponent, that will carry conviction to the mind of
every candid man."

Now, sir, I say I propose, by the very witnesses he has
brought before the Senate, to prove that he was wholly unsus-
tained in his aspersion; and I expect him as a just man—not to
say a generous and benevolent man, as I said before—to withdraw that defamation, or else to find himself in a position, which
he has himself described as one "it would excite his scorn to
occupy." The facts in this case are quite the reverse from the
view which the Senator from Texas has thought proper to
present. The letter to which he refers, and from which he
makes a quotation of the opinion expressed by the commanding general of the army of the Rio Grande, that the militia
of Texas were too far from the border, and their aid could not,
therefore, be depended upon—that assertion was no defamation, as he says, of the character of the people of Texas, no
reflection upon their gallantry. Nor was the expression in relation to the Texans made by the General, when, as the Senator
says, not one of them had ever been placed under his command, and not a solitary corps or individual of them had he then
ever seen ranged under his banner.
Sir, before the war commenced, specific authority was given
to that general to call upon the people of Texas for forces, if
he required them. The indication was that Texas was to have
priority in any demand for troops. In a letter from the War
Department of August 16, 1845, he was instructed to look to
Texas for such auxiliary force as he might require. In keeping with my promise not to read more extensively than was
necessary, I will not read that letter, unless the reading be called
for; but before the receipt of that authority, a correspondence
had commenced with the President of Texas, in relation to the
defence of her settlements. The commanding general, writing

from his headquarters at Corpus Christi, to the then President of Texas, Anson Jones, says as follows:

"HEADQUARTERS, CORPUS CHRISTI, *August* 16, 1845.

"You have undoubtedly received intelligence of the hostile steps taken by Mexico, and the probable declaration of war against us by that power. Under these circumstances, I do not deem it prudent to detach any portion of my force at present; and it is the principal object of this communication to recommend that any volunteers or spies now in the service of Texas be continued in employment, should you consider it necessary for the defence of the frontier. If you concur in this view, I will, at your instance, dispatch an officer to muster into the service of the United States any companies which you may designate as necessary for the security of the frontier, to conform in numbers and organization to the laws of the United States. Should such musters be made, I will recommend that the officers and men, while in service, continue to receive the same rate of pay which they have drawn from the Texan government.

"My presence, and that of my command, is now imperatively required on this frontier. When our relations with Mexico and the state of the service in this quarter shall permit my absence, I will take great pleasure in proceeding to the seat of Government, and conferring with you personally in relation to the proper dispositions to be made for the permanent occupation of the frontier."

This was done on his own responsibility, as appears by the following extract from a letter to the Adjutant General at Washington, D. C.:

"HEADQUARTERS, CORPUS CHRISTI, *August* 26, 1845.

"In regard to employing volunteers from Texas, you will perceive that I have in part anticipated the wishes of the Government in my letter of the 16th instant to President Jones, a copy of which was furnished you on the 19th. In that communication, I looked only to the defence of the frontier against Indian aggressions; but I shall now communicate with President Jones, and ascertain the number of volunteers that can be called into service in case of an invasion by Mexico, and shall take the necessary steps to arm and employ that force, should the safety of the country require it."

In answer to his letter the President of Texas, Anson Jones, informed him of three hundred rangers then in the service of Texas. These rangers were mustered into the service under the command of General Taylor. One company of these rangers was serving with him at his headquarters at Corpus Christi, where he found them when he arrived in that country. They were under the command of Captain Bell, now, I believe, the Governor of Texas; so that if he had written anything in that letter of March 29, 1846, which expressed any opinion in relation to the troops of Texas, it was subsequent to the time that they had been mustered in under his command, and after a portion of them had served at his headquarters. It was not, then, without any personal knowledge of them. It was not, then, when, as the Senator assumes, he was bound to form his opinion entirely from their military history, and "the bright lustre of their own lone star." The conclusion that their remoteness rendered it improper that he should rely upon the people of Texas for volunteers was fully justified by subsequent facts, which will be presented. The Senator from Texas, who has seen service himself, knows as well as any one that a general standing with his command almost in contact with an opposing army before hostilities had commenced, and when the hope was still entertained that he might avoid collision—I say that, under such circumstances, he knows as well as any one that militia are not the most desirable force; he knows as well as any one why a general, instead of volunteers, should ask for regular recruits to strengthen his command, when it was necessary to preserve the strictest order in his own camp; when, to carry out the policy of conciliation, it was essential to have troops who would implicitly obey orders, both in sight and out of sight, and that he should have troops whom, if necessary, he could detach in full assurance that if they fell in with any of the inhabitants of the country, they would neither wantonly offend nor maltreat them. These were considerations which fully justified him in asking for recruits rather than volunteers. These were considerations, however, that he did not present. Confined to the view which the Senator from Texas has presented in an extract—the fact that the militia of Texas were too remote from the border to be depended upon—there is nothing to have provoked an attack or to have warranted even a complaint. That opinion was fully verified by the delay which followed his call upon Texas for troops when collision became inevitable. When it was apparent to him that conflict must ensue, then, as early as he became convinced of that fact, (April 26, 1846,) he wrote to the Governors of Texas and of Louisiana, and called upon each of them to furnish him with four regiments. Now, see what follows. Did the Texans, as the Senator says they would have done, rally to his standard in a moment? Did they come before the troops of Louisiana? Upon the answer to this question I rely for a decision as to the justice or the injustice of the conclusions to which the Senator from Texas has arrived. This call was made upon the same day both upon Texas and Louisiana—was answered by the arrival of part of the Louisiana troops upon May 20th, and on the 24th the other detachment arrived. But the first notice that I find of the arrival of any Texan troops was on June 24th, one month after the arrival of the Louisiana troops, and then only as being encamped at Point Isabel for purposes of organization:

"HEADQUARTERS, CITY OF MATAMOROS, *May* 24, 1846.

"Sir: I have to report the arrival this day of Gen. Smith, with the battalion of the first infantry, the Washington regiment of the Louisiana volunteers, and a company of volunteers from Mobile. Another regiment of Louisiana volunteers is below, and will probably arrive this evening or to-morrow. This command was accompanied from the mouth of the river by the steamboat "Neva," which succeeded without difficulty in reaching this place."

"HEADQUARTERS, MATAMOROS, *June* 24, 1846.

"Some volunteers have arrived at Brazos Santiago from Tennessee, presumed to be of the twelve months' quota; but I have received no report from their commander. The volunteers who previously arrived from New Orleans have nearly all moved to Barrita, except two regiments at this place; and I shall bring them up the river as soon as I can procure transportation, which I am impatiently awaiting, and for want of which I am still unable to make a forward movement. The volunteers from Texas are encamped near Point Isabel, and are now organizing under the direction of the governor.

"We have no authentic intelligence from the interior of Mexico. The army at Linares is believed to be moving towards Monterey, much reduced in numbers by desertion and sickness. It is rumored that Bustamente is at the head of the government, and that Paredes is advancing with a large force to this frontier. Another report places Herrera at the head of affairs, but there seems to be no intelligence on which we can safely rely."

Now, must not the Senator from Texas on this point withdraw every reflection that he has made? Does he not, in the first place, find that that letter was not written before the

General had command of the Texan troops? Does he not find, that instead of reluctance to exercise the authority conferred upon him, he ordered Texan troops to be mustered into service before he had received the authority from the War Department? Does he not find, further, that he called upon Texas at the same time that he called upon Louisiana, and that about a month intervened between the arrival of the troops of those States? Then I ask him, in the face of all these facts, whether he will still persist in his assertion that the opinion quoted by him was unfounded, that it was a reflection upon Texan troops, and that the Texans were waiting to join at a moment's warning the General's standard, and to punish the Mexicans? The Senator, who well knows that the statement in the letter pointed to a fact which subsequent events established most fully, yet converted it into a stigma upon the people of Texas. Why, sir, it required ingenuity of the highest order to find any reflection in this upon the people of Texas. It required a proneness to censure to see in it anything else than a simple declaration of a fact which the world knew then, and which subsequent events have established, if it was then unknown, that Texas was sparsely settled, her borders constantly invaded by savage foes—that she was occupied in the defence of her northern and western frontiers when the army of the United States was ordered to Texas to protect her from invasion by Mexico. But out of this simple extract from a letter which was supported by facts such as I have mentioned, he not only draws the construction of a stigma upon the people of Texas, but he makes it a basis for glorification of his constituents of Texas which I am sure the people would never have applied to themselves. Who are they? Are they not emigrants from States of this Union? Did not the revolution of Texas spring from the energy, the courage, and the free principles which emigrants from the United States had carried into Texas? And if they differed in any respect from the people of the United States, it must be by the infusion of that blood which the Senator from Texas seems so much himself to despise—that of the original Mexican inhabitants. In this alone can they differ from other people of the United States. It is strange to me that a Senator who himself was at the head of the revolution, had the glory to have been the leader of that last great battle which terminated so gloriously for the flag of Texas—that he, who cannot fail to remember that his ranks were filled by emigrants who came to aid their brethren in their struggle, and who had never been residents in Texas—strange that he should attempt to make invidious distinctions between the people of Texas and other citizens of the United States.

But, sir, of these four regiments which I have stated did not arrive until after the Louisiana regiments, there is another fact somewhat indicative, which comes in as supplementary to the arguments of the Senator. But three of these regiments ever arrived—two of mounted troops, and one of infantry; the fourth regiment never came. Let no one suppose I say this with any view to cast reflection upon the people of Texas. Far otherwise. I refer to it but to establish the fact, which the General knew before, that they were not in a condition to furnish large quotas to his army; it was a sparsely settled country, and it would take a long time to raise and organize troops; and, under such circumstances, to detach large bodies of men from the demands which their condition creates, for the purpose of war, it is necessary that the inducement should be strong, and the term of service short.

The Senator from Texas said that the Texans were kept at Point Isabel, the most unhealthy situation—that they occupied it for weeks without tents, and that tents were lying at Fort Brown, &c. It would have been very hard for the Senator to have condensed in a sentence of the same length a greater number of errors. Point Isabel was a high point, the highest point in the neighborhood, the only one exempt from drifting sand. It was selected as a site for the general hospital, and remained such till the conclusion of operations in that quarter. An arm of the sea swept its base, and it was the only high hill in the neighborhood that was covered with grass. It was a very desirable position, as far as health and comfort were concerned. Then he says they were kept without tents. Perhaps that is the point that makes it so grave an accusation. It could not be the position itself, for the Senator but a short time ago was describing to us the great importance of Point Isabel, its superiority over other positions in the neighborhood of the mouth of the Rio Grande. Then, however, he was arguing for a garrison to be sent there to guard the custom-house. When it was to be described as the encampment of the Texan troops, it was at once converted into the most unhealthy position in the neighborhood. Now, sir, for the statement about the tents. He selects Fort Brown as a depôt from which tents might have been drawn. My opinion is, that from Nova Scotia to the Isthmus of Panama, he could not have selected a place to which he might not as well have gone for tents as to Fort Brown. The gallant and obstinate defence that the garrison had made deprived it of its camp equipage. They cut up their tents to make sand-bags to form ramparts against the enemy. They were without tents themselves; instead of being the storehouse from which tents were to be drawn, the brave defenders were themselves unsheltered. In this letter of May 20, nearly a month after the call upon Texas for troops, the General, writing from Matamoros, says in relation to the volunteers from Texas:

"HEADQUARTERS, MATAMOROS, *May* 20, 1846.

"In my communication to the Governor, the organization was very exactly prescribed—being that indicated from your office on the 25th of August, 1845. I find, however, that this organization has been exceeded; and, moreover, that General Gaines has called for more volunteers than I deemed necessary, extending the call to other States besides Louisiana. It will of course be for the Government to decide whether the future operations in this quarter will require the amount of force (entirely unknown) which is coming hither. * * * * I fear that the volunteers have exhausted the supply of tents deposited in New Orleans for the use of this army. We are greatly in want of them, and I must request that immediate measures be taken to send direct to Brazos Santiago, say one thousand tents for the use of the army in the field. The tents of the 7th infantry were cut up to make sand-bags during the recent bombardment of Fort Brown.''

Sir, the Senator from Texas, an old soldier, should have looked still further into this question. The depôts of tents in the United States had all been exhausted. A war had suddenly come upon the country, and the ordinary supplies were quite insufficient, and soon were entirely exhausted—not only of tents, but of all the necessary camp equipage. The Quartermaster General, with that energy and fertility of resource which so eminently distinguish him, resorted to every expedient—among others, the use of a new material for tents, the material ordinarily used for their manufacture being exhausted. Of this material substituted, tents were manufactured and transported to the army as rapidly as the transportation would allow. Where, then, sir, is the foundation for this charge which would insinuate, if it does not specify, inhumanity upon the part of the General—that he kept troops in the most unhealthy exposure, wholly unprovided with tents, while he had a depôt of tents at a short distance from their encampment? Vanished, sir —vanished under the application of the touchstone of fact. I have a right to appeal to the justice of the Senator to withdraw this reflection also.

But again: that Senator, in the same temper of self-glorification, refers to the battles of Palo Alto and Resaca de la Palma, and says: "Why, sir, two hundred and fifty Texan rangers, if 'he had applied for them, would have repulsed any attempt 'that might have been made to cross the Rio Grande by the 'Mexican troops, and the song of peace would have been heard 'uninterrupted up to the present day." Yes, sir, two hundred and fifty Texan rangers, or at most five hundred, he says, would have been sufficient for that purpose. Yet, sir, a squadron of dragoons, before hostilities had commenced, was sent out to observe the river, and reconnoitre above the headquarters of our army. It was commanded by a soldier whose gallantry was never questioned or suspected, and whose daring finally cost him his life upon the plains of Mexico, while his junior captain was one of the most accomplished soldiers in our army, whose education had been perfected abroad. These officers, at the head of their companies—Captains Thornton and Hardee—were captured in the neighborhood of the American encampment by a detachment of that very army which he supposes two hundred and fifty Texan rangers could have held in check, and tamed into peaceful desires.

But, Mr. President, is it to be presumed or asserted that this whole country was thrown into one general burst of joy—is it probable that our towns were illuminated when the little army on the Rio Grande repulsed, beat on two fields, a Mexican army which could have been held in check by two hundred and fifty Texan rangers? Is it true, sir, that those soldiers who had spent their lives in acquiring their profession, with an army of two thousand men—than which none was ever more favorably composed for desperate service, old soldiers and young leaders—performed only what two hundred and fifty Texan rangers could have done so much more effectually? Shades of Ringgold and McIntosh, Barbour, Ridgely, and Duncan, and thou, the hero of the Mexican war, let not your ashes be disturbed! The star of your glory will never be obscured by such fogs and empty clouds as that. It will continue to shine brighter and brighter as long as professional skill is appreciated or bravery is admired, and patriotism has a shrine in the American heart.

But, sir, it was not alone in the United States that the military movements and achievements on the Rio Grande were viewed with admiration. The greatest captain of the age—the great Duke of Wellington—the moment he saw the positions taken and the combinations made upon the Rio Grande—the moment he saw the communication opened between the depôt at Point Isabel and the garrison at Fort Brown by that masterly movement of which the battles of Palo Alto and Resaca de la Palma were a part—exclaimed that General Taylor is a general indeed. And yet, sir, all history is to be rewritten, all the rapture and pride of the country at the achievements upon those bloody fields are to disappear, and the light of science to pale before the criticism of that Senator, by whom we are told that a little band of mounted riflemen could have done that which cost so many American lives and hecatombs of Mexicans. The Senator from Texas spoke in language well calculated to feed the vanity of his State, but not as a historian, nor, as it seems to me, quite as an American Senator might, and in a manner still less becoming to an old soldier. The Senator goes on to express the ferocious impatience of the Texans to pursue the Mexicans, but says ''they were restrained, 'and lieutenant colonels from the interior were permitted to 'lead our troops through the dense chaparrals and jungles of 'Mexico, whilst the brave Texans were restrained or taken to the 'southern plains, there to meet beneath burning suns a linger- 'ing death by disease.''

Mr. President, who restrained them? They came not till the enemy had gone. They came not until he had concentrated his forces at Monterey. They came not till the troops of Mexico, far beyond the Sierra Madre, and even from San Luis Potosi, were reported to have made a junction with the retreating army at Monterey. Who, then, restrained them? Who sent them to southern plains? What lieutenant colonel led the troops through the jungle and the chaparral? Sir, the fact is that these troops were led by the highway, the only way by which infantry could have been marched. The column of march followed a plain wide road. There was no jungle and no chaparral. The only detour made from the great route pursued by the army was made by Texans themselves. They took the route through China, which is probably the route referred to by the Senator, and they lost some two or three of their men. But he says they could have got to the city of Monterey in June, and that they could have taken the city or been killed. They could not have got there in June. I doubt whether they could have got there at any time alone. The outposts of the enemy retired before the advance guard of our army. They no doubt would have fought a smaller force.

But if they had finally got there, then the Senator has put

in a very good alternative, "or they could have been killed." They were brave men. I have no doubt they would have dared to go wherever their chief would have ordered; and if he had been unwise enough to have ordered them to Monterey, I have no doubt they would have attempted it, and that they could have and would have been killed in the attempt.

Then the Senator from Texas, in his second speech, attempts to account for the refusal of the Texan infantry to proceed to Monterey, they having been discharged at Camargo, about one month before the battle at Monterey. He says that the reason why the Texans declined was the unpopularity of the officers, and that there was no prospect of further action.

Now, sir, to take up the reasons one at a time: The leader of that infantry regiment had served with distinction in the army of the United States, and was well known as one of the best officers in it. He was the adjutant general of General Atkinson in the Black Hawk campaign of 1832. It was General Johnson, than whom there is nowhere to be found a braver, and rarely a more skillful soldier. How, sir, did he get into the command of the Texan regiment of infantry? He was elected to the office, I suppose. They elected their officers, as I understand it. Then it was by their own choice that he got the command.

In the next place, was there any apprehension that he would keep them out of dangerous service, or any fear that they would not get into a fight if there was one? No one who knows anything of that officer will ever believe it. When his regiment was discharged, and left him at Camargo, General Johnson remained, and offered his services as an individual; they were accepted, and he was distinguished in the battle of Monterey, and complimented in the general orders. Then, as to the prospect at the time of any further action: The prospect about that time was imminent. The report was, that Bustamente was already in the vicinity, and that Paredes was on his way with reinforcements, and General Ampudia was reported to be, with greatly augmented force, at or near Monterey. The commanding general, when he corresponded with the department, said, indeed, that he placed no confidence in the reports of the Mexicans. He did not know where they were, nor when they would arrive—whether they would give him battle at Monterey or not; it might be before reaching that place, or it might be beyond it, at the Pass of Los Muertos—correctly named, if intended to promise death to an attacking column—for it is one of the strongest places by nature, against an army going from the north, which is in the country.

He had been corresponding with the department from time to time, informing them of his want of transportation, of his inability to advance, and also announcing his purpose, as soon as he should have made a depôt at Camargo, to march upon Monterey and take it. That town had the reputation for the greatest strength of any in the country. It was believed by the Mexicans to be impregnable. In all the domestic struggles, the Indian incursions, and various wars of Mexico, it had never been taken. General Ampudia, the military commandant of the town, pledged himself to its inhabitants that, unless driven to extremity, he would give us battle outside of Monterey.

The Senator says that the fortifications were not commenced before September. Now, the great fortification at Monterey— that called the New Citadel, which, among the volunteers, had the *sobriquet* of the Black Fort—was dusky with age. Its stone battlements stood, and still stand, proof against any strength we ever had, and, against the assaults of mounted riflemen, might stand a thousand years. That never was taken, sir, and we never had the power to take it, save by capitulation. Admirably situated as it was, and having all the massive strength of Spanish fortification, it commanded the town, which it had the power to demolish. The town itself was a fortification from one end to the other. The houses being built of stone, with stone walls three or four feet thick, with balustrades fitted for the exact purposes of a breastwork, made the whole town a fortification. The houses, for the most part, are only one story high, and immediately overlooking the narrow streets. This was no place, sir, for the charge of horsemen. This error may have resulted from another, which was indicated when the Senator referred to the fact that the heavy ordnance was kept behind. He supposes it was left by choice. Not so, sir. It was left behind solely from necessity, and for the want of transportation. The deficiency of heavy artillery was supplied by an extraordinary amount of effort. Unbroken horses were taken and harnessed in to supply the means of transportation. The commanding general had to depend on the enemy for the transportation of the provisions to supply his troops. The transportation was, to a great extent, obtained from the Mexicans themselves. That march was an extraordinary one. It was hurried, as the General's correspondence shows, in order to aid the Government in concluding negotiations and a peace, and with the hope of preventing the necessity of a general war. The march was therefore undertaken, all unprepared as the army was. It became necessary for him, therefore, to reduce his army by leaving behind every inefficient man—regiments of 900 or 1,000 men were cut down to 500. With this picked force, he commenced his march, which it was believed at the time would terminate in one of the most severely contested battles ever fought. And, sir, the struggle was as to who should be permitted to go. The letters read by the Senator from Maryland, and which I will not read again, show that the General offered the Texan infantry an opportunity to go on with the army, But, sir, they did not want to go. I do not say that they were afraid to go, but they did not want to go on foot. It was with difficulty that one regiment was induced to consent to go on foot, and that regiment declined at the eleventh hour.

But, sir, the Senator says these Texas troops did good service —that is, the mounted men; that they took the plaza, took the heights, and took the Bishop's palace. Well sir, I am at a loss to know upon what grounds the Senator rests these statements. The plaza was never taken. There is, therefore, no question as to who took that. It was never taken. No one ever saw it even except at one corner, and that at a distance, until after the capitulation. It remained in the hands of the Mexicans. They had concentrated their troops on it. They covered with troops the roofs of the neighboring houses, which surrounded the plaza, over which they hung as black clouds up to the time when it was finally surrendered by capitulation. Therefore, it is useless to argue about who took the plaza.

Then, as to the Bishop's palace, which the Senator seems to invest with all the charms once attached to the "Halls of the Montezumas:" He evidently supposes that Bishop's palace to have been a most formidable place. Probably he considers it a fortified castle, with moat, and drawbridge, and tower, and garrisoned battlements. On the contrary, that Bishop's palace was the remains of a house once commenced but never finished, never garrisoned, and never susceptible of being defended. It stood then as unappropriated and as unfit for defence as the remains of the burnt theatre upon Pennsylvania avenue. Even the little redoubt at the end of the palace was built upon the opposite side to that which was attacked. That redoubt was not built to resist an attack, but to cover the army if it should retreat, being driven out of the town. It was a work of defence for a retreating army, and not a work of resistance to an invading one. It was on the wrong side of the palace for that, looking to the town of Monterey, and not towards the troops who attacked. As to the heights, the taking of which he ascribes to the Texans, they were taken by all the troops of Worth's division; and that gallant soldier to whose memory we have recently paid a tribute—the soldier who bore to his grave the wound honorably received at Lundy's Lane—that soldier most competent to command a division composed of various arms, led veteran troops tried at Palo Alto and Resaca de la Palma. With those troops the Texans in brave and generous rivalry struggled, and a modest man would be slow to say that they achieved the feats on which rests the fame of that field. General Worth was never accused of prejudice against the Texans, though he was sometimes accused of favoring them too much. I will read extracts from his report touching each event, and it will be seen how the heights were carried, and by whom:

Extracts from General Worth's Report of the battle of Monterey.

"On the morning of the 21st the division was put in motion, and with such formation as to present the readiest order of battle on any point of assault. At six the advance, consisting of Hays's Texans, supported by the light companies, first brigade, under Captain C. F. Smith, (both extended as the valley widened or contracted,) closely followed by Duncan's light artillery and battalion heads of columns, on turning the angle of the mountain, at a hacienda called San Jeromino, came upon a strong force of cavalry and infantry, mostly the former. A conflict immediately ensued. The Texans received the heavy charge of cavalry with their unerring rifles and usual gallantry; the light companies opened a rapid and well-directed fire. Duncan's battery was in action in one minute, (promptly supported by a section of Mackall's,) delivering its fire over the heads of our men. Ere the close of the combat, which lasted but fifteen minutes, the first brigade had formed to the front on the right and left, and delivered its fire. The second brigade was held in reserve—the ground not admitting of its deployment. The enemy retired in disorder.

"At twelve, m., a force was detached under Captain C. F. Smith, with orders to storm the batteries on the crest of the nearest hill, called Federacion; and, after taking that, to carry the fort called Soldada, on the ridge of the same height, retired about six hundred yards. The two effectually guarded the slopes and roads in either valley, and consequently the approaches to the city. This command consisted of four companies (K 2d, B 3d, and G and H 4th artillery) of the artillery battalion, and

Green's, McGowan's, R. A. Gillespie's, Chandlis's, Ballows's, and McCulloch's companies of Texas riflemen, under Major Chevalier, acting in coöperation—in all about three hundred effectives.

"The appearance of heavy reinforcement on the summit, and the cardinal importance of the operation demanding further support, the 5th, under Major Scott, and Blanchard's company of volunteers, were immediately detached, accompanied by Brigadier General Smith, who was instructed to take direction in that quarter. On reaching the advance parties, General Smith discovered that, under favor of the ground, he could, by directing a portion of the force to the right, and moving it obliquely up the hill, carry the Soldada simultaneously with the Federacion. He accordingly very judiciously pointed, and accompanied the 5th, 7th, and Blanchard's company in that direction. Captain Smith's command having most gallantly carried the first object of attack, promptly turned the captured gun—a nine pounder—upon the second, and moved on with his main body to participate in the assault upon Soldada, which was carried in gallant style by the forces under Scott, Miles, Blanchard, and Hays, (who had been detached on special service, but who returned in time to share with fifty of his men in the first assault, and take a prominent part in the second)— the whole directed by General Smith.

"Lieutenant Colonel Childs was assigned to lead this storming party, consisting of three companies, (J and G 4th, and A 3d, artillery battalion,) three companies 8th infantry, (A, B, and D,) under Captain Screven, with two hundred Texan riflemen, under Colonel Hays, and Lieutenant Colonel Walker, (captain of rifles,) acting in coöperation. The command moved at three, conducted to its point of ascent by Captain Sanders, military, and Lieutenant Meade, topographical engineers. Favored by the weather, it reached by dawn of day within about one hundred yards of the crest, in which position, among the clefts of rocks, a body of the enemy had been stationed the previous evening in apparent anticipation of attack. The enemy's retreating fire was ineffectual, and not returned until Colonels Childs' and Hays' commands had reached within a few yards of the summit, when a well-directed and destructive fire, followed by the bayonet of the regulars and rush of the Texans, placed us in possession of the work. The cannon having been previously withdrawn, no impression could be made upon the massive walls of the palace or its outworks without artillery, except at an enormous sacrifice.

"After many affairs of light troops and several feints, a heavy sortie was made, sustained by a strong corps of cavalry, with desperate resolution to repossess the heights. Such a move had been anticipated and prepared for. Lieutenant Colonel

Childs had advanced, under cover, two companies of light troops, under command of Captain Vinton, acting major, and judiciously drawn up the main body of his command, flanked on the right by Hays's and left by Walker's Texans. The enemy advanced boldly; was repulsed by one general discharge from all arms; fled in confusion, closely pressed by Childs and Hays, preceded by the light troops under Vinton; and while they fled past, our troops entered the palace and fort. In a few moments the unpretending flag of the Union had replaced the gaudy standard of Mexico.''

Due credit was given for what they did; and I am one of the last to deprive them of a single feather in their plumes. I grant they deserved what they got; and no one claimed for them more, until the Senator from Texas discovered that the army was derelict or unemployed, and that Texans came in and took the town for them.

The honorable Senator from Texas tells us that Texans did all this. They took the palace. I am well assured that no one of the brave men who struggled in that contest could ever make any such pretensions. They know too well the difficulties of the performance. They know too well by whom they were led, by whom they were supported, by whom they were covered, and by whom they were directed ever to make such a claim. It could only be made by one who did not see and who has most carelessly read the history of that contest.

The Senator from Texas, after these high claims, complains that the Texans were denounced as the refuse of the army, and he must rescue them from obloquy. I ask him who has cast obloquy upon them? Who denounced them as the refuse of the army? I ask him still further, if he intends to assert that General Taylor withheld from the Texans due credit for their services in any battle? General Taylor was a man of few words. He usually said what he thought, and always thought what he said, and he expressed it briefly. He was never extravagant in the commendation of any man, and never withheld justice from any. I will recur to various places in his report, to show the equal notice taken of all who were alike entitled to notice.

Extracts from the report of General Taylor after the battle of Monterey.

''Major General Henderson, commanding the Texan volunteers, has given me important aid in the organization of his command, and its subsequent operations.

''Colonels Mitchell, Campbell, Davis, and Wood, commanding the Ohio, Tennessee, Mississippi, and second Texas regiment respectively—   *   *   *   *   *   *   *

"I have noticed above the officers whose conduct either fell under my own immediate eye, or is noticed only in minor reports which are not forwarded. For further mention of individuals, I beg leave to refer to reports of division commanders, herewith respectfully transmitted."

Here the colonels of Texas were commended in common, and equally with those of other regiments who were longer under fire, and reference is made to the reports of division commanders. But this was not all; and I call the Senator's attention to two general orders:

General Order, }   HEADQUARTERS, CAMP NEAR MONTEREY,
   No. 123.   }   *September,* 27, 1846.

"The Commanding General has the satisfaction to congratulate the army under his command upon another signal triumph over the Mexican forces. Superior to us in numbers, strongly fortified, and with an immense preponderance of artillery, they have yet been driven from point to point, until forced to sue for terms of capitulation. Such terms have been granted as were considered due to the gallant defence of the town, and to the liberal policy of our own Government.

"The General begs to return his thanks to his commanders, and to all his officers and men, both of the regular and volunteer forces, for the skill, the courage, and the perseverance with which they have overcome manifold difficulties, and finally achieved a victory shedding lustre upon the American arms.

"A great result has been obtained, but not without the loss of many gallant and accomplished officers and brave men. The army and the country will deeply sympathize with the families and friends of those who have thus sealed their devotion with their lives."

General Order, }   HEADQUARTERS, CAMP NEAR MONTEREY,
   No. 124.   }   *October,* 1, 1846.

"The mounted troops from Texas, having expressed a desire to return home during the present cessation of active service, will be mustered out of service and discharged to-morrow.

"The Commanding General takes this occasion to express his satisfaction with the efficient service rendered by the Texas volunteers during the campaign, and particularly in the operations around Monterey; and he would especially acknowledge his obligations to General Henderson, Generals Lamar and Burleson, and Colonels Hays and Wood, for the valuable assistance they have rendered. He wishes all the Texas volunteers a happy return to their families and homes.

"Col. A. S. Johnson, who has served in the campaign as inspector-general of the volunteer division, is hereby honorably discharged from the service. He will receive the thanks of the Commanding General for the important services rendered by him in that capacity."

Now, sir, where does the Senator stand? These are the facts, which, as I said before and now repeat require the Senator to withdraw his accusation. But the language of the Senator would induce one to suppose that there had been denunciation for acting well at Monterey. After claiming the capture of the town as the work of the Texans he says:

"Even after that they were denounced and stigmatized as the veriest refuse of the community, and as a dishonor to the army." "Even these deeds were not sufficient to rescue them from obloquy and defamation."

The fact is, that they were commended highly, and specially commended for their services in battle, but were censured for their irregularities, which was the duty of the General, and he would have done it without instructions. It had, however, been made his particular duty by the special orders he had received, to conciliate the people of Mexico in every quarter in which he marched.

The Senator treats the subject of the murders about the town of Monterey after the capitulation, as though it had been simply a Mexican killed in battle, and as a fair retaliation. A retaliation upon whom? He says a Texan was killed, and it was a fair retaliation to kill a Mexican. Did they kill the man who committed the murder? If he had been found, there would have been no necessity for violating orders, in order to retaliate. But the retaliation was the killing of innocent persons—it might be helpless women and children—by firing upon a house, or by killing some peaceful Mexican coming with supplies to market, because some of the robbers from the mountains had killed a Texan.

The Senator from North Carolina near me [Mr. BADGER] reminds me that this is the Indian rule; but it would be as impolitic, if applied by an invading general attempting to conciliate the people, as it would be inhuman. The people were disarmed, and whilst we held the country there was an obligation to protect them. If we failed in that protection, and permitted the robbers from the mountains to come among them, and then they should kill one of our own men, the failure was ours, and the crime was not that of the helpless inhabitants. We were bound to punish the robbers who violated their property, and were the terror of the country. We became their guardians, and our neglect of that duty could not justify us in killing one of the innocent people of the town because these marauders in their visits should murder one of our people. But this the Senator from Texas calls retaliation, as though the unarmed inhabitants were to protect the troops, instead of the reverse.

But he says that after the capitulation of Monterey the Mexicans were not disarmed, but went armed about the town. If the Senator will turn to the articles of capitulation, he will find not only the number of arms that they were permitted to retain, but the number of rounds of ammunition which they were allowed, and the conditions of the grant. When they crossed the plains to San Luis Potosi, the retiring troops were allowed for defence against the Indians these arms, and with them in their hands they marched out of the town, under the supervision of our troops. I never saw an armed Mexican riding about the town after the capitulation. There was an armed lancer shot in the street, and that was the atrocity to which reference was made. An officer of their army upon parole was present in Monterey, and with him he had an orderly. They were about to start from Monterey to go to Saltillo. He was riding out of the town, and the orderly was following. That orderly was armed because he was going into the country, and he was shot from a window as he rode through the street. The immediate commander and military governor of the town of Monterey, the lamented General Worth, told me that that officer on parole, on leaving town, had just shaken hands with him; and before his hands were yet entirely cool from the parting grasp, he was informed that the officer's orderly had been shot in the streets by the Texan Fitzsimmons. The brave, honorable Texans who were there never countenanced the act. The brave and good men of the Texas regiment were as indignant as others at the infamous atrocity. Colonel Hays was the first to arrest the offender; and if he had been allowed to deal with him, that individual would probably have met summary punishment. This is but a sample. The true soldiers of the Texas regiments, and of every other, denounced these irregularities of their own troops or of any other. They supported the commanding general in all that he did for the honor of his country, for the honor of the army, and of the flag he bore. The complaint which he makes is unjust to the better class, the great majority of the Texan troops, who never countenanced or defended these atrocities.

He must have heard of Mexicans shot at other places, and at an anterior period. The Senator surely cannot intend to justify such an act as that which is fully reported in the document before me, and to which I have referred. The testimony in relation to it was taken by the captain and colonel, and this constituted one of the atrocities of which complaint was made. Or does he refer to that respectable citizen of Linares, murdered by a party remote from the camp of the commanding general, to whom the complaints of the murdered man's family came? That is another case, which you Mr. President, [Mr. SHIELDS being in the chair,] who served in the Mexican war, so well understand, which marks the distinction between a murder and the killing of an enemy in battle. You, sir, know also why it so often occurs that undisciplined cavalry commit these irregularities.

But the Senator reads from a letter of June 16, 1847:

"The volunteers for the war, so far, give an earnest of better conduct, with the exception of the companies of Texan horse. Of the infantry I have had little or no complaint.'

If the General had gone further, and said that irregular cavalry always produce disturbance in the neighborhood of a camp, he would have said no more than my experience would confirm. With their freedom from fatigue at the close of a march, they are restless; and when in camp, while their horses stand in tether, they are always ready to avail themselves of a chance to wander far from the camp, and, thus removed from restraint they commit more irregularities than other troops, from this very reason.

The Senator went on to say, in relation to the statement that some shameful atrocities had been perpetrated in Monterey after the capitulation of the town, "What high encomiums are these, in acknowledgment of valorous and chivalric deeds! What encouragement to cheer a veteran! What encouragement to offer to a young and ardent patriot?"

What had atrocities after the capitulation of the town to do with gallant feats in battle? Nothing, sir; nothing. And what could the veteran feel but indignation at knowing that shameful atrocities were being committed upon an unarmed people? How could the ardent hope of a young patriot be chilled, when told that he was to support and defend his country's flag, and not to commit rapine and murder? What high-toned gentleman would not feel, the very instant you convinced him that such acts were to be allowed in the army, that it was no place for him? It would be to him an inducement to enter the army to believe that it was to be governed by considerations of honor and morality, and propriety of demeanor, wherever it went, and that he was to be with men who would not tarnish the fame of his country—men who would not commit acts unworthy of a gentleman and an honest man. These are my views of the feelings of the veteran and of the young patriot, and I find nothing in these extracts either to offend the one or to chill the ardor of the other.

The Senator read another extract:

"One company of Texas foot volunteers, which has rendered excellent service in the campaign, is now on the march to Camargo, there to be mustered out of service."

In commending the troops in the general order, no regiment had been mentioned. The mounted regiments of Texas had been noticed and commended in the order for their discharge; but this was the first time that these men of the foot company had been specially noticed. If the Senator chooses to torture it into injustice because a foot company is commended which had not before been noticed, while the mounted regiments were not again mentioned in connection with it, though they had before been commended, I will leave it for him to do so, but will first tell him that the foot company deserved special commendation, not only for the service in Monterey, but for the circumstances connected with its being there. It went mainly from the State of Mississippi. I know how it got there. Though it fought in the army under the standard of Texas, it was raised chiefly in the State of Mississippi, and in the county adjoining that in which I reside. Unable to get into the service from Mississippi, they went to Louisiana; unable to get into the service in Louisiana, they went to Texas. They there served to make up the complement of that one foot regiment which Texas furnished; and when that regiment declined to remain in service at Camargo, that one company offered their services, were accepted, and performed duties in the siege and attack on Monterey for which they were commended.

And here, sir, we touch the spring of the Senator's declamation, which makes him so prompt to notice any commendation of that single company, although the whole of the Texan mounted regiments had been commended. The Senator repeats in his first and in his second speech that the Texans had command of the city and had possession of all its fastnesses—that they had taken the heights and the Bishop's palace and the plaza, and that they with difficulty could be restrained from destroying the town.

Now, sir, the main battle in the storming of Monterey, as you sir, [Mr. SHIELDS in the chair] well know, was fought at the east end of the town. There their great defences were erected. When General Taylor approached the town and reconnoitered, his observations, and that military genius which won for him the fame which he acquired, and which gave him the confidence of the army he led, proved to him the great advantage which would result from making a flank movement, turning the position of the enemy upon the other side of the town, attacking it the same time upon both extremities, and cutting off the communication with Saltillo. He ordered that gallant soldier, Major Mansfield, of the engineers, to make a reconnoisance, which was done under the enemy's guns, and reported, with a map of the route and positions. Upon that report he ordered a division of tried troops, under command of that able soldier, General Worth, to take their position and attack the enemy on the heights. But the hard work, sir, was at the other end of the town—there their principal field fortifications were erected. They flanked each other according to the well-known rules of war; and if these should be taken it was but to encounter the stone walls of the massive houses on each side of the streets, and the barriers across them. There, sir, was the heart of the battle. These were men to do deeds of valor, and that was the place to which the old chief went himself. He always went where hardest blows were to be given and received.

Now, sir, in the battles of Monterey there were about five hundred men lost, counting the killed, wounded, and missing. Of those five hundred casualties four hundred occurred at the east end of the town and on the first day of the battle. And at the east end of the town, and on the first day of the battle, how many Texans do you suppose were engaged? Just one, sir—and he the late Colonel Johnston, of the foot, who, as inspector general, served in General Butler's division. The Texans were not there, because that was not the post assigned them. They would have been there if they had been ordered, and would have behaved themselves no doubt like the rest of the men. Of that there is no question in my mind. They were on duty at their posts— places far less dangerous than that. It was in that first day's

hard conflict, where, without a battery train, and under fire
of that new citadel which commanded the whole plain, and
under command of three works well garnished with artillery,
and flanking each other, the volunteers of the army, and a very
small part of the regulars, stormed the enemy's advanced works,
and drove them into the interior of the town. It was that first
day's hard fighting which subsequently compelled them to concentrate on the plaza; and it was not till after that, on the third
day, when these forces were concentrated in the town, that the
Texans were dismounted, and, serving on foot, entered it with
other troops. Then, sir, on the third day, one of the Texan
regiments upon the west end and the other at the east end, performed good service in the town. That regiment which came
from the red lands of Texas entered the town with the Mississippi regiment, and the two regiments struggled together
throughout the day, side by side, advancing alternately upon
one side of the street and the other, scaling the walls, and
climbing houses. With fraternal feeling and generous rivalry,
they fought together; and there were the Texans, the only Texans, who ever saw the plaza before the capitulation. I well remember, Mr. President, the gallantry of those Texans on that
day. I feel for them now an attachment which they understand,
and which they well know would never permit me to detract in
any degree from their fame. Ready for every adventure—
prompt, even reckless in the presence of danger—they bore
themselves through all the dangers of the day; and with the
Mississippi regiment they occupied a house from which they
saw one corner of the plaza, but they looked over a Mexican barricade to see it. They were the only troops that ever saw it
before the capitulation. Now, sir, when the order was received to withdraw from that point, to vacate the town, because the General had received notice of a desire for capitulation on the part of the enemy, they felt, as the Senator from
Maryland said very justly the other day, that there was greater
danger in returning than in maintaining their position. More
than this: their minds had been intent on retaining their present
position or advancing. They and the Mississippians had constructed a species of hurdle, under cover of which they expected
to pass the barrier of the enemy which commanded the street,
and to gain a position from which they could fire into the plaza.
They were intent upon their object, and unwilling to retire.
They knew the danger of retiring, it was true. But in the
speech of the Senator from Maryland, if it was intended to say
that they did not wish to retire, because they feared the danger

of retiring, he did them less than justice. They had gained a strong place, and they wanted to advance. We all wanted to advance, and believed we saw speedy success. When the act of retiring commenced, it was quite as critical as the advance had been. The support of the troops in the rear had been withdrawn —the general in command of that division having supposed that we of the advance were retiring also. Under these circumstances, every street was swept by the fire of the Mexicans, as these Texans and Mississippians retired across them. This was the service on which any claim to taking the plaza must rest; it was participated in by Colonel Wood's regiment—Major General Henderson, an old soldier, tried and true, commanding in person. None who were there will ever deny to them one particle of that praise which has been accorded to them, and they, like ourselves, will laugh at the extravagant claim which the Senator has set up for them.

But the Senator was struck with surprise at the employment of these Texans to garrison Laredo, when they had behaved so badly; and from the purpose of their employment he drew the argument that the General in the field had one boundary for Texas, and the President of the United States had another. Now, sir, I can very readily understand such a case. I can very well understand how, as the President, acting on his own convictions, he should pursue a different policy from that of the General in the field, acting under orders, which required him to consider the Rio Grande the boundary of Texas. We all recollect the extensive correspondence, the explicit orders which he received to consider the Rio Grande the boundary; after which he advanced to the Rio Grande. In this order, which directed General Lamar to hold possession of Laredo, it was announced as a purpose to protect the Texans from Indian incursions, and to facilitate the extension of the jurisdiction of Texas to the Rio Grande. Such were the orders and duties of the General, and he was carrying them out in his instructions to Lamar. He was incurring a responsibility in employing Texans without being so authorized. And on this question, as he had done before, he took the hazard of employing Texans without having received authority from the War Department. The other case was, when he mustered in the mounted regiment for a second tour of three months; while all other volunteers were refused for less than a year, under a law which specified that term. When he did so he complimented them in advance of service by a confidence in their efficiency which formed the justification of his act.

He stated his anxiety to have these mounted troops—his

necessity for them; and, under that necessity, he took the responsibility of mustering them in under conditions which were denied to all the other States by the War Department. Sir, it was deemed advisable to station a small garrison at Laredo, and he preferred men who fought at Monterey, to be placed under command of a soldier he had seen tried. Therefore, General Lamar was authorized to recruit a company from the men who had served under Hays and Wood, and to proceed to the frontiers of Texas. Sir, whenever a general of the army of the United States shall take upon himself such a heavy responsibility as this, for the benefit of the State of Mississippi—whenever a general of the army of the United States shall incur such hazard as this to protect the frontier of the State of Mississippi—may my tongue be paralyzed before it speaks in his defamation! Others have different rules by which to measure their gratitude for services done. I have no wish to prescribe for them a standard, but I have a right to speak for myself.

Then, Mr. President, to follow the Senator in his main points—for I will not take up the details—he refers to a letter in which the commanding general said he had mustered in the company of Captain Baylor, and in that letter mentioned that he had sent Major Chevallie's battalion from Monterey to Saltillo, and said again, what he and many other officers had previously noticed, that outrages were committed upon the peaceful inhabitants of Mexico. He mentions, too, the change in the character of those troops which he had mustered in for the war over those which had been mustered in for a year. He speaks of the discipline of those mustered in for the war, and speaks of it favorably. He says: "Of the infantry I have had little or no complaint." He does not say he makes no complaint, but that he had little or no complaint. "The mounted men of Texas have scarcely made an expedition without unwarrantably killing a Mexican." Now, sir, all the tirade into which the Senator breaks out when he says "What an atrocity to kill a Mexican!"—all this is answered by the word unwarrantably, which precedes it. That indicated the nature of the killing—the killing of peaceful, unarmed people.

Then the Senator talks as though he had taken an attitude against which no man could ever offer resistance. How does it happen that these men, so wanton and outrageous "that the commanding general could not control them in the face of a large army, were sent to Saltillo, where there was none to control and restrain them from outrages?" I will tell you how it was. At Monterey, which was more an interior post, there were five or six hundred men—a wide spread, thickly-settled country, where temptations to plunder and outrage were presented in every direction. At Saltillo, General Wood commanded a division of more than two thousand men, who were stationed in a country sparsely settled, and where the inhabitants had less claim upon our protection, and where, the neighborhood being more infested by robber bands, the people had been to a greater extent driven in to the limits of the town, and the chances were greater that if the soldiers killed a Mexican they would kill some one of a party of robbers. It was, then, not as stated, but that they were sent into the presence of a large force—into a country where, if they committed irregularities, they would probably be fewer, and could be better restrained. It is known to all who hear me that, even after hostilities ceased—after the towns were in possession of our troops—the robber bands hung about that district, and attacked individuals who wandered too far from the chain of sentinels. They committed trespasses upon those peaceful inhabitants who had furnished supplies; and against these it was necessary to send out expeditions of mounted men. Then, sir, it was a transfer to a place where they could not do so much harm, and might do more good. There is the answer. Nor am I compelled to stop there. The Texans themselves condemned the atrocities committed by some of their countrymen, and a company of them, as I understand, were refused companionship by this battalion, and were, by force of moral influence, compelled to withdraw. I have no wish to dwell on cases, and have not charged my memory with them; but I say to the Senator, go to any Texan, brave and honorable, as many are known to him to be, who served then and there, and ask him about the facts: I doubt not he will tell him that the reports, if too general, nevertheless were tempered to the last degree.

The Senator the other day referred to one of these brave soldiers who served in that particular battalion, and who is now in this ctiy. I do not know that the Senator knew all the points which he might gain in his reference. Perhaps he was not aware that that gentleman was a publisher of a newspaper after General Taylor entered Matamoros; and in that position he was induced to take notice of him rather harshly. But, sir, that gentleman, gallant as he always was—dashing, daring, unmanageable to some extent—after his press was broken up, became a soldier. Ask him, as a soldier, whether he ever received anything but justice from General Taylor. Ask him whether he received anything but kindness and consideration when he approached him. Ask him whether he will indorse any of the charges which the Senator from Texas made. I think I know him well enough to anticipate his answer.

But the Senator finds in this letter a request to the effect that no more troops may be sent from Texas, and upon this he breaks out again into rapturous declamation. Now, sir, it was known that no more troops, except mounted troops, were expected from Texas; if more were drawn that they would be mounted men; and, taken in connection with this known fact, it meant no more than that General Taylor wanted no more volunteer cavalry. If I should ever have the fortune to command an army, or, what is much more probable, if you, Mr. President, [Mr. SHIELDS,] should ever be placed in that responsible situation, our experience in Mexico would tell us that we wanted none but regular cavalry—no irregular mounted men of any kind.

Then, Mr. President, passing over that—of which perhaps I should not have taken so much notice—the senator introduces the gallant, lamented Walker, who, he says, was mainly instrumental in saving the army at Palo Alto. Now, sir, he was a very good officer. He performed rather a desperate adventure in bearing an express to Fort Brown, when the troops had marched to Point Isabel; but I never before heard that any event resulted from that express which would not have occurred if it had been captured. That express, so far as I know anything of it, was to inform the garrison of Fort Brown that the troops at Point Isabel, were to return as soon as they could. They would have held out if they had not heard from them, and if they had not returned for a period much longer than elapsed. They never would have surrendered, had they known that it would have been a month before the troops would arrive. And, sir, this very express was guarded by Captain May, with some of his dragoons, who went within sight of Fort Brown, passing the camp of the enemy. He there waited for the express men to return, and delayed so long that he was compelled to pass the enemy's camp, in returning, by day-light; and the delay came very near doing an immense amount of harm, in cutting off a portion of the cavalry force, already very small.

Then, sir, the Senator from Texas introduced another, a highly meritorious, probably more distinguished soldier from Texas—Captain McCullough—a man to whom we all accord high qualities as a partisan officer, and credit for valuable services wherever employed. He was highly esteemed by all portions of the army. But for Captain McCullough he claims the fact of the defence being made at Buena Vista. The Senator says: "Instead of saying in that report that Captain McCullough gave information at Encarnacion which saved the army, he merely remarks that he was of great service on that occasion.'' Yes, sir, it was McCullough who reconnoitered the enemy's camp, and gave the first information of the advance of Santa Anna; and this enabled our troops to fall back from Agua Nueva to Buena Vista, where a gallant defence was made. It was very true McCullough was detached to reconnoitre the advance of the Mexicans at Encarnacion, and reported the fact. It was a fact that he saw a body of Mexicans there, but a fact which in itself was worth so little that it was necessary to make another reconnoissance, and the next one was made two-fold. Colonel May reconnoitered in the direction of Hedionda, McCullough in that of Encarnacion. Colonel May met the enemy by a for- tuitous advance of a portion of his reconnoitering party, and it was necessary for them to return by different routes. Colonel May came in during the night, and reported the presence of a large force at Hedionda. His lieutenant came in the next morning, and reported the direction of another encampment. This, sir, was the reconnoissance which compelled us to fall back on Buena Vista. Had it been known there that Santa Anna would come from Encarnarcion with his whole force through the pass of Carnero, General Taylor would probably, with his tents standing, have fought the battle on that field, and have beaten them more entirely, if possible, than at Buena Vista. They would have been compelled to lay down their arms, and beg for water, of which they could obtain none short of eighteen miles in their rear. But, sir, the fact being known that there were two passes in his rear, which rendered it probable, from the report of Colonel May, that if he stood where he was the Mexican army would turn his position, and take the whole of his supplies at Saltillo, compelling him to fight the enemy in position, perhaps at the very ground he had himself selected for defence, it became necessary, to avoid this contin- gency, that he should fall back.

I dislike, Mr. President, to speak as an eyewitness, and yet I cannot tell the whole of this transaction without speaking of it as such.

The morning that Colonel May came in with the report of his observation, there was among the troops some speculation and much feeling against falling back. I well remember that the regiment that I had the honor of commanding was then under arms for inspection. I was then ordered to strike my tents, and hold myself in readiness to march to Buena Vista that morn- ing. We hoped that Captain McCullough would bring in some news. We were afraid, however, after the time passed when he was expected, that he was lost; for we well knew that he was as daring as he was skillful, and, though we had great confidence in his resources, we had great fear that he had made his reconnoissance too closely and lost his life. Before his return the movement to the rear was made. This service and the other were fully recognized in the reports of Palo Alto and Buena Vista. The Texans are spoken of there, not as having won the battle, not as having decided the fate of the army, not as having instructed General Taylor in the art of war, but as having done their duty, and done it well. That was the only commendation that he gave to those who did most. It is from such material as this that the Senator has built his fabric of prejudice against the State of Texas. If, sir, some Senator from another State had undertaken to prove that Texas was treated with special consideration and favoritism, it would have been much better done. He would at least have had the opportunity to show that, while the Louisiana troops were discharged because they would not enter the term of reëngagement required by the act of Congress—that is to say, for one year—the Texan troops were received with the privilege of being mustered out at the end of three months. They might have pointed out the arrangement of Camargo, where permission was freely given to the Texan infantry to advance to Monterey, if they would reëngage. From any other State this charge could have come better. It would not have been true from any. The answer is ready for each. But it would have been more fully sustained from any other. The report and correspondence fully show that due justice was given to the troops that served in battle; and it was given in that brief, positive style that was his own. He never dealt in superlatives or superfluities, but in brief, positive, and pointed language, and gave to each the credit that was his due, and condemned in all the irregularities which they committed. It was not, as the Senator's research seems to have induced him to suppose, that Texas alone received condemnation for breach of orders and good conduct. In harsher terms than were ever bestowed upon the troops of Texas, the troops of Arkansas were censured in the very letter from which he quoted of June 16, 1847, which the Senator quoted to show how bitter the General was against the Texans. That letter referred to everybody else but the troops of Texas; it referred to the twelve-months' men —those who had just been mustered out. He said that the peaceful inhabitants of the villages along the road complained of the outrages of these returning volunteers. That the complaint

was made and the outrages were committed, I have no more doubt
of the one than of the other. The Mississippi regiment went
down at the same time, and was the same character of troops
described in the letter. But I have never "winced" under
that letter, because my "withers were unwrung." I have never
felt that it had any application to the Mississippi troops, and
therefore I have felt nothing, and had nothing to say about it.
Let any Texan, approved at home and approved abroad, be
consulted by the Senator from Texas on this point, and he will,
I think, find that he will agree with me mainly in what I have
said. On no important point do I believe there would be any
difference. Go to those who served under him in battle, where
his form, like the white plume of Henry, was a guide to point
the bravest to the hottest of the fight—to those who received his
cheerful, unaffected greeting, whenever they approached him—
go to him whose private affairs led him to seek a counsellor in
his general; or further still, go to the wounded man who received
his care, and ask him whether pride, or selfishness, or coldness
was in his heart, and you will receive from each and all the
same answer—No! The renown of his public career, the fame
that he gained in battle, was a column for the public admiration, more perishable, less desirable, than that impression which
was made in the hearts of those who knew him. It was his sterling private virtues that made every soldier he commanded his
friend; it was this which, combined with confidence in his military skill, gave him that power to lead his thousands on where
thousands bleed.

It was this that always made his subordinates ready to serve
him, and never willing to leave him. It was this beautiful trait
in his character which caused him to scorn all those whose want
of morality led them to commit aggressions upon the unarmed
and defenceless. It was this which caused the pride of his
triumphant followers to mingle with the gratitude of the people
he conquered. It was this which caused the victorious shout to be
mingled with the blessings of the downtrodden, whom he raised,
the defenceless, whom he protected, and brought leaves beside
the laurel to hide the cypress of his triumphal arch. His character may be very briefly stated; just, sincere, resolute, true
to his friends, charitable to his enemies, and just to all men,
save where benevolence turned justice aside. Of all the accusations that could be thrown upon any man none could be more
unfounded than that which is now made against him—the man
whose eagle eye shone through the smoke of battle, yet would

feel a mother's softness over it creep when he looked upon a wounded comrade.

When the Senator reiteratedly charges him with prejudice against a State, it but shows how little he understood his character. So far from being well founded, I can say, if I ever knew a man who was entirely above sectionality, he was one. To this his education conduced; he had grown up in the army, and served his country in every portion of it. His fame was identified with his whole country, and his affections were as broad as his whole country. I never heard a sectional remark made to him that it was not checked or rebuked, as it might deserve one or the other. How could it be supposed that a State for which he had taken such high responsibility, to secure the volunteers of which he had incurred still higher responsibility—the most helpless State in the Union, and therefore, from his known character, the one with which he would be most prone to side would, through every portion of its representatives, have spoken thus of him?

But the Senator, having run over all these private traits, then called in question his military endowments. He said that the battalions fell at Monterey; and he would not say how they were disposed—he spares criticism on General Taylor, whose movements are said to have been pronounced above criticism by the first soldier of Europe. He is over-kind. Criticism is defied. But I hope the Senator will learn the localities of the town first. Then let him try it at any point, from the commencement of the siege to the close of the capitulation. All criticism is equally defied of his more remarkable battles—those of Palo Alto and Resaca de la Palma; those battles which set upon our armies the seal of invincibility, and which led the way —yes, made the future victories a consequence. Or, if he choose, he may go to the last, that was filled with so many crises, so important in its results; fought against such numerical odds without an erroneous order, either as to position or time. So fortuitous was every event in that remarkable contest, that I hold it surpassed human wisdom, and must be assigned to the superintending care of Providence.

It has taken longer to explain some of the points to which I felt bound to refer than I expected. I therefore will omit a great number of them, to which I had intended to refer. Imperfectly I have discharged a duty which I felt it incumbent on me to perform. If I had died last night, it would have caused me to die with a feeling of regret that I had left it undone. I have done it as a simple duty, not from any unkindness to the

Senator, far less from any disposition to detract from or depreciate in any degree the soldiers of Texas. But it was that I might do justice to many of my comrades, whose dust now mingles with the earth upon which they fought—that I might not seem to leave unredressed the wrongs of the buried dead. I have endeavored to suppress all personal feeling. It is true that sorrow sharpens memory, and that many deeds of noblest self-sacrifice, many tender associations, rise vividly before me. The rude assault on my old commander, whose deeds as a soldier were a thing apart from his political life, has pointed the defence especially to that assault. I remember the purity of his character, his vast and varied resources, which made him always the best-informed man in his camp of all which was passing about him. I remember the immense responsibility under which he acted at the battle of Buena Vista, where he was recommended by his senior general to retire to Monterey. He then found himself with a handful of men, opposed to twenty-one thousand veterans marshalled against him. The struggle between the duties of the soldier, what might be the feelings of the soldier, and the sympathies of the man, were terrible. Around him stood those whose lives were in his charge, whose mothers, fathers, and children would look to him for their return—those there who had shared his fortunes on other fields—some who were eager for the combat, without knowing how direful it would be—immediately about him those loving and beloved, with such confidence in their commander that they but waited his beck and will to do and dare. On him, and on him alone, rested the responsibility of meeting the crisis. It was in his power to avoid it by retiring to Monterey, there to be invested and captured, and then sheltering himself under his instructions. He would not do it, but cast all upon the die to maintain his country's honor, and save his country's flag from trailing in the dust of the enemy he had so often beaten, or close the conqueror's career as became the soldier. His purpose never wavered—his determination never faltered; his country's honor, his country's flag to triumph, or to find an honorable grave, was the only alternative presented. Under these circumstances, on the morning of the 23d, that glorious but bloody conflict commenced. It won for him a chaplet that it would be a disgrace for an American to mutilate, and which it were an idle attempt to adorn. I leave it to a grateful country, conscious of his services, and with a discrimination not to be confounded by the assertions of any, however high in position. It is just to myself and the Senator from Texas for me to say, that I have been mainly induced, under such circumstances, to notice his remarks, because of the value they receive from his own historical character—the fact that, with such value attached, they are to go on the congressional record of the country, and because of the high position he holds, and from which he scatters these opinions over the land.

Remarks of Jefferson Davis on Bill to admit California Aug. 6, 1850.

Mr. DAVIS, of Mississippi. Mr. President, it seems to me to be in very bad taste, not to say very bad judgment, at the very beginning of a question, to commence sitting it out, when the subject has scarcely been entered upon, and an amendment is now before the Senate, and under debate, of which not one Senator except the mover can have any information, and when the measure is in itself a new one so far as debate in the Senate goes, for it now for the first time stands alone; and it is well known that Senators are to be found opposing it who sustained it when united with other measures. I say that under the circumstances, I consider it ill-judged in the majority to be pressing it through on the third day of its consideration. There is something ominous in it. It is part of the early indications of what the minority in this Government is to expect, and it may very well excite the feelings of that minority, and some disposition to show the majority who it is that will have to wait. I am not one of those who, on this occasion, or any other, are disposed to test that great matter who can sit the longest at night; and if these be the qualities which a Senator should possess, instead of taking the oldest and wisest men in the country to sit in this Chamber, the country had better get young and stout men of unbroken constitutions. They could sit here more hours undoubtedly. The whole practice is decidedly wrong. It is lowering the tone and standing of the body, and it is an extreme remedy, only properly to be resorted to when the measure has been fully discussed, and has reached a point where the minority strive only for delay. It is not to be resorted to when amendments are offered in good faith, and when several gentlemen deliberately state to the Senate that he who addresses it not only addresses the Senate in good faith, but with the announcement that his notes being but partially prepared, he can address it with more effect and in less time to-morrow. I do think there should have been no opposition to an adjournment under the circumstances. I propose to sit here certainly as long as the Senate requires, and it may be that those who are now pressing us so unreasonably to a night session, may become weary of it sooner than those who are thus pressed. Upon them, whatever consequences from fatigue and over-exertion may fall upon the Senate, will rest the responsibility. If, sir, their purpose was to feed the present excitement of the country, and to disturb the fraternity which should exist among members of the body, and which, unhappily, is ceasing, they could not have taken a more direct plan than that which they have adopted—calling the yeas and nays upon every petty motion—refusing to adjourn under every remonstrance—and refusing to go into executive session when assured that the public business requires it. It is known to everybody that a large amount of executive business is collected, and that we have wasted time in fruitless and exciting discussions. This body has other duties to perform besides those which are done in open session, and let each Senator remember how little this session we have attended to these other duties. These are my views.

Remarks of Jefferson Davis on the Texas Boundary, Aug. 9, 1850.

Mr. DAVIS, of Mississippi. Mr. President, I feel constrained to take a very different course from that of either of my friends who have last addressed the Senate. I shall follow the dictates of my own conscience and my own sense of right; and believing, as I do, that this amendment expresses what is true, I shall vote for it. They agree with me as to the fact, but vote against it. Such seems to be the difference between us. This amendment but asserts that for which we have been for years contending—that which the Government has constantly maintained from the beginning of this question down to a very recent period, when the last message was received from the President of the United States. Any attempt now to throw doubt upon the title of Texas by the Government of the United States is untrue to their history and faithless to Texas. Any attempt now to rob Texas of one acre of her soil, under the pretence that she does not own it, is to take advantage of an exercise of authority which the United States first usurped and afterwards held by the permission of Texas, and with the express disclaimer that it was not to rob her of her right.

On January 4, 1847, the then Governor of Texas, General Henderson, learning that the Government of the United States was about to establish a territorial government at Santa Fé, addressed a letter to the Secretary of State of the United States, from which I will read a single sentence:

"Inasmuch as it is not convenient for the State at this time to exercise jurisdiction over Santa Fé, I presume no objection will be made on the part of the government of the State of Texas to the establishment of a territorial government over that country by the United States, provided it is done with the *express* admission on their part that the State of Texas is entitled to the soil and jurisdiction over the same, and may exercise her right whenever she regards it expedient.

"I remain, with very high regard, your most obedient servant,

J. PINCKNEY HENDERSON.

"Hon. JAMES BUCHANAN,
    "Secretary of State."

The then Secretary of State, the medium of Executive correspondence, replied (February 12th, 1847) to this letter; and from it I will read a paragraph also:

"In that you have already perceived that New Mexico is at present in the temporary occupation of the troops of the United States, and the government over it is military in its character. It is merely such a government as must exist, under the laws of nations and of war, to preserve order and protect the rights of the inhabitants, and will cease on the conclusion of a treaty of peace with Mexico. Nothing, therefore, can be more certain than that this temporary government, resulting from necessity, can never injuriously affect the right which the President believes to be justly asserted by Texas to the whole territory on this side of the Rio Grande, whenever the Mexican claim to it shall have been extinguished by treaty. But this is a subject which more properly belongs to the legislative than to the executive branch of the Government.

"I am, &c.,   JAMES BUCHANAN.

"To his Excellency J. PINCKNEY HENDERSON,
    "Governor of Texas, Austin."

When the late Executive was called on, during the present session of Congress, in relation to this subject, he referred in his reply to the letter of Mr. Buchanan, and he there sustains the opinion contained in that letter. He remarks as follows:

"I have not been informed of any acts of interference by the military forces stationed at Santa Fé with the judicial authority of Texas, established or sought to be established there.

I have received no communication from the Governor of Texas on any of the matters referred to in the resolution; and I concur in the opinion expressed by my predecessor, in the letter addressed by the late Secretary of State to the Governor of Texas, on the 12th day of February, 1847, that the boundary between the State of Texas and the Territory of New Mexico 'is a subject which more properly belongs to the legislative than to the executive branch of the Government.'   Z. TAYLOR.

"WASHINGTON, January 30, 1850."

These facts were reaffirmed in two subsequent messages, and, under the opinion thus expressed, the exercise of any authority by officers commanding in the district of Santa Fé was prevented from acquiring or maturing any title.

I heard, with great surprise and equal regret, the opinions contained in the message of President Fillmore on Texan affairs, and in the letter of his Secretary of State, which accompanied it, read at that table the other day. I was surprised that a letter which had been addressed to an officer of the army about to join his regiment at Santa Fé, and to serve under the officer then stationed there, and exercising civil and military authority, should be considered an order for the establishment of a territorial government at Santa Fé. It was no order, and not even a letter, to the military governor of Santa Fé. The spirit of that message is, from beginning to end, an abandonment of the whole course of this Government towards Texas, changing front absolutely; and it is one of the highest federal documents ever promulgated in the United States. It assumes to settle that which all his predecessors had claimed to be a legislative question—to settle it without commissioners, without postponing it to a judicial tribunal, or any arbitration. It calls for the immediate action of Congress; in default of which we are to understand the Executive will determine the balance by throwing the sword of the United States into the scale.

In this state of things, we are now told by southern Senators that the proposition of the Senator from Virginia, which but asserts what previous Administrations have heretofore acknowledged—which but asserts that which the whole people of the United States affirmed in the war with Mexico—that that resolution must be opposed, because it cannot be adopted. Sir, this has been the doctrine which has made southern Senators retire from the assertion of southern rights, and driven from us those of our northern friends who would most willingly have supported us. After southern men have refused to support a measure of southern right, how can they expect support from northern men? It is only when the South is united, and when she speaks in terms which show at least that one section of the Union requires this measure, that the northern men can justify themselves for departing from the policy which their constituents have indicated, and for granting to the South more than they otherwise would concede. Surely we cannot get this, nor anything else, if we do not assert our rights and maintain them.

Mr. President, it was this same course which divided southern men when the late compromise bill was before the Senate. It was that constant endeavor on the part of southern men to find what they could get, rather than that which they should have; that species of canvassing everywhere else except within a man's own judgment to find the rule of his conduct; that species of canvassing which I regret to see others adopt, and which for myself I can never resort to. That compromise bill was supported by southern men, not because it was all to which they were entitled, but because it was all we could get. We who adopted a different principle, and under its guidance opposed the so-called compromise bill lately rejected by the Senate, have been referred to as having acted with Abolitionists. When the friends of that measure spoke under the excitement of disappointment, whilst their anguish was fresh, that allowance was made which was due to an outbreak of feeling. But when the plaint is continued beyond a reasonable limit, and accusations are renewed which, always unfounded in truth, should have ceased if they were not withdrawn after the excitement of the occasion had passed away, it becomes proper to answer by the facts and the history of the case. What was the position of southern men who opposed that bill? We stood upon the convictions of our duty and the rights of our constituents. We met, conferred together, and pursued that course which to us seemed best calculated to sustain these rights; and we, with a portion of the northern Senators, defeated the bill. What was the position of those southern men who advocated the bill? They met and held consultations out of the Senate with northern Senators whose opposition to slavery was practically the same as that of those who voted with us. The difference, then, was this: We, without holding private conferences, voted in the Senate with those northern Senators who chose to vote with us. They consulted in secret conclave with other northern Senators, occupying, on the only question at issue—the rights of the slaveholding States in the Territories— the same ground, and then voted with them in the Senate. To illustrate, I ask what was the difference in the creed of the

Senator from Maine, who sits on my left, [Mr. BRADBURY,] and that of the other Senator from Maine, [Mr. HAMLIN]? One was taken into the association of the "omnibus," and became a leading member. He it was who came forward with an amendment to resuscitate the measure when it seemed to be in *extremis*. The other steadily opposed it. The other, therefore, I suppose, is among the persons called abolitionists. What is the difference between them on any question relating to slavery? Is there any? I have never seen the evidence of it in their votes. And what is the difference between the Senator from New Hampshire, who sits before me, [Mr. NORRIS,] and the one who sits upon the other side of the Chamber, [Mr. HALE]? One is called an Abolitionist; the other, perhaps, is not. But upon every vote we have had touching the slavery question, I should like to see the difference pointed out. Which of them is willing to allow the South to extend the institution of slavery into any territory of the United States? Which of them is willing to recognize the right of the South to introduce slave property into the recently-acquired territory. Neither of them; and if he who sits upon the other side of the Chamber is more vehement in anti-slavery declamation, he is also more good-natured in his manner. The difference is one which I have not been able to estimate as at all important to the South. What, then, is the value of all this? Where is the essential distinction between the classes? On whose shoulders does the heaviest responsibility rest, if any attach, to acting with northern Senators on the so-called compromise bill—the southern Senators who opposed or those who supported it? We held no caucus with them; we acted on our own judgment. We had meetings, so far as we had them, out of the Senate, with southern Senators alone; and we voted here with whomsoever chose to vote with us.

I had hoped that when that bill which had drawn so many southern men to its support was dead, we should have no more dissension in our own camp—that we should have quiet from that time onward; and I regret the indication now given, that upon this proposition, upon which the South has stood with unusual unanimity from the beginning, a proposition which recognizes the Rio Grande as the boundary of Texas, the same division which has heretofore existed reappears. One would suppose from the argument that that proposition rested for its authority upon the Senator from Virginia alone, instead of beginning, as it did, from the date of the annexation; instead of being sustained as a principle in every southern State; instead of being the basis on which we went to war with Mexico, and the distinctly recognized feature of the treaty by which the war was closed; instead of being the position sustained and emphatically avowed by the late southern convention at Nashville.

I shall not, for one, because there is a majority against me, abandon the position which I have maintained from the beginning of the question. I shall not, from a dread of being in the minority, surrender what I think is the right of Texas and the right of the South. I will not tarnish the fair fame of my country by presenting and maintaining for the United States against Texas a claim for boundary, the assertion of which by Mexico led us into a war with that Republic. The United States so far as they extinguished any claim of Mexico to territory east of the Rio Grande, must have extinguished it for the benefit of Texas. Even if the United States in their own right had acquired all the claim that Mexico had, it could not be used by them against Texas. They would stand falsified before the world—disgraced by the assertion of such a claim against a State of the Union, in whose defence and for whose benefit they waged war with Mexico, and vindicated the territorial right it is now proposed to invalidate.

Mr. DAVIS, of Mississippi. Mr. President, I rise for very little other purpose than to say that I hope no Senator to whom I alluded considered me as calling him an Abolitionist. I called no Senator an Abolitionist. I spoke of northern Senators, and made a comparison, as to their creed, on the only point at issue connected with the rights and privileges of slave owners—between those northern Senators who voted for and those who voted against the compromise or adjustment bill, thus referring to those who were called Abolitionists. I called nobody such. I think it probable that if you will summon, one after another, every one of those so denominated, they will tell you they are not Abolitionists. They have a great many names at the North among those who hold the same opinions in relation to slavery. I doubt, very much, I repeat, whether there is one Senator in this hall who would call himself an Abolitionist.

I certainly never intended to say that any should be ashamed of holding counsel with a northern Senator, or with a Senator because he came from the North. On the other hand, I but stated what is the fact. Our conferences were among southern men who were in coincidence of opinion, and I wish it had been in my power to say that there was one northern man who had coincided with us. I should have rejoiced over it more than over many southern men. I should have hailed it as a harbinger of that good feeling, that appreciation of our institutions at the

North, of which I may state I have seen so little evidence during the present session. I certainly, Mr. President, in making what I held to be a distinction due to the position which I and some others had occupied, did not intend to go into the arraignment of northern Senators, still less those who acted with them. The arraignment had been made by others as against us. We had been, from time to time, referred to as acting with Abolitionists; and this morning I have stated briefly, in reply to such insinuations, what I believed to be the truth, the whole truth, and nothing but the truth.

Remarks of Jefferson Davis on the admission of California, Aug. 10, 1850.

Mr. DAVIS, of Mississippi. From the time my attention was first directed to the subject of the land in California and Oregon, I have hoped that whenever we reached the consideration of the subject, Congress would adopt a different course from that which has heretofore been applied to two or three of the Territories of the United States. I thought that the mountain character of the country, the large amount of mineral land known to exist there, increasing the ordinary difficulty of surveying with a chain and compass, and rendering it easier to survey by the geodetic method, clearly pointed out that mode as the one by which that portion of the United States should be surveyed. All of our map is founded on that land survey, which contains just that amount of error due to the difference between an oblate and spheroid and a plain. That is an error which increases as we go north, and will be very great on the northern part of California and Oregon. The method of granting donations of land has been on the supposition that it is to be laid out in square sections and towns, according to the ordinary mode. I make this statement, because I intended to introduce a new mode of surveying these lands; and I did hope that at some future day the same mode would be extended across to the Atlantic, so that we might have, what other countries have, a correct topographical map of the country we inhabit.

Mr. DAVIS, of Massachusetts. I wish to say, for one, that I am not prepared to vote upon this question at all, at present, and for this reason: These lands are not surveyed, and the country has not been explored. We all know that it is a country of extraordinary features. It has thus far developed itself as a region remarkable for its mineral wealth. It seems to me that this business of granting land should be postponed till this country has been explored, and we can understand a little better what we are doing when we make the grant. I think it is a matter that calls for the serious consideration of Congress. Some portions of the country are filled with valuable minerals to a remarkable extent, and some better knowledge of the general features and general character of the country ought to be possessed by us before we undertake to grant it away.

Mr. FOOTE. The donative proposition would be equally satisfactory to me, under any circumstances that can be imagined. I do not care how valuable or how widely opposed the character of the lands is. My own opinion is that the people of California are entitled to as much land as this amendment proposes to confer upon them; and I concur with the Senator from Missouri that it is by no means a liberal provision.

Mr. DAVIS, of Mississippi. I would inquire what number of sections the amendment proposes to embrace? Does it cover all after the sections relating to the judiciary?.

The PRESIDENT. It does; all of them.

Mr. DAVIS. I would then call the attention of my colleague to the last section, which contains a proviso, which I understood my colleague to explain to the Senator from Missouri as being a negative proposition in its character. I would rather, if it be a negative, that it should be struck out.

Mr. FOOTE. It is not a matter of great importance to me, but I believe, and I think I have good reason to believe, that it will tend to secure additional support to the amendment, on the principle that I have stated. I am anxious that the amendment should be adopted. I know that some members of this body, as well as of the House of Representatives, would be disinclined to vote for the amendment if they thought the effect would be to prevent the Senators and Representatives from California from taking their seats. With that object in view I have drawn the amendment so as to leave the matter precisely as it is, so that the qualifications of the members of each House will be decided upon in each House respectively.

Mr. DAVIS, of Mississippi. This seems to carry a conclusion somewhat in addition to any argument which has been given before for the admission of the Senators and Representatives to their seats. I have held, and stated before to the Senate, that the people of California had, in my opinion, no right to form a State government and send Senators and Representatives here until they had the consent of Congress. My objection is radical and covers both cases. I move to strike out that part which relates to the Senators and Representatives taking their seats.

Same bill Aug. 13, 1850.

Tuesday, *August 13, 1850.*

The Senate resumed the consideration of the bill. The question was on the passage of the bill.

Mr. DAVIS, of Mississippi. I do not propose, Mr. President, at this stage of the bill, and in the known temper of the Senate, to enter into any argument upon its merits or demerits. Although there is a wide field of facts not yet explored, it is not my purpose to enter upon it. I feel that it would be useless. More than that; I should fear to expose myself to an exhibition of that restlessness which has on this question marked the majority of the Senate, and which I do not wish to encounter. But I ask why, and among whom, is the spirit of impatience manifested? Does it proceed from a desire to provide a government for California? No, sir; the records deny that. This impatience is most exhibited by those who, at the last session of Congress, refused, unless with the slavery restriction, to unite with us to give the benefits of a territorial government to California; such a government as was then adapted to their condition; nay more, such a government as is best adapted to their condition now. Then, sir, among that class of Senators the great purpose of giving a territorial government to the people of California was held subordinate to the application of the Wilmot proviso to the bill. Then, and for that reason, Congress failed to give the protection to this people which they had a right to expect at the hands of a just Government, and which they had a right to demand under the treaty of peace with Mexico.

Now, sir, when the people inhabiting that Territory have formed a Constitution, one of the clauses of which prohibits the introduction of slaves, those who refused to give a government under the circustances just named, and, as we have a right to infer, for the reason stated, are now found most earnest in pressing upon us, in violation of all precedent, its admission as a State into the Union. Then are we not compelled to conclude that their policy, both then as now, was governed by the single desire to exclude slaveholders from introducing that species of property into any of the recent acquisitions from Mexico? Is that in accordance with the provision of the Constitution, which secures equal privileges and immunities to all the citizens of the several States of the Union? Is it in accordance with the principle of even-handed justice, if there had been no constitutional obligations? These acquisitions were made by the people of the whole United States, and we are bound to remember that those whom this bill proposes to exclude, contributed more than their fair proportion, both of blood and treasure, to obtain that territory. No, sir, the Constitution forbids; justice condemns the course which is pursued, and patriotism and reason frown indignantly upon it. Is it, then, a matter of surprise that we, the suffering party, have shown resentment and made determined opposition? Is it not rather a matter of surprise that that indignation which has blazed throughout the southern States should have been received with such calm indifference by the majority of Congress; that Congress has not only refused to listen, but has treated with scorn the appeal which has been made? Such, however, has been the history of this debate.

But if the motive be denied, then I ask, if not for the reason I have given, why are northern Senators pressing with such eagerness the admission of California? Is it to secure a benefit for their manufactures or navigation? No, sir. They know that when the inhabitants of California become a State they will be a people in favor of free trade, and that their policy will be to invite the shipping of the world, and secure for themselves the cheapest transportation. It is not, then, for purposes of their own interest that they seek her admission. Is it to preserve their political rights under the Constitution? No sir, Now they are in the majority, and they need no addition for such a purpose as that. Then we are forced to conclude that it is for the purpose of aggression upon the people of the South—that it is an exhibition of that spirit of a dominant party which regards neither the Constitution nor justice, nor the feelings of fraternity which bind them to us, but treads with destroying and relentless step on all considerations which should govern men, wise, just, and patriotic.

And this is the evidence of that love for the Union which is constantly presented to us as a reason why we should abandon the rights, why we should be recreant to the known will of our constituents, why we should disregard the duties we were delegated to perform, and submit to aggression such as freemen have never tamely borne. But, Mr. President, is this the way to avoid danger from the indignation which has been aroused; is this the way to avert the danger of disunion, if such danger exist? That indignation, and that danger, so far as it has been excited, is the offspring of injustice, and this is the maturing act of a series of measures which lead to one end—the total destruction of the equality of the States, and the overthrow of the rights of the southern section of the Union. We, sir, of the

South, are the equals of the North by compact, by inheritance, and the patriotic devotion and sacrifices by which the territory from which it is proposed to exclude us was acquired. And when such an outrage excites a manly remonstrance, instead of bringing with it a feeling of forbearance and a disposition to abstain and reflect, it is answered by the startling cry of disunion, disunion! What constitutes the crime of disunion?

This, sir, is a Union of sovereign States, under a compact which delegated certain powers to the General Government, and reserved all else to the States respectively or to the people. To the Union the South is as true now as in the day when our forefathers assisted to establish it; against that Union they have never by word or deed offered any opposition. They have never claimed from this Federal Government any peculiar advantages for themselves. They have never shrunk from any duty or sacrifice imposed by it, nor sought to deprive others of the benefits it was designed to confer. They have never spoken of that constitutional Union but in respectful language; they have never failed in aught which would secure to posterity the unincumbered enjoyment of that legacy which our fathers left us.

Those who endeavored to sap and undermine the Constitution on which that Union rests are disunionists in the most opprobrious understanding of that term; such being the crime of disunion, I ask by whom, and how is this spirit of disunion promoted? Not by those who maintain the Constitution from which the Union arose, and by adherence to which it has reached its present greatness; not those who refuse to surrender the principles which gave birth to the Union, and which are the soul of its existence; not those who claiming the equality to which they were born, declare that they will resist an odious, unconstitutional, and unjust discrimination against their rights. This, sir, is to maintain the Union by preserving the foundation on which it stands; and if it be sedition or treason to raise voice and hand against the miners who are working for its overthrow, against those who are seeking to build upon its ruins a new Union which rests not upon the Constitution for authority, but upon the dominant will of the majority, then my heart is filled with such sedition and treason, and the reproach which it brings is esteemed as an honor. But, sir, if gentlemen wish to preserve the constitutional Union, that Union to which I and those whom I represent are so ardently attached, I have to say the way is as easy and plain as the road to market. You have but to abstain from injustice, you have but to secure to each section and to all citizens the provisions of the Constitution under which the

Union was formed; you have but to leave in full operation the principles which preëxisted, created, and have blessed it. Then, sir, if any ruthless hand should be raised to destroy the temple of this Confederacy, with united hearts and ready arms the people will gather around it for its protection; then, sir, it would be indeed a Union of brethren, and not that forced Union which it is sought now to establish and maintain by coercing sovereign States at the point of the bayonet, and reducing the free spirit of the people to submission by the terror of marching armies. By virtue, by confidence, by the unpurchasable affection of the people, by adherence to fundamental principles, and under the direction of the letter of compact and Union, this Republic has grown to its present grandeur, has illustrated the blessings and taught to mankind the advantages of representative liberty. As a nation, it is, though yet in the freshness of youth, among the first Powers of the globe, and casts the shadow of its protection over its citizens, on whatever sea or shore, for commerce or adventure, they may wander. When we see a departure in the administration of the Government from the fundamental principles on which this Union was founded, and by adherence to which it has thus prospered, we have reason to believe the virtue and wisdom of our fathers have departed from the people, or that their agents are unworthy of those whom they represent.

We stand on the verge of an act which is to form an era in the history of our country. Now, for the first-time, we are about permanently to destroy the balance of power between the sections of the Union, by securing a majority to one, in both Houses of Congress; this, too, when sectional spirit is rife over the land, and when those who are to have the control in both Houses of Congress will also have the Executive power in their hands, and by unmistakable indications have shown a disposition to disregard that Constitution which made us equals in rights, privileges, and immunities. When that barrier for the protection of the minority is about to be obliterated, I feel we have reached the point at which the decline of our Government has commenced, the point at which the great restraints which have preserved it, the bonds which have held it together, are to be broken by a ruthless majority, when the next step may lead us to the point at which aggression will assume such a form as will require the minority to decide whether they will sink below the condition to which they were born, or maintain it by forcible resistance.

Such are the momentous consequences which are foreseen as possibly flowing from this event; nor are these forebodings, in any degree, reduced; or these injuries at all tempered by the spirit in which it is done. They are rather aggravated by the concurrent declarations which are made; the scoffing superiority assumed towards those who are your equals in every constitutional sense; the foretaste which has been given us of the arrogance of political supremacy. It is this which has served to create, and which has fully justified the extreme opposition exhibited by southern Senators. I was prepared to go to any possible limit in opposition to this measure, because I felt and feel that the fate of my country might depend upon it, and therefore, as a patriot, as one devoted to the Union, here as readily as elsewhere, I was and am ready to sacrifice myself in such a cause. It is not, therefore, for want of will, but for the want of power, that I have not offered further opposition than I have.

In that temper to which I have alluded, as manifested on this occasion, we are forewarned of the fate of the minority when the South becomes such permanently in both Houses of Congress. In that spirit of aggression and reckless disregard of the rights of the minority when the power is possessed to execute its will, I believe we may see, like the handwriting on the wall, the downfall of this Confederacy. The occasion, therefore, to my mind, is one which may well justify all the feeling which has been exhibited, and claims of the patriot whatever sacrifice may be demanded. For myself, actuated by such motives, and controlled by such opinions, I required nothing to prompt, nothing to justify, nothing to direct me to the opposition I have made. But, if I had needed any or all of these, they were at hand in the expressions of popular will, by primary meetings and legislative action. The Legislature of my State have instructed me to resist this bill for the admission of California, under the circumstances of the case, by all proper and honorable means. The same Legislature made an appropriation of money to enable the Governor to offer proper resistance to the Wilmot proviso, if it should be passed by Congress and approved by the President. And in this bill, as it is proposed, I see nothing in any essential degree differing from the Wilmot proviso. What matters it to me whether Congress has declared that within certain limits of the old territory of California slavery shall be prohibited, or whether Congress shall give validity to an act of an unauthorized people within that territory, and thus exclude us from it? If there be any difference, it would be in favor of the action of Congress; because the injustice and oppression would be the same—certainly no greater—without having added thereto the outrage of a revolutionary seizure of public domain, under the expectation of finding favor by declaring hostility against the extension of the limits of slave property; it would be the fraud or usurpation of an agent, by which we would be deprived, instead of the seizure of another subsequently sustained and justified by the agent.

But the effect of an act of Congress would be less permanent; it might be repealed, and might more probably than the provision of a State constitution, be reversed by the decision of the inhabitants of the Territory. It can bring no soothing to me to say the act is that of the people. There was no organized permanent body of persons, such as constitute a people. Those who acted but registered the well-known will of the majority of Congress on the subject of slave property; and if their unauthorized acts are approved, breathed into life by this Government, it will be because they have served its purpose in excluding the South from equal participation in the territory.

There is a great difference between the organized inhabitants of a Territory, a political community authorized by legislative action, and the assemblage, however large and respectable, of an unorganized mass of adventurers. The former could not, without the consent of the United States, erect a State out of the Territory of which they were the people, and unauthorized, assume to themselves sovereign power over it. But if this be doubtful, it cannot be claimed that, without any such organization, without any evidence as to numbers or qualifications, an unorganized band of adventurers can set at naught the sovereignty of the United States, convert the public domain to their own use, and claim therefrom the right to be admitted as a State into the Union; that goldhunters and fur-traders, fishermen or trappers, may rush on to newly-acquired domain, and for purposes general or special, temporary or permanent, appropriate the territory which belongs to the United States to their own exclusive benefit; or, as in this case peculiarly, to that of a particular section, with an insulting discrimination against one half of the people of the Confederacy to whom the territory belongs.

But the case presented to us is even worse than this. The people thus found as sojourners or adventurers on the territory were not themselves the prime movers in this matter. They were prompted to it. It is a fact, sir, which has come to my knowledge, that the military governor who succeeded after the peace of Queretaro sent out messengers to ascertain whether the people of California desired to have a civil instead of the existing military government; and that he received such an answer as caused him to refuse to issue the proclamation previously prepared. That the proclamation remained until his successor, who issued it, came into power, when, with a few additions and slight modifications, it was sent forth. There had been no material change in the state of the country. It is true that there was an additional influx of population, and an additional reason to suppose that a territorial government would not be provided for them; but the population was as unstable as before, and not much better prepared to support a State government. Under these circumstances, this governor sent out his proclamation, calling on the people to meet and hold a convention to form a constitution for their own government. The last sentence of the proclamation expressed the hope that it would be acceptable to the people. The paper itself bore internal evidence that it was not the action of the people, but the prompting suggestion of a military governor, claiming to exercise civil authority over them.

I say the case is worse than if the transient inhabitants should, at their own volition, claim to snatch the territory from the United States and appropriate it to themselves. It was not dignified by the impress of popular purpose. If the consequences which are likely to result from this movement were not so grave, we should look upon all the action which occurred anterior to the assembling of that convention, the manner in which the elections were conducted, and in which the ratification of the constitution was expressed, as a farce. In that series of letters, thought to be worthy of being incorporated into a book, written by Bayard Taylor, we are informed that while traveling in one district just before the election, he came near being seized on and elected to the convention *nolens volens*—like Teague O'Regan, the hero of Modern Chivalry. That which was intended as a satire on our popular elections might here have been verified.

I do not propose to detain the Senate by entering into evidence of that kind. These and graver facts are abundant, but I know it is useless to produce them. My purpose now, Mr. President, is to make a serious appeal to the Senate against the act which there is but little doubt they are about to perform. In the name of equality, of constitutional right, of peace, of fraternity, I call upon the majority to abstain. I utter no menace, I foretell no violence; now, as heretofore, I refuse to contemplate or speak of disunion as a remedy. But, sir, "in sorrow rather than anger," at the empty threats which have been made against us, I solemnly warn the majority that they do not look to the South as a field on which victories are to be won without cost, and where the emoluments of conquest are to be obtained without sacrifice. We, sir, are the descendants of those who united with the men of the North in the revolutionary struggle upon what was to them an abstract principle; we are the descendants of those who cast behind them considerations of safety and interest—who looked danger in the face, and united with your father because they were oppressed. Then, sir, unless it is believed that we are degenerate sons of our glorious sires, in that fact should be found a warning against presuming too far upon the loyalty which, by the sons as by their sires, has been exhibited to the Union. That loyalty is to the Union as established by the Constitution. Sir, they are not bound to the mere form that holds the States together. If I know their character, and have read their history with understanding, they would reject it as a worthless weed whenever the animating spirit of the Constitution shall have passed from the body.

Then, Senators, countrymen, brethren—by these, and by other appellations, if there be others more endearing and impressive than these, I call upon you to pause in the course which pressed by an intemperate zeal, you are pursuing, and warn you, lest blinded by the lust for sectional dominion, you plunge into an abyss in which will lie buried forever the glorious memories of the past, the equally glorious hopes of the future, and the present immeasurable happiness of our common country. It is not as one who threatens, nor as one who prepares for collision with his enemies, but as one who has a right to invoke your fraternal feeling, and to guard you against an error which will equally bear on us both; as one who has shared your hopes and your happiness, and is about to share your misfortunes, if misfortunes shall befall us; it is as an American citizen that I speak to an American Senate—it is in this character that I have ventured to warn you; it is with this feeling that I make my last solemn appeal.

Mr. CLEMENS. I must ask a few minutes of the time of the Senate to express my opinions on the subject now under consideration. I know, sir, that this bill is to pass; I know that anything I can say here will have no effect to prevent its passage; and, under these considerations, I had determined to content myself with giving a silent vote against it. Some of my friends, however, have this morning suggested that a few remarks from me might not be altogether out of place.

In obedience to their wishes, I propose to state, rather in the form of a protest than a speech the reasons why I object to the passage of this bill. Those reasons have been heretofore stated and argued at length by myself and others. I shall do nothing more to-day than recapitulate the main points, reserving for another time, and another theatre, any lengthened discussion of topics which cannot now be otherwise than wearisome here.

I object to the passage of the bill because there has been no census taken of the inhabitants, either by Federal or territorial law, and this Senate has no evidence that at the formation of the constitution there was a number of free inhabitants within the limits of California sufficient to entitle her to one Representative, much less two. I object to it because no territorial government was ever established in California by law. I object to it because there was no law of Congress fixing her boundaries, and no law authorizing the formation of a constitution and State government. Above all, I object to it because it is the offspring of Executive usurpation. The convention was called together, organized, and completed its sittings under military auspices. That clause of the constitution which prohibits slavery was notoriously adopted expressly to exclude one half of the States of this Union from an equal participation in the fruits of a war in which southern and northern blood was freely mingled, and southern and northern treasure lavishly expended.

These objections are not stated for the first time. I urged them long ago. And in all the debate which has followed, I must be permitted to say, they have not been answered. On the contrary, they have been admitted. The force of them, however, is sought to be evaded by the assertion, that, although many irregularities have unquestionably attended the application of California for admission as a State, yet these irregularities may be, and ought to be, overlooked in consideration of the extraordinary circumstances of the case. That Congress having failed to provide a government for California, it was the right of the people to establish one for themselves, which we are now bound to recognize. This argument would not be altogether without force if California and the majority in Congress were the only parties in interest. If the rights of no one else were affected, the majority might atone for a former wrong by dispensing with the usual guards and securities. Such, however, is not the case. There are, unfortunately, two interests in this Government—a northern and a southern interest.

It becomes necessary, therefore, to know which one of these interests perpetrated the first wrong, and which is to be benefited by that now proposed. If it be true that both sections are equally to blame for refusing to give a territorial government to California, or if it be true that the southern States alone are guilty, then, sir, we would have no right to complain if that wrong should be urged as an argument against us now. The record however, shows that such was not the case. In addition to that record, if more were needed, we have the published declarations of the Senator from New York, [Mr. SEWARD,] that he himself was mainly instrumental in causing the defeat of a territorial bill. The northern interest denied a government to California, and now, when they are to be benefited by the admission of California, this outrage is converted into an argument, and we are gravely asked to assent to the doctrine that two wrongs make a right.

The failure to give California a government was no fault of ours. Upon what principle, then, is the North to be *rewarded* for a sin she did commit, and the South punished for earnestly endeavoring to prevent its commission? Sir, I feel bound to say that Loyola never had more ingenious or more unscrupulous disciples than those who reason after this fashion. A wrong was done to California, and to us, in refusing a territorial government. Now, another wrong is to be heaped upon us because of the first. The story of the scape-goat, to which we listened not long since, has found its prototype in the history of the southern people. We have been dragged to the verge of a precipice, and are about to be hurled down backwards for the sins of others, not our own.

It is necessary that I should refer here, Mr. President, to a few remarks which were made by the Senator from Michigan yesterday, and I regret that the honorable Senator is not now in his seat; but as this is the only opportunity which I shall have of adverting to those remarks in connection with this bill, he must pardon me for disregarding the usual courtesy extended to absent Senators. He told us yesterday that the people of California had a right to establish a government, with or without our consent; that we, having failed to establish a government for them, they had an inherent right to establish one for themselves. This, sir, is not the doctrine which I learned from a speech of that Senator, delivered a few years ago. I propose to read what were his sentiments in 1847. I read from his speech on what is called the three million bill:

"But no territory hereafter to be acquired *can be governed* without an act of Congress providing for the organization of its government."

Now, sir, this is precisely my doctrine, and the doctrine of the South. We believe that an act of Congress is indispensable to the government of any Territory, and when we find that no such act has passed in relation to California, we can recognize no government established by those who may happen to be upon her soil as legitimate.

Again the Senator says:

"That is the very first step in its progress, in the new career opened to it. TILL THEN no legitimate authority can be exercised over it."

Again, sir, I agree with the Senator, and I am happy to be able to quote his high authority against the new doctrine of squatter sovereignty which is beginning to pervade the land. The right of a few individuals to seize upon the public domain, and erect themselves into a sovereignty, is something which, in my judgment, cannot be too strongly reprobated. If I had no other reason for opposing the admission of California, this alone would be sufficient, and I might appeal to the Senator from Michigan to go with me in that opposition if he still adheres to the opinions I have quoted.

Mr. President, other Senators have spoken of the probable action of the States they represent upon the passage of this bill. I do not know what Alabama may do. That her action will be characterized by wisdom and firmness I have not the least doubt. I am not here to indicate to her what she ought to do. I am the servant, not the leader of her people. Whatever they do, I shall do in despite of Executive menaces, and of all the bloody pictures other hands may exhibit to our view. Born upon the soil of the State while it was yet a Territory, we have grown up together. Time after time she has committed her honor and her interests to my hands. Again and again she has trusted and promoted me, and I recognize no allegiance to any power higher than that I owe to her. Whenever she commands I will obey. If she determines to resist this law by force, by secession, by any means, I am at her service, in whatever capacity she desires to employ me. If this be treason, I am a traitor—a traitor who glories in the name.

I know, sir, that the President, in his late letter to the Governor of Texas, has assumed the right of the Government to coerce a sovereign State. I deny that there is anything in the Constitution—anything in the laws, to justify such an assumption. The law is plain and clear—individuals, not States, are the subjects of coercion. If any State should secede, let him if he dare attempt to employ military force to compel her return. He will soon find, in that event, that he has more than one State to deal with, and that the powers and resources of this Government are wholly inadequate to the task he has undertaken. The federal doctrine that all power lodges here has been somewhat widely repudiated, and the denial of State sovereignty, either North or South, can bring to the Executive nothing but contempt.

I hold that my first allegiance is due to my State, and that treason cannot be committed against any power while obeying her mandates. Such opinions have recently been unsparingly denounced, but let me warn those who resort to such weapons that they may be used by more than one side. There are more traitors than traitors to the Union. Sir, I impugn no man's motives who lets mine alone. I question the purity of no man's conduct who does not provoke retaliation by assailing others; but when men intimate that obedience to the mandates of my State is treason, they must expect to hear in return that, in my opinion, there are those in this land, and about this Capitol, who would sell their souls to Satan for the privilege of having a hand in President making, Cabinet making, and the consequent distribution of the public offices. There are those who would sell their Saviour, were he again upon earth, for half the price that Judas accepted to betray him. Denunciations, sir, are weapons that two can use, and if any one expects to employ them against me with impunity, he miscalculates sadly the character of the man he assails.

I have said all I think it necessary to say. I did not mean to argue the bill here. I shall, if necessary, argue it at home.

Mr. DAVIS, of Mississippi. I regret that there are some remarks of the Senator from Texas [Mr. HOUSTON] which seem to require me to make a very brief reply. An ordinary man, in the position of a representative of so wide-spread a State as Texas, and with so many important questions as are now involved in our legislation, would find objects sufficient to occupy his attention, without taking upon himself the charge of a neighboring State. The Senator, however, has thought proper to take Mississippi under his wing, and now, as on a former occasion, to arraign the conduct of that State, and to institute a comparison between the primary convention of the people and the resolutions of her Legislature, injurious to the latter. On a former occasion I found it necessary to correct some errors into which the Senator had fallen in relation to the action of the people of Mississippi, and though not a great while has passed, it seems to have been swept from his memory, as the returning tide of the sea sweeps names that are written in the sand. They are wholly obliterated; and he comes forward now as though the question was an entirely new one. Without reiterating to him all that I said on a former occasion, in relation to the convention of Mississippi, I propose now to correct the egregious error into which he has fallen; when he says that the convention excluded the consideration of California, but the Legislature, fearing the prospect of an adjustment and probable settlement, introduced it when they convened. Now the facts are simply these. The central meeting and convention met in May and October, 1849, when the question did not exist, and a proposition, as I explained on a former occasion, was introduced to consider how far it was advisable in the slaveholding States to permit the creation and admission of new free States before a certain period without counterbalancing slaveholding States, and the proposition was withdrawn for the sake of unanimity. Not that it could not have been adopted—for three-fourths of the convention were in favor of it—but there was some opposition to it, and it was therefore withdrawn. Now, sir, long after that convention adjourned, and after Congress had assembled, the Representatives and Senators from Mississippi addressed a joint letter to the Governor, who laid them before the Legislature, and upon that letter the Legislature adopted certain resolutions, and among these resolutions was included one in opposition to the admission of California. Now, sir, the difference was not in the temper, but in the state of facts—and that state of facts produced by the intervening time between May, 1849, and March, 1850. The Senator will see, therefore, that any conclusion which he attempts to draw from a dissimilarity of action between the Convention and the Legislature, is not founded on the opinions of the people, but belongs to the state of facts at the different times at which the action was taken. So much for that point.

But the State of Mississippi is somewhat prominent in this matter compared to her age—certainly prominent in the matter of the Nashville Convention; and for that reason, I suppose it was, that the honorable Senator thought proper to comment upon the course of that State. Now, I should think if ever there was a convention which claimed consideration from the Senator from Texas, and which might have expected from him kinder considerations than anybody else, it was the Nashville Convention. Prominent among its acts was the assertion of the title of the State the Senator represents to those very boundaries which he, more than any other individual, had aided in establishing and heretofore asserting. I well remember the Senator's opinion, and that, formerly, in explaining to me the boundaries of Texas, he only varied from those now asserted by the Nashville Convention, by claiming that the line did not follow the main branch of the Rio Grande, but the northwest branch to its source, and thence due north to the 42d parallel. This Convention then asserted, with that exception, what the Senator himself claimed under the treaty which he himself negotiated, and which the Congress of Texas had asserted when an independent State; and taking this position in defence of the rights to Texas, I think it might have claimed very kind consideration from that Senator. It was to these matters of the past alone I intended to refer. As to the prophecies, because they foretell future peace and happiness for the country, I trust his vision is more correct of the future than it has shown itself of the past, for not only is he wrong in this matter of the supposed action of the Mississippi Convention, but he is equally wrong in relation to the action of this body and the House on the Clayton compromise. He says it was not the North who defeated the Clayton compromise. Now, sir, the South supported it in this Chamber against northern opposition, and passed it, and they supported it in the House. It was laid on the table, it is true, by the motion of a southern member, but there were only seven or eight—certainly not exceeding eight—southern members who voted to lay it on the table; the rest were northern votes. Northern power, with this very small addition of seven or eight southern men aiding them, carried the bill to the table, and it was then against the South, and by the power of the North, that the Clayton compromise was defeated.

Now, sir, as to the whole argument which the Senator bases upon the proposition, that if the South has lost the balance of power it does not call for disunion I have to say that no one has asked that. We have pointed to the loss of the balance of power as bringing with it another thing. We have pointed to the state of facts in regard to the action of Congress to show that in our opinion that Constitution is already disregarded; and when the temper exists to disregard the Constitution, and the power is possessed to carry that temper into effect, that man must shut his

eyes to the future who does not see at once that the consequence
is disunion. It is not that one has more power than the other,
but the reckless exercise of the power, which authorizes the
apprehension of danger; for, sir, if the Constitution had not
been disregarded, this new question of the balance of power
would never have been introduced. The idea of the balance
of power, as it existed originally, was between the States, between
the great and monopolizing States and the small ones, and not
between sections. This sectional agitation is the growth of
a subsequent generation to that which formed the Constitution.
The danger is one of our own times, and it is that sectional
division of the people which has created the necessity of looking
to the question of the balance of power, and which carries with
it, when that balance is disturbed, the danger of disunion.

Mr. DAVIS, of Mississippi. As I said before, I shall not
follow the gentleman in his prophecies; though I hope, as they
promise future happiness to the country, they will be realized.
Nor, like him, shall I pretend to be a judge of popular opinion.
Not even in my own county would I pretend to tell to an exact
vulgar fraction how many people agree on any one thing. I
have no pretension to the possession of any such knowledge.
But when the Senator speaks of facts, and in my own State,
I will correct him as long as he makes misstatements. I do not
know where he found his authority, but wherever he found it,
it is untrue. A majority of the counties were represented
in that convention; and let me tell you why they were not all,
or nearly all, represented there. A meeting was held in May,
and this convention met in October, as it was known, but to
carry out the spirit of the plan presented in May, and therefore it was that many of the remote counties did not send delegates, though more than half of them were represented. Now
I know, and every other Senator knows, how easy it is to manufacture a statement that a meeting, however large and respectable, was only composed of seven or eight persons. And an old
politician, like the Senator, whom it was my pleasure to know
before I entered upon manhood as a successful politician in the
State where he then resided, it is strange that he should catch
up reports by the way-side, about the size of meetings, where,
perhaps, the reporter was not, and retail them here. There
was great unanimity among the people, and it was tested by
the fact, that although at the time the canvass went on for the
election of State officers, the question rose above all party considerations, and the candidates touched it not as a thing upon
which to ride into office. It was held to be above all party con-

siderations, and was so recognized for a period long subsequent to that. It is true, that some party division has since arisen. It arose in the Legislature, and it has extended from there, but it did not exist at the time the Senator says he got his information. There was great unanimity, great concurrence of opinion; and the only reason why the convention was not more fully attended, was that no man doubted what the convention would do. Now, in my reference to the Nashville Convention, I did not bring it up as an endorsement of paper that was not current; and the Senator knows, feeble though my advocacy may have been, that I have always maintained the title of Texas. But when the bill is protested; when the paper is not passing current; when the majority were pronouncing it worthless, then I thought that the Senator owed some consideration to the Nashville Convention when it came forward and set its seal to vouch for the correctness of that title. In this view I held that the Convention, and all others who advocated the title of the State of Texas, when it was disputed, and advocated it too against a dead majority, had a right to the consideration and not the reprobation of the Senator from Texas.

Mr. HOUSTON. I have not said that the Senator from Mississippi did not advocate the rights of Texas; on the contrary, I feel grateful to him and to every other gentleman who has sustained her title. Nor has Texas taken any course condemnatory of the position assumed by those gentlemen. She supported the boundary bill, with the view of harmonizing matters and removing what appeared to be an obstacle in the way of restoring peace and quiet to the country. As she came into the Union on the principle of concession, she was willing still further to extend her action on that principle, in the hope that great good might result from it. Hence it was that the Senators from Texas supported that bill, and I entertain the hope that the Legislature of the State will ratify our action, and that the very unpleasant circumstances standing in the way of harmony and peace will soon be removed. We yielded no right whatever which Texas possessed, but we conceded, as Texas has done since her inception, much to the United States for the preservation of the quiet of the Union.

The Senator from Mississippi contends that I am wrong in relation to the fact that a majority of the counties were not represented in the convention at Jackson. It is true, although I obtained my information from respectable sources, that it may be erroneous, but my informants were men of respectable character, and I took it for granted that what they said was correct, not expecting to make use of it at the time. Since the subject has come up, I must advert to the statement of the gentleman, made at the time this subject was incidentally alluded to by me, and he called on me for explanations in regard to it—in February last, I think it was. The honorable gentleman then stated that if it was alleged that there was any interference in the State of Mississippi by persons not residing in that State, it was a most erroneous one. He said the whole movement depended upon the people there; that a few leading men, known in all portions of the State, met and had a consultation, and then recommended to the people the meetings that were subsequently held to send delegates to the convention; that delegates were accordingly sent, being gentlemen of the highest respectability, and that all this was done, not by the politicians or political leaders of Mississippi, but by the people alone, the said politicians, influenced by high considerations of patriotism, all the while holding the people back. Now, I should like to know if a number of prominent men—half a dozen, or a dozen say, of leading politicians in the State—get together and consult and recommend the holding of primary meetings to the people of the State, which meetings are subsequently held, if that should be termed restraining the people from action? Does that look as if the people were ahead of the politicians, or does it not rather look as if the politicians were ahead of the people? And I would ask also, if an agreement among leading and intelligent gentlemen to ride through the State and get up public meetings does not look much more like giving tone to popular sentiment than it does of restraining it?

Mr. DAVIS, of Mississippi. I wish merely to correct an error of the Senator, and put him in the train of his argument. As to the meeting of half a dozen persons—I do not recollect the precise number now—it was one anterior to that of which I spoke to the Senator. There was a conventional meeting, of which I spoke to-day, which occurred in May, composed of delegates from the counties, and that was the meeting which put forth the address and resolutions recommending to the people of the State to hold primary meetings. I repeat that the first meeting spoken of was a mere personal gathering, claiming no authority at all. The first meeting to which I referred was a conventional meeting, composed of delegates from the counties, and of men whom I said were known throughout the State.

Mr. HOUSTON. Well, then, it appears that a few individuals

gave the impulse to all this excitement in Mississippi, and the other States also. If such be the fact, I believe it will be confined to those individuals, and will not pervade the mass of the people; and hence it was that I guarantied the fidelity to the Union. And I repeat, if their constitutional rights are fairly carried out, and there be no infraction of them, you will find the people of the South ever loyal to the institutions of the country. I am contending that had not the people been excited in the manner and by the means to which I have once before referred, they would never have talked of, much less taken up as a solemn question for debate, the idea of estimating or calculating the value of the Union. That is what I said; and it was denied in the little controversy that took place between the Senator from Mississippi and myself, that any one out of the State of Mississippi had any agency in these occurrences. Sir, subsequent events have proved that there was a mighty spirit from abroad operating in those conventions, and that this course was suggested from another State, with a view of leading directly to this Nashville Convention. So, sir, I was correct in my assertion of this fact, though the proof was not fully developed at the time. The eagle, sir, seeks his prey at a distance; he does not seek it about his eyrie; and I apprehend, sir, there was a master spirit at work there. I met it here in all its power, and, feeble as the array was, I opposed myself to it. I felt the violence of its resentment; but still, sir, this did not cause me to falter in the discharge of my duty, and, as one of the representatives of the State of Texas, I placed my foot upon and trampled upon all the movements and agitation which suggested and led to the Nashville Convention. And, sir, such will ever be my course. I speak not for other gentlemen; they have a right to do as they please; their duties are their own, and their consciences will alone control them. I have my constituency to account to, and I have my duty to perform, not only as a Senator, but as a citizen, which is a higher distinction. It is not one State, but the whole Union which is interested in this matter. Strike down the rights of one man, and you lead to the destruction of the whole fabric. Therefore, I am not for permitting the Government to destroy either the rights of the States, as such, or the rights of individuals. These rights are protected by solemn guarantees, and whether of person, liberty, or property, they are rights the disturbance or destruction of which will ever meet my unyielding opposition.

Mr. DAVIS, of Mississippi. The Senator seems to recollect very well when he first commenced this attack. He says it was in February.

Mr. HOUSTON. The 9th, I think.

Mr. DAVIS. I think I read to him a series of resolutions adopted in that Mississippi Convention, which resolutions, if he needed anything to confirm him in the belief of the attachment of the people of Mississippi to the Constitution under which we live, would have given it to him. I read, then, these resolutions to show the fact that we have an abiding attachment to the Union, and desire to vindicate and sustain it upon its ancient principles. But what is the use of declaring that the people adhere to the Union as long as the Constitution is disregarded? The first of this series of resolutions declares what the Senator has chosen to present in other words. But they speak of the Union which rests upon the Constitution; to that the people of Mississippi adhere; and I state again, so that now the slander which has been put forth that the action of that people arose from a letter of Mr. Calhoun may be nailed to the wall, that it was a movement of the people above politicians and above parties. It never rested on any better foundation than that of that letter, written after the event. I think it more proper to suppose that the convention dictated the letter, rather than the letter dictated the action of the convention. All this has been called forth and answered in Mississippi, and the letter itself has been published by the very man to whom it was addressed. Formerly some misrepresentation went abroad, because a respectable gentleman from South Carolina, traveling on the Mississippi river, landed at Jackson, and went out to that convention, although he had not seen that distinguished statesman Mr. Calhoun, and had no knowledge of his views. If the Senator knew who composed that convention, it would be unnecessary to tell him that no man would be required to prompt them. There were men there who needed no dictation. The movement was one of the people, and the convention but reflected it. It is not true in any sense that the character of it was ever fashioned by Mr. Calhoun.

Mr. HOUSTON. It is very strange that that letter was at the convention, and had no influence upon its deliberations.

Mr. DAVIS. It did not arrive during the convention.

Mr. HOUSTON. Was it not in the convention?

Mr. DAVIS. I understood that it was not.

Mr. HOUSTON. I understood that it was received by

Colonel Tarpley in the convention, and there exhibited. It was a singular coincidence that a gentleman from South Carolina should have been passing down the river and visited the convention, and should be invited within the bar of the house, and that he should have met with the assembly during the time of the sittings, and remained to the close of their deliberations, and then departed. Now, this all looks suspicious. I do not say there was anything in it; but it would have led my mind to the conclusion that this letter had suggested the course pursued, as the convention was subsequent and fully in accordance with the suggestions contained in that letter. And the fact that that gentleman happened at that particular time to be traveling there seems to me to be somewhat suspicious. I do not know but that he thought that would be an agreeable time to meet the professional gentlemen of Mississippi. But it would all lead to the suspicion that he knew something about the letter, and as he left at the time he did, it would seem as though it was all a matter of concert, and that concert had much to do with the deliberations of that convention.

Mr. DAVIS. I merely want to tell the Senator that all his speculations about the gentleman from South Carolina can be answered upon application to a gentleman in the House of Representatives.

Resolution offered by Jefferson Davis, Aug. 10, 1850.

MILITARY RECONNOISSANCE.

Mr. DAVIS, of Mississippi, submitted the following resolution, which was considered and agreed to:

Resolved, That the report of the Secretary of War of the 3d of June, communicating the reports and reconnoissances by Captain French and Lieutenant Simpson, be printed, with the map and such of the accompanying sketches as in the opinion of the chief of the Topographical Bureau may be necessary; and that the said report be printed in connection with the report of the Secretary of War of the 23d of July, communicating the reports of the other reconnoissances called for by the resolution of the Senate of the 8th of June last; and that 3,000 additional copies be printed, 300 of which for the use of the Topographical Bureau; and that the said reports be bound, provided the cost thereof shall not exceed twelve and a half cents each.

Protest against the California Bill.

(From Monroe Democrat, Sept. 4, 1850.)

We, the undersigned Senators, deeply impressed with the importance of the occasion and with a solemn sense of the responsibility under which we are acting, respectfully submit the following protest against the bill admitting California as a State into the Union, and request that it may be entered upon the Journal of the Senate. We feel that it is not enough to have resisted in debate alone a bill so fraught with mischief to the Union and the States which we represent, with all the resources of argument which we possessed, but that it is also due ourselves, the people whose interests have been entrusted to our care, and to posterity, which even in its most distant generations may feel its consequences, to leave, in whatever form may be most solemn and enduring, a moral of the opposition which we have made to this measure, and of the reasons by which we have been governed. Upon the pages of a Journal which the Constitution requires to be kept so long as the Senate may have an existence, we desire to place the reasons, upon which we are willing to be judged by generations living and yet to come, for our opposition to a bill whose consequences may be so durable and portentous as to make it an object of deep interest to all who may come after us.

We have dissented from this bill because it gives the sanction of the law, and thus imparts validity to the inhabitants of California, by which an odious discrimination is made against the property of the fifteen slaveholding States of the Union, who are thus deprived of that position of equality which the Constitution so manifestly designs, and which constitutes the only sure and stable foundation on which the Union can repose.

Because the right of the slaveholding States to a common and equal enjoyment of the territory of the Union has been defeated by a system of measures which, without the authority of precedent, of law, or of the Constitution, were manifestly contrived for that purpose, and which Congress must sanction and adopt should this bill become a law. In sanctioning this system of measures, this Government will admit, that the inhabitants of its territories, whether permanent or transient, whether lawfully or unlawfully occupying the same, may form a State without the previous authority of law, without even the partial security of a territorial organization formed by Congress, without any legal census or other efficient evidence of their possessing the number of citizens necessary to authorize the representation which they may claim, and without any of those safeguards about the ballot box which can only be provided by the law and which are necessary to ascertain the true sense of a people. It will admit, too, that Congress having refused to provide a Government, except upon the condition of excluding slavery by law, the Executive branch of this Government may, at its own discretion, invite such inhabitants to meet in convention, under such rules as it or its agents may prescribe, and to form a constitution affecting not only their own rights but those also of fifteen States of the Confederacy, by including territory with the purpose of excluding those States from its enjoyment, and without regard to the natural fitness of the boundary or any of the considerations which should properly determine the limits of a State. It will also admit that the convention, thus called into existence by the Executive, may be paid by him out of the funds of the United States without the sanction of Congress, in violation not only of the provisions of the Constitution, but of those principles of obvious propriety which would forbid any act calculated to make that convention dependent upon it; and last, but not least in the series of measures which this Government must adopt and sanction in passing this bill, is the release of the authority of the United States by the Executive alone to a government thus formed, and not presenting even sufficient evidence of its having the assent of a majority of the people for whom it was designed. With a view of all these considerations, the undersigned are constrained to believe that this Government could never be brought to admit a State presenting itself under such circumstances, if it were not for the purpose of excluding the people of the slaveholding States from all opportunity of settling with their property in that Territory.

Because the vote for a bill passed under such circumstances would be to agree to a principle which may exclude forever hereafter, as it does now, the States we represent from all enjoyment of the common territory of the Union; a principle which destroys the equal rights of their constituents, the equality of their States in the Confederacy, the equal dignity of those whom they represent as men and as citizens in the eye of the law, and their equal title to the protection of the Government and the Constitution.

Because all the propositions have been rejected which have been made to obtain either a recognition of the right of the slaveholding States to a common enjoyment of all the territory of the United States, or to a fair division of that territory between the slaveholding and non-slaveholding States of the Union; every effort having failed which has been made to obtain a fair division of the territory proposed to be brought in as the State of California.

But, lastly, we dissent from this bill, and solemnly protest against its passage, because, in sanctioning measures so contrary to former precedent, to obvious policy, to the spirit and intent of the Constitution of the U. States for the purpose of excluding the slaveholding States from the territory thus to be erected into a State, this government in effect declares that the exclusion of slavery from the territory of the United States is an object so high and important as to justify a disregard, not only of all the principles of sound policy, but also of the Constitution itself.   Against this conclusion we must now and forever protest, as it is destructive of the safety and liberties of those whose rights have been committed to our care—fatal to the peace and equality of the States which we represent—and must lead, if persisted in, to the dissolution of that Confederacy in which the slaveholding States have never sought more than equality, and in which they will not be content to remain with less.

> J. M. MASON,
> R. M. T. HUNTER,
> A. P. BUTLER,
> R. B. BARNWELL,
> H. L. TURNEY,
> PIERRE SOULE,
> JEFFERSON DAVIS,
> D. R. ATCHISON,
> JACKSON MORTON,
> D. L. YULEE

Senate Chamber, 13th August, 1850.

Remarks of Jefferson Davis on the protest of certain Senators against the admission of California. Aug. 15, 1850.

Mr. DAVIS, of Mississippi. Mr. President, those who have protested against the passage of the bill admitting California by the paper now before the Senate are certainly very much indebted to their opponents for the importance they have given this protest. I might have doubted whether so few raising their voice against so great a measure would have attracted public attention. But that doubt has been removed by the bitter opposition that the opponents of this protest have made to its reception. Now, I am sure the country will have their attention drawn to it. And if it shall produce those great effects which some have attributed to it, it will be, not on account of the paper itself, but because of the opposition which has been made by the majority of this body to its reception, and because of the great importance of the subject to which it relates. Had I, sir, for one, not believed the importance of that subject to be great beyond any which had preceded it, I never should have entered into a proposition to place a protest upon the Journal. It was because I believed that upon the measure which has passed by this body hung the fate of the country; because I believed that it would carry to remote generations its influence, that I have sought, in this grave and imposing manner, to spread upon the Journal of the Senate my opposition to the measure.

If, sir, the Senator from Missouri, [Mr. BENTON,] with all the learning which he usually brings to the discussion of any subject, has failed to convince the Senate that parliamentary law, and the safety of the country, should induce them to reject this protest, the rule of the Senators from Maryland would certainly effect that object. He says it ought not to be received because a majority of the Senate are opposed to the opinions it contains. If that is to be the rule, how, in the name of common sense, would a protest ever be received, and whence could it originate? Would it be after a measure had passed that a majority would protest against it? If not, how would a protest ever contain that which a majority would approve? The whole argument, I say, with great respect to that Senator, was idle. It is because the minority appeal against the ascertained will of the majority that the protest is offered. And it therefore must contain opinions which the majority do not approve, unless it be considered as a new mode of reconsideration for a reversal of the decision which had been made. But have we asked you to establish a rule to be applied in all cases, when any Senator may object to a law, or have we claimed it as a right? Neither, sir; both were early disavowed. We have presented this protest because we believed the importance of the occasion justified it. It is for you, Senators, to decide whether you will reject or receive it. I, as one who signed that protest, certainly do not intend to vote upon the question of its reception. You may receive it or reject it, at your option. You have given it great importance aleady by your opposition. Increase that importance if you will by refusing to receive it. I have nothing to lose by further opposition to its reception. The power of the majority has no terrors for me. I have stood heretofore as one of the minority, contending for the rights of my constituents against a majority; upon that ground I am proud still to stand. And when that minority sinks down to one-half the number of those who signed that protest, my pride will be doubled and my determination in no degree diminished. We had a right to appeal to the Senate on such a great occasion as this, for leave to spread upon the Journal our reasons for resisting what we believed to be an invasion of the constitutional rights of our constituents. But, notwithstanding the argument of the Senator from Maryland, I say there is not in that paper one single statement which goes to deny the constitutional power to admit a State. I know that Congress have the power of admitting new States into the Union; and that they can exercise it at discretion. But the obligation is not the less to exercise that plenary power with a sound discretion, and with due regard to the rights of the States. You are bound to exercise it in the spirit of the instrument from which the power is derived. Some of us believe that it has now been exercised in a manner which violates our constitutional rights. And that is the argument of the protest. We do not deny the constitutional power but we deny that it has been exercised as is required by the controlling principles and paramount purposes of the Constitution; that is, in violation of the equality of the States, and the equal privileges and immunities of their citizens.

But the Senator, as strangely as another Senator, [Mr. HOUSTON,] who sits on my left, has found in that protest a recommendation to the States for resistance. I have heretofore stated to the Senate, and now repeat, that I stand here as a representative to the Federal Government. For that reason, if there were none stronger, I could not recommend any measure for its destruction. More, sir: I know my relative position towards those whom I represent too well to assume the attitude of an adviser. I am their servant. They instruct me. I have never assumed and never can assume to be their tutor or their master, and to instruct them.

Is it not true, as stated in the protest, that the anti-slavery feeling of Congress led to the admission of California? Does any deny that a territorial government was refused to that country because gentlemen could not impose the Wilmot proviso upon it? Is any man now so reckless as to say that California could have been admitted if her constitution had contained a recognition of slavery? And if not, is not the argument of the protest on that point established?

Sir, the representatives of southern States here have but poor encouragement to struggle for what they believe to be the rights of their constituents; and can have but small hope of maintaining them when the greatest opposition comes from those representing the same interest as themselves. Our friends from the slaveholding States, if they did not choose to act with us, might at least have had the grace to keep their seats and let us have a fair though unequal contest with the northern majority, known to be against us. The error of excess of zeal in a common cause might have claimed toleration if not favor. But, instead of this, their voices have been the first to be raised in opposition; have rung loudest in the conflict, and now are the last to be heard.

The South never can get her rights until represented by those who will unite in maintaing them. If she had been so represented at this session, we had friends from the non-slaveholding States who would have joined in giving us that to which we are entitled. I am weary of the constant complaint of the friends of the so-called compromise bill—this eternal wailing after its death, like Rachel weeping for her children, and would not be comforted because they were not. That measure met with the doom which I thought it deserved. I glory in being one of those who inflicted its death upon it. Now, as a part of that bill, it is declared that they could have got a division of the territory by the line of 36° 30'. However this may be, the votes taken on various propositions gave the uninitiated no reason to expect it. When that assertion was first made, after the defeat of the bill, I asked, if so, why it could not be done then, on the measure which was before us. Those bills are yet before the House, why may it not still be done? If, instead of reproaches there had been union among those who had the same interest to defend; if, when the Senate consisted of but fifty-seven members, the representatives of fourteen slaveholding States had united for the extension of the Missouri compromise line to the Pacific, in the sense and spirit in which it was originally adopted, I could have laid my hand on at least one northern man who would have joined with us, and then the question would have been settled forever. The stone which marked the end of the line would have also stood as a monument to record the termination of this discord. It was the recreancy of our own brethren, of southern representatives, and not the impracticability of their demands, which has brought us to the condition in which we now stand.

The PRESIDENT. The Senator is not permitted to speak of "recreancy."

Mr. DAVIS. I am sure that we are entitled——

The PRESIDENT. The Chair is under the necessity of preventing the Senator from going on, if he continues that course of remark.

Mr. DAVIS. I will then turn my attention to another point, withdrawing whatever is considered a violation of order. It has been argued as a novelty in this Government, that we have had sectional meetings, and have established a sectional press at the seat of Government. Sir, if there have been sectional meetings, it has been because there has been oppression upon a section. If there had been no sectional organization to deprive another section of its rights, there would have been no sectional meetings to resist it. And with whom, when a section was arrayed against us, were we to meet? Certainly not with those who represented that section. Our purpose was resistance to wrong, and we necessarily met with those who would act with us.

But, sir, a sectional press is no novelty. An Abolition paper has been established for years in this city, and gone unrebuked. And when a part of the southern representatives, for the manner in which they advocated the rights of the South, found themselves without any medium through which they could speak to the country; when both the great political papers of this city were upon one side, against those to whom I have referred; then were they not reduced to the necessity of providing the means by which they could speak to the country, and disabuse the public of the misrepresentations constantly made of their purposes and opinions through the public press? It was not, then, sectional feeling, or if so, it does not lie as a charge at our door, which produced either the meetings or the paper. It was sectional aggression on us; and because we required combination to discharge our duties with effect, and a press to protect our cause from perversion.

But, sir, the Senator from Texas, [Mr. HOUSTON,] reading this protest through glasses not furnished to those who signed it, finds in it the assertion that the South has sustained wrongs for which disunion is the only remedy. There is no such assertion in the paper. It recommends no measure to the southern States. It suggests nothing. It merely points out our wrongs, and points them out in language more temperate, not to say subdued, than the Legislatures of southern States themselves have used. Facts are presented, the case is laid bare, and the protest then leaves it in the hands of our masters. We have found ourselves unable to preserve their constitutional rights; it is for them to decide on whom is the censure, and what measures they will adopt for their protection.

I repeat, what I have often said, that I do not attempt to influence the opinions of those whom I represent; but I seek to know and reflect them. If it be a crime to acknowledge allegiance to my State as superior to that I owe the General Government, it is one which it will not be found difficult to establish, but which, while this Government remains the agent of the States, whilst the States themselves shall continue, it will be impossible to any great extent ever to punish. And if the attempt shall be made, then, sir, disunion and disunionists will be seen in their true colors. Then the act which destroys the Confederacy will have been perpetrated.

No charge was ever less founded, no charge was ever more unjust, than that those who resist aggression, who strive to maintain the Constitution, on which alone the Union can rest, are those who are seeking its destruction.

I, sir, have not gone so far as the Senator from Texas has this morning. He said the South was his country. I, sir, am an American citizen. My allegiance, I know, is first due to the State I represent. My feelings and my honor both bind me in the first and last resort. But this Union is my country. I am a citizen of the United States, it is true, because I am the citizen of a State. My affections begin in, but are not bounded by the limits of that State. I belong to no State and no section, when the great interests of the Union are concerned; I belong to the State which is my home when the Union attempts to trample upon her rights; when outrage and oppression shall drive those affections now extended over the broad Union back to their more narrow circle, then heart and hand I am wholly her own.

Mr. DOWNS. Mr. President, I did not intend to say another word on this subject, but my friend from Mississippi [Mr. DAVIS] used a very remarkable expression, which I cannot pass over. The gentleman rejoices and takes great credit to himself for having assisted effectually in destroying the compromise bill. It seems to me that the exultation of my friend is a little out of date. It might have been very well ten days ago. But I cannot for the life of me see how it has much application now, inasmuch as every single feature of the compromise bill, with no material alteration, has obtained the sanction of the Senate. Gentlemen may take exultation from such triumphs as that, if they please or can, but I can only say that I do not see how they have triumphed. Every material feature of the compromise has passed. The Texas feature was modified more than any other, but it passed, giving Texas more territory than she got by the compromise bill as reported by the Committee of Thirteen. But the remark of the gentleman which chiefly called me up was an expression which he made use of, in such general terms that it might be applied to a great many persons—that the South had failed in obtaining her rights because of the "recreancy" of certain southern gentlemen. Now, I ask the gentleman to state how far he extends that remark. Does he extend it to me?

Mr. DAVIS, of Mississippi, (in his seat.) What reason has the Senator to suppose that I applied the remark to him?

Mr. DOWNS. I only supposed it possible because the remark was general, and I differed with the gentleman on some points relating to the interests of the South.

Mr. DAVIS, (in his seat.) When the Senator concludes his remarks I will reply to him.

Mr. DOWNS. Sir, I have voted with the Senator on almost all the material amendments that were offered in the progress of these measures.

Mr. BENTON. There is evidently going to be a misapprehension between these two gentlemen.

The PRESIDENT. The Chair is not aware of it. The Chair called the Senator from Mississippi [Mr. DAVIS] to order when he made use of an expression improper to be used in debate. The Senator was understood to withdraw it, and there the Chair supposed the matter rested.

Mr. BENTON. There is likely to be a misapprehension between the Senators. When the Senator from Mississippi has said that he will answer the Senator from Louisiana after he is done, I am unwilling to avoid preventing any ill-feeling and any misapprehension which may arise in the mean time. For that reason, I really desire that the thing might be dropped, and that the gentleman should not speak here on that point until they have talked with one another as gentlemen and friends should talk with each other.

The PRESIDENT. The Senator is not in order. The Chair would state that when he called the Senator from Mississippi to order for using an improper expression he understood that the expression was withdrawn by that Senator.

Mr. PRATT, (in his seat.) There the Chair is mistaken.

Mr. DAVIS, of Mississippi. My only objection to answering the inquiry of the Senator from Louisiana promptly, was the manner in which his question was put, and the fact that that Senator must have known full well that my remark could not have applied to him. I thought, when the Senator put the question, that he should have remembered the kindly feelings which have subsisted between us, and that therefore he ought to have known that I did not refer to him. Therefore it was that I did not answer his question. But a moment has passed, and I have now no objection to telling the Senator that my remark did not apply to him.

Mr. DAVIS, of Mississippi. Mr. President, I will inform my friend from Louisiana why it is that I triumph in the defeat of that so-called compromise bill. First, we have saved something of the rights of Texas, something of that which that bill proposed to take from her. But, more than that, we have presented each proposition in its own naked deformity. We have saved the legislation of the country from adopting as a new rule a species of bargain and barter, by the combination of things wholly dissimilar into one great bill. So that, by the rejection of that omnibus bill, the country has been saved from that which I consider a great evil. My triumph consists in that bill not having been enacted. But, sir, my triumph will cease whenever the lamentations of the omnibus bill men shall cease. Whenever they cease from day to day to din in our ears their lamentations over the loss of that "great healing measure," then shall I cease to think of it, and certainly to speak of it. This morning I compared them to Rachel who was weeping for her children, and would not be comforted because they were not; because the friends of the omnibus bill are constantly dinning in our ears their lamentations over the loss of that measure. It was in that connection that I noticed the matter.

Now, as to the distinction in relation to constitutional power. I thought I stated it briefly to be an admission on my part that Congress had the power to admit new States at their discretion; but that that power might be exercised, and in this case I thought it was exercised, in violation of certain other constitutional rights of citizens of the United States. That was the whole distinction which I proposed to make, and I believe it is the distinction made in the protest before the Senate.

Remarks of Jefferson Davis on the recapture of Fugitive Slaves.
Aug. 19, 1850.

Mr. DAVIS, of Mississippi. The Senator from Ohio has remarked that, in that part of Ohio in which he resides, there have been frequent cases of "kidnapping." I presume he refers to Cincinnati. Sir, I quite agree with him, if he means that persons traveling with servants who are slaves, very frequently suffer loss by kidnapping at Cincinnati; but it is on the other side of the case from that which he is understood to sustain: it is the kidnapping of servants from persons who are traveling on one of our national highways. Here and elsewhere this constitutes a source of great annoyance to persons traveling with their slaves from the States of the South. If any other species of kidnapping has been practiced, I have yet to see the first proof of it. My knowledge of the southern people, of more than one community living in the slaveholding States, will justify me, and the testimony of others here will, I am sure, bear me out in saying, that if any man go from a slave State and arrest a free person of color, and bring him to a slaveholding State as his property, he would be liberated at once and the thief arrested. It is a felony which the people there would not tolerate for a moment.

A SENATOR. And the kidnapper would be severely punished.

Mr. DAVIS. And the kidnapper, as a Senator has just remarked, would be severely punished. It would be a felony in the eye of the law, the least of all likely to be shielded by public sympathy.

But the Senator from Massachusetts [Mr. WINTHROP] makes an argument in favor of trial by jury, in the case of fugitive slaves, on the ground that the execution of a law depends upon the will of the people by whom it is to be executed. I grant the force of his arguments; but it strikes me that, so far as his argument has force, it goes exactly against his conclusion, the argument being that the law cannot avail anything, because the people do not approve it; and, therefore, we are called on to submit it to the test of a jury trial. If it is admitted that the law cannot be executed because of the opposition to it, growing out of the popular feeling, the jury reflecting that popular feeling will decide against it, in accordance with preconceived opinions.

Mr. WINTHROP. Will the Senator from Mississippi allow me one word of explanation?

Mr. DAVIS. Certainly.

Mr. WINTHROP. I think the Senator from Mississippi confounds two entirely distinct ideas—the one, the idea of conforming the law to what may be the sentiment of the community in regard to slavery; the other, the idea of conforming the law to what may be the opinion of the community in regard to the propriety and justice of the law itself. What I said was this: That all laws depend for their execution and efficiency, in no small degree, upon the opinion of the community that they are just and reasonable laws; and that if this law should go forth to the people of any of the free States with an idea that it is arbitrary, oppressive, and regardless of the great principles of justice, it would be much less likely to be faithfully executed than if it was more in conformity with the public sentiment of those States. This is only an amplification of the old classical saying—*leges vand sine moribus*—and is too familiar to every one to require another word of remark.

Mr. DAVIS. That is the "higher law" spoken of by the Senator from New York——

Mr. WINTHROP, (in his seat.) No.

Mr. DAVIS. That public sentiment which requires that the provisions of the Constitution should not be carried out when they happen to conflict with its abstract notions of justice. That provision of the Constitution was for the rendition of fugitives from justice, and fugitives from service; they were placed on the same basis, and I wish that that provision of the Constitution had stood unaided by Congressional legislation till the present day, and that the moral sense of the community had been relied on, and State legislation left to provide for its execution, instead of hedging it round by acts of Congress, which serve, it seems, but little other purpose than to relieve from the moral obligation to preserve and maintain the Constitution.

What is this question of jury trial? Is it to try the offence of escaping from service or labor to which the individual was held in another State, or is it to supervise the judicial proceedings of a sister State. Why, then, should you not have a jury trial before you give up the man charged with murder? The wrong of the proposition is as plain as the justice and reason of the rule of the settled practice, which is to hold the trial where the facts can best be established; to try the right to service or the criminality of one accused where the identity can be most certainly proved, instead of where the popular feeling is against the right asserted, and where it would be most difficult to prove the facts. This is the fruit of yielding to that feeling, which is not a commendable respect for the trial by jury, but a prejudice against the right recognized by the Constitution to own slave property. It is that which has made the northern States the refuge of fugitive slaves, and which causes them to be shielded and concealed. Neither, sir, is it the result of philanthropic feeling for the African race. Recently, in exemplification of this, I have seen published in a northern paper a caution to all persons to be on their guard against a woman who was going about and deceiving the public by passing herself off as a fugitive slave, for the purpose of obtaining the aid and comfort which, in that character, would be bestowed upon her; conclusively showing, as an admitted fact, that if she was a fugitive from service, she was to have a home and succor, but being free she was not entitled to public sympathy. The violation of the rights of private property and of constitutional obligation, seems to be the well from which alone this sympathy can be drawn. But to return to the point of jury trial.

Who, Mr. President, is best qualified to judge whether the person arrested is a fugitive from service, or is a freeman who has been kidnapped? A wanderer is found in a village or city, and a claim is made that he is a fugitive slave. Are the inhabitants of that village or city the best judges whether he is a slave, or the inhabitants of the place whence he is said to have fled? Let him be taken to the neighborhood from which he is said to have escaped, and who is there who does not know whether he is a fugitive slave or not? Sir, it is but justice to the South to say that in no community could stronger feelings exist than would be found there against him who would kidnap a freeman for the purpose of making him a slave.

Mr. President, like the Senator from South Carolina, I feel no great interest in this law, because I have no hope that it will ever be executed to any beneficial extent. But if the border States—those most interested in the question—hope to derive any benefit from it, I am willing, within the limits of my opinion as to what Congress may do, and what the Constitution imposes, to leave them to frame the law as they think will best protect them, and to let it be tested by time. I do not believe that they will ever succeed, in those States which now offer obstacles, in the recovery of fugitive slaves by an act of Congress providing for their restoration and delivery; and still less, if the act should provide for trial by jury, would there be in my mind a probability of such success. I should be opposed to the proposition to require a jury trial, even if it were to be held in the State from which the fugitive escaped, because I hold it to be an assumption of power not granted to the Federal Government, a violation of State rights, by attempting to direct their legislation and forms of proceeding. The right of jury trial, if there be any question as to the condition of a person of color in regard to freedom or slavery, already exists in every slaveholding State. They can appeal to that under the laws of the State to which they belong or may be carried, and I shall not feel disposed to dictate to any State what its laws should be.

On the recapture of fugitive slaves, Aug. 22, 1850.

Mr. DAVIS, of Mississippi. I very reluctantly voted against the amendment of the Senator from Maryland. I did it, however, from a conviction that it was a proposition departing from that principle now recognized in our legislation. So reluctantly did I vote against it, that I listened to every argument in its favor, to see if I could consistently vote for it. But, in the cases that were stated as analogous, I could see no analogy. I could find no semblance in the case of indemnity demanded from foreign Governments, and nothing which had a relation to this case in that of losses sustained from the depredations of Indians when there is a failure to execute the law within the limits of the United States. I cannot put the States of this Union in the same condition as a foreign country or an Indian tribe, and therefore the analogy fails in my opinion. The same principle contained in the amendment of the Senator from Maryland, now remains in the bill before the Senate. Before the vote is taken on the motion of the Senator from Kentucky to strike out the whole bill, I move to strike out from the word "law," in the thirty-ninth line, down to the end of the seventh section. The portion proposed to be struck out is as follows:

"And should such fugitive at any time after being arrested as aforesaid, by warrant as aforesaid, be rescued by force from those having such fugitive in custody, then it shall be lawful for such claimant, his agent or attorney, to exhibit proof of such arrest and rescue before any judge of the circuit or district court of the United States for the State where the rescue was effected; and upon such arrest and rescue being made to appear to him by satisfactory proof, and that the same was without collusion; and further, that the service of labor claimed

516 JEFFERSON DAVIS, CONSTITUTIONALIST

of such fugitive was due to such claimant in the State, Territory, or District whence he fled, it shall be the duty of such judge to grant to such claimant, his agent or attorney, a certificate of the facts so proved, and of the value of such service or labor (in the State, Territory, or District whence the fugitive fled) to said claimant, to be proved in like manner; which certificate, when produced by such claimant or his attorney, shall be paid at the Treasury, out of any moneys therein not otherwise appropriated; and the same shall be filed in the Treasury as evidence of so much money due from the State or Territory where such rescue was effected to the United States, and shall be by the Secretary of the Treasury reported to Congress at the next session ensuing its payment: *Provided,* That not more than $—— in case of a male, or $—— in case of a female fugitive shall be so allowed or paid.''

Mr. FOOTE. I have heretofore announced that I should take but little part in this discussion, because the people whom I represent, though they have some little interest in the pending question, are by no means so extensively interested in a measure providing for the restoration of fugitives from service as are the border States of the Union. But we are, notwithstanding, anxious that some efficient law should be adopted securing the rights of property so specially guarded and guarantied by the Constitution itself. I have, therefore, coöperated cordially with the Senators from Maryland, Virginia, and Missouri, in support of the proposition offered by the Senator from Maryland, which has been voted down. I regret that the amendment of that Senator was not adopted, because I am perfectly satisfied that the only efficient manner in which we can provide for the recapture and restoration of fugitives from service is by one substantially similar to that proposed by the Senator from Maryland. All other remedies having heretofore proved ineffectual, we are bound now to resort to some new expedient for the removal of a great and growing evil. The amendment of the Senator from Maryland, though, was voted down, and I fear that the proposition of the Senator from Virginia, which is almost equivalent to it, will share the same fate to-day. The defeat of the amendment of the Senator from Maryland is quite a remarkable fact; it is, indeed, one of a mortifying and melancholy character in some of its bearings. I regret to be constrained to say that the vote of yesterday, upon the amendment referred to, when analyzed, shows that if all the southern Senators had voted for it, it would have been adopted, have become the law of the land, and have efficiently provided for the recapture and restoration of fugitives from service. Such, I say, is the result of an analysis of the vote of the Senate upon this amendment. Thus, but for an unfortunate division of sentiment in the South, or at least among southern Senators here, producing the defeat of the amendment of the Senator from Maryland, the South would have been secured effectually in regard to one of her most vital interests, and in relation to which she has been fated to suffer heretofore the most serious injustice. Sir, is the South thus to suffer eternally from the discordant opinions and conflicting action of her own chosen representatives? I fear, sir, that to-day we shall again realize the scene of discord and division among southern Senators once before realized. I fear that the amendment of the Senator from Virginia will presently share the fate of its predecessor. For one, sir, I rejoice to have the opportunity of voting for the amendment of the Senator from Virginia, feeling very anxious indeed to participate in the enactment of an efficient law, such as the plain language of the Constitution seems to me to demand. I do most confidently believe, that if the proposition of the Senator from Virginia is defeated, it will be impossible to provide for the South any efficient law upon this subject. I fear also that hereafter, if this amendment should be defeated, the South will have little reason to complain of the failure of Congress to perform its constitutional duty in regard to the recapture and restoration of fugitives from service, since this failure will be attributable, in part at least, to the acts of southern Senators here. It is not my intention to call in question the motives of any one, but simply to state a condition of facts actually existing, and which I do most profoundly deplore. I do hope that the day is not far distant when southern Senators, communing more freely and more amicably with each other, will be able to agree together as to the measures necessary to the safety and repose of the southern States, and of the whole Confederacy. It shall not be, as it has not heretofore been, my fault, if more harmony should not prevail among those who represent the slave States of the Union.

Mr. DAVIS, of Mississippi. The last remark of my colleague would seem to point to southern men who act with myself in——

Mr. FOOTE. Not in the least degree. I did not allude to my colleague at all.

Mr. DAVIS. If the remark was not intended to apply to me, I have nothing to say in answer to it.

The misfortune of southern men not agreeing upon this bill, if it be a misfortune, is one which results from a different interpretation of the Constitution—from the not unusual fact, that, though viewed from the same point, we do not see the thing in the same light. I shall be compelled to vote against such a proposition as this, which would hold the Treasury of the United States responsible, as underwriter, to secure a particular species of property from loss. The proposition is to secure payment by the United States for the value of runaway slaves, when they are not restored; a proposition which I am not able to derive from the obligation to protect it against the hostile action of the States or of the people, and which is, to my mind, likely to lead to consequences not to be desired by any southern man. Our safety consists in a rigid adherence to the terms and principles of the federal compact. If, for considerations of temporary or special advantage, we depart from it, we, the minority, will have abandoned our only reliable means of safety. If we admit that the Federal Government has power to assume control over the slave property; if we admit that it may interpose its legislative and financial power between the individual owning that property and the property itself, where shall we find an end to the action which anti-slavery feeling will suggest? We know that in the other end of the Capitol a proposition already exists to transport free negroes from this country to Africa, in steamers owned by the United States. If such a proposition should prevail, we relieve the non-slaveholding States from the best check we have upon the popular feeling in favor of runaway slaves, their unwillingness to have negroes among them, and charge the whole country with the expense of removing this practical, wholesome restraint upon the growing disposition to violate our property right, in disregard of the constitutional obligation which we are now, by other means, endeavoring to enforce.

But what will be the operation of the proposition before us, and where is it to stop? If we adopt the principle of indemnification, which has been suggested, we of the South will have to pay a disproportionate amount of the contributions made, not to enforce the Constitution by restoring fugitives from service or labor, but to acknowledge our inability to protect the property of citizens within the limits of the United States, and to compound, by paying for it when it is stolen. The obligation imposed by the Constitution is not this; it is not to purchase, but to return the property. How far the proposition before the Senate would be effectual for the purpose proposed, I cannot tell. My belief is, not to a very great extent; because, in most instances, it would be, if not impossible, extremely difficult to find the property. I recently read of a case of a traveler passing through Pittsburgh where a servant went off, taking with him his master's baggage, whilst he was at dinner in the hotel at which he had stopped. A police officer, who was employed, traced the fugitive to his concealment, but did not make the arrest; and when asked by the owner to give him the information, answered in substance, that "he dared not inform; it would be as much as his life was worth to point out the house." The slave was not found, and under the proposed remedy there could be no indemnity in that case. Where a slave can be found, I think we may provide by law remedies adequate for his restoration; and where there is danger from the violence of mobs, I think it is the duty of the Government to make such provision as may be necessary not only to secure the citizen in the arrest of his property, but also to give him a safe conduct to his own State. That, I think, is a remedy which may and should be made efficient whenever a fugitive slave can be captured.

Mr. DAVIS. Men oftener differ about terms than about things. My colleague has made an argument in favor of a proposition to expend money to restore slaves who have fled from their owners. To that I have no objection; my opposition is to a proposition, not to carry out the constitutional provision for the restoration of fugitives, but to pay for such slaves as cannot be restored. My colleague argues, and very conclusively, that the Government of the United States never can constitutionally undertake to transport free negroes from the United States to Africa, there being no grant in the Constitution of any such power. Thus, sir, we argue against this proposition, and ask where is the grant in the Constitution of any power on the part of Congress to pay money for runaway negroes. The power is given to levy taxes and to raise money by imposts for enumerated purposes, from none of which can I derive the power or application claimed. A provision of the Constitution requires that runaway slaves shall be restored to their masters; but, sir, not that if they are not restored they shall be paid for. Those who have argued it heretofore have done so on a supposed analogy in the case, to the infraction of the rights of property by a foreign nation, or by Indian tribes. I see no analogy from which such a conclusion can be drawn. The application cannot be carried out, unless a State can be treated as an enemy or held in such subordinate condition as a savage tribe. I cannot suppose one or the other.

I have not assumed that if this bill should be passed here, another bill will be passed in the House of Representatives for the transportation to Africa of slaves who may be emancipated by it. In speaking of a proposition which had been made at the other end of the Capitol, I referred to what I supposed was well known; and whether this bill should pass here or not, the bill to which I alluded may pass there. It is well known that the non-slaveholding States object to the presence of free negroes among them; and if the evil may not now be sufficiently great to drive them to an act which strict constructionists would regard as a palpable violation of the Constitution, I do think that, whenever it shall happen that they shall have free negroes enough among them to constitute a serious and general annoyance, our brethren have ingenuity enough to find reasons which will justify, in their estimation, the use of such means for getting rid of them; that in such case they will resort to those means; the Treasury will be called upon to transport them to Africa, and we of the South would have to pay a disproportionate part of the money with which our slaves were liberated, and with which they were subsequently removed, for the benefit of those by whose action our property was originally taken from us.

As to what the South will feel of irritation or otherwise, in relation to the bill, I shall say that, so far as the vote of the Senate is an indication, we should expect the South to object to the exercise of the proposed remedy, because it is not for the purpose of giving effect to the requirement of the Constitution, and it is not among the objects for which the taxing power was granted. To show how far it will find favor, I will present a hypothetical case. Suppose that in any State of this Union a proposition was made in the State Legislature to tax the whole people of the State for the guarantee of any particular species of property. Is there any legislative body in this Union that would pass such a law, or a State in the Union that would submit to it except for protection against a foreign enemy? I suppose there is not one. And the tax-payers of the country would be as little likely to believe it just out of their own States respectively as in them. If the remedy, then, could be made effectual, how long should we enjoy it?

Allusion has been made to the State of Mississippi being but slightly interested in this matter of fugitive slaves. She is not so slightly interested in this question as the Senator from Maryland supposed. Negroes do escape from Mississippi frequently, and the boats constantly passing by our long line of river frontier furnish great facility to get into Ohio; and when they do so escape it is with great difficulty that they are recovered; indeed, it seldom occurs that they are restored. We, though less than the border States, are seriously concerned in this question. We are interested in having such laws passed as will compel their return. Those who, like myself, live on that great highway of the West—the Mississippi river—and are most exposed, have a present and increasing interest in this matter. We desire laws that shall be effective, and at the same time within the constitutional power of Congress; such as shall be adequate, and be secured by penalties the most stringent which can be imposed.

On the recapture of Fugitive slaves Aug. 23, 1850.

Mr. DAVIS, of Mississippi. I would merely say, that believing the constitutional provision applied solely to the restitution of the fugitives, my mind has been intent on that purpose alone. I think a provision for the payment of the slave, if he is not returned, would have a tendency rather to prevent than increase the probability of getting him restored; because, though there may be no sense of justice, in a few fanatics, there is a sense of justice in the great body of the people everywhere, which might be stifled by the assurance that the owner of the property would lose nothing by his failure to recover his slave. The sense of justice of the people might be checked, by being told that the owner would not suffer if he did not recover his property, because if he did not he would receive the value of it in money. I think, therefore, the provision would rather prevent than aid in the delivering up of the fugitive. I also propose, if this amendment of mine shall prevail, to amend another section of the bill, so as to give the power to recover $1,000 for each slave, the delivery of whom is prevented, by civil actions against those who do rescue and conceal the fugitive. With that remedy, and with another amendment which I shall offer, requiring the delivery of the slave into the State of the owner, under the hands of a marshal, and the summoning of a posse to aid him at the expense of the Government, the bill, I think, will be effectual. Thus where a slave is recaptured he will be delivered; where he is not, the indemnity clause will avail nothing.

The question was then taken on the amendment, and it was agreed to.

Mr. DAVIS, of Mississippi. I now move to amend the bill in the fourth section, by inserting after the word "dollars," in the 28th line, the words "for each fugitive so lost as aforesaid."

The amendment was agreed to.

Mr. DAVIS. I move further to amend the sixth section, by striking out the proviso which extends from the 20th line to the end of the section. The object is to cause the delivery to be made at the expense of the Government.

The words proposed to be stricken out are as follows:

"*Provided,* That before such charges are incurred the claimant, his agent or attorney, shall secure to said officer payment of the same; and in case no actual force be opposed, then they shall be paid by such claimant, his agent or attorney."

The amendment was agreed to.

Mr. DAVIS. I move further to amend, by inserting in the 6th line of the 7th section, after the words "court of record therein," the words "or judge thereof, in vacation."

The amendment was adopted.

Mr. DAVIS, of Mississippi. When I spoke of that ignorance to which the Senator from Massachusetts has referred, I did not speak of the ignorance of constitutional law on the part of the Senator from Massachusetts or the people of Massachusetts; but when the Senator chose to put that construction upon my remark, I allowed him to proceed. I might have answered him, when he was referring to the history of his action in 1843, as the Vicar of Wakefield said to the man who sold Moses the green spectacles: "I ask pardon, sir, for interrupting so much learning; but I think I have heard all this before."

Now, I still hold, as I did before, that such excitement can only be produced by ignorance of the facts in the case, can only be generated by those who manufacture such anecdotes as that which the Senator related, and by announcing to the people of Massachusetts that mariners are taken from vessels to be incarcerated on shore. I would ask any gentleman here or elsewhere to point to a case where, at any southern port, the steward of a vessel has been seized from the vessel, and carried on shore? But does not every gentleman perceive, at the same time, that unless the process can be executed on board the vessel, such steward will go ashore and commit the outrages which this law was created to prevent, and then fly to the deck of his vessel for protection, and claim immunity? It must be competent to arrest him there. But if he stays on board, where and when was ever a search instituted to ascertain whether he was there or not? It is well known that the stewards of our armed vessels of the navy of the United States are generally black. They go into every port in the United States, and who ever interfered with them? So, sir, the vessels which are constantly entering into the port of New Orleans have the same class of stewards. If they remain on board they are not interfered with. If they go ashore they are likely to do mischief; they have done it, have been the means of getting slaves on board the vessel, and having them shipped to ports where their abolition masters can protect them. For this reason, it has been necessary to exclude them by law. Ignorance with respect to the practical operation of the law in the southern States, may be well expected even in the most learned in Massachusetts, especially when they are led to that ignorance by those who seek to cater to it in order to promote their own designs of mischief. Had the truth been told by every man, the unhappy excitement which has arrayed section against section could never have existed. It has been falsehood, as well with regard to our own domestic affairs as with regard to those points of difference between the institutions of the different States, which has produced the excitement. And this is why I should deem it a blessing to have the fraud exposed, and why I desire the Senator from Georgia should have an opportunity to proceed. It was because I knew of the very able opinion he had given, and how it had been assailed, that I wished to hear him; because I believe that the people of Massachusetts might listen to him and learn how they have been deceived. However wise they may be in constitutional law, they may be ignorant of the facts that exist, and their ignorance may be practiced upon by those who abuse it.

Committee Report by Jefferson Davis, Aug. 20, 1850.

REPORTS FROM COMMITTEES.

Mr. DAVIS, of Mississippi, from the Committee on Military Affairs, to which were referred the proceedings of a meeting of the Medical and Chirurgical Faculty of Maryland, at the annual convention held at Easton, in that State, relative to the rank of surgeons in the army and navy, asked to be discharged from the further consideration of the same, on the ground that the rank of surgeons in the army was already established by law, and that it be referred to the Committee on Naval Affairs; which was agreed to.

Also, from the same committee, to which was referred the "Joint resolution from the House of Representatives explanatory of certain acts therein mentioned," reported back the same with an amendment, striking out, in the 17th line, the words "or from disease contracted"; thus making the provisions applicable only to those who may hereafter die of wounds received while in service.

Resolution offered by Jefferson Davis, Aug. 27, 1850.

Mr. DAVIS, of Mississippi, submitted the following resolution for consideration:

Resolved, That, 1,500 additional copies of the message of the President of the 17th of July last, communicating, in compliance with the resolution of the Senate, a report of Lieutenant Webster, of a survey of the Gulf coast of the mouth of the Rio Grande, together with the supplemental report, communicated the 26th instant, be printed.

Remarks of Jefferson Davis, Aug. 28, 1850.

SURVEY OF THE RIO GRANDE.

The Senate proceeded to consider the resolutions on the table; and the following, which was submitted by Mr. DAVIS, of Mississippi, yesterday, came up in its order:

Resolved, That 1,500 additional copies of the message of the President of the 17th of July last, communicating, in compliance with the resolution of the Senate, a report of Lieutenant Webster, of a survey of the Gulf coast of the mouth of the Rio Grande, together with the supplemental report communicated the 26th instant, be printed.

Mr. DAVIS, of Mississippi. The Senate have ordered the printing of this document, and it is for the Senate to decide whether they will print extra copies or not. If they intend to do so, they had better order them at once, so that the printers may not have to reset the type. I will also say that this is a topographical survey of the lower Rio Grande. If it had been submitted to the Senate last year I think it would have saved them from a very great blunder, which they made in the establishment of a custom house. I consider it very valuable to the Senate and the country.

The resolution was adopted.

Remarks of Jefferson Davis on the Military Academy bill,
Aug. 29, 1850.

Mr. DAVIS, of Mississippi. I think the Senator from Maine
has made a very good speech, if he had appended it to something to which it had a useful application; but I think it is out
of place here, because the whole increase of expenses proposed
is only something over $700. It is a diminution of the salary of
one of the professors, his salary having been accidentally higher
than that of the professor of the senior chair of the academy.
The object is to put all the salaries of the principal professors
upon the same scale. The Senator from Maine has not inquired,
I am sure, or he would not have given the reasons which he has
offered against the passage of this amendment. He seems to
suppose that he can obtain competent men to fill these chairs
anywhere, and for a less sum of money. His remarks remind
me of a saying of William Cobbett. He said he could obtain
an able-bodied man to perform the duties of king for fifty
pounds a year. I have no doubt he can get able-bodied men to
take these chairs for such salaries as he supposes; but I think he
is mistaken if he supposes he can get competent men to do it
who will not require a salary as high as it is proposed to give.
The instruction at this institution is peculiar. In mathematics
it is more extensive and thorough than elsewhere; and the
science of war and of military engineering is taught in no other
institution in the country. Therefore these chairs must necessarily be filled by officers drawn from the army, and must be
men of the highest attainment in their profession. On being
appointed professors, they surrender the right of promotion
in the army and all prospects of professional distinction. It is
only those of the highest attainments in science, and of the best
capacity, who are selected for these duties. The Senator from
Maine was never more mistaken than in the supposition that the
salaries are higher than those given to men of similar occupation and standing in other institutions of the country. They
are below what is received in many institutions—greatly below
that which they could elsewhere obtain; but the professors have
a pride in the progress and success of the institution, some of
them having been connected with it more than twenty years.
Having grown up with the institution, they feel that attachment
which binds them to it, and is superior to pecuniary temptation,
but it may not be to depreciation and neglect by the country
whom they have so long and so advantageously served.

Again, the Senator from Maine is mistaken in supposing there has been no complaint on the part of the professors, and that the position is favorable to low salaries. The place is one where the living is expensive, and, as they have to entertain much company, their salaries barely support them. There are many places where they could be supported for much less, and where they could obtain higher salaries. The institution has borne good fruit, and I think it is a poor economy to strike at the source of the army's glorious reputation by parsimony in the salaries of the professors, such as will deprive the academy, not only of the present experienced professors, but render it impossible hereafter to obtain like ability. The proposition is not to any amount worthy of consideration to increase the expenses of the academy, but to place it on a basis with respect to these salaries which will relieve it hereafter from the cavils to which it has been exposed in consequence of the manner in which the salaries have been paid. It is to place the amount paid distinctly and fairly before the country, so that demagogues may not have any handle to lay hold upon in connection with the compensation made to the professors. It is that the salaries may be fixed, so that every man may know what is received. The standard fixed upon is below that of the colleges generally in the country. If these men are, as I think they are, entitled to the gratitude of the country for all they have bestowed upon it, both in peace and war; if they have by their instructions at this academy given efficiency to the army, and greatly increased the science which has been spread broadcast over the land, it is but a poor return for such benefits to be caviling at the proposition to raise the salaries of these professors a few hundred dollars. I regret that these objections have occurred. I should have expected every Senator to favor the proposition, seeing it is but little more than to change the mode of compensation by fixing the amount to be received by commutation of allowances into a salary. I expected to see it adopted at once, and that it never would be changed until some one should propose to increase the salary to such amount as they could elsewhere receive. An increase, I believe, they should have.

Mr. BRADBURY. Mr. President, the manner of the Senator from Mississippi partakes more of the camp than the Senate. He undertakes to decide *ex cathedra* whether my remarks are applicable to the question or not. Of that the Senator must permit me to judge. I do not choose to submit to his decision when he undertakes to pronounce upon the pertinency of my remarks. I am the judge of that matter, whether they are applicable or not to the subject before the Senate, and not that Senator. If he sees fit to call me to order, to that mode of testing the point I am ready to submit. I made the suggestion that here was a proposition to increase salaries without necessity disclosed to the Senate. I saw fit to call the attention of the Senate to that subject, because I saw, on every hand, an indication of increase of expenditures. I remarked that I thought proper to call attention to this subject in all cases, whether large or small. This is no great matter; but it involves an increase of salaries, as I think, without necessity, and I have done my duty in noticing the fact. I think we should look into every case, and see that the expenditures of the Government are not unnecessarily increased. I leave the subject with the Senate. It is of itself, of but little consequence, and I will not consume further time, remarking only that it is time to stop the unnecessary increase of expenditures in all cases.

Mr. DAVIS. If I had ever supposed that I could gain anythink by lecturing the honorable Senator from Maine, I should give it up now as hopeless, and come to the conclusion that he was unteachable. The remarks of the Senator were not applicable, because they were directed to a state of facts which did not exist; and now he takes issue with me because I tell him so. He cannot alter the facts. They are there; and I have a right, and every other man has a right, to judge of the applicability of his arguments, when he argues as to the facts.

Whether my manner belongs to the camp or the forum, I trust that my arguments will always be founded on truth. The Senator has committed an error as to the facts. If he did not commit an error, he must have known that he was attacking that which did not exist. I supposed that he was committing an error, because the facts did not exist so as to justify the attack. If he takes issue on that, let him do so and make the most of it. But he winds up by saying that it is a matter of such small importance that he leaves it to the Senate——

Mr. BRADBURY. Without further remark.

Mr. DAVIS. Exactly; and he leaves it precisely where he found it. I think it is probable that he has not changed the opinion of any one; nor even given sufficient reasons to justify his own. And if the matter is one of such small importance, it is a great pity the Senator did not think of that before, and allow the question to be taken without giving rise to this debate.

The question was then taken on the adoption of the amendment, and it was agreed to.

Mr. HUNTER. I hope the question will be taken on the

remaining amendments altogether, as they follow as a matter of course from the adoption of the last amendment. They are merely verbal, so as to make the several parts of the bill agree.

The question was then taken on the remaining amendments proposed by Mr. HUNTER, and they were agreed to.

Mr. DAVIS, of Mississippi. I offer an amendment to come in at the end of the tenth line, as a proviso to that clause of the bill.

The amendment was then read, as follows:

"*Provided,* That the superintendent shall have rank by lineal grade or brevet not below that of lieutenant colonel, and that the commandant of cadets shall have rank by lineal grade, or brevet, not below that of a major."

Mr. DAVIS. I will state in a few words the reasons which induce me to offer that amendment. The compensation of the superintendent, if he have lower rank than is there provided, is too small. No officer can consistently with his own interest hold the office unless he have higher compensation than is allotted to the rank of the present superintendent. The late war with Mexico has given to that corps several brevets. They have several officers above the rank indicated by the amendment. Those officers may be taken by their brevet rank given for brilliant service, and such a compensation be thus given as is necessary to support the officer holding that station. That is the reason for the first branch of the amendment. The second is that which relates to the commandant of cadets. He should have the rank of major, and, as young officers may hereafter expect to be selected for both posts—the old officers of engineers having been already detailed for the post of superintendent, and a great many of the old officers of other corps for the post of commandant—I wish to give effect to brevet rank in both cases for the post of commandant. I have especial reasons.

The commandant should not only be a soldier of such character and experience as to enable him to teach the strategy of war with advantage, but also to impress his character on those who are to be taught. To effect this, it is essential that he should be a soldier tried in the war. Young officers who have acquired no higher rank than lieutenant by lineal grade may be selected for the post of commandant by having been breveted for distinguished services; their experience will be useful, and their character will be more useful than their experience, by inspiring military ardor in the youths under his command. That position is one which immediately and entirely regards the military branch of instruction in the academy—the rest regards the scientific. The commandant has charge of the military instruction of the cadets, and, more than others, forms their military character.

Mr. DAVIS. The object of the Senator from Florida [Mr. YULEE] could only be attained by creating what is termed "local rank," a species of rank known in the British service, but entirely unknown in our own. Increasing the compensation alone would not suffice. A local rank might be given to the superintendent equal to any grade which Congress might adopt. Any officer might be selected; and holding the post would give him, for the time he held it, a local rank. Then the compensation follows of course; otherwise it would be likely that the superintendent would be of lower grade than the commandant, and that would destroy the whole organization of the academy. The commandant, by the operation of the rules of war, takes command. It would, therefore, be necessary that a law should be enacted to create a local rank in the academy. If the amendment were so shaped as to make such a proposition, I think it would very likely lead to a long debate. I will therefore withdraw that amendment, and offer another to be added to the end of the bill.

"For the completion of the riding hall, $8,000."

The late Secretary of War, in considering the estimates of the last year, struck out the estimate for the completion of the riding hall, which is unfinished. The one now in use is poor and badly constructed. In a letter from the instructor of the artillery class, who is also instructor of the riding class, it is stated that, from the construction of the building, it is difficult to impart instruction properly, and that in many instances there is danger of the cadets losing their lives. It appears that this appropriation for the finishing of the riding hall is essential to the communication of instruction, and equally essential for the safety of those who are to be instructed.

Committee Report by Jefferson Davis, Sept. 3, 1850.

Mr. DAVIS, of Mississippi, from the Committee on Military Affairs, to which was referred the memorial of Joseph J. Graham, asking authority to raise a regiment of dragoons from the young men of the southwestern part of Virginia and the eastern part of Tennessee, to serve on the frontier, and at the expiration of their term to be allowed a half section of land, asked to be discharged from the further consideration of the same; which was agreed to.

Also, from the same committee, to which was referred certain resolutions of the Legislature of the State of Texas, relative to the payment of certain companies for services on the western frontier, submitted a report, which was ordered to be printed, accompanied by a joint resolution for the settlement of the accounts of certain companies of Texas volunteers, which was read and passed to a second reading.

Remarks of Jefferson Davis concerning the credentials of the Senators from California, Sept. 10, 1850.

Mr. DOUGLAS. Mr. President, I have been requested to present the credentials of WILLIAM M. GWIN as a member of the Senate elect from the State of California. I move that they be read, and that the oath of office be administered to Mr. GWIN.

The Secretary read the credentials accordingly.

Mr. BARNWELL. Mr. President, I have been requested to present the credentials of JOHN C. FREMONT as a Senator from California. It is well known, sir, that I entertained the strongest constitutional objections to the admission of California into the Union. But Congress having passed an act for her admission, Mr. FREMONT's admission could not be otherwise than very acceptable.

The credentials were read by the Secretary.

Mr. DAVIS, of Mississippi. Mr. President, if I were governed by either personal or party considerations, I certainly should make no objection to the ordinary course which is pursued when the credentials of Senators are received here. But believing, as I do, that the constitutional provisions for the election of Senators could not have been complied with in this case, it is with me a sacred matter of duty to interpose such objection as requires me to move the reference of these credentials to the Committee on the Judiciary, with instructions to report on the law and the facts. I make that motion.

The Secretary read the motion, when it was reduced to writing, as follows:

Resolved, That the credentials of the Senators elect from the State of California be referred to the Committee on the Judiciary, with instructions to report on the law and the facts.

Mr. DOUGLAS. Mr. President, I see no necessity for taking up time by this reference. If this were the forepart of the session I would interpose no objection to the reference. But now less than three weeks of the session remain, and much legislation must take place for California. Hence it is important that these Senators should take their seats. In order that they may do so, there being many precedents for this case, certainly one or two precisely in point, as no one can doubt, I hope the motion will not prevail.

Mr. DAVIS called for the yeas and nays on his motion, and they were ordered.

Mr. DAVIS. If it be in order, and if the chairman of the Judiciary Committee thinks he will be then ready to report, I would move, as additional instructions, that the committee report to-morrow morning.

The PRESIDENT. Such instructions are not in order.

Mr. DAVIS, of Mississippi. I do not consider that California was a State out of the Union, but that it was a Territory of the United States—territory obtained by conquest and purchase—over which the United States had full authority, and over which Congress failed to exercise that authority, from considerations, as I believe, discreditable to the Government itself. It was this failure of the Government to take charge of this Territory which constituted the best argument for the action of the people of California themselves. California became a State by the action of Congress, and the action of the President approving the bill which Congress passed; and she was not a State before that action was had. The Constitution provides that Senators shall be elected by the Legislature of a State, and, if there was no State, there could be no Legislature of a State. I do not propose to go into an argument upon this subject, and I only moved the reference to a committee which I thought might best judge of a constitutional question, and I do not believe now that the committee would have detained us more than one or two days. I seek for no delay—I wish the question fairly presented, and I took this mode of reaching it. I am one of those who opposed the admission of California—who sought to restrict its boundaries; but I am not one of those who at any time was prepared to enter into a compact to admit her with reduced boundaries. I considered the defect in the whole proceeding to be inherent and radical, and beyond any reduction of the boundaries. I am one of those who stand here instructed by my State Legislature to resist the admission of California by all honorable and constitutional means. This is taken as an incident to State existence prior to the admission of California, and this is the ground taken by the Senator from Kentucky. If, then, I am under instructions to use all honorable and constitutional means to resist the admission of California as a State, I am also necessarily instructed to oppose everything which is an incident to the assertion of State existence prior to our action for admission.

I did not wish to be drawn into any remarks on this subject and personal considerations rendered me very reluctant to do so; nor did I wish to consume the time of the Senate by debate. Whatever views I have entertained on this subject have been heretofore expressed, and I have merely sought now to refer the question to that committee to whom we have supposed we might entrust the examination of questions of constitutional law.

Remarks of Jefferson Davis on the slave trade in the District of Columbia, Sept. 10, 1850.

Mr. DAVIS, of Mississippi. I find little controversy between those who have spoken on this bill, except as to the punishment which should be visited upon him who introduces his slave property into the District of Columbia. It is assumed to be an offence, and is treated as though the only question were whether the individual who introduces a slave into the District shall be fined, or whether the slave shall be manumitted. The power to do this is not referred to any particular grant of the Constitution, but it is attempted to draw it from the fact that like power has been exercised by a State, which, being sovereign over its own territory, may have for public purposes refused, under certain conditions, to allow slaves to be introduced within its borders. Yet what State ever legislatively refused to allow a citizen of the United States to pass through its borders with a slave? And that is the nature of the prohibition presented here. No one expects that slaves are to be brought into the District for sale and residence here, and the whole argument directs itself to the traders who may bring slaves here, and keep them in depot with the intention of sending them elsewhere. It is then the right of transit over the District against which this bill is directed, and this is one step further than any State, even in the exercise of its sovereign power, has gone. But is it to be inferred that because a sovereign State may exercise certain powers, that Congress possesses the same? The States, as sovereign, possess all the powers which they have not delegated; the Federal Government as a trustee has only those which have been granted to it. Are powers to be usurped? are all the limitations of the Constitution to be forgotten? and are we in fact now a consolidated Government, to be controlled by the will of the majority? The Constitution confers on Congress the power to exercise exclusive legislation over the District— exclusive, in order that its legislation might not come in conflict with that of the States who should surrender a certain amount of their territory to form a seat of Government. That was to give to Congress the control of the District, within which it might meet for purposes truly and clearly connected with a seat of Government. It was not to confer on Congress the absolute or unlimited power of legislation, but to prevent any one else from legislating in a District ceded for use as the seat of Government. Therefore it must have been that exclusive power was granted. But to this exclusive power there are two limitations: first, the restrictions of the Constitution; and secondly, the intent, the motive, the purposes for which the grant was made. I deny that Congress has the power to pass any law in relation to the District of Columbia, except so far as that law may be connected with objects of the grant; and if there be a reasonable doubt as to the constitutional power, the necessity should be immediate and absolute, such as involved the purpose of the grant, which would warrant its exercise.

But if the proposition which is now before us, and which is to prohibit any citizen of the United States from bringing a slave into the District, with a view thereafter of taking him into another State of the Union, be within the power of Congress, it is not derived from such necessity as I have described. If it be drawn from the power of exclusive legislation in the District, why may we not adopt a like provision in relation to every arsenal, custom-house, fort, and dock-yard? The same section of the Constitution which gives to Congress exclusive legislation over the District of Columbia gives it over the forts, arsenals, custom-houses, and dock-yards. Then if a citizen of Georgia, wishing to go to Mississippi with a slave, which he should subsequently sell, passed through a dock-yard of the United States, his slave would be emancipated by general legislation. To this extent would the power here asserted reach, whenever it should please the majority to exercise it.

This, sir, is a species of property recognized by the Constitution of the United States, and the same instrument guaranties to every citizen of the United States the right, unobstructed, to pass with every species of property through any portion of the United States. A sovereign State may forbid the introduction of a certain species of property within its limits, there to remain, whether for sale or use. But I do not believe a State has the right to prevent a citizen of the United States from exercising the right of transit with any property which he may legally hold; this is one of the results of our free-trade Constitution. If, then, no State has the right to obstruct or abolish, even on her own domain, that privilege, how can it be supposed that it was intended to confer such power upon their agent? Yet we have before us a proposition to deprive citizens of the United States of the right of transit over territory surrendered to the Government of the United States solely for the purposes of a seat of Government.

Sir, instead of intending to confer unlimited power on Congress, I would rather suppose that it was intended to make it exclusive, with a view that whatever territory should be held for a seat of Government should be neutral; that the rights of all citizens should be equal in such district; that property should not be affected by the legislation of the States which had ceded the territory. If the State of Maryland should choose to abolish slavery, I can well understand that this provision of the Constitution was intended as a shield over the District, so that every citizen of the United States might come here to this as common ground, bring with him any species of property he might own, and enjoy the rights he had in the State of his residence. I am opposed to both the proposition of the bill and that of the amendment; not equally, however, for one is more abhorrent to me than the other; but I am utterly opposed to both. I cannot consent to prohibit a citizen of the United States from exercising the right he has to pass through the United States, or any part of it, with any species of property recognized by our Constitution or laws. I shall oppose this and all kindred measures, however ineffectual may be such opposition to that anti-slavery majority around which sycophants, deserters, and ambitious demagogues gather. Least of all, in this District, which was neutral ground of our fathers, and has descended as such to us, can I agree to discriminate against a particular species of property, and the rights of a certain class of the citizens of the United States. I will not argue the general question, but content myself with denying now, as I have denied at all times, the power of Congress to discriminate in relation to property or to declare what is or is not property. There were certain specific powers granted to the Federal Government, and beyond these it can have none. The rights of property were never surrendered to the decision of the Federal Government, and it has no right to attempt a discrimination by which the use of a particular property is to be restricted, its value diminished, or its possession destroyed.

Mr. DAVIS, of Mississippi. I think I understood the language of the bill before the Senator from Maryland explained it to me; however, I do not see anything to affect my position in the difference between the construction he places on it, and that which he ascribes to me. What matters it that the condition is annexed of an intent to sell the slave at some future time, and some other place, as that on which forfeiture shall attach? I deny the power; it was not granted; it was prohibited by the clause which forbids this Government to take private property, except for public use, and on making due compensation therefor. What I ask is, where does this Government get the right to ask the citizen what he is going to do with his property, and where does it get the right to discriminate or decide, by his future intentions, on the right of possession and transit with such property?

Mr. PRATT. I did not intend to argue the constitutional question; I merely stated that the Senator had extended the effect of this law beyond what its provisions would really warrant. I stated particularly, that he was right in supposing that it did prohibit the slave-dealer from carrying slaves here, or establishing a depôt for them as merchandise; but that in regard to citizens coming here, or passing through with their servants, it did not include them. I did not attempt to argue the constitutional power at all.

Mr. DAVIS, of Mississippi. What right has Congress to inquire for what purpose a man has brought his property here? Can you entertain that question?

Mr. PRATT. That is not the question.

Mr. DAVIS, of Mississippi. That is the whole question. The provision is against those who bring slaves here to be transported and sold elsewhere. How is that to be determined? Now, it might occur that the Senator himself, however improperly, would be called a slave-dealer in some sections of the Union. If names are to determine the application of the law, it will extend to all who own slaves. It is a provision which never can seriously affect the property of my constituents. My opposition is to the principle rather than to the value of the interest involved, though I believe that interest to be much more general than the property of slave-dealers. The people of Mississippi are little if at all interested in such trade. I do not know how soon they may find it to their advantage to prevent further introduction of slaves into their limits, and I believe that it is the policy of all the southern States to check the further emigration from those States who do sell slaves. I spoke of the constitutional power, and against that my whole argument was directed. But the Senator supposes that an individual may come here with his servant, and not be interfered with. Why not? What constitutes placing him in depôt? The slave being in a State of involuntary servitude, is always in a species of confinement. He has not the right to go without the leave of his master, and thus is under duress. The depôt is a comfortable looking house, in which, I understand, a trader keeps his slaves before going to some market. Rather a boarding-house in its aspect than a prison. I had been here long after I heard of the slave-pens in this city, before I knew what was meant by the term, and I have asked some of the oldest inhabitants of the District if they had ever seen a gang of slaves passing manacled through their streets, and they have all answered me "No!" I have never seen anything of the kind during the various sessions I have served here. I finally discovered, by accident, what this slave-pen was, so often spoken of in Congress, by having my attention drawn to a dwelling-house, by the spacious yard and growth of poplar trees around it. That, I was told, was the "slave-pen." It is a house by which all must go in order to reach the building of the Smithsonian Institution, and looking as little like a jail as any residence in the city of Washington.

But if you deprive the owner of a gang of slaves from having his own house in which to board them, and keep them separate from other people, what is the necessary consequence? Why, that for the time he stays here he lodges them in jail for safe keeping. It is an act of inhumanity rather than of kindness on our part, therefore, to deprive him of the right of keeping the slaves in his own house, where he could keep them comfortably, as it would be on the trader's part an act of fatuity voluntarily to put them in confinement so as to affect their comfort or health. He regards them as property, and he takes care of them as such, governed by the same motives which actuate dealers in any other species of property. I know the odium which exists against this class of traders; I have grown up in a community which feels it, and partake of it myself; they are usually northern men, who come among us but are not of us. But I did not intend to direct my remarks to that aspect of the question. It was the question of power to which I invited the attention of the Senate, and it was this proposition, by one long stride to pass the barriers of the Constitution, and cater to an anti-slavery feeling by trampling upon constitutional rights in a species of property against which the Government seems now to be arrayed in hostility, that formed the basis of my argument, and prompted the opposition I have offered.

Mr. PRATT. The Senator from Mississippi reiterates the opinion that a citizen of the United States other than a slave-dealer could not, while in transit, while he was going through this District, put his servants in depôt for safe-keeping under the provisions of this bill. Now the difference between us is, that in the first place, under the clear construction, as it appears to me, which the Senator must place on this bill, if he had read it attentively, a citizen of the United States, not a slave-dealer, would have the right to put his servants in depôt here, unless he intended to carry them elsewhere, to be sold as merchandise. But, independent of that, there is the fourth section of the Maryland act to which I have referred, and which is the law of the District, in which there is an express legislative agreement that the citizens of the United States may bring their servants here, provided they do not design to sell them. First listen to the bill itself:

"It shall not be lawful to bring into the District of Columbia any slave whatever for the purpose of being sold, or for the purpose of being placed in depôt, to be subsequently transported to any other State or place to be sold as a slave."

It will be seen that the inhibition is not on the placing them in depôt, but on the placing them in depôt when the intention of the party is to carry them to some other place, there to sell them as merchandise. There is no inhibition against any citizen bringing his servants here and placing them in depôt, unless his further design is to carry them elsewhere for the purpose of selling them as merchandise. That, I submit to the Senate is the clear and manifest construction of this bill. Then comes the law of the District, as it now stands, being the fourth section of the Maryland act to which I have referred:

"Nothing in this law shall be so construed as to affect the rights of any person or persons traveling or sojourning with any slave or slaves within the State, such slave or slaves not being sold or otherwise disposed of in the State, but carried by the owner, or attempted to be carried by the owner out of the State."

Thus, when the owner shall bring a slave here and place him in depôt, if the object is not to sell him as merchandise, he has a perfect right to do so, and to carry him away when he proposes to go elsewhere.

Mr. DAVIS, of Mississippi. That is not the point of difference between us. I ask the Senator how we are to ascertain whether the individual intended to sell his negro or not? It is his property, and this law will require every man that shall come here to go and enter into bonds that he will not sell his servant. It is his property, and he has the right to sell it as such if he pleases. Is Congress then to require the arrest of every man who comes here, and make him enter into bonds that he will not sell his property here, or that when he transports it here it shall not be sold? That is the only mode of reaching it? These men do not come here and put up a sign thus: "Negroes taken in depôt and sold as merchandise." Such a law may cause the arrest of one of the Senator's own constituents, who may come here on his way to Virginia, and require him to give bonds that he will not sell his servant when he gets there. That is the point.

Sept. 11, 1850.

Mr. DAVIS, of Mississippi. While temporarily absent from my seat, I was informed that the Senator from Massachusetts read a letter referring personally to myself. Now I lay no claim to the amount of intelligence which his correspondent seems to award to me, but I do claim to have used due caution in getting information. Before I made that statement here, I made inquiry among those best informed on the subject, and I learned that the arrests of free persons of color, coming in vessels to the ports named, had been of those persons who had been on shore, and thus violated the police regulations which the absolute necessity of the case had required these cities to establish—police regulations to prevent the murder of the inhabitants, and the burning of the city by incendiaries, prompted by fanatics baser than the slaves whom they use as instruments for arson and murder. The Senator from Massachusetts reads the letter; I ask him does he indorse it?

Mr. WINTHROP. I do not understand what the Senator means by indorsing it.

Mr. DAVIS, of Mississippi. Does he adopt the statement as his own?

Mr. WINTHROP. Certainly not. I know nothing of the statement or the person, further than the letter itself furnishes evidence. I read the letter as I received it by due course of mail. And I showed it to the Senator from Mississippi before I read it to the Senate, and therefore I have taken no advantage of his absence.

Mr. DAVIS, of Mississippi. I am not in the habit of reading letters to the Senate unless I can vouch for the truth of what they contain. I am not in the habit of parading my private correspondence before the Senate, or of attempting to impugn the statements of my brother Senators here by letters from those who I am not prepared to indorse.

With a modicum of intelligence only, I had not so much credulity as to credit the statements on which the Senator relies. I therefore made inquiries in quarters I believed to be most reliable, and arrived at the conclusion that the statements of the letter which was read by the Senator were unfounded, absolutely false. I know something personally of a portion of what is involved in this assertion. I reside so near to New Orleans, and visit it so often, it being my market town, as to have some opportunity to know what is done there. There are two Senators upon this floor who know more about it than myself. There are two Senators who can speak for Charleston, and the Presiding Officer can speak for Mobile. I believe the whole statement to be a groundless aspersion, put forth by an Abolitionist, and I am sorry that the Senator from Massachusetts has so far forgotten what was due to this body, and to himself, as to introduce it upon this floor.

The PRESIDENT. The Senator will observe order.

Mr. DAVIS, of Mississippi. There are times, sir, when men might be excused for forgetting to measure their language. When the moral character of one entire section of the Union is assailed, it is time for those who value it to speak in language not to be misunderstood. I will, however, endeavor to remember the rules of debate.

The charge, not now for the first time brought forward, involves a multitude of crimes. It is an attempt to pervert a necessary police regulation into a system for the capture of freemen, that they may be reduced into slavery. Whatever faults the people of the South may have, I speak confidently when I say kidnapping is not among them.

Sir, there is no community more entirely opposed to reducing any freemen to slavery than that which I have the honor to represent. There is no man of standing in that community who would not contribute from his purse to relieve any human being, however black, whom the vicissitudes of the sea should drive to their shore, instead of taking advantage of his misfortune to reduce him to bondage. There is not a lawyer in that community who would not step forward and voluntarily advocate the cause of any free man thus arrested. Sir, when vessels come into any of the ports that have been named, and lie at anchor, or steamboats come to at the landing of that river which bears on its bosom the wealth of the great valley of the West to its depôt, New Orleans, I am well assured that no civil officer would step upon their decks to inspect the crew, that he might arrest any free colored man found on board; and am still more certain that such arrest would never be made to reduce him to slavery. But when the safety of our towns is endangered, when the peace of our citizens is involved by the free negroes sent among us as emissaries to instigate the slave population to insurrection, then the highest law of nature, the law of self-preservation, requires that the civil officer should interpose and arrest such dangerous persons.

I do not know how far the Senator from South Carolina has considered this question, as connected with the city of Charleston, but it is a matter of history that the second delegate from Massachusetts to South Carolina was one who was sent for the purpose of counteracting those regulations designed to prevent the instigation of the slaves to arson and murder. The first was sent when brave men, resolved to resist oppression by power, unmindful or regardless of right, sought for aid in the generosity and fraternity of the southern colonies. The difference in the purpose and spirit of these missions is typical of the political and moral change which time and circumstances have wrought.

Disregarding the necessity to meet which this police regulation was enacted, they sent the second ambassador to Charleston to see whether that regulation could not be annulled, and to institute private and insidious inquiries into the domestic institutions of the city, for purposes which it was the part of prudence to suspect.

If, Mr. President, these States are united as one family—if, indeed, we are to view each other as a confederated people, it is necessary that this hostility to southern interests—this war upon the domestic peace and security—this constant outrage on the feelings of the South, should cease. Were we without the restrictions of the Constitution—were we a people relying upon our own hearts and hands for the preservation of our rights, these invasions would not probably have gone so long unredressed. Thus have sectional rivalry and fanatic hate, instead of restraint, found shelter and pretext in our Union. The enmity is rendered worse by the fact of brotherhood. They would not have been able to do so much harm as a foreign nation. As aliens, they must have observed the terms of the treaty, or incur the responsibilities of war; now they aggress under the forms of the Constitution. That which was made to unite all for the protection of each, is bent to the purpose of the dominant party. They disregard the comity of nations, instead of observing the fraternity of confederated States. It is time these things should cease.

I am sorry, Mr. President, that the Senator from Massachusetts, a ripe scholar and a gentleman, who knows what is due to others as well as what is due to himself, has produced his private correspondence before the Senate, and without being willing to adopt the statements, reads them in reply to the remarks he had elicited by his course on a former occasion. Why bring forth a preserved letter from, as it appears, an unknown correspondent, referring by name to a Senator, and bearing testimony in a case much too important to be thus decided? I repeat, sir, that I have inquired into the matter, and believe that what has been stated with regard to the arrest and sale of free persons in the southern ports, is entirely untrue.

Mr. DAVIS. If the Senator from Massachusetts will permit me, before he leaves that subject, I will say another word.

Mr. WINTHROP. Oh! certainly.

Mr. DAVIS. I did not consider the Senator from Massachusetts dishonored by receiving that letter any more than I considered myself dishonored by reading it. I read it when it was handed to me, as the Senator has just stated. On that occasion I thought his conduct entirely proper. I made my comments, as he has stated, in a friendly manner; but I did not expect that would parade such poor testimony before the Senate and the country.

Bill reported by Jefferson Davis, Sept. 14, 1850.

PENSION BILL.

Mr. DAVIS, of Mississippi, from the Committee on Military Affairs, to which was referred the resolution of the Senate, directing the Committee on Military Affairs to inquire into the expediency of granting a pension to the widow of Lieutenant Colonel Æneas Mackay, reported a general bill entitled "A bill to provide pensions for the widows and orphans of deceased officers and soldiers," and asked that it might have its second reading at this time. There being no objection, the bill was read a second time, and considered as in Committee of the Whole.

The bill provides for five years' pensions to the widows and orphans of officers and soldiers of the United States.

The first section provides that if any officer, non-commissioned officer, artificer, farrier, blacksmith, musician, or private belonging to the army of the United States, or to the militia in the service of the United States, whether by draft or by voluntary enrollment shall be killed, or die by reason of a wound received, or disease contracted, or injury received while in the line of their duty, leaving a widow, or if no widow a child or children, under sixteen years of age, such widow, or if no widow, such child or children shall be entitled to receive half the monthly pay to which the deceased was entitled at the time of his death, the allowance to continue for the term of five years thereafter.

The second section provides that if, before the expiration of the said term of five years, the widow should marry again, or die, leaving no children, or there being no widow, if the child or children should die before the expiration of the term of five years, then, in either case, the half-pay allowance shall cease. But if the widow, having been placed on the pension roll, should die before the expiration of the term of five years, leaving a child or children, the half pay shall be allowed for the remainder of the term to the child or children of the deceased soldier, as thereinbefore provided.

The third section provides that if any officer, non-commissioned officer, artificer, farrier, blacksmith, musician, or private of the army of militia, whilst in the service of the United States, shall, since the seventh day of May 1845, have been killed in battle, or have died of wounds received in the line of his duty, his widow or children shall be entitled to the provisions of the foregoing sections, subject to all the restrictions and limitations therein contained.

Remarks of Jefferson Davis on bill to suppress the slave traffic in the District of Columbia, Sept. 16, 1850.

Mr. DAVIS, of Mississippi. Whilst gentlemen are dividing the honors that result from the passage of these bills, either in a joint or separate form, I have only to say that, so far as I am concerned they are welcome to the whole, I do not represent that public opinion which required the passage of them, either jointly or separately.

If any man has a right to be proud of the success of these measures, it is the Senator from Illinois, [Mr. DOUGLAS.] They were brought before the Senate by the Committee on Territories, and this Committee of Thirteen, which it is claimed has done so much for the honor of the Senate and the peace of the country, merely stuck together the work of other men, save and except the little bill to suppress the slave trade in the District of Columbia. I merely wish to say that, so far as the public opinion of the community which I represent has been shadowed forth in public meetings, and in the public press, it has been wholly adverse to the great body of these measures. I voted for one—that which the Senator from Virginia originated, and which was modified in the Senate till I thought, as far as we could make it so, it became efficient for the protection of our rights. That was the only one which met my approval.

Mr. FOOTE. I will detain the Senate but a moment longer. I was not one of the Committee of Thirteen, but I was one who most cordially applauded their labors; and I think they did a great deal. Certain it is that these bills were reported by the Committee on Territories; but it is equally certain—and I believe I may say that without egotism—that the report of the Committee on Territories was based upon bills introduced by myself.

Mr. DAVIS, of Mississippi, (in his seat.) Oh, yes, I am willing to give you all the credit for that.

Mr. FOOTE. But the fact is, the labors of the committee were independent of all that. The committee was raised for the consideration of the whole subject of slavery, at least for the purpose of taking into consideration the questions growing out of slavery. They modified some measures that had been originated by other committees, and originated others, and matured a new system—a system of pacification and adjustment, which has now become part of the law of the land, with the exception of the present bill; and they brought it in, incurring all the responsibility of reporting it, and stood by it with a manly resolution and persevering energy which finally triumphed over all obstacles. Although these bills did pass separately, I maintain, and shall ever maintain, that but for the fact of their being combined by the committee originally, and being blended here in discussion, and being united in the public mind; but for there having been a general understanding in both Houses of Congress, at the time of the passage of these bills, that each of them should pass as a part of a scheme of adjustment, most of them never would have passed in any form. Therefore it is that I say that the labors of the Committee of Thirteen were not small— they were not light—they were not inconsiderable. They were great and arduous labors, involving high and fearful responsibility, calling for the greatest abilities, the most noble moral qualities, and resulting in such consequences as will cause the friend of freedom to rejoice, in all countries, now and forever. So much for the committee.

Now I feel bound to say, in reply to my colleague, that I differ with him much upon a certain delicate point which he has brought to our notice this morning. We differ, sir, now, as we always differ—*as friends;* and whatever difference of opinion may exist between us, I take pleasure in uniformly referring to him as a gentleman whose motives are as good as my own, though his judgment with regard to certain measures is not in accordance with mine. He has concluded by saying that he does not represent that public opinion which is in accordance with this plan of adjustment. I am gratified at having it in my power to say that I do represent that precise state of public opinion which he repudiates. I feel bound to say, in addition, (and I say it with my hand on my heart, and with a solemn determination to tell the truth about this matter, as I understand and believe it,) that my opinion is that nine-tenths of the enlightened freemen of the State of Mississippi are now, and have been all along, cordially in favor of this much-abused plan of adjustment; and I predict that they will deliberately and formally sanction hereafter all that the committee have done. I believe they will declare their approbation of all the labors of the committee, and avow their concurrence in all that I have done and said at any time, as one of their Senatorial representatives. Such is my opinion. My colleague entertains a very different opinion. We shall soon be at home among our constituents, where we shall confer together as friends, and where we shall consult our mutual constituents also as friends. I go for consulting them, and if they decide against me, I shall be no longer an occupant of a seat in this body.

Mr. HALE. Mr. President, I rise to inquire what is the question before the Senate?

The PRESIDENT. It is on the passage of the bill "to suppress the slave trade in the District of Columbia."

Mr. HALE. I thought it was who should have the most glory for defeating the "compromise bill." [Laughter.] I had something to say on that subject. I wish to say nothing on this.

Mr. DAVIS, of Mississippi. Mr. President, I have heretofore declined to state by vulgar fractions the opinions of the State I represent. I do not intend to do so now. I have heretofore stated that I believed I represented the opinions of my constituents in opposing these measures. I am firm in that belief. But I do not intend to argue with my colleague about his opinions. I am well assured that he will find no nine-tenths in any one county, still less in the State of Mississippi, favoring his course on these measures. The language expressed by my colleague here on other occasions excited surprise in Mississippi and has been remarked upon in the public press. I know of no community in Mississippi, not a single town or county, where I believe he can find a majority in favor of all these measures— and nine-tenths is such a majority as scarcely leaves a show of opposition. That nine-tenths of the people of the State are in favor of a system of measures which nearly every prominent man in the State has condemned, is an assertion which marks clearly how far the warm impulses of the gentleman, when pursuing any measure to which he attaches himself, will lead him from the calmer conclusions of his maturer judgment.

As to the opinions of my colleague, I know him too well to doubt that he says what he thinks. I know him well enough to be assured that his excitability has led him into an error in relation to this matter. When he and I visit our constituents, at the short period to which he refers, he will find what the public opinion is.

Mr. FOOTE. Mr. President, a single word.

The PRESIDENT. The Chair is under the necessity of stopping this course of debate. It is not at all relevant to the question under consideration.

Mr. FOOTE. I hope the Chair will bear with me while I make a single remark. I am perfectly willing to abide by the decision to which my colleague refers. And I am willing to leave it to the Senate, and to the country to decide whether he or I am the more "excitable" man of the two.   [Laughter.]

Committee report by Jefferson Davis, Sept. 16, 1850.

Mr. DAVIS, of Mississippi, from the Committee on Military Affairs, to which were referred the following memorials, to wit: The memorial of the Legislature of Missouri, in favor of a grant of land to teamsters who served in the war with Mexico, and the memorial from General Hugh W. Dobbin, asking remuneration for services in the war of 1812, submitted a report in each case, which was ordered to be printed, and asked to be discharged from the further consideration of the same; which was agreed to.

Also, from the same committee, to which was referred the memorial of C. J. Cook and A. A. Lockwood, asking compensation for their property, destroyed by a party of United States soldiers in the town of Fredericksburg, in the State of Texas, submitted a report, asking to be discharged from the further consideration of the same; which was agreed to.

Remarks of Jefferson Davis on the bill creating the office of surveyor general of public lands in Oregon, and making donations of land to actual settlers, Sept. 17, 1850.

PUBLIC LANDS IN OREGON.

On motion by Mr. DOUGLAS, the Senate proceeded to the consideration of a bill entitled "An act to create the office of surveyor general of the public lands in Oregon, and to provide for the survey, and to make donations to settlers of the public lands."

The pending amendment was one offered by Mr. DAVIS, of Mississippi, when the bill was last under consideration on the 3d instant, as follows:

"Add to the bill the words: And that such portions of the public lands as may be designated under the authority of the President of the United States for forts, magazines, arsenals, dock-yards, and other needful public uses, shall be reserved and excepted from the operation of this act."

Which was modified, on the suggestion of Mr. BADGER, by the addition of the following:

"Provided, That if it shall be deemed necessary, in the judgment of the President, to include in any such reservation the improvements of any settler made previous to the passage of this act, it shall in such case be the duty of the Secretary of War to cause the value of such improvements to be ascertained, and the amount so ascertained shall be paid to the party entitled thereto, out of any money in the Treasury not otherwise appropriated.''

Mr. DAVIS, of Mississippi. When this matter was last under consideration some statements were made in relation to the military reservations proposed to be made by the Government, and trespasses were said to have been made upon the rights of the settlers. Since that time I have made some further inquiries, and I find that not only what I then stated is correct, but that the proofs are more conclusive than I supposed it possible to obtain. I find from the official correspondence, and the statements of the officer sent here in connection with this matter, that in no instance has any one been driven from his possessions; and that in every instance where the Government has selected land on which there were improvements, a careful estimate has been made of the value of the improvements found upon the land, with a view to making therefor full compensation. I have learned what is probably the foundation of the story of the store-house at Astoria. An officer direct from that country informs me that the commanding officer of the garrison desired to obtain a store-house which was the property of the Hudson's Bay Company, and that he sent a proposition to an agent of the company in relation to it. It had not been taken possession of when this officer left the country, but he met the agent of the Hudson's Bay Company on his way, in order to agree upon the terms of rent to be paid by the commanding officer. I have learned, also, that the town of Astoria is situated upon four claims, each one mile square, with houses scattered along the bank of the river, having a small strip of land along the margin of the river cleared; and that the lot intended to be reserved is a high point of land, overlooking the channel of the Columbia river. On this two or three, or at most four inferior houses, had been erected, and the value of the improvements were estimated to be worth about two thousand dollars. I learn, also, that this tract is claimed by the Hudson's Bay Company. How far the treaty of Washington, which determined the boundary of Oregon, confirmed the possessory title of the Hudson's Bay Company in Oregon, it

is not now for the Senate to decide. It is a question settled
by international agreement. Their right may be extinguished
by purchase, but we can no more allow citizens of the United
States to dispossess them by settlement than we could send
troops to turn them off from the lands by force. There is, then,
to be considered in this connection, first, the title of the Hudson's
Bay Company, and then the reversionary title of the United
States, as standing in the way of these locations. We may
grant to the settlers of that country whatever right we possess.
We may go further, and grant whatever rights we may hereafter acquire, but they have no claim by settlements; we have
no power to make grants on lands previously occupied, and
now possessed by the Hudson's Bay Company. I understand,
also, that there has been some attempt at fraud in relation to
this matter; that the Hudson's Bay Company permitted its
servants, as individuals, to locate on its tracts of land, under
the impression that the company's title to their possessions in
the country could not be permanently held; and I have also
been informed that sometimes the employés of the company have
made locations against the claim of the company, so as to secure
its improvements for their own benefit, under operation of the
anticipated law for grants to actual settlers.

The reports of the officers in relation to the proposed reservations are very full. I have many before me, being originals
and copies, showing the position and extent of the particular
locations selected. That at Astoria is the lower one of these
four sections, claimed as settlement rights, and which constitute the so-called town of Astoria. It is a high point of
land, overlooking the river, and is represented as essential for
military purposes. The other reservations proposed to be made
for military purposes, at the mouth of the Columbia river, are
Point Adams, two square miles; Cape Disappointment, about
six hundred and forty acres; and Sand Island, containing about
twenty acres. These points I understand have now no occu-
pants upon them, and that there is no private claim upon them.
The Astoria point has already been noticed. Six miles above
Astoria there is another point of land overlooking the river,
which is also considered desirable for military purposes, and at
that point it is supposed that six hundred and forty acres might
be requisite. Next in order is the site for an ordnance depôt on
the Willamette river. And here, sir, I will say a few words
in answer to the argument made by the Senator from Illinois,
and founded especially upon this case, which he treated as an
invasion of the private rights of Mr. Meek, on the Willamette

river. I have sought, and acquired, I believe, very full information in relation to this claim. I have a map before me of the survey which was made for a reservation at that place. That was the point selected by the commanding general for an ordnance depôt, because, it being on the south side of the Columbia river, and on the north side of the Willamette, it was supposed to be most secure from attack, either by approach through the Puget Sound, or by the Columbia river, or by land routes from other points. It also possesses the water power necessary to drive the machinery required for an arsenal of construction. The private interest of the resident was treated as property in selecting the site, and from the estimate made seems very small compared with the idea suggested by the Senator's argument. One would suppose from his representation that it was an extensive cultivated estate, and that it had been laid waste; that it was over wide-spread fields of grain and clustering vines that the iron-shod hoofs of the cavalry had ruthlessly trodden. Now, all that appears by the map and report is one acre of cleared and fenced land, and a log cabin, which is estimated at a hundred and eighty dollars—one hundred dollars being the high rate allowed for clearing the acre of land, and eighty for the fence and cabin. And as to the horses running destructively over the grain-fields, the reply is contained in the statement made to me of the manner in which the survey was made. The officers and two soldiers were sent to make the survey; they went by way of the river in a boat, and had no horses with them. There was, according to my information, no dispossession of the resident. These officers went to his house, stated the object of their visit, gave assurances that his property should be fairly estimated, and if taken for public use would be paid for; they made the survey, and left in the most friendly manner. No troops have ever been stationed there, nor any other action by the military officers of the Government than that of the surveying party who marked the bounds of the proposed reservation, and returned, as they had gone, in a boat. Instead, therefore, of troops dispossessing this resident, and converting his fields into a pasture for the cavalry horses, it was only a surveying party who went there for the purposes of designating a reservation which it was proposed to make, and who, when they had done so, left the place. It is not intended, if the reservation be authorized, to take immediate possession. It was a mere selection and survey of a site, that hereafter, when it may become necessary to construct arms and ammunition in that country, we might have a reservation on which we could erect an ordnance depôt and arsenal of construction without paying an exorbitant price for a proper site. In making this survey, too, the greatest care was exhibited to avoid collision, and not needlessly to interfere with any settlement. There is a saw-mill on the stream, the water power of which it was expected to use; and in making the selection they treated with the owner of the mill in relation to the water privilege. There was also a settlement where there were some valuable fruit trees planted, and other improvements. They avoided that settlement, and made their location around this cabin, with its single acre of cleared land.

I will be very brief in the remainder of my remarks, as the Senator from Illinois informs me he intends to withdraw his objection. I will, therefore, say only so much as may be due to the officers whose conduct has been called in question. The location at the Dalles is in the Indian country, where the natives subsist upon the fish which they take from the river at that very favorable point for this pursuit—salmon fishing. If white men were allowed to go there, with the superior fishing apparatus and skill they possess, they would deprive those Indians of their only means of support. These are, I suppose, the fisheries from which the white men are said to have been excluded. If they went there, they were trespassers on the Indian land, and ought to have been driven off.

The military reservation at this point cannot interfere with settlers' rights, pretensions, or reasonable expectations. The missionary location will be, I doubt not, duly respected, and the reestablishment of the mission would be promoted by the presence of troops. It was long since abandoned by the missionaries, on account of the hostility of the surrounding tribes.

A reservation is proposed at Puget's Sound. This is, I believe, all except such places as may from time to time be found necessary in the Indian country. I will state further, that it is not intended that any reservation within the settled part of Oregon should be more than a mile square; and wherever private claims are required to give way to the public service, the property which is taken is to be estimated and paid for at its full value. Such is the character of the amendment, and such has been the expectation and conduct of the officers on the part of the Government in relation to these proposed reservations.

Mr. DOUGLAS. The statements that I made the other day on this subject were made on the authority of the Delegate from Oregon. He believed them. I believed them. I do not choose now to enter into a controversy as to whether the information received by the Senator from Mississippi or the information I have received is correct. Neither of us can settle that point at present. But I deem it so important, and the Delegate from Oregon deems it so important that this bill should pass now, that I do not propose to say one word in reply. But I hope we may now vote.

The amendment was adopted.

Mr. DAVIS, of Mississpppi, moved to strike out the third section of the bill, and insert in lieu thereof the following:

"'The surveys in said Territory shall be made after what is known as the geodetic method, under such regulations and upon such terms as may be provided by the Secretary of the Interior, or other department having charge of the surveys of the public lands, and that said geodetic surveys shall be followed by topographical surveys, as Congress may from time to time authorize and direct.''

Mr. DOUGLAS. Mr. President, I merely rise to express the hope that the amendment will not prevail; not with reference to its merits, but because its introducing a new system of surveying may endanger the bill in the House. If it is a better plan we can adopt it hereafter. But it is a new system, which requires investigation, and may at this time operate to defeat the bill.

Mr. DAVIS, of Mississippi. Mr. President, I should be sorry if the amendment should have that effect. Some time since I gave notice of my intention, whenever the subject of surveys in California and Oregon came up, to make this proposition. I am convinced that the geodetic is the only mode by which a strictly accurate survey can be made anywhere; and that there never was a country where it was more necessary than in Oregon and California. This is the result of the mountainous and mineral character of the country. Its narrow valleys being included between mountain ridges, afford the highest facilities for geodetic surveys, and the greatest difficulty to the mode now in use. There are also districts of country entirely worthless, and which lie contiguous to places where a single acre would be worth more than the thousand acres adjoining. We require, then, the highest degree of accuracy in the survey.

The present system is one which is wrong in theory. It has inherent errors, and those errors do not compensate each other, but constantly accumulate. When the present system is attempted to be applied to a mineral country, these errors increase to such a degree that surveys made in the old mode cannot be in any degree reliable. So they must prove in either Oregon or California. I believe, also, that the mode which I propose, in a country such as this, if the minute survey, the small triangulation, be confined to the fertile valleys and mines, can be adopted at less expense than a survey by the present mode of the whole country, as this mode requires.

As we advance to the north the errors of the present mode of survey increase. Between the 40th and 41st degree of north latitude there would be an error of 476 feet—nearly one-tenth of a mile to a degree of latitude. This is because the system of survey which we now use is founded on the supposition that the earth is a plane instead of being spheroidal, as it is known to be.

Mr. President, I have no more interest in this matter than any other member of the Senate must have. It is a matter of history that we adopted the present mode of survey from the fact that our first system of land survey had to be applied to a flat and heavily wooded country, where the more scientific method could not be advantageously adopted. Mr. Ellicott, a man of high attainments, was well aware of its defects, when the system was introduced. If the Senator's own prairie State of Illinois had been surveyed by the geodetic and the topographical manner, she might now present a map as accurate as that of the garden, at a cost little if anything more than the imperfect plats which have been obtained by the system pursued. Still more is this true of the mountain districts and the higher latitudes to which we are now going. We have been acting on an unsound theory and the theory being unsound, no errors which result from practice can ever compensate for themselves.

Mr. President, I see that there is not a disposition to enter into the merits of this question, and it is disagreeable, under such circumstances, to press its consideration. But I scarcely know how to avoid it. If we adopt the old mode of survey for Oregon, there is an end of the matter. If we commence upon that system because we are pressed for time, I do not see how we are to escape the same evil in the adjoining country. It will then be applied to California, as I suppose we will adopt some mode of survey for California at this session. If there is a mode by which the relative merits of the two methods of survey can be tested, whether by a committee of the Senate or otherwise, I should be very glad to see that course adopted. I have no wish to press discussion on the Senate at this time. But I believe that we should not surrender this, the only opportunity we can have to adopt a system which is true in itself, and which can so favorably be applied to the country for which we are about to order surveys. It is to begin with the mode with which we must sooner or later end, if we are to have accurate maps. I believe it should now be adopted there, hereafter to be extended thence to the Atlantic. This mode, once inapplicable, can soon, if not now, be applied to the whole country, as the dense, heavy woods which prevented us in the valley of Ohio from commencing with this mode of surveying are now in a great measure removed. Then we may present a a map of the United States, such as France now presents of her territory— such as Switzerland has given to geography. We are in this matter behind the civilization of the nineteenth century; and it is time we should come up to it; its advantages should appear in our public acts, and be conferred on our infant colonies.

Remarks of Jefferson Davis, Sept. 19, 1850, on appropriations for certain custom-houses.

Mr. DAVIS, of Mississippi. I am somewhat afraid of commencing this building of custom-houses in the interior towns; and I think the true rule by which we are to decide whether a place is worthy of a custom-house or not, is the amount of duties that is collected in that place. Now, I take it for granted that the amount collected in St. Louis is very small. It must be so; for though steam has brought St. Louis very near to the Gulf, the amount of water in the river is not increased, and it is doubtful whether a sailing vessel could get to St. Louis. Therefore, I take it for granted that goods will continue to be delivered at New Orleans, and then sent up to St. Louis in a different class of vessels. We have a port of entry much lower down, at Vicksburg, to which sea-going vessels can run, but they do not often do so. We had a vessel for that purpose, but it was hogged on a bar. Now, by every argument that has been used here, we require an appropriation for Vicksburg, to which sea-going vessels *can* ascend. That place should be considered before St. Louis. Now, I think the true rule to be employed in judging of this matter is, the amount of duties on imports that is collected.

The question being taken upon the amendment, it was lost.

Mr. DAVIS, of Mississippi. I objected to the appropriation

for the city of St. Louis; and yet the honorable Senator from Ohio urges that all the arguments in favor of the appropriation for that city apply to Cincinnati. His argument, therefore, would not be conclusive to me. Again: I think that all the arguments which apply to St. Louis do not apply to Cincinnati; for there are periods when sea-going vessels might get to St. Louis, but I do not think they' ever could get to Cincinnati. They certainly could not get through the canal, and it very seldom, if ever, happens that they could go up over the falls. I do not think all the arguments could be applied to Cincinnati that apply in favor of St. Louis; and for that reason I should be more opposed to this appropriation.

Mr. DAYTON. Cincinnati is also situated fifty or one hundred miles further up the river from the gulf than St. Louis. They have two persons employed in St. Louis, and but four at Cincinnati; yet it is asked to erect a custom-house there!

Mr. DAVIS. Mr. President, gentlemen have struck at last upon the true explanation of this matter. Goods imported to supply every portion of the West are imported into New Orleans; the duties are received there, and consequently the labor is performed at that place. Now, sir, I could not give a more striking proof of this, than to look into the Blue Book, and see what is done at St. Louis. There is a receiver at St. Louis, who receives for his services $174. There is an assistant, who receives $50. I suppose this is a full compensation for all the duties they perform. Nothing can be more apparent to me than that most of their duties relate to the internal commerce of the country. There is, I know, a large, a very large tonnage, but it is a tonnage engaged in the internal trade—a tonnage not registered, but licensed. When a vessel arrives from a foreign country with goods intended for the interior consumption, the duties are assessed at the port of New Orleans. They are seldom taken up the river upon the same vessel, but are generally shipped upon other kinds of craft. Now, I am willing to vote for measures like this, whenever there is an emergency shown. I am as willing to vote for a custom-house in the West as in the East, if there is any evidence before me that it is necessary to build one at all; but I have no evidence before me that there is any demand for such an appropriation at present. I shall therefore vote against it. It is a subject that ought to be inquired into. The business should be understood before we adopt a measure of this description.

Mr. DAYTON. This bill is now in Committee of the Whole. I give notice to the Senator from Maine, [Mr. HAMLIN,] that when this bill is reported to the House, I shall move to strike out the appropriation for the custom-house in Bangor.

Mr. DAVIS, of Mississippi. The Senator from Maine has argued, from the extent of tonnage registered and licensed the necessity for a custom-house. I think we have no occasion to build a custom-house for purposes of registry and license. A single room twenty feet square would, I apprehend, be sufficient to discharge all the duties connected with those transactions. You want a custom-house as a depôt for goods; and it will be recollected that last year the Senate was much occupied with the question of the warehousing system; and I think the conclusion of the Senate then was, that it was more advantageous to the United States to hire warehouses belonging to other persons than for the United States to build and own them. I have no doubt that, with the progress of settlement, a large amount of goods will pass up the Mississippi river, and many of its tributaries, to be stored for future consumption; and some time hereafter it may come to pass that the trade will reach that point that custom-houses may be necessary; but that will not depend so much upon the amount of goods consumed as it will upon the amount and location of capital engaged in the foreign trade. For the present, I have no doubt that it will be better to abstain from these appropriations.

Remarks of Jefferson Davis on the civil and diplomatic bill. Sept. 23, 1850.

Mr. DAVIS, of Mississippi. I doubt very much the propriety, and indeed the power, to make such an appropriation. I doubted its propriety when the first appropriation was made. It will be seen that the increase of the appropriation asked for is quite as rapid as the increase of the power described by the Senator from Missouri. Twenty thousand dollars was first given for experiments, and $40,000 is asked now to carry them out; and the next session, perhaps, $80,000 will be asked to apply them. Where does Congress get the power to make this appropriation? for that is the question we should ask ourselves in the exercise of our legislative power over any subject. It is surely not in the Constitution, and I know no other source of power to which Congress can apply. The Constitution gives Congress power "to promote the progress of science and useful arts, by securing, for limited times, to authors and inventors the exclusive right to their respective writings and discoveries." That was the whole grant of the Constitution. To carry out that grant we established a Patent Office, and grant patents and copyrights, and the exclusive right to books and discoveries. But, sir, the proposition of the Senator from Missouri is to make this Government, not the guardian of the rights of authors and discoveries, but the patron of arts and inventions. We are to run the hazard of the utility of a supposition of some inventor, and appropriate the money, without the possibility of deriving that benefit from it which every capitalist requires in his own case. Indeed, I see no limit. The Senator from Missouri very graphically described the thirsty craving of the sand that was going to drink up the water drawn from the reservoirs on the Ohio; but the thirst of the sand would be quenched when kept covered with water, and they would not demand further drink; but how, and in what mode, can we suppress the constant uprising of inventors to demand appropriations from Congress? It may come to pass that speculating men, *chevaliers d'industrie,* will seek it as a mode of drawing money from the Treasury, without any expectation that their experiments would succeed. Are we to sit here as a body of examiners, to ascertain the merits and to decide upon the probability of each proposition submitted, and determine whether we shall advance money upon it or not? Surely this would be diverting us from our legitimate course; and surely, too, the whole matter is in direct violation of the constitutional provision. But, as to the question of merit, I deny nothing to Professor Page for any invention or discovery which I suppose he may claim; but it must be recollected that this invention was familiar to the country some years ago, when an obscure blacksmith, I think, from Vermont exhibited a little model machine in the various cities in the northeastern part of the United States. As long ago as the winter of 1837, I saw it worked by this very mode of applying electro-magnetic power. But, sir, there is another idea; and the public press, in recent articles, must have attracted the attention of every Senator to it. A young man, known a few years ago very favorably as an artist and painter of portraits and historical pieces, has for years been experimenting upon this same subject. He has made an engine in Baltimore; and, if we may credit the statement in regard to it, he has obtained a higher power than has Professor Page. Poor and friendless, he yet struggled alone, and against Professor Page with an appropriation of $20,000 from the Government to aid him. Some time ago he filed his *caveat* in the Patent Office for his invention, and since then he has been perfecting it, with a view to obtain a patent. Now, he has at least the right to ask from Congress "hands off," and that, in this fair struggle between rival genius, he may be allowed, poor and without aid, to enter the contest with Professor Page to the final goal of a patent.   If Congress, however, shall decide to make this appropriation, I claim that he shall be put on an equality; but I make no such claim now, for I am opposed to the whole principle of voting money for any species of experiments, and particularly at this time, when we see that the first abuse leads to such results.

Remarks of Jefferson Davis on the bill granting lands to the several states for the benefit of the indigent insane.
Sept. 26, 1850.

Mr. DAVIS, of Mississippi. I look upon this as a proposition to make the United States Government a mere source of charity. There is no class that would more appeal to the humanity of right-minded persons than the indigent insane; and the statistics of the memorials show how great is the necessity for some kind of provision for that class of our population. But, sir, there are questions higher than those of humanity, considerations higher than our feelings, to govern us in this and all other questions of legislation. This Government was intended to be one of specific, enumerated powers. The purposes for which money was to be raised were enumerated, and beyond those enumerated there are only such as are necessary to carry the enumerated powers and grants into effect. If we can found an institution for the indigent insane, why can we not establish one for the orphans of the country? If we can establish hospitals to cure the insane, why not for the diseased of the country? Why may we not establish common schools at the expense of the Government all over the land, to teach those who are ignorant but of sound mind? All these things would appeal to the feelings of the public; and if Senators forget the Constitution in consulting one case, I would ask what limits are there to the appropriations we are to make? Heretofore we have made appropriations from the public lands of all the States in which they lie, under the claim that it was done on the principle of proprietorship—that the grant was made to increase the value of the property that remained after the grant. But no such plea can be set up here. This is a professed charity. This land is to be sold, and the Government is to take stock, create a perpetual fund to supply these eleemosynary institutions for the indigent insane. Next the blind and deaf will be appealed for, and every class of the community suffering from poverty and want have equal claims. This is a departure from that principle which alone can maintain this Government in its purity, that we shall refer constantly to our grant of power, and ask whether this power is conferred or not. Now, will any Senator undertake to show me a grant in the Constitution which gives to Congress the right to appropriate money to establish institutions of charity? If not, then I ask why should we try to avoid that by appropriating the public lands to be converted into money, to be applied to the same purpose? Surely no Senator would seek to do that indirectly which he could not do directly. And hence no argument is to be made except those powers of proprietorship which are said to be vested in and possessed by the United States.

If the Senator had displayed himself less impatient when I first offered an objection to taking up this bill, I should have said very little more than I then said; and I will not be tempted into protracting my remarks now on account of the impatience then shown. The whole thing is upon the surface. We have no power to make such grants. It is a departure from the sound principles to which we have heretofore adhered in the administration of the Government—a departure, the end of which no man can tell. Our appropriations this year do far more than swallow up all the revenue. Step by step we are squandering the patrimony we inherited. I call upon Senators, then, to contemplate the end to which they are rushing, and to point out to me the grant of power under which they do this, and tell me why, if they may exercise this power now, it should not be exercised, and the public funds and property expended to entertain every other class of our population.

Mr. DAVIS, of Massachusetts. I have a few words which I wish to say. In the first place, we by a general law reserve every sixteenth section for purposes of general education. By what power and authority is that done? We have been granting here millions upon millions of acres for the purpose of promoting the erection and establishment of railways and canals throughout the country. Under what authority have we done this? We grant to new States lands to establish colleges. By what authority is that done? We grant to the new States, uniformly, not less than 500,000 acres of land, which we place at the disposal of those States. Under what authority is that done? We granted a township of land to Connecticut many years ago, by an act of Congress, for the benefit of a deaf and dumb asylum. We granted, within my own recollection, one

township of land for a like institution in the State of Kentucky.
Some gentleman says it was in 1804. I recollect it very well.
I think it was somewhat later. Now, sir, we are asked, under
what authority is all this done? It is done, sir, under the
general power and authority vested in this Government to dispose of the public domain. If I could distinguish between this
case and those cases to which I have referred, there might be
some force in the argument. It seems to me there is no substantial distinction between them. But as this subject was
taken up with the understanding that there should be no
debate, I will not extend my remarks.

Mr. DAVIS, of Mississippi. The Senator makes an argument
that because something has been done heretofore without the
authority of the Constitution, therefore we may do the same—
that we have, for that reason, authority to make similar grants
in similar cases. The other cases which he alludes to stand
upon very different grounds. The school sections in the different States are granted as a part of that compact which exists
between the United States and the State sovereignties. It is
done upon the same principle as that upon which we grant
them a percentage upon all the public land sold in a State.
The State forbears to tax the land owned by the United States
for the first five years after it is sold. In consideration of this
forbearance, the United States grants to the State certain lands
for colleges and schools. So far as we have granted lands for
railroads and canals—so far as I am concerned at least—we
have always endeavored to limit the grants to a principle which
would naturally govern any large landholder to grant a portion
of his lands towards improvements in order to increase the value
of that which remains. I have always sought to govern my
votes by that principle. I will follow the Senator's example
not to debate the question.

Mr. DAVIS, of Mississippi. The State of Mississippi has
done something towards this species of institution, and the people of Mississippi have shown that they are interested in for-
warding as much as they can the establishment of such an institution; but what they have done they have done from their
own resources. The State of Mississippi is committed to no
such policy as this. The State of Mississippi has expressed
no opinion, so far as I am informed, in favor of the
Federal Government taking any such step as is now proposed. The action of the Legislature of Mississppi was in behalf of the indigent insane of the State of Mississippi. She
appropriated money for their relief; but how did that affect

the question whether the Federal Government has the constitutional power? The States are sovereign. The Federal Government is only the agent of the States, authorized to raise and appropriate money for certain specific purposes, and for none other. Let each State, therefore, take care of its own indigent insane.

Remarks on the bounty land bill. Sept. 2, 1850.

Mr. DAVIS, of Mississippi. I think we should keep in view two things: first, the classification of the men, and second, the character of our land surveys. It would be inconvenient to have fractional parts not laid out on the maps at the land offices. The classification of the men may be easily made into twelve months men, six months men, and three months men. A slight modification of the language of the amendment, I think, would cover the whole difficulty. The difficulty which the Senator from Illinois finds will be remedied, I think, by providing one hundred and sixty acres of land as the amount of the grant to twelve months men, and further providing that, if any soldier shall have engaged for twelve months and served out the term of his engagement, or until honorably discharged, he shall have one hundred and sixty acres of land. Such was the phraseology of the law which granted bounty lands to the soldiers in the Mexican war. Men who were discharged for wounds or disease, or any other honorable cause, got the whole amount of land which was due to the term for which they engaged. It requires, therefore, but a slight modification of the language of the amendment to make it cover all those who were honorably discharged within the term for which they were engaged. The twelve months man, who was discharged for wounds before his term of service expired, would get the amount graduated for the term of service for which he was engaged. He having broken up his business for that time, is fairly entitled to the amount. I would further suggest to the Senator that all the men who were called out as militia men, or engaged as volunteers, and have been actually engaged in battle, shall be put on the same footing as the three months men. The services of those who only served ten days before they were discharged, or lost their lives in battle, (in which case the land should be given to their widows,) might perhaps be worth more than the service of the whole three months.

Mr. DAVIS, of Mississippi. I supposed in the cases referred

to by the Senator, the volunteers had enlisted for during the war, and that is a period longer than twelve months.

Mr. UNDERWOOD. That would be an indefinite period, and would be worse than ever; for then, according to my construction of the amendment, they would only get forty acres. I want the amendment to be so framed, if it is the pleasure of the Senate, as to include the class of cases mentioned by Captain Cox.

Mr. DAVIS, of Mississippi. ''For twelve months or during the war'' will do it.

Mr. SHIELDS. Yes, that will cover everything.

The PRESIDENT. Does the Senator from Illinois so modify his amendment?

Mr. DOUGLAS. Yes, sir; I will modify it so as to read ''for twelve months or during the war,'' instead of ''for twelve months or more.''

Mr. DAVIS, of Mississippi. I think the Senator from Illinois provides for a danger that is more imaginary than real. The twelve months' men, who were discharged just before the expiration of their service, were all mustered out at the date which completed their twelve months, and very few of them if you compute the rate of travel at twenty miles a day from the place they were mustered out to their residences, would have reached their homes within the twelve months. They may have reached home before that; but they had a right to travel at the rate of twenty miles a day to the place of their original enrollment; and at that computation I think you will find that, in most cases, if not in all, the soldier was twelve months in service. Then the only voucher for the length of time of actual service is the final muster roll, on which they were discharged, and that would should show twelve months in service. But there is a great number of cases excluded by the amendment proposed by the Senator from Illinois, [Mr. DOUGLAS] —cases in which they enrolled for twelve months, and perhaps in the first three months were wounded and discharged for disability. The merit is as high, surely, as if they had served twelve months, if, by casualty in battle, they were wounded and necessarily discharged. Now, I am not willing to exclude this class; and I think the period of engagement is the only true period by which to measure the amount of land to be given. If a man was engaged for twelve months, he must have broken up his business at home, and made his arrangements for twelve months; and if he returns within that period, wounded, he will probably linger an invalid during the whole twelve months. I, for one, am entirely opposed to reducing the quantity of land to be granted to him, if it is to be granted at all. I think he should receive the same quantity as his comrades, whose better fortune may have preserved them for the whole term.

Mr. UNDERWOOD. I would like to ask the Senator from Mississippi, or those better informed on the subject than I am, whether there were any persons who entered the service for a period between twelve and nine months, or if they all entered the service for as long as twelve months? The amendment, as it now stands, would embrace the cases Captain Cox speaks of here precisely; but if there was any such thing as entering the service for between nine and twelve months, and all those spoken of in the letter served nine or ten months, they would still be excluded. But I suppose there is no such thing as entering for an intermediate time.

Mr. DAVIS, of Mississippi. The law enacted soon after the declaration of the war with Mexico required that the volunteers should be raised for twelve months. Previous to that, some volunteers, enlisted some for six and some for three months, had gone out, but they could not be received, because the law said specifically that they must be engaged for twelve months. Consequently they were discharged, except such as were retained under the old militia act for three months, and renewed their engagement so as to serve for six months. But there was no such term as six months; only the old militia term of three months, and the term provided for by the law raising volunteers for the Mexican war of twelve months or during the war. These were the only terms.

Remarks of Jefferson Davis on the Indian appropriation bill. Sept. 26, 1850.

Mr. DAVIS, of Mississippi. The statement of the chairman of the Committee on Indian Affairs is one of the most extraordinary I have ever heard. The idea that Indians have been drawn upon a building by the presence of the troops of the United States is to me altogether incomprehensible. He says that these troops were there, and that being there drew upon the building those Indians who destroyed them. Why, the thing is impossible. The troops being there might keep them away from it; it could not bring them on. If they failed to secure the property which their presence was designed to protect, it certainly constitutes no just foundation for a claim against the United States. It is enough that they did what they might to protect this property. It is quite out of the question that the presence of the troops drew the savage enemy to the place. The Senator has not been guarded in his statement. The troops, unless they took possession of this warehouse for the purpose of defending it, took possession of it by rent. Now, why the whole claim is set up by the chairman of the Committee on Indian Affairs is to me incomprehensible.

Mr. ATCHISON. That an old soldier, and such a distinguished one——

Mr. DAVIS, of Mississippi. Oh, no; not that.

Mr. DAVIS, of Mississippi. I must say something in answer to my friend from Missouri, who has put in a *caveat* in my favor for a patent. But if it was permitted for the Senator or any one else to make his own case, and give his own answers, he would undoubtedly win the case. But the misfortune in this case was that I guarded my language. I spoke of the *savage* foe, and the case cited by the Senator from Missouri can have no analogy with my remarks. In the progress of civilization the cultivated nations avoid the destruction of private property. They march their armies against the armies of the enemy, and fight battles to decide issues between nations. Not so with the savage foe. They attack private property where it is not guarded. They assail hamlets because they find them defenceless. There is no analogy between the cases. The Senator, therefore, has drawn a conclusion which does not apply to my proposition, which proposition confines itself to the savage foe. He refers to the case of Buena Vista. There is no analogy between the two cases. The Mexican army marched against the American army. If they beat the American army, they of course would have the stores which the Americans then possessed. If they conquered the Americans, they would gain one point of honor for their nation; and it was well understood that, if they could overcome the American army once, they were then willing upon that trophy to treat. There is, however, not the slightest analogy between the cases which have been classed together. The Senator draws his conclusion from an argument which I never presented.

Now, the Senator may have precedents to give to our consideration. If there are precedents, so much greater the necessity for our examining every case. If he is going to bring me the case in Florida, where we have paid for damages which never existed, because troops were at the places, I tell him beforehand that one wrong does not justify another. I tell him beforehand that there are precedents which lead more to the devastation of the Treasury of the United States than they do to the devastation of the property of private individuals. I shall concede no such case as this because one wrong has been done at a former time.

Mr. DAVIS, of Mississippi. The Senator from Texas has only stated the question at issue between the Senator from Missouri and myself. The Senator from Missouri says that I misunderstood his precedent. Why, sir, that which he quoted was equally unfortunate, if not more so. He quotes the case of Tippecanoe. Now, the Indians did not go to attack the troops at that place. General Harrison went to the Indians; he went past their village. In that very country I have heard the particulars of that attack, from an officer under General Harrison, who told me that he went through the Indian village before the attack, and saw these Indians with their faces blacked; and black faces among the Indians always signify war to the knife. He went into the encampment of General Harrison. The gentleman is one of the constituents of my friend from Indiana. [Mr. WHITCOMB.] He says that he expected an attack from the Indians. The encampment had been pointed out to the Indians, as it was close to the village. In the other case that the Senator referred to, they were all little advanced fortifications—stockades thrown into the Indian country to hold them in check, and which the Indians felt it was necessary for them to take, in order to make a safe inroad into the country behind. But let the Senator show, if he can, that the Indians have selected a place fortified and held by troops, instead of one undefended, as a matter of choice. Let him show that Indians have gone past an undefended village, to attack a place held by troops. Let him show this, or anything approaching to this, and he will put our savage foes on the footing of civilized nations in waging war; but not till then will his pretension have a solid foundation.

Mr. DAVIS, of Mississippi. The Senator from Georgia appeals to my justice and magnanimity. I find myself unfortunately between two fires. The Senator from Missouri—who has disclaimed being a military man, but who has made a speech that shows that Nature designed him for one—is on the one side, and the Senator from Georgia, who should hold the seals of the Treasury, is making an attack on the other side. Now, sir, whether I have made a sufficient answer to one attack, I will leave for others to decide.

LETTERS, PAPERS AND SPEECHES   565

Very briefly I will endeavor to answer the second attack. We have appropriated money to Georgia to cover claims for spoliations committed by the Creek Indians at a former period. But the amount, as far as my information goes, greatly exceeds the depredations yet proved. I doubted very much the propriety of turning over the whole fund to Georgia without receiving any statement showing that the depredations were equal to that amount. So it is, however, that money has been transferred, and if a citizen of Georgia has suffered Indian depredations, they have the fund of the United States in their possession, and let them pay it. Far more money has been paid over to Georgia than depredations have yet been shown to balance it. I speak of the old spoliations.

On Indian appropriation bill, Sept. 27, 1850.

Mr. DAVIS, of Mississippi. This proposition was discussed, I believe, on a former day, and I then took occasion to offer some objection to it. I entertain the same opinions now as I expressed then. I will not go over the whole again, because I never address the Senate unless with some object, and if my poor opinion is worth anything it has been already given. In the treaty extinguishing the title of the tribe to this Territory a reservation was made to these half-breeds, and the president was authorized to subdivide the country among them. These half-breeds are now considered citizens of the United States, voting, and, I believe, some of them members of the Legislature of Minnesota. I think, therefore, that it is quite unjust to these half-breeds who have parted with their tribe and character to make a treaty now with the tribe to buy out their possession or reservation again. These half-breeds hold the land, and have incorporated their labor in it and made improvements, and now an average value of land to be distributed *per capita* among the half-breeds will be altogether unjust to those who have made valuable improvements. It is their property on the faith of the Government. They have improved it, and they should be allowed to retain it. If the crowding white population makes it desirable that the half-breeds should be removed, let each man sell his own land which he has improved, and if half what is said of their intelligence and of their rapid advancement to civilization be true, we hazard nothing in leaving it to themselves to dispose of their own possessions. I am, therefore, altogether opposed to the purchase by the United States. Let the half-breeds sell what is their own to those who will give them for it what they believe to be its value. The United States have necessarily no connection with the transaction.

The cost is a thing into which I will not enter further than to say to the Senator from Iowa that the cost of surveying the land must be greatly over that of the ordinary survey of public lands, for there can be no just survey save that which will award to each of the inhabitants there that which he now claims. Their settlement has not been made under sections and township lines, and the consequence would be that it would very often happen that in subdividing according to the ordinary mode of survey you would put the house on one side and the field on the other. You would have to survey, therefore, with a view to the settlement, and not in the ordinary mode of surveying the public lands of the United States.

I think this whole thing objectionable. As I said before, I do not propose to go into the question of the rate we are to pay. These half-breeds have incorporated their labor in the land. It is, then, theirs. Let them sell it for their own advantage, or, if they do not choose to sell it, leave them where their condition and local attachment render them anxious to remain.

Mr. DAVIS, of Mississippi. We ought to ask ourselves where these Indians would be removed to if they were removed from these lands. They now extend to the Red river, on the north —to Lord Selkirk's settlement; and beyond that is the British possession. West of that is the country which we have reason to believe would be assigned to them; and it is not at all suited to their wants. There is no pressing population in this country which requires that the Indian title should be extinguished at once; and I see no reason why we should place at the discretion of the President a treaty which we have a right to reject from the beginning, and have not determined to accept. It is a strange proposition that we reflect upon the discretion of the President because we do not wish him to form this treaty. We have a right to decide whether we wish the treaty made or not; and to give the authority to the President is nothing more nor less than directing him to make the treaty. I do not wish the treaty made at all. Let the Indians alone until Minnesota shall be in need of this territory. The Indians are becoming civilized as the settlers extend beyond them. I have always doubted the policy of crowding a great number of Indian tribes upon a single territory. They have their hereditary feuds and causes of quarrels with other tribes, with which they will be brought into juxtaposition in the territory. I doubted the policy at the time it first commenced. My intercourse with the Indians upon the frontiers has since led me to doubt it still more strongly. I believe that we are now following out a policy which will result in more evil than good.

Committee report by Jefferson Davis, Sept. 27, 1850.

Mr. DAVIS, of Mississippi, from the Joint Committee on the Library, to whom had been referred the memorial of William E. McMaster, praying that he may be authorized to paint full half-length portraits of all the Presidents, to be placed in the President's House, asked to be discharged from the further consideration of the same.

Mr. D. said: In making this motion, I wish to state that this motion is not to be considered as a criticism on his style or a decision on his merits. It merely implies that the Library Committee prefer taking portraits already completed to authorizing the making of them.

The motion was agreed to; and the committee were discharged from the further consideration of the subject.

Mr. DAVIS, of Mississippi, from the Joint Committee on the Library, reported the following joint resolution; which was read a first and second time by unanimous consent, and considered as in Committee of the Whole:

A joint resolution authorizing the Joint Committee on the Library to purchase certain portraits of the first five Presidents of the United States, now in the Congressional Library.

Resolved by the Senate and House of Representatives of the United States of America in Congress assembled, That the Joint Committee on the Library be and hereby is authorized to purchase the portraits of the first five Presidents of the United States, now in the Congressional Library: *Provided,* That they do not cost more than $500 each.

Mr. D. I would state that the committee reported in favor of the purchase of these portraits some years ago, at a cost not exceeding $1,000 each. The memorial of the executor of Mr. Stuart refers to that, and he says he would consider $1,000 a fair price. They are known to be genuine portraits by Stuart. Mr. Adams, when a member of the Committee on the Library, gave some information on that point. The Joint Committee have no doubt that these are genuine portraits by Stuart, though they do not consider them the best of his style. But the Joint Committee have thought proper to limit the price which shall be paid for these portraits to $500 each.

No amendment having been offered, the resolution was reported to the Senate.

Remarks of Jefferson Davis, Sept. 28, 1850.

Mr. DAVIS, of Mississippi. I wish to offer the following amendment:

"That the Secretary of War be and he is hereby authorized to pay the unexpended balance of the appropriation made by the act of March 3, 1849, for publishing a new edition of the Ordnance Manual, to the officer of the United States army employed in compiling, arranging, superintending, and publishing the same, as provided by the terms of said act."

The Secretary of War at that time (Mr. Marcy) recommended to the Senate a new edition of the Ordnance Manual to be printed, the old one being exhausted. A communication was sent from the Ordnance Bureau to the Committee on Military Affairs, which recommended that to defray the expense of publishing a new edition of a thousand copies, including compensation to be allowed to Captain Mordecai for compiling, arranging, and supervising, there should be appropriated $6,000. The Committee on Military Affairs reported an amendment to the appropriation bill, which left out the name of Captain Mordecai, and increased the number of copies to 1,500. The number of copies was increased for reasons which it is unnecessary at this time to detail, and the name of Captain Mordecai left out, because the committee believed it was improper to make appropriation for an individual, and that for some cause or other it might be advisable or desirable to change the order —that the officer might die, and if the appropriation were made in his name, no other officer could take charge of the work, and it would fail to be executed. For that reason the committee recommended that there should be appropriated $6,000 to defray the expenses of publishing 1,500 copies. When the work was completed, the balance on hand was, of course, the compensation for the officer. As all the bills had to be paid, the balance was the compensation for the compiler; but Secretary Crawford (in a communication which lies before me, believed he had no authority to pay the compiler for the work, because he was an officer of the army—the act of 1842 prohibiting all extra allowances to officers of the army; and he therefore recommended additional legislation upon the subject. The Committee on Military Affairs, recollecting the whole history of the transaction, informed the Secretary that it was the intention to pay the officer of the army, who was, in fact, the compiler of the work. He, however, decided that he would not pay the money without some legislation to authorize him; and the amendment which I now offer is to authorize the unexpended balance to be allowed to the compiler, in accordance with the intention of the act of 1849. It is not to make a new appropriation of money, but to allow the unexpended balance of a former appropriation to be paid to the individual for whom it was intended in the first place.

The question being taken on the amendment, it was agreed to.

SUPERINTENDENT OF MILITARY ACADEMY.

Mr. DAVIS, of Mississippi. I have another amendment, which I will explain as briefly as I can:

"*Provided*, That the pay and emoluments of the superintendent of the United States Military Academy shall in no case be less than the pay of a professor of natural and experimental philosophy."

When the appropriation bill for the Military Academy was before the Senate, I made a proposition to increase the rank of that officer to the grade of lientenant colonel, either by linear commission or by brevet. It was with a view to secure to him the pay of lieutenant colonel, believing that amount was necessary to maintain the station which he occupied, and further, because that is the pay of the professors of natural and experimental philosophy. At that time, on account of another proposition being entertained by my friend from Florida, [Mr. YULEE,] I abandoned the proposition, in order that it might be disposed of in this bill. We now find ourselves at the close of the session, without any ability to consider a new mode of providing for the increase of rank of that officer. I therefore offer this amendment, in order that he may escape from the anomalous condition in which he is placed as superintendent of that academy, being in fact the commanding officer of that institution. As his case now stands, he receives but the pay of a captain. A junior in rank, therefore, receives the same pay as the superintendent, who has all the care of the institution. The whole thing is an anomaly, and is therefore unjust. We have no time now to adopt a more acceptable plan, and I offer this amendment as the only mode of escaping from the condition in which we are placed.

Mr. HUNTER. I only ask my friend whether the effect of the amendment will not be to turn out the man who already occupies the post?

Mr. DAVIS, of Mississippi. Not at all; it is merely to increase his pay from that of captain to that of a lieutenant colonel.

The amendment was adopted.

Remarks of Jefferson Davis on the Naval Appropriations bill Sept. 28, 1850.

THE NAVAL APPROPRIATION BILL.

The Senate then resumed the consideration of the naval appropriation bill.

Mr. DAVIS, of Mississippi. I have an amendment which I wish to offer after the 124th line, as follows:

"Provided, That ten appointments of midshipmen may be made by the President, without reference to residence or congressional recommendation.''

I will state that, as at present provided, the officers of the army not having residence have had very little opportunity to get their sons into the navy. We have a provision of this kind for the army, allowing the President to appoint cadets *at large,* as it is termed—boys without residence, and without influence —sons of officers who have spent their lives in the army and navy, and have had no opportunity to enter the service.

Mr. BUTLER. I concur with my friend from Mississippi in that amendment. I will state an instance in which an officer found it impossible to get an appointment in the navy for his son. Col. Eugene, not having a claim upon his country by hereditary right, presented his son to the Navy Department for a midshipman's warrant, and the late Secretary told him that he was not so far a citizen of South Carolina as to claim the privilege of presenting his son, though, in my opinion, the

Secretary made a blunder there. I do not know that the present Secretary would hold that the same strictness, that men going into the army and navy are to forfeit the right of giving their sons an equal right with others. I hold that would be unjust.

Mr. DAYTON. May I be permitted to ask whether that is to extend the number of midshipmen provided for by law,

Mr. DAVIS, of Mississippi. It is not contemplated to increase the number—ten appointments being the whole number that the President can make, the number of midshipmen to be appointed being wholly controlled by law. A certain number are recommended by members of Congress for the filling of places as vacancies occur. This gives the President the power to recommend ten himself.

Mr. DAVIS, of Massachusetts. If I understand it aright, some district or other is to be vacated for every one of these appointments. Now, I protest against that. I have found the application of that principle to my own part of the country repeatedly; and when I have made application for the appointments for certain districts, I have been answered that the appointments at large excluded them, and the consequence has been that we have not been represented in that branch of the public service. The districts have been kept open and vacant on that account.

Mr. DAVIS, of Mississippi. Does the Senator say "midshipmen?"

Mr. DAVIS, of Massachusetts. Cadets.

Mr. DAVIS, of Mississippi. That is a different thing.

Mr. DAVIS, of Massachusetts. Well, it applies to midshipmen also. These appointments *at large* are made to the exclusion of congressional districts. I shall vote against it. I am quite willing to vote upon the question of increasing the number, provided there can be appointments as there used to be.

Mr. DAVIS, of Mississippi. I wish to reply briefly to the remarks of the honorable Senator from Massachusetts. The proposition which I have submitted to the Senate, would, of course, if entertained by the Senate, look to the postponing of some appointments from some congressional districts, but not to vacate any one of them. I was surprised at the answer that the Senator from Massachusetts said he had received on his application for cadets. A cadet appointed by the President *at large* as it is termed, does not vacate any congressional district. He is appointed generally from those who have no residence, and cannot stand in bar of an appointment from any congressional district. Now I propose to give to the navy the advantage of the same system that is operating in the army. I am sure the Senator from Massachusetts has not understood the reply given to him, or he who gave the answer was ignorant of the rules which govern the department.

Mr. DAVIS, of Massachusetts. I meant to refer to midshipmen. I suppose I said "cadet" by mistake.

Mr. DAVIS, of Mississippi. If the Senator meant to refer to midshipmen, he was mistaken, for the President has no such power at all. All midshipmen are now appointed by recommendation.

Mr. DAVIS, of Massachusetts. If the Senator will allow me, perhaps I can place myself right in regard to that. There was, at a period of the Government, some two years ago, so large a number of midshipmen appointed, that the districts in my portion of the country were kept open, because they were filled up from other portions of the country.

Mr. DAVIS, of Mississippi. All that has been regulated. But there has been this fact in the system, that the son of an officer of the navy, who one might naturally suppose would be the best qualified for appointment in the navy, is excluded from it, because his father has lost his citizenship, and his son must take a residence in some congressional district to get an appointment. Now, I wish to remedy that by giving to the President ten appointments at large for the navy, as he has for the army.

Mr. DAYTON. I beg leave to ask whether any official of this Government has ever held that an officer in the army or the navy has lost his residence from the fact of his being in the army or navy, or that his son has lost his residence on that account?

Mr. DAVIS, of Mississippi. That has been the construction placed upon the law.

Mr. DAYTON. Now, if we are to legislate upon any such construction as that, we had better legislate upon the construction itself; for it is opposed to law, to common sense, and common feeling, that a naval officer or an army officer should thus lose his residence.

Mr. DAVIS, of Mississippi. The Senator from New Jersey, perhaps, did not hear the case stated by the Senator from South Carolina, which covered this very point.

Mr. DAYTON. This is one of those matters in reference to which I would not legislate upon any special case. Every lawyer knows very well that no officer can lose his residence by being afloat, or at a military station, and his family cannot lose residence in that way. Now, in point of fact, I submit that it is in the knowledge of us all, that the sons of these naval officers get into the service in some way—I do not know how—with much more facility than any other class of our citizens.

Mr. DAVIS, of Mississippi. Not now.

Mr. DAYTON. That is my knowledge. And in my part of the country there is hardly a naval officer, within my knowledge, who has not a son if he be of age, in the naval service. I am very much afraid that, if you enact that the President is to appoint ten midshipmen, you will create a jealousy; for on what part of the country is the President to quarter them?

Mr. DAVIS, of Mississippi. On none.

Mr. DAYTON. Then you must increase the number of midshipmen.

Mr. DAVIS, of Mississippi. Not so. You do not quarter them upon any part of the country, nor do you increase their number. It seems to me to be a very simple proposition. The midshipman is appointed at large, and the fact that he is appointed to fill some vacancy will, of course, only delay the appointment in some congressional district, but not fill it.

Mr. DAYTON. It is the same thing whether they are quartered upon the district, or you delay the appointment from the district by reason of the other appointment.

Mr. DAVIS, of Mississippi. You do not prevent it, but only delay it.

Mr. WHITCOMB. It occurs to me that the Senator from Mississippi can obtain his object, and obviate all objection, by framing his amendment so as to change that mode of illiberal construction, and leave the sons of naval and military officers to be considered as residents of the places where their fathers actually reside when not performing duty.

Mr. DAVIS of Mississippi. There are many cases that cannot be reached by any such provision. If the officers come on shore when off duty, they may be in one place or in another; and even if they go to one place all the time, they are still absent so much that they have lost all their interest, and are unable to get congressional recommendation. Now, I can very well understand that every naval officer who came from the State of New Jersey, should, when he was on shore, prefer to reside there, and thus preserve his residence. Not so with the interior States. The cases are entirely different. The honorable Senator judges from his experience in his locality; we judge from ours, and it is directly the reverse. But, suppose that an officer of the navy was appointed from the District of Columbia, how is he to get his son into the navy? Or suppose a citizen of the District of Columbia desires to enter the navy, how is he to enter it? Formerly, I know, they were sent out to be quartered upon some congressional district, and to remain there a short time, and then be appointed from it. But I understand that the construction of the law is now very rigid, and it is altogether impossible for any such thing to be done under the construction that is now made. My proposition is to remedy a great defect. If Senators wish to increase the number of midshipmen, they can make that proposition. I believe the number of midshipmen is now very well balanced for the size of the navy. But if some congressional district were to be delayed one or two years, the evil would be less than the one which I wish to remedy.

The question being taken upon this amendment, it was not adopted.

Mr. HALE. I wish to offer an additional section by way of amendment. It is to prevent the appointment of any more captains in the navy, until the present number shall be reduced to fifty.

[The amendment could not be obtained by the Reporter.]

Now, one remark in regard to that. We have now sixty-eight captains in the navy, and forty-two out of the sixty-eight are waiting orders—some of them having been waiting twenty, and some of them thirty years. I find more than one waiting orders for thirty years; some of them twenty; some eighteen, and so along down. Forty-two out of sixty--eight waiting orders at a salary of $2,500 a year! Now, my amendment proposes to keep fifty, twice the number now employed, lacking two—twenty-six being in the service. I do not propose to turn anybody out of the navy, but simply not to appoint any more until the number is reduced to fifty.

The question being taken on the amendment, it was rejected.

The bill was then reported to the Senate as amended.

The PRESIDENT stated that the question would be taken upon all the amendments together, unless some Senator wished to reserve some one or more of them.

Mr. DICKSON said he preferred that they should all be rejected.

Mr. GWIN said that he wished to reserve all the amendments with regard to the docks in California.

The question being then taken on the other amendments, they were concurred in on a division—ayes 32, noes not counted.

Mr. YULEE. As the amendment which has been reserved

involves so large an appropriation, as we are to meet again so soon, and as I deem it a very important provision, I deem it my duty to move again in the Senate to strike out the whole that relates to the dock there, and ask the yeas and nays upon it.

The yeas and nays having been ordered, the question was taken upon this amendment, and it was not agreed to—yeas 20, nays 26.

The amendments were then ordered to be engrossed for a third reading of the bill, and the bill was read a third time, and passed.

ARMY APPROPRIATION BILL.

On motion by Mr. HUNTER, the Senate proceeded, as in Committee of the Whole, to the consideration of the bill making appropriations for the support of the army of the United States for the year ending June 30, 1851.

Mr. HUNTER. I will state that the Committee on Finance have reported this bill without amendments. By doing so, we have by no means intended, however, to dictate anything to the Senate in relation to it. We reported it without recommending amendments, because we had not time to give that critical examination to the bill which it properly required. I stand here ready to vote for any amendment which may be offered, and which may commend itself to my judgment.

Mr. HALE moved an amendment in behalf of Charlotte Lynch; which was not agreed to.

Mr. DAVIS, of Mississippi. The Committee on Military Affairs have some amendments to offer. It is not our fault that this bill has been reported at the end of the session. The responsibility rests upon others. Upon the Committee on Military Affairs only rests the responsibility of drafting appropriations which the interests and wants of the service require.

The first amendment was to increase the pay of officers in Oregon.

Mr. D. said: I have received memorials and various statements, both from officers commanding in Oregon and other persons fully informed. They say that the price of rent, the price of bread, and the price of every species of supplies, is so extravagantly high, that no officer can live upon his pay. It is the same case in California. The men also are tempted, by the great demand for labor and the high rates that are offered for it, to such a degree that a man who is serving at $7 a month may desert his post, throw down his musket, and take up a shovel or a pick and earn $7 a day. The consequence is, that in order to pursue deserters and bring them back, or to send out new troops to take their place, it costs the Government much more than it would to give a liberal compensation, such as would retain them in the service. The mode I have adopted is, for commissioned officers, to give the same extra pay to all the officers, no matter what may be their grade—the increased expenditure bearing about equally upon all. Officers of an inferior rank would not be benefited as the exigencies of the case require, if they received extra pay in proportion to their pay as established by law. I have, therefore, thought that this method of increase would be more equitable than any other.

Mr. HUNTER. I would ask the chairman of the Committee on Military Affairs whether this increase of pay has received the sanction of the department?

Mr. DAVIS, of Mississippi. Oh, yes; certainly. I was only sparing the Senate. If it is desirable, I will commence reading. I have got the estimate of the Postmaster General, the Secretary of War, and of almost everybody else that the Senate would like to hear from. [Laughter.]

The question being taken upon this amendment, it was agreed to.

Mr. DAVIS, of Mississippi. The next amendment is, to insert in the 119th line, after the word "already," the following:

"*Provided*, That the principal assistant in the Ordnance Bureau of the War Department shall receive a compensation not less than that of ——, under the fifth section of an act approved the 23d of August, 1842, from and after the date thereof."

If there is any doubt about the amendment, I can explain it in a few moments. In the Ordnance Bureau it is necessary to have an assistant, who must be one of the most accomplished and instructed ordnance officers, upon whom is devolved the chief responsibility of that bureau. If he be a captain in the army, he is detailed to discharge the duties; and as the interests. of the service will generally require that he should be a captain, his pay is about $600 a year. It is proposed, then, to put this officer upon the same footing as to pay, so that it shall not be a sacrifice for him to enter the Ordnance Bureau.

The question being taken upon this amendment, it was agreed to.

Mr. DAVIS, of Mississippi. In the provision to supply the deficiency occurring at the Military Academy at West Point, the

Senator from Virginia has called my attention to the fact that there are only $600 appropriated, where the amount required is $1,090.83. I therefore move to strike out $600 to defray the expenses of the board of visitors at West Point, and to insert $1,090.83.

The question being taken upon this amendment, it was agreed to.

Mr. DAVIS, of Mississippi. Another amendment. I will state to the Senator that last year, in the appropriation bill, after examination, and in accordance with the bill lying on the table, the Senate's provision was made to pay all additional rations to officers of the army, as being within their construction of the law, fixed for permanent posts in the army. But a different construction has been put upon it by the Auditor, who has decided that it must be renewed this year. I have also put in an engineer.

The amendment was read, and, the question being taken, it was agreed to.

Mr. DAVIS, of Mississippi. I have a letter from the Chief of the Bureau of Topographical Engineers, asking for an appropriation to pay a draughtsman, who has been employed in the lettering and bordering and some of the minute typography of a map. He estimates the labor of this draughtsman to be worth $5 a day. The whole amount asked for is $1,040, which he says is for service in the months of October, November, December, January, February, March, April and May—219 days, amounting to $1,040. A Senator asks me if there was any authority for employing him. None at all I believe, other than the fact, that his services were needed to complete a work which Congress had imposed upon the bureau. I will read an extract:

Extract from page 5 of Report of the Colonel of the Corps of Topographical Engineers to Congress, dated

"NOVEMBER 20, 1849.

"One officer (Brevet Colonel J. McClellan) is engaged in compiling from the best authorities, under a resolution of the Senate, a map of the country between the Mississippi and the Pacific, embracing all our territory on that sea. This map is in a great state of forwardness, but is yet detained in order to take advantage of the new information which is daily received. *It was found necessary that he should have an assistant draughtsman;* but the bureau, having no officer to spare, and no appropriation out of which a draughtsman could be paid, no person could be assigned. An able draughtsman, (Mr. J. W. Butler,) however, being unemployed, has agreed to lend his services to the work, trusting to such remuneration as Congress may, in its wisdom, and upon a judgment of his services, think proper to allow.''

I have other statements from various parties upon the same subject, if the Senate is desirous of hearing them read.

The question being taken upon the amendment, it was agreed to.

Mr. DAVIS, of Mississippi. I move a reconsideration of the resolution by which the Senate determined to take a recess, in order that we may go on and complete this bill.

The question being taken upon this motion, it was not agreed to.

Jefferson Davis to Charles P. McIlvain.[1]

Washington D. C.
16th. Sept. 1850

My dear Sir:

Your kind letter of April 3d. 1849, without postmark, has just reached me and gives me great gratification in the evidence it bears that you still remember me. Like others who had the good fortune when cadets to be under your instruction I have followed your course and rejoiced in the public appreciation you have commanded, but supposed from my position that I had been forgotten by you long since. I thank you for the interest you feel in my history, the paternal affection you show for me as one of your cadets, it awakens many recollections and prompts me to say, if the seed sown by you has not borne fruit in my case, I yet trust that the germ is not dead.

So much time has elapsed since the writing of your letter that I suppose the case of your brother to which you refer is not probably now before the Dept. If you will advise me it will give me real satisfaction to serve you as you propose or otherwise to the extent of my ability.

As ever very truly and gratefully your friend

JEFFN. DAVIS.

[1] Protestant Episcopal bishop (1799-1873), born in Burlington, N. J., died in Florence, Italy; professor of ethics and chaplain at the U. S. Military Academy 1825-27; elected bishop of Ohio, 1832; president of Kenyon College; author of many theological works.

Jefferson Davis to B. Pendleton and others.

(From Mississippi Free Trader, Nov. 30, 1850.)

Brierfield, Warren county,
November 10th, 1850.

Gentlemen:—In the "Free Trader," of the 2d October, I find the proceedings of a public meeting, held at Natchez, on the 23d September, 1850, to which my attention is directed by a resolution which instructs the President of the meeting to forward a copy of the proceedings "to the Hon. H. S. Foote and, also, to our (your) other Senator," etc, etc.

As my name was not mentioned, and as I have not received a copy of the proceedings, as ordered it is admissible to conclude that my address was not known; therefore I avail myself of the information in the form in which it is presented, to show my respect for the meeting, by replying to the resolutions through the same channel which has conveyed them to me. By implication, it appears that my constituents assembled, as above, disapprove of my course on the measures of the last session of Congress, in relation to the "controversy between the North and the South." I can not, gentlemen, adopt your views on those measures; and the inequality between us consists of the importance I attach to the opinions of any portion of my constituents and the want of value which my conclusions will, probably, have in your estimation. Believing, however, that you have fallen into grave errors, which a reference to the records will correct, and that those errors are likely to injure, rather than promote, the interests and rights in which we have a common fortune, I plead, even if it be to unwilling ears, for the cause in which I have unsuccessfully labored, but which is as dear to me in this hour of defeat as it could have been if, happily, it had triumphed.

That cause is the equality of the Southern States, as members of the Union, and the maintenance of their constitutional rights, as such. It has been painful to me to perceive in any, however few, of the Southern people a disposition to consider those who have steadily maintained the rights and interests of the South as the promoters of agitation, whose influence should be destroyed by attaching to them the odious designation of disunionists. Our Union is a compact, its terms, the Federal Constitution, form the bond of its connection, and breathed into it the breath of its existence.

Who, then, are the disunionists? Are they those who sternly insist on a rigid adherence to the Constitution, or those who disregard its principles? But one answer can be given by any who, when they speak of the Union, mean the Confederacy of the Constitution, the inheritance which our revolutionary fathers left us. The question has been frequently asked those who used the term "ultra Southern men" in what any Southern man had claimed for his section more than its constitutional right. That question has never been so answered as to fix upon men of the South even the wish to violate the contract their fathers made and transferred to their sons. Who then are truly the disunionists? Surely those who agress or encourage aggression on those rights and principles which the Union was formed to secure, and on which, as a foundation, it was erected. The framers of the Constitution were those who preferred revolution and separation from the mother country to submission—to taxation by others than their own representatives; they never would have consented to found a new government, in which the minority should be subject to the discretionary legislation of a majority. The Government they instituted was one of specific grants and enumerated objects; all else was reserved to the States and the people. To allow one department of this Government, or common agent, to usurp undelegated powers, subject only to the restraint which another department of the Federal Government may impose, would be to render the reservation not absolute, but conditional, in the end, probably, to become nugatory.

If the rights of the States are held subordinate to the decision of the co-ordinate branches of the Federal Government, the principal has changed places with his agent, the creator with the creature. If the Constitution can be warped and wrung until its nature is altered, and the States still be coerced to adhere to the Union, they have lost the sovereignty they won by the battles of the revolution, and the possession of which enabled them to enter into a confederation. The Union was the result of the liberty and independence of the States, not the converse, and such being my opinion, I cannot agree to the proposition of your first resolution, that the liberty we inherit from the heroes and patriots of our revolution is one and inseparable from the Union. The institutions of the States were established, their independence was achieved before the Union was formed, and, if the sons be worthy of their sires, might be maintained, though the Union should perish. That their prosperity has been promoted, their usefulness developed by the Union, is not to be questioned; and as little is it to be doubted, that by dissolution, all sections would be injuriously affected; but I do not think the institutions of the South would be destroyed by that event, or our State Governments materially altered. Not only do I believe our liberty would be preserved, but that our form of Government would remain, and our commercial interests, if not promoted, would be far less impaired than any other section of the Union.

The second resolution approves the series of measures adopted by Congress in relation to the controversy between the North and the South, as founded on the principles maintained and relied on by the South in the assertion of her rights of property and the protection of her interests; and as a settlement which rejects and puts to rest the "Wilmot Proviso," and leaves the territories equally open to all citizens, with their property of every species guaranteed by the Constitution; and as a recognition of the right of the people of a territory, in organizing themselves into a State, to settle the question of slavery for themselves in their organic law. If I could see all this in those measures, I would certainly agree that there was much to approve, and should not have returned to Mississippi with the depression which attached to the feeling that I came as a messenger who returned with none other than evil tidings to relate. Your construction is certainly not that which I placed upon them when I opposed their enactment, and, what is important, is not that given by the Congress which passed them. To secure the rights of property, and protection for interests which had been asserted by the South, I offered two amendments. The first, referring to the territorial governments proposed to be established for Utah and New Mexico, was in these words: "Provided, that nothing herein contained shall be construed to prevent said territorial legislature from passing such laws as may be necessary for the protection of the rights of property of any kind which may have been or may be hereafter, conformably to the Constitution and laws of the United States, held in, or introduced into said territory." After full debate, and modification of language, so as to avoid the objections made by some, the vote was taken on the amendment in the above form, and it was defeated—yeas 25, nays 30—but one Senator from a Northern State (Dickinson) voting for it. The second amendment was in these words: "And that all laws or parts of laws, usages or customs, pre-existing in the territories acquired by the United States from Mexico, and which, in said territories, restrict, abridge or obstruct the full enjoyment of any right of person or property of a citizen of the United States, as recognized or guarantied by the Constitution or laws of the United States, are hereby declared and shall be held as

repealed." This amendment, after debate, was defeated—yeas
18, nays 30—not one Senator from the non-slaveholding States
voting for it. Thus it is shown that the majority of the Senate
did not construe their action as you have done. A like reference
to the House of Representatives will show the same state of the
case in that body. The principle of equality of right, and protection by the federal government of those rights, was not the
basis on which the bill was founded. There were not wanting,
even among those who admitted the equality of right, persons
who objected to the claim for protection as a violation of the
principle of non-intervention. In vain was it answered, that the
federal government was established by the States to afford,
within its prescribed sphere, common and equal protection and
security to all. The plastic, variously defined, intangible doctrine of non-intervention formed a shelter for all who, eschewing
the tent of abolitionism, were nevertheless hostile to the institution of slavery.

The third resolution assumes that the admission of California
was a mere matter of Congressional discretion, and asserts that
those who opposed it were willing to admit her with limited
boundaries, thereby acknowledging they had no constitutional
objection. The last position is an error of fact; as your Senator,
I did not, could not offer or accept any such proposition; my
objections were fundamental, and had my course in any moder-
ate degree attracted your attention, you could not have attributed to me a disposition to enter into such a contract. I did
not consider the admission of California as a thing wholly within
the discretion of Congress. Every question of legislation is a
constitutional question, and should be distinctly referable to a
prescribed duty or a granted power. Congress may admit new
States into the Union. This is not an authority which would
warrant that body in the creation of a State, or would justify
it in waiving an inquiry into the facts, and requiring adequate
proof of the existence of a State, and of its competency to take
its place in this union of equals, and properly to discharge its
duties as a member of the confederacy.

The right of "the people of a territory" in organizing themselves into a State, to determine its organic law is not disputed,
has not been opposed by Southern men—but the unorganized,
unauthorized adventurers in California were not "the people of
a territory" as the phrase is applied and understood in the
United States. There was not the local, the social, the political
relation which would fulfill the definition of "a people" or "a
territory"—the inhabitants, except the Mexicans remaining

there, were by law trespassers on the public domain, which was not "a territory" but an undefined part of the territory belonging to the United States. The States of the Union were the sovereign owners, not those who first might reach the new acquisition in the race of the gold hunters. The ultimate sovereignty could be acquired but in one of two modes, by withdrawal of the authority of the States to whom the territory belonged, or by successful revolution. No one will contend that it was acquired in either mode, that essential requisite therefore did not exist. There having been no census, there being no officer who could hold an election, or affix an official signature to a return; and no prescribed qualifications for voters: the information was so imperfect, so wholly unofficial, and the defects so radical, as to constitute a case which in my opinion did not come within the constitutional power of Congress, conferred for the admission of new States. The necessity of the case required the establishment of government and a review of the action of Congress at the last and two preceding sessions will show why the mode of admitting California as a State was adopted instead of following the oldest and safest mode of establishing a territorial government, preparatory to a transfer of the eminent domain to the people of the territory, for the organization of a State. It will be seen that the Southern members as a class had for years past desired and attempted to organize a territorial government, but that the effort failed because of the determination of Northern members not to allow such government unless with the condition that involuntary servitude should be excluded from the territory. The inhabitants of California were driven to the formation of a State as the only mode of obtaining a government, and could not have doubted, as it appears by the debates of their convention they did not, that in order to be admitted as a State it was necessary that they should conform to the views of the anti-slavery majority in Congress. This furnishes an explanation for the extended, unnatural boundaries they claimed, including in one section a population whose Representatives protested against the act, in another an unknown inaccessible desert, with the prohibition of slavery in the whole, that the agitating question of slavery might (by their action) be kept out of Congress. Thus the inhabitants of California are relieved from the censure which would have attached to the attempt of aliens and citizens to prohibit other citizens from sharing with them the harvest offered by a country filled with hidden treasure, which every freshet threw to the surface. But just to the extent that the inhabitants are excused the responsibility attaches to the anti-slavery majority represented in the Federal government, which refused the mode best suited to the condition of California and adopted another because thus the slaveholder of the South could be excluded. Had there been no such influence, and an equal opportunity for emigration from the South as from the North, the resulting population might have decided differently as to the introduction of slaves; but if not, there would have been no cause to complain when in due time and manner the decision was made against it.

Though the Missouri compromise was not within the constitutional powers of Congress, it may have derived validity from the acquiescence of the States, and certainly should not have been repudiated by the North for whose benefit it was introduced and by whose votes it was almost unanimously supported. Two Senators from Indiana, one member from New Hampshire, and one from New York, and three from Massachusetts, being the Northern vote against the Missouri compromise.

Whilst, then, I agree with the strictures contained in your fourth resolution on the Missouri Compromise, as an original proposition, I thought and still believe the question, as presented to us, wears a very different aspect from that which it bore in 1820. Though time cannot sanctify wrong, it may establish acquiescence, and thus it may be considered a compact between the States, whose powers are not, like the Congress, restricted to the grants of the Constitution. In the action of the Nashville Convention on this subject, I see but a laudable anxiety to avoid sectional strife, and a fraternal spirit of concession. After asserting, in their sixth resolution, the duty of the federal government to recognize and maintain the equal rights of the citizens of the several States in the territories of the United States, their eleventh resolution sets forth: "That in the event a dominant majority shall refuse to recognize the great constitutional rights we assert, and shall continue to deny the obligations of the federal government to maintain them, it is the sense of this Convention that the territories should be treated as property, and divided between the sections of the Union, so that the rights of both sections be adequately secured in their respective shares. That we are aware this course is open to grave objections, but we are ready to acquiesce in the adoption of the line of 36 deg. 30 min. North latitude, extending to the Pacific ocean, as an extreme concession, upon considerations of what is due to the stability of our institutions." I had taken a position in the Senate which was equivalent to this, and though my action may not have received your notice, your reprobation of this proposition of the

Nashville Convention carries censure to me as your Senator. You treat it as a surrender to Congress of the right to unlimited legislation over slave property in the territories, and as presenting, as the only alternative, *disunion*. It was certainly not all to which I considered the South entitled, but I do not perceive how it is deemed the subject of censure on that account by those who approve the measures of Congress, a part of the history of which is a refusal to give that much.

When Senator King, of Alabama, proposed to limit California on the South by the parallel of 35 deg. 30 min., I offered an amendment to his amendment, substituting the line of 36 deg. 30 min., which then, as now, I believed to be the line indicated by nature and best suited to the population. The amendment to the amendment was rejected—yeas 23, nays 32. The question then recurred on the amendment, and it was also rejected— yeas 20, nays 37. Neither proposition got a Northern vote. Would this have been the case, if the desire had been to secure to the South that equality which you consider is recognized in the measures adopted?

On another occasion, when the proposition was to fix the Southern boundary of Utah at the 37th degree of North latitude, I offered an amendment substituting the parallel of 36 deg. 30 min. It was opposed in debate as containing an implication with regard to slavery, and was lost—yeas 26, nays 27—only two Northern Senators (Dickinson and Douglass) voting for it. The second proposition of your resolution pronounces disunion as the only alternative presented by the demand of the Nashville Convention. Why so? It is true that the men of the North held the Union so lightly that they would rather dissolve it than abide by a compromise which in former years they forced upon the South—would rather destroy it than permit the South to enjoy in a part of the territory those rights which, constitutionally, they have in the whole? If so, neither their justice, patriotism or fraternity have much claim to our consideration. Or is it that those who claim equality of right would not submit to be confined to a part—to be, in any degree, shorn by the federal government of the interests it was formed to protect? If this be the source from which disunion is expected to flow, our danger is imminent, indeed, when we are denied recognition or protection in the whole.

Will I be answered, that we can appeal to the Courts? If so, I reply, we could have appealed to the Courts against the "Wilmot Proviso." The security, and protection, and equality asserted could not, I suppose, have meant the right to appeal to the Supreme Court against a hostile discrimination.

That the North has not abandoned the claim of power to legislate in relation to slavery in the territories, is shown by the report which accompanied the bills when jointly brought in by the Committee of Thirteen; by the declarations of prominent members of both houses of Congress, and by the action of some Northern members after the bills had finally passed. The argument which prevailed against the Wilmot Proviso was that it was unnecessary; that slavery was excluded by the law of nature and the law of Mexico. If, then, it should be found that the law of nature invites rather than excludes slave labor, and if it should be decided that the law of Mexico withered beneath the shadow of our Constitution, those, who, under the above supposition, opposed the prohibition of slavery, would not merely be relieved from any obligation to adhere to their position, but if, like Mr. Clay, opposed to "the extension of slavery into those new territories, either by the authority of Congress or by individual enterprize," would be called on by their previous declarations to unite in obstructing the entrance of slavery into the territories.

It is not by a change of the phraseology or avoidance of the issue that the Wilmot Proviso is to be put to rest; it is the index of an energetic spirit, a wide spread sentiment, which wars, as it has warred for years, against our slave property, and which is now united to a sectional party, struggling for political dominion over us. Such unwavering purpose and sleepless energy does not seek repose when flushed by recent triumph, and cheered by the near prospect of final success. When the Wilmot Proviso shall be beaten by Northern members, who avow, as their reason, that the South possesses equal rights in the territories, and should be protected in their enjoyment, then I will believe that the Wilmot Proviso is put to rest, and will be prepared to rejoice with you in the consummation of that desirable event. That which has been done is by no means the equivalent of this, and I but discharge the duty of your sentinel on the out-post, when I state my belief, that the measures enacted in relation to the territories were expected and designed by the majority, to exclude slaves from the territories, and restrict them to the States in which they are now held.

In your fifth resolution you say, in effect, that a part of Texas, by the terms of the annexation, was placed within the reach of prohibitory enactment by Congress, in relation to slavery, and that the power has been abandoned. I suppose the reference was to the third guarantee of the second section of the joint resolution for annexing Texas to the United States, in which it was provided that new States, not exceeding four in number, in addition to the State of Texas, might, by the consent of said State, and under other conditions enumerated, be admitted into the Union.

It was further provided, that such States as were formed out of territory lying south of the parallel of 36-30 of north latitude, commonly known as the Missouri compromise line, should be admitted into the Union, with or without slavery, as the people of each State asking admission might desire.—"And in such State or States as shall be formed out of said territory, north of said Missouri compromise line, slavery, or involuntary servitude, (except for crime,) shall be prohibited."

I cannot find in this a grant of power to the Congress to make prohibitory enactment against slavery in any part of the territory of Texas. The conditions began only at the point at which it ceased to be a part of Texas; it applied to a new State, and if the portion of Texas north of 36-30 should remain permanently a part of that State then the provision would remain a dead letter. The day must be very remote, if it ever should arrive, when that part of Texas which is north of the Missouri compromise line will have the requisite population to form a State, which was the condition on which it was to be separated. As part of the State of Texas it was secure from the assault of Abolitionism, at least until it assert, what has been heretofore denied, the intent to interfere with slavery within the States where it exists. What then have they abandoned, what have we gained, or rather what have we not lost? If Texas accept the proposition how will the true boundary of Texas, as annexed, ever be established, and if there be rights in the territory sold, as having been part of Texas, who will determine, exactly, what that territory was? You will remember that the boundary, claimed the Rio Grande, was disputed, and that neither by or before the proposition to purchase the claim of Texas to the country west and north of her newly defined boundary, was the Rio Grande admitted to be the true limit of that State?

I agree with you in your commendation of the bill for the recovery of fugitive slaves, yet we had reason to fear that those who disregarded a plain provision of the Constitution, who had nullified it, as well as the act of 1793 intended to enforce it, would render the act of 1850 equally void. But whatever be the merit of that law, by examination of the proceedings of

Congress you will find, that it was not originally framed, or subsequently amended to its present form, or mainly advocated by those to whom you return thanks.

The measure known as the bill to abolish the slave trade in the District of Columbia, which is the grossest usurpation of power and most palpable violation of constitutional right, is not alluded to by you, I am therefore permitted to hope you do not approve of the power asserted by Congress in that bill to emancipate a slave because his owner brings him into the district of Columbia to keep him there until his interest or convenience shall induce him to remove his slave elsewhere for sale. A right not denied to the owners of other property, and a penalty in violation of the prohibition against taking private property except for public use, and by making due compensation therefor.

I have at greater length than was originally intended sought to meet the issue presented to me of approval or disapproval of the measures passed at the last session of Congress in relation to slavery and the territories. It was the exact issue which a representative could not decline. My opposition was earnest, because I confidently believe it my duty, your interest, and because I thought the public voice of Mississippi and the resolutions of her legislature so instructed. That I am not peculiar in the opinion that the measures as a whole were wanting in the compensation or equality which would entitle them to the name of compromise appears by the remarks of the two most eminent among their advocates. Mr. Webster said, the North lost what the South gained, nothing. Mr. Clay said, directing his remarks to Mr. Hale, "let him tell me if the North does not get almost every thing and the South nothing but her honor—* * * * show what sacrifices, what is sacrificed by the North in this bill. That is what I want."

Well might a Northern man be challenged to show the concession, or sacrifice which his section was to make, and though some Northern members in Congress required even more than "almost every thing," yet since their return to their constituency I have seen no evidence of public dissatisfaction towards any of the measures, except that which required a compliance with the provision in the Constitution for the delivery of fugitive slaves.

If the measures enacted require redress, it is for the people to prescribe the mode and measure of it; it does not become their Representative to suggest them, and nor does the issue presented by your resolutions involve that question.

By the admission of California the South is in a minority in both branches of the National Legislature. By the dismemberment of Texas and the addition of the East to the West side of the Rio Grande the United States have there a territory which may at no remote period become a State. Though the much-lauded ordinance of 1787 limited the number of States to be made out of the Northwest territory to five, that number has been already carved out, and a territory remains from which another may be formed. With all the departments of government in the hands of an unfriendly majority what hope can the minority have unless the government be restrained to the *principles* of the Constitution, and how can the weaker party expect justice if it oppose a broken front to the onward accelerated march of their more powerful opponent. Had the South been united we should not have been forced into our present condition, were it united now all which is not irretrievable might be recovered. But if at the moment of assault we are found wrangling one against another, if the doctrine of passive obedience shall prevail, we shall receive the contempt of the enemy, our supposed spirit has held in check for so many years; and merit the pity of our friends at the North who have sacrificed themselves by maintaining the principles which it was thought the South would never surrender.

We have, gentlemen, a common interest, a common fortune, and must reach the same conclusion wherever we take the same view of the facts. There is now a wide difference of opinion between us; of the correctness of the one and the error of the other let the records of the past and the transactions of the future decide. Yours is the more pleasing hope, and, if I know myself, none would be more gratified at its fulfilment than

Your obedient servant, etc., etc.,

JEFFERSON DAVIS.

Messrs. B. Pendleton and others, President and members.

Petition to Jefferson Davis, signed by State Senator T. Jones Stewart and 317 other citizens of Wilkinson county.

(From Woodville Republican, Nov. 19, 1850.)

Dear Sir: We, the undersigned citizens of Wilkinson, hold it to be our duty under the circumstances, as well as it is our highest pleasure, to assure you of the great approbation and admiration with which your course in the recent struggle between Northern *might* and Southern *right,* has been viewed by us.

We have seen you in every attack, and though surrounded by defection, stand up manfully and with judgment for our rights and honor.

When the Compromise bill of the Committee of Thirteen was brought in as the deceptious instrument for our destruction, we beheld you, searching out its fallacies, exposing its cunningly concealed snares, and overturning the arguments built up with skill and labor for its support. The bill was defeated, but the measures composing it have since, in effect, become laws. We regret that there was so little sense of justice left in the American Congress; but your efforts, dear sir, deserve still the same praise. What will be the course of the Southern People remains to be seen.

Had it been necessary or proper for us, during the contest, to have expressed these our sentiments, we would unhesitatingly have done so; but we were conscious that you have instructions from the Legislature; that you acted, guided by unerring principles; and that to encourage you to continue on your course would be unnecessary, and to instruct you, improper.

With assurances of augmented confidence and esteem,

Your Fellow-Citizens,

T. Jones Stewart, Felix Embree, John Roberts, Alexander E. Wall, J. L. Jones, J. C. Reiley, Hiram McGraw, W. M. Pacquinette, Wm. Alexander, E. McGraw, J. M. Anderson, W. R. Scudder, S. R. McDowell, G. W. Mayes, F. S. Richardson, A R. Brown, Geo. P. Richardson, G. W. Keller, L. S. Johns, Wm. T. Jones, E. McNeil, Henry Perry, Chas. McNeil, John Shropshire, Robt. O. Love, I. H. King, John L. Hayes, James A. Combs, Jno. C. Alexander, Overton Bell, James Stephens, G. H. Scudder, D. Hovey, W. M. Crisp, Sam'l Caston, Wm. A. Sims, Wm. H. Benton, Wm. C. McLean, James H. Burt, G. P. Netterville, J. F. Robinson, Maunsel White, Wm. J. Netterville, Jno. B. Draughan, Thos. Brannan, Wm. D. White, W. J. Hodge, Thomas I. Lanier, Robert Watson, Florida Ford, James Martin, Jacob Curry, J. B. Fenner, Thos. S. Dawson, H. Hampton Smith, Presley Berry, James Clayton, Henry H. Bell, W. Dowty, Const. Wilmerua, John T. Lelsh, Moses Paris, Benjamin Rogers, William Wilson, John Williams, John Stricker, Jacob Stutmann, Edward Duff, A. J. Stephenson, John H. Calmes, W. J. Nock, O. F. Meeker, C. F. Pierce, L. L. Babers, J. Buckley, Peter Sutherland, Wm. C. Donnell, Douglas H. Cooper, W. P. Burton, M. Creswell, H. R. Hampton, Christian Miller, Henry

E. Curtis, F. B. Haynes, Wm. H. Herrin, John F. Dameron, T. C. Sargent, F. G. Nichols, M. E. Saunders, Abram Saunders, M. W. Chrestman, A. McFarland, Carnot Posey, W. A. Holmes, W. M. Wood, S. W. Hazlep, Dennis Bunch, Robt. H. Davis, Geo. W. Brown, Seth Kline, John W. Burgess, Sam'l Bell, Geo. W. Jones, I. D. Gildart, L. K. Barber, W. E. Gildart, J. Schwartz, Henry Burgower, Leopold Henry, Wm. J. Feltus, J. H. Leatherman, Wm. Hays, Wm. J. Bryant, Daniel Miller, George H. Gordon, Wm. L. Frazier, N. Humphreys, J. M. Morris, R. S. Morris, I. Cohen, N. Scudder, John Richardson, Gilbert Sinclair, J. A. Smith, Fred Conrad, J. J. McMorris, Peter Smith, Joseph Snyder, M. Simon, A. J. Edie, H. D. Robinson, Joseph Ewing, H. H. Jeter, S. H. Stockett, John S. Holt, Jr., Thos. W. Hays, P. H. Joor, Adam Lanehart, Henry S. VanEaton, David L. Jeter, Charles Sims, William Baker, Hiram Ashley, J. H. Ferguson, Wm. Netterville, Sterling L. Jeter, B. T. Conner, Thos. Shropshire, W. C. Green, J. A. Ventress, George B. Collier, Thomas Johns, Willis Hunter, B. C. Stuart, T. B. Helmer, Joseph Embree, Isaac D. Stamps, Thos. H. Curry, B. C. Rogers, Michael Crist, P. W. Ferguson, Mayers Levi, Wm. Deloach, C. Netterville, Nehemiah Carter, Patrick J. Curtin, B. F. Sibley, T. Kingsbury, R. S. Tillery, John McCrea, Wm. T. Bining, J. J. McCrea, Thomas F. Scott, J. B. Chambers, Charles C. Cage, G. Blanchard, Jehu Holland, H. H. Herbert, M. Ferguson, George W. Cage, Nic. Freshon, W. O. Rodney, B. G. Dorsey, Samuel Leek, Davis H. Sanders, Sterling Jeter, J. H. Read, Alex. Newman, Thos. Brannan, Jr., Thomas J. White, F. V. Stephens, Benj. Kilgore, Wm. Clark, Absalom Liggit, John Kirkland, David Johns, C. E. Cammack, R. M. Newman, Wm. S. Newman, A. W. Johns, Joseph Smith, Robt. McReady, Joseph Alexander, Arglas Jeter, Arglas W. Jeter, B. F. Ives, M. M. Love, H. R. Davis, B. S. Groom, L. H. Bryan, W. J. Dove, N. Norwood, A. T. Moore, Wm. L. Cage, T. G. Conner, Theo. W. White, H. S. White, Jonas Platt, George Morris, G. S. Morris, M. J. Morris, F. Gildart, James Riddle, J. Lindemann, T. M. Kincade, Francis Best, G. B. Newell, Wm. Henly, Benedict Wolf, H. M. Farish, G. Ellis, R. Allen, J. M. Westrope, N. C. Gordon, D. Holt, C. Farish, James Hays, James Dunckley, Jas. M. Miller, H. J. Butterworth, J. M. Iler, M. G. Caston, B. S. Knight, Wm. Rule, Vincent Row, Wm. H. Rowley, S. R. Harrison, John L. Rogers, William L. Jeter, R. R. Richardson, D. L. Carter, Benjamin Bass, Wm. Shropshire, Thos. H. Oswald, H. J. Feltus, Jr., G. W. Leatherman, Wesley Chambers, W. Beach, R. B. Newell, W. E. L. Baum, David Murray, Wm.

Stamps, Wm. A. A. Chisholm, S. B. Morris, R. Clampitt, J. B. Therrell, Samuel Thomas, A. J. Westrope, George W. Noland, Jeremiah Netterville, H. Smith, W. K. Prater, Wm. Hastings, S. J. Richardson, J. R. Leek, Pulaski Cage, Josiah A. Knight, Daniel H. Prosser, G. W. Hitchcock, Thos. Wilkinson, S. W. Stafford, T. B. Ewell, P. Higdon, B. W. Wright, A. W. Partin, J. W. Holloway, D. L. Flinn, C. Kaigler, John W. Kaigler, V. V. Kaigler, Tandy A. Walker, J. B. Walker, William Walker, Thomas E. Ogden, Charles Mackay, Joseph Collins, W. N. Patterson, P. F. Keary, James H. Nicholson, W. B. Netterville.

Jefferson Davis to S. Cobun and others.[1]

(From Port Gibson Herald, Nov. 29, 1850.)

Briarfield, Nov. 7, 1850.

Gentlemen :—Yesterday I returned from a visit to some of the Counties North of us, and received your letter of the 19th October, inviting me on the part of the friends of the Nashville Convention and of Southern Rights, to meet them at Eldwood Springs on the 2d of November. By the above statement you will perceive that the day appointed had passed before the invitation was received. I had anticipated the pleasure of seeing my friends and neighbors of Claiborne county, and sincerely regret the combination of circumstances which will deprive me of an opportunity to do so. I deem it always a privilege to state fully to my constituents the course I have pursued as their Representative, and to learn their views and wishes as to the future, but in the present crisis of our fate it is peculiarly desirable that the most perfect cointelligence should exist between the people and their Representatives. On the measures which mainly occupied the Congress at its last session, it was my happy fortune to find in the action of primary meetings and in the resolutions of the legislature instructions which accorded with my individual opinion in relation to our true policy and with my conviction of constitutional right and governmental obligation. The South may confidently point to her history and present attitude to prove her fealty to the compact our Fathers made, and to answer the slander of those who undermining the temple of the Constitution arraign those as its destroyers who have rallied round it for its defence. As

---

[1] Influential citizens of Claiborne county, Mississippi.

sovereigns, each above the control of the other, the States laid the foundation of the Union, as equals they wrought and finished the structure, that, as equals they might enjoy the protection it was designed to afford. To that Union an allegiance is due, to that Union it has been and will cheerfully be rendered; but if its foundation be changed, if it be dedicated to another use, the obligation then no longer exists. Of that fact the States as sovereign members of the confederacy must judge. Entertaining this opinion I have not hesitated to avow my readiness to abide by the issue whenever Mississippi should make it, and to acknowledge her right to claim my entire allegiance whenever she chose to assert it. As her Representative I did not believe it became me to pledge her to any line of policy or to make any issue for her, I have not attempted to do either one or the other. As an accredited agent of Mississippi to the Federal Government, I have felt it due to her honor as well as my own, that so long as I retained such position the duties and obligations pertaining to the station should be faithfully observed.

When, therefore the purpose of "Disunion" has been charged upon those who have acted as I have done, and held the opinions which I entertain in relation to the legislation of the last session of Congress, I have expected those who knew me best to anticipate me in the answer I have given to the charge—that so far as it was intended to apply to myself, it was slanderous and false.

The importance of the principal measures discussed and enacted during the long session of Congress which has recently closed, and the excitement which the sectional character of the debate created, give assurance that your information is so full that to enter into details concerning them could not be otherwise than wearisome. But it may not be inappropriate as this is the only opportunity I shall probably have to offer a few general reflections as connects with our present position in the Confederacy.

At the formation of the Union the equality between the navigating and agricultural States was such that Mr. Madison said the Northern States would be reconciled by their greater number of States, and the Southern States from their larger area by the prospect of greater population. The idea of equilibrium of power thus early entertained continued and appears from time to time in the admission by pairs of slaveholding and non-slaveholding States. The opposition to the admission of Missouri, applying in due form and in entire observance of precedent, exhibited in addition to the old feature of preserving the balance of power, a new element of strife, the domestic institution of slavery. Then the South in generosity and confidence rather than wisdom agreed to pacify the sectional hostility to the further increase of political power in the slaveholding region, that slavery should be prohibited in all the territory North of 36 deg. 30 min. of North latitude. This together with the cession by Virginia of the Northwest territory secured to the Northern section a permanent majority in the Union, and has led to a train of events in which we are realizing the wisdom of the opinion of Mr. Jefferson, that paper guaranties were only valuable when the power existed to enforce their observance. The South has become a permanent minority in both Houses of Congress, and in the electoral colleges, if she possesses the power to enforce the observance of her constitutional rights it must be elsewhere than in the Halls of Congress, and at the ballot box.

It does not suffice to say that the Supreme Court is the judge in all questions of the constitutionality of a law, because constitutional rights may be lost by withholding protection, by refusing legislation, or by fraudulently concealing the purpose of a law.

An instance of the first is presented in the failure to give Government power to extend the laws and provide for the execution of constitutional requirements in the territories acquired from Mexico. And more recently in the refusal to remove all doubt as to the existence of an obstruction in the Mexican law to the introduction of slave property into New Mexico and Utah, or to throw the shield of the United States laws over emigrants who should take slaves into those territories. Governments are formed and supported to give protection, ours has no power, or right to discriminate between citizens and different kinds of property. To all citizens belong equal privileges and immunities, and all property has equal claim to protection, but there has been discrimination against slaveholders and their property, and even Southern men have been its apologists by urging that to claim protection was to concede the power to destroy. A position which would render it fatal to a people to give any power to their Government. The equivalent of which would be to say, that if the army of the United States can defend the frontier of a State, they can also change its boundary. The doctrine of non-intervention in the institutions of a State or of a people forming a State constitution has no application to a territory belonging to the States, or to inhabitants not organized or possessed of those attributes which in a political sense would constitute them a people. The Federal Government is the agent of the States and possesses certain powers over the territory belonging to the United States conferred like all others for the common good. The discretion permitted in their use must be subordinate to the principles of the constitution, not in violation of them. It seems then plain to me that there is an obligation to protect, and that there is no power to destroy property which any citizen of the United States may choose to carry with him when he claims the right of a citizen to equal enjoyment in the common property of the States.

This was a right which I understood our State to assert when taking her stand against the "Wilmot Proviso." If to be deprived of equal enjoyment of the territories was the wrong contemplated, if security and adequate protection was the right claimed; if it was for the substance, not against the shadow, that our efforts were directed, then the contemplated case has arisen. It was the action of the Congress which gave vitality to the "Constitution" of California, the clause prohibiting the slaveholder of the Southern States from migrating to that country with his property derives its binding force from the action of the Federal Government, as it was dictated by the known will of the anti-slavery majority which controls and directs it. In the law to abolish the slave trade in the District of Columbia we have a palpable violation of the rights of private property and the principle of free transit and trade between the States, which may be called the bed stone in the foundation of our Union. The power to discriminate against slave property and legislate so as to destroy it if it be admitted in one case will be exercised in others. It was the assertion of the right to tax the colonies which produced the revolution, the amount was not the consideration it was for the principle that Washington and Franklin and Adams and their compeers resolved to sacrifice all the proud and hallowed associations which bound them to the mother country.

In the past action of Mississippi I find the indication of her future course; may the union of the South and the sober sense of the North produce a return of that sense of justice, and faithful observance of the principles of our federal compact which will enable a minority to live as equals in the confederacy, but if this, the first wish of an American heart cannot be gratified, if our Union as formed by the men of the Revolution cannot be preserved, the responsibility will be with those who drive us for the sake of security, peace, and the equality to which we were born, to look out of the Union for rights denied to us

in it. The North can preserve the Union, easily preserve it by
the observance of constitutional obligations and a due regard
for the principles from which the Union arose, the South may
possibly preserve the Union by union and the firm maintenance
of their rights; not by submission to wrong, not by blind worship of a name, not by peans over the corpse when the animating
spirit has fled.

Accept, gentlemen, my thanks for the very grateful manner
in which you have communicated the invitation to which this
is a reply; like yourselves I am a friend of the Nashville Convention, indeed it has been strange to me that whilst Conventions are constantly held at the North to destroy our security,
our prosperity, our character, and pass to a great extent
unrebuked, the first proposition to prepare for defence, to
counteract the assailants is met by wide spread condemnation,
and even some in the South join in the unjust cry. When Abolitionists convene for our destruction it is the sacred right peaceably to assemble, but if Southern men convene for defence, it
is denounced by the ignorance and hollow hearted as treason.
Such is too apt to be the fate of a minority in a Government as
powerful to reward as our own. From the aroused attention of
the people I hope for a just appreciation of our condition; from
their patriotism and judgment for the proper measures in the
present and all future contingencies. Please, gentlemen, present
me in acceptable terms to those with whom you are associated,
and believe me very truly, your friend and fellow-citizen,

JEFFERSON DAVIS.

To messrs.

S. Coburn, J. B. Thrasher, Jno. C. Humphreys, Dr. S. F. R.
Abbay, R. T. Archer, J. J. Wood, J. Jeffries, D. Cameron,
J. M. Magruder.

(Introduction to questions and answers in the two letters following.)

The letter of Col. Jefferson Davis, copied below, is in reply
to the following questions, lately propounded to him at Jackson. Let every true Southerner carefully read it, and then
ask himself if Col. Davis does not, in this letter, set forth the
true and proper cause to be pursued by the Southern States:

B. D. Nabors and others to Jefferson Davis.

(From Woodville Republican, December 3, 1850.)

1st. Are you in favor of dissolution of the Union now or hereafter, because of the legislation at the late session of Congress?

2nd. Are you in favor of the establishment of a Southern Confederacy, now or hereafter, because of the late session of Congress?

3d. Are you in favor of a secession of the State of Mississippi from the Union now or hereafter, because of the legislation of the late session of Congress?

4th. Are you in favor of resistance, of any and what kind, to the recent acts of Congress? If so, please state the character, the manner and time of such resistance.

Signed.

B. D. NABORS,
CHAS. B. AMES,
C. F. HEMINGWAY,
W. D. LYLES,
C. R. CRUSOE,
GEO. H. FOOTE,
W. BROOKE,
JAS. E. SHARKEY,
A. M. WEST.

Jefferson Davis to B. D. Nabors and Others.

(From Mississippi Free Trader, Nov. 30, 1850.)

Jackson, Nov. 19, 1850.

Gentlemen: I have the honor to acknowledge the receipt of your letter of yesterday, which came to hand last night, under circumstances which you must have known precluded anything more than a brief reply. The questions you propound, except the last, seem to have been copied from a letter addressed to a Senator of Louisiana, by a citizen of that State, which, I trust explains the nature of the enquiries. No one, who has taken so much interest in my opinions as gravely to ask for them, could have failed to find, in my public course, sufficient reason for the modification of those questions, so as to conform to my well known position, had he been preparing questions for my own particular case. If any have falsely, and against the evidences before them, attempted to fix on me the charge of wishing to dissolve the Union, under existing circumstances, I am sure your information and intelligence has enabled you to detect the shallow fraud. If any have represented me as seeking to establish a Southern Confederacy on the ruins of that which our revolutionary fathers bequeathed to us, my whole life, and every sentiment I have ever uttered, in public or private, give them the lie.

If any have supposed, gratuitously, (they could not otherwise,) that my efforts in the Senate were directed to the secession of Mississippi from the Union, their hearts must have been insensible to the obligations of honor and good faith, which I feel are imposed upon me, by the position of an accredited agent from Mississippi, to the Federal Government. Your fourth question, therefore, is the only one which I feel you could have addressed to me, as your Representative, for any other *kind* purpose, than to give me an opportunity thus summarily to dispose of baseless slanders against me.

The responsibility of a Representative is for the course he has pursued; the issue between him and his constituents must be, that of approval or disapproval; the inquiry it involves is, did he truly represent those for whom he acted? was he right or wrong? To know what he would do in the future, the case must be distinctly stated; otherwise, he might answer to one supposition, when the inquiry was directed to another. It would require the gift of prophecy to tell what remote consequences may flow from the acts of the late session of Congress, and, without such gift, no one could assume to say what he might hereafter believe should be done. When a people lose the power to maintain their rights and protect their interests under the existing form of government, ordinary prudence requires that they should seek such change as will secure them against the destruction of both. The character of the aggression, the degree and imminence of the danger, will prescribe the means and indicate the necessity. To the debates of the Senate, and such of my public addresses as you may have heard, since my return to Mississippi, I refer you for the cause and reasons of my opposition to the measures adopted at the last session of Congress. You ask me if I am "in favor of any and what kind of resistance" to those acts. As your Representative, I declined to enter on that branch of the question in the U. S. Senate; in that capacity, I took the position that it was not for me to make an issue for the State. Your question is not, I think, one which directs itself to my official position; but, as I intend to answer, it is unnecessary to argue that point, and I mention it as leading to the statement that it is as a citizen, not as a Senator, of Mississippi, that I give you my opinion of our duty in the present crisis.

I am in favor of the execution of the plan indicated by the State Convention of October, 1849, the address of that Convention to the slaveholding States, and by the Legislation of the State at its last session, which I consider may be stated thus: to submit the question to the people, in a law, for the assembling of a Convention of the State, to consider of and decide on our present condition and future prospects, and the measures which should be adopted. To prepare for the defence of the State, armed if need be. To propose a convention of the slave-holding States, to be composed of formally elected delegates, which should unite all those States who were willing to assert their equality, and right to equal protection in, and equal enjoyment of, the common property. The States thus united should, in my opinion, demand of the other States such guarantees as would secure to them the safety, the benefits, the tranquility which the Union was designed to confer. If granted, the minority could live in equality under the temple of our federal compact; if refused, it would be conclusive evidence of the design of the majority, to crush all paper barriers beneath the heel of power; the gulf of degradation would yawn before us. The equality to which we were born being denied, and the alternative of slavish submission or manly resistance being presented to us, I shall be in favor of the latter. Then, if full provision has been made, in the preparation of arms, of munitions of war, of manufacturing establishments, and all the varieties of agriculture to which our climate and soil are adapted, the slaveholding States, or even the planting States, may apply the last remedy —the final alternative of separation, without bloodshed or severe shock to commercial interests. Painful under any circumstances it must be to those who have through life cherished the hope of perpetuity to our Union, to see it destroyed; but faithful history will record our many sacrifices to preserve it, and the responsibility of its destruction must attach to those who, by assailment of the constitution, which they had the power to violate and not the will to observe, have stifled in the Union the breath of its existence. A most unfair attempt has been made to put in the foreground the question of Union or Disunion, by those who were violating or surrendering our constitutional rights. To yield to aggression is to produce, certainly in the future, that condition from which dissolution must, and civil war probably will spring; unless it be assumed, that the Southern minority will hereafter consent to occupy such position, towards the Northern majority, as the colonies of North America, on the 4th of July, 1776, determined not to hold towards the Kingdom of Great Britain. The destruction of that equilibrium, which would have prevented the overthrow of the constitution by the construction of an interested majority, may be charged to the generous concessions of the South in ceding the North West territory, in permitting the Missouri Compromise, and by other less noted acts which accumulated power in the North, by transfer from the South. Concession and sacrifice have not secured to us the good feeling of the North; submission to wrong will not more probably command their respect. To preserve the Union, the principles, the spirit of the Constitution must be preserved. I do not think the North has given us reason to expect this service from that quarter; how shall the South effect it? This, to my mind, is the question to which we should direct our investigation.

Whatever can effect that end will give perpetuity to the Union; if it cannot be reached, then the Government changes its character; there might remain *an* Union but not *the* Union.

For myself, I have no hesitation to inform you, that I prefer to go out of the Union, with the Constitution, rather than abandon the Constitution, to remain in an Union.

I believe, gentlemen, I have answered your inquiry, as far as it was possible for me to do so, without further information than your letter affords; and have the pleasure to subscribe myself, very respectfully, your fellow-citizen, etc.,

JEFFERSON DAVIS.

Messrs. B. D. Nabors, Charles B. Ames, C. F. Hemmingway, W. D. Lyle, C. R. Crusoe, Geo. H. Foote, W. Brooke, James E. Sharkey, A. M. West.

Resolutions of the Mississippi Legislature commending the conduct of Senator Davis and censuring the conduct of Senator Foote. Dec. 19, 1850.

Mr. FOOTE. Mr. President, I hold in my hand certain resolutions of censure upon my own course as a member of this body, adopted recently by the Legislature of the State of Mississippi, which I will submit with a single remark. I have no feeling at all relative to the proceedings of that body. The gentlemen who compose it are doubtless very respectable gentle-

men, but I think they are little acquainted with the public
sentiment, and before the next Autumn they will find that these
resolutions were wholly unnecessary and undeserved. These
resolutions, however, I was requested to present to the Senate,
and I have done so. I have nothing more to say, but my colleague may take such course as he may think proper.

Mr. DAVIS, of Mississippi. I hope they will be read and
printed for the use of the Senate.

The resolutions were accordingly read and laid upon the
table. The motion to print was referred to the Committee on
Printing:

The resolutions are as follow:

EXECUTIVE CHAMBER, JACKSON, *Dec.* 6, 1850.

SIR: Complying with the last resolution enclosed, I have
the honor to transmit a "preamble and resolutions of the Legislature of the State of Mississippi in relation to our Senators
and Representatives in Congress," with a request that they be
presented to the Senate of the United States.

I am, very respectfully, your obedient servant,

J. A. QUITMAN.

To the Hon. JEFFERSON DAVIS, Senator, &c.:

*Preamble and Resolutions of the Legislature of the State of
Mississippi, in relation to our Senators and Representatives
in Congress.*

Whereas, in a special message of the Governor of this State,
bearing date the 11th of February, 1850, the following communication from the Senators and Representatives of Mississippi in
the Congress of the United States was presented to the Legislature then in session, to wit:

WASHINGTON, *January* 21, 1850.

His Excellency JOHN A. QUITMAN, Governor, &c.:

SIR: We, the Senators and Representatives in Congress from
Mississippi, feel it incumbent upon us to advise you, and through
you our common constituents, that we have a well defined
opinion that California will be admitted as a State of this
Union during the present session of Congress. The President
earnestly recommended it, and we cannot be mistaken in supposing that a majority of both Houses of Congress will be
found to vote for it. Our individual positions have undergone no change. We regard the proposition to admit California as a State, under all the circumstances of her applica-

tion, as an attempt to adopt the "Wilmot proviso" in another form. But separated as we are from our constituents, and having no convenient means of consulting them as to their views on the new phase of this perplexing question, we desire through you to submit the single fact to the people and the Legislature, that California will most likely obtain admission into the Union with her constitutional prohibition of slavery; and we beg leave to add that we shall be greatly pleased to have such expression of opinion by the Legislature, by the Governor, and if practicable by the people, as shall clearly indicate the course which Mississippi will deem it her duty to pursue in this new emergency.

Very respectfully, your obedient servants,

> JEFF. DAVIS,
> H. S. FOOTE,
> J. THOMPSON,
> W. S. FEATHERSTON,
> WM. McWILLIE,
> A. G. BROWN.

And whereas the Legislature, after mature consideration of the subject-matter of said communication, adopted, in accordance with the suggestions therein contained, among others, the following resolutions, as instructions to the Senators, and as expressive of their opinions to the Representatives in Congress from this State, to wit:

"*Resolved,* That the policy heretofore pursued by the Government of the United States in regard to said Territory, (of California,) in refusing to provide territorial government therefor, has been and is eminently calculated to promote, and is about to effect indirectly, the cherished object of the Abolitionists, which cannot be accomplished by direct legislation, without a plain and palpable violation of the Constitution of the United States.

"*Resolved,* That the admission of California into the Union as a sovereign State with its present constitution, the result of the aforesaid false and unjust policy on the part of the Government of the United States, would be an act of fraud and oppression on the rights of the people of the slaveholding States, and it is the sense of this Legislature that our Senators and Representatives should, to the extent of their ability, resist it by all honorable and constitutional means."

And whereas the Hon. JEFFERSON DAVIS, one of the Senators, and the Hons. A. G. BROWN, WILLIAM McWILLIE, W. S. FEATHERSTON, and JACOB THOMPSON, members in Congress from this State, in accordance with said resolutions, and with the interest and will of the people of Mississippi, did, by their action in

Congress, resist by all honorable and constitutional means the admission of California, with her existing constitution, into the Union as a sovereign State; and whereas the Hon. HENRY S. FOOTE, one of the Senators in Congress from this State, in violation of the spirit and intent of said resolutions, and in opposition to the interest and will of the people of Mississippi, did not resist, by all honorable and constitutional means the admission of California into the Union as a sovereign State with her existing constitution, but by giving his support to the miscalled compromise, reported by the Committee of Thirteen in the United States Senate, violated the instructions of the Legislature as contained in said resolutions, based upon his own request, and disregarded the interest and will of the people of Mississippi: therefore,

Resolved by the Legislature of the State of Mississippi, That the course of the Hon. JEFFERSON DAVIS, as Senator, the Hons. A. G. BROWN, WM. McWILLIE, W. S. FEATHERSTON, and JACOB THOMPSON, as Representatives in Congress from this State, on the question of the admission of California, is approved, as representing the interest and will of the people of Mississippi; that the course of the Hon. HENRY S. FOOTE, on this question is not approved, being, in the judgment of the Legislature, opposed to the interest and will of the people of Mississippi.

Be it further resolved, That the course of the Hon. JEFFERSON DAVIS, as Senator, and Hons. A. G. BROWN, WM. McWILLIE, W. S. FEATHERSTON, and JACOB THOMPSON, as Representatives in Congress from this State, in their firm and consistent support, and able advocacy of the rights and honor of Mississippi and the South, in all the questions before Congress at its late session involved in the slave controversy, is approved; that the course of the Hon. HENRY S. FOOTE on all these questions is not approved; and this Legislature does not consider the interests of the State of Mississippi committed to this charge safe in his keeping.

JOHN J. McREA,
Speaker of the House of Representatives.

JOHN I. GUION,
President of the Senate.

Approved, November 30, 1850.

J. A. QUITMAN.